Fundamentals
of Human
Sexuality

Fundamentals of Human Sexuality
third edition

HERANT A. KATCHADOURIAN, M.D.
DONALD T. LUNDE, M.D.
Stanford University

HOLT, RINEHART AND WINSTON
New York   Chicago   San Francisco
Dallas   Montreal   Toronto   London   Sydney

Library of Congress Cataloging in Publication Data

Katchadourian, Herant A
  Fundamentals of human sexuality.

  Bibliography: p. 495
  Includes indexes.
  1. Sex. I. Lunde, Donald T., joint author.
II. Title. [DNLM: 1. Sex behavior. HQ21 K185f]
HQ31.K36 1980   612.6   80-10603
ISBN: 0-03-042941-2

Foreword

It is a curious and poignant fact that some of the subjects that affect human lives most powerfully receive little attention in scientific research or in higher education. Sex is such a subject. This situation is beginning to change for the better, and this book is a remarkable contribution to the improvement. I know of no other book on human sexuality that matches it in clarity, cogency, and dependability of information.

Five years ago it was my privilege to invite Herant Katchadourian to join the faculty of the Stanford University School of Medicine. Shortly thereafter, I asked him to replace me on a committee on university health. The members of this committee were quickly impressed with his extraordinary qualities and asked him to undertake an innovative course on human sexuality for Stanford undergraduates. The third time the course was offered, with Donald Lunde as collaborator, over a thousand students enrolled, making it the largest single course at Stanford. This textbook grew out of that course, which continues to attract an enthusiastic response from the student body.

The scientific literature on sex is in its infancy. Although popular books abound, full of flashy claims and disputable speculations, there is a striking lack of adequate textbooks on human sexuality for college-level instruction. This is in pronounced contrast to the large number of excellent textbooks in such subjects as biology and psychology. No doubt this reflects the fact that sex has always been a delicate subject, a not quite respectable field for scientific inquiry or scholarly analysis. Similarly, there has been concern that sex education will lead to sexual promiscuity or aberration. By now it should be apparent to any reasonable person that there is no scarcity of interest in sex nor in exploring the avenues of sexual experience. What is lacking is accurate information and thoughtful consideration of alternative courses of action.

So far as I know, this book is the first successful attempt to produce a textbook on human sexuality that, in scope, reliability, and level of sophistication, compares favorably with the better textbooks in the biological and social sciences. The availability of this book should greatly facilitate the teaching of human sexuality in colleges and may prove to be a potent incentive to start such courses where none exists now.

The primary emphasis in this book is on information, not advice. The information has been selected with care and the reader is clearly told when he is being presented with empirical data, what are the limitations of the evidence, and when one must rely upon hypothetical constructs. Whenever pertinent, alternative explanations are offered for the same behavior or phenomenon. The material is presented in a fashion that should make it readily comprehensible for beginning college students, yet the information is sufficiently sophisticated to make the book valuable for advanced students as well. Since people of all ages have generally lacked scientifically based education about sex, this book can be useful to a broad range of readers.

There are few topics where the need for an integrated view is as great as in the area of sex. Although much remains to be learned about the biological, psychological, and cultural aspects of sex, we know enough to realize that these elements cannot be separated from each other, nor can one be ignored in favor of the other. One of the major strengths of this book is that it approaches human sexuality as a comprehensive and integrated topic by thoughtfully distributing emphasis across different areas, and by viewing sexual behavior in an evolutionary, historical and cross-cultural perspective.

The authors have ranged widely across biological sciences, social sciences, and clinical medicine in arriving at their assessment of the current state of knowledge about sex. They are not inhibited by the narrow confines of a single discipline, nor are they preoccupied with any doctrinaire ideological position. They are open-minded, broadly informed, and freely inquisitive. They often find present evidence inadequate to answer questions definitively, yet they do not avoid difficult issues. Their assessment of evidence is consistently judicious and useful. Moreover, their appraisals are expressed with wit and grace and the book is enjoyable to read.

Finally, it is significant to note that this textbook on human sexuality for college instruction is written by two psychiatrists, both members of the faculty of Stanford University, who have broad backgrounds in the behavioral and biological sciences. During the past decade, this university has made a deep commitment to pooling the strengths of various disciplines to achieve a deeper understanding of man. In the Department of Psychiatry of the School of Medicine, where the authors teach and do their research, specialists come from a variety of disciplines: psychiatry, clinical psychology, developmental psychology, physiological psychology, endocrinology, biochemistry, genetics, anthropology, and statistics. In the undergraduate Human Biology program, where the Human Sexuality course is now given, the Departments of Biology, Genetics, Pediatrics, Sociology, and Psychiatry play leading roles. The problems of man do not come in neat packages that fit the traditional academic disciplines. They are far-reaching, complex, and fascinating. Drs. Katchadourian and Lunde have approached human sexual behavior in this spirit and the book they have produced is thus hard to classify, easy to read, and a genuine contribution to our understanding of man.

David A. Hamburg, M.D.

Department of Psychiatry
Stanford University
1972

Acknowledgments to the Second Edition

In the acknowledgments to the first edition we indicated that the text was an outgrowth of our course on human sexuality at Stanford University and went on to say that it is appropriate that we first give due recognition to those who helped initiate and sustain the course. Robert M. Moulton, Jr., chaired the committee on university health where the need for such a course was first discussed. His interest and support, along with that of Robert R. Sears (who was at the time Dean of Humanities and Sciences at Stanford and a member of the committee) were crucial. Since then help and encouragement have come from many quarters. David A. Hamburg's broad conception of psychiatry legitimized our involvement in this field. The university unfailingly provided the necessary financial and administrative support. We have been the grateful recipients of much encouragement from the faculty as well as from other members of the Stanford community. Ultimately our most important supporters have been our students, for without their enthusiastic response neither the course nor this book would exist today.

During the early phases of the preparation of this book we profited greatly from visits to the Institute for Sex Research at the University of Indiana. Director Paul Gebhard and others on his staff have been helpful in numerous ways. The Institute is well known for its publications, but deserves wider recognition for the informal, yet important, educational job it fulfills.

A number of colleagues and friends read parts of the manuscript and made specific, as well as general, comments. We are particularly grateful in this regard to Anthony Amsterdam, Frank A. Beach, Paul and Anne Ehrlich, Fred Elmadjian, Julian M. Davidson, Paul H. Gebhard, H. Duane Heath, Raeburne Heimbeck, Donald Laub, Erich Lindemann, John Messenger, George L. Mizner, Karl Pribram, Stephen A. Robins, John Romano, Leslie Squier, Judge George W. Phillips, Jr., Sherwood L. Washburn, Archdeacon John Weaver, and Lee H. Yearley.

H.A.K.
D.T.L.

January 1975

Preface to the Third Edition

In the five years since the publication of the second edition, *Fundamentals of Human Sexuality* has found wide use in human sexuality courses in the United States and Canada. During this period the authors and the publisher have received many letters of comment from instructors who have taught from the book. While these comments generally have been favorable, they have contained useful suggestions for revision. Many of the changes made in the third edition stem from these suggestions.

While retaining the three-part organization—Biology, Behavior, Culture—the authors have made a number of additions, deletions, and changes in organization.

Chapter 12 in the second edition, Sexual Disorders, has been divided into two chapters: Diseases of the Sex Organs (new Chapter 7) concludes Part I, and Sexual Malfunctions and Treatment (Chapter 12) concludes Part II. This permits a logical separation of diseases of sex organs from sexual malfunctions and their treatment.

Chapter 7 (Sexual Behavior) and Chapter 8 (Psychosexual Development) from the second edition have been combined in new Chapter 8, Sexual Behavior through the Lifespan. In this combined chapter the flow of sexual development over a lifetime is effectively presented and there is increased coverage of sexuality in the later years.

Chapter 11, Homosexuality and Other Sexual Behaviors, in this edition provides expanded coverage of homosexuality as well as a fuller discussion of rape.

Chapter 13, Sex and Society (the first chapter of Part III), new to this edition, deals with changing sexual attitudes and behavior from a sociological perspective.

Three chapters, The Erotic in Art, The Erotic in Literature, and The Erotic in Film have been deleted in this edition. The decision was made as a result of considerable soul-searching and controversy and with real regret. It was based upon two concerns: length and the priority of usefulness in teaching. The third edition could not be longer than the second and to accommodate new material some cutting had to be done. In view of user comments indicating that these three chapters were often not assigned, the decision was made to delete them. In addition, Chapter 18, Human Sexuality: Current Trends, has been deleted and the material that it included has been added to the appropriate chapters.

All chapters have been substantially brought up to date, including reference to the most recent research findings.

Recognizing the difficulty that male writers have in reflecting the woman's as well as the man's experience and perception of human sexuality, particular heed has been paid to the suggestions of women reviewers. Their comments have been an invaluable aid in balancing the picture.

A new feature in this edition is the addition of boxed material throughout. The boxed material is designed to highlight particularly interesting information, to provide expanded documentation, and to amplify points in the text.

The division of labor between the co-authors was as follows: Katchadourian wrote the introductory chapter, the chapters on anatomy, physiology, sexual behavior through the lifespan, autoeroticism, sexual intercourse, and sexual malfunctions and treatment. Lunde was responsible for chapters on hormones, conception and pregnancy, contraception, diseases of the sex organs, homosexuality and other sexual behaviors, sex and society, law, and morality. In the revision of his chapters Lunde received invaluable assistance from John and Jan-ice Baldwin of the University of California, Santa Barbara. The revised chapters and the new sex and society chapter were planned by Lunde and the Baldwins, the Baldwins revised the chapters, and then on the basis of Lunde's critiques prepared final drafts. The Baldwins, sociologists by training, and experienced in teaching the human sexuality course, bring a fresh perspective to the chapters that they prepared.

The Publisher

January 1980

Contents

Chapter 1

Fundamental Questions about Human Sexuality

Given the universality of sex, we would expect a great deal to be known about it. But this is not the case, partly because sexual behavior is variable and partly because all societies regulate sexual activity. This control restricts both the observation of sexual behavior and the access to information about it. We can therefore neither generalize from personal experience nor investigate freely.

Of the innumerable questions that can be asked about the sexual life of humans, three are of primary importance: Why do we behave sexually? How do we behave sexually? And how should we behave sexually?

Our task in this book is to provide information to help answer these questions.

Why We Behave Sexually

There are certain physiological functions, like eating, whose primary purpose is immediately obvious. Even though food preferences vary widely among individuals and groups, everyone must eat something: fish or fowl, raw or cooked, with or without fork and knife, and so on. Similarly, unused food matter must be eliminated from the bowels regardless of the social customs attached to the process. No society can interfere with the physiological functions of eating and elimination without jeopardizing life.

What about sex? Can it be compared to either of these two functions? Both comparisons have been tried, but neither is quite adequate. We can, of course, refer metaphorically to "sexual hunger." In fact, at certain times people and animals may prefer copulating to eating. Nevertheless, sex is not an activity necessary to sustain life, except in the broad sense of species preservation. In fact, there is no generally agreed on evidence that abstinence from sexual activity is even necessarily detrimental to health.

The comparison to elimination also has some superficial validity, as most men do ejaculate periodically. But women experience orgasm and do not ejaculate, so the comparison is not appropriate. At best, therefore, we can speak only of periodic neurophysiological "discharge" through orgasm, with the understanding that sexual activity is not literally the "discharging" of anything that would otherwise be "dammed up."

Although comparisons to other body functions may be inadequate, we can hardly deny that the origins of human sexual behavior are rooted in biological makeup. But we must also consider other factors because, although indispensable, biology is not all there is to sex. All behavior is ultimately the interactional outcome of three types of forces—

biological, psychological, and social. In discussing these determinants of sexual behavior, we do not intend to imply that a choice among these factors is necessary; it is understood that they are complementary and integrated rather than mutually exclusive.

Biological Origins of Sexuality

Biological explanations of sexual behavior have generally been based on the concept of instinct. This notion of an innate force has proved quite useful, but scientists have so far failed to define specifically enough what terms like "instinct" and "drive" mean.

As sex and reproduction are so intimately linked in most living beings, we tend to forget that there are also asexual modes of reproduction and organisms that duplicate themselves merely by dividing into two identical "daughter cells." Sexual reproduction, in which two dissimilar cells (sperm and egg) combine to form a new being, is nevertheless the reproductive mode of most animals, including humans.

It is thus understandable that one explanation of sexual behavior is simply the need to reproduce. Sex, in this sense, is part of a larger reproductive "instinct," a deep-rooted biological incentive for animals to mate and perpetuate their species. But lower animals cannot possibly know that mating results in reproduction. For that matter, we do not know who made the momentous discovery, at some point in prehistory, that coitus leads to pregnancy. As lower animals are ignorant of this association, what mysterious force propels them to mate?

Although the reproductive consequences of copulation are obvious to us, sexual behavior cannot be scientifically explained in teleological terms, as behavior in which animals engage in order to reproduce. Besides, a great deal of animal and especially of human sexual activity serves no reproductive function.

A simpler and more likely explanation is that humans and other animals engage in sex because it is pleasurable. The incentive is in the act itself, rather than in its possible consequences. Sexual behavior in this sense arises from a psychological "drive," associated with sensory pleasure, and its reproductive consequences are a by-product (though a vital one). We are only beginning to understand the neurophysiological basis of pleasure. It has been demonstrated, for example, that there are "pleasure centers" in the brain (in the thalamus, hypothalamus, and mesencephalon) that, when electrically stimulated, cause animals to experience intense pleasure. (Stimulation of certain adjacent areas causes extreme discomfort or pain.) When an animal has the opportunity to stimulate these pleasure centers, it will persist in doing so to the exclusion of all other activity: It will not take time to eat even when starving.

What about sex hormones? They are a fascinating but currently problematic subject of study. We know, for instance, that they begin to exert their influence before birth and are vital in sexual development. Yet, in the mature animal they seem relatively dispensable to the maintenance of sexual functioning. Although these hormones are intimately linked to sexual functioning, the link is clearly not a simple one, and we have yet to discover a substance that might represent a true "sex fuel."

Thus, the biological basis of our sexual behavior involves certain physical "givens," including sex organs, hormones, intricate networks of nerves, and brain centers. How these components are constructed and how they work will occupy us in Part I of this book.

Psychological Determinants of Sexual Behavior

If biological explanations of sexuality were totally satisfactory, it would not be necessary for us to go farther. But, as they do not at this time suffice, we must look for additional factors to explain sexual behavior.

In discussing psychological determinants of behavior, we often must deal with different levels of analysis of the human organism. In one sense, psychological or social forces are merely reflections and manifestations of underlying biological processes. For example, Freud argued that the libido, or sex drive, is the psychological representation of a biological sex instinct.

In another sense psychological factors are independent of the biological, even though they must be mediated through the neurophysiological mechanisms of the brain, for neither thought nor emotion can occur in an empty skull. But these mechanisms are considered only as the intermediaries through which thought and emotions operate, rather than as their primary determinants. Let us again use hunger as an example. When the brain motivates a person to eat, in response to a feeling of hunger (due to certain sensations in the gastrointestinal system or to a decrease in blood sugar), the response of the individual is relatively independent of psychological and social considerations. Although such factors have some influence on the individual's behavior, they are not the main determinants. Yet if a person dislikes pork or is expected to abstain from eating it, he acts from personal preference or religious conviction. His motivation is still mediated through the brain, but it originates in learned patterns of behavior rather than in biological factors. We have used the example of hunger, rather than of sex itself, because in the latter the biological imperative is less clear.

Theories of the psychological motivation for sexual behavior are fundamentally of two types. In the first, which includes psychoanalytic theory, psychological factors are considered to be representations or extensions of biological forces. In contrast, many learning theories assume that patterns of sexual behavior are largely acquired through a variety of psychological and social mechanisms. In Chapter 8 we shall discuss this issue in greater detail.

While the causes or determinants of a given type of behavior must not be confused with the purposes that it serves, and though such distinctions are not always easy to recognize, it is also useful to examine the various aims of sexual behavior. For instance, when a person engages in sex expressly to satisfy physical desire or to relieve "sexual tension," we may say that sex occurs "for its own sake." But for most people sex has an emotional component as well; it takes on added significance as an expression of affection or love for the partner. We can argue whether this affective component ought to be a basic part of sex or a desirable addition to it, and this question will be considered later in this chapter.

If we assume that the primary goals of sexuality are reproduction and the attainment of pleasure, a number of secondary, though by no means unimportant, goals can be discerned that are "nonsexual." Paramount among these is the use of sex as a vehicle for expressing and obtaining love. This may involve deep and genuine affection or its shallow and stereotyped parodies. Women have been traditionally more likely to barter their bodies for such emotional security and reassurance. Adolescent girls may indulge in promiscuous but joyless sexual encounters to maintain popularity and acceptance by their peers. Underneath such behavior is a defense against loneliness, which is effective at best for a brief period and must therefore be frantically repeated and sustained. Similar considerations apply to males who are also likely to be driven to sexual exploits to defend against self-doubts about masculinity and power. The contribution of sex to self-esteem is most important. Each of us needs a deep and firmly rooted conviction of personal worth. Although no one can hope to be universally loved and admired, we must receive some appreciation from "significant others" and from ourselves. An important component of a person's self-esteem is his sexual standing in his own eyes, as well as in the eyes of others. The role of sex in self-esteem varies among individuals and groups, and some sexual attributes have more widespread significance than others. A man who is impotent is likely to lose confidence in himself and to feel uncertain and incompetent even in areas in which sexual virility has no direct bearing. Others may be driven to compensate for their sexual weaknesses by acquiring political power, wealth, or knowledge, or through antisocial behavior.

In contrast, women have traditionally been much less concerned about their ability to experience orgasm, though this attitude is changing, at least in the West. In some conservative groups in the Middle East, for instance, a woman who fails to reach coital orgasm may be aware of a lack, but her self-esteem is not affected by it. The disaster for her is not frigidity but sterility.

The more striking changes in female awareness of orgasm have been occurring in the West, particularly in countries long influenced by the "Victorian ethic." Respectable Victorian women, for instance, risked actual loss of self-esteem if they experienced sexual pleasure (at least, so the predominantly male chroniclers of the age tell us). In contrast, the sophisticated modern Western woman is rapidly becoming as preoccupied with orgasm as males are, and as vulnerable to loss of self-esteem at failure.

For some women, however, the association between sex and self-esteem has always seemed less direct than for men. Women have tended to be more concerned with being attractive, desirable, and lovable, and deficiencies in these attributes are more apt to damage their self-esteem than sexual responsiveness as such. Also, these attributes and sexual responsiveness are often mutually enhancing: A woman who feels admired and desired is more likely to respond sexually, and a responsive woman in turn is more ardently desired. Currently, for increasing numbers of women, the importance of being a sexually alive and responsive person is becoming more central to their lives.

Sexuality is clearly an important component of an individual's self-concept or sense of identity. Awareness of sexual differentiation precedes that of all other social attributes in the child: The child knows the self as a boy or girl long before it learns to associate the self with national, ethnic, religious, and other cultural groupings.

Although developing an awareness of one's biological sex is a relatively simple matter, the acquisition of a sense of sexual identity is a more complex culturally relative process. Traditionally we have assumed that biological sex (maleness and femaleness) and its psychological attributes (masculinity and femininity) are two sides of the same coin. In traditional and stable societies this assumption may have been (and may still be) valid. But in the technologically advanced and structurally more fluid societies such direct correspondence between biological sex and psychological attributes is being challenged more and more vigorously as occupational and social roles for men and women become progressively blurred. There is an extensive literature on the topic of sex differences to which we shall make further references, and we shall discuss the entire topic more fully in Chapter 8.

Finally, sex figures prominently in an individual's moral or spiritual identity. At least in Western cultures it is used as a moral yardstick more consistently than any other form of behavior, at both the personal and public levels. Many of us feel greater guilt and are often punished more severely for sexual transgressions than for other offenses. Common as sexual themes are in our mass media, the level of tolerance is nowhere near that for aggression and violence.

Although both personal and public attitudes are changing in this regard, a common first reaction as to whether or not a person (particularly a woman) is moral or "honorable" is to think in sexual terms. We are not implying that this should or should not be so, but are merely pointing out the enormous influence that sex has on our standing as individuals and members of society.

Social Factors in Sexual Behavior

Just as psychological functions are intimately linked with biological forces, so they are equally tied to social factors. In fact, distinctions between what is primarily psychological and what is social often tend to be arbitrary. As a rule, in referring to social or cultural factors the emphasis is on the interpersonal over the intrapsychic and on group processes over internal ones.

Sexuality is often considered a cohesive force that binds the family together. In this sense it is subservient to a social goal, and social organizations reciprocally facilitate sexual aims by providing sexual partners and contacts. Sexuality can also have a divisive influence, and this potential may be one reason for the ambivalence with which sex is viewed in many societies.

Sex also functions as a form of communication. The very act of giving oneself to another fully, willingly, and joyfully can be an exquisite means of expressing affection. But sex can also be used as a weapon to convey dominance and anger. When, after coming home from a party, a wife who is sexually aroused refuses to sleep with her husband because he has been flirting with other women, she may be using sex to communicate a message ("I am angry") and a lesson ("Next time behave yourself"). In a similar situation a husband may impose sex on his wife or even discreetly entice her into it primarily to show his mastery over her. Similarly, promiscuous sexual activity may communicate messages like "I am lonely," "I am not impotent," "I dare to misbehave," and so on.

Sex also symbolizes status. Like male animals in a troop, men with power in society have had first choice of the more desirable females. Beauty is naturally pleasing to the eye, but beyond this attraction the company of a beautiful woman is taken as a testimony and a tribute to a man's social standing. A woman's status is more often enhanced by the social importance than by the looks of the man. The value of sex as an indicator of status prompts men in some cultures to keep mistresses; similarly, in prison a dominant male inmate may have a "girl" (a sexually submissive male). In both instances, the actual sexual interest may be quite desultory.

As women gain true parity with men, these attitudes obviously undergo profound changes. Apart from the consequences of sexual discrimination, it is worth reflecting on what it means to use another person for purposes of self-aggrandizement.

The association of sex and aggression is very broad and encompasses biological, psychological, and social considerations. We need only point out here that aggressive impulses may be expressed through sexual behavior and vice-versa, and that there is a fluid and intimate relation between these two powerful "drives" in all kinds of sexual liaisons.

For some people sexual activity is a form of self-expression in a creative, or esthetic, sense. What matters most is not simple physical pleasure, but the broadening of sensual horizons with each experience, and the opportunity to express and share these experiences in a very special and intimate way with another person. Such feelings, though very real, are difficult to describe.

In various places and at various times sex has been used for the loftiest, as well as for the basest, ends. Although sexuality is foreign to the major Western traditions of religious worship, other religions have had distinctly sexual components, as the erotic statuary adorning Indian temples and phallic monuments from Classical times attest.

On balance, sex has been more crassly and mercilessly exploited than any other human need. The female body in particular has been used as a commodity since remotest antiquity. Although women have benefited financially from prostitution, men have had more than their share of profits from this commerce. Prostitution is the most flagrant example of the use of sex for practical gain, but it is by no means the only one. Sexual favors are exchanged for other services between spouses and friends. Sex is used to maintain social standing, to gain popularity, to ensnare and hold spouses and mates, and so on. The overt and covert use of sex in advertising hardly needs to be pointed out.

Other uses of sex are legion. The ancient Romans wore amulets in the form of male sex organs. Some people use sex to cure headaches, to calm their nerves, or to end insomnia. Sex can thus be used for "nonsexual" as well as "sexual" ends. Conversely, sexual gratification can be achieved through orgasm as well as by the displacement and sublimation of the sexual drive with countless ordinary and extraordinary "nonsexual" activities.

How We Behave Sexually

As causation is complex, it is understandable that we do not have satisfactory answers to our first question. We might hope, however, that answers to our second question would be relatively easy, for all that is theoretically required is the observation of behavior rather than attempts to fathom human motivation. But, in fact, we are frequently in the dark on questions of how we behave sexually as well, and this ignorance may be an important cause of our ignorance of causation. After all, if we do not know enough about *how* people behave, how can we investigate *why* they behave as they do?

A comprehensive view of human sexual behavior would require knowledge of current sexual behavior in our own society, the history of sexual behavior and how it has changed over the centuries, sexual behavior in other cultures and its historical roots, and, finally, the sexual behavior of animals.

Although it is customary (for good reason) to decry our ignorance in these matters, we actually do have a great deal of information (and a great deal more misinformation) on human sexual behavior, even though it is uneven and scattered. Most of this information can be found in three sources: art and literature, clinical reports, and ethnographic and statistical surveys.

Since the Paleolithic cave painters of *c.* 15,000 years B.C., artists have portrayed sexual activities. As a result we have a wealth of information, despite repeated and often successful attempts to conceal, distort, and destroy it.

Writers of all periods have also recorded descriptions, observations, and speculations on the sex life of humans. More recently, films have become an important vehicle for the portrayal of sexual behavior.

Clinical interest in sexual functioning also goes back to antiquity, but more intensive (some people think excessive) concern with sexual behavior is a twentieth-century phenomenon. The primary interests of the clinician have been aberrations and malfunctions. We can also learn a great deal about the normal through studies of the abnormal, as long as inferences are made with full awareness of the potential pitfalls.

Surveys of sexual behavior are generally of two types. In the first, observations are primarily descriptive. Anthropologists and travelers have, for instance, provided fascinating accounts of sexual activities in distant lands. The second type of survey is more systematic in attempting to describe sexual behavior in quantifiable terms, relating the activities of specially selected samples to other significant characteristics. The Kinsey studies are the best-known examples of this type of survey. In Chapters 8 through 12 we shall make extensive use of data from both types of surveys, as well as from clinical sources. The more important sources of information that we have used are discussed later in this chapter.

Interest in animal behavior has until recently been restricted to zoologists. Now, however, we are becoming more aware of the relevance of data on animal behavior (particularly that of primates) to the understanding of human behavior. Just as cross-cultural data provide us with comparisons of how various societies organize certain behaviors, cross-species comparisons may eventually permit us to trace the biological roots of our behavior. We can also learn about biology from cross-cultural studies and about social systems from cross-species comparisons, for there are biological constants in all cultures, and social organization is not an exclusively human characteristic.

How We Should Behave Sexually

Our third question is primarily, though not exclusively, a moral one. In addition to more strictly moral judgments, we must take into account, for instance, health considerations, factors that will enhance sexual satisfaction, and social customs and conventions that carry no moral weight but define courtesy, decency, and so on. At worst these codes are hollow rituals that needlessly complicate life, offer arrogant badges of status, and serve as tools of intimidation. At best they make social intercourse more comfortable and gracious. Although we must bear in mind these wider implications of the question, we shall be concerned here mainly with the more specifically moral aspects of sexual behavior.

Assessments of behavior, sexual or otherwise, are generally made according to four criteria. First is the statistical norm: How common is the behavior? Second is the medical norm: Is the behavior healthy? Third is the

ethical norm: Is the behavior moral? Fourth is the legal norm: Is the behavior legitimate?

It would be helpful if these four criteria were mutually reinforcing, or at least not contradictory. For instance, unprovoked murder during peacetime is infrequent, obviously unhealthy for the victim, morally inadmissible by almost everyone, and illegal in practically all societies. It would be difficult, however, to find other examples that are quite so clearcut. In actual practice we must judge behavior primarily according to one or another of these criteria, but there is a strong tendency to seek corroboration from the rest. In fact, one set of judgments is often predicated on another. For example, an act is considered immoral or illegal because it is unhealthy or offends the majority (or the reverse). In addition, we seek to strengthen arguments against behavior that we wish to suppress: An activity that we consider immoral seems worse if it is indulged in by only a few, is unhealthy, and is also illegal.

The application of such judgments to sexual behavior in heterogeneous and pluralistic societies has resulted in much confusion. The meaning of the statistical norm has been distorted, partly through ignorance and partly deliberately. Medical judgments have often lacked scientific support. Morality has been confused with tradition and the idiosyncrasies of those in power. Statutes and ordinances have frozen into law many dubious factual claims and moral conclusions. Not infrequently the original determination that an act is unhealthy or uncommon turns out to be incorrect or no longer applicable, but the moral and legal judgments based on it persist.

Sexual morality requires judgments on a wide range of specific activities. Some activities are exceedingly rare. Others are so destructive or disruptive that no society, no matter how tolerant, can possibly condone them. We certainly cannot have "free rape" and so far no society has managed widespread "free love" (in which anyone can sleep with anyone else whenever they choose).

Even if morality could be set aside, it would be unrealistic to believe that we could always benefit from such arrangements without paying any price for them. For practical purposes, moral issues become matters of general concern when disapproved behavior are attractive to many people and not barred by overwhelming practical considerations.

According to an old saying, a stiff penis has no conscience. The world, however, is not populated by penises and vaginas but by men and women, and they do have consciences. In fact, the moral questions related to sex, as well as to any other area of life, may well be the most critical ones. They certainly are the most difficult.

There are several well-known approaches to the discussion of sexual ethics. First is the straitlaced attitude, which at its worst stands for dullness, hypocritcal double standards, tedious lists of ''don'ts'' with a few ''dos'' (that are hardly worth doing), and an outlook that generally inhibits all that is spontaneous, imaginative, and exciting in sex.

The opposite alternative is the callously libertine approach advocated by assorted sexual ''liberators.'' Their central message is a cavalier insistence on discarding sexual shackles and casting off all inhibitions. The proponents and practitioners of this ethic are not always concerned with the consequences of their acts and even less bothered by offending the sensibilities of others.

Then there is the intermediary stance that is becoming increasingly prevalent, whereby permissiveness is tempered with consideration. There is little concern with abstract principle in this stance; the attitude is rather one of ''as long as it gives pleasure to all concerned and hurts no one, it is moral.''

In the search for a sexual ethic it is tempting to bypass basic moral issues by dismissing them as ''philosophical'' abstractions of no practical immediacy and instead to try to go directly to the specifics of sexual behavior. This shortcut usually fails, for before we can sensibly discuss whether premarital sex, for example, is right or wrong, we must agree on what ''right'' and ''wrong'' mean. Nor can we be satisfied with the mere enunciation of moral generalities, for the specifics of sexual acts must also be recognized: Agreeing that sexual exploitation is wrong is insufficient to determine whether or not certain episodes of premarital sex are wrong. Premarital sex may or may not be exploitative, and, besides, exploitation is not the only basis of moral judgment.

The answer to a given moral question is dependent on the content and application of specific principles. For example, the following considerations could enter into judgments about heterosexual intercourse: Children are best raised by their parents; sex is most satisfying in the context of stable relationships; and secrecy is inimical to honest relationships. In a particular sexual act these components (*content*) of moral judgment are then *applied* to the specific act. In the case of extramarital intercourse it is likely that children resulting from the union will not be reared by both parents or that children in an existing marriage will lose a parent; that the relationship will be unstable; and that the relationship will have to be kept secret. Therefore such acts could be judged morally wrong on any or all counts.

In contemporary Western society, however, neither the content of moral judgment nor their applications are agreed on. In this example, some people would argue that it is preferable to raise children in communes, that casual sexual encounters can be satisfying and need not result in pregnancy, that it is possible to have stable relationships without benefit of marriage, and that what you do not know will not hurt you. There are marked differences of opinion in these matters between groups divided along generational, educational, and socioeconomic lines. Even within the clergy of the same denomination opinions are likely to be conflicting.

Faced with these uncertainties we are forced to reconsider basic ethical issues. But we cannot do that in a book of this kind. We could take a "neutral" position and raise many questions and answer none, which would offer no practical help. To take a polemical stance in defense of one or another moral code would be inconsistent with the basic purpose of this book. The least objectionable solution to the dilemma appears to us to present various ethical alternatives and argue for "common sense" positions which, although lacking the force of moral truth, may serve as workable points of reference. We shall, therefore, next examine certain features of moral judgments that are especially pertinent to sexual behavior. These include the distinctions between private and public morality, absolute and relative moral stands, and changes in moral values.

Private and Public Morality

Moral principles seem to derive their authority from various sources: divine revelation, social customs, legal statutes, and so on. When religious institutions are strong, they tend to enforce their moral codes through the civil authorities. As the industrial West has become progressively more secularized, church and state have, at least in principle, separated their spheres of influence. In other cultures the law of the land is still based on religious documents (for example, the Koran in Saudi Arabia). Even in the West there are wide differences on this point, depending on particular religious institutions and political systems: The Catholic Church in Italy and the Lutheran Church in Sweden exercise different kinds of influence.

In the realm of sexual behavior there is increasing awareness of the need to distinguish between private and public behavior, especially when the former involves acts between consenting adults conducted in private. The trend now is toward viewing such behavior as beyond the right of society to regulate it. But because a behavior is legal does not necessarily mean it is healthy or moral.

Sexual behavior becomes public when it is carried out before others or when others' individual rights are violated. Although standards obviously vary, all societies attempt to regulate public sexual behavior in one way or another. There is no record of a totally "free" community in this respect. Judgments, moral as well as legal, are important in both private and public life, but they should not be confused.

Our intent here is not to equate morality with legality but rather to draw attention to how and why we discriminate between certain forms of behavior. In some cases, such as marital coitus, the act may be viewed as immoral and illegal only if it is performed in public. Yet, oral-genital contact is, at least to some, deemed morally and legally objectionable even if engaged in in private.

Absolute versus Relative Standards

Should moral judgments be absolute and independent of all other considerations, or should they be relative depending on circumstances? This question has been debated for centuries, yet each thoughtful person must face it for himself or herself.

Absolute moral stances are usually based on religious conviction, but may also be supported by universal philosophical principles. For example: "You shall not commit adultery" (Exodus 20:14) is an absolute command that makes no allowances for "special situations."

Absolutist standards are clear and unambiguous, assuming one understands the basic premises. They obviate soul-searching on every occasion, and help people to live according to their beliefs by minimizing personal choice and the likelihood of self-deception. While thus doing justice to the spirit, however, they tend to neglect the flesh. They may be useful as reminders of the basic weakness of humans, but they do not function effectively as regulators of human behavior, or do so only at the cost of severe sexual deprivation.

Another difficulty with absolute codes is their rigidity. There are special circumstances in which most people are inclined to forgive if not to condone certain behavior. For instance, to use an extreme example, what does one say to a mother in the ghetto who prostitutes herself to feed her children? Hypothetically there may be other solutions to her poverty, but what if practically there are none? In condemning such a woman are we obeying the letter of the moral law but violating its spirit? Because of such considerations even absolutist doctrines frequently make tacit concessions to circumstance, and thus become to some degree relative.

The more frankly relativistic approach, it is argued, provides the individual, male or female, with a sense of autonomy, without so many stifling rules and regulations. The moral absolutist who believes that premarital intercourse is wrong must face each opportunity with gloom. He or she is damned with guilt if he yields and damned with frustration if he does not. The moral relativist faces frustration too, should he decide to abstain, but otherwise he is free to yield with joy. He thus approaches each opportunity with spontaneity and hope, for he can decide on the merits of the situation. A devout religious believer would shake his head at this logic, for it makes of morality a purely human enterprise. A cynic would shake his head because it seems unrealistically optimistic.

At worst a relativistic morality can be purely self-serving. One does what one wants to do and then rationalizes it. Justifications may be serious ("He/she loves me") or trivial ("Let's do it because it's New Year's Eve"). At its most responsible, relative morality is conditional on some profound principle like *agape* or selfless love. But even then it is not clear how we can be certain that the necessary conditions are fulfilled or what happens

to sexual desire in their absence. What if the consequences of an act performed for the loftiest of motives prove harmful to one or the other participant or to a third party?

Morality and Change

That individuals and institutions change their moral views over time can hardly be disputed. Furthermore, change is usually initiated by the young, and often appears bewilderingly rapid to those experiencing its effects. The following statement is more than forty years old, but for some could as well have been written today:

The younger generation is behaving like a crazy man who for one lucid moment has suddenly realized that the physicians in charge are all demented, too. The elders who have for so long been the sacred guardians of civilization have bungled their task so abominably as to have lost irrevocably their influence for sobriety and sanity with the youth of the world. The failure of the church to treat sex and natural impulse with dignity and candor is the largest single fact in that disintegration of personal codes which confronts us in these hectic times: the inevitable swing of the pendulum from concealment to exhibitionism, from repression to expression, from reticence to publicity, from modesty to vulgarity. This revolutionary transition is inevitable and essentially wholesome, for all its crudity and grotesquerie.[1]

Members of the "younger generation" to which this paragraph refers are now the grandparents of the contemporary college population.

It is also possible to argue, however, that today we are going through a particularly rapid and far-reaching process of change in our attitudes toward sex. For instance, a 1969 poll of 1,600 Americans in various walks of life revealed that 81 percent considered a policeman who takes money from a prostitute

---

[1]Calverton and Schmalhausen (1929), p. 11.

to be more immoral than the prostitute; 71 percent thought that a doctor who refuses a house call to a seriously ill patient is less moral than a homosexual; 54 percent regarded a politician who accepts bribes as more reprehensible than an adulterer.[2]

More recent polls show that while there may have been distinct changes in moral attitudes towards some aspects of sexual behavior, a substantial majority of Americans still profess their belief in the traditional values of family life. For instance in a nationwide poll of 1,044 registered voters, almost four out of five persons condemned extramarital sex and two out of three disapproved of teen-agers having sex relations. This is of course what people say; what they do may be another matter.[3]

There is no doubt that the availability of reliable and reasonably safe contraceptives has already had a major influence on sexual behavior, for moral and legal codes of sexual behavior have probably originated in large measure in concern about illegitimate offspring. The integrity of the family unit has had to be fiercely protected, for no culture can trifle with the upbringing of its progeny and hope to survive very long. It is possible, however, that such worries have now become less realistic and that certain traditional values, like reproductive fertility, are beginning to be viewed negatively.

As changes in deep-rooted sexual mores tend to be slow, no matter how dizzying they may appear, we have yet to experience the full impact of the new separation of sex from reproduction. Montagu ranks the significance of "the Pill" with that of the discovery of fire, learning how to make tools, the development of urbanism, the growth of scientific medicine, and the harnessing of nuclear energy.[4]

[2]Changing morality . . . (1969).
[3]*The New Morality* (1977). Based on Yankelovich poll.
[4]Montagu (1969), p. 11.

Fundamental Standards for Sexual Behavior

Given the uncertainties about why and how people behave sexually and the confusion between judgments of private and public behavior, the dilemma of absolute versus relative moral standards, and changing moral values, how do we decide how we should behave sexually here and now?

Most of us do not regulate our sex lives formally. At best we have general feelings about how we should behave sexually. Most of us conform out of inertia or fear and break rules mainly on impulse. We reject some activities totally because of the enormity of their social consequences or the threats that they pose to our self-esteem. We find others unappealing or difficult of access. When we change our moral views, we usually do so with guilt and primarily to justify acts already committed. Hopefully, some of us also grow wiser with time.

Our behavior and attitudes are determined by complex and often unconscious processes that explain the apparent irrationality with which we conduct our lives. That is "human nature," and little can be done to change it. We are not, however, totally helpless in this respect, even though it may be convenient to assume that we are. At some point every thoughtful and responsible person must exercise "free will" and make choices. The first, and basic, choice is whether he wants to be a "moral" person, by whatever standard, or to take what he can for himself and the rest of the world be damned. The ambiguities and difficulties in making ethical judgments can be used as an excuse for avoiding them altogether: As no one really "knows" what constitutes right and wrong, why pay attention to them at all? Why not do as we please and let other people fend for themselves?

Unless we begin with a readiness at least to make reasonable efforts to act "morally," it is pointless to engage in discussions of sexual ethics. Yet, even such honest willingness to be moral may be insufficient by itself without additional guidelines. The Golden Rule[5] or some version of it, is probably as universal an ethical yardstick as any available. Its central purpose is to make us concerned about how our acts influence the welfare of others as well as our own. In the philosopher Emmanuel Kant's terms, it forces us to consider the consequences of our behavior if everyone else were also to behave likewise.

The Golden Rule is nevertheless no moral panacea. Its literal application would obviously be relativistic; in the extreme it would lead to absurd situations: A masochist, for example, would be entitled to hurt someone else because he presumably welcomes such treatment himself. Since we often do not know what is in our own best interest, how can we treat others in the light of how we would want them to treat us? Thus, even if we all agreed to act on such a rule, we would still need to know how to behave in actual practice under ambiguous and changing social conditions. Such "Golden Rules" therefore are not blueprints for action, but "a point of view from which to consider acts."[6]

A corollary test of moral intent, aside from observation of the Golden Rule, is to test how far a person is willing to extend his area of concern. Some avowed criminals have loyalties to limited circles of friends, perhaps simply as extensions of their own self-interests. To qualify as a moral code, concern must extend beyond such self-seeking attachment to circumscribed groups. In general, the wider the circle of concern, the more genuine is the moral awareness. Ultimately, some recognition must be extended to everyone, on the basis of his humanity alone and regardless of social or psychological characteristics and

affiliations. It takes very little effort to be considerate of those whom we love, need, or fear. The value of morality is in influencing behavior when such factors are not operative. Willingness to be a "moral" person is a necessary first step, but does not automatically resolve the problem of morality. We also have to know how to act morally. Given the strength of sexual needs, the multiplicity of sexual aims, and the pressures of specific situations, it seems reasonable to seek a fundamental standard to guide us in satisfying our sexual needs in pleasurable yet "moral" ways. Our choice of such a standard is likely to reflect (through agreement or rebellion) the values of our families and culture. But, in order to be meaningful and workable, the standard must be a basically personal set of principles, self-enforced. Such standards cannot therefore be either proposed or adopted wholesale. They must be evolved over time and through experience. The most that other people can do for us is to suggest certain considerations that may be useful in this process, and that is what we intend to do here.

In order to do justice to sexual needs, as well as to realistic limitations on sexual expression, a fundamental standard must be located at a sensible point between absolute and purely relative on the moral continuum. Furthermore, this position must be fairly stable without being rigid. Bohannan differentiates between ethical principle, which is absolute, and morality, which is relative.[7] The standard of behavior should be a workable combination of ethical and moral principles.

These recommendations are easier to offer than to follow. When yesterday's sin becomes today's virtue, what do we say to those (or ourselves) who after years of self-denial discover that the rules of the game have changed? How do we learn discipline and teach it to our children, knowing that standards may change once again?

---

[5]Matthew 7:12. "Whatsoever ye would that men should do to you do ye even so to them."

[6]Dewey (1960), p. 142. *See also* p. 2 of Dewey for a list of works that have strongly influenced the development of the theory of morals.

[7]Bohannan (1969), Chapter 13.

There are no ready answers to these questions. Above all, we must be at peace with our own consciences. But we also must learn to live in society, and it is not always easy to reconcile these two imperatives.

To live in society in reasonable peace we have to know its rules and to be able to differentiate between those that can be broken with relative impunity and those that cannot. But what if the rules are irrational or unfair? Is adjustment to society the ultimate goal? The answers again involve personal choices. Most people follow the main trends of sexual behavior, and this majority provides stability. Many people, however, refuse to conform, and some attempt to change others' behavior as well. Those who do should remember that deviation from the norm and forging ahead of one's time are the prerogatives of prophets and fools: Since the ratio appears to be in favor of the latter, one must be sure of his calling. Despite these imponderables, can we isolate some components of a fundamental standard of sexual behavior? There are at least five that seem worthy of major consideration.

Acceptance of Sexual Realities

Knowledge and acceptance of sexual realities are indispensable to sexual fulfillment and honesty. First comes the willingness to recognize biological facts, including practical knowledge (not necessarily from formal study) of the sexual organs and their functions. More important is acceptance of sexual feelings as legitimate biological and psychological manifestations, rather than as afflictions that must be exorcised or only grudgingly tolerated.

Next is a willingness to accept behavioral facts, to recognize how people behave, regardless of how we think that they ought to behave. People have remarkable capacities for self-deception. When an investigator reports statistics on the prevalence of some socially unacceptable behavior, there is always a public outcry. People object not because

they have more reliable data but because the findings "don't make sense." "There cannot be so many homosexuals," they may say; but what they mean is that there should not be so many homosexuals. The tendency to think in stereotypes is often as strong as the tendency to deny: According to some people, for example, any artist or intellectual, any man who is refined or gentle is a homosexual.

The behavioral realities are there, whether we recognize them or not. By ignoring, distorting, or denying them we merely fool ourselves. On the other hand, recognizing reality does not necessarily require condoning it.

Of all the various phases of our sex lives perhaps the most crucial is how well we face up to our own sexual thoughts and feelings. It is not possible to come to terms with ourselves as long as we refuse to confront our own sexuality. Some extraordinary individuals willingly recognize their sexual needs, yet delay or inhibit satisfying those needs for what they consider to be higher causes. That is one thing; simply to look away is another. We must be honest with ourselves and others in all things, but especially in sex, for in this area pretense wears thin, bravado sounds hollow, and in bluffing others we bluff ourselves.

Enhancing Sexuality

Sexuality is not a wild horse that must be tamed and then exercised periodically. It is a potential with which we are born and which must be developed and nourished. It is every bit as important to be concerned about fulfilling our sexual capabilities as about fulfilling our intellectual or artistic capabilities.

The biological origins of sexual functioning do not insure its automatic operation. Monkeys raised in isolation, for instance, do not know how to interact sexually. They are physically healthy and the sex drive is present, but the behavior that would lead to gratification is disorganized. Sexuality thus requires a certain milieu in which to develop. It needs warm contacts with other people, and it needs nurture.

To start with, there must be acceptance of the fundamental value of sex, in addition to acceptance of its reality. Such acceptance must come early and be incorporated into the personality structure of the child. His intimate relationships must enhance this feeling and permit the growth of his sexuality while instilling the restraints required for successful social living.

A fundamental standard must therefore include incentives as well as prohibitions. There is at times the assumption that one can do no wrong sexually as long as one does nothing at all. This approach is too negative and makes sexuality appear a necessary evil at best.

When a person enters a relationship that has a legitimate sexual component, is he not obligated to act effectively in a sexual way? When a parent does not provide for the family to the best of his or her ability or fails to care for the children, we rightfully condemn such a parent. But what about the spouse who makes no effort to maintain and improve his or her sexual attractiveness, who is lazy and inept in bed, and who tries to pass off sexual incompetence as innocence or decency?

Integrating Sex into Life as a Whole

Ultimately, sex must make sense in the context of one's overall life. At certain periods sexual pressure is overwhelming, and sometimes we go to great lengths for its sake. But these instances are unusual and transitory and generally give way to more prosaic but steady sexual needs.

The place that sex occupies in our overall lives varies from one person to another. It is possible that we are born with different genetic predispositions in drive strength. Physical characteristics certainly have great influence on personality development and sexual

behavior. For example, a pretty child discovers very early the impact of that fact on others. The families that rear us and the community values that we learn to share or reject combine to shape our sexual behavior.

For some people sex becomes the pivot of their lives. Others hardly seem to care. The important point is not how many orgasms we achieve during a week or in a lifetime but whether or not our sexual needs are satisfied in a manner consistent with the strength of our desires, the requirements of our consciences, and the basic goals and purposes of our lives.

As we shall discuss in Chapter 12 some sexual dissatisfactions are caused by false or excessive expectations. Gratifying as sex may be, we can derive only so much from it. It cannot be substituted for all other needs, just as substitution of other satisfactions for those of sex can also be stretched only so far.

A fundamental standard that does not facilitate the integration of sexuality into life as a whole has limited usefulness. There are those who feel or act morally in all respects but sexually; sex is thus their secret vice. To a degree such schisms may be unavoidable, but beyond certain limits they constitute points of weakness that are vulnerable to stress.

The Relation of Sex to Marriage

The aspect of heterosexual intercourse that raises the most frequent moral concern is whether it occurs within or outside of marriage. Marriage in its various forms is a universal institution. Sex almost always plays a part in it, but, of course, marriage involves much more than sex. At least in principle, however, there are important cultural differences in whether or not sex is restricted to marital partners.

In the West the traditional expectation has been that sex will be restricted in this way. In practice there have been many departures from this expectation, particularly among men. Currently the trend is toward less rigidity on this point for both sexes, particularly in relation to premarital sex. Statistical estimates of the incidence of virginity have been one of the more popular forms of sex research on university campuses. Extramarital coitus poses different kinds of problems, for it involves consideration of the spouse's feelings as well as of one's own conscience.

Because of the long-term mutual commitments of married couples, marital sex has particular significance. The marital relationship entails much more than sex. Nevertheless, sexual imcompatibility is a frequent cause of marital discord. Marital discord arising from other sources also leads to sexual problems. The issue is not how much sex is necessary or ''good'' for the couple but whether or not sex plays a mutually satisfactory role in the relationship.

These areas are the ones to which a fundamental standard must apply. The matter has been discussed time and again and continues to be a major topic.[8] We shall have occasion to return to it in Chapter 10.

Sex and Love

Each era and culture has had its views on love, and many of man's most eloquent expressions have been those of love. It is a tribute to the enduring strength of the sentiment to which it refers that the word ''love''—hackneyed, abused, and exploited as it has been—still retains so much meaning.

A common, and justified, criticism of ''sex manuals'' is that they neglect appropriate consideration of love: Either they omit mention of it altogether, or they include only insipid platitudes. By the same token, essays on love tend to neglect or etherealize sex to a point at which it seems more suited to angels than to human beings.

The relation of sex to love, like that of sex to marriage, is a frequent source of controversy. The well-known Western ideal attempts to combine all three: sex, love, and marriage. But relatively few people seem able to attain this ideal or to sustain it over periods of years. Currently, some people are willing to settle for love and sex alone, and love too may be on its way out as a necessary condition for sex. This change is viewed as moral degeneration by some people and as sexual regeneration by others.

There is a vast literature on love, as well as many historical and analytical studies of the concept of love.[9] Love is generally viewed as a complex emotion. There are different kinds of love, and each act of love has a number of components. Thus, we differentiate *sex* (or lust), *eros* (or the urge toward higher states of being and relationships), *philia* (friendship, or brotherly love), and *agape* (or *caritas,* selfless love as exemplified in the love of God for man), and so on.[10]

Should sex, which is equally complex, not be viewed as an entity in its own right? If we can have love with or without sex, why can we not legitimately have sex with or without love? Everyone must ultimately face this question, and a well-thought-out individual fundamental standard may be preferable to the usual compromises reached under the pressures of the moment.

Sexuality in Historical Perspective

Part of the confusion regarding sexual behavior arises from our inability and unwillingness to view sexual matters in an historical and cross-cultural context. We become so bound up in our immediate needs and fears that we lose perspective both at the personal and the

[8]See Farnsworth and Blaine, eds. (1970), pp. 133–151; Student Committee on Human Sexuality (1970).

[9]For a study of love in the Western world, *see* De Rougemont (1956). Some books on love have attracted wide attention; *see,* for example, Russell (1968), Fromm (1956), Lewis (1960), Maslow (1968).
[10]May (1969).

societal level. The adolescent has little inclination to remember how he felt about sex as a child or how he is likely to view it as an adult. Adults likewise readily forget what it was like to be an adolescent. When a longitudinal view is finally forced on us in old age, there is relatively little time or energy left to do very much about it.

We are just as shortsighted and ahistorical as a society. Our views of history are often at the level of homilies about the "good old days" or how "the more things change, the more they remain the same." We learn about ancient times and remote places in school, but such knowledge is rarely seen as having any immediacy for our lives.

We are pressed by the present and preoccupied with the future. As a consequence we have difficulty in determining whether changes we see in sexual behavior constitute regular installments in the normal course of events or if a process of more drastic change is afoot. It is altogether easy under such circumstances for some to cry "sexual revolution" in the face of any startlingly real, just imagined, or wished-for change; and for others to placidly sit through profound upheavals in sexual attitudes and behavior as if nothing new were happening.

There will be a sustained effort throughout this book to keep in mind the need for historical and cross-cultural frames of reference. The proper starting point for the narrative thread of sexual behavior is in our primate ancestry. Biological history in this regard is just as important as cultural history. Ideally, we should be mindful of all human experience at all times in all cultures. A practically more feasible goal is to know at least something about one's own culture during the more recent past.

Arthur Schlesinger, Jr., in an informal essay on the history of love in this country, has outlined some of the major shifts that have occurred in sexual attitudes over the past three centuries.[11] We often think of the Puritan founders of this nation as prudes. Yet the Puritans in the seventeenth century were quite open about sex and viewed it as a natural and joyous part of marriage. One James Mattock was expelled from the First Church of Boston for refusing to sleep with his wife. Puritan maidens with child were married by understanding ministers, as is indicated in the town records of the time. The Puritans were stern and God-fearing people, who could be very harsh with adulterers. Yet their wrath was aroused not because of the sexual element but because such behavior threatened the sanctity and stability of marriage. The lack of a general sexual repressiveness was even apparent to outsiders. A visitor from Maryland who was in Boston in 1744 reported: "This place abounds with pretty women who appear rather more abroad than they do at [New] York and dress elegantly. They are for the most part, free and affable as well as pretty. I saw not one prude while I was there."

With the coming of national independence in the eighteenth century, there was a reaction to romantic notions that were associated with Old World feudalism and aristocracy. The republic was pledged to liberty, equality, and rationality. Marriage became more and more a service institution geared to populate the nation and strengthen the labor force. Native as well as visiting observers were quick to comment on this victory of rationality over romantic love. "No author, without a trial," complained Hawthorne, "can conceive of the difficulty of writing a romance about a country where there is no shadow, no antiquity, no mystery, no picturesque and gloomy wrong, nor anything but a commonplace prosperity, in broad and simple day-

---

[11]Schlesinger (1970). For a more extensive historical review of changing attitudes to sex since the Middle Ages, *see* Taylor (1970).

light, as is happily the case with my dear native land." The French writer, Stendhal, observed that Americans had such a "habit of reason" that abandonment to love became all but impossible. In Europe, he wrote, "desire is sharpened by restraint; in America it is blunted by liberty."

In the nineteenth century American men became progressively more obsessed with achievement and making money. American women, on the other hand, had become quite self-assertive, having successfully used the leverage provided by their scarcity when the country was being settled and later during its expansion to the West. Between male preoccupation and female coolheadedness, love and romance seem to have been more and more dissociated from the relationship between the sexes.

To further complicate matters the nineteenth-century marriage attempted to make up for the lack of passion with a certain gentility and oppressive inhibitedness. Men and women could not visit art galleries together in Philadelphia because of the potential embarrassment that classical statues would cause. Prudery was carried to extraordinary lengths and Victorian standards of decorum seem to have been more oppressively enforced in this country than even in England.

The separation of sexuality from respectable relationships resulted in increasing reliance by men on the services of prostitutes to satisfy urges that were considered too beastly to impose on their wives and the mothers of their children. This is not to say that many individuals did not achieve a workably harmony between sex and affection within their marriages. But the tendency, at least among the financially better off classes, was toward an idealizing of women on the one hand and robbing them of their sexuality on the other.

There were occasional voices of protest raised by women, but these usually involved extreme feminists. Victoria Woodhull, for instance, proclaimed in one public lecture: "Yes, I am a free lover! I have an inalienable, constitutional, and natural right to love whom I may, to love as long or as short a period as I can, to change that love everyday if I please!"

The upheaval of World War I accelerated dramatically the changes that were already in ferment at the turn of the century. Wars have a jarring impact, since people under stress are driven to and allow themselves behaviors that they ordinarily would not engage in. In the postwar period additional influences, including the spread of the tenets of psychoanalysis and the social sciences, further secularized and liberalized the common culture. Other important influences that helped liberalize sexual attitudes were related to increasing leisure and prosperity and the availability of contraceptives. The development of the automobile and the movie industry also had widespread impact, since the former provided a certain mobile privacy and the latter reached large numbers of individuals and often dwelt on romantic and, for the time, sexually explicit themes.

The changes following World War II have further eroded traditional sexual attitudes. With the spread and entrenchment of psychoanalytic views in psychiatry and the social sciences the notion that sex is a central moving force in life came to be more widely accepted. The studies of Alfred C. Kinsey and his associates in the late 1940s and early 1950s, as well as the writings of the anthropologist Margaret Mead, combined to force people to reconsider their traditional views about how people behave or ought to behave sexually. Further advances in the development of contraceptives made the separation of sex and reproduction more feasible for a wider sector of the population. The discovery of penicillin virtually eliminated the threat of syphilis and gonorrhea for a while. Children reared according to permissive standards grew up to be parents themselves and allowed more latitude in behavior to their own children, so that by the early 1960s a new generation of youth developed a distinctive life style, a more radical political philosophy, and more liberal sexual attitudes.

Common observation indicates that during the past decade and a half there have been sweeping changes in public attitudes toward the expression and discussion of sexual themes. The publications of Masters and Johnson brought sex into sharp focus both within the professions and the general public. The astonishing success of numerous books on sex indicates an apparently insatiable interest in such literature by the reading public.

In the literary world sexually explicit themes are becoming commonplace. There have always been such books on the market, but now the authors are established writers like Roth and Updike. Nor is such literary license any longer the prerogative of male writers, as witness Anais Nin's *Delta of Venus*. The theater, too, has stretched the boundaries of the acceptable to include explicit scenes of coitus (*Oh! Calcutta!*), oral-genital sex (*The Beard*), and homosexual acts (*Fortune and Men's Eyes*). *The Last Tango in Paris* represents this same trend in film, which in the more "hard core" variety is already suffering from the boredom of redundancy.

Problems in Sex Research

Beside the multitude of problems inherent in the investigation of any complex human function, there are additional difficulties in sex research, notably questions about the propriety of such research itself. As usual, the polar positions in the controversy are most easily stated. One is that sex is a natural biological function and that its physiology must be elucidated by the most effective methods available. The scientific study of other body functions has been most effectively conducted in the laboratory, and sexuality is no exception.

This approach involves observing, recording, and quantifying data in ways that can be readily understood and replicated. Even though sex has well-known emotional components, its physiology is still best studied under the glare of laboratory lights rather than in the glow of moonlight. As far as behavioral research is concerned, we must likewise ascertain the facts in the most expeditious manner possible.

The objections to this approach originate from a variety of sources. One argument is that sex is more than just another physiological function and that certain moral considerations ought to regulate its study. For example, though a woman may experience the same physiological changes during orgasm with her husband or with a stranger, the fact is secondary to the issue of her committing an "immoral" act in the latter instance. Some people argue that it is indecent to watch others making love, regardless of the purpose of the observation or the relationship of the pair.

Another type of objection is that the statistical and laboratory approaches miss the essence of sex by focusing on its physiological or quantifiable aspects; that it is appropriate to think in terms like "total outlet" and "sexual-response cycle" in connection with animals and machines but not with human beings.

Proponents of sex research correctly reply that people have fought progress in this area every inch of the way. There was a time when physicians even had to deliver babies under cover because exposing the mother's genitals would have seemed indecent. If this particular standard of decorum had been sustained we would not have the science of obstetrics today. Many people who were shocked by Kinsey's work were not offended by Havelock Ellis, who had shocked his own contemporaries however. Many of those who now object to physiological sex research accept Kinsey's work because he only inquired about what people did and did not ask them to perform for him. Such is progress. The pioneers blaze the trail, and the rest of us must be dragged behind, some kicking and screaming all the way.

The questions about sex research that are being raised today may result from public outcries but also come from concerned individuals. This concern is not directed exclusively at sex research but at the larger issue of contemporary sexual attitudes. Are we losing our capacity for shame? Is the price of free public sexual expression a diminution of our sensitivities to the point of an irrevocable loss? Are we taking the mystery out of sex, and even its meaning?[12]

Some critics claim that a new sexual tyranny is arising, as men, and more especially women, now feel shame and guilt at failing to experience orgasm (or orgasm at certain levels of intensity)—a reversal of the traditional pattern. Is there an inverse relation between the emphasis on sexual technique and the experiencing of sexual passion? As the Victorians sought love while avoiding sex, do we seek sex while avoiding love? Are we turning our sex organs into machinery in our already highly mechanized world?[13]

These questions are disturbing to sophisticated and sensitive men and women; they are not like the objections of assorted turn-of-the-century prudes and censors like Anthony Comstock. There are no ready answers, and these questions will continue to be asked. But the real problem is not whether sex research should continue (or whether free sexual expression ought to be permitted in the arts and in literature). Most reasonable people will agree that sex research should go on if we wish to continue the quest for truth. The relevant questions are how we should best study sex and what to do about the use and abuse of the resultant data.

The remarks of Alan Gregg in his introduction to the first Kinsey volume in 1948[14] are equally applicable now, more than three decades later:

Certainly no aspect of human biology in our current civilization stands in more need of scientific knowledge and courageous humility than that of sex. The history of medicine proves that in so far as man seeks to know himself and face his whole nature, he has become free from bewildered fear, despondent shame, or arrant hypocrisy. As long as sex is dealt with in the current confusion of ignorance and sophistication, denial and indulgence, suppression and stimulation, punishment and exploitation, secrecy and display, it will be associated with a duplicity and indecency that lead neither to intellectual honesty nor human dignity.[15]

---

[12]Tyrmand (1970).
[13]May (1969).

[14]Gregg was then Director for Medical Sciences of the Rockefeller Foundation, the major financial supporter of the Kinsey study.
[15]Kinsey et al. (1948), p. vii.

Part One

Biology

Chapter 2

Anatomy of the Sex Organs

Praise be given to God, who has placed man's greatest pleasure in the natural parts of woman, and has destined the natural parts of man to afford the greatest enjoyment to woman.

—The Perfumed Garden

The human body has no other parts as fascinating as the sexual organs. Venerated and vilified, concealed and exhibited, the human genitals have elicited a multitude of varied responses. They have been portrayed in every art form, praised and damned in poetry and prose, worshipped with religious fervor, and mutilated in insane frenzy.

Many of us combine a lively interest in the sex organs with an equally compelling tendency either to deny such interest or to be ashamed of it. There are men and women who have been married for years, who have engaged in sexual intercourse countless times, but who have never looked frankly and searchingly at each other's genitals. Nor is this aversion merely a matter of prudishness. To many people the sex organs appear neither beautiful nor sexy when viewed directly. Unfortunately, although concealment may promote desire, it also perpetuates ignorance.

The performance of basic procreative functions obviously does not require any formal knowledge of anatomy. For most people, however, some knowledge of sexual anatomy, particularly of the genitals, is helpful in understanding sexual functions. Anatomy, the study of structures, is related to physiology, which deals with functions, as geography is related to history: It is the description of the theater where the action takes place.

The genitalia are part of the reproductive system, and procreation is their most fundamental function. But humans also engage in sex for many other purposes. We cannot procreate without sex, but we do not always engage in sex in order to procreate. This separability of sex and reproduction is an issue of far-reaching psychological and social consequence, one still unresolved in most human societies.

An objective approach to anatomy would

deal with each bodily structure in its own right, and anatomists do just that. But most of us are likely to approach parts of the body with far more subjective attitudes. We find some organs more fascinating or think of them as more important than others, sometimes without adequate physiological justification for such views.

To think of the heart as the seat of emotions is a harmless fiction. But our attitudes towards the genital organs have not been so innocuous. Male perspectives on sexuality that have been socially dominant have held an ambivalent view of the female genitals. Men are fascinated, aroused, and preoccupied by them, but simultaneously they are feared and deprecated as defective copies of the male. Males often have ambivalent views about their own genitals as well, alternately imbuing them with exaggerated importance and being anxious about their size, shape, and capacity for performance.

Female attitudes towards the genitalia, be it their own or those of males, have had much less occasion for public expression, but women too seem to have feelings of shame, confusion, or ambivalence. Women also tend to be even less knowledgeable than men about sexual anatomy because their own organs are more concealed and they have been expected or assumed not to be interested in the genitals of males. These attitudes have recently become more open and accepting, but there is still much variability in people's views on the subject.

The Basic Plan of the Reproductive System

There are obvious and concealed differences between the reproductive tracts of the two sexes. But before we dwell on these, it is important to understand the fundamentally similar plan on which the two are built.

In both sexes the reproductive system can be thought of as consisting of three parts. First are a pair of gonads or reproductive glands (ovaries in the female; testes in the male) that produce the germ cells (ova, or eggs, and sperm). Second are a set of tubes (a pair of fallopian tubes and the uterus in the female; epididymis, vas deferens, ejaculatory duct—in pairs—and the urethra in the male) that transport these germ cells. Third are organs for the delivery and reception of the ejaculate containing sperm (penis and vagina). In addition, the gonads produce hormones in both sexes and the uterus houses the growing embryo. There are also a number of accessory sex organs (a pair of bulbourethral glands in both sexes and a pair of seminal vesicles and the prostate gland in the male) and covering structures that form part of the genitalia (scrotal sac in the male, major and minor lips in the female).

The reproductive systems of both sexes have the same embryological origin. In fact, very early in life it is not possible to tell them apart by examining the immature reproductive structures. Although the sex of the infant is decided at the moment of fertilization, this does not become manifest until later in development. The differentiation of the male from the female is dependent on the genetic contribution of the fertilizing sperm (the Y chromosome) and on hormones produced by the developing testes (androgens). Although normally these events progress quite predictably, anatomical maleness and femaleness are not immutably fixed by genetics. It is possible to push development toward the female or male side despite the fundamental genetic sex of the person. In abnormal conditions like hermaphroditism, this is precisely what happens. We shall have occasion to discuss these matters more fully in later chapters.

From this common embryonal origin the reproductive organs differentiate in the two sexes to fulfill their complementary functions. Sexual organs can thus be compared usefully in two ways. One is in terms of their embryonal origins. Every reproductive organ in one sex has its developmental counterpart or *homologue* in the other.[1] These organs can also be compared as functional counterparts. For example, the clitoris and penis are homologous. Functionally, they are also comparable by being highly responsive to erotic stimulation. But the clitoris has no direct reproductive function. It does not mate with the penis; that is done by the vagina, which is thus the counterpart of the penis in coital terms.

One could conclude from what has been said so far that we seem to consider heterosexual intercourse for reproductive purposes the standard or normative unit for sexual functions. This is and is not the case, depending on what one means. The anatomy and physiology of the reproductive system has evolved in ways to maximize its reproductive potential. Its design, as it were, would therefore make most sense in reproductive terms. But this is not to say that the only or even best use of sex for a given individual is necessarily for procreation. But even if sex is not to be used for reproduction, the structure and function of the sex organs can be best understood within that biologically fundamental framework.

We shall now turn to the main purpose of this chapter by examining first the bony framework which houses the reproductive system. Then we shall deal with the anatomy of the female and male sex organs and close the chapter with a consideration of the developmental processes. The reason that we shall consider the female first is not because she is more or less "important" than the male, but because the female reproductive system is somewhat less convoluted than that of the male and thus probably easier to understand for most.

---

[1]In biology the term "homologous" refers to organs or parts that correspond to each other in evolutionary origin and are basically similar in structure but not necessarily in function. By contrast, "analogous" organs or parts resemble functionally but have different origins or structure.

The Bony Pelvis

The reproductive system in either sex is located partly inside the body cavity and partly outside it. Although all the sex organs belong to a single system, the internal ones are regarded as primarily organs of procreation, whereas the external ones, the genitals, are associated more closely with sexual activity itself. The external organs are thus more likely objects of erotic and social interest.

The internal sex organs are housed in the *pelvis* (*see* Figure 2.1). The bones of the pelvis consist of the triangular end of the vertebral column (*sacrum*) and a pair of "hip bones," which are attached to the sacrum behind and to each other in front (at the *symphysis pubis*), thus forming a circle at their rim. Each "hip bone" actually consists of three separate bones (*ilium, ischium, pubis*) that are fused together. The components of the bony pelvis are in turn fixed and permit no movement.

Comparison of the female pelvis with that of the male in Figure 2.1 shows that even though the male pelvis has a heavier bone structure, the female pelvis is broader and its outlets wider. This allows for easier passage of the infant's head during birth. Women with narrower or male-type pelvic outlets sometimes cannot give birth naturally, and their children must be delivered through abdominal (cesarean) section of the uterus (discussed in Chapter 5).

The pelvic cavity is a bottomless basin crowded with organs belonging to the reproductive, urinary, and digestive systems. Figure 2.2 and Figure 2.3, respectively, show the relationship of the female and male reproductive organs to the pelvis.

Separating these organs from one another and supporting and attaching them to the bony framework of the body are various tough fibrous structures analogous to canvas sheets (*fasciae*) and cords (*ligaments*). These structures, along with the various muscles in the area, form a multilayered "hammock" in

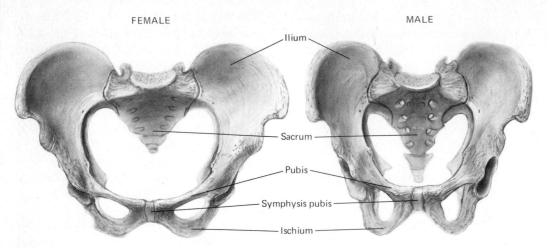

FEMALE

MALE

Ilium

Sacrum

Pubis

Symphysis pubis

Ischium

Figure 2.1 The bony pelvis. From Dienhart, *Basic Human Anatomy and Physiology.* Philadelphia: Saunders, 1967, p. 35. Reprinted by permission.

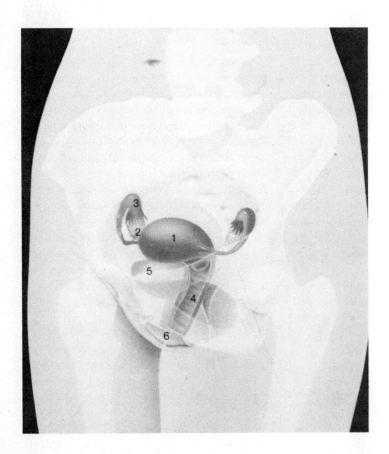

Figure 2.2 Female reproductive organs. (1) Uterus, (2) ovary, (3) Fallopian tube, (4) vagina, (5) bladder, (6) labia majora and labia minora on the right side. From Nilsson, *A Child Is Born.* New York: Delacorte Press, 1977, p. 21. Reprinted by permission.

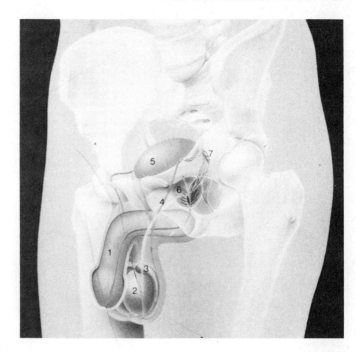

Figure 2.3 Male reproductive organs. (1) Penis, (2) testicle, (3) epididymis, (4) spermatic cord, (5) bladder, (6) prostate, (7) seminal vesicle. From Nilsson, *A Child Is Born*. New York: Delacorte Press, 1977, p. 17. Reprinted by permission.

which the genital organs are embedded and suspended.

Because of the anatomical peculiarities of the reproductive organs in the two sexes, the particular arrangements of these supporting fascia, ligaments, and muscles are somewhat different, as will become clear when these structures are described.

Female Sex Organs

External Genitals

The external genitals of the female are collectively called the *vulva* ("covering"). They include the *mons pubis* (or *mons veneris*, "mount of Venus"), the *major* and *minor lips*, the *clitoris*, and the *vaginal introitus*, or opening.

The mons pubis is the soft, rounded elevation of fatty tissue over the pubic symphysis. After it becomes covered with hair during puberty the mons is the most visible part of the female genitals.

The Major Lips

The major lips (*labia majora*) are two elongated folds of skin that run down and back from the mons pubis. Their appearance varies a great deal: Some are flat and hardly visible behind thick pubic hair; others bulge prominently. Ordinarily they are close together, and the female genitals appear "closed."

The major lips are more distinct in front. Toward the anus they flatten out and merge with the surrounding tissues. The outer surfaces of the major lips are covered with skin of a darker color, which grows hair at puberty. Their inner surfaces are smooth and hairless. Within these folds of skin are bundles of smooth muscle fibers, nerves, and vessels for blood and lymph. The space between the major lips is the *pudendal cleft*;[2] it becomes

[2]*Pudendum*, a term no longer in general use, refers to the female external genitalia and means "a thing of shame."

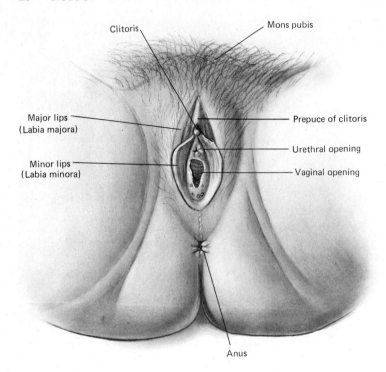

Clitoris

Mons pubis

Major lips
(Labia majora)

Minor lips
(Labia minora)

Prepuce of clitoris

Urethral opening

Vaginal opening

Anus

Figure 2.4 External female genitalia. From Dienhart, *Basic Human Anatomy and Physiology.* Philadelphia: Saunders, 1967, p. 217. Reprinted by permission.

visible only when the lips are parted (see Figure 2.4).

The Minor Lips

The minor lips (*labia minora*) are two lighter-colored hairless folds of skin located between the major lips. The space that they enclose is the vaginal *vestibule* into which open the vaginal and urethral orifices, as well as the ducts of the Bartholin's or greater vestibular glands. The minor lips merge with the major lips behind. In front each divides in two: The upper portions form a single fold of skin over the clitoris and are called the *prepuce of the clitoris;* the lower portions meet beneath the clitoris as a separate fold of skin called the *frenulum of the clitoris.*

From front to back the structures enclosed by the minor lips are the clitoris, the external urethral orifice, the vaginal orifice, and the openings of the two greater vestibular glands. The anus, which is completely separate from the external genitals, lies farther back.

The Clitoris

The clitoris ("that which is closed in") consists of two masses of erectile spongy tissue (*corpora cavernosa*), the tips (crura) of which are attached to the pubic bone. Most of the clitoral body is covered by the upper folds of the minor lips, but its free, rounded tip (the glans) projects beyond it. The urethra does not pass through it.

The clitoris becomes engorged with blood during sexual excitement. Because of the way it is attached, however, it does not become erect as the penis does. Functionally it corresponds more closely to the glans of the penis: It is richly endowed with nerves, highly sensitive, and a very important focus of sexual stimulation, which is its sole function.[3] The clitoris has also been subjected to ritual mutilation (*see* Box 2.1).

[3]Given its importance to female sexual arousal, the clitoris has recently become the focus of more professional attention. For a detailed study of clitoral anatomy, function and related considerations, see Lowry and Lowry (1976). Also of interest is Lowry (1978).

Box 2.1   Female "Circumcision"

The practice of female "circumcision" is far less known generally than its male counterpart. Yet the practice has been widespread in many cultures and continues to be practiced in the Near East and the African continent where currently there are an estimated 30 million women who have undergone one or another version of this mutilating procedure.[1]

To be precise, the term female "circumcision" should be restricted to the removal of the prepuce of the clitoris only, which is the common practice among Moslems. Other procedures include the amputation of the clitoris (*clitoridectomy*), sometimes with the additional removal of the labia minor and the labia majora. When the edges of the excised vulva are made to heal together (*infibulation*) the procedure is referred to as "Pharaonic circumcision." This obliterates access to the vaginal area except for a small opening to allow urine and menstrual blood to come out. When the woman becomes entitled to engage in coitus the orifice is enlarged by tearing it down (*introcision*).

These practices have ancient roots like male circumcision. But while male circumcision in no way incapacitates the individual, what is done in the female beyond excision of the clitoral prepuce are mutilating procedures that seriously interfere with sexual function. With all due respect to the right of cultures to fashion their own rituals, it is hard to find reasonable justification for the perpetration of these brutal practices on helpless young girls.

The Western world has had its own version of female genital mutilation. Early in the nineteenth century, "declitorization" was a medical procedure for the treatment of masturbation and "nymphomania" and was used both in Europe and the United States. Such surgery became discredited with the advent of the present century.[2]

Currently some sex therapists advocate the freeing up of clitoral adhesions in the treatment of orgasmic dysfunction. The only medical justification for clitoral excision is for conditions, such as cancer, that require radical surgery.

[1]Remy (1979).
[2]For more detailed accounts of these practices, see Hayes (1975), Huelsman (1976), and Paige (1978).

Urethral Opening

The external urethral orifice is a small, median slit with raised margins. The female urethra conveys only urine and is totally independent of the reproductive system.

Vaginal Opening

The vaginal orifice or *introitus* is not a gaping hole but rather is visible only when the inner lips are parted. It is easily distinguishable from the urethral opening by its larger size. The appearance of the vaginal orifice depends to a large extent on the shape and condition of the *hymen*. This delicate membrane, which only exists in the human female, has no known physiological function, but its psychological and cultural significance has been enormous (*see* Box 2.1). It varies in shape and size and may surround the vaginal orifice (annular), bridge it (septate), or serve as a sievelike cover (cribriform) (*see* Figure 2.5). There is normally always some opening to the outside.[4]

Most hymens will permit passage of a finger (or sanitary tampon), but usually cannot accommodate an erect penis without

[4]In rare instances the hymen consists of a tough fibrous tissue that has no opening (*imperforate hymen*). This condition is usually detected after a girl begins to menstruate and the products of successive menstrual periods accumulate in the vagina and uterus as an enlarging mass. It is corrected by surgical incision, usually without aftereffects.

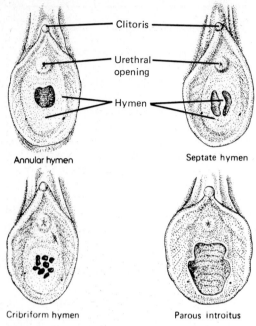

Annular hymen

Septate hymen

Cribriform hymen

Parous introitus

Figure 2.5 Types of hymens. From Netter, p. 90. © 1954, 1965 CIBA Pharmaceutical Company, Division of CIBA-GEIGY Corporation.

tearing. Occasionally, however, a very flexible hymen will withstand intercourse. This fact, coupled with the fact that the hymen may be torn accidentally, makes the condition of the hymen unreliable as evidence for or against virginity. In childbirth the hymen is torn further and only fragments remain attached to the vaginal opening (*see* Figure 2.5).

When the major and minor lips are removed, a ring of muscular fibers are revealed to surround the external vaginal opening (*see* Figure 2.6, in which it is shown to the left of the vagina only). Such muscular rings that act to constrict bodily orifices are known as *sphincters*. The *bulbocavernosus muscle* in this case acts as a vaginal sphincter even though it is not as highly developed as, for instance, the anal sphincter. Both voluntarily and sometimes without being aware of it, women flex this muscle and thus narrow the opening of the vagina. In normal function and in some pathological conditions, the level of

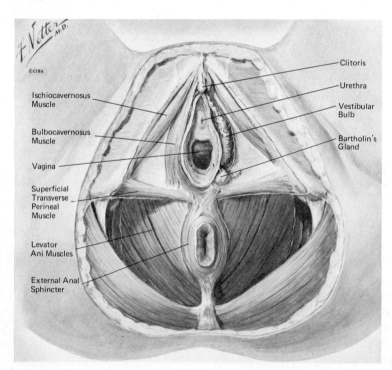

Figure 2.6 Female external genitalia (skin removed). From Netter, *The Ciba Collection of Medical Illustrations:* Volume 2, Reproductive System, p. 92. Reprinted by permission. © 1954, 1965 CIBA Pharmaceutical Company, Division of CIBA-GEIGY Corporation.

Box 2.2 Defloration

The tearing of the hymen during the first coitus received a great deal of attention in "marriage manuals." Under ordinary circumstances it is an untraumatic event. In the heat of sexual excitement the woman feels minimal pain. Bleeding is generally also slight. What makes first intercourse a painful experience for some is the muscular tension that an anxious, unprepared, or unresponsive woman experiences in response to clumsy attempts at penetration. In anticipation of such difficulties some women with no premarital sexual experience used to have their hymens stretched or cut surgically before their wedding nights with the knowledge and consent of their grooms to avoid doubts of virginity or disappointment at being "cheated" of the experience of defloration. The current frequency of this practice is unknown.

The hymen is an exclusively human body part. Other primates and lower animals do not have it. Why and how the hymen evolved is not clear, but most human societies seem to have "made the most" of it. There is hardly a culture that has not been preoccupied with its proper disposal. Where defloration has been thought to pose a magical threat, special men or women have been assigned to carry it out. Among the seminomadic Yungar of Australia girls were deflowered by two old women a week before marriage. If a girl's hymen was discovered at this time to be not intact, she could be starved, tortured, mutilated, or even killed. The old custom of parading the bloodstained sheets on the wedding night as proof of the bride's chastity is well known. In various cultures, horns, stone phalluses, or other assorted implements have been used in ritual deflorations.

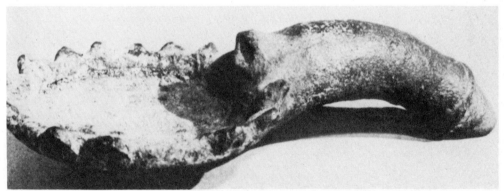

Lamp, of terracotta, used in the defloration of girls. Bastar state. Modern. From Philip Rawson, *Erotic Art of the East.* New York: G. P. Putnam's Sons, 1968. By permission.

tension exerted by these muscles is of prime importance, as we shall discuss.

Underneath the bulbocavernosus muscles are two elongated masses of erectile tissue called the *vestibular bulbs.* These structures are connected at their upper ends with the clitoris and like that organ become congested with blood during sexual arousal. They too play an important function in the female sexual response cycle and, together with the muscular ring, determine the size, tightness, and "feel" of the vaginal opening.

Internal Sex Organs

The internal sex organs of the female consist of the paired ovaries and uterine (*fallopian*) tubes, the uterus, and the vagina, along with a few accessory structures. The ovaries have a dual function: the production of germ cells or *ova* ("eggs") and of female sex hormones (*estrogen* and *progesterone*). As hormones are secreted directly into the bloodstream, glands that produce them need no ducts and are known as *ductless,* or *endocrine,* glands.

The ovary is an almond-shaped, small (1½ × ¾ × 1 inches), and rather light organ (¼ ounce), which shrinks further in old age. In their usual positions the ovaries lie verti- cally (*see* Figure 2.7) flanking the uterus (*see* Figure 2.8). They are held in place by a number of folds and ligaments, including the *ovarian ligaments,* which attach them to the sides of the uterus. These ligaments are solid cords and are not to be confused with the uterine tubes, which open into the uterine cavity.

The ovary has no tubes leading directly out of it. The ova leave the organ by ruptur- ing its wall and becoming caught in the fringed end of the fallopian tube. To permit the exit of ova, the ovarian capsule is thus quite thin. Before puberty it has a smooth, glistening surface. After the start of the ovar- ian cycle and the monthly exodus of ova, its

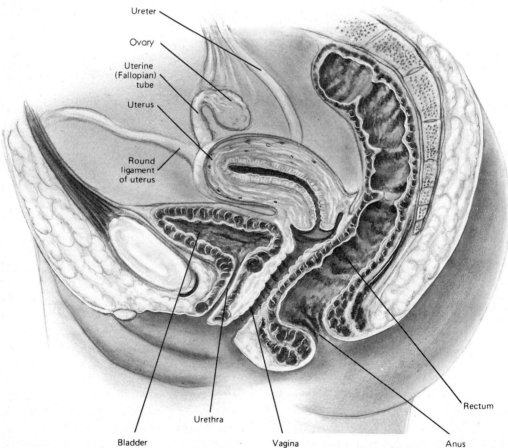

Ureter
Ovary
Uterine (Fallopian) tube
Uterus
Round ligament of uterus
Bladder
Urethra
Vagina
Anus
Rectum

Figure 2.7 The female reproductive system. From Dienhart, *Basic Human Anatomy and Physiology.* Philadelphia: Saunders, 1967, p. 213. Reprinted by permission.

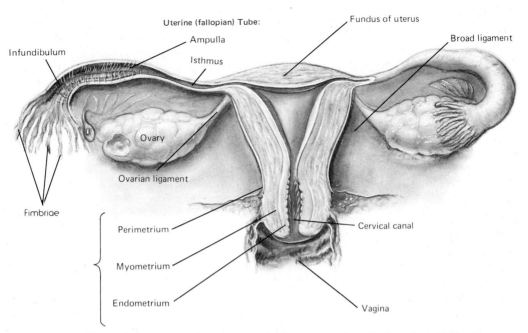

Uterine (fallopian) Tube:

Ampulla

Isthmus

Infundibulum

Fundus of uterus

Broad ligament

Ovary

Ovarian ligament

Fimbriae

Perimetrium

Myometrium

Endometrium

Cervical canal

Vagina

Figure 2.8 Internal female reproductive organs. From Dienhart, *Basic Human Anatomy and Physiology.* Philadelphia: Saunders, 1967, p. 215. Reprinted by permission.

surface becomes increasingly scarred and pitted.

The ovary contains numerous capsules, or *follicles*, in various stages of development, embedded in supporting tissues; these are located toward the periphery of the organ (the *cortex,* or "bark") (*see* Figure 2.9). The central portion of the ovary, the *medulla* ("marrow"), is rich in convoluted blood vessels.

Each follicle contains one ovum. Every female is born with about 400,000 immature ova (*oocytes*). No additional new ova are generated during the rest of a woman's life. At puberty only about 40,000 of these oocytes are left. Some of them start maturing, and each month one follicle ruptures, discharging the ovum. This process is repeated monthly and some 400 oocytes reach maturity during a woman's reproductive lifetime. The empty follicle becomes a yellowish structure (*corpus luteum*). This ovarian cycle has great reproductive and hormonal significance and will be discussed in

detail under those respective headings in Chapters 4 and 5.

The two uterine, or fallopian,[5] tubes are about 4 inches long and extend between the ovaries and the uterus. The ovarian end of the tube, the *infundibulum* ("funnel"), is cone-shaped and fringed by irregular projections, or *fimbriae,* which may cling to or embrace the ovary but are not attached to it. After leaving the ovarian surface, the ovum must find its way into the opening of the uterine tube. Although not every ovum succeeds in doing so, the process seems to be aided by a mysterious attraction between the uterine tube and the ovary. There have been instances in which women missing an ovary on one side and a uterine tube on the other have nevertheless become pregnant—all the more remarkable considering that the ovum is about the size of a needle tip and the opening

[5]Named after a sixteenth-century Italian anatomist, Gabriello Fallopio, who mistakenly thought that the tubes were "ventilators" for the uterus.

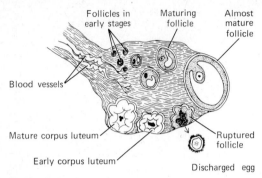

Figure 2.9   Composite view of ovum. From Crawley, Malfetti, Stewart, and Vas Dias, *Reproduction, Sex, and Preparation for Marriage.* Englewood Cliffs, N.J.: Prentice-Hall, 1964, p. 16. Reprinted by permission.

of the uterine tube is only a slit about the size of a printed hyphen.

The second portion of the tube (the *ampulla*) accounts for over half its length. It has thin walls and is joined to the less tortuous *isthmus,* which resembles a cord and ends at the uterine border. The last segment of the tube (the uterine part) runs within the wall of the uterus itself and opens into its cavity (uterine opening).

The cavity of the uterine tube becomes progressively smaller between the ovarian

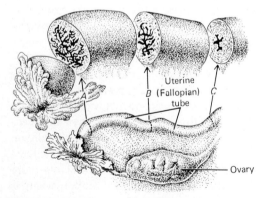

Figure 2.10   Uterine tube. (A) Infundibular, (B) ampullar, (C) isthmic. From Eastman and Hellman, *Williams Obstetrics,* 13th ed. New York: Appleton–Century–Crofts, 1966, p. 31. Reprinted by permission.

end (2 millimeters) and uterine end (1 millimeter); the numerous folds projecting into the cavity also gradually disappear (*see* Figure 2.10). The lining of the uterine tube has a deep velvety texture because of the numerous hairlike structures (*cilia*) lining it. If the ovum were the size of an orange, these cilia would be comparable in size to eyelashes.

The function of the fallopian tubes is more than mere storage and conveyance of germ cells. The fertilization of the ovum usually occurs in the infundibular third of the uterine tube, where sperm that have traversed the vagina and the uterus meet the ovum. Passage of the ovum through the tube takes several days, and, if fertilization has occurred, the structure that reaches the uterine cavity is already a complex, multicellular organism.[6]

The ovum, unlike the sperm, is not independently motile; its movement depends on the sweeping action of the cilia lining the tube and the contractions of its wall during the passage of the ovum.

Although the fallopian tubes are nowhere as surgically accessible as is the vas deferens of the male, they are still the most convenient targets for the sterilization of females. The usual procedure is to tie or sever the tubes (*tubal ligation*) on both sides. The result is sterility without concomitant impairment of sexual characteristics, desire, or ability to reach orgasm.

The uterus, or womb, is a hollow, muscular organ in which the embryo (known as the fetus after the eighth week) is housed and nourished until birth.[7] The uterus is shaped

[6]On rare occasions the fertilized ovum becomes implanted in the wall of the uterine tube itself, causing one form of ectopic ("out of normal place") pregnancy, which ultimately results in the death of the fetus and may cause the tube to rupture, with potentially serious consequences for the mother.

[7]The Greek word for uterus is *hystera,* a term that supplies the root for words like "hysterectomy" (surgical removal of the uterus) and "hysteria" (a condition believed by the ancient Greeks to result from the uterus wandering through the body in search of a child).

like an inverted pear and is usually tilted forward (anteverted) (*see* Figure 2.7).[8] The uterus is held, but not fixed, in place by various ligaments. Normally 3 inches long, 3 inches wide at the top, and 1 inch thick, it expands greatly during pregnancy. There is no other body organ that ordinarily undergoes a comparable adaptation.

The uterus consists of four parts (*see* Figure 2.8): the *fundus* ("bottom"), the rounded portion that lies above the openings of the uterine tubes; the *body* which is the main part; the narrow *isthmus* (not to be confused with the isthmus of the fallopian tube); and the *cervix* ("neck"), the lower portion of which projects into the vagina.

The cavity of the uterus is wider at the point at which the uterine tubes enter, but narrows toward the isthmus; the *cervical canal* then expands somewhat and narrows again at the opening (the *external os*) into the vagina (*see* Figures 2.8 and 2.11). Because the anterior and posterior uterine walls are ordinarily close together, the interior, when viewed from the side (in sagittal section), appears to be a narrow slit (*see* Figure 2.7).

The uterus has three layers (*see* Figure 2.8). The inner *mucosa*, or *endometrium*, consists of numerous glands and a rich network of blood vessels. Its structure varies with the period of life (prepubertal, reproductive, and postmenopausal) and the point in the menstrual cycle. We shall discuss these variations later in connection with sex hormones and pregnancy. The second, or muscular, layer (*myometrium*) is very well developed. Intertwined layers of smooth muscle fibers endow the uterine wall with tremendous strength and elasticity. These muscles are vital for propelling the fetus at the time of birth by means of a series of contractions. The

<hr/>

[8]Attempts at self-abortion or abortion by untrained individuals often end in disaster because of this anatomical feature. When a probe or long needle is introduced, the tendency is simply to push it on into the uterus; instead, the instrument pierces the roof of the vagina and penetrates the abdominal cavity.

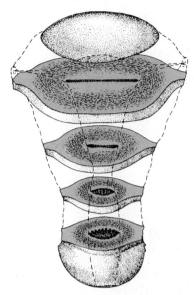

Figure 2.11 Reconstruction of uterus showing shape of its cavity and cervical canal. From Eastman and Hellman, *Williams Obstetrics,* 13th ed. New York: Appleton–Century–Crofts, 1966, p. 44. Reprinted by permission.

muscular layer of the uterus is continuous with the muscular sheaths of the fallopian tubes and the vagina. The isthmus of the uterus and the cervix contain fewer muscle fibers and more fibrous tissue than do the body and the fundus. The third layer, the *perimetrium* or *serosa,* is the external cover.

The vagina ("sheath") is the female organ of copulation and the recipient of the semen. Through it also pass the discharge during menstruation and the baby during birth. It does not serve for the passage of urine.

The vagina is ordinarily a collapsed muscular tube—a potential, rather than permanent, space. Its main surfaces are formed by the anterior and posterior walls, which are about 3 and 4 inches long respectively. Its side walls are quite narrow. It also appears as a narrow slit in sagittal section (*see* Figure 2.7).

The vaginal canal is slanted downward and forward. At its upper end it communicates with the cervical canal (usually open only the width of the lead in a pencil), and the lower end opens into the vestibule between the minor lips.

The inner lining, or vaginal *mucosa,* is like the skin covering the inside of the mouth. In contrast to the uterine endometrium it contains no glands, although its appearance is affected by hormone levels. In the adult premenopausal woman the vaginal walls are corrugated, but fleshy and soft. Following menopause they become thinner and smoother. The middle vaginal layer is muscular, but far less developed than is that of the uterine wall. Most of these fibers run longitudinally. The outer layer is also rather thin. The vaginal walls are poorly supplied with nerves so that the vagina is a rather insensitive organ except for the area surrounding the vaginal opening, which is highly excitable.

Behind the vestibular bulbs are two small glands (*Bartholin's* or *greater vestibular glands*), the ducts of which open on each side of the lower half of the vestibule in the ridges between the edge of the hymen and the minor lips. Their function is also somewhat obscure. Formerly assumed to be central in vaginal lubrication, they are now considered to play at most only a minor role in this process. The primary source of the vaginal lubricant has been shown to be the vaginal walls themselves (discussed in Chapter 3).

Size of the Vagina

Because of its function in sexual intercourse, the vagina, like the penis, has been the subject of great interest and speculation.[9] Popular notions differentiate between tight and relaxed vaginas, those that grasp the

penis and those that do not, and so on. Some aspects of these notions are demonstrable, and others are purely mythical. Functionally it is more meaningful to consider the introitus separately from the rest, for in many ways it differs from the remainder of the organ as much as the glans of the penis differs from its body.

The vagina beyond the introitus is a soft and highly distensible organ. Although it looks like a flat tube, it actually functions more as a balloon. Thus there is normally no such thing as a vagina that is permanently "too tight" or "too small." Properly stimulated, any adult vagina can, in principle, accommodate the largest penis. After all, no penis is as large as a normal infant's head, and even that passes through the vagina.

The claim that some vaginas are "too large" is more tenable. Some vaginas do not return to normal size after childbirth, and tears produced during the process weaken the vaginal walls. Even in these instances, however, the vagina expands only to the extent that the penis requires. When we add to its anatomical features the relative insensitivity of the vaginal walls, we can reasonably conclude that the main body of the vaginal cavity does not either add to or detract from the sexual pleasure of coitus in any major way. Most of the time there is no problem of "fit" between penis and vagina.

The introitus is another matter. First, it is highly sensitive. Both pain and pleasure are intensely felt there. Second, the arrangement of the erectile tissue of the bulb of the vestibule and, more important, the presence of the muscular ring of the bulbocavernosus around it make a great deal of difference in how relaxed or tight it will be. It must be emphasized that these muscles permit a significant degree of voluntary control over the size of the opening. A woman can relax or tighten the vaginal opening as she can relax or tighten the anal sphincter (though usually to a lesser extent). Furthermore, in common

[9]The many colloquial names for the vagina attest to the interest elicited by this organ. In *The Perfumed Garden* it has been called the "crusher," "the silent one," "yearning one," "glutton," "bottomless," "restless," "biter," "sucker," "the wasp," "the hedgehog," "the starling," "hot one," "delicious one," and so on. (Nefzawi, 1964 ed.). For more current terms see Haeberle (1978), p. 491.

with all other muscles of the body, those around the introitus can be developed by exercise.

There is continuing controversy as to whether the penis can be "trapped" inside the vagina. The prevalent view is that this is a misconception arising from the observation of dogs, in which this phenomenon occurs. The penis of the dog expands into a "knot" inside the vagina and cannot be withdrawn until ejaculation or loss of erection occurs. But, then, occasionally reports are published of the same phenomenon occurring in humans.[10]

There are other, purely psychological horrors that haunt some men: Fantasies that the vagina has teeth (*vagina dentata*) or is full of razor blades or ground glass are known and understandably influence sexual functioning.

Breasts

The *breasts* are not part of the sex organs; however, because of their erotic significance, we shall discuss them briefly here. Breasts are characteristic of the highest class of vertebrates (mammals), which suckle their young and are therefore called *mammary glands*. Their structure and development are similar to sweat glands.

Although we generally associate breasts with females, males also have breasts that have basically the same structure but are normally not as well developed. If a male is given female hormones, he develops female-looking breasts.

The adult female breasts are located in front of the chest muscles and extend between the second and sixth ribs and from the midline of the chest to below the armpit. Each breast consists of lobes or clusters (about fifteen to twenty) of glandular tissue, each with a separate duct opening on the nipple. The lobes are separated by loosely packed fibrous

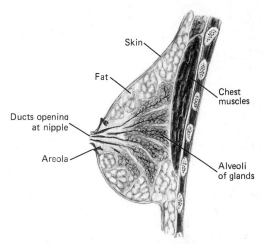

Figure 2.12 Vertical section of the breast. From Dienhart, *Basic Human Anatomy and Physiology.* Philadelphia: Saunders, 1967, p. 217. Reprinted by permission.

and fatty tissue, which gives the breast its soft consistency (*see* Figure 2.12).

The *nipple* is the prominent tip of the breast into which the milk ducts open. It consists of smooth muscle fibers that, when contracted, make the nipple erect. The area around the nipple (*areola*) becomes darker during pregnancy and remains so thereafter. The nipple, richly endowed with nerve fibers, is highly sensitive and plays an important part in sexual arousal.

The size and shape of breasts have no bearing on their sensitivity or responsiveness. Nor is a smaller-breasted woman necessarily any less capable of breast-feeding than a larger-breasted woman. Many, but not all, women find stimulation of the breasts and nipples sexually arousing.[11]

Although the size and shape of female breasts have no physiological significance, such attributes tend to greatly influence their erotic appeal and a woman's esthetic image

---

[10]For a clinical account of a case of "penis captivus" see Melody (1977), p. 111.

[11]In addition to personal idiosyncrasy, the sensitivity of the breasts has been shown to be dependent on the hormonal levels, which fluctuate with the menstrual cycle and in pregnancy.

Box 2.3   Breast Augmentation through Surgery

For some years plastic surgery has been used to correct breast differences and deformities that occur naturally or follow breast surgery.

The earlier techniques of breast enlargment relied on liquid silicone injections. Since these have proved unsatisfactory and have tended to lead to numerous complications, this method currently is not used by reputable surgeons. Instead, a far superior technique has been developed utilizing soft silicone implants, whereby the materials introduced into the breast are encapsulated in an inert sac and do not come into direct contact with the breast tissue. This reasonably safe approach quite successfully accomplishes the task of endowing a woman with breasts that appear and feel more satisfactory to her. There is no interference with lactation. However, such surgery is expensive, carries certain risks as do all major surgical procedures, and is objectionable to some women on ideological grounds.

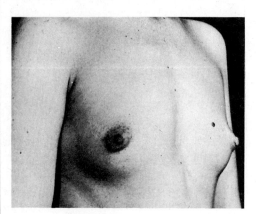 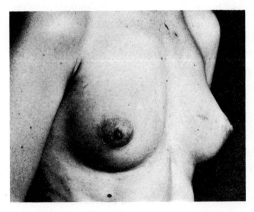

Breast augmentation through the implantation of silicone gel prosthesis. Courtesy of Dr. Donald R. Laub, Division of Reconstructive and Rehabilitation Surgery, Stanford University School of Medicine.

of herself. Such cultural judgments are of course quite arbitrary, but generally extremes in size in either direction tend to cause self-consciousness.

The female breasts develop during puberty and sometimes one grows faster than the other. The resulting asymmetry may be disturbing, but eventually the two sides become equal in size. Also, among older women, the breasts undergo other natural changes. As their supporting ligaments stretch, they tend to sag. Following menopause they become smaller and less firm. Such changes, though physiologically normal, may have psychological repercussions for some.

What to do, if anything, about these issues is a matter of personal choice. Exercises, creams, and other popularly advertised methods do not demonstrably augment breast size (apart from exercises developing the underlying chest musculature), but plastic surgery can be quite effective (see Box 2.3).

Male Sex Organs

External Genitals

The external sex organs of the male consist of the *penis* and the *scrotum* (see Figure 2.13).

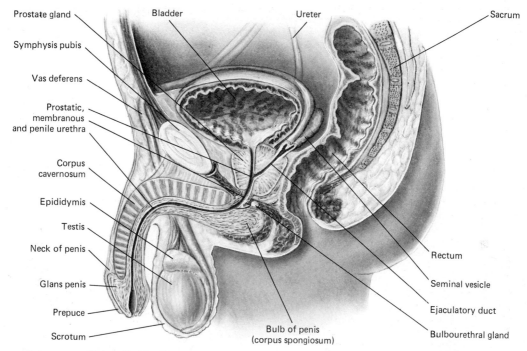

Prostate gland

Bladder

Ureter

Sacrum

Symphysis pubis

Vas deferens

Prostatic, membranous and penile urethra

Corpus cavernosum

Epididymis

Testis

Neck of penis

Glans penis

Prepuce

Scrotum

Rectum

Seminal vesicle

Ejaculatory duct

Bulbourethral gland

Bulb of penis (corpus spongiosum)

Figure 2.13 The male reproductive system. From Dienhart, *Basic Human Anatomy and Physiology.* Philadelphia: Saunders, 1967, p. 207. Reprinted by permission.

Penis

The penis ("tail") is the male organ for copulation and urination.[12] It contains three parallel cylinders of spongy tissue (*see* Figure 2.14) through one of which runs a tube (*urethra*) that conveys both urine and semen. The portion of the penis that is attached to the pelvis is its *root;* the free, pendulous portion of the penis is known as its *body.*

The three cylinders of the penis are structurally similar. Two of them are called the cavernous bodies (*corpora cavernosa*), and the third is called the spongy body (*corpus spongiosum*). Each cylinder is wrapped in a fibrous coat, but the cavernous bodies

have an additional common "wrapping" that makes them appear to be a single structure for most of their length. When the penis is flaccid, these bodies cannot be seen or felt as separate structures, but in erection the spongy body stands out as a distinct ridge on the underside of the penis.

As the terms "cavernous" and "spongy" suggest, the penis consists of an agglomeration of irregular cavities and spaces very much like a dense sponge. These tissues are served by a rich network of blood vessels and nerves. When the penis is flaccid, the cavities contain little blood. During sexual arousal they become engorged, and their constriction within their tough fibrous coats causes the characteristic stiffness of the penis. We shall discuss the mechanism of erection further in subsequent chapters.

At the root of the penis the inner tips (*crura*) of the cavernous bodies are attached to the pubic bones. The spongy body is not

[12]*Phallus* is the Greek name for "penis." Many colloquial terms refer to the erect penis as a pricking, probing, piercing instrument. Nefzawi's *The Perfumed Garden* has more exotic descriptions like "housebreaker," "ransacker," "rummager," "pigeon," "shamefaced one," "the indomitable," and "swimmer." (1964 ed., pp. 156–157). For more current terms see Haeberle (1978), p. 491.

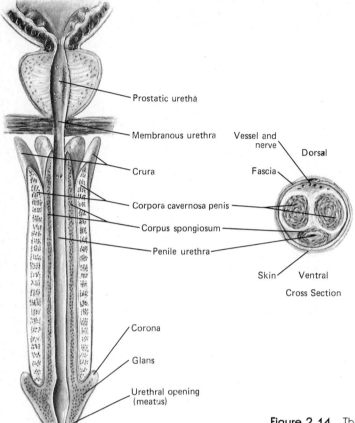

Prostatic urethá

Membranous urethra

Crura

Corpora cavernosa penis

Corpus spongiosum

Penile urethra

Corona

Glans

Urethral opening
(meatus)

Longitudinal Section

Vessel and
nerve

Dorsal

Fascia

Skin   Ventral

Cross Section

Figure 2.14   The penis. From Dienhart, *Basic Human Anatomy and Physiology*. Philadelphia: Saunders, 1967, p. 211. Reprinted by permission.

attached to any bone. Its root expands to form the *bulb* of the penis, which is fixed to the fibrous "hammock" that stretches in the triangular area beneath the pubic symphysis. The crura and the bulb constitute the root of the penis.

The smooth, rounded head of the penis is known as the *glans* ("acorn") *penis*. This structure is actually formed entirely by the free end of the spongy body, which expands to shelter the tips of the cavernous bodies. The glans penis has particular sexual importance. It is richly endowed with nerves and extremely sensitive. The rest of the penis is far less sensitive. Although the glans as a whole is highly excitable, its underside, where

a thin strip of skin (*frenulum*) connects it to the adjoining body of the penis, is particularly sensitive, as is its rim, or crown (*corona*), which slightly overhangs the superficial constriction called the *neck* of the penis. This neck is the boundary between the body of the penis and the glans. At the tip of the glans is the longitudinal slit for the urethral opening (*meatus*).

The skin of the penis is hairless and unusually loose, which permits expansion during erection. Although the skin is fixed to the penis at its neck, some of it folds over and covers part of the glans, forming the *prepuce*, or *foreskin*. Ordinarily the prepuce is retractable and the glans readily exposed. Circum-

Box 2.4 Male Circumcision

Circumcision ("cutting around") is the excision of the foreskin and is practiced around the world both as a ritual and as a medical measure. In the circumcised male the glans and the neck of the penis are completely exposed (*see* Figure 2.17).

As a ritual, circumcision was performed in Egypt as long ago as 4000 B.C. It thus long antedates the practice among Jews, Moslems, and other groups.[1] Circumcision for medical purposes in the United States dates back to the nineteenth century. Its original justification was to help combat masturbation. After this rationale was discredited, its advocates endorsed the practice on the grounds that after circumcision smegma does not accumulate under the prepuce and that it is therefore generally easier to keep the penis clean. Also, cancer of the penis was reportedly less frequent among the circumcised and cancer of the cervix less common among their spouses. Review of the evidence has shown these associations to have been highly questionable. Nevertheless,

physicians are currently still divided as to the advisability of routine circumcision in infancy.

Circumcision is medically obligatory if the foreskin is so tight that it cannot be easily retracted over the glans (*phimosis*). But this condition is rare and impossible to predict in infancy since it takes several years for the foreskin to become retractable among the majority of boys.[2]

It is generally assumed that the circumcised male is more rapidly aroused during coitus because of his fully exposed glans penis. Circumcision is also believed to cause difficulty in delaying ejaculation. Current research has failed to support these beliefs: There seems to be no difference between the excitability of the circumcised and uncircumcised penis.[3]

[1]The basis for the practice among Jews is set forth in Genesis 17:9–15. "You shall circumcise the flesh of your foreskin, and it shall be the sign of the covenant between us."
[2]For a critical review and discussion of the function of circumcision see Paige (1978).
[3]Masters and Johnson (1966), p. 190.

cision is the excision of the prepuce. In the circumcised penis, therefore, the glans is always totally exposed (*see* Box 2.4). Through more radical surgery it is also possible to form male and female genitalia through transsexual surgery (*see* Box 2.5).

Under the prepuce and in the corona and the neck are small glands that produce a cheesy substance (*smegma*) with a distinctive smell. This is a purely local secretion of no known function that must not be confused with the semen that is discharged through the urethra.

The human penis (unlike that of all other carnivora) has no bone. Nor does it have muscles within it. The *bulbocavernosus* and *ischiocavernosus* muscles surround the bulb and the crura, respectively, but their

function is primarily in helping eject urine and semen through the urethra (*see* Figure 2.15). Although these muscles may have an indirect role in contributing to venous congestion, the process of erection does not directly involve muscles, nor can the penis be moved voluntarily except for slight jerking motions.

The scrotum is a multilayered pouch. Its thin outermost skin is darker in color than is the rest of the body. It has many sweat glands, and at puberty it becomes sparsely covered with hair. The second layer consists of loosely organized muscle fibers (*dartos muscle*) and fibrous tissue. These muscle fibers are not under voluntary control, but they do contract in response to cold, sexual excitement, and a few other stimuli. Under such conditions the scrotum appears compact and

Box 2.5 Transsexual Surgery

During the past few decades increasing attention has been attracted to individuals who for deeply felt reasons wish to undergo a radical sex change. Most often this involves males who want to become females. Much of the public interest in this connection has focused on the more dramatic physical changes brought about by surgery. Actually, where such programs are responsibly conducted, the surgiccal procedure is only one aspect of the total process of sex reassignment.

In the change from male to female the testes and most of the penile tissues are first removed. In a subsequent stage the labia and vagina are constructed to approximate as closely as possible the appearance of the female genitalia. These persons can then engage in sexual intercourse, and some of them are able to attain orgasm.

The surgical transformation from female to male is more complicated, and none of the various techniques so far devised have been as successful as the

procedures for conversion of male to female. The penis and scrotum in these cases are constructed from tissues in the genital area. The artificial penis may appear convincingly "real" in successful cases, yet it is nonfunctional in the sense of being incapable of erection. In one approach a skin tube is fashioned at the underside of the new penis where a rigid silicone tube can be inserted permitting intromission and coitus. (For a more detailed discussion of these procedures and other aspects of transsexual changes, see Laub and Gandy, 1973).

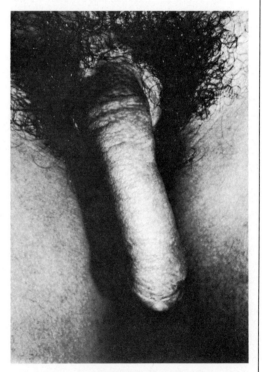

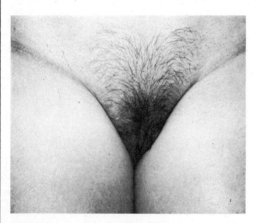

Postoperative result of male-to-female sex-change surgery. Courtesy of Dr. Donald R. Laub, Division of Reconstructive and Rehabilitation Surgery, Stanford University School of Medicine.

Postoperative result of female-to-male sex-change surgery. Courtesy of Dr. Donald R. Laub, Division of Reconstructive and Rehabilitation Surgery, Stanford University School of Medicine.

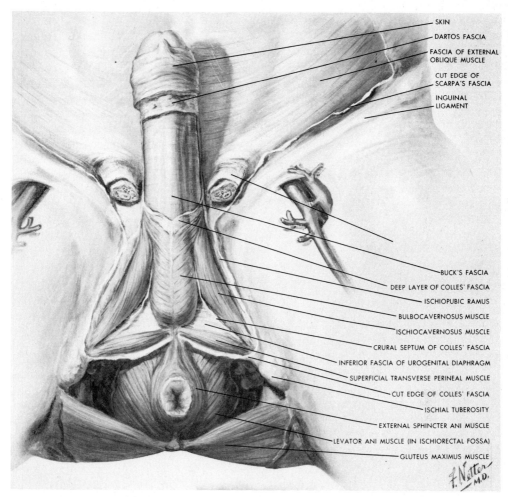

SKIN
DARTOS FASCIA
FASCIA OF EXTERNAL OBLIQUE MUSCLE
CUT EDGE OF SCARPA'S FASCIA
INGUINAL LIGAMENT

BUCK'S FASCIA
DEEP LAYER OF COLLES' FASCIA
ISCHIOPUBIC RAMUS
BULBOCAVERNOSUS MUSCLE
ISCHIOCAVERNOSUS MUSCLE
CRURAL SEPTUM OF COLLES' FASCIA
INFERIOR FASCIA OF UROGENITAL DIAPHRAGM
SUPERFICIAL TRANSVERSE PERINEAL MUSCLE
CUT EDGE OF COLLES' FASCIA
ISCHIAL TUBEROSITY
EXTERNAL SPHINCTER ANI MUSCLE
LEVATOR ANI MUSCLE (IN ISCHIORECTAL FOSSA)
GLUTEUS MAXIMUS MUSCLE

Figure 2.15 Male external genitalia (skin removed). From Netter, *The Ciba Collection of Medical Illustrations*: Volume 2, Reproductive System, p. 11. Reprinted by permission. © 1954, 1965 CIBA Pharmaceutical Company, Division of CIBA-GEIGY Corporation.

heavily wrinkled. Otherwise it hangs loose and its surface is smooth. When the inner side of the thigh is stimulated, the dartos muscle contracts slightly (the *cremasteric reflex*).

The scrotal sac contains two separate compartments, each of which houses a testicle and its *spermatic cord* (see Figure 2.16). The spermatic cord is a composite structure from which the testicle is suspended in the scrotal sac. It includes the tube (*vas deferens*)

that carries the sperm from the testicle, as well as blood vessels, nerves, and muscle fibers. When these muscles contract, the spermatic cord shortens and pulls the testicle upward within the scrotal sac.

The spermatic cord enters the abdominal cavity from the scrotal sac by traversing a region of the abdominal wall called the *inguinal canal*.

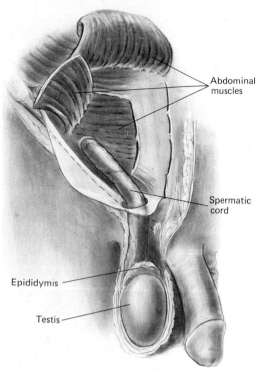

Figure 2.16 *Spermatic cord in the inguinal canal. From Dienhart, Basic Human Anatomy and Physiology. Philadelphia: Saunders, 1967, p. 209. Reprinted by permission.*

Size of the Penis

Variation in size and shape from individual to individual is the rule for all parts of the human body. Nevertheless, the size and shape of the penis are often the cause of curiosity and amusement as well as apprehension and concern. Representations of enormous penises can be found in numerous cultures, including some from remote antiquity (*see* Figure 2.17). These anatomical exaggerations are generally not mere caricatures or monuments to male vanity but symbols of fertility and life.

The average penis is 3 to 4 inches long when flaccid and somewhat more than 6 inches in erection. Its diameter in the relaxed state is about 1¼ inches and increases another ¼ inch in erection. Penises can, however, be considerably smaller or larger.

The size and shape of the penis, contrary to popular belief, are not related to a man's body build, race, virility, or ability to give and receive sexual satisfaction. Furthermore, variations in size tend to decrease in erection: The smaller the flaccid penis, the proportionately larger it tends to become when erect. The penis does not grow larger through frequent use.

Symbolic representations of the penis have been used for religious and magical functions (*see* Boxes 2.6 and 2.7).

Figure 2.17 *Mochica pottery. Courtesy of William Dellenback, Institute for Sex Research, Inc.*

Box 2.6 Phallus Worship

The worship of the male genitals is one of the oldest religious practices known. It is usually interpreted as related to fertility cults: the expression of man's desire for the perpetuation of the race and his identification with the reproductive powers of nature. In ancient Greece phallic worship centered around Priapus and the Dionysiac cults. Priapus was the son of Aphrodite (goddess of love) and Dionysus (god of fertility and wine). Usually represented as a grinning little man with an enormous penis, Priapus was very much in evidence during the many festivals honoring Dionysus, which were occasions for orgiastic abandon.

Under the Roman Empire phallic worship took on a less festive, rather grim form. During the yearly festival the notorious Day of Blood, some frenzied participants actually mutilated their own genitals. In fact, self-castration during this festival became a prerequisite for admission into the priesthood.

In India, Shiva (or Siva), one of the three supreme gods of Hinduism, was symbolically represented and worshipped as an erect penis (the lingam).

The phallic symbol could stand above or combined with a symbol of the female vulva (the yoni) as shown in the accompanying figure. Offerings of milk would be poured on the lingam, then drained off from the surrounding basin and used for various ritual purposes. Phallus worship has also been prominent in Japanese and some American Indian fertility rites.

Lingam-yoni altar. Stone. Eastern India. Modern. From Philip Rawson, *Erotic Art of the East.* New York: G. P. Putnam's Sons, 1968.

Internal Sex Organs

The internal sex organs of the male consist of a pair of testes or testicles, with their duct system for the storage and transport of sperm (epididymis, vas deferens, and ejaculatory duct in pairs and the single urethra) and accessory organs (a pair of seminal vesicles and bulbourethral glands and the prostate gland).

The testes ("witnesses": from the ancient custom of placing the hand on the genitals when taking an oath) are the *gonads*, or reproductive glands, of the male. They produce sperm, as well as the male hormone testosterone.

The two testicles are about the same size (2 × 1 × 1¼ inches), although the left one usually hangs somewhat lower than the right one. The weight of the testicles varies from one person to another, but averages about 1 ounce and tends to lessen in old age.

Box 2.7 Magical Uses of Genital Symbols

Since paleolithic times, various symbolic representations of the male and female genitalia have been put to magical uses. The Romans used phallic symbols in numerous guises to ward off the "evil eye." Sometimes these consisted of small stone phalluses embedded in a wall or larger free-standing representations placed at the boundary of the property. Commonly, they took the form of amulets showing the penis in naturalistic or fantastic forms. The magical thinking behind the practice was that such objects would fascinate the person with the evil eye and divert his gaze from the wearer of the amulet, thus sparing the person.[1] Similar practices in more or less obvious form can be discerned in other past and present cultures.

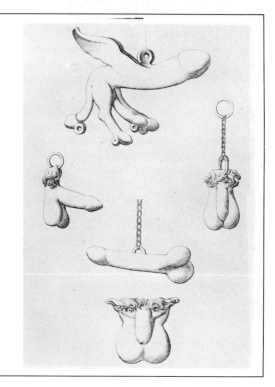

[1]For further details, see Grant (1975).

Each testicle is enclosed in a tight, whitish fibrous sheath (*tunica albuginea*, "white tunic")[14] which at the back of the organ thickens (*mediastinum testis*) and penetrates the testicle. Its ramifications (*septa*) then spread out within the organ and subdivide it into conical *lobes* (*see* Figure 2.18). Each lobe is packed with convoluted *seminiferous* (sperm-bearing) *tubules*. These threadlike structures are the sites at which sperm are produced. Each seminiferous tubule is 1–3 feet long, and the combined length of the tubules of both testes measures several hundred yards.

[14]This anatomical feature is responsible for the sterility that may follow mumps in adulthood. When this virus infection involves the testicles, the swelling organs push against their unyielding covers, and the pressure destroys the delicate tubes in which the sperm develop. When the same virus infects the female ovaries, the organs simply swell up and then return to their normal size and function.

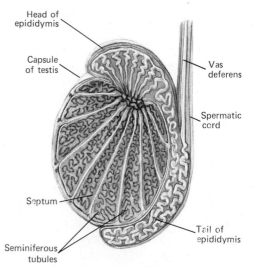

Figure 2.18 Testis and epididymis. From Dienhart, *Basic Human Anatomy and Physiology.* Philadelphia: Saunders, 1967, p. 207. Reprinted by permission.

This elaborate system of tubules allows for the production and storage of hundreds of millions of sperm. The process of *spermatogenesis,* or sperm production (discussed more fully in Chapter 5), takes place exclusively within the seminiferous tubules: Microscopic cross sections thus shown sperm at various levels of maturation. The first or earliest cell in this maturational chain is the *spermatogonium,* which in subsequent stages of development is successively called a *spermatocyte* (primary and secondary); *spermatid;* and fi-

nally, when mature, *spermatozoan,* or sperm. The seminiferous tubules of the newborn are solid cords in which only undifferentiated cells are evident. Following puberty, the tubules develop a hollow center into which the sperm are released (*see* Figure 2.19).

The second major function of the testes is the production of the male sex hormone. The testicular cells that produce the male hormone are found between the seminiferous tubules and are therefore known as *interstitial cells* (or *Leydig's cells*): They are scattered in

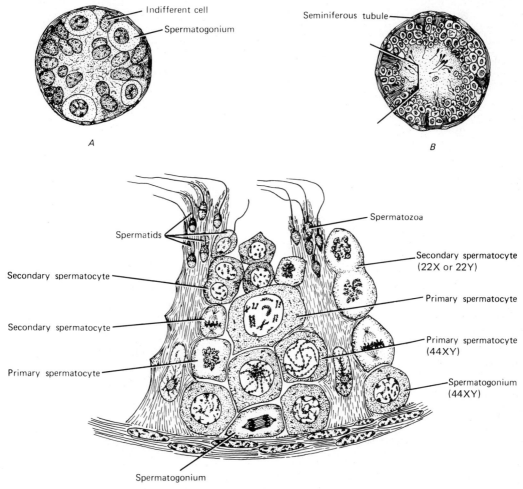

Figure 2.19 Human testis tubules, in transverse section. (*A*) Newborn (×400); (*B*) adult (×115); (*C*) detail of the area outlined in (*B*) (×900). From Arey, *Developmental Anatomy,* 7th ed. Philadelphia: Saunders, 1965, p. 41. Reprinted by permission.

the connective tissue in close association with blood vessels. The cells responsible for the two primary functions of the testes (reproductive and endocrine) are thus quite separate and never in contact.

The seminiferous tubules converge in an intricate maze of ducts, which ultimately leave the testis and fuse into a single tube, the epididymis. Figure 2.20 shows the route that sperm follow through these larger ducts during ejaculation.

The epididymis ("over the testis") constitutes the first portion of this paired duct system. Each is a remarkably long tube (about 20 feet) that is, however, so tortuous and convoluted that it appears as a C-shaped structure not much longer than the testis to whose surface it adheres (see Figure 2.18).

The vas deferens, or *ductus deferens* ("the vessel that brings down"), is the less tortuous and much shorter continuation of the epididymis. It travels upward in the scrotal sac for a short distance before entering the

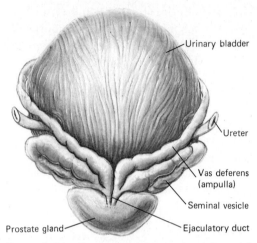

Figure 2.21 The bladder, seminal vesicles, and prostate gland—posterior view. From Dienhart, *Basic Human Anatomy and Physiology.* Philadelphia: Saunders, 1967, p. 210. Reprinted by permission.

abdominal cavity; its portion in the scrotal sac can be felt as a firm cord.[15]

The terminal portion of the vas deferens is enlarged and once again tortuous; it is called the *ampulla* ("flask"). It passes to the back of the urinary bladder (see Figure 2.21), narrows to a tip, and joins the duct of the seminal vesicle to form the *ejaculatory duct.* This portion of the paired genital duct system is very short (less than 1 inch) and quite straight. It runs its entire course within the *prostate gland* and opens into the prostatic portion of the *urethra* (see Figures 2.13 and 2.21).

The *urethra* has a dual function in the

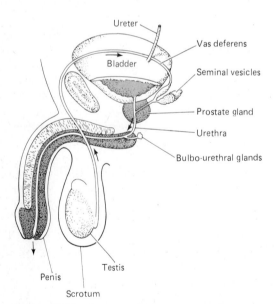

Figure 2.20 Passage of spermatozoa. From McNaught and Callander, *Illustrated Physiology.* Baltimore: Williams & Wilkins, 1972, p. 178. Reprinted by permission.

[15]That the vas is so easily located and surgically accessible makes it the most convenient target for sterilizing men. The operation (vasectomy, "cutting the vas") is very simple: under local anesthesia, a small incision is made in the scrotum, and the vas is simply either tied or cut. To stop all passage of sperm, the operation must, of course, be performed on both sides. The man is then sterile, but his sex drive, potency, and ability to have orgasms are not affected. He will continue to ejaculate, but his semen will contain no sperm. It is sometimes possible to reestablish fertility by untying or suturing the severed vas. This procedure is, however, very delicate and not always successful.

male, conveying both semen and urine. It begins at the bottom of the urinary bladder and periodically empties accumulated urine. (It must not be confused with the two *ureters,* each of which begins in one kidney and carries urine into the bladder.) The urethra is about 8 inches long and is subdivided into prostatic, membranous, and penile parts (*see* Figures 2.13 and 2.14).

The prostatic portion of the urethra is more easily dilated than are the others. In its posterior wall are the tiny openings of the two ejaculatory ducts. The multiple ducts of the prostate gland also empty into the prostatic urethra like a sieve (*see* Figure 2.14).

Voluntary control of urination is made possible by the muscle fibers (*urethral sphincter*) surrounding the short membranous urethra. When sufficient urine has accumulated in the bladder, the resulting discomfort prompts the person to relax the urethral sphincter to allow the passage of urine. The external urethral opening has no sphincter, which is why at the end of urination the urine left in the penile portion must be squirted out through the contraction of the bulbocavernosus and ischiocavernosus muscles.

The penile part of the urethra has already been discussed. It pierces the bulb of the corpus spongiosum, traverses its whole length, and terminates at the tip of the glans in the external urethral opening (*see* Figure 2.14). The *bulbourethral glands* (to be discussed later) empty into this portion.

Accessory Organs

Three accessory organs perform auxiliary functions in the male. They are the prostate gland, two seminal vesicles, and two bulbourethral glands.

The prostate is an encapsulated structure about the size and shape of a large chestnut and consisting of three lobes. It is located with its base against the bottom of the bladder. It consists of smooth muscle fibers and glandular tissue whose secretions account for much of the seminal fluid and its characteristic odor. As we have described, it is traversed by the urethra and the two ejaculatory ducts, and prostatic fluid is conveyed into this system through a "sieve" of multiple ducts.

The prostate is small at birth, enlarges rapidly at puberty, but usually shrinks in old age. Sometimes, however, it becomes enlarged and interferes with urination, necessitating surgical intervention. (It may be removed piece by piece through the urethra or in open surgery.) The size of the prostate is determined clinically by means of rectal examination.

The seminal vesicles are two sacs, each about 2 inches long. Each ends in a straight, narrow duct, which joins the tip of the vas deferens to form the ejaculatory duct. The function of the seminal vesicles was once assumed to be the storage of sperm (each holds about 2 to 3 cubic centimeters of fluid), but it is currently believed to be primarily involved in contributing fluids that initiate the motility of sperm through the action of their tails.

The bulbourethral glands (*Cowper's glands*) are two pea-sized structures flanking the penile urethra into which each empties through a tiny duct. During sexual arousal these glands secrete a clear, sticky fluid that appears as a droplet at the tip of the penis (the "distillate of love"). There usually is not enough of this secretion to serve as a coital lubricant. As it is alkaline, however, it may help to neutralize the acidic urethra, which is harmful to sperm, in preparation for the passage of semen. Although this fluid must not be confused with semen, it does often contain stray sperm, which explains pregnancies resulting from intercourse without ejaculation.

Developmental Anatomy of the Sex Organs

The study of the developmental anatomy of the various systems and organs of the body is a separate science (embryology). A com-

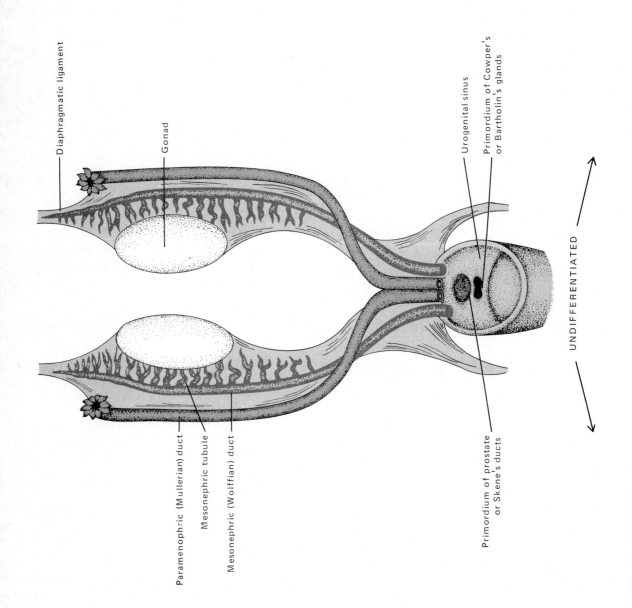

Diaphragmatic ligament

Gonad

Urogenital sinus

Primordium of Cowper's or Bartholin's glands

Paramenophric (Mullerian) duct

Mesonephric tubule

Mesonephric (Wolffian) duct

Primordium of prostate or Skene's ducts

UNDIFFERENTIATED

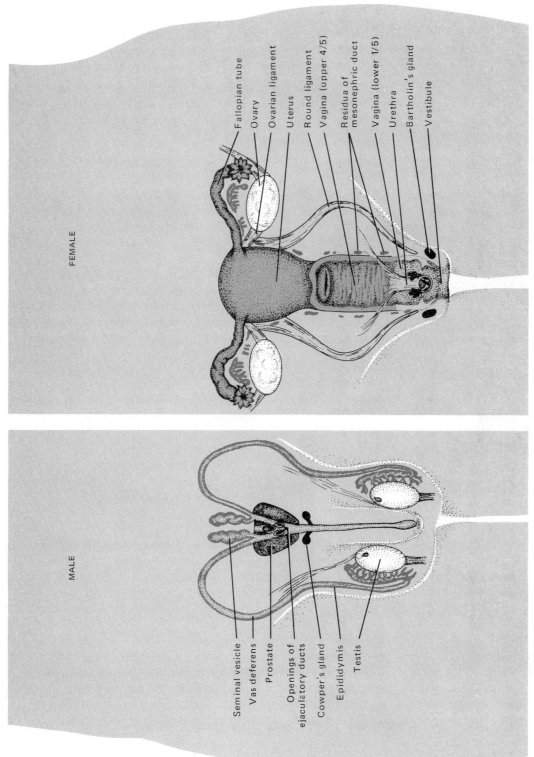

Figure 2.22 Homologues of internal male and female genitalia; development from undifferentiated stage. From Netter, *Reproductive System*, The Ciba Collection of Medical Illustrations, vol. 2 Summit, N.J.: Ciba, 1965, p. 2. Reprinted by permission. © 1954, 1965 CIBA Pharmaceutical Company, Division of CIBA-GEIGY Corporation.

MALE

Seminal vesicle
Vas deferens
Prostate
Openings of ejaculatory ducts
Cowper's gland
Epididymis
Testis

FEMALE

Fallopian tube
Ovary
Ovarian ligament
Uterus
Round ligament
Vagina (upper 4/5)
Residua of mesonephric duct
Vagina (lower 1/5)
Urethra
Bartholin's gland
Vestibule

prehensive survey of the development of the reproductive system is far too complex an undertaking for us to attempt here. We shall therefore select only a few aspects of this process to illustrate how sex organs develop and to emphasize the basic *structural* similarities between the male and female reproductive systems. Intrauterine growth and development in general will be discussed in conjunction with conception and pregnancy.

The genital system makes its appearance during the fifth to sixth week of intrauterine life, when the embryo has attained a length of 5 to 12 millimeters. At this undifferentiated stage the embryo has a pair of gonads and two sets of ducts (*see* Figure 2.22), as well as the rudiments of external genitals (*see* Figure 2.23).

At this time one cannot reliably determine the sex of the embryo by either gross or microscopic examination. The gonads have not yet become either testes or ovaries, and the other structures are also undifferentiated. This lack of visible differentiation does not mean that the sex of the individual is still undecided; sex is determined at the very moment of fertilization and depends on the chromosome composition of the fertilizing sperm. If the fertilizing sperm carries a Y chromosome, the issue will be male. Otherwise it will be female. These mechanisms that determine the process of sex differentiation will be discussed in Chapters 4 and 5.

Differentiation of the Gonads

The gonad that is destined to develop into a testis gradually consolidates as a more compact organ under the influence of the Y chromosome. Some of its cells are organized into distinct strands (*testis cords*), the forerunners of the seminiferous tubules. Other structures form the basis of the future internal duct system. By the seventh week (when the embryo is 14 millimeters long) enough differentiation may have occurred so that the organ is recognizable as a developing testis. If by this time

the basic architecture of the future testis is not discernible, it can be provisionally assumed that the undifferentiated gonad will develop into an ovary. More definitive evidence that the baby will be a girl comes somewhat later (about the tenth week), when the forerunners of the follicles begin to become visibly organized. After these basic patterns are set, the testis and ovary continue to grow accordingly. These organs do not attain full maturity until after puberty. The differences between the gonads of the newborn and the adult of each sex, briefly outlined above, will be further elaborated in Chapters 4 and 5.

Descent of the Testis and Ovary

Concomitant with the development described, both the testis and the ovary undergo gross changes in shape and position that are of special significance. At first the testis and the ovary are slender structures high up in the abdominal cavity. By the tenth week they have grown and shifted down to the level of the upper edge of the pelvis. There the ovaries remain until birth; they subsequently rotate and move farther down until they reach their adult positions in the pelvis.

In the male this early internal migration is followed by the actual descent of the testes into the scrotal sac (*see* Figure 2.24). After the descent of the testes, the passage is obliterated.

Two clinical problems may arise during this process. First, one or both of the testes may fail to descend into the scrotum before birth, as happens in about 2 percent of males born. In most of these boys the testes do descend by puberty. However, if they do not do so spontaneously, hormonal or surgical intervention becomes necessary. Otherwise the higher temperature of the abdominal cavity would interfere with spermatogenesis, resulting in sterility if both testes have failed to descend into the scrotum. Undescended testes are also more likely to develop cancer.

The second problem arises when the

UNDIFFERENTIATED

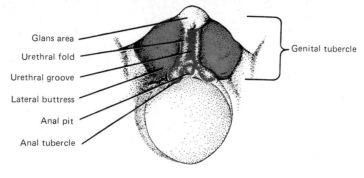

Glans area

Urethral fold

Urethral groove

Lateral buttress

Anal pit

Anal tubercle

Genital tubercle

45-50 MM.

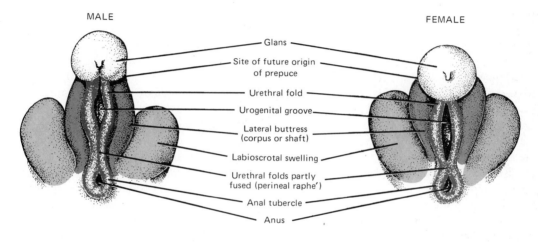

MALE

FEMALE

Glans

Site of future origin of prepuce

Urethral fold

Urogenital groove

Lateral buttress (corpus or shaft)

Labioscrotal swelling

Urethral folds partly fused (perineal raphe')

Anal tubercle

Anus

FULLY DEVELOPED

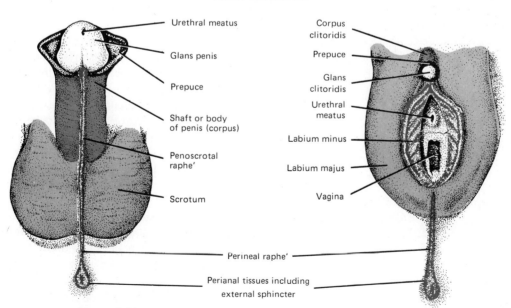

Urethral meatus

Glans penis

Prepuce

Shaft or body of penis (corpus)

Penoscrotal raphe'

Scrotum

Corpus clitoridis

Prepuce

Glans clitoridis

Urethral meatus

Labium minus

Labium majus

Vagina

Perineal raphe'

Perianal tissues including external sphincter

Figure 2.23 Homologues of external male and female genitalia; development from undifferentiated into differentiated stage. From Netter, *Reproductive System*, The Ciba Collection of Medical Illustrations, vol. 2 Summit, N.J.: Ciba, 1965, p. 3. Reprinted by permission. © 1954, 1965 CIBA Pharmaceutical Company, Division of CIBA-GEIGY Corporation.

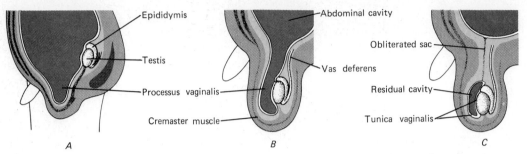

Figure 2.24 Descent of human testis and its subsequent relations shown in diagrammatic hemisections. From Arey, *Developmental Anatomy,* 7th ed. Philadelphia: Saunders, 1965, p. 333. Reprinted by permission.

passage traversed by the testes is not eliminated or reopens when the tissues become slack in old age. An abnormal passage is created, and intestinal loops may find their way into the scrotal sac creating a condition known as *inguinal hernia,* or *rupture* (*see* Figure 2.25). It too can readily be corrected by surgery.

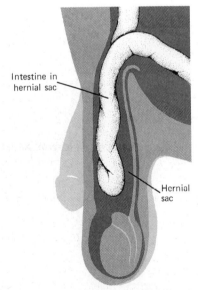

Figure 2.25 Inguinal hernia. From Arey, *Developmental Anatomy,* 7th ed. Philadelphia: Saunders, 1965, p. 334. Reprinted by permission.

Differentiation of the Genital Ducts

In the undifferentiated stage the embryo has two sets of ducts: the *paramesonephric* or *Müllerian* (the potential female) and the *mesonephric,* or *Wolffian* (the potential male) ducts (*see* Figure 2.24).

Just as the Y chromosome directs the development of the undifferentiated gonad to become a testis, the embryonal testis in turn determines the future development of the genital ducts. It accomplishes this by producing two substances: fetal androgen, which promotes the further differentiation of the Wolffian system, and a second substance that inhibits the further development of the Müllerian ducts. As a result the Wolffian duct on each side eventually becomes the epididymus, vas deferens, and seminal vesicle, and the Müllerian ducts degenerate.

In the absence of these testicular hormones (and without the need of ovarian hormones) the Wolffian ducts degenerate and the Müllerian ducts form the fallopian tubes, uterus, and the upper two-thirds of the vagina.

The lower third of the vagina, the bulbourethral glands, and the urethra in both sexes and the prostate gland are derived from the urogenital sinus which is part of the urinary system.

The precise mechanisms involved in the

above process are not entirely clear, but the general principle holds that differentiation of the reproductive tract is dependent on the Y chromosome first and then on testicular hormones. Otherwise the undifferentiated system will develop into the female pattern. Thus, irrespective of genetic makeup, if the gonads are removed early in life, the organism will develop into a female.

Differentiation of the External Genitals

The external genitals, like the internal, are at first sexually undifferentiated (*see* Figure 2.23). As we have indicated, by the seventh week the sex of the embryo can be ascertained provisionally by means of a microscopic study of the gonads. Several more weeks are necessary for the more distinctive development of the external genitals. The sex of the 4-month-old fetus is unmistakable. Differentiation of male and female external genitals is illustrated in Figure 2.23.

As with the differentiation of the internal duct system, it is testicular hormones that convert the undifferentiated precursors of the external genitalia to the male pattern. Otherwise it is the female pattern that develops.

This process of differentiation usually proceeds in a predictable and orderly manner. However, anomalies of development occasionally result in paradoxical conditions of bisexuality or hermaphroditism (discussed in Chapter 4).

With the aid of Figures 2.22 and 2.23 it is now easier to match the homologous pairs of organs in male and female. In principle it should be possible to identify the homologue to every part; however, since the degenerated remnants of theWolffian ducts in the female and the Müllerian ducts in the male are inconsequential structures, there is no point in attempting this for our purposes. The homologous pairs of significance are as follows: seminiferous tubules–ovarian follicles; Bartholin's gland–Cowper's gland; glans penis–glans of clitoris; corpora cavernosa of penis–corpora cavernosa of clitoris; corpus spongiosum of penis–bulb of the vestibule; underside of penis–labia minora; scrotum–labia majora.[16]

---

[16]A complete listing of all homologous pairs may be found in Moore (1973), p. 216.

Chapter 3

Physiology of Sexual Functions

The physiological goal of sexual activity is the attainment of orgasm. A great deal of such activity falls short of this goal, and the frequency and means by which orgasm is achieved through a lifetime vary tremendously. In studies of sexual behavior, orgasm is used as a quantitative unit, for it can be easily recognized and its occurrence counted.

In this chapter we are primarily concerned with physiological processes. There is an inherent danger in this approach, and it can be legitimately asked whether or not it is ever possible to separate the physiological functions of the body from their psychological concomitants. We do not intend to claim a dichotomy between mind and body, but practical considerations dictate that we examine the various facets of human sexuality a few at a time. Furthermore, as Kinsey has stated: "Whatever the poetry and romance of sex and whatever the moral and social significance of human sexual behavior, sexual responses involve real and material changes in the physiologic functioning of an animal."[1]

It is common knowledge that an episode of sexual experience begins with mounting excitement, which culminates in orgasm and is followed by a period of relaxation and sexual satiety. In more formal descriptions various stages have been ascribed in this process. Havelock Ellis envisaged two phases: tumescence and detumescence. More recently Masters and Johnson have proposed four phases: excitement, plateau, orgasm, resolution. The purpose of such subdivisions is to facilitate observation and description. Such classifications are not intended to obscure the basic unity of sexual activity, which proceeds in a continuous manner with manifestations of various phases overlapping and merging into one another imperceptibly.

Sexual Stimulation

The ability to respond to sexual stimulation is a universal characteristic of all healthy beings. Although the nature of the stimulus varies widely, the basic physiological response of the body is the same. The varieties and intensity of sexual arousal that each person experiences during a lifetime are, however, legion. Sometimes this excitement achieves full expression in orgasm; most of

[1]Kinsey et al. (1953), p. 594.

the time it progresses no farther than lingering thoughts or vague, evanescent yearnings.

What triggers such responses? Potentially, anything and everything. The stimuli may be "sexual" in the ordinary sense of the term; or they may involve factors that have no erotic interest for most people. The number and variety of sexual stimulants are bewildering. To impose some order, it is usual to classify erotic stimuli on different parameters: physical versus psychological, those to which responses are innate versus those to which they are learned, and so on. Such classification attempts are, however, of limited usefulness, for most stimuli have both physical and psychic components, and all behavior has internal and external determinants.

All modalities of sensation can be and usually are involved in erotic arousal, but for most human beings touch predominates, followed by vision. Among other animals other sensory modalities, like smell and taste (as in insects), may be more potent.

Stimulation through Touch

Tactile stimulation probably figures in most instances of sexual arousal leading to orgasm. Though other modalities are also important, touch remains the predominant mode of erotic stimulation. It is, in fact, the only type of stimulation to which the body can respond reflexively and independently of higher psychic centers. Even a man who is unconscious or whose spinal cord is injured at a point that prevents impulses from reaching the brain (but leaves sexual coordinating centers in the lower spinal cord intact) can still have an erection when his genitals or inner thighs are caressed.

The perception of touch is mediated through nerve endings in the skin and deeper tissues. These end organs are distributed unevenly, which explains why some parts (fingertips) are more sensitive than others (the skin of the back): The more richly innervated the region, the greater is its potential for stimulation.

Some of the more sensitive areas are believed to be especially susceptible to sexual arousal and are therefore called *erogenous zones*. They include the clitoris; the glans penis (particularly the corona and the underside of the glans); the shaft of the penis; the labia minora and the space they enclose (vestibule); the vaginal canal; the area between the anus and the genitals; the anus itself; the breasts (particularly the nipples); the mouth (lips, tongue, and the whole interior); the ears (especially the lobes); the buttocks; and the inner surfaces of the thighs.

Based on questionnaire responses, the primary nongenital erotic zones are reportedly the thighs (32 percent males, 14 percent females), the lips (10 percent males, 6 percent females) and the breasts (36 percent females, 5 percent males).[2]

Although it is true that these areas are most often involved in sexual stimulation, they are not the only ones by any means. The neck (throat and nape), the palms and fingertips, the soles and toes, the abdomen, the groin, the center of the lower back, or any other part of the body may well be erotically sensitive to touch. Some women have reached orgasm when their eyebrows were stroked or when pressure was applied to their teeth alone.[3]

The concept of erogenous zones is not new: Explicit or implicit references to them are plentiful in "love" manuals, and the practical value of such knowledge is self-evident.[4] A knowledge of erogenous zones may greatly enhance one's effectiveness as a lover. It must be noted, however, that these zones are often indistinct and do not correspond to any given pattern of nerve distribution. Also, the ultimate interpretation of all stimuli by the brain is profoundly affected by previous ex-

[2]Goldstein (1976), p. 130
[3]Kinsey et al. (1953), p. 590.
[4]The *Kama Sutra* refers to the armpit, throat, breasts, lips, "middle parts of the body," and thighs as suitable locations for stimulation (Vatsyayana, 1963 ed., p. 99). Also see Box 3.1.

Box 3.1 "Of the Various Seats of Passion in Women"

In classical Hindu erotic manuals, such as the *Ananga Ranga,* detailed instructions are given on the erogenous female zones and how and when to stimulate them. In addition to the general table reproduced

From Richard Burton and F. F. Arbuthnot, Trans., *The Ananga Ranga or the Hindu Art of Love of Kalyana Malla.* New York: Putnam, 1964.

below, more specific tables give instruction for the arousal of women of different classes of temperament. Although such prescriptions have no demonstrable physiological validity, they show the concerted effort to bring together various beliefs on human nature and cosmic forces in the service of sexuality.

Shuklapaksha or light fortnight; right side		The touches by which passion is satisfied	Krishnapaksha or dark fortnight; left side	
Day	Place		Place	Day
15th	Head and hair	Hold hair, and caress the head and fingertips	Head and hair	1st
14th	Right eye	Kiss and fongle	Left eye	2nd
13th	Lower lip	Kiss, bite and chew softly	Upper lip	3rd
12th	Right cheek	Do.	Left cheek	4th
11th	Throat	Scratch gently with nails	Throat	5th
10th	Side	Do.	Side	6th
9th	Breasts	Hold in hands and gently knead	Breasts	7th
8th	All bosom	Tap softly with base of fist	All bosom	8th
7th	Navel	Pat softly with open palm	Navel	9th
6th	Nates	Hold, squeeze and tap with fist	Nates	10th
5th	Yoni	Work with friction of Linga	Yoni	11th
4th	Knee	Press with application of knee and fillip with finger	Knee	12th
3rd	Calf of leg	Press with application of calf and fillip with finger	Calf of leg	13th
2nd	Foot	Press with toe, and thrust the latter	Foot	14th
1st	Big toe	Do.	Big toe	15th

perience and conditioning. A specific "erogenous" zone may thus be quite insensitive in a given person, or it may be sensitive to the point of pain. One cannot therefore approach another person in a mechanical, push-button manner and expect to elicit automatic sexual arousal.

Although it is true that one is more likely than not to respond to stimulation of the usual erogenous zones, the subtle lover will seek to learn the unique erogenous map of his or her partner, which is the result of both biological endowment and life experiences.

The frankly erotic component in being touched must be understood in the broader, more fundamental need for bodily contact that stems from our infancy. A crucial component in infant care is the touching, caressing, fondling and cuddling that is carried out by the adult caretakers. The dire effects that result from the deprivations of such care have been well documented for humans[5] and other primates.[6] Indeed, tactile communication plays such a major part in primate life

[5]Spitz and Wolf (1947), Harrow and Harmon (1975).

[6]Harlow (1958). We shall discuss some of Harlow's work in Chapter 8.

that the practice of grooming has been called the "social cement of primates."[7] The use of touch is a good example of how an ostensibly sexual process, in this case arousal, is embedded in the more fundamental human needs for contact, security, and affection.

Stimulation through Other Senses

Vision, hearing, smell, and taste are to varying extents also important avenues of erotic stimulation. These modalities, in contrast to touch, do not operate reflexively. We learn to experience certain sights, sounds, and smells as erotic and others as neutral or even offensive. We are not born with the notion that roses have an attractive odor or that feces (particularly those of others) smell bad. Regardless of the claims of cosmetic manufacturers, there are no scents and colors that are "naturally erotic," but scents and colors can be exciting if we have been conditioned to associate them with sexual arousal.[8]

The reflexive basis of tactile stimulation does not prevent its being subject to experiential modification. As discussed earlier, any part of the body surface may be rendered erotically sensitive or insensitive through experience and mental associations. Yet usually the reflexive aspect of tactile stimulation continues to operate. With vision, hearing, and smell, all responses are learned.

There is consequently boundless diversity in the sexual preferences and dislikes of individuals, as well as of cultures. This diversity makes it impossible to generalize about the effectiveness of any one source of stimulation. Why a certain female profile or a male sexual characteristic should be found exciting in one culture but not in another or only during a certain period of a given culture is cause for endless speculation.

The sight of the female genitals is probably as nearly a universal source of excitement for heterosexual males as any that exists. Paradoxically, viewing the male genitals does not seem to excite females as much, but this may simply be due to cultural inhibitions. There certainly are women who are just as fascinated by male genitals as men are by female genitals. In cultures in which nudity is acceptable, open preferences for certain features of external sex organs develop. Among some peoples of South Africa, for instance, large, pendulous minor lips ("Hottentot aprons") were considered very attractive in women. By pulling and stretching these parts during childhood and adolescence women caused them to hypertrophy. Alteration and mutilation of the genitals do not, however, always have erotic purposes, but may serve magical or religious functions.

Even though erotic standards differ and change, the impact of visual stimuli are unmistakable, as our preoccupation with physical attributes, cosmetics, and dress indicates. We could argue whether or not esthetic concerns are erotically motivated in all instances. Furthermore, the ability to experience and elicit sexual feelings does not necessarily depend on shape and form, as experience with beautiful but unresponsive women or handsome but inept men readily demonstrates.

The effect of sound is perhaps less telling but nevertheless quite significant as a sexual stimulant. The tone and softness of voice as well as certain types of music (with pulsating rhythms or repeated languorous sequences) can serve as erotic stimuli. But since these responses are learned, what stimulates one person may simply distract or annoy another.

The importance of the sense of smell has declined in man, both generally and in sexual terms. Nevertheless, the use of scents in many cultures, as well as preoccupation with body odors, attests to its considerable influence.[9]

---

[7]Jolly (1972), p. 153).

[8]An intriguing possibility exists that humans, like some other animals, secrete pheromones, in which case the above statement will have to be modified. Pheromones are discussed in Chapter 4.

[9]For further discussion of the role of olfaction, see Schneider (1971).

We would expect the smell of vaginal secretions and semen to have erotic properties. Yet most people do not openly admit to recognizing such properties—possibly because of inhibitions about discussing sexual matters. Observation of sexual behavior among animals indicates not only that our sense of smell has declined but also that we have lost our enjoyment of whatever body smells we do perceive. Sexual stimulants will be discussed further in connection with aphrodisiacs in Chapter 4.

Emotional Stimulation

Despite all the fascinating information that we have about the physical basis of sexual stimulation, the key to understanding human sexual arousal remains locked in emotional processes. Sexual arousal is an emotional state that is greatly influenced by other emotional states. Even reflexive sexual elements are normally under emotional control. Stimulation through any or all of the senses will result in sexual arousal if, and only if, accompanied by the appropriate emotional concomitants. Certain feelings like affection and trust will enhance, and others like anxiety and fear will inhibit erotic responses in most cases.

Given our highly developed nervous systems, we can react sexually to purely mental images, which makes sexual fantasy the most common erotic stimulant. Our responsiveness is thus not solely based on the characteristics of the concrete situation, but includes the entire store of memory from past experience and thoughts projected into the future. What arouses us sexually is in the last analysis the outcome of all these influences.

As human beings we all share to some extent a common history, as well as a common biology. For example, we are all cared for as infants by older persons who become the first and most significant influences in our lives. But we are also unique in numerous ways. The earlier remarks about erogenous zones can therefore be applicable to the psychological realm as well as to the physical.

Just as most of us are likely to respond to gentle caressing on the inside of our thighs, we are also likely to respond positively to the expression of sexual interest in us. In both cases the response will depend on the person involved and on the circumstances, and is hardly an automatic reaction.

Much of what is being said here is rather obvious, but it needs to be reiterated because we often find it easier and less threatening to rely on physical forms of arousal than on emotional expression. The role of psychological factors in sexual arousal and responsiveness will preoccupy us often in the rest of this book. Our primary concern at this point is with the physiological mechanisms underlying these emotional processes, and we shall deal with these at the end of the chapter.

Gender Differences in Sexual Arousal

Do women and men react differently to sexual stimuli? Are men "turned on" more easily than women? Are such differences, if they exist, innate or culturally determined?

Despite obvious and widespread interest in such questions, amazingly little research exists concerning differences among males and females as to what they generally consider to be erotically stimulating. Let us consider, for instance, the effect of viewing potentially prurient visual material. Kinsey reported that men are generally more stimulated than women by viewing sexually explicit materials (such as pictures of nudes, genitals, or sexual scenes) but that women are as equally stimulated as men by viewing motion pictures and reading literary material with romantic content. Most people would tend to agree to this claim on the basis of common observation. After all, the readership of "girlie" magazines, collectors of "dirty pictures," audiences at "stag films" and burlesque shows are predominantly male; and there seems to be no comparably intense interest among women.

But what about experimental rather

than reported evidence (which was the basis for Kinsey's conclusion) in this regard? A group of 50 male and 50 female students at Hamburg University matched for various background characteristics were shown sexually explicit pictures under experimental conditions.[10] In general, men did find pictures with sexual themes more stimulating when this involved isolated scenes (male subjects looking at pictures of attractive women in bikinis or exposing their genitals; female subjects looking at pictures of men in bikinis or showing naked men with erect penises). Where the scene had an interpersonal or affectionate component (kissing couple) women were equally if not more responsive. Scenes of coitus were somewhat more arousing to men, but not much more so than to women.

When looking at these pictures, the most frequent physiological reactions of the women were genital sensations (warmth, itching, pulsations), and about a fifth of the women reported vaginal moistening. Men usually responded with an erection.

In terms of the prevalence of these physiological responses, there was no significant overall difference between the sexes: 35 women and 40 men (out of 50 in each group) had some genital response. Nor was there any significant difference in the sexual aftereffects of the test: About half the subjects in each group reported increased sexual activity during the next 24 hours, involving masturbation, petting, or coitus. Increased sexual desire that was not acted on was also reported in comparable terms by both sexes.

A larger sample (128 males and 128 females) were shown films featuring male and female masturbation, petting, and coitus.[11] Once again, men responded more readily, but the difference with women was slight. There were no significant differences in the

prevalence of physiological reactions while viewing the films. Among the women 65 percent experienced genital sensations—28 percent felt vaginal moistening and 9 percent had sensations in the breast. Among men 31 percent had full and 55 percent had partial erections. About one in five men and women reported some masturbatory activity while viewing the film, and in four cases, all of them male, this was carried to the point of orgasm. During the following 24 hours there was some increase in sexual activity for both sexes, especially masturbation.

These findings tend to confirm the notion that males seem to respond more readily than females to erotic visual material. But this statement must be immediately qualified. First, the difference between the sexes is nowhere as impressive in this regard as is generally assumed. The apparent contrast is to a large extent due to social expectations and cultural convention: Women are not supposed to react as men do to explicit sexual material. This is often sufficient to inhibit their responses. In the event that their responses are not inhibited, women are likely to keep quiet about their true feelings so as not to risk social censure.

Second, whatever actual differences may exist generally between the sexes, they are superseded by the differences among the members of each sex. Thus, one will find many women who will react more positively to erotic visual stimuli than the "average" man. When this occurs, it is misleading to conclude that some women "respond like men," as if there were a fixed male standard of response. It is preferable to think of a variety of responses that men and women share in variable degree, but none of which is exclusive or characteristic of either sex.

There are at least two additional pitfalls in such comparisons. One is related to the biased selection of the erotic stimulus. Most erotic art, for instance, is produced by men. When we use these male-preferred sexual

[10]Sigusch, et al. (1970).
[11]Schmidt and Sigusch (1970). For a more comprehensive discussion of this research, see Chapter 7 by these same authors in Zubin and Money (1973).

representations and symbols as the standard stimuli, and women do not respond as actively as men do, it hardly follows that women are generally less responsive to erotic visual materials.

The second problem is even more fundamental and is based on sex discrepancies in the self-perception of sexual arousal. Most investigations of erotic stimulation used to rely on the verbal reports of subjects on viewing photographs of nudes and verbal descriptions or motion pictures of sexual activity.[12]

More recently, when physiological measures of arousal have been combined with verbal reports, a whole new dimension has been added to our understanding of these issues. In one study subjects listened to tape-recorded stories with erotic and romantic themes. In addition to reporting how they felt, the male subjects were monitored with a penile strain gauge and the females with a vaginal photoplethysmograph.[13] Both sexes reacted similarly in finding the tape with explicit erotic content more stimulating than those with romantic or erotically neutral content. Particularly arousing were the tapes where the female was the initiator of the encounter. There was however an interesting discrepancy between the verbal reports of the women and their physiological reactions: Only half of the women who were physiologically aroused reported this fact. The men on the other hand never failed to perceive the evidence of their physiological arousal.[14] There is no reason to believe that the female subjects were willfully concealing the fact of their being aroused. Their relative failure to per-

ceive sexual arousal must be explained therefore by anatomical differences (it is harder to miss an erection than the female counterpart such as vasocongestion) or perhaps by unconscious psychological mechanisms repressing such perception.[15]

Currently, women are becoming more willing to reveal their sexual preferences, and they tend to oppose the traditional practice of being measured by male criteria. As stereotyped views of sex-linked differences diminish, one can actually see a convergence in sexual response patterns. This has already taken place to some extent among the younger generations in the West.[16] As these changes become more generalized, we shall see what differences will remain, if any, among the responses of women and men to erotic visual stimuli.

These remarks notwithstanding, it would be premature to conclude that all currently perceived differences are due to "sexist" bias. There is ample evidence for discrepancies in the patterns of sexual arousal among animals. In the case of animals, communication of sexual interest predominantly occurs through physiological processes (like the secreting of pheromones) or morphological changes (such as the swelling and redness of the anogenital region of the female in estrus). Animals also engage in certain set behavioral courtship patterns. These processes are usually quite sex-specific.

What complicates matters further is the fact that such declarations of sexual interest may also serve to communicate other messages. For example, among primates rump presentation and mounting are both preludes to coitus, as well as a demonstration of submissive and dominant status respectively. To

---

[12]See, for example, Clark (1952); Byrne and Sheffield (1965); Schmidt and Sigusch (1970); Byrne et al. (1973).

[13]The penile strain gauge is a flexible loop, similar to a rubber band, that fits at the base of the penis and measures blood volume and pressure pulse, both of which reflect the degree of vasocongestion. The photoplethysmograph is an acrylic cylinder that contains a photocell and a light source. It is placed at the entrance of the vagina and detects evidence of vasocongestion.

[14]Heiman (1975).

[15]For more information on physiological measures of sexual arousal, see Zuckerman (1971), McConaghy (1967), and Heiman (1978).

[16]For references related to this trend in northwestern Europe and the United States, see Schmidt and Sigusch in Zubin and Money (1973), p. 140.

what extent such primate patterns of sexual stimulation persist among humans is not clear. The effect of hormones on libido is discussed in Chapter 4 and is obviously pertinent to the issue of sexual arousal.[17] As for other aspects of sexuality, we are just beginning to seriously view human behavior in primate perspective. There is a major shift in humans to more subtle behavioral patterns and verbal communication of sexual intent. Cultural diversity in this regard is wide, and a great deal of such behavior is barely realized consciously even by the person manifesting it.[18]

We have only dealt here so far with the question of erotic response to visual stimuli. The means of sexual arousal are so many and their underlying processes so complex that these brief references should be viewed as no more than illustrative examples. We must keep in mind that arousing sexual interest goes far deeper than mere sexual coquetry and forms the first step in the reproductive endeavor through which a species maintains itself.

Sexual Response: General Characteristics

In response to sexual stimulation the body reacts as a whole. The components of this total response are, however, many and varied. To facilitate description we shall first outline the general behavioral characteristics of sexual response patterns and then deal with the physiological changes in the sex organs and various body systems.

We shall be dealing throughout with the ordinary patterns of human sexual response. Our descriptions are not, however, intended as standards of "normality" or "healthiness." There are innumerable variations on these patterns, and they are also perfectly "nor-

mal" and "healthy." The biological basis of sexuality does not imply that its manifestations are relentlessly uniform.

Since sexual excitement and orgasm are widely experienced phenomena, we may wonder about the need to describe them. But most of us cannot generalize from only our own experiences. There is far too much variation among individuals to permit generalization, and, furthermore, most of us are in no mood for dispassionate observation at times of sexual stimulation. There is in fact a blurring of our perceptual ability during sexual arousal, as a result of which we are not quite fully conscious of our own sensations and physiological responses.

Approach to Orgasm

In response to effective sexual stimulation a sensation of heightened arousal develops. Thoughts and attention turn to the sexual activity at hand, and the person becomes progressively oblivious to other stimuli and events in the environment. Most people attempt to exert some control over the intensity and tempo of their mounting sexual tensions. They may try to suppress it or to ward it off by diverting their attention to other matters. Or they may deliberately enhance and prolong the feeling by dwelling on its pleasurable aspects. If circumstances are favorable to fuller expression, these erotic stirrings are difficult to ignore. On the other hand, anxiety or strong distractions may easily dissipate sexual arousal during the early stages.

Although excitement sometimes intensifies rapidly and relentlessly, it usually mounts more unevenly. In younger people the progression is steeper, whereas in older ones it tends to be more gradual. As the level of tension rises, external distractions become less effective, and orgasm is more likely to occur.

The prelude to orgasm is pleasurable in itself and can be quite satisfying. In fact, following a period of sustained excitement one may voluntarily forgo the climax. But linger-

---

[17]Also see Dmowski et al. (1974).
[18]For an anthropological review of sexual signaling, see Hewes (1973).

ing tensions usually do create irritability and restlessness if unrelieved by orgasm.

It is generally believed that men respond more rapidly to sexual stimulation and are capable of reaching orgasm more rapidly than women are. A great deal of advice in marriage manuals revolves around this very point: Because women supposedly respond more slowly, they must be stimulated for longer periods if they are to reach orgasm. This belief has a certain validity, for in clinical practice the "slower" wife usually does complain that she is "left behind." Yet there is no known physiological basis for this claimed difference, and females can respond more or less as quickly as males do to effective sexual stimulation.

The average female, for example, takes somewhat less than four minutes to reach orgasm during masturbation, whereas the average male needs between two and four minutes. Some women may achieve climax, however, in as little as 15 to 30 seconds. The disparity between the sexes in achieving coital orgasm is therefore related not to fundamental physiological differences but to the mechanical and psychological components of sexual intercourse.

The behavioral and subjective manifestations of sexual excitement vary so widely that no one description can possibly encompass them all. With mild sexual excitement, relatively few reactions may be visible to the casual observer; on the other hand, in intense excitement behavior may be quite dramatic.

The person in the grip of sexual excitement appears tense from head to toe. The activities of the muscles, though dramatic, are by no means the only sexual responses of the body. The skin becomes flushed; salivation increases; the nostrils may flare; the heart pounds; breathing grows heavy; the face is contorted and flushed; the person feels, looks, and acts quite unlike his or her ordinary self.

These phenomena may be quite mild. The results of muscular tension and vaso-

congestion are inevitably present, but are not always reflected in a highly visible manner. The person may remain still or show only occasional and minimal overt responses. Movements may be deliberate and gentle. Changes in facial expression may be minor. But, no matter how attenuated his or her behavioral manifestations, the person must experience distinct increases in heart rate and heavier breathing; otherwise arousal is simply not present.

We have so far omitted all reference to changes in the sex organs, for we shall deal with them in detail later. We have also left out idiosyncratic manifestations: Some stutterers, for instance, speak more freely when sexually aroused. The gagging reflex may disappear, which explains the ability of some people to take the penis deep into their mouths. Spastics may coordinate better; those suffering from hay fever may obtain temporary relief; bleeding from cuts decreases. The perception of pain is markedly blunted during sexual arousal, which partly explains masochistic endurance of sadistic practices.

Orgasm

Orgasm (from the Greek *orgasmos,* "to swell," "to be lustful") is one of the most intense and profoundly satisfying sensations that a person can experience. In physiological terms it consists of the explosive discharge of accumulated neuromuscular tensions. More subjectively defined, it is a high pitch of tension in which time seems to stand still for a moment. There is drive toward release and utter helplessness to stop it. In a matter of seconds it is all over, but while it lasts it seems an eternity.

The patterns of response during orgasm vary among individuals and according to age, fatigue, length of abstinence, and context. On strictly physiological grounds there is no reason why men and women should react differently during orgasm. However, psychological factors and different standards of propriety

Box 3.2   Varieties of Female Orgasm

The formal differentiation between types of female orgasm was originally proposed by Freud[1] and reiterated by other psychoanalysts.[2] It has thus been a tenet of orthodox psychoanalytic theory that females experience two types of orgasm: clitoral and vaginal. The term *clitoral orgasm* means orgasm attained exclusively through direct clitoral stimulation. Likewise, *vaginal orgasm* means orgasm attained through vaginal stimulation.

This dual orgasm theory assumes that in young girls the clitoris, like the male penis, is the primary site of sexual excitement and expression. With psychosexual maturity the sexual focus is said to shift from the clitoris to the vagina, so after puberty the vagina emerges as the dominant orgasmic zone. Should this transfer not occur, the woman remains incapable of experiencing vaginal orgasm and is restricted to the "immature" clitoral type.

[1]*New Introductory Lectures on Psychoanalysis* (1933), in Freud (1957–1964), Vol. XXII.
[2]For example, Ferenczi (1936), Abraham (1948), Knight (1943), Fenichel (1945), Deutsch (1945), Benedek (1952). In more current psychoanalytic literature there is a shift away from the dual orgasm hypothesis. See, for instance, Salzman (1968).

Kinsey and his associates raised doubts about the whole concept of dual orgasm. They pointed out that the vagina is a rather insensitive organ; during pelvic examinations many women simply cannot tell when the vaginal wall is being gently touched, and in surgical practice the vagina has been found to be rather insensitive to pain. Also, microscopic studies fail to reveal end organs of touch in most vaginal walls.

The data from Masters and Johnson's study supported the Kinsey point of view: Physiologically there is one and only one type of orgasm. The clitoris and the vagina respond in identical fashion, regardless of which is stimulated or, for that matter, even if neither one is directly involved (as when orgasm occurs after breast manipulation only). This finding does not mean that the subjective experience of orgasm, elicited by whatever means, is always the same. The similarity is in the physiologic manifestations only. The subjective experience of orgasm resulting from masturbation or coitus, or from coitus in a given position or with a specific person, can certainly vary tremendously. But the basis of these differences is psychological.

The initial impact of the Masters and Johnson research was so striking that the whole controversy of clitoral versus vaginal

may markedly alter the behavior of the two sexes. Differences in orgasmic response may also arise from physical considerations, such as whether the person is experiencing orgasm when lying down or standing up, and so on.

At one extreme, the overt manifestations of orgasm may be so subdued that an observer may hardly be able to detect them; on the other hand, the experience may be like an explosive convulsion. Most commonly there is a visible combination of genital and total body responses: sustained tension or mild twitching of the extremities while the rest of the body becomes rigid; a grimace or muf-

fled cry; and rhythmic throbbing of sex organs and pelvic musculature before relaxation sets in. Less commonly reactions are restricted to the genitals alone. The pelvic thrusts are followed by subdued throbbings, and general body response seems minimal.

In intense orgasm the whole body becomes rigid, the legs and feet extended, the toes curl in or flare out,[19] the abdomen becomes hard and spastic, the stiffened neck is thrust forward, the shoulders and arms are

[19]In Japanese erotic art curled toes indicate sexual excitement. The characteristic posture of the stiffened and extended feet and hands is called *carpopedal spasm*.

Box 3.2   Continued

orgasm appeared to have been laid to rest once and for all. But this has in fact not happened and the issue continues to be debated.[3]

Part of the problem is in the difficulty of separating physiological effects from the totality of the experience.

Currently women who are aware of the Masters and Johnson findings continue to assert their perception of subjective differences, as is illustrated in Box 3.3.

The controversy actually goes beyond the matter of subjective sensation. Singer and Singer, for example, have attempted to review the issue of whether or not convulsive contractions of the vaginal introitus and the surrounding area are a necessary element in the female orgasm.[4] They argue that they are not, and instead propose that there are three types of female orgasm.

First is the "vulval orgasm," which is characterized by involuntary rhythmic contractions of the vaginal introitus ("orgasmic platform"). They claim that this is the orgasm observed by Masters and Johnson (which we shall discuss in detail in the following section). This type does not

depend on the nature of sexual activity, whether it is coitus or masturbation, and has consistent physiological properties.

Second, there is the "uterine orgasm," which does not involve contractions of the vulva but is characterized by a special type of breathing: The woman takes in a series of gasping gulps of air and then momentarily stops breathing before forcefully exhaling the held breath, sometimes uttering forced sounds or incoherent words. This is followed by a feeling of relaxation and sexual satiation.

The reason that this second type of orgasm is called "uterine" is because it presumably results from the repetitive displacement of the uterus and consequent stimulation of the peritoneum (which consists of sensitive folds of tissue that cover the abdominal organs). Unlike the vulval orgasm, the uterine variety is dependent on coitus (or a close substitute), since clitoral stimulation, for example, would have no direct physical impact on the uterus.

The third type is the "blended orgasm," which, as the terms suggests, combines elements of the previous two kinds.[5]

[3]*See*, for example, Clark (1970), Robertiello (1970), Fisher (1973).
[4]Singer and Singer (1972).

[5]Also of interest in this female orgasmic controversy are the views of Sherfey (1973) and Fisher (1973).

rigid and grasping, the mouth gasps for breath, the eyes buldge and stare vacantly or shut tightly. The whole body convulses in synchrony with the genital throbs or twitches incontrollably.

At the climax the person may moan, groan, scream, or utter fragmented and meaningless phrases. In more extreme reactions there may be uncontrollable laughing, talking, crying, or frenzied movement. Such climaxes may last several minutes.

Orgasm is experienced by both men and women as intense pleasure, though its subjective components do vary somewhat

between the two sexes.[20] In adult males the sensations of orgasm are linked to ejaculation,[21] which occurs in two stages. First,

[20]An interesting way of conceptualizing the orgasmic experience is to view it as an "altered state of consciousness." For an exposition of this view, see Davidson (in press).
[21]Ejaculation and orgasm are two separate processes. Orgasm can be experienced in both sexes and probably at all ages. It consists of the neuromuscular discharge of accumulated sexual tensions. Ejaculation on the other hand is experienced only by males following puberty, when the prostate and accessory glands become functional. Females do not ejaculate. The fluid that lubricates the vagina is produced during arousal and does not correspond to the male semen.

Box 3.3 Female Experiences of Orgasm

The first of the following selections is from a Doris Lessing novel. The second description is provided by a married pair of physiologists who monitored their sexual responses in the privacy of their own bedroom:

When Ella first made love with Paul, during the first few months, what set the seal on the fact she loved him, and made it possible for her to use the word, was that she immediately experienced orgasm. Vaginal orgasm that is. And she could not have experienced it if she had not loved him. It is the orgasm that is created by the man's need for a woman, and his confidence in that need.

As time went on, he began to use mechanical means. (I look at the word mechanical—a man wouldn't use it.) Paul began to rely on manipulating her externally, on giving Ella clitoral orgasms. Very exciting. Yet there was always a part of her that resented it. Because she felt that the fact he wanted to, was an expression of his instinctive desire not to commit himself to her. She felt that without knowing it or being conscious of it (though perhaps he was

conscious of it) he was afraid of the emotion. A vaginal orgasm is emotion and nothing else, felt as emotion and expressed in sensations that are indistinguishable from emotion. The vaginal orgasm is a dissolving in a vague, dark generalised sensation like being swirled in a warm whirlpool. There are several different sorts of clitoral orgasms, and they are more powerful (that is a male word) than the vaginal orgasm. There can be a thousand thrills, sensations, etc., but there is only one real female orgasm and that is when a man, from the whole of his need and desire takes a woman and wants all her response. Everything else is a substitute and a fake, and the most inexperienced woman feels this instinctively. (From *The Golden Notebook* (London: Michael Joseph Ltd., 1962), p. 186. Reprinted by permission of Simon and Schuster and Michael Joseph Ltd. Copyright © 1962 by Doris Lessing.

This female usually experiences two orgasms during coitus, one before the male ejaculates and a second about half a minute after ejaculation commences, and these are qualitatively different. The first sometimes tends

---

there is a sense that ejaculation is imminent, or "coming," and that one can do nothing to stop it. Second, there is a distinct awareness of the contracting urethra, followed by fluid moving out under pressure.

Orgasm in the female starts with a feeling of momentary suspension followed by a peak of intense sensation in the clitoris, which then spreads through the pelvis. This stage varies in intensity and may also involve sensations of "falling," "opening up," or even of emitting fluid. Some women compare this stage of orgasm to mild labor pains. It is followed by a suffusion of warmth spreading from the pelvis through the rest of the body. The experience culminates in characteristic throbbing sensations in the pelvis. The female orgasm, unlike that of the male, can be interrupted.

Are all orgasms the same? The question

is impossible to answer categorically. At one level, no two experiences are ever the same because each of us is unique and because even the same person is different in some ways at different times. But for practical purposes we do consider certain experiences to be identical if in most aspects they replicate themselves.

In the latter sense the male orgasmic experience physiologically and psychologically seems to be fairly standard. There are wide differences in intensity and other aspects, as we shall discuss in connection with sexual intercourse, but all these differences are understandable as departures from a generally recognized common experience.

The situation is more complex with women. They experience the same variations as men do, but in addition there is the possibility that women experience qualitatively

Box 3.3 Continued

to be fairly laboured, and the second occurs almost automatically. The second is very much more intense in feeling and occurs much more reliably than the first. The first orgasm is considerably more variable and inconstant than the second, occurring sometimes soon after the beginning of coitus, sometimes after a considerable time has elapsed and sometimes not at all. During periods of heightened excitement, the first orgasm might be intentionally eliminated, or alternatively could develop into multiple orgasms, i.e. about six or seven minor orgasms, if coitus lasts long enough. This depends on the responsiveness of the penis for when the penile reactions are swift, coitus ends quickly. The most noteworthy characteristic of the first (pre-ejaculatory) orgasms is their failure to satisfy. Whether one or six occur, the sensation of incompleteness and dissatisfaction remains. These orgasms seem to serve the purpose of ensuring a satisfactory state of excitement or responsiveness for the final (post-ejaculatory) orgasm, especially if the opportunity for foreplay is limited. With the final (post-ejaculatory) orgasm complete satisfaction is obtained, irrespective of the number of orgasms which preceded it.

. . . With the final contractions of ejaculation, the male begins to relax his hold and become inert. At this point a compulsive abdominal and vaginal straining and heaving begins in the female. The penis seems to be pushed into the vaginal outlet, the shaft is gripped just below the glans by the muscles at the vaginal outlet, until the glans is made to form a tight-fitting plug in the vagina. At this stage the heaving reaches its maximum intensity and heralds the orgasmic contractions in the vagina and uterus at intervals of approximately 1 sec. The vaginal reaction to ejaculation is so automatic that it seems to have almost the quality of a reflex, and thus could, in times of stress, presumably fail. The vaginal contractions alternate with inward heaves, which carry with them a sensation of inward suction, though the intensely pleasurable orgasmic sensations are more allied to the contractions and the sense of relief these bring. The sensation of suction does not usually accompany clitoral or extra-coital orgasm. (From C. A. Fox and Beatrice Fox, "Blood Pressure and Respiratory Patterns during Human Coitus," *Journal of Reproductive Fertility*, 19:3 (August, 1969), p. 411. Reproduced by permission of Blackwell Scientific Publications Ltd.)

different orgasms that also involve differences in physiological mechanisms (*see* Boxes 3.2 and 3.3).

The theoretical fascination of this subject notwithstanding, the practical issue to bear in mind is that clitoral stimulation seems to be a crucial component in eliciting erotic responses in the majority of women. Until proved to the contrary, there would seem to be little to be gained and much to be lost to handicap women with the view that clitoral stimulation is somehow a crutch to be relied upon if "vaginal," "authentic," or some other presumably higher orgasmic response is not forthcoming.

Aftereffects of Orgasm

Whereas the onset of orgasm is fairly distinct, its termination is more ambiguous. The rhythmic throbs of the genitals and the convulsions of the body become progressively less intense and less frequent. Overwhelming neuromuscular tension gives way to profound relaxation.

The manifestations of the postorgasmic phase are the opposite of those of the preorgasmic period. The entire musculature is relaxed. The person feels an overwhelming need to rest. The head feels too heavy for the neck to support. The grasping hands and curled toes relax, and the arms and legs can be moved only with effort. The pounding heart and accelerated breathing revert to normal. Congested and swollen tissues and organs resume their usual colors and sizes. As the body rests, the mind reawakens, and the various senses regain their full acuity gradually.

The quiescent state of body and mind following sexual climax has given rise to the belief that all animals are sad following coitus.[22] Actually, for most people the predominant sensation is one of profound gratification, or peace and satiation. The contorted expression yields to one of calm. The eyes become luminous and languid, and a subtle flush lights the face.

The descent from the peak of orgasm may occur in one vertiginous sweep, or more gradually. Particularly at night the profound postcoital relaxation contributes to natural weariness, and the person may simply fall asleep. Others feel relaxed but perfectly alert or even exhilarated.

It is not unusual to feel thirsty or hungry following orgasm. A smoker may crave a cigarette. Often there is a need to urinate, sometimes to move the bowels. Idiosyncratic reactions are myriad: Some people feel numb or itch; some want more physical contact; and others want to be left alone. It is difficult to separate physiologically determined responses from psychological, or learned, patterns of behavior in this area.

Regardless of the immediate postorgasmic response, a healthy person recovers fully from the aftereffects of orgasm in a relatively short time. Protracted fatigue is often the result of activities that may have preceded or accompanied sex (drinking, lack of sleep), rather than of orgasm itself. When a person is in ill health, however, the experience itself may be more taxing.

Orgasm in Lower Animals

The expressions of orgasm are clearly discernible among mammals. In the male animal there is no question that orgasm occurs regularly, and ejaculation marks it clearly. Female animal orgasm is more difficult to detect. In female mammals, other than humans, neuromuscular tensions do not seem to subside abruptly following coitus but rather dissipate slowly. Furthermore, female animals in heat remain responsive to sexual stimulation after coitus, rather than losing interest as males do.

Even though most infrahuman females seem to be orgasmically nonresponsive, there are records of specific instances in which female chimpanzees have seemed to exhibit all the signs of orgasm. Physiological measures of blood pressure in these animals during sexual activity also demonstrate similar elevations and depressions for both sexes, which constitute indirect evidence for the occurrence of sexual climax. The evidence from animals indicates that orgasm evolved late for females. Whereas orgasm in males is clearly the continuation of mechanisms present in infrahuman species, the human female is unique in her ability to reach orgasm so readily and unmistakably.[23]

The Sexual Response Cycle

The physiology of sexual function has been sadly neglected in medical research. In the fourth century B.C., Aristotle observed that the testes are lifted within the scrotal sac during sexual excitement; more than 20 centuries passed before this fact was confirmed under laboratory conditions.

So far there has actually been only one extensive investigation of the physiology of orgasm, the one conducted by Masters and Johnson.[24] Their work is widely known, and numerous summaries of it are available.[25] We shall therefore outline it only briefly here.

Research Background

Masters and Johnson were primarily interested in investigating the physiology of orgasm in a laboratory setting. Their subjects were 694 normally functioning volunteers of

---

[22]The original remark, ascribed to Galen (A.D. 130–200) was *Triste est omne animal post coitum, praeter mulierem gallumque* ("Every animal is sad after coitus except the human female and the rooster").

[23]Ford and Beach (1951), p. 30.
[24]Masters and Johnson (1966); (1979).
[25]See, for example, Brecher and Brecher (1966), Part I, and Belliveau and Richter (1970), Chapter 4.

both sexes between the ages of 18 and 89 years. These subjects thus did not constitute a random sample of the general population, and in this sense they were not "average people." Nor were they specifically selected for their sexual prowess; the only such requirement was that they be sexually responsive under laboratory conditions. In socioeconomic terms the group was as a whole better educated and more affluent than is the general population, though there was some representation across social classes.

The research procedure was to observe, monitor, and sometimes film the responses of the body as a whole and the sex organs in particular to sexual stimulation and orgasm. Both masturbation and sexual intercourse were included in the experiment. In order to observe vaginal responses, a special penislike object was used; it was made of clear plastic, which permitted direct observation and filming of the inside of the vagina.

The laboratory in which the research took place was a plain, windowless room containing a bed and monitoring and recording equipment. The subjects were first left alone to engage in sex, and only when they felt comfortable in this setting were they asked to perform in the presence of investigators and technicians monitoring the equipment (recording heart rates, blood pressures, brain waves, and so on). It was the type of setting in which hundreds of experiments of all kinds are conducted in medical centers all over the world. The only unique element was the specific physiological function under study.

During almost a decade (beginning in 1954) at least 10,000 orgasms were investigated. Because more of the subjects were women and because females registered more orgasms than males under the circumstances, about three-quarters of these orgasms were experienced by women. The same investigators have reported more recently their physiological findings in the sexual response cycle of homosexual males and females as well as those with bisexual ("ambisexual") orientation.[26]

Although no one has yet attempted to fully replicate Masters and Johnson's research, the scientific validity of their physiological findings has been widely accepted. There have been some questions raised about minor aspects of their findings, which we shall point out further on.[27]

Response Patterns

The sexual response patterns shown in Figure 3.1 and 3.2 summarize observations by Masters and Johnson. They represent generalized patterns rather than consistent reactions of individuals. These graphic summaries do not show the common deviations from basic responses. Such deviations, however, occur mostly in the durations of phases rather than in the sequence of response in each. We can therefore view these curves as typical, while keeping in mind the wide range of variation within them.

The sexual response pattern for males (Figure 3.1) and the three patterns for females (Figure 3.2) include the same four phases: excitement, plateau, orgasm, and resolution.

These response patterns are generally independent of the type of stimulation or sexual activity that produces them. The basic physiology of orgasm is the same, regardless of whether it is brought about through masturbation, coitus, or some other activity. Differences resulting from the type of stimulation do not affect the fundamental changes manifested by the body, but may affect the intensity of responses to some extent.

We shall repeatedly emphasize the subjective experience of the fundamental similarity of sexual responses in the two sexes. There are, however, a number of differences between male and female responses that

[26]Masters and Johnson (1979).
[27]For a critique, see Fox and Fox (1969).

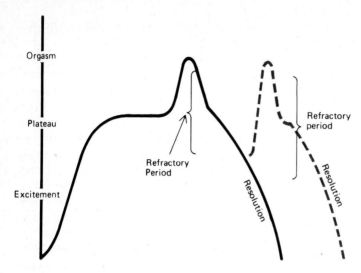

Figure 3.1   The male sexual response cycle. From Masters and Johnson, *Human Sexual Response* (Boston: Little, Brown and Company, 1966), p. 5. Reprinted by permission.

must be noted. Some result from anatomical differences; others cannot be explained structurally and possibly reflect variations in nervous system organization.

The first major difference is in the range of variability. It is already apparent from Figures 3.1 and 3.2 that whereas a single sequence characterizes the basic male pattern, three alternatives are shown for females. Even this diagram does not fully convey the richer variety of female responses. But this does not mean that the male response is the basic norm and the female responses variant forms of the male.

The second difference between the sexes involves the presence of a refractory period in the male cycle. (A cell, tissue, or organ may not respond to a second stimulation until a certain period of time has elapsed after the preceding stimulation. This period is known as "refractory.") As is indicated in Figure 3.1, the refractory period immediately follows orgasm and extends into the resolution phase. During this period, regardless of the

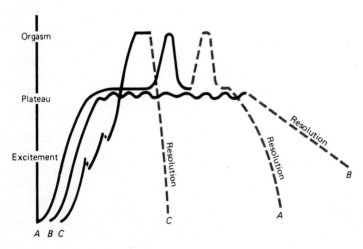

Figure 3.2   The female sexual response cycle. From Masters and Johnson, *Human Sexual Response* (Boston: Little, Brown and Company, 1966), p. 5. Reprinted by permission.

nature and intensity of sexual stimulation, the male will not respond. He cannot achieve full erection and another orgasm. Only after the refractory period, the duration of which has not yet been specified with precision, can he do so.[28]

Females do not have such refractory periods (Figure 3.2). Even in the pattern closest to that of the male (line A), as soon as the first orgasm is over the level of excitement can mount immediately to another climax. Women can thus have multiple orgasms in rapid succession.

Men have been considered to be very limited in their capacity for multiple orgasm due to their refractory period. Among the subjects studied by Masters and Johnson only a few males seemed capable of repeated orgasm and ejaculation within minutes. More recent evidence suggests that multiple orgasm is not that rare if orgasm and ejaculation are considered separately from each other.[29] We shall return to this issue shortly when we discuss orgasm in greater detail.

Apart from these differences, the basic response patterns in the two sexes are the same. In males (Figure 3.1) and females (Figure 3.2, line A) excitement mounts in response to effective and sustained stimulation, which may be psychogenic (erotic thoughts and feelings) or somatogenic (physical stimulation), but usually involves both. Excitement may mount rapidly or more slowly, depending on various factors. If erotic stimulation is sustained, the level of excitement becomes stabilized at a high point: the plateau phase. Sometimes during this stage the point of no return is reached, and orgasm follows. This abrupt release is succeeded by a gradual dis-

persion of pent-up excitement during the resolution phase.

The lengths of these phases vary greatly, but in general the excitement and resolution phases are the longest. The plateau phase is usually relatively short, and orgasm usually takes only a minute or less. Although the diagrams do not indicate them, there may be several peaks in the plateau phase, each followed by a return to a lower level of excitement. It is also possible that excitement may not reach the point of orgasm. The overall time for one complete coital cycle may range from a few minutes to much longer.[30]

The two other female patterns (Figure 3.2, lines B and C) represent opposite alternatives to the more common pattern. In pattern B the woman attains a high level of arousal during the plateau phase but these peaks of arousal do not quite culminate in orgasmic release. Instead sexual tension is gradually dissipated through a protracted period of resolution.

In contrast, pattern C shows a more explosive orgasmic response, which bypasses the plateau phase and is followed by a more precipitate resolution of sexual tension. This form of orgasm tends to be both more intense as well as more protracted.[31]

During the various phases of the sexual response cycle numerous specific physiological changes occur, some in the genitals, some in other parts of the body. As we describe these reactions we must keep in mind that not all of these responses continue through the entire cycle. Some physiological responses (like erection of the penis) set in right away and persist throughout the entire cycle,

---

[28]The length of the refractory period seems to vary greatly among different males and with the same person on different occasions. It may last anywhere from a few minutes to several hours: The interval usually gets longer with age and with successive orgasms during a given sexual episode (Kolodny et al., 1979).

[29]Robbins and Jensen (1977).

[30]Among the Kinsey subjects, men reported reaching orgasm generally within 4 minutes, whereas it took women 10 to 20 minutes to do so. But when women relied on self-stimulation, they too could reach orgasm within 4 minutes or so.

[31]Such sustained orgasms have been labeled *status orgasmus,* or "orgasmic states," in contrast to single orgasms. This is analogous to the distinction between single convulsions and convulsive states in epilepsy.

whereas the others occur only during part of a given phase (for instance, additional coronal engorgement late in the plateau phase).

Physiological Mechanisms of Sexual Response

Two underlying mechanisms explain how the body and its various organs respond to sexual stimulation: *vasocongestion* and *myotonia*.

Vasocongestion is the engorgement of blood vessels and increased influx of blood into tissues. Ordinarily the flow of blood through the arteries into various organs is matched by the outflow through the veins, and thus a fluctuating balance is maintained. When under various conditions blood flow into a region exceeds the capacity of the veins to drain the area, vasocongestion will result. Blood flow is primarily controlled by the smaller arteries (arterioles), whose muscular walls constrict and dilate in response to nervous impulses. The ultimate causes may be physical (for example, heat) or psychological (for example, embarrassment). Congested tissue, because of its excess blood content, becomes swollen, red, and warm. Sexual excitement is accompanied by widespread vasocongestion involving superficial and deep tissues. Its most dramatic genital manifestation is the erection of the penis. (Erection has been called the "blushing of the penis.") The response varies in different organs and at different times, but is necessarily present in sexual excitement.

Myotonia is increased muscle tension. Even when a person is completely relaxed or asleep, the muscles maintain a certain firmness or "muscle tone." From this baseline muscular tension increases during voluntary flexing or involuntary orgasmic contractions. During sexual activity myotonia is inevitable and widespread. It affects both smooth and skeletal muscles and occurs both voluntarily and involuntarily. Although evidence of myotonia is present from the start of sexual excitement, it tends to lag behind vasocongestion.

Vasocongestion and myotonia are the underlying sources of practically all physiological manifestations during sexual activity, and the reader should keep them in mind during our discussion of general and specific physiological responses.

The physiological manifestations of the sexual response cycle do not change in any fundamental way in older individuals. Aging does bring about definite anatomical and physiological alterations, but the differences in this regard between the older person and his or her former self are mainly differences in the intensity and not in the nature of the physiological response.[32]

The original findings reported by Masters and Johnson were derived from observations of orgasm attained by self-stimulation and coitus. These have now been supplemented by reports of the physiological reactions of homosexual and bisexual males and females. This evidence shows that there is no fundamental difference in sexual physiology between heterosexuals and those with homosexual orientations.[33]

Reactions of Male Sexual Organs

Penis

Of all the male sex organs the penis undergoes the most dramatic changes during sexual excitement and orgasm. Erection is correctly regarded as evidence of sexual excitement. Nevertheless, there are instances in which erections occur in the absence of sexual stimulation or erotic feelings and vice versa.

Erection is experienced on innumerable occasions when awake or while asleep by practically all males and may occur in earliest infancy (some baby boys have erections right after birth), as well as in old age. Erection is not an all-or-none phenom-

---

[32]Sexuality and aging, including changes in physiology, are discussed in more detail in Chapter 8.
[33]For more details, see Chapter 7 in Masters and Johnson (1979).

enon; there are many gradations between the totally flaccid penis and the maximally congested organ immediately before orgasm.

Erection occurs with remarkable rapidity. In men younger than 40 years of age, less than 10 seconds may be all the time required. There are tremendous differences among individuals, as well as among occasions for the same individual. Younger men generally respond more rapidly, but slowing down with age is not inexorable.

The excitement phase may be short, and activity may rapidly proceed to the more stable plateau phase. More often the earlier phase is quite protracted, and the varying firmness of erection reflects the waxing and waning of sexual excitement and desire. During this period a man is quite vulnerable to loss of erection. Even if sexual stimulation continues uninterrupted, distraction can cause partial or total detumescence.

During the plateau phase the penis undergoes two further though relatively minor changes. Although full erection is achieved at the end of the excitement phase, further engorgement occurs, primarily in the corona of the glans. Erection is then more stable, and the man may temporarily turn his attention away from sexual activity yet remain tumescent.

During orgasm the characteristic rhythmic contractions begin in the accessory sexual organs (prostate, seminal vesicles, and vas), but very soon extend to the penis itself (*see* Figure 3.3). Orgasmic contractions involve the entire length of the penile urethra, as well as the muscles sheathing the root of the penis. At first they occur regularly at intervals of approximately 0.8 second, but after the first several strong contractions they become weaker, irregular, and less frequent.

Ejaculation ("throwing out"), though not precisely synonymous with orgasm, is its cardinal manifestation in the adult male. The fluid, which flows in variable amounts (usually about 3 cubic centimeters, or a teaspoonful), is known as "semen," "seminal fluid," or "spermatic fluid." It consists of sperm (which account for very little of its volume) and the secretions of the prostate (which impart to it a characteristic milkiness and odor), of the seminal vesicles, and to a much lesser extent of Cowper's glands.

Ejaculation consists of two distinct phases. During the first (emission, or first-stage orgasm) the prostate, seminal vesicles,

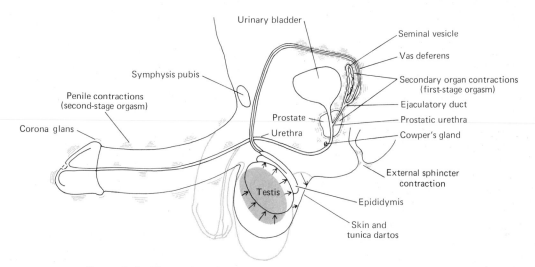

Figure 3.3 The male pelvis: orgasmic phase. From Masters and Johnson, *Human Sexual Response* (Boston: Little, Brown and Company, 1966), p. 184. Reprinted by permission.

and vas deferens pour their contents into the dilated urethral bulb. At this point the man feels the inevitability of ejaculation. In the second phase (ejaculation proper, or second-stage orgasm) the semen is expelled by the vigorous contractions of the muscles surrounding the root of the penis and the contractions of the genital ducts. The subjective experience at this point is one of intense pleasure associated with orgasmic throbs and the sensation of spermatic flow.

The amount of fluid and the force with which it is ejaculated are popularly associated with strength of desire, potency, and so on, but these beliefs are difficult to substantiate.

There is also a popular notion that semen is generated entirely by the testes, for during arousal the testes may feel tense and full, and this feeling is relieved by ejaculation. Nevertheless, the contribution of the testes to semen is restricted to sperm and the minimal fluid that carries them. The pelvic sensation of fullness before orgasm results from vasocongestion and sustained muscular tensions. Women have similar experiences even though they do not ejaculate.

In the resolution phase the changes of the preceding stages are reversed, and erection is lost. Detumescence occurs in two stages: First, there is a relatively rapid loss of erection, which reduces the organ to a semi-erect state; then there is a more gradual decongestion in which the penis returns to its unstimulated size. In general, the longer the excitement and plateau phases (and the more marked the vasocongestion process), the longer the primary stage of resolution, which in turn delays the secondary stage.

After ejaculation, if sexual stimulation continues (if the penis remains in the vagina or even if the man remains close to his sexual partner), the penis remains tumescent longer. If, on the other hand, he withdraws, is distracted, or attempts to urinate, detumescence is more rapid. A man actually cannot urinate with a fully erect penis because the internal urinary sphincter closes reflexively during full erection to prevent intermingling of urine and semen.

Scrotum

During the excitement phase the scrotal skin contracts and thickens with a resulting loss of the normal baggy appearance. The initial response of the scrotum to sexual excitement is thus similar to its reaction to cold (and also to fear and anger). If the excitement phase is quite prolonged, the scrotum relaxes, even though the sexual cycle is not yet completed. During the plateau and orgasmic phases there are no further changes. In the resolution phase there is usually a rapid loss of the thickening of the scrotal skin. The scrotum shows no color changes.

Testes

The changes undergone by the testes, though not visible, are quite marked. During the excitement phase both testes are lifted up within the scrotum (see Figure 3.3), mainly as a result of the shortening of the spermatic cords and the contraction of the scrotal sac. During the plateau phase this elevation progresses farther until the organs are actually pressed against the body wall. Full testicular elevation is necessary for orgasm for reasons that are unclear.

The second major change is a marked increase in size (about 50 percent in most instances) because of vasocongestion. During orgasm there are no further changes.

In the resolution phase the size and position return to normal. Again the process may be rapid or slow (the pace is usually consistent for a given person) and, the longer the plateau phase, the more protracted is the process of detumescence.

Cowper's Glands

The bulbourethral (Cowper's) glands show no evidence of activity during the excitement phase. If tension is sustained, a drop or so of clear fluid, probably produced by these glands, appears at the tip of the penis. These tiny structures are rudimentary in men. By contrast, in some animals (for example, stallions, rams, bears, and goats) these glands secrete profusely during sexual arousal.

Men vary a great deal in the production of this mucoid material. Although most secrete only a drop or none at all, a few produce enough to wet the glans or even to dribble freely. The presence of this fluid is reliable evidence of a high level of sexual tension, but its absence does not ensure the opposite. Its association with voluptuous thoughts has been well known. Medieval scholars called it the "distillate of love" and correctly distinguished it from semen. It has also been mentioned in ancient literature.[34]

It has been assumed sometimes that this secretion acts as a lubricant during coitus. Because of its usually scanty and inconsistent presence, however, this function is unlikely. A more plausible explanation is that it neutralizes the urine-contaminated acidic urethra, protecting the sperm during their passage.

Although quite unrelated to semen, this secretion sometimes contains stray sperm that have seeped out before ejaculation. Intercourse may thus result in pregnancy even though the male withdraws his penis before orgasm, which often explains unexpected pregnancies when the participants vehemently maintain that coitus stopped before intravaginal ejaculation.

Prostate and Seminal Vesicles

The responses of the prostate gland and the seminal vesicles are similar and will therefore be described together. Overt changes are restricted to the orgasmic phase (see Figure 3.3), during which they play a major role. As indicated earlier, ejaculation actually begins with the contractions of these accessory structures as they pour their secretions into the expanded urethra. The admixture of sperm from the throbbing vas deferens with the secretions of the seminal vesicles (whose walls also pulsate spasmodically) occurs in the ejaculatory duct, and sperm are thus propelled through the duct into the urethra. These accessory organs actually participate in the rhythmic convulsions of orgasm. Their contractions, along with the filling of the urethra, are responsible for the sensation that orgasm is imminent.

Reactions of Female Sex Organs

Vagina

In reproductive terms, the vagina corresponds functionally to the penis and the physiological responses of the vagina and penis to sexual stimulation are complementary: As the penis prepares for insertion, the vagina prepares to receive it; however, these reactions are not limited to sexual intercourse. Effective stimulation, or whatever origin, brings about the standard vaginal and penile responses.

The vagina exhibits three specific reactions during the excitement phase: lubrication, expansion of its inner end, and color change. The warm, moist vagina reveals sexual desire, and the term "lubricity" is an appropriate synonym for it. Moistening of the vaginal walls is actually the very first sign of sexual response in a woman and usually occurs within 10 to 30 seconds after erotic stimulation.[35]

The lubricatory function of the clear, slippery, and mildly scented vaginal fluid is

---

[34]The *Priapeia,* epigrams on Priapus by various Latin poets, includes the following poem (quoted in H. Ellis [1942], Vol. II, Part One, p. 153):

> You see this organ after which I'm called
> And which is my certificate, is humid;
> This moisture is not dew nor drops of rain,
> It is the outcome of sweet memory,
> Recalling thoughts of a complacent maid.

[35]However, the fact of vaginal lubrication is not always sufficient evidence by itself that a woman is ready for coitus. There are psychological factors beyond mechanical considerations to be taken into consideration.

self-evident. As the fluid is alkaline, it has also been assumed to help neutralize the vaginal canal (which normally tends to be acidic) in preparation for the transit of semen. The source of this fluid was, however, unknown until recently.

In the past it was assumed that the fluid was a female ejaculate, analogous to male semen and therefore essential to conception. This misunderstanding, which was prevalent until the seventeenth century, had some unusual repercussions. It formed the basis for theological tolerance of female masturbation if orgasm did not occur naturally during coitus; the argument was that, unless the woman complemented male semen with her own ejaculation, conception could not occur. Such a failure would negate what was considered the primary function of coitus.

Inasmuch as the vaginal wall has no secretory glands, it was assumed also that the lubricant emanated from either the cervix, the Bartholin glands, or both. It has recently been convincingly demonstrated, however, that this fluid oozes directly from the vaginal walls. The secreting mechanism is as yet unclear, but in all likelihood it is related to vasocongestion in the vaginal walls.[36]

The Bartholin glands produce a discharge, but, in analogy to the secretion of the male Cowper's glands, it tends to be scanty, erratic, and of lubricating value only in the area of the introitus, if at all. Incidentally, the clear vaginal fluid that results from sexual excitement must not be confused with the chronic vaginal discharges produced by various infections (see Chapter 12). Some secretions from the cervix may also be normally present, but they too do not contribute substantially to vaginal lubrication.

The second major vaginal change during the excitement phase is the lengthening and expansion of the inner two-thirds of the vagina. The ordinarily collapsed interior vaginal walls expand to create a space where the ejaculate will be deposited. The stretched walls of the vagina thus lose some of their normal wrinkled appearance.

Finally, the ordinarily purple-red vaginal walls take on a darker hue in response to sexual stimulation. This discoloration, initially patchy, eventually spreads over the entire vaginal surface. These color changes reflect the progressive vasocongestion of the vaginal walls.

During the plateau phase the focus of change shifts from the inner two-thirds to the outer one-third of the vagina. In the excitement phase the outer end of the vagina may have dilated somewhat, but in the plateau phase it becomes congested with blood and the vaginal lumen becomes at least a third narrower. These congested walls of the outer third of the vagina constitute the *orgasmic platform*. It is there that rhythmic contractions during orgasm are most evident. During the plateau phase the "tenting effect" at the inner end of the vagina progresses still farther, and full vaginal expansion is achieved. Vaginal lubrication tends to slow down, and if the excitement phase is unduly protracted, further production of vaginal fluid may cease altogether in the plateau phase.

During orgasm (see Figure 3.4), the most visible effects occur in the orgasmic platform. This area contracts rhythmically (initially at approximately 0.8-second intervals) from 3 to 15 times. After the first three to six contractions the movements become weaker and more widely spaced. This orgasmic pattern varies from person to person and in the same person from one orgasm to another. The more frequent and intense the contractions of the orgasmic platform, the more intense is the subjective experience of climax. At particularly high levels of excitement these rhythmic contractions are preceded by spastic (nonrhythmic) contractions of the orgasmic platform that last 2 to 4 seconds. The inner portion of the vagina does not contract but

---

[36]Masters and Johnson (1966), p. 70.

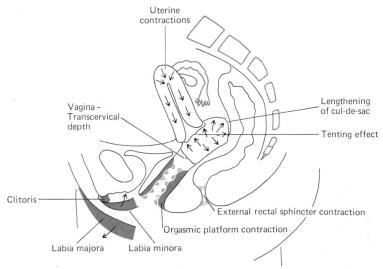

Figure 3.4   The female pelvis: orgasmic phase. From Masters and Johnson, *Human Sexual Response* (Boston: Little, Brown and Company, 1966), p. 77. Reprinted by permission.

continues its "tenting." These observations confirm that the vagina is not a passive receptacle for the penis but an active participant in coitus.

During the resolution phase the orgasmic platform subsides rapidly. The inner walls return much more slowly to their usual form. With decongestion the color of the vaginal walls lightens over a period of 10 to 15 minutes. The process of lubrication may in rare instances continue into this phase, and such continuation indicates lingering or rekindled sexual tension. With sufficient stimulation, a second orgasm may follow rapidly.

Clitoris

The clitoris is an exclusively sexual organ, and in contrast to its male homologue, the penis, it plays no part in reproduction and is totally independent of the urinary system. In response to sexual excitement the clitoris becomes tumescent through vasocongestion, just as the penis does. The overhanging prepuce of the clitoris does not, however, permit it to stand erect. That the clitoris does not function exactly as a miniature penis is also

apparent from its relatively slow response to stimulation. The immediate counterpart to penile tumescence is vaginal lubrication, rather than clitoral vasocongestion.

The clitoris is highly sensitive. Practically all women perceive tactile stimulation in this area, and most women respond erotically to such manipulation.[37] Its shape and ability to trigger voluptuous sensations have led to comparisons with an electric bell button.[38]

During the excitement phase both the glans and the shaft of the clitoris become congested. This response is more consistent for the glans and may result in the doubling of its diameter. The vasocongestive response is more rapid and more marked if the clitoris and adjoining areas of the mons are stimulated directly. The fundamental sequence of

[37]In gynecological examinations conducted for the Kinsey study, 98 percent of the subjects were able to perceive tactile stimulation of this organ; in contrast, less than 14 percent could detect being touched in the interior of the vagina (Kinsey et al., 1953), pp. 574 and 580.

[38]" . . . a veritable, electric bell button which, being pressed or irritated, rings up the whole nervous system" (quoted by H. Ellis, 1942, Vol. II, Part One), p. 130.

changes, however, is independent of the method of stimulation.

The shape, size, and position of the clitoris in the unstimulated state and its visible tumescence during the excitement phase have no relation to the likelihood of orgasm. Important as it is for sexual stimulation, the clitoris gives no reliable clues to the subsequent course of the sexual cycle. Visible tumescence of its glans, when it does occur, coincides with the vasocongestive response of the minor labia and comes quite late in the excitement phase (when the penis has been erect for some time and the vagina is fully lubricated). The clitoral glans, once tumescent, remains so throughout the sexual cycle.

During the plateau phase the entire clitoris (glans and shaft) shows a peculiar response. It is retracted under the clitoral hood and almost disappears from view. This reaction is particularly rapid and striking in response to direct stimulation and may result in the clitoris' receding to half its unstimulated length. As the initial enlargment of the organ indicates sexual excitement, its subsequent retraction may understandably be misinterpreted as indicating loss of sexual tension. When excitement abates the clitoris reemerges from under the hood. During a protracted plateau phase there may be several repetitions of this retraction-emergence sequence, which may confuse the uninformed male who is attempting to stimulate his partner's clitoris.

During orgasm the clitoris remains hidden from view. Following orgasm it promptly (in 5 to 10 seconds) reemerges from its retracted position. The rapidity and timing of this response are comparable to the first postorgasmic loss of penile erection. Final detumescence of the clitoris, on the other hand (like the second stage of penile erection), is much slower (usually taking 5 to 10 minutes but sometimes as long as half an hour). When orgasm has not occurred, the engorgement of the glans and shaft of the clitoris may persist for hours and cause discomfort.

Major Lips

The labia of women who have not given birth (nulliparous labia) are anatomically somewhat different from those of women who have (parous labia). These structural alterations influence the types of physiological response during the sexual cycle, especially in the major lips.

Nulliparous major lips become flattened, thinner, and more widely separated, "opening" and exposing the external genitals. This slight opening reveals the congested moist tissues between. During the plateau and orgasmic phases nulliparous major lips show no further changes. During the resolution phase they return to their decongested size and shape and resume their midline contact. Resolution proceeds rapidly if orgasm does occur. Otherwise the changes brought about during excitement take longer to dissipate. Following a protracted period of arousal, congestion may be so intense that the labia remain swollen for several hours after all sexual stimulation has ceased.

Parous major lips are larger and more pendulous and may contain permanently distended (varicose) veins. Instead of flattening, they become markedly engorged, and may double or triple in size during arousal; but they do nevertheless expose the entrance to the vaginal orifice. There are no changes during the next two phases. Resolution is more rapid if orgasm occurs. Otherwise this phase takes longer, depending on how distended the labial veins have become and how effectively they can be drained.

Minor Lips

The alterations in the minor lips during the sexual cycle are quite impressive and remarkably consistent. As the excitement phase progresses to the plateau level, they become severely engorged and double or even triple in size in both parous and nulliparous women. These tumescent lips project between the overlying major lips and become quite apparent, which may explain the parting of the major lips during excitement.

Color changes reflect the extent of venous congestion and are therefore affected by any existing venous distension in parous women. During the plateau phase the minor lips become progressively pink, or even bright red in light-complexioned women. In parous women the resulting color is a more intense red or a deeper wine color.

This vivid coloration of the minor lips has been observed so consistently that they have been called the "sex skin" of the sexually excited woman.[39] If erotic stimulation continues beyond this point, orgasm is inevitable; but if stimulation is interrupted, orgasm will not occur. Orgasm does not occur unless labial congestion first reaches this peak. In this sense the "sex skin" is comparable to the full testicular elevation of the male: Both herald impending orgasm.

Bartholin's Glands

Bartholin's glands respond to sexual stimulation by secreting a few drops of mucoid material rather late in the excitement phase or even in the plateau phase. They appear to be most effectively stimulated by the action of the copulating penis over a long period of time, and parous women have a more generous production of the secretion. The contribution of these glands to vaginal lubrication or to neutralizing the acidic vaginal canal is relatively minor.

Uterus

Despite its being hidden from view the uterus has long been known to participate actively in the changes of the sexual response

cycle. It has often been assumed that the contractions of the uterus during coitus cause the semen to be sucked into its cavity. Masters and Johnson found no evidence to support this assumption.[40] One also encounters references in literature to a woman's enjoyment resulting from the penis ramming against the uterine cervix. This too is totally unsubstantiated. In fact, the cervix is remarkably insensitive; it can even be cut without pain.

The uterus responds to sexual stimulation initially by elevation from its usual position. (This reaction does not occur if the uterus is not resting in its normal anteverted position.) This reaction pulls the cervix up and contributes to the tenting effect in the vagina. Full uterine elevation is achieved during the plateau phase and is maintained until resolution, when the organ returns to its usual position over a period of 5 to 10 minutes.

In addition, the uterus clearly shows the effects of the two main physiological phenomena: vasocongestion and myotonia. The former is manifested in a distinct increase in size during the earlier phases, which returns to normal following orgasm; the latter is apparent in the activity of the uterine musculature, culminating in distinct contractions.

Orgasmic contractions start in the fundus and spread downward. Although they occur simultaneously with those of the orgasmic platform, they are less distinct and more irregular. The cervix shows no specific change until the resolution phase, when the external cervical opening may dilate to some extent immediately after orgasm. The more intense the orgasm, the greater is the likelihood of this cervical reaction. Because of inevitable changes in the cervix during child-

---

[39]Masters and Johnson (1966), p. 41.

[40]This is contradicted by Fox et al. (1970), who found that a pressure gradient exists between the vagina and uterus immediately following female orgasm. Their proposed explanations for the reason why Masters and Johnson failed to find evidence for uterine suction are in Fox and Fox (1967).

birth, this reaction is best seen in the nulliparous woman.

Extragenital Reactions

As was indicated earlier, the responses of the body to sexual stimulation are not restricted to the sex organs. As extragenital manifestations are quite similar in the two sexes, we shall describe them together.

Breasts

Even though male breasts also respond to sexual stimulation, changes during the sexual cycle are far more striking in the female. Our description, therefore, refers primarily to the latter.

Erection of the nipple is the first response of the breast to sexual stimulation. It occurs in the excitement phase and is the result of the contraction of "involuntary" muscle fibers rather than vascular congestion. Engorgement of blood vessels is, however, responsible for the enlargement of the breasts as a whole, including the areolae.

In the plateau phase the engorgement of the areolae is more marked. As a result, the nipples appear relatively smaller. The breast as a whole expands farther during this phase, particularly if it has never been suckled (it may increase by as much as a fourth of its unstimulated size); a breast that has been suckled may change little in size or not at all. During orgasm the breasts show no further changes. In the resolution phase, along with the rapidly disappearing sexual flush, the areolae become detumescent, and the nipples regain their fully erect appearance ("false erection"). Gradually breasts and nipples return to normal size.

Changes in the male breast are inconsistent and restricted to nipple erection during the late excitement and plateau phases. Male nipples are rarely stimulated directly during heterosexual activity (sometimes they are during homosexual contact), but the nipple

reactions nevertheless appear in more than half the instances observed.

Skin

The significance of skin changes accompanying emotional states is well known. We blush in embarrassment, flush in anger, turn pale in fear. These surface reflections of inner feelings are manifest in the infusion or draining of blood from the vessels in the skin and are controlled by the autonomic nervous system. It is thus hardly surprising that sexual activity results in definite skin reactions, consisting of flushing, temperature change, and perspiration.

The flushing response is more common in women. It appears as a discoloration, like a rash, in the center of the lower chest (epigastrium) during the transition from the excitement to the plateau phase. It then spreads to the breasts, the rest of the chest well, and the neck. This sexual flush reaches its peak in the late plateau phase and is an important component of the excited, straining, and uniquely expressive physiognomy of the woman about to experience the release of orgasm. During the resolution phase the sexual flush disappears very quickly; the order reverses its spread so that discoloration leaves the chest last.

Temperature changes during the sexual response cycle have not yet been measured. Although there is no evidence that the temperature of the body as a whole changes, people do frequently report feelings of pervasive warmth following orgasm; and there are popular references to sexual excitement as a "glow," "fever," or "fire." Superficial vasocongestion is the likely explanation of this sensation.

Perspiration (apart from that caused by physical exertion) occurs fairly frequently during the resolution phase. Among men this response is less consistent and may involve only the soles of the feet and the palms of the hands. There may be a great deal of physical activity during a sexual encounter and, when the atmosphere is warm, sweating is greatly increased and may occur throughout the sexual cycle. Perspiration is one of the means by which the overheated body cools itself.

Cardiovascular System

Just as the heart races and pounds during fear, anger, and excitement, it also responds to sexual stimulation by beating faster. This reaction is usually not immediate; and mild, transient erotic thoughts may not alter the heart rate. But significant levels of sexual tension and certainly orgasm do not occur without some elevation of the pulse rate.

In the plateau phase the heart rate rises to 100 to 160 beats a minute (the normal resting heart rate is 60 to 80 beats a minute). The blood pressure also registers definite increases parallel to that in the heart rate. These changes are quite significant, and are comparable to levels reached by athletes exerting maximum effort. They entail considerable strain on the cardiovascular system, which is easily handled most of the time; people with heart disease, however, require medical guidance in this regard.

Respiratory System

Respiration and heart rate are interrelated through complex physiological mechanisms, so they respond concurrently to demands on the body. The most common example is physical exercise. Changes in respiratory rate lag behind those in heart rate. Faster and deeper breathing becomes apparent in the plateau phase, and during orgasm the respiratory rate may go up to 40 a minute (the normal rate is about 15 a minute, inhalation and exhalation counting as one). Breathing, however, becomes irregular during orgasm, when the individual may momentarily hold his breath and then breath rapidly. Following orgasm he may take a long deep breath or sigh as he sinks into the resolution phase. Along with the pulse and

blood pressure, respiration returns to normal rate and depth.

The flaring nostrils, heaving chest, and gasping mouth that accompany sexual experience are popularly known and caricatured in the stylized panting of comedians to suggest erotic excitement. Some of the panting and grunts uttered during orgasm result from involuntary contractions of the respiratory muscles, which force air through the spastic respiratory passages. Following orgasm the soft palate relaxes, and the person may make snoring noises.

The changes manifested by the cardiovascular and respiratory systems are partly caused by muscular exertion and are nonspecific to sex. Apart from these changes, however, are some that occur in response specifically to sexual stimulation. Changes in facial expression and gasping for breath during orgasm raise the possibility that the individual suffers a lack of oxygen (anoxia), but this surmise has not been conclusively documented.[41]

Digestive System

The response of the digestive tract to sexual stimulation can best be observed at its beginning and end: the mouth and the anus. During sexual arousal the secretion of saliva increases and the person may literally drool. During intense erotic kissing (or mouth-genital contact) increased salivation is very apparent.

The anus is a sensitive area, which, apart from its proximity to the genitals, appears to be intimately involved in both eliciting and responding to sexual stimuli. Some people react to anal stimulation erotically, whereas others are indifferent or disgusted. Anal stimulation is not an exclusively male homosexual practice; it occurs in heterosexual relations also.

[41]For a review and discussion of blood pressure and respiratory patterns during human coitus, see Fox and Fox (1969).

Box 3.4   Reactions of Sex Organs during the Sexual Response Cycle

Male	Female
Excitement Phase	
Penile erection (within 3–8 seconds) *As phase is prolonged:* Thickening, flattening, and elevation of scrotal sac *As phase is prolonged:* Partial testicular elevation and size increase	Vaginal lubrication (within 10–30 seconds) *As phase is prolonged:* Thickening of vaginal walls and labia *As phase is prolonged:* Expansion of inner ⅔ of vagina and elevation of cervix and corpus *As phase is prolonged:* Tumescence of clitoris
Plateau Phase	
Increase in penile coronal circumference and testicular tumescence (50–100% enlarged) Full testicular elevation and rotation (orgasm inevitable) Purple hue on corona of penis (inconsistent, even if orgasm is to ensure) Mucoid secretion from Cowper's gland	Orgasmic platform in outer ⅓ of vagina Full expansion of ⅔ of vagina, uterine and cervical elevation "Sex-skin": discoloration of minor labia (constant, if orgasm is to ensue) Mucoid secretion from Bartholin's gland Withdrawal of clitoris
Orgasmic Phase	
Ejaculation Contractions of accessory organs of reproduction: vas deferens, seminal vesicles, ejaculatory duct, prostate Relaxation of external bladder sphincter Contractions of penile urethra at 0.8 second intervals for 3–4 contractions (slowing thereafter for 2–4 more contractions) Anal sphincter contractions (2–4 contractions at 0.8 second intervals)	*Pelvic response (no ejaculation)* Contractions of uterus from fundus toward lower uterine segment Minimal relaxation of external cervical opening Contractions of orgasmic platform at 0.8-second intervals for 5–12 contractions (slowing thereafter for 3–6 more contractions) External rectal sphincter contractions (2–4 contractions at 0.8-second intervals) External urethral sphincter contractions (2–3 contractions at irregular intervals, 10–15% of subjects)
Resolution Phase	
Refractory period with rapid loss of pelvic vasocongestion Loss of penile erection in primary (rapid) and secondary (slow) stages	Ready return to orgasm with retarded loss of pelvic vasocongestion Loss of "sex-skin" color and orgasmic platform in primary (rapid) stage Remainder of pelvic vasocongestion as secondary (slow) stage Loss of clitoral tumescence and return to position

---

Box 3.5 General Body Reactions during the Sexual Response Cycle

Male	Female
Excitement Phase	
Nipple erection (30%)	Nipple erection (consistent)
	Sex-tension flush (25%)
Plateau Phase	
Sex-tension flush (25%)	Sex-tension flush (75%)
Carpopedal spasm	Carpopedal spasm
Generalized skeletal muscle tension	Generalized skeletal muscle tension
Hyperventilation	Hyperventilation
Tachycardia (100–160 beats per minute)	Tachycardia (100–160 beats per minute)
Orgasmic Phase	
Specific skeletal muscle contractions	Specific skeletal muscle contractions
Hyperventilation	Hyperventilation
Tachycardia (100–180 beats per minute)	Tachycardia (110–180 beats per minute)
Resolution Phase	
Sweating reaction (30–40%)	Sweating reaction (30–40%)
Hyperventilation	Hyperventilation
Tachycardia (150–180 beats per minute)	Tachycardia (150–180 beats per minute)

Stimulation of the anus has well-known repercussions in the body: Stretching the anal sphincter induces inhalation, but contraction makes exhalation difficult. The rhythmic contraction of the anus, along with the flexing of the buttocks, induces sexual tension. Some women are able to reach orgasm through this maneuver alone.

Sexual activity elicits anal responses (noted by Aristotle). During the excitement and plateau phases, the rectal sphincter contracts irregularly in response to direct stimulation. The more striking reactions, however, occur during orgasm, when involuntary contractions can be seen to occur at approximately the same 0.8-second intervals as do the throbs of the orgasmic platform and the penile urethra. Anal contractions, which do not always occur, usually involve only two or four spasms. The rectal sphincter relaxes while the manifestations of orgasm are still in progress elsewhere.

Urinary System

The male urethra is an integral part of the penis, and its changes during the sexual response cycle have already been described in that connection. In some women the urethra undergoes a few irregular contractions during orgasm. Unlike the anal spasms these contractions are asynchronous and quite feeble. The urge to urinate after orgasm has already been mentioned.

The multiplicity of changes involving various males and females organs makes is difficult to maintain an overall view of the progression of events during each phase of the sexual response cycle. Boxes 3.4 and 3.5 are intended to highlight the temporal interrelations of the reactions of different body parts and should convey an impression of the orderly yet variable progression of events.[42]

[42]The tables are adapted from Beach, ed. (1965), pp. 517 and 522. A more detailed set of tables can be found in Masters and Johnson (1966), pp. 286–293.

Neurophysiological Basis of Sexual Functions

Most of the information presented so far in this chapter has been descriptive. Underlying the patterns of sexual stimulation and response that we have considered, there exist complicated mechanisms of control. Some of these are hormonal in nature and will be discussed in the next chapter. Others are neurophysiological and, though closely integrated with endocrine functions, can be discussed separately for our purposes here.

All sensory input must ultimately be interpreted in the brain before a particular sensation is experienced. But, apart from this process, the brain can use memory and imagination to initiate sexual excitement without external sensory stimuli. Thus every form of behavior we observe has a corresponding set of events that silently unfold in the nervous system. No thought, however trivial, and no emotion, however ethereal, can exist in an empty skull. Therefore all sexual experience must be finally understood at the level of neurophysiological activity. This is not to say that the neurophysiological component is the most "important" or that such understanding in itself will be an adequate substitute for other ways of conceptualizing human experience, such as in psychological or philosophical terms. But neither can we ever dispense with the physical basis of these mental events if we aspire to comprehend them fully.

Unfortunately we have only a rudimentary knowledge at this time of the neuroendocrinological aspects of sexual functions and behavior. Until recent years virtually nothing was known about the parts of the brain involved in the control of even such basic functions as erection and ejaculation.[43] During the past several decades a good deal of research has changed this. But much of this work is still in an experimental stage. Because of this and the fact that even an elementary understanding of these matters would require more background in neuroanatomy and physiology than can be reasonably expected, we shall not attempt to discuss this area in any depth here. Enough will be said, however, to illustrate some of the basic neurophysiological processes at work in sexual functions and point out the awesome complexity of what remains to be discovered.[44]

Our primary interest here is in the neural control of sexual function. Sexual activity entails a great deal more than just genital function and involves virtually every system of the body. A great many of the components of sexual activity are thus specific or exclusive to sexual functions. For instance, touch receptors (Meissner's corpuscles) embedded in the skin merely inform the brain that a certain area of the skin is being stimulated; it is up to the brain to interpret this touch as a lover's caress.

There are special nerve endings and end organs that respond specifically to cold, warmth, pain, touch, and the like; but none that is specialized to respond selectively to sexual stimulation. The nerve endings in the glans penis are thus no different from those in the fingertips. Also, sensory messages are transmitted from the body to the brain and spinal cord, and responses are transmitted to the body parts through the same networks of nerves regardless of whether or not the activity is sexual. In this sense nerves, like telephone cables, are ignorant of the content of the messages they carry.

The nervous control of sexual functions is coordinated at two levels: in the spinal cord and in the brain. Normally, control at these levels is closely coordinated, but some functions like erection and ejaculation can also occur independently of the brain.

[43]MacLean (1976).

[44]For a review of animal studies in neural control of sexual behavior see Bermant and Davidson (1974). Brain mechanisms of sexual functions are discussed in MacLean (1976) and Whalen (1977). For a broader introduction to neuropsychology see Thompson (1967) and Pribram (1977).

Spinal Control of Sexual Function

Sexual functions are controlled at their most elemental level by spinal reflexes. Reflexes are the basic units of nervous organization and at their simplest have three components: a receptor, a conductor or transmitter, and an effector. The receptor can be any nerve that detects and conveys sensory information (such as touch, pressure, or pain) to the transmitter neurons in the spinal cord, which interpret the sensory input and convey the appropriate response to the third component, the end organs ("effectors"), thus completing the reflex arc. The end organ may be a muscle that contracts or a gland that secretes in response to such stimulation. An example of a simple reflex is withdrawal of the hand after touching a hot object. Another well-known example is the knee-jerk response to tapping the patellar tendon. Reflexes are involuntary in the sense that their response is automatic and does not require a "decision" by the brain. The brain is conscious of these responses and may be able to inhibit the reflexive response to a variable extent.

The examples of the reflex acts given above involve the sensory motor system. There are other reflexes, including those involved in sexual functions, that belong to the autonomic part of the nervous system. This system operates involuntarily to control many of the internal functions of the body. Its activities are normally carried out below the level of consciousness.

The autonomic nervous system has two main subdivisions, both of which are involved in sexual function: the parasympathetic and the sympathetic. Stimulation of one or inhibition of the other has the same overall effects.

One of the basic functions of autonomic nerves is to control the flow of blood by constricting or dilating arteries. In the case of genital blood vessels the effect of parasympathetic stimulation is arterial dilation and the effect of sympathetic stimulation is arterial

construction. The reflexive processes in sexual functions have been better elucidated in the male. Hence we shall first discuss penile erection and ejaculation.

Mechanism of Erection and Ejaculation

The three major spinal components that control erection and ejaculation are easier to comprehend when considered separately. The first component in the process of erection consists of the sensory (afferent) nerves, which convey a variety of stimuli from the genitalia to the spinal cord. As shown in Figure 3.5 there are two nerves that transmit such stimuli to the sacral portion of the spinal cord (segments S2 to S4): The *pudendal nerve* carries impulses elicited by the stimulation of the surface of the penis, and the *pelvic nerve* transmits impulses elicited by pressure and tension deep within the penile structures (*corpora cavernosa* and *corpus spongiosum*).

The second division of the reflex mechanism consists of the spinal cord centers for erection and ejaculation (Figure 3.6). As described above, the pudendal and pelvic nerves convey sensory impulses to the S2 to S4 seg-

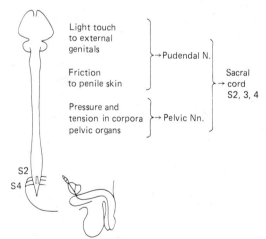

Figure 3.5   Peripheral afferent stimuli. From Tarabuley, "Sexual Function in the Normal and in Paraplegia." *Paraplegia 10* (1972), 202. By permission.

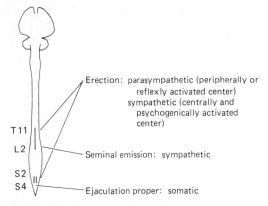

Figure 3.6 *Spinal cord centers. From Tarabuley,* "Sexual Function in the Normal and in Paraplegia." *Paraplegia 10* (1972), 204. By permission.

ments of the spinal cord, which contain the primary parasympathetic "erection center," activated reflexly by external or peripheral stimulation. A second spinal center located higher up (segments T11 to L2) is part of the sympathetic system, which also plays a role in the process of erection. This center is thought to mediate psychogenically or centrally induced stimulation from the brain and results in erection. This apparently contradictory situation in which parasympathetic and

sympathetic stimulation seem to produce the same reaction will be clarified shortly.

The spinal ejaculatory centers also have dual locations. The main autonomic center is in the sympathetic segment of the spinal cord (T11 to L2). This is where the first phase of orgasm, seminal emission, is triggered. The second component, ejaculation proper, is controlled by the sacral portion of the cord (S2 to S4), but this time not by its autonomic component but rather by the somatic or voluntary part.

The third division of the reflex arcs, consisting of the effector (or efferent) nerves, is shown in Figure 3.7. Note that the same nerves (pelvic and pudendal) that were shown in Figure 3.5 to transmit impulses to the spinal cord also convey impulses from the cord to the tissues. This is because what appears as a single nerve has a large number of component nerves that, like a cluster of telephone cables, communicate different messages to and fro.

The efferent or outgoing nerves to the tissues carry the messages that result in the final outcomes of erection and ejaculation. These involve the parasympathetic, sympathetic, and somatic parts of the nervous sys-

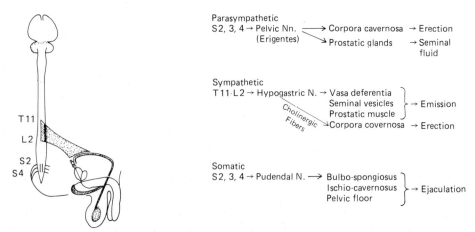

Figure 3.7 *Peripheral efferents. From Tarabuley,* "Sexual Function in the Normal and in Paraplegia." *Paraplegia 10* (1972), 204. By permission.

tem, all of which work in a closely integrated fashion. The parasymphatic system is primarily responsible for erection (but also for the stimulation of the prostate gland, which discharges seminal fluid). The sympathetic system is primarily responsible for ejaculation in concert with the somatic component (but also is involved in the process of erection). To clarify these variously overlapping and sequential activities, we shall next consider what transpires physiologically during an entire sexual orgasmic cycle.

When stimulated by appropriate incoming sensations the parasympathetic reflex erection center in the spinal cord responds by sending out impulses through parasympathetic nerves to the arteries conveying blood to the spongy tissue of the penis. Ordinarily cavernous and spongy bodies receive modest amounts of blood from the arteries, which are then drained by the veins. Under parasympathetic stimulation these arteries dilate. With the onrush of blood, the penile tissues rapidly fill up as the veins of the penis, hampered by their valves and the compression of their thin walls by the swelling organ, cannot handle the outflow of blood. The penis is thus rapidly engorged so that it stiffens and stands erect. Loss of erection results from a reversal of this process: Sympathetic nerve fibers constrict the arteries, cutting down the inflow of blood, and drainage through the veins increases until the organ returns to a flaccid condition.

To understand how sympathetic stimulation can also produce erection we need to digress briefly to consider further how these two divisions of the autonomic system operate. The major differences between the effects of these two systems depend on the type of hormones secreted by their nerve cells (neurons). In the case of the parasympathetic system the chemical secreted is acetylcholine, and therefore these neurons are called *cholinergic*. The sympathetic neurons secrete norepinephrine (also called noradrenaline) and are therefore said to be *adrenergic*. Al-

though this distinction generally holds, some sympathetic neurons are cholinergic and therefore their effect mimics that of parasympathetic stimulation. As shown in Figure 3.7, the sympathetic fibers (in the hypogastric nerve) that act on the corpora cavernosa are cholinergic; hence their effect, similar to parasympathetic stimulation, is to promote vasocongestion and thereby result in erection.

When sexual stimulation is effective to the point of triggering orgasm then another reflexive mechanism comes into play. The first phase of orgasm, emission, is triggered by the sympathetic center (T11–L2) through the sympathetic fibersin the hypogastive nerve. This results in the contraction of the vas deferens, seminal vesicles, and prostate gland, and the emptying of their contents into the urethra. In the next phase, impulses through somatic nerves to the muscles surrounding the penis (bulbospongiosus, ischiocavernosus, and other pelvic muscles) result in their contraction and the ejaculation of semen.

Emission and ejaculation are thus two closely integrated yet separate physiological processes. Ordinarily they occur together, but under some conditions one or the other may be experienced separately. Thus emission may take place without ejaculatory contractions, in which case semen simply seeps out of the urethra. Or ejaculatory contractions occur without having been preceded by the emission of semen.

The mere fact that there is no expulsion of semen during ejaculation does not necessarily mean that emission has not occurred. It is possible for ejaculation to be retrograde. That is, instead of the ejaculate being forced out of the urethra, it may be pushed in the opposite direction and empty into the urinary bladder.[45]

The processes described so far are the reflexive aspects of penile erection. They are

[45]For further discussion of the spinal sexual mechanism, see Tarabulsi (1972), Weiss (1973), Hart (1978), and Davidson (in press).

independent of the brain, in the sense that they can occur without assistance from higher centers. For instance, a man whose spinal cord has been severed above the level of the spinal reflex center may still be capable of erection. He will not "feel" the stimulation of his penis; for that matter, he may even be totally unconscious. But his penis will respond "blindly" as it were.

The independence of reflex centers does not mean that they cannot be influenced by the brain, however. Intricate networks link the brain to the reflex center in the spinal cord. Purely mental activity may thus trigger the mechanism of erection without physical stimulation, or it may inhibit erection despite persistent physical stimulation. Usually the two components operate simultaneously and complement each other. Spurred by erotic thoughts, the man initiates physical stimulation of the genitals; conversely, physical excitement inspires erotic thoughts.

The instances in which erection seems to be nonsexual in origin involve tension of the pelvic muscles (as when lifting a heavy weight or straining during defecation). Irritation of the glans or a full bladder may have the same effect. Erections that occur in infancy are explained on a reflex basis also. An additional gruesome example is erection experienced by some men during execution by hanging.

Reflexive Mechanisms in Women

It is generally assumed that there are spinal centers in women that correspond to the erection and ejaculatory centers of men. The reflexive centers in the female spinal cord are less well identified in part because the manifestations of orgasm are relatively more difficult to ascertain among female experimental animals.

The vasocongestive response that underlies male erection results in comparable tumescent changes in the clitoris and the rest of the genital tissues as we have seen. Likewise, the orgasmic response is similar, although there are some important differences as was discussed earlier.

The vasocongestion response, which results in the swelling of genital tissues and vaginal lubrication, is under parasympathetic control. The orgasmic phase in women does not have an emission component and therefore corresponds to the second or ejaculatory phase of orgasm of the male consisting of the rhythmic contractions of the musculature of the genital organs and the muscles surrounding them. Women of course do not ejaculate in the sense of emitting some counterpart of semen.[46]

Brain Mechanisms

We have made repeated references to the influence of the brain on sexual function without specifying how this works and which portions of the brain are involved. We have avoided this issue so far because relatively little is known about the representation of sexual functions in the brain, and what is known is so complex that it is difficult to deal with it adequately within the confines of this book.

It is important to realize at least that we already know enough about the sexual functions of the brain to go beyond the usual generalities that the brain is the "most important erogenous zone." The following examples will indicate the nature of the research done in this field and some of its salient findings.

During the past several decades, many neurophysiologists and psychologists have been investigating the neurophysiology of sexual functions and emotional states using experimental animals as subjects.

There are three general investigative approaches to the study of sexual neurophysiological mechanisms in the brain. First is the use of electrical stimulation, whereby erection, ejaculation, and copulatory behavior are elicited by activating various areas in the

---

[46]For a contradictory view claiming that women do ejaculate, see Sevely and Bennett (1978).

Box 3.6   The Klüver-Bucy Syndrome

In 1937 two investigators reported that removal of the temporal lobes of the brain in the monkey resulted in striking behavioral changes, including increased sexual activity involving autoerotic, heterosexual, and homosexual behavior.[1]

This phenomenon, now named after the two investigators, Klüver and Bucy, has been reproduced in man by bilateral removal of the temporal lobes. The change in sexual behavior was manifested as follows:

. . . Fifteen days after the operation the patient's attention was attracted by the sexual organs of an anatomic scheme hanging on the wall of the examining room. On that occasion he displayed to the doctor, with satisfaction, that he had spontaneous erections followed by masturbation and orgasm. From then on the patient gradually became exhibitionistic. He wanted to show his sexual organ erect to all doctors. He never manifested any sexual aggressiveness toward persons of the female sex for whom, on the contrary, he showed indifference in contrast with his behavior before the operation. Homosexual tendencies, clearly expressed by verbal invitations to some doctors, were soon noticed. Although monotonously insistent, he did not manifest the slightest aggressiveness either verbally or with gestures. At present, about two years after the operation, the patient is now in a mental hospital, practices self-abuse several times a day, but shows no aggressiveness either toward the male or female sex. The homosexual tendency still persists.[2]

Further evidence implicating the temporal lobe in sexual function comes from the observation of hypersexual episodes in temporal lobe epilepsy when sites in the temporal lobes cause the abnormal stimulation.[3]

[1]Klüver and Bucy (1937).
[2]Terzian and Calle-Ore (1955).
[3]Blumer (1970).

brain. The second approach is through destruction of specific brain areas that affect sexual behavior. It is possible for instance to eliminate copulation in male rats, cats, dogs, and rhesus monkeys by medical prioptic lesions. Similarly, sexual behavior may be eliminated in female animals through hypothalamic lesions.[47] If stimulation of a brain area results in a given sexual reaction, such as erection, and destruction of the region eliminates such response, then the inference is that the brain area in question is at least one link in the chain of brain mechanisms controlling that function.

A complementary approach is to identify brain areas that have an inhibitory effect on a given function. How we act is the outcome of the "push" to behave in a certain way as well as the inhibitory "pull" restraining us from doing so. The effect of inhibitory mechanisms becomes manifest by the activities that appear or are modified as a result of the removal or destruction of the parts of the brain exerting the inhibitory effect. An example involving the temporal lobes is provided in Box 3.6.

Many of the sites that seem to be linked to sexual function (including parts of the temporal lobes) are part of a set of structures deep within the brain that are referred to as the *limbic system*. These parts of the brain belong to the phylogenetically older part of the brain in contrast to the cerebral hemispheres, which are newer structures in an evolutionary sense. The limbic system is not a single anatomical entity. Rather, as is shown in Figure 3.8, it has a number of discrete components with numerous pathways to other centers in the brain. But taken as a whole, these structures constitute an integrated network. The components of the limbic system are arranged in the form of a ring, one in

[47]Davidson (in press).

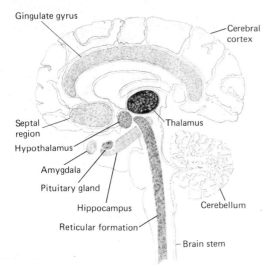

Figure 3.8 The limbic system of the human brain. The thalamus, hypothalamus, pituitary gland, and the reticular formation are interrelated with the limbic system but are not a part of it. From Harlow, et al., *Psychology*. San Francisco: Albion Publishing Company, 1971, p. 156. Reproduced by permission.

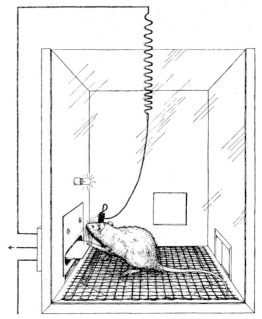

Figure 3.9 Self-stimulation circuit allowing the rat to excite "pleasure centers" in the brain electrically by pressing on a treadle. From James Olds, "Pleasure Centers in the Brain." Copyright © 1956 by *Scientific American, Inc.* All rights reserved.

each cerebral hemisphere. Together, they surround the brain stem (which is the continuation of the spinal cord into the brain) and the paired cluster of nuclei called the thalamus.[48]

Stimulation of various parts of the limbic formations elicits alimentary, agressive, defensive, as well as sexual responses. For example, stimulation of the septal region, among other parts, elicits penile erection, mounting, and grooming in the male animal. However, the limbic formations are not the only ones involved in sexual behavior. For instance, excitation of thalamic sites results in seminal emissions and ejaculatory sites have been located along the spinothalamic tract.[49] It is also now possible to monitor the activity

of brain waves during orgasm (*see* Box 3.7).

So far we have dealt with the more specific components of the brain mediating sexual functions. How, through all this, does the brain experience pleasure? An interesting research approach has led to the location of "pleasure centers" in the brain. This research was initiated by Olds, working with rats.[50] Microelectrodes were implanted in the brain of the animal and attached to a circuit allowing the rat to stimulate its brain electrically by pressing on a treadle (*see* Figure 3.9) Ordinarily, rats under such an experimental setup will spontaneously press the lever several times in an hour. But when the electrodes were placed in certain portions of the brain (located in the hypothalamus, thalamus, and mesencephalom), the experimental rat would go on pressing the lever as often as 5000

[48]The term "limbic" is derived from the Latin for "fringe" or "border."

[49]For further discussion of brain mechanisms, see Chapter 4 by MacLean in Zubin and Money (1973), and MacLean (1976).

[50]Olds (1956).

Box 3.7   Brain Wave Manifestations of Orgasm

The electroencephalogram (EEG) is the record of the electrical activity of the brain. The record reflects the voltage fluctuations between two points on the scalp. The EEG

From H. D. Cohen, R. C. Rosen, and L. Goldstein, "Electroencephalographic Laterality Changes during Human Sexual Orgasm." *Archives of Sexual Behavior* 5:3 (1976), 189–199.

tracings below are from the right and left parietal channels of a male subject. They successively show brain activity prior to sexual arousal (baseline), 30 seconds prior to orgasm, during orgasm, and 2 minutes following orgasm. Note that the change in amplitude in brain waves is more marked in the right hemisphere than in the left.

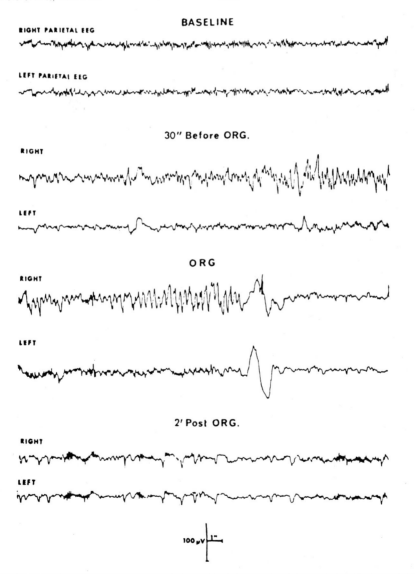

BASELINE

RIGHT PARIETAL EEG

LEFT PARIETAL EEG

30" Before ORG.

RIGHT

LEFT

ORG

RIGHT

LEFT

2' Post ORG.

RIGHT

LEFT

$100 \mu V$

times an hour, and would do this despite hunger and thirst until it was exhausted.

Since the stimulation of these locations appeared to be so rewarding, Olds called them "pleasure centers." Curiously enough, the same areas or perhaps systems inexorably interwoven with the pleasure mechanism turned out to be highly unpleasant when stimulated, so that the rat would avoid exciting them as vehemently as it would persevere in stimulating the rewarding parts. In addition, definite pathways in the brain are involved in the sensation of pain as such.

More recently, the presence of pleasure and pain systems has been shown among humans. The subjects were two patients with electrodes implanted in their brains for therapeutic purposes (one was a psychiatric male patient, the other an epileptic woman). The areas that yielded pleasure or stimulation corresponded roughly to the same regions in the animal brains. Pleasure was clearly of a sexual nature when the septal region or the amygdala of the limbic system was stimulated. Furthermore, whenever the patient was sexually aroused, brain wave changes emanating from the septal region could be detected. Such arousal could be elicited by external erotic stimuli (pictures, films), by having the subject fantasize, through the direct delivery of chemicals to the septal region, or through the administration of euphoria-producing drugs. Arousal could also be accomplished by electrical stimulation carried out by either the experimenter or the patient.

In addition to verbally reporting feelings of sexual arousal and appearing to be aroused, one of the patients, just like the experimental rat, stimulated himself incessantly (1500 times over three hours on one occasion) and begged to stimulate himself a few more times whenever the stimulating apparatus was to be taken away from him.[51] However, there is as yet no drug that when taken orally or by injection will reliably stimulate these parts of the brain and produce pleasurable sensations.[52]

These pleasure centers in man are in areas that lie close to the regions where stimulation leads to erection. They are also interconnected with other thalamic areas which receive sensory input from the body surface. One can thus begin to see the various bits and pieces fitting together to provide a neuroanatomical basis which would explain how incoming erotic tactile stimuli would activate sexual behavior and reinforce it with pleasurable feelings.

Our discussion so far has focused on various types of brain centers. Although the localization of physiological functions in the brain provides very valuable information, the final answers to how the brain regulates sexual functions is not likely to come from the identification of "sex centers" but from a broader understanding of the integrated brain systems that are involved with sexuality and other related processes. As Beach has stated, "Instead of depending on one or more 'centers,' sexual responsiveness and performance are served by a net of neural subsystems including components from the cerebral cortex down to the sacral cord. Different subsystems act in concert, but tend to mediate different units or elements in the normally integrated patterns."[53]

Another major consideration to bear in mind is that the nervous and endocrine systems work in close coordination in regulating sexual functions. The hypothalamus, for instance, is an important "headquarters" for both neural and endocrine control of sexual activity. The discussion of hormones in the chapter that follows is thus a logical succession to our consideration of the physiology of sexual function.

---

[51]For further discussion of this work see Heath (1972).

[52]Cox (1979).
[53]Beach (1977), p. 216.

Chapter 4

Sex Hormones and Reproductive Biology

Sex hormones play a very important role in reproductive biology. The internal and external differences in anatomy between males and females are a direct result of the effects of sex hormones. X or Y sex chromosomes program the sex glands to produce female or male sex hormones, and these hormones lead to the development of female or male reproductive organs in the fetus. At puberty the sex hormones are responsible for the maturation of these organs as well as the development of additional anatomical features like breast enlargement in females and enlargement of the larynx (voice box) in males. Sex hormones also play an essential role in all aspects of reproductive physiology, including ovulation and pregnancy in females and sperm production in males.

Although the effects of sex hormones on anatomy and physiology in humans are well established, their role in human sexual behavior is not clear. In most animals sex hormones play a critical role in mediating both sexual and aggressive behavior. Removal of the sex glands in animals leads to the rather striking differences in behavior seen, for example, between a bull and its castrated counterpart, a steer. A spayed cat shows little interest in sex, and a chicken given shots of male sex hormones will quickly rise to the top of the pecking order. There are no comparably dramatic or predictable behavioral effects of sex hormones to be found in humans.

Although the effects of sex hormones on the human brain are not well understood, important discoveries in recent years have proved that the brain regulates the production of sex hormones by the sex glands. These discoveries have provided new insights into such phenomena as infertility caused by emotional stress. In this chapter we shall discuss the role of sex hormones in reproductive biology and, more cautiously, we shall describe some possible effects of sex hormones on human behavior.

Basic Endocrinology

A brief review of what hormones are and how they work should facilitate the reader's understanding of the topics covered later in this chapter. *Endocrinology* is the study of the secretions of endocrine, or *ductless,* glands. In contrast to some glands (like the sebaceous or salivary glands) the endocrine glands secrete their products directly into the bloodstream. Hormones are chemical compounds produced by the endocrine glands; they exert profound physiological effects on specific tissues or organs to which they are transported by the bloodstream. The endocrine glands include such structures as the thyroid, parathyroid, adrenal, and pancreas glands. For our purposes, however, we shall concentrate on the sex glands (the ovaries and testes), the *pituitary* gland, and the *hypothalamus*.

The Pituitary

The pituitary gland (known also as the *hypophysis*) is the most complex of all endocrine glands. It is a pea-sized structure located at the base of the brain and connected to a part of the brain called the hypothalamus by a system of microscopic blood vessels and nerve fibers (*see* Figure 4.1). A variety of hormones are produced by the pituitary, and their chemical structures resemble protein molecules. The actions of the pituitary hormones include stimulating other endocrine glands to produce their hormones and stimulating the growth and maturation of various tissues.

Two pituitary hormones, called *gonadotrophins,* are of particular interest because they stimulate the sex glands: the *follicle-stimulating hormone* (FSH) and the *luteinizing hormone* (LH). A third pituitary hormone, *prolactin,* stimulates milk production in the female breast and is discussed in Chapter 5. In the female, FSH and LH stimulate the ovaries to manufacture and secrete the female sex hormones, *estrogen* and *progesterone*. In the male, LH is usually called *interstitial-cell-stimulating hormone* (ICSH) because it stimulates the interstitial (Leydig's) cells of the testes to manufacture and secrete the male sex hormone, *testosterone*. All the sex hormones belong to a group of chemical substances called *steroids,* which resemble in structure (but not in activity) that well-publicized chemical culprit, cholesterol. Steroid hormones are widely used compounds in medicine. Birth control pills consist of mixtures of synthetic female sex steroids. The drug cortisone, identical to a steroid hormone manufactured by the adrenal glands, is used for the treatment of a wide variety of ailments from arthritis to poison oak.

The early history of endocrinology is essentially the history of the discovery of the effects and the chemistry of steroid hormones. Classical methods of studying hormone activity involve depriving the organism of the hormone and observing the changes that occur; then administering doses of the hormone to demonstrate reversal of the effects noted during deprivation.

The effects of testosterone deprivation were first recorded among castrated males in ancient Egypt, China, and elsewhere. Aristotle noted the effects of castration on men and birds in the fourth century B.C. Castration of a rooster prevents growth of the cock's comb; in 1849 Berthold showed that this effect could be reversed by transplanting testes from another rooster to a castrated one. In 1889 the French physiologist Charles Brown-Sequard claimed to have experienced increased potency after treating himself with a testicular extract. This, and other highly publicized dramatic effects (longevity, youthful appearance, energy, and virility) attributed to extracts of the sex glands, tended to give endocrinology a somewhat disreputable flavor among the more conservative members of the medical profession.

In recent years, however, there has been a resurgence of interest in the study of hormones and, in particular, the mechanisms by which the brain can influence the timing and extent of hormone secretions. The study of these mechanisms is now a separate field called *neuroendocrinology*. Two anatomical sites in the head are of primary interest to neuroendocrinologists, the pituitary gland and the *hypothalamus*. Direct nerve connections from the brain to the *neurohypophysis* (posterior portion of the pituitary) have been known to exist for some time, but no nerve fibers have direct connections with the *adenohypophysis* (anterior portion of the pituitary). Since the sex gland stimulating hormones (*gonadotrophins*)[1] are produced

---

[1]Also called gonadotropins.

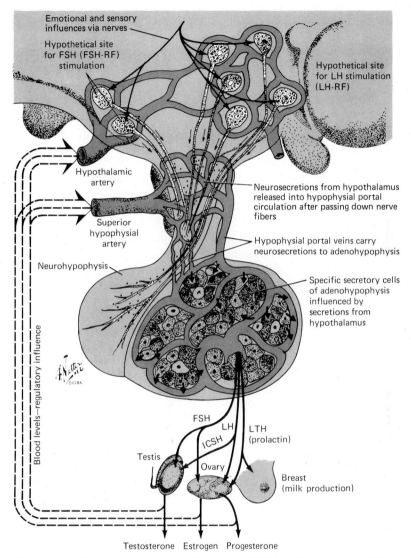

Emotional and sensory
influences via nerves

Hypothetical site
for FSH (FSH-RF)
stimulation

Hypothetical site
for LH stimulation
(LH-RF)

Hypothalamic
artery

Neurosecretions from hypothalamus
released into hypophysial portal
circulation after passing down nerve
fibers

Superior
hypophysial
artery

Hypophysial portal veins carry
neurosecretions to adenohypophysis

Neurohypophysis

Specific secretory cells
of adenohypophysis
influenced by
secretions from
hypothalamus

Blood levels—regulatory influence

FSH

LH

LTH
(prolactin)

ICSH

Testis

Ovary

Breast
(milk production)

Testosterone   Estrogen   Progesterone

Figure 4.1   The pituitary gland. © Copyright 1953, CIBA Pharmaceutical Company,
Division of CIBA–GEIGY Corporation. Reproduced, with permission, from The Ciba Collection of
Medical Illustrations by Frank H. Netter, M.D. All rights reserved.

exclusively by cells in the adenohypophysis,
the anatomical facts seemed to dictate a
model in which the anterior pituitary and the
sex glands are an autonomous system operating on a simple feedback principle; that is,
gonadotrophins are released until the sex
glands produce sufficient sex hormones to
"turn off" the pituitary gonadotrophin secre-

tion. The pituitary monitors the level of sex
hormones passing through it in the bloodstream, much as a thermostat monitors the
temperature in the surrounding air and turns
off the furnace when the temperature reaches
the thermostat setting. This model is consistent with numerous observations in animals,
where increasing the amount of circulating

sex hormones (for example, by injection) decreases pituitary gonadotrophin output and, conversely, where decreasing the sex hormones (for example, by castration) stimulates gonadotrophin output. However, other observations do not fit this simple feedback model.

The cyclic secretions of hormones during the menstrual cycle indicate rhythmic variations in the messages being sent via the bloodstream from pituitary to ovaries. Furthermore, physical and psychological stress, which are perceived and appreciated via the brain and nervous system, have long been known to alter pituitary-dependent events, such as menstruation. The implication seems clear—the pituitary is subject to regulation by the brain, just as the thermostat in the feedback model is subject to changes in setting based on "outside" information (for instance, one might raise the temperature setting in anticipation of unusually cold weather, and so forth).

The Hypothalamus

It has now been firmly established that the part of the brain that controls the pituitary is the hypothalamus. Located just above the pituitary, the hypothalamus receives sensory inputs from virtually every other part of the central nervous system. The hypothalamus is very small in relation to the rest of the brain, weighing about 5 grams and comprising only about 1/300 of the whole brain. (The small size of this important part of the brain is one reason why research has been difficult and painstaking.) Some of the first experiments that demonstrated the significance of the hypothalamus involved the stimulation or destruction of discrete groups of cells in various animals. It was shown that selective stimulation or ablation in specific areas of the hypothalamus will cause alterations of estrus cycles, lactation (milk production), and a number of other bodily functions such as temperature regulation, growth, and sleep.

Although initially puzzled by the absence of nerve connections between the hypothalamus and the anterior part of the pituitary (which produces gonadotrophins), researchers began to focus on the *portal* system of blood vessels linking the pituitary and hypothalamus (*see* Figure 4.1).[2] By the 1960s the generally accepted theory of neuroendocrinology was that the hypothalamus controlled the anterior pituitary by means of substances transmitted through the portal blood vessels, rather than by nerve impulses. Proof of the theory involved isolating these substances, purifying and identifying them, and demonstrating that they in fact stimulated the pituitary when administered experimentally. By the 1970s several hypothalamic hormones (also called "releasing factors") had been isolated, identified, and shown to be pituitary stimulants. In 1977 the Nobel prize in medicine was awarded to three scientists who were responsible for much of this research.[3]

The hypothalamic hormones are short-chain polypeptides, resembling fragments of larger protein molecules in chemical structure. The two factors of greatest significance for reproductive functions are known as the follicle-stimulating hormone releasing factor (FSH-RF) and the luteinizing hormone releasing factor (LH-RF).[4] As the terms imply, these brain-generated chemicals stimulate the release of FSH and LH from the pituitary gland. Hypothalamic hormones are extremely potent chemicals and are present in

---

[2]These vessels were first identified by a Hungarian pathologist in 1927, who noted that they were enlarged in people who died suddenly and violently. Their significance was not realized until many years later.

[3]A. V. Schally, R. S. Yalow, and R. Guillemin. For a detailed review of this work see Schally (1978).

[4]There is a trend toward using the term "releasing hormone" (RH) rather than "releasing factor" (RF). Thus, FSH-RF and FSH-RH are synonyms, as are LH-RF and LH-RH. It has been suggested that FSH-RF and LH-RF are identical compounds (Schally, 1978) but this view is disputed by others.

only minuscule amounts in the brain.[5] Research using naturally occurring extracts is therefore slow, but the possibility of synthetic versions of these hormones is on the horizon. Synthetic hypothalamic hormones would not only facilitate research but also clinical applications to problems like infertility.

Neuroendocrine Control Mechanisms

We have already introduced the concept of feedback in the context of the thermostat model of pituitary function. This basic concept is still valid in many respects, but recent discoveries have shown that control of hypothalamic and pituitary hormone secretions is more complex than was previously thought to be the case. Furthermore, the hypothalamus is now viewed as the "ultimate" regulator, rather than the pituitary.[6] Figure 4.2 is a diagrammatic representation of current understanding of neuroendocrine control mechanisms, using LH-RF and LH as examples.

The hypothalamus receives information from two general sources: the nervous system and the circulatory system. Information from the environment as well as internally generated information (including, perhaps, emotions like anxiety) reach the hypothalamus via the nervous system. Information regarding the levels of various hormones in the body reaches the hypothalamus via the bloodstream (including, perhaps, the specialized network of vessels called the portal system). The hypothalamus responds to these inputs by either increasing or decreasing its production of hormones (releasing factors). In the

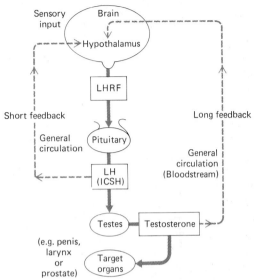

Figure 4.2 Diagrammatic representation of the neuroendocrine feedback mechanisms. LH-RF, LH, and testosterone are used as examples.

case shown in Figure 4.2, the hypothalamus sends LH-RF to the pituitary via the portal system. The pituitary responds by releasing LH (also known as ICSH) into the bloodstream. LH reaches the testes and stimulates the release of the male sex hormone, testosterone, which travels (also via the bloodstream) to various target organs. The increased level of testosterone in the bloodstream reaches the hypothalamus (and pituitary) via the general circulation and, in effect, conveys the information that the order for more testosterone has been received and obeyed. LH-RF and LH production then slows or stops until the testosterone levels start to drop off, signaling a need for more LH-RF (and LH). This loop between the hypothalamus and the testes is called the *long feedback* loop and is probably the primary control mechanism for sex hormone production. There is some evidence for a *short feedback* loop between the pituitary and hypothalamus via the bloodstream whereby increased LH levels

---

[5]It takes millions of animal hypothalami to yield a few milligrams of LH-RH. (The hypothalami are removed from animal brains supplied by meat packing companies.) In humans, doses of 25 micrograms (25 millionths of a gram) of LH-RH have been shown to be physiologically effective. (Schally, 1978).

[6]Until the past decade the pituitary was often referred to as the "conductor of the endocrine orchestra." It is now referred to as the "concertmaster" (Tepperman, 1973, p. 36).

"turn off" LH-RF production even before testosterone gets there.[7]

Two general observations should be clear at this point. First, to the extent that normal reproductive biology depends upon sex hormones, more is required than normal sex glands. (In fact, as we shall see shortly, conditions like precocious puberty are often caused by disorders of the pituitary or hypothalamus, not the sex glands.) Second, it is possible to "fool" the hypothalamus and pituitary by taking hormones in pill form. This raises the blood level of circulating hormones and turns off the production of LH-RF or FSH-RF (depending on which hormones are ingested). This is the principle involved in birth control pills (*see* Chapter 6).

Female Reproductive Endocrinology

Puberty

A girl's first menstrual period (menarche) occurs several years after the beginning of the physical changes that define puberty. Puberty begins somewhere between the ages of 9 and 12 for most girls. Menarche usually occurs between the ages of 11 and 14. Reasons for the timing of these events are not well understood (*see* Box 4.1).

External Changes

The most obvious change in the outward appearance of a girl during puberty is the development of the rounded contours that distinguish the adult female profile from that of the male. This process begins with an increase in secretion of FSH by the pituitary gland.

FSH stimulates the ovaries to produce

---

[7]There is suggestive evidence to indicate the possibility of an *ultrashort feedback* loop, which involves direct reflux of LH back to the hypothalamus via the portal system. For more detailed information on endocrinology see Reichlin et al. (1978), Ganong and Martin (1978), Tepperman (1973), and Austin and Short, vol. 3 (1972).

estrogen (a collective noun referring to a group of chemically related female sex hormones produced in the ovaries). The estrogen, in turn, travels through the bloodstream to the breasts, where it stimulates growth of breast tissue. (This and other hormonal pathways at puberty are summarized in Figure 4.3.) The pigmented area around the nipples (the areola) becomes elevated, and the breasts begin to swell as the result of development of ducts in the nipple area and an increase in fatty tissue, connective tissue, and blood vessels. The milk-producing part of the breast (*mammary gland*) does not develop fully during puberty and indeed does not become fully mature and functional until childbirth.

At the same time that estrogen is inducing the development of fatty and supporting tissue in the breasts of the young girl, a similar process is occurring in the hips and buttocks. These changes may be more pronounced in one region than in another in a particular woman. In some cultures the size and shape of the buttocks are important indices of femininity. In others greater emphasis is placed upon the breasts.

Another visible change at puberty is the appearance of *pubic* and *axillary* (underarm) *hair*. This hair is coarser and has more pigment than does that of the scalp, and its growth is stimulated partly by estrogen and partly by hormones secreted by the adrenal glands, also in response to a stimulating hormone (adrenocorticotrophic hormone, or ACTH) from the pituitary gland.

The adrenal glands are paired glands situated just above each kidney. In the female they produce small amounts of *androgens* (male sex hormones), which stimulate growth of pubic and axillary hair and are perhaps related to the female sex drive. In addition, the adrenal glands produce cortisone, adrenaline, and other substances. Excessive secretion by the adrenal glands, a pathological condition known as "Cushing's disease," may result in excessive growth of facial hair.

Box 4.1   The Onset of Puberty

Puberty refers to the maturation of the reproductive organs and associated changes in body structure and appearance. One of the greatest unsolved mysteries in developmental biology is the question of what triggers the events of puberty. The sex glands are capable of producing the required sex hormones much earlier, and yet they do not (with rare exceptions). Attention has focused on the hypothalamus and the pituitary, since their production of stimulating hormones has been found to increase at the onset of puberty. The result is increased production of sex hormones and the resultant developments described in this chapter.

But the next question posed by this evidence is what triggers this increased stimulation on the part of the hypothalamus (and pituitary)? Current theory is that the hypothalamus gradually becomes less sensitive to the small amounts of sex hormones in the bloodstream during childhood. In feedback terms, it takes larger amounts of sex hormones to "turn off" the hypothalamic "gonadostat," with the result that the hypothalamus sends

messages to the pituitary to increase FSH and LH production until, finally, adult levels of sex hormones are circulating in the bloodstream (Grumbach et al., 1974). Even if this theory is correct, it does not explain why puberty occurs when it does. One possible explanation is based on evidence that achievement of a certain critical weight (rather than age) triggers the events of puberty (Frisch, 1974). This evidence helps to explain the phenomenon of puberty occurring at earlier ages during the last century, since children now are bigger sooner. This theory and evidence have been criticized on various grounds, however, and are not yet generally accepted (Falkner, 1975).

In brief, we understand the sequence of events and the role of hormones during puberty, but we still do not know for certain what triggers the onset of puberty. Given the amount of learning that must take place before humans are capable of becoming competent parents, it does make sense for the reproductive system to mature late in development, whatever the mechanism.

A frequent source of embarrassment at puberty is the appearance of facial *acne,* a condition that is generally transient and seems to be related to changes in hormones occurring at this time of life. Although it generally presents no more than a cosmetic problem, acne may sometimes be severe and require medical treatment, particularly if accompanied by infection of the skin, which can lead to permanent scars. These scars can sometimes be satisfactorily removed later by various plastic surgery techniques, which should be performed by a competent physician. Acne tends to be more severe in girls whose menstrual cycles are very irregular.[8]

[8]Lloyd (1964), p. 184.

Estrogen also causes accelerated growth of the external genitals at puberty, including enlargement of the labia and associated structures. The clitoris enlarges under the stimulation of androgens from the adrenal glands. At the same time there is a noticeable increase in skeletal size, which is related to increased secretion of the growth hormone by the pituitary gland.

Internal Changes

Estrogen specifically stimulates growth of the uterus and vagina during puberty. The muscular wall of the uterus enlarges and its glandular lining also develops. The lining of the vagina is extremely sensitive to estrogen, and its thickness is proportional to the amount

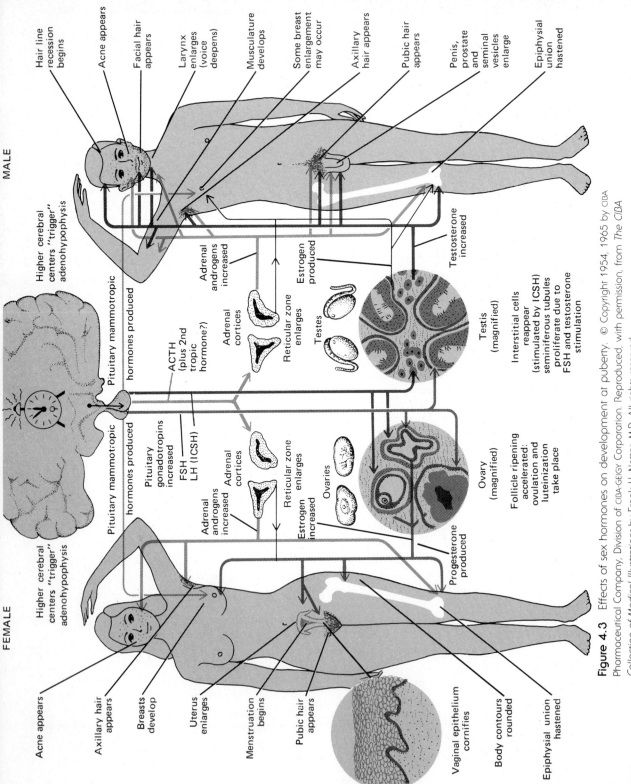

Figure 4.3 Effects of sex hormones on development at puberty. © Copyright 1954, 1965 by CIBA Pharmaceutical Company, Division of CIBA-GEIGY Corporation. Reproduced, with permission, from *The CIBA Collection of Medical Illustrations* by Frank H. Netter, M.D. All rights reserved.

of this hormone present at any given time. Examination of a mucus smear containing cells from the vaginal walls is a simple and clinically useful test for determining how much estrogen is present. As the vaginal wall matures, the pH of the secretions that moisten its surface changes from alkaline to acid.[9]

Under the influence of estrogen the female pelvis enlarges during puberty and assumes contours different from those of the male pelvis. Ultimately, estrogens also prevent further growth of the long bones of the skeleton (counteracting the effects of the growth hormone), and usually no further increase in height occurs after about age 17 in girls. An estrogen deficiency in late puberty may cause great height in a girl, for estrogen normally applies brakes to skeletal growth. Many other factors are also involved in determining the height of a given individual.

Estrogen secretion increases in quantity during puberty, mediating the various external and internal physical changes that we have just described. Moreover, it takes on a cyclical pattern of secretion, which results in certain cyclical phenomena in the female, the most obvious of which is the menstrual cycle.

Becoming an Adult

In many societies menarche has been regarded as the time when a girl becomes a woman, and girls often marry shortly after the first menstruation. Puberty rites often occur at the time of the first menstruation. These rites are sometimes only family affairs, but in other societies the ritual is quite elaborate. Among some California Indian tribes, for instance, a girl was segregated from the rest of the tribe during her first menstrual period. She lived in a special hut built for this purpose and had to eat and bathe in a prescribed

manner, using special implements. The Chiricahua Apaches also had elaborate ceremonies at menarche and believed that at this time girls possessed certain supernatural powers, including the power to heal and to bring prosperity.

In U.S. culture puberty does not mark the entrance into adulthood. Nevertheless, girls are quite sensitive in responding to the physical maturity of others in the peer group. Studies have shown, unexpectedly, that girls who mature late score highest on peer-group ratings of popularity and prestige.[10]

An interesting but unexplained observation is that the average age of menarche in Western countries has been gradually declining. In 1860, for example, a girl usually had her first period between 16 and 17 years of age, whereas in 1960 it usually occurred between 12 and 13. This phenomenon is usually attributed to better nutrition, but other factors may also be involved. Animal studies do not entirely support the notion that better nutrition alone hastens the beginning of puberty. In any event, recent evidence shows that the trend toward earlier menarche is now leveling off in Western countries.[11]

The Menstrual Cycle

Menstruation (from the Latin word for "monthly") is the periodic uterine bleeding that accompanies the ovarian cycle and the shedding of the lining of the uterus. Menstruation is regulated by hormones and is seen only in female humans, apes, and some monkeys. An ovarian, or estrus, cycle occurs in other mammals but is not accompanied by bleeding. The length of the ovarian cycle is specific for each species. It is approximately 28 days in the human, 36 days in the chimpanzee, 20 days in the cow, 16 days in sheep, and five days in mice. Dogs and cats usually ovulate only twice a year.

---

[9]The pH scale is a commonly used index of acidity and alkalinity based on hydrogen ion concentration. The scale runs from 0 to 14; the neutral point is 7. Values from 7 to 14 indicate an alkaline state, from 7 to 0 an acid state.

[10]Hamburg and Lunde (1966), p. 3.
[11]Marshall (1977), p. 70.

Box 4.2 Sex Differences in Physical Ability

Many people believe that males are naturally superior to females in athletics due to biological advantages in strength and endurance. The fact that 70 to 80 percent of world-class athletes in strength events use anabolic steroids (which are similar to male sex hormones) further reinforces the idea that testosterone (a male sex hormone) gives men a major advantage over women in athletics. Numerous studies on average males and females appear to confirm these ideas. Before puberty girls and boys of the same age have almost identical strength and endurance. However, after puberty, most males improve significantly in physical ability while most females either make only minor gains or actually lose strength and endurance.

In the past two decades, however, exercise physiologists have begun to study woman athletes, and a new view of female athletic ability has emerged.[1] With adequate physical training, women can develop considerable athletic ability. It has only been in recent years that many

females have been encouraged to develop their athletic abilities. Most girls have been discouraged from pursuing vigorous physical activity once they reach menarche. They have been pushed toward a sedentary life-style in which their physical fitness can only deteriorate. As women have become more serious competitors in the world of sports, they have begun to close the gap that has long separated female and male athletes, at least in some sports. For example, the Olympic records of women's and men's times in the 400-meter free style swimming events reveal that the men were 16 percent faster than the women in 1924, 11 percent faster in 1948, and only 7 percent faster in 1972. Both women and men have been improving their times throughout this period, but the women have been improving faster. The female record in 1970 was faster than the male record in the mid-1950s.

When comparing highly trained female and male athletes, there are many indications that women may have the same potential for strength and endurance that men do. Part of the difference in

[1]Wilmore (1975, 1977) and Mathews and Fox (1976).

The first menstruation occurs usually between the ages of 11 and 14 years, as has been noted, and may come as a shock to the girl who has not been prepared for it. For the first few years after the menarche the girl's menstrual periods tend to be irregular, and ovulation does not occur in each cycle. For some time after her first period, then, the girl is relatively infertile, but she can nevertheless become pregnant.

For the first few years after menarche a young woman's menstrual cycles may be very irregular in length, but by age 18 or 20 her periods usually assume a certain rhythm. Although there is considerable variation among

mature women in the frequency of menstrual periods, most cycles fall into the range of 21 to 35 days, with a mean of about 28 days.

The occurrence of irregular menstrual cycles in women after the age of 20 may be related to various factors, some of which are not well understood. Certainly, psychological states are important, particularly a prolonged or severe emotional stress. It was not uncommon for women to cease menstruating while imprisoned in German concentration camps during World War II (often before malnutrition or physical illness had developed). Gynecologists also report that some women cease menstruating or menstruate irregularly while

Box 4.2   continued

female and male performances results from the fact that males are larger and heavier than females. When one compares the performance of well-trained females and males of the same weight, many differences disappear. The strength of the lower extremities is virtually identical when comparing women and men athletes of similar weight. Females' legs are actually 5.8 percent stronger than males' legs when comparing people with the same lean body weight (i.e., total weight minus fat). This indicates that women's muscles are not inferior to men's. It is true that men show a distinct superiority in upper body strength. Well-trained female athletes are only 30 to 50 percent as strong in the upper body as well-trained males; but it is difficult to know how much of this relates to biological differences or to training. At present very few women have attempted to develop their upper bodies to the extent that males do. Measures of endurance reveal no significant differences between highly trained women and men long distance runners when comparisons are made relative to lean body weight.

The anabolic steroids used by male athletes do increase muscle bulk and body weight, and this would be expected to help the athlete who depends on size and brute strength. Scientific studies of strength changes in athletes who use these steroids have produced inconsistent findings. Some show increases in strength in comparisons with control groups, but others do not. Male athletes often take 5 to 10 times the recommended daily dosage of these steroids; hence the effects should be more prominent than the effects of testosterone in the normal male. (Men who use anabolic steroids run the risk of liver damage and possible tissue damage in the testes and prostate.)

At present, it is impossible to predict how close female athletes will come to closing the performance gap that has traditionally separated the sexes. It is clear that many of the current physical differences between females and males result from cultural and societal restrictions that channel most females into sedentary roles after puberty. When males adopt sedentary life-styles in their thirties, they too show a similar loss of strength and endurance.

at college but have regular cycles when they are home for the summer.

Sometimes an unmarried woman who has intercourse and fears pregnancy will have a "late" menstrual period. This delay seems related to her emotional state, but we cannot usually rule out the possibility that she has indeed conceived but has spontaneously aborted very early.

Proliferation

The menstrual cycle can be divided into four phases: the proliferative phase, ovulation, the secretory phase, and menstruation. The phases of the menstrual cycle, like the

events of puberty, are essentially under the control of hormones. The proliferative phase begins when menstruation ceases and lasts for about 9 or 10 days in a 28-day cycle (*see* Figure 4.4). During this time the endometrium that was shed during the preceding menstruation grows and proliferates. The proliferative phase is sometimes called the *preovulatory phase* signifying that it occurs before the release of a mature egg from the ovary. During menstruation and proliferation the pituitary gland secretes FSH, which stimulates several of the ovarian follicles to mature (*see* Figure 4.5) and stimulates these follicles to produce estrogen. The estrogen is

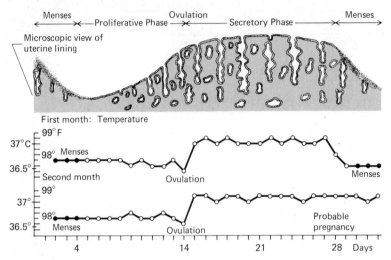

Figure 4.4 The phases of the idealized 28-day-menstrual cycle. The last four days represent the beginning of a new menstrual cycle. Adapted from Benson, *Handbook of Obstetrics and Gynecology,* 3rd ed. (Los Altos, Calif.: Lange Medical Publications, 1968), p. 27. Reprinted by permission.

responsible for the regrowth of the endometrial lining. All but one of the follicles decompose and are reabsorbed by the body. The one remaining follicle will ultimately rupture during ovulation in response to the stimulus of increased production of LH by the pituitary gland.

Estrogen stimulates the growth of the glandular surface of the endometrium, and a thickness of about ⅛ inch (3.5 millimeters) is attained during this phase. In addition, estrogen stimulates the size and productivity of the mucous glands of the cervix. Cervical mucus produced under estrogen stimulation is plentiful, thin, and highly viscous; it has an alkaline pH and contains nutrients that can be used by the sperm. As mentioned previously, rising estrogen levels also stimulate growth of the vaginal lining so that maximum thickness is achieved at ovulation.

Ovulation

The amount of fluid within the maturing follicle increases steadily during the proliferative phase, and ultimately the follicle ruptures and the mature egg (ovum) is released into the fallopian tube. This process is *ovulation,* which occurs about 14 days before menstruation. In a 28-day cycle ovulation thus occurs on about the fourteenth day; but

in a 34-day cycle it occurs on about the twentieth day. The significance of these schedules to those depending on the "rhythm method"[12] for birth control is obvious.

Secretion

The period after ovulation is called the *secretory,* or *postovulatory,* phase of the menstrual cycle. The pituitary gland, responding to the stimulus of increased estrogen levels in the bloodstream, produces more LH, which travels through the bloodstream to the recently ruptured ovarian follicle and stimulates the remaining cells of the follicle to develop into a microscopic glandular structure called the *corpus luteum.* The corpus luteum, under continued FSH and LH stimulation, produces progesterone, along with estrogen. This new source of estrogen accounts for the second peak in the estrogen level seen in Figure 4.5. (Figures 4.6 shows FSH and LH levels.) Under the combined influence of estrogen and progesterone, the glands of the endometrium that have developed during the proliferative phase become functional and *secrete* nutrient fluid by the eighteenth day of a 28-day cycle, corre-

---

[12]Abstinence from intercourse during the presumed fertile period of the menstrual cycle.

sponding to the time when the ovum is free within the uterine cavity and dependent on uterine secretions for nourishment. In addition, there is increased proliferation of blood vessels within the uterus during this phase.

Progesterone inhibits the flow of cervical mucus that occurs during ovulation and diminishes the thickness of the vaginal lining.

If fertilization does not occur, the pituitary gland responds to the increased blood levels of estrogen and progesterone much as a thermostat responds to an increase in temperature and shuts off production of FSH and LH, depriving the corpus luteum of the chemical stimulation to produce estrogen or progesterone. The corpus luteum then withers away.

Menstruation

The final phase of the menstrual cycle is actual menstruation, or *menses*, the shedding of the endometrium through the cervix and vagina. Menstruation represents the results of the hormonal changes that happened during the last menstrual cycle. It also signifies the beginning of the next menstrual cycle. The trigger for menstruation appears to be the fall in the estrogen level at the end of the cycle. (The change in progesterone level that

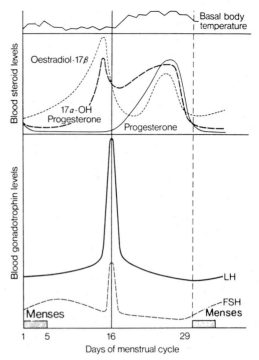

Figure 4.6   Hormone changes in the human menstrual cycle.

occurs simultaneously is not necessary for menstruation.)

The menstrual discharge consists primarily of blood, mucus, and fragments of en-

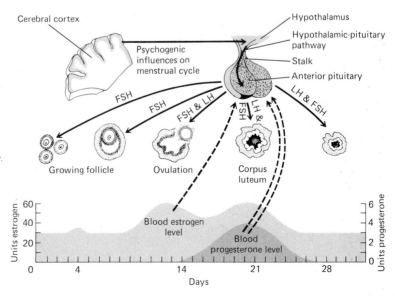

Figure 4.5   Ovulation during the menstrual cycle. The long feedback loops are shown by broken lines. Adapted from Benson, *Handbook of Obstetrics and Gynecology,* 3rd ed. (Los Altos, Calif.: Lange Medical Publications, 1968), p. 26. Reprinted by permission.

dometrial tissue. About 2 ounces (60 milliliters) of blood are lost in an average menstrual period. For a woman on an adequate diet, such blood loss can be easily tolerated. Heavy menstrual bleeding in a woman on a deficient diet can, however, lead to anemia. The duration of menstrual bleeding is usually from three to seven days, and periods longer than one week usually indicate some abnormal condition.

Traditionally, women have used externally worn sanitary napkins to absorb the menstrual discharge, but the trend now is toward internally worn tampons—cylinders of absorbent cotton that are inserted into the vagina and removed by an attached string. When tampons were first introduced in 1933, the public and some church leaders became very concerned about possible abuses of the tampon and claimed for some years that it was an instrument of contraception, masturbation, or defloration.[13] It is now realized that these claims are all untrue, and tampons are becoming increasingly popular. Tampons can be used whether or not a woman has had intercourse, since most hymens will easily allow their insertion.

As the estrogen level continues to fall, the pituitary gland again responds as a thermostat would and turns on its secretion of FSH, which increases ovarian production of estrogen that is needed for proliferation of the endometrial wall to begin again. The timing of menstrual cycles, however, is not determined solely by internal hormonal events (*see* Box 4.3).

Menstrual Problems

There are two common problems related to menstruation: premenstrual tension and painful menstruation. The degree to which these problems are caused by biological or psychological factors has not been determined. Probably both biological and psychological factors are complexly interwoven, affecting

[13]Delaney et al. (1976).

each woman to different degrees. At present the relative importance of the two factors for each woman cannot be known.

Biological Effects

Painful menstruation (*dysmenorrhea*) is the most common problem related to the menstrual cycle. Considering the number of changes that a woman's body goes through each month, it is not surprising that problems sometimes accompany these changes. Almost all women at one time or another experience discomfort in the pelvic area during a menstrual period, and for some women the pain can be frequent and severe. Some women have no symptoms, others continue their normal activities with little more than the help of aspirin, and a few may be forced to stay in bed for a day or two during each menstrual period. The basic complaint of women with this condition is cramps in the pelvic area, but there may also be headaches, backaches, nausea, and general discomfort. In women for whom dysmenorrhea is a monthly problem, it usually begins at an early age; it is relatively uncommon for a woman to have her first painful menstrual period after the age of 20. Those women who do suffer from menstrual cramps often notice a great improvement after childbirth, but the reason for this "cure" is unknown.

The cause of menstrual cramps seems to be related to uterine spasms. It seems that these spasms are caused by chemicals in the menstrual fluid known as *prostaglandins* (*see* Chapter 6).[14] Masters and Johnson reported that some women also use orgasm as a means of helping relieve dysmenorrhea. The

[14]Some women's health care centers use "menstrual extraction" for women with painful or difficult periods. The menstrual fluid and tissue are removed shortly after the onset of the menstrual flow by means of a flexible plastic tube inserted via the cervix. Suction is provided by a syringe attached to the end of the tubing. This so-called "five-minute period" carries with it certain hazards and is contraindicated in women with a history of uterine infections, tumors, and a number of other conditions. The medical profession tends to take a dim view of this procedure as practiced by self-help groups.

Box 4.3   Vaginal Odors as Reproductive Signals

The vaginal odors of some animals play an important role in communicating to the male information about the female's level of sexual receptivity. The female hormone cycle determines which odors are present at which time. Recent studies have shown that women secrete chemical signals—in the form of volatile fatty acids—similar to those of other primates.[1] As shown in the illustration, there is a peak output of the volatile fatty acids shortly before ovulation—except in pill users, who have no peak. People who are allowed to smell odors from various parts of the menstrual cycle can tell the difference between the odors from various points in the cycle. The peak odors are cheeselike due to butanoic acid. When men and women evaluate the vaginal odors, they tend to find them most pleasant during the ovulatory period.[2]

Women are clearly influenced by the odor cycles of other women, although the influence does not operate at a conscious level. Women who live together in college dormitories or other close quarters often begin to menstruate close to the same time.[3] Odor cues are implicated. When a "donor" woman wears cotton pads under her arms for 24-hour periods and other women are exposed to the odors, the menstrual periods of the recipient women shift to become closer to the periods of the donor.[4] Recipients who began an experiment with menstrual periods 9.3 days away from the donor gradually shifted to be only 3.4 days away from the donor after 4 months of odor exposure. It appears that odors from many parts of the body are influenced by the monthly hormonal cycles and can serve to synchronize other women.

Why do women's menstrual cycles become synchronized? In the evolutionary past, reproductive synchrony paid off in terms of survival. In many primate groups, females bear their offspring in one restricted period of the year, when food abundance is optimal for the survival of the young. By having all the females in a group bear infants at the same time of year, all the females are lactating and attentive to infant care at the same time. Because none of the females is sexually receptive, the disruptive influences created by intrusive males and copulatory activity are minimal.[5] Mechanisms that allow females to respond to environmental cues and to each other increase the precision of reproductive synchrony.

Are men influenced by women's odor cycles? Males of many mammalian species are most attracted to females who transmit odors associated with ovulatory and pre-ovulatory periods.[6] The mere presence of sexually cycling females increases spermatogenesis and testosterone production. Although current research has not demonstrated such effects in human males, it is possible that minor effects may still be discovered.

Volatile fatty acids in the vaginal secretions of 47 women (86 cycles). Redrawn from Michael et al. (1974).

[1]Bonsall and Michael (1978).
[2]Doty et al. (1975).
[3]McClintock (1971).
[4]Russell et al. (1977).
[5]Rowell (1972), p. 115.
[6]Michael et al. (1976).

contractions of orgasm increase the rate of menstrual flow, and some women have reported that orgasm experienced shortly after the onset of menstruation not only increases the rate of flow but reduces pelvic cramping when present and frequently relieves menstrually associated backaches.

In addition to pelvic pains, a few women experience so-called "menstrual migraines" with their periods. These headaches are essentially the same as are other migraine headaches, except that they occur particularly during menstruation or just before the beginning of menstrual flow.

During the four to seven days preceding menstruation most women experience symptoms that make them aware of their coming period. When these symptoms are particularly severe they are known as *premenstrual tension,* or the *premenstrual syndrome.* Fatigue, irritability, headache, pain in the lower back, sensations of heaviness in the pelvic region, and a weight gain of as much as several pounds (due to retention of fluids) are among the symptoms. For some women these problems can contribute to emotional and psychological upset at this time. Women who commit crimes or suicide do so more often in the week just before their periods or during their periods. (This is not to say that women are prone to commit crimes or suicide, however, since males commit more than three-fourths of serious crimes and their suicide rate is three times higher than the female rate.) In France a woman who commits a crime during her premenstrual period may use this fact in her defense, claiming "temporary impairment of sanity." The symptoms of premenstrual tension are probably related to the shift in hormone levels occurring at this time, but other factors are also involved.

A separate condition also related to cyclical changes in hormones and retention of fluid is premenstrual pain and swelling of the breasts, known as *mastalgia.* This condition is less common than, but may occur in conjunction with, premenstrual tension.

An unexplained phenomenon is *Mittelschmerz,* pain occurring in midcycle during ovulation. This symptom is most common in young women. It consists of intermittent cramping pains on one or both sides of the lower abdomen lasting for about a day. Occasionally the symptoms of ovulation have been mistaken for appendicitis, much to the embarrassment of the surgeon who decides to operate and finds a healthy appendix.

Psychological Effects

Throughout history the causes of menstruation have not been understood. As a consequence, beliefs about this normal bodily process have become intermingled with cultural myths as various peoples have tried to explain and cope with a process that seemed to them to be a strange and even mystical or evil occurrence. In most cultures the menstruating woman has been restricted in her activities, and in some societies she has been completely segregated from other people in order to protect them, especially the men, from the harmful influence of menstrual bleeding.

The writings of Pliny, a Roman historian, reflect many prescientific beliefs about menstruation.

Contact with it turns new wine sour, crops touched by it become barren, grafts die, seeds in gardens are dried up, the fruit of trees falls off . . . the edge of steel and the gleam of ivory are dulled, hives of bees die, even bronze and iron are at once seized by rust, and a horrible smell fills the air; to taste it drives dogs mad and infects their bites with an incurable poison.[15]

Today many societies still consider women to be "unclean" during menstruation. Strict menstrual taboos are commonly practiced among some groups in India.[16] These people believe that a man can become polluted simply by touching a menstruating

[15]Pliny (77 A.D. [1961]).
[16]Ullrich (1977).

woman. A priest is needed to purify him. A woman must warn the man of her condition if he might come closer than three feet of her. If a menstruating woman touches certain substances such as wood, rope, or cloth, the pollution is passed to another person who touches the object at the same time. Thus people cannot cross a bridge until a menstruating woman is off the bridge. Other societies impose different restrictions on women during their periods. The women may have to follow special diets and they may be forbidden to participate in specified activities.

The Old Testament and the Koran and Hindu law books all specifically prohibit intercourse during menstruation because women are presumed to be polluted and dangerous at this time and will defile anyone who has contact with the menstrual discharge. Orthodox Jewish women are not permitted to have sex while menstruating and for seven days afterwards. They must take a ritual bath before they are considered to be "clean" again. Several South American and African tribes believe that a man would become physically ill if he had sexual relations with a menstruating partner. Some nomads of northeast Asia believe that a woman would become sick and eventually sterile if she copulated while bleeding. Other tribes believe that a menstruating woman who had any physical contact with a man could cause him to lose his virility and his hunting ability. In such societies women are physically isolated from their communities during menstruation.

There is no medical reason why a woman should refrain from intercourse while she is menstruating. In fact, the taboos against intercourse during menstruation are declining. A recent survey of 575 married men and women revealed that even though 71 percent of people 55 years old and over had never had intercourse during menstruation, only 28 percent of the people 35 and younger could make the same statement.[17]

A menstruating woman is often thought of as having a sickness or a handicap. In fact, many menstruating women are not completely comfortable with their bodily processes. Most women would feel quite embarrassed if some menstrual blood were to "soil" their outer clothing. If the source of blood were a cut they would be much less embarrassed. Women learn from their culture that menstruation is something about which to feel uncomfortable.

A study of 298 college women found differences in menstrual problems in women of different religious groups.[18] Catholic women often felt that menstrual difficulties were part of their role. The Catholic women (especially virgins) who thought a woman belonged in the home and who had no career desires were most likely to have severe menstrual distress. Among the Jewish women, those who followed the Orthodox Jewish teachings regarding menstruation were most likely to have menstrual difficulties. The Protestant group studied was too diverse for any correlations to be evident. Another finding of the study was that women who reported physical pain and psychological stress during menstruation tended to report more problems at other times, too.

A recent study suggests that to some degree psychological factors are operating in the reporting of premenstrual symptoms.[19] Forty-four college women who were approximately one week from menstruation were led to believe that an electroencephalogram (EEG) could predict the timing of their next menstrual period. After undergoing an elaborate "test" that was supposed to predict the onset of the next period, all the women filled out a Menstrual Distress Questionnaire, the standard questionnaire used in menstrual research. The women who were told that their period was due in one or two days were much more likely to report the following

[17]Paige (1978).

[18]Paige (1973).
[19]Ruble (1977).

problems—water retention, pain, and changed eating habits—than women who were told that their period would be ten days away. (A follow-up on the women found that the average number of days before the onset of the next period did not differ between the two groups.) Studies such as these indicate that to some extent there is a psychological component to menstrual problems.

Hormonal Control of Sexual Behavior

The degree to which sexual behavior in monkeys and apes is under hormonal control is not entirely clear, but the relation of sexual behavior to sex hormones in lower mammals is well known. Females come into estrus—that is, become receptive to the sexual advances of males—at specific points in their cycles that coincide with ovulation and maximum levels of female sex hormones. Mating at this time obviously enhances the probability of reproduction, and there is essentially no sexual activity in lower mammals except when the females are fertile and likely to conceive. Removal of the ovaries of a guinea pig or hamster has been shown to eliminate sexual activity, but the female can be made sexually receptive again with injections of estrogen and progesterone.

The human female is unique in that her sexuality is not limited to one particular part of the menstrual cycle; that is, human sexual activity is not linked to specific periods of the female's cycle, as it is in most other mammals. Studies have shown, however, that there are predictable variations in the frequency of intercourse and orgasm during the menstrual cycle in many women, with peaks occurring at midcycle and just before menstruation.[20] A similar pattern for self-rating of sexual arousal in young women during the menstrual cycle has also been found.[21] Other

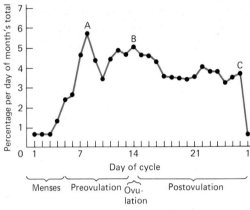

Figure 4.7 The distribution of intercourse for 52 women on 1123 occasions during the menstrual cycle. Redrawn from McCance et al. (1952).

studies indicate that the frequency of intercourse is highest after menstruation ceases, with minor peaks occurring around the time of ovulation and perhaps right before menstruation (*see* Figure 4.7).[22] The pattern in which coitus peaks after menstruation and declines thereafter may reflect a rebound of sexual activity after abstinence during menstruation. Interestingly a study that measured female-initiated coitus did not find a large peak occurring after menstruation in those women who engaged in intercourse during their menstrual period. The minor peak before the menstrual period may reflect preparation for the time when the likelihood for intercourse is reduced.

It is possible that changes in coital frequencies may be influenced by variations in sex hormones. The increased frequency of intercourse may be related to the increased levels of estrogen, although it may be related to androgens, which some data indicate may also peak at this time. There is evidence that the androgens secreted by the adrenal glands influence the sex drive of women: Surgical removal of the adrenal glands has a more

[20]Udry and Morris (1968).
[21]Moos, Lunde, et al. (1969).

[22]McCance et al. (1952), James (1971), Gold and Adams (1978).

predictable effect on sexual interest than does removal of the ovaries. Women who receive androgenic hormones for medical reasons sometimes also report dramatic increases in sexual desire while under treatment. Three possible mechanisms have been suggested to explain this result:

1. Androgens cause heightened susceptibility to psychic and somatic sexual stimulation.
2. Androgens produce increased sensitivity of the external genitalia.
3. Androgens induce greater intensity of sexual gratification (orgasm).[23]

Menopausal Problems

There are several common problems that women experience during menopause. As with menstruation, these symptoms are probably caused by a complex mixture of biological and psychological factors. At present, the relative influence of the various factors is not known.

Biological Effects

The term *menopause* refers to the permanent cessation of menstruation due to the physiological changes associated with aging. A broader term, encompassing the various changes that occur in connection with the altered functioning of the ovaries is *climacteric* ("critical period"). The latter generally includes the years from 45 to 60, the years of the "change of life."

Menstruation most commonly ceases between the ages of 46 and 50. Menstrual periods usually become very irregular several years before menopause, and this interval is one of relative infertility, as is that just after menarche. Pregnancy beyond age 47 is rare, but it has been medically documented as late as 61.

There is evidence that menopause comes at an earlier age in women who smoke than

[23]Greenblatt et al. (1972).

in nonsmokers. In a study of 3500 women in seven countries researchers found that at ages 48 to 49, a woman who smokes a pack a day or more is nearly twice as likely to be past menopause as is a woman who never smoked. The researchers suggest that nicotine may have an effect on the secretion of the hormones involved in menopause or on the way the body handles sex hormones.

The mechanism of menopause, unlike that of puberty, is not related to the pituitary gland. The latter continues to pour out FSH, but for some reason the ovaries gradually fail to respond and very little estrogen is produced.

The best known symptom of the climacteric is the *hot flash* or *flush,* caused by the dilation of blood vessels resulting in the experience of waves of heat spreading over the face and the upper half of the body. It may be followed by perspiration or chills and may last for a few seconds or longer. Other physical symptoms include headaches, dizziness, heart palpitations, and pains in the joints. Severe depression (*involutional melancholia*) may occur at this time in women with no previous history of mental illness. The cause is unknown. Less severe depression during menopause may be partly related to the hormonal imbalance of this period.

Some of the symptoms of the climacteric will affect about three-fourths of women to some degree, but only about 10 percent of them are obviously inconvenienced by these problems. Doctors have prescribed estrogens to relieve these symptoms, but in 1976 the U.S. Food and Drug Administration warned that women who take female hormones to relieve menopause symptoms run a "marked increase" in the risk of cancer of the uterus. The agency cautioned that women should be given the lowest possible doses for the shortest possible time.

Certain changes in the genitals occur during the years after menopause, including a gradual shrinking of the uterus and vaginal lining. Some women experience a new awakening of sexual desire after menopause, perhaps because they no longer need worry about pregnancy or contraception.

Psychological Effects

Historically, menopause has been a little-understood phenomenon. In some cultures women are given special privileges and status when they cease menstruating and bearing children. In other cultures menopause has been stereotyped as a difficult and trying time. Indeed, women in *Inis Beag,* a rural community in Ireland (*see* Chapter 13) believe that menopause can produce madness, and many withdraw from life when they reach that age. Some even spend the rest of their lives in bed. A century ago in the United States and England some doctors treated women with menopausal complaints by bleeding them or by applying leeches in order to rid them of excess blood. Clearly, if people believe that menopause is a difficult life transition, the belief can become a self-fulfilling prophecy.

It is difficult to determine exactly what role psychological factors play in causing or exacerbating the problems women experience during the climacteric.[24] Depression in particular appears to be influenced by both the hormonal changes and psychological difficulties associated with this period of life. Part of these difficulties can be traced to the problems some women experience in coping with their loss of reproductive capacity, their changing role within the family and society, and their own aging. Although some women have problems when children leave home, several studies have found that middle-aged women whose children no longer live at home report being happier than women of about the same age who still have a child at home.

[24]For a comprehensive review of the biological and psychological causes of menopause see Tucker (1977).

It is clear that menopausal problems result from more than hormonal causes alone. Several studies report no correlation between emotional problems and estrogen levels (as judged from vaginal smears). Estrogen therapy is not an automatic cure for menopausal depression. At present the role of estrogen therapy in relieving depression is controversial. Some studies report very positive results and other studies give more mixed findings. In addition, research has shown that certain social and psychological factors play a key role in determining whether a woman will experience problems during the climacteric. For example, women who overspecialized in the motherhood role experience more problems at menopause than other women. Women who have not been pregnant report fewer problems than women who have. Women from higher economic groups report fewer problems than women from lower economic groups. Better educated women report fewer problems than women with a grade-school education.

In general, it must be emphasized that most women cope successfully with the biological and psychological problems they experience during menopause. The stereotype that menopause is a very difficult period for most women is not true.

Male Reproductive Endocrinology

Puberty

Puberty begins somewhat later and lasts longer in boys than it does in girls. It is initiated at age 10 or 11 in boys by the same pituitary hormones that mediate it in girls, FSH and LH. But in males, as was noted earlier, LH is called "interstitial-cell-stimulating hormone" (ICSH) because of the difference in the site of its action.

ICSH reaches the interstitial cells of the testes through the bloodstream and stimulates them, initiating the process of puberty. Little is seen in the way of striking external changes, but the interstitial cells begin producing the primary androgen (male sex hormone), a compound known as *testosterone*. This one substance is essentially responsible for the development of all the physical changes (including development of *secondary sex characteristics*) that occur during puberty (*see* Figure 4.3).

External Changes

The first noticeable changes resulting from testosterone stimulation include enlargement of the testes and penis and the appearance of fine straight hair at the base of the penis. At first the penis increases in circumference more than in length. By age 12 it is still, on the average, about 1.5 inches (3.8 centimeters) long in the relaxed state and less than 3 inches (7.6 centimeters) long in erection.

As the testes enlarge, however, their capacity to produce testosterone increases, and at age 13 or 14 rapid growth of the penis, testes, and pubic hair begins. By this age most girls will have had their first menstrual period,

although they will not necessarily be ovulating as yet.

Axillary hair does not appear until about age 15 in most boys, and at the same time some fuzz appears on their upper lips. Adult beards do not appear for two or three more years, however, and indeed by age 17 about 50 percent of boys in the United States have not yet shaved and many others shave only infrequently. Continued development of facial and chest hair under androgen stimulation continues beyond age 20 in many young men, along with recession of the hairline (*see* Figure 4.8).

A very noticeable change that occurs during puberty—though strictly speaking an internal change—is the deepening of the voice, related to growth of the *larynx* ("voice box") in response to hormonal stimulation. The deepening of the voice may be gradual or fairly abrupt, but on the average it occurs by age 14 or 15.

Acne becomes a source of embarrassment to many boys at age 15 or 16, as does another transient phenomenon, enlargement

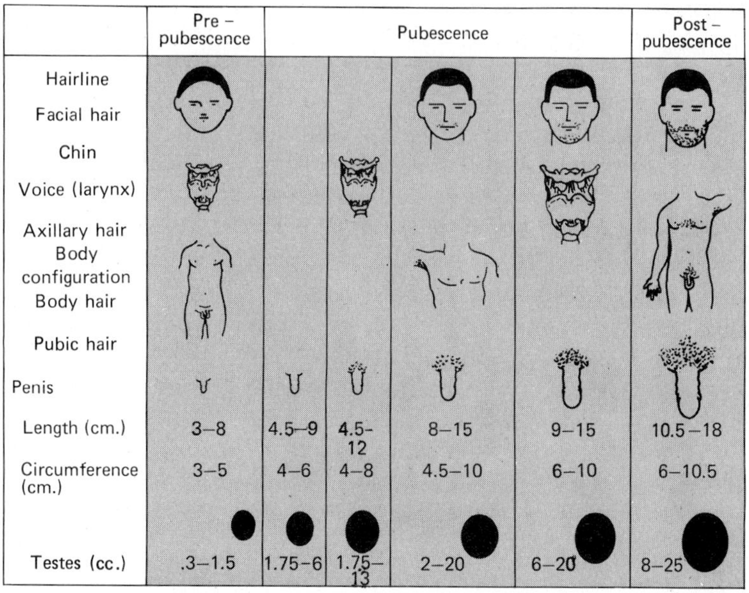

Figure 4.8 Development of some secondary sex characteristics in men. From Wilkins, Blizzard, and Migeon, *The Diagnosis and Treatment of Endocrine Disorders in Childhood and Adolescence,* 3rd ed. (Springfield, Ill.: Charles C Thomas, 1965), p. 200. Reprinted by permission.

	Pre-pubescence	Pubescence				Post-pubescence
Hairline / Facial hair / Chin						
Voice (larynx)						
Axillary hair / Body configuration / Body hair						
Pubic hair						
Penis						
Length (cm.)	3–8	4.5–9	4.5–12	8–15	9–15	10.5–18
Circumference (cm.)	3–5	4–6	4–8	4.5–10	6–10	6–10.5
Testes (cc.)	.3–1.5	1.75–6	1.75–13	2–20	6–20	8–25

Box 4.4   Premature Puberty

Although puberty normally begins at about age 12 and 13 for girls and boys, it can begin much earlier. If the changes begin before 8 in girls and 9 in boys, the condition is called precocious puberty.[1] Girls are twice as likely to have precocious puberty as boys. There are cases of menstruation beginning in the first year of life. The youngest known mother was a Peruvian girl who began menstruating at 3 years and gave birth (by cesarean section) at the age of 5 years and 7 months. There are cases in which penile development began at 5 months and spermatogenesis at 5 years. Boys as young as 7 years of age have reportedly fathered children. In many cases, especially in girls, precocious puberty does not indicate any major problem: The early puberty merely reflects a natural variation in the body's timing mechanisms. However, 20 percent of girls and 60 percent of boys with precocious puberty have a serious organic disease. Tumors in the hypothalamic region of the brain, the gonads, or the adrenals can trigger the production of gonadotrophins or sex hormones, which in turn lead to the early sexual maturation of the body.

In some cases, a child may undergo incomplete precocious puberty. There may be early breast development or early growth of pubic hair, but no other changes. These changes are less likely to be related to major organic disorders than is complete precocious puberty.

[1]Katchadourian (1977), pp. 128 ff.

of the breasts, or *gynecomastia*. The latter occurs in about 80 percent of pubertal boys and is probably related to small amounts of female sex hormones produced by the testes.

Overall growth in both height and weight occurs during puberty. But, whereas the girl develops fat deposits in breasts and hips at this time, the boy's new weight is in the form of increased muscle mass and he consequently develops a quite different physique.[25] Whereas the female pelvis undergoes enlargement at puberty, more striking expansion occurs in the boy's shoulders and rib cage at this time. There is also a definite spurt in the linear growth rates of boys at puberty, and this process continues until age 20 or 21, when the male hormones finally put the brakes on growth in the long bones of the skeleton. As previously noted, female sex hormones induce this "braking" process more rapidly, which accounts for the generally smaller height of women.[26]

Internal Changes

Whereas the changes in external appearance just described give the appearance of biological maturity to the growing boy, significant internal changes must also occur before the capacity for reproductive activity is actually achieved.

The pituitary hormone FSH, which stimulates maturation of the ovum in the female, is also essential in the production of mature sperm in the male. With the increase in FSH secretion during puberty, germ cells in the lining of the seminiferous tubules of the testes (*see* Chapter 2) begin to divide and

[25]The use of supplemental androgens ("anabolic steroids") to increase the muscle mass of Olympic athletes (particularly shotputters) and professional athletes (particularly football players) has become widespread and controversial in recent years.

[26]This statement does not imply that a tall girl has a deficiency of female sex hormones or that a tall boy has a deficiency of male hormones. Other factors, including heredity and nutrition, influence stature. Americans of both sexes have been getting progressively taller with each successive generation during the last century, a phenomenon usually ascribed to a better diet.

Box 4.4   continued

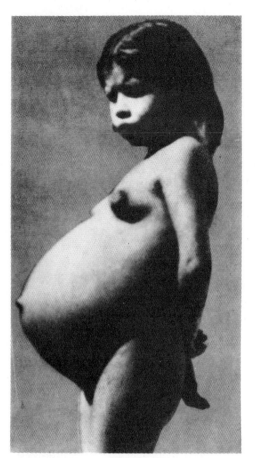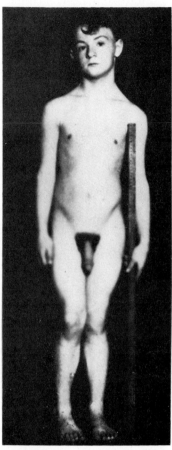

Lina Medina (left) is the youngest mother known in the medical literature. She gave birth in 1939 at the age of 5 years and 7 months. A 5-year-old boy with an unusual adrenal development (right) has the height of an 11.5-year-old and precocious penile development. From Wilkins, Blizzard, and Migeon *The Diagnosis and Treatment of Endocrine Disorders in Childhood and Adolescence*, 3rd ed. (Springfield, Ill.: Charles C Thomas, 1965). Reprinted by permission.

differentiate into mature sperm. Mature sperm are first present in the ejaculatory fluid at age 15, on the average, but, as with the other changes at puberty, there is wide variation among individuals, encompassing the range from ages 11 to 17.

FSH is a necessary but not sufficient stimulus for the production of mature sperm. Other hormones, particularly thyroid hor-mone, must also be present in sufficient con-centrations. In addition, a temperature lower than normal body temperature is essential to mature sperm production. In undescended testicles, which are still in the abdominal cav-ity, mature sperm cannot be produced be-cause of the warmth of the environment.

The organs that supply fluids for the se-men enlarge significantly during puberty. The prostate gland is particularly sensitive to the stimulation of testosterone. By age 13 or 14 the prostate gland is producing fluid that can be ejaculated during orgasm, but this fluid will probably not contain mature sperm. Just as the menarche does not necessarily indicate that a girl has ovulated, so the ability to ejaculate does not indicate that a boy is fertile.

At about this same age a boy begins to have "wet dreams," or *noctural emissions* of seminal fluid (*see* Chapter 9).

Becoming an Adult

Many societies have specific puberty rites for boys, generally to signify that they have reached adulthood. As there is no event for boys comparable to menarche, an arbitrary age like 13 may be taken as the time for initiation. In some societies, however, particular manifestations like the appearance of facial hair or the first "wet dream" are required for adult status. Women are often excluded from such male puberty rites, and sexual information is often transmitted to boys during these ceremonies. In addition, circumcision may be performed at this time (*see* Chapter 2). Many tribal peoples require the performance of certain acts of physical strength, skill, and endurance; in addition, a boy may be required to participate in certain sexual activities.

With the exception of the bar mitzvah among Jews, our society does not have formal puberty rites for boys. Nevertheless, like girls, boys are very sensitive to the physical transformations that occur in their peers during puberty and respond accordingly. Early-maturing boys have thus been found to have greater peer-group prestige and are most often ranked as "leaders" among boys of pubertal age. It should be noted, however, that in adulthood the late maturers are often found to be more adventurous, flexible, and assertive than are early maturers.[27]

[27]Hamburg and Lunde (1966), p. 4.

Hormones and Fertility in the Male

There is no fertility cycle in men as there is in women. Sperm are normally produced throughout the reproductive years, and the healthy man is consistently fertile at all times of the month and year. This phenomenon corresponds to the fairly consistent secretion of testosterone by the testes, in contrast to the cyclical secretion of sex hormones in the female.

In the animal world there are some exceptions to this continuous male fertility. Some species, like deer and sheep, have specific "rutting seasons" during which the males are fertile and sexually active. For the rest of the year these animals are infertile and generally uninterested in sexual activity. In certain wild rodents the testes are actually drawn into the body cavity except during the mating season, when they descend into the scrotum. During the period that the testes are inside the abdominal cavity they produce neither sperm nor male sex hormones.

Although testosterone secretion and spermatogenesis are generally constant in men, variations may occur in certain situations. Severe emotional shock has been known to cause temporary cessation of sperm production in some men. Studies of soldiers in combat show that testosterone levels rise and fall in response to the degree of stress to which men are exposed.[28] Recent studies have also shown that intercourse in males is followed by an increase in the level of testosterone in the bloodstream.[29] These findings should not seem surprising in light of the interrelations of sex hormones, pituitary hormones, and the brain, which we described earlier in this chapter.

Other factors may also affect fertility in men, either temporarily or permanently. Certain drugs, including some used in the treatment of cancer and at least one antibiotic

[28]Rose (1969), p. 136.
[29]Fox et al. (1972).

Box 4.5   Eunuchs

Castration, the removal of the testes, can occur before puberty or after, by accident or by plan. Although castration is rare in modern times (except as a result of accidents, disease, or war), it used to be a much more common practice.

Eunuchs who are castrated before puberty retain their high voices and do not develop the secondary sex traits of beards and body hair.[1] They develop subcutaneous fat deposits that follow the feminine pattern. Men who were castrated before puberty can have erections, much the same as prepubertal boys can. Once prepubertal castrates reach adulthood some of them may marry and have regular sexual intercourse and satisfying erotic feelings.[2]

Early castration was most common in the Near East, and probably first performed in ancient Egypt where hundreds of young boys would be castrated in a single religious ceremony and their genitals offered as sacrifices to the gods. A eunuch (from Greek *eunoukhos*, "guardian of the bed") is a castrated male; and eunuchs have perhaps been most famous as harem guards. Although most eunuchs were slaves to Muslim rulers, they occasionally worked themselves into positions of great influence and power. The sex drive varied greatly among eunuchs, but some were apparently very active sexually.

The practice of using castrates in choirs spread to the West from Constantinople.

Castrati were used in the papal choir until the early nineteenth century. Because women were not allowed to perform in the opera up into the eighteenth century in parts of Europe, talented boys were castrated to produce the sopranos who would eventually play women's roles.

Eunuchs played a powerful role in Chinese imperial govenments for more than 2000 years and through 25 dynasties.[3] At the peak of their influence, there were over 70,000 eunuchs in the service of the Ming dynasty. They gained great power and wealth by manipulating the emperors and were in part responsible for the decline and fall of every dynasty. The eunuch system was not completely abolished until 1924, when the final 470 eunuchs were driven from the last emperor's palace.

Men who are castrated after puberty do not lose the secondary sex traits they gained during puberty, nor do they lose the sexual knowledge and psychosexual orientation they developed in prior years. There is a great deal of variability among these men in their sexual interest and performance. The ability to ejaculate is lost, since it is hormonally dependent; but orgasm without ejaculation feels much the same as the normal orgasm. Most men lose their sexual potency, but some do not.

[1]Money and Ehrhardt (1972).
[2]Money and Alexander (1967).
[3]Mitamura (1970).

(*Furadantin*), may cause temporary sterility. A prolonged exposure to high temperature, as in an illness involving a high fever or in frequent and prolonged hot baths, may inhibit sperm production. Mumps may cause permanent sterility in men through the mechanism described in Chapter 2. Severe or prolonged radiation can cause sterility or the production of abnormal sperm. In the days when

fluoroscopes were commonly used in fitting shoes, some shoe salesmen were rendered sterile by prolonged exposure to radiation.

Aging in the Male

There is no male equivalent of the menopause in the female. The term *menopause* means the cessation of the menses. Thus, males do not have a menopause in the true

Box 4.6   Hormonal Errors

Individuals who exhibit external genital characteristics of both sexes have traditionally been called *hermaphrodites*. Ancient Greek and Roman art and literature are replete with images and reference to the deity Hermaphroditus. Herodotus and Plato both referred to an ancient tribe living north of the Black Sea said to be ambisexual. Plato theorized that such people represented a third sex, which had died out over time. To other writers, however, hermaphrodites seemed to have supernatural qualities. From the time of Theophrastus (382–287 B.C.) through the Roman Empire, Hermaphroditus was considered a god, the offspring of Hermes (god of occult science) and Aphrodite (goddess of love).

In medical terminology a true hermaphrodite (*hermaphroditus verus*) is an individual who has both ovarian and testicular tissue. The condition is extremely rare: Only 60 cases have been reported in the entire world medical literature of the twentieth century. Such an individual may have one ovary and one testicle or sex glands that contain mixtures of ovarian and testicular tissues. This combination of tissues and hormones is usually accompanied by a mixture of masculine and feminine characteristics, but hermaphrodites usually have masculine genitals and feminine breasts. There often is some sort of vaginal opening beneath the penis, and many hermaphrodites menstruate. Development of the uterus is often incomplete—with, for instance, only one fallopian tube present. True hermaphrodites are usually genetic females (XX). They can be raised as males or females and the decision is often made based on their appearance at birth. The first picture shows a hermaphrodite who is a genetic female, with a right testis and left ovary. This person has always lived as a male. He is married and a stepfather.

In addition to true hermaphrodites, there are also male and female pseudohermaphrodites. Unlike the true hermaphrodite, the pseudohermaphrodite does not have both ovarian and testicular tissue. But pseudohermaphrodites do have some sex organs that resemble the organs of the opposite sex. The development of both male and female sex organs is caused by the simultaneous presence, in significant amounts, of male and female sex hormones during embryological development (*see* Chapter 2).

Since male sex hormones can also be produced by the adrenal glands, a female may present a masculine appearance because of a genetic defect in the adrenal glands that results in the pouring forth of large amounts of androgens. This condition is known as the adrenogenital syndrome

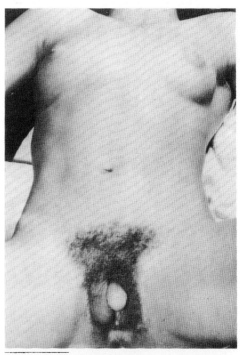

A true hermaphrodite, who is a genetic female that has always lived as a male. He has one ovary and one testis. From Money *Sex Errors of the Body*. (Baltimore: Johns Hopkins Press, © 1968), p. 121. Reprinted by permission.

Box 4.6   continued

(AGS). Such individuals not only have masculine-appearing external genitals at birth, but they also become further masculinized at puberty due to the continued secretion of large amounts of androgens.

Although such a woman may have normal internal female genitalia, including ovaries, her clitoris is often enlarged and resembles a penis as can be seen in the picture below. In addition, the folds of the labia may be fused in such a manner as to resemble a scrotum, with the result that such a female may be reared as a male.

There are other conditions that can produce a female pseudohermaphrodite. If a mother has an androgen-producing tumor while pregnant or the mother is given progestin (synthetic progesterone, which sometimes has male effects) while pregnant, the fetal genitals may be masculinized, and a female pseudohermaphrodite may be created. Unlike the female with AGS, there is no excess of male hormones present in the female's

body after birth; thus no further masculinization will take place.

Male pseudohermaphrodites are produced during intrauterine development if the male does not produce sufficient male hormones or if these hormones are not biologically active. For example, some male pseudohermaphrodites have androgen insensitivity. In this case a genetic male (XY) with androgen-secreting testes (usually undescended) has the external

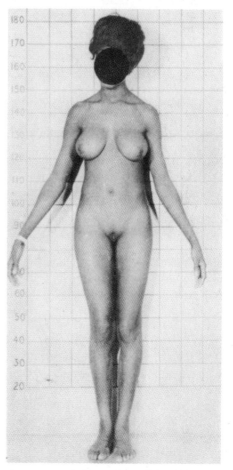

A woman with the androgen insensitivity syndrome. She is a genetic male. From Money Sex Errors of the Body. (Baltimore: Johns Hopkins Press, © 1968), p. 113. Reprinted by permission.

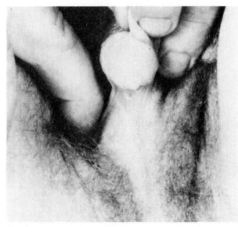

Characteristic external genitalia of a female pseudohermaphrodite. From Jones and Scott, Hermaphroditism, Genital Anomalies and Related Endocrine Disorders (Baltimore: Williams & Wilkins, 1958), p. 212. © 1958 by The Williams & Wilkins Co.; reprinted by permission.

Box 4.6   continued

appearance of a female, a vagina, but no uterus. It would appear that receptor sites for androgens, located on the X chromosome and/or other chromosomes, are blocked by some unknown mechanism, thereby rendering the male hormones inactive.[1] Such males are sometimes raised as females. Others are raised as males, but they do not develop the secondary sex traits of the male since their bodies do not respond to androgens. Instead their bodies respond to the female hormones present and breasts develop. The third picture is of a female who is actually a genetic male who has the androgen-insensitivity syndrome.

There are many variations among male pseudohermaphrodites, from males with androgen insensitivity to males with almost completely normal appearances. For example, a male may have normal external genitals but also have a uterus. A male may have a clitoris-like penis with the urethra opening at the base. The testes may be undescended and a vaginal opening may be present.

In most cases the gender identity and gender role of hermaphrodites and pseudohermaphrodites corresponds to the sex they were raised to be. Also, the sexual activity of both true and pseudohermaphrodites reflects their assigned gender roles—those reared as males usually choose female sexual partners, and vice versa. (There is one unusual case on record, however, of a hermaphrodite who had intercourse alternately with men and women, using the vaginal opening or the enlarged clitoris to suit the occasion.)

Most types of pseudohermaphroditism can be corrected by surgical or hormonal and surgical treatment; but it is important that the proper diagnosis be made early. Psychological difficulties are quite common in individuals who have lived for several years or more with mistaken or ambiguous sexual identities, as might be expected.

[1]Mittwoch (1973).

sense of the word. Whereas the ovaries essentially cease to function at a fairly specific time in a woman's life, the testes continue to function in men indefinitely, though there may be gradual declines in the rates of testosterone secretion and sperm production (*see* Figure 4.9). There are well-documented reports of men of 90 years of age having fathered children, and viable sperm have been found in the ejaculations of men even older.

Although older men do not technically experience a biological menopause, there are certain problems that become more common in men with age. The most common biological problem is enlargement of the prostate gland, which occurs in 10 percent of men by age 40 and in 50 percent of men by age 80.

This enlargement interferes with control of urination and causes frequent nightly urination, but it can usually be corrected. It also causes men to worry about their aging and sexual ability (*see* Chapter 7).

Men may experience psychological changes in their fifties and sixties.[30] Any of a variety of life experiences that are common at that age can cause some men problems, although other men will not be affected. By their fifties, people are often aware of growing old, and thoughts of death may be painful. It may hurt to see younger men moving into exciting jobs while the older men—past their prime—are being put out to pasture. Many

[30]Rubin (1977).

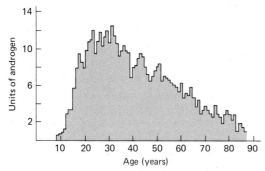

Figure 4.9 The quantities of biologically active androgens excreted by boys and men. Redrawn from Pedersen-Bjergaard and Tónnesen (1948).

men who once had high aspirations begin to realize that they had not accomplished as much in life as they had hoped. Changes in the family structure—as the children leave home—may leave the husband and wife alone together, often aware that they have grown apart during the child-rearing years.

Naturally, not all men experience these changes or find aging to be problematic. Numerous factors can help make aging easier to cope with: among these are a good marital and family relationship, health and vigor, and a realistic appraisal of one's abilities and acceptance of that which is inevitable. There is no change related to hormone levels that need interfere with sexual activities in men or women as they grow older. Both men and women can continue to have fulfilling sex lives well into old age.

Chapter 5

Conception, Pregnancy, and Childbirth

For centuries the "miracle of birth" must have seemed just that—a miracle. No one could fully explain how it happened, and in some societies people did not even make the connection between sexual intercourse and pregnancy. Two South Pacific tribes, the Arunta and the Trobrianders, believed that intercourse was purely a source of pleasure unrelated to pregnancy. Natives of these tribes believed that conception occurred when a spirit embryo entered the body of a woman. The spirit was believed to enter the uterus either through the vagina or through the head. In the latter instance, it was thought to travel through the bloodstream to the uterus.

Other people, though recognizing that intercourse is essential to conception, believed that supernatural powers determined whether or not specific acts of intercourse would cause pregnancy. The Jivaro tribesmen in the Amazon region believed that women were particularly fertile during the phase of the new moon. Perhaps this belief reflects association of the lunar cycle with the menstrual cycle, both of which are about the same length.

A few tribes, like the Kiwai of New Guinea and the Baiga of India, believed that a woman could become pregnant from something that she had eaten, implying that a substance taken in through the mouth may have contained semen, which then found its way to the uterus.

Today we know that it is the union of sperm and egg that results in conception, pregnancy, and the birth of a child. Even though there are still aspects of these processes that have yet to be fully explained, the miracle of birth is no longer quite as mysterious as it once must have seemed.

Conception

The moment when sperm and egg unite is the moment of conception. In order to understand exactly what this means, it is necessary to have some basic knowledge of the cells involved—sperm and eggs.

Sperm

The persistence of myths and misconceptions about conception is understandable when we realize that sperm were not discovered until 300 years ago, and even then there was little agreement on what sperm were. The discovery was made in the laboratory of Anton van Leeuwenhoek (1632–1723), a Dutchman who did some of the first scientific investigations of life forms with a microscope. He noted that sperm resembled other microscopic organisms he had seen swimming

Box 5.1   Where Do Babies Come From?

People have always been curious about the origins of human life. Early observers often allowed their imaginations to carry their theories beyond the facts.[1] Over 2000 years ago Aristotle speculated that the human fetus originated from a union of menstrual blood and male seminal fluid. After the microscope was developed in the late 1600s, scientists could see the sperm in the seminal fluid for the first time. Naturally, sperm did not resemble humans in appearance. Nor could any structures with human form be found inside the female body. The absence of human form in either the sperm or the ovaries created more questions than answers: How could a human baby develop from formless origins?

Two schools of thought emerged to explain the inexplicable. The ovists claimed that a minuscule, but fully formed, baby was contained in the eggs and that the sperm functioned only to activate the growth of the preformed baby. The homunculists held the opposite view, that the preformed baby resided inside the head of the sperm but did not begin to develop until it arrived in the fertile environment provided by the uterus. Looking through their crude early microscopes, several of the homunculists claimed to have seen a homunculus—or little man—inside the sperm, which served

[1]Meyer (1939).

as evidence for their theory. Large sperm were presumed to produce male children, and small sperm to produce females.

The logic of both the ovist and homunculist theories led to the incredible conclusion that all generations of humans had been preformed from the beginning and that each generation was stacked inside either the ova or sperm of all previous generations, like Chinese boxes!

Of course, these early scientists could not know that fetal development is under control of genetic information. This modern theory was not developed until the early 1900s.

A homunculus as drawn by Niklaas Hartsoeker in 1694.

about in pond water, and he named them *spermatozoa* ("seed animals"). Van Leeuwenhoek was convinced that sperm were involved in human reproduction, but others at the time thought that sperm were only miscellaneous organisms contaminating the seminal fluid. A hundred years later Lazaro Spallanzani (1729–1799) demonstrated that seminal fluid from a male dog that had been filtered (thus removing the sperm) was incapable of causing pregnancy when injected into the vagina of a female dog.

From the union of male and female germ cells one new cell is formed. It divides into two cells, then into four cells, then into eight cells, and so on. If all goes according to plan, the result after approximately nine months is a fully formed human infant. The process of cell division is called *mitosis*. The information that guides cells in their division and multiplication is contained in the *chromosomes*, threadlike bits of material in the nucleus of each cell.

Human body cells contain 46 chromosomes: 22 pairs and two "sex chromosomes" that determine the sex of an individual (*see* Figure 5.1). The body cells of females have two X chromosomes, and those of males have one X and a smaller Y chromosome. Human germ cells (sperm and egg) are different from other cells. Instead of containing the usual 46 chromosomes, they contain only 23. Thus, when sperm meets egg and their chromosomes combine, the result is one cell with the usual 46 chromosomes. Germ cells have only half the normal number of chromosomes because they go through a special type of reduction division called *meiosis* (from the Greek word for "less").

Sperm Production

Sperm are produced in the seminiferous tubules of the testes, and they go through several stages of development beginning with cells called *spermatogonia* that lie along the internal linings of the tubules. The spermatogonia divide into *spermatocytes*, which in turn undergo reduction division, so that the resulting *spermatids* have only 23 chromosomes. Because this process begins with normal male cells (having both an X and a Y chromosome), half of the spermatids will have an X and half will have a Y chromosome after meiosis. In females there are two X chromosomes in each cell. So, when meiosis occurs during the maturation of eggs, each egg ends up with one X chromosome.

It is the spermatid that eventually becomes a mature sperm. Its pear-shaped head contains the nucleus of the cell. The spermatid has a cone-shaped middlepiece and a tail that enables it to swim (*see* Figure 5.2). The head of the sperm is about 5 microns long, the middlepiece another 5 microns, and

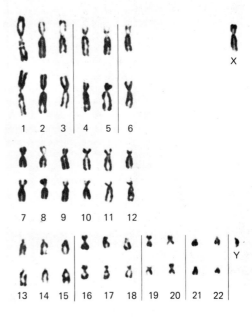

Idiogram of Human Male

Figure 5.1 The human chromosomes (autosomes 1–22, sex chromosomes X and Y) from a male cell in culture. The 46 chromosomes are from a photomicrographic print (cut single) arranged in pairs, and grouped according to sizes and relative lengths of the arms. From Tjio and Puck, *P.N.A.S.* 44 (1958), 1232.

the tail 30 to 50 microns (1 micron equals 0.000039 inch or 0.001 millimeter). Enough sperm to repopulate the world would fit into a space the size of an aspirin tablet.

As these tiny sperm cells are produced they move up the seminiferous tubules to the epididymis (*see* Figure 2.18) and are stored there until they are ejaculated. If ejaculation does not occur within 30 to 60 days, the sperm degenerate and are replaced by the new ones that are being produced continuously.

The Journey of the Sperm

Billions of sperm are ejaculated by most men during their lifetimes, but few sperm ever

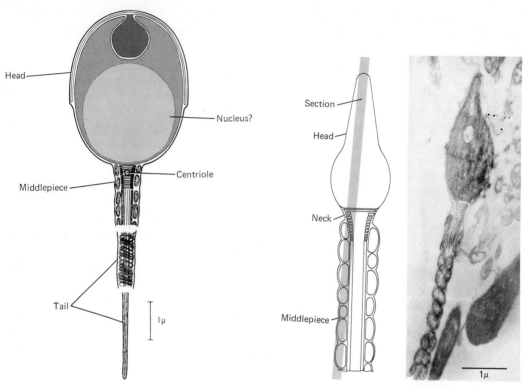

Figure 5.2   A human sperm. (*Left*) A "frontal" section (based on electronmicroscopic studies). Sperm diagram from Schultz-Larsen.
(*Right*) Electronmicrograph of a somewhat tangential "longitudinal" section through head and middlepiece. Diagram shows approximate plane of section. Head and middlepiece diagram from Lord Rothschild, *British Medical Journal*, 1 (1958), p. 301.

unite with an egg. Most sperm die. This is due to the use of contraceptives as well as to the fact that intercourse frequently occurs when the woman is not fertile. Also, sperm are ejaculated during activities such as nocturnal emissions and masturbation when there is no possibility of fertilization.

The spermatic fluid in a normal ejaculation has a volume of 2.5–5 cubic centimeters, approximately a teaspoonful. This small amount of fluid contains 150–600 million sperm, which comprise only a very small proportion of the total volume of semen. The ejaculated fluid is whitish and semigelatinous. If a male ejaculates frequently the fluid may have a more watery consistency.

If ejaculation has occurred during intercourse, the sperm will be deposited in the woman's vagina and will begin to make their way to the uterus. One of the first obstacles they face is the force of gravity. If intercourse has taken place while the woman was lying on her back, and if she has remained in that position for sometime afterward, there is a greater chance that some of the sperm will travel toward the cervix and on into the uterus. But if the woman has been in an upright position during intercourse or if she has arisen immediately afterward, the force of gravity will cause the sperm to flow away from the uterus. Even when the woman lies on her back, sperm may be lost through the vaginal opening, especially if this opening has been widened during childbirth. However, as explained in Chapter 3, the engorgement of the blood vessels around the vaginal opening during sexual arousal creates a temporary orgasmic platform that helps keep seminal fluid in the vagina.

The position and structure of the penis may also affect the journey of the sperm. Continued in-and-out thrusting of the penis after ejaculation, for instance, tends to disperse the sperm and hinder them on their journey. The semen also may fail to reach the cervix because of incomplete penetration of the vagina by the penis. This may be unavoidable in the case of extreme obesity or because of a condition known as *hypospadias,* in which the opening of the urethra is located under rather than at the tip of the glans. In such cases artificial insemination may be used to impregnate the woman. In this process the male ejaculates into a container to which a chemical preservative (glycerine) has been added. This fluid is then injected into the vagina or directly into the uterus. Sperm can also be quick-frozen in a glycerine solution and stored for later use [1]

Even if coitus occurs during a fertile period, there are still many obstacles on the sperm's journey to meet the egg. If the sperm does reach the area of the cervix and is allowed to remain there, it still has another problem to face—acidity. As mentioned in Chapter 4, the pH of cervical secretions varies, and sperm are extremely sensitive to acidity. If the secretions of the cervix and vagina

[1]Sperm may be quick-frozen in a glycerine solution and stored for years. When pregnancy is desired, it is thawed and insemination is performed as described in the text. The use of "sperm banks" as "fertility insurance" for men who have had vasectomies has become somewhat popular in recent years. Present evidence indicates there is at least a 50 percent chance of pregnancy by this method if the sperm is less than five years old. With increasing age, frozen sperm specimens show decreased motility upon thawing. (For further discussion of vasectomy, see Chapter 6).

are strongly acidic, the sperm are destroyed quickly. (This is why for contraceptive purposes a vinegar or acetic acid douche is sometimes used to wash out the vagina after intercourse; see Chapter 6). Even in a mildly acidic environment (a pH of 6.0, for instance) the movement of sperm ceases. The best pH for sperm survival and movement is between 8.5 and 9.0 (alkaline). In such an environment the natural tendency of sperm is to swim toward the cervix against the flow of the fluid coming from the cervix.

Sperm swim at a rate of 1 to 2 centimeters (about 1 inch) an hour, but once they are through the cervix and inside the uterus they may be aided in their journey by muscular contractions of the wall of the uterus. Sexual stimulation and orgasm are known to produce contractions of the uterus, a phenomenon of which pregnant women in particular are often acutely aware. Whether or not these contractions aid the sperm in their journey through the uterus is not known for sure; but it is known that sperm may arrive in the fallopian tubes much sooner than would be expected from their own unassisted rate of propulsion—within an hour to an hour and a half after intercourse, in fact.

Once through the uterus and into the fallopian tube, the sperm complete the final 2 inches or so of their journey by swimming against the current generated by small, waving, hairlike structures (cilia) that line the tube. Even if the woman has ovulated, only about half of the sperm that make it through the uterus end up in the fallopian tube that contains the egg (except on rare occasions when a woman ovulates from both ovaries at the same time).

If one considers all the obstacles that sperm face on their journey, it is not surprising that of the several hundred million sperm in the original ejaculation only about 2000 reach the tube that has the egg. And then only one actually unites with the egg.

The Egg (Ovum)

The egg (ovum) is much larger than the sperm and much larger than the other cells of the body, but it still is quite small compared to the eggs (ova) of other species—scarcely visible to the naked eye (*see* Figure 5.3). It is a spherical cell about 130 or 140 microns in diameter (about 1/175 inch), and weighs about 0.0015 milligram or approximately one-twenty-millionth of an ounce.

The discovery of the human egg has been attributed to Karl Ernst von Baer (1792–1876), generally recognized as the father of modern embryology. Von Baer studied a group of female dogs in various stages of pregnancy and succeeded in finding minute specks of matter in dogs in which the embryos had not had time to develop. He noted that these small objects in the fallopian tubes were smaller than the follicles of the ovaries, which had previously been thought to be the eggs themselves. Von Baer then

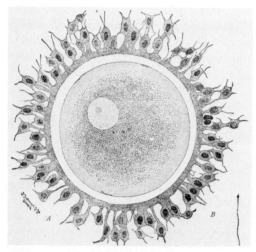

Figure 5.3   A picture of the human egg, close to maturity. The zona pellucida is the clear circle. The corona radiata is still present in this figure. It is the outer layer of cells. A human sperm is in the lower right-hand corner, showing the relative size of the two cells. From Arey, *Developmental Anatomy*, 7th ed. (Philadelphia: W. B. Saunders Company, 1974.) By permission.

verified that the follicles contained minute bodies identical with those he had previously observed in the fallopian tubes, which had been assumed to represent the actual germ material essential for reproduction. Later studies of humans confirmed these findings.

We noted in Chapter 2 that at birth the ovaries contain about 400,000 primitive egg cells (*primary oocytes*), and it is generally believed that no new egg cells are produced by the human female after birth, in significant contrast to the continuous production of sperm in the male throughout his life. Although only about 400 eggs are essential to provide one a month during a woman's reproductive life, exposure to radiation or drugs may alter all the germ cells at once and do permanent damage.

Possibly related to the "aging" of eggs is the increased incidence of certain defects, particularly Down's syndrome (mongolism), in children born to older women. A woman in her forties is a hundred times more likely to have a Down's child than is a woman of 20. This finding has been clearly correlated with the mother's age, although it is not known what causes chromosome defects as women grow older. For these and other reasons, the age at which it is best for a woman to have a child, biologically speaking, is usually said to be between 20 and 35 years.

Egg Maturation

An egg matures while still in the ovary, encased in a larger spherical structure known as a *graafian follicle*. The egg divides while still within the follicle, producing a large *secondary oocyte* and a minute *first polar body*, each containing 46 chromosomes. The final step in maturation of the egg occurs after ovulation, within the fallopian tube when division of the genetic material in the cell occurs, resulting in an egg containing 23 chromosomes and a second polar body containing 23 chromosomes. The latter is extruded and disintegrates. Thus the egg contains half of the chromosomes that might be a part of a new being.

The mature egg is a spherical cell containing, in addition to the genetic material (chromosomes), fat droplets, protein substances, and nutrient fluid (*see* Figure 5.3). It is surrounded by a gelatinous capsule (*zona pellucida*), the final obstacle to the sperm cell seeking to fertilize the egg. (A layer of small cells, the *corona radiata*, that surrounds the egg within the follicle has usually disappeared by this time.)

Ovulation and Migration of the Egg

The hormonal mechanism that stimulates ovulation has been described in Chapter 4. At the time of ovulation the graafian follicle has reached 10 to 15 millimeters in diameter and protrudes from the surface of the ovary. It is filled with fluid, and its wall has become very thin. The egg has become detached within the follicle and is floating loose in the fluid. At ovulation the thinnest part of the follicle wall finally bursts, and the egg is carried out with the fluid. Although the fluid does build up a certain amount of pressure within the follicle, the process of ovulation is less like the explosion of an air-filled balloon and more like leakage from a punctured sack of water.

Occasionally a follicle fails to mature and rupture; the result is a *follicle (retention) cyst,* one of the most common forms of *ovarian cysts* (a fluid-filled sac in the ovary). Such cysts may vary from microscopic size to 1 to 2 inches in diameter. It is possible for several cysts to be present simultaneously in one or both ovaries. If large they may produce pain in the pelvis and cause painful intercourse, and the ovary may be tender to external pressure. Cysts of this kind rarely present serious problems and usually disappear spontaneously within 60 days.

The exact mechanism by which the egg finds its way into the fallopian tube is still a mystery. Although the fringed end of the tube is near the ovary, there is no direct connection that would ensure that the egg did not simply fall into the abdominal cavity (*see* Figure 2.8). Indeed, it sometimes does, but even more fascinating, it has clearly been established that an egg from an ovary on one side of the body can somehow reach the tube on the other side. There is a well-documented instance of a woman who had her right tube and left ovary removed surgically yet succeeded in having two normal pregnancies afterward.

In any event, once the egg has entered the fallopian tube it begins a leisurely journey to the uterus, taking about three days to move 3 to 5 inches. The egg, in contrast to the sperm, has no means of self-propulsion but is carried along by the current of the small cilia lining the tube. There are also periodic contractions of the muscles in the walls of the fallopian tubes, which are believed by some investigators to aid in transporting the eggs, although this belief has not been definitely confirmed.

If the egg is not fertilized during its journey through the fallopian tube, it disintegrates.

Fertilization

The moment when sperm and egg unite is the moment of conception, and, though it is commonly believed that conception occurs within the uterus, it actually takes place about halfway down the fallopian tube. If intercourse has taken place within about 72 hours or less before ovulation, viable sperm may be present in the tube, swimming about in apparently random fashion when the egg arrives on the scene. Conception must occur within about 48 hours after ovulation or the egg will be incapable of being fertilized. Assuming that the time of ovulation is known and the woman has intercourse within three days before or two days after this time, she may become pregnant.

Although many sperm surround the egg

Box 5.2   The Preformationist View

A medieval medical manuscript illustrates the preformationist's beliefs about the fetus's position in the uterus. The preformationists held that the fetus was perfectly preformed from the moment of conception. The only changes that they presumed to occur during pregnancy were growth and shifts in position. The pictures represent the fetus in the uterus as a fully formed human being with adult proportions. (Artists of the period typically drew children as if they were small-scale adults, too.)

at the time of fertilization only one sperm actually penetrates it. This sperm adds its 23 chromosomes to the 23 in the egg, providing the necessary complement of 46 for one fertilized human cell. It is believed that the additional sperm assist conception by secreting a particular enzyme (*hyaluronidase*) that aids in eliminating excess cellular material that may still cling to the outside of the egg.

The mechanism by which a sperm actually penetrates the capsule of the egg is unknown, but apparently it bores through this capsule somehow. In some animals sperm have been observed to enter the eggs and to continue to move well into the interior with the aid of their tails. In other animals only the heads and middlepieces enter the eggs.

By means of another unknown mechanism the wall of the egg becomes impervious to sperm once the first one has successfully penetrated. Whether or not this

sperm represents the "best" of the available specimens is a matter of conjecture; in any event the particular genes that it carries will determine the sex and many other characteristics of the child. If it carries an X chromosome the child will be a girl. If it carries a Y chromosome the child will be a boy.

Attempts to predetermine the sex of offspring are as old as recorded history. Aristotle recommended having intercourse in a north wind if boys were desired, intercourse in a south wind for girls. A more recent formula includes engaging in intercourse two to three days before ovulation and then abstaining if a girl is desired. To conceive a boy the couple must limit intercourse to the time of ovulation. The timing is combined with an acid douche, shallow penetration, and no orgasm for the woman to conceive a girl, or with an alkaline douche, deep penetration, and orgasm for the woman to conceive a boy. While one study found this method to be fairly successful, another study reported conflicting results: Engaging in intercourse several days before ovulation and then abstaining resulted in a higher incidence of boys (not girls); when coitus occurred close to the time of ovulation there was a higher incidence of girls (not boys). These conflicting results reveal problems in the current methods of sex selection.[2] Although there have been numerous attempts to separate X-containing from Y-containing sperm by centrifugation, sedimentation, filtration and other laboratory procedures, none has been notably successful.

A study of 5981 married women in the United States indicates that if sex selection were practiced by this sample, the long-term effect on the ratio of male to female births (currently 105 male to 100 female) would be negligible. However, there was a strong preference for the first child to be male, so that the short-term affect would be a preponderance of male births, followed several years later by a preponderance of female births. When asked their opinions about the actual practice of sex preselection, 47 percent of the women in the sample were opposed, 39 percent were in favor, and 14 percent were neutral.[3]

Amniocentesis

The most accurate method for finding out the sex of an unborn child is amniocentesis, but this procedure usually is not performed until the fourteenth or sixteenth week after the last menstrual period.[4] Although amniocentesis can be used to find out the sex of a fetus, it is most often used to test the chromosomal or biochemical makeup of the fetus when some abnormality is suspected.

[2]For a further discussion of these methods see Shettles (1972) and Guerrero (1975).
[3]Westoff and Rindfuss (1974).
[4]Researchers are developing several promising techniques for determining the sex of the fetus before 12 weeks of pregnancy.

The procedure of amniocentesis is simple. First, sound waves are used to make a picture (an ultrasonic scan) of the fetus in the womb. Once the position of the fetus is known, it is possible to insert a hollow needle through the abdominal wall into the pregnant uterus without harming the fetus (*see* Figure 5.4). Some of the amniotic fluid that surrounds the fetus (and contains cells of the fetus) is then removed and analyzed. The condition and number of the chromosomes as well as the presence of either an X or Y chromosome can be determined with a high degree of accuracy.

Amniocentesis is a relatively safe procedure for both mother and fetus. In a study sponsored by the National Institutes of Health of more than 1000 amniocenteses there were no major complications. Only three sex determinations and six diagnoses of chromosomal abnormalities were incorrect. About 5 percent of all infants born live have some sort of serious birth defect or will develop mental

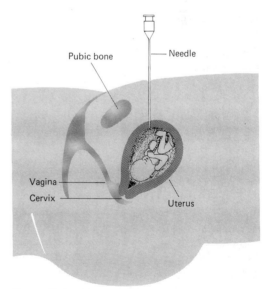

Figure 5.4   Amniocentesis involves removing a few milliliters of amniotic fluid to test for cellular abnormalities. Redrawn from *Resident & Staff Physician* (1977). By permission.

retardation. Among the serious abnormalities that can be detected by amniocentesis are Down's syndrome (mongolism), neural tube closure defects (open spine), Tay-Sachs disease, cystic fibrosis, and Rh incompatibility. When abnormalities are diagnosed, women can legally choose to have an abortion—although by the time the chromosome analysis is complete (the twentieth week to twenty-fourth week of pregnancy) abortion is no longer a simple, risk-free operation (*see* Chapter 6).

Because a woman in her forties is 100 times more likely than a woman in her twenties to have eggs with abnormal chromosomes, amniocentesis is currently recommended for all women who become pregnant after the age of 35 and for women who have previously had a child with a chromosome abnormality or with some other problem that can be detected by analysis of fetal cells. It is also recommended for couples with family histories of certain heritable problems. "Genetic counseling" is an important medical obligation, but it can also be distorted into a political and racist weapon.[5]

Infertility

Even in overpopulated societies failure to conceive is often a problem of great concern to individuals involved. Between 10 and 15 percent of all marriages in the United States are involuntarily childless. Although it is common in many societies to attribute sterility to females, about 40 percent of infertile marriages result from sterility in the male partners. Therefore it is important that, whenever a couple wishes to have children and is unsuccessful for about a year, both the husband and wife should see a physician, for either or both may have disorders that can be treated.

[5]For instance, sickle-cell anemia is an incurable, and often fatal, hereditary disease of the blood that occurs almost exclusively in black people. The racial implications of counseling people with this disease not to have children is obvious, as is the medical dilemma of knowingly perpetuating the illness.

Conditions that interfere with a man's ability to ejaculate into the depths of the vagina are one cause of infertility and have been described earlier in this chapter. More commonly, the problem is a low sperm count, which can result from many factors. An ejaculation that contains fewer than 35 million sperm per cubic centimeter (a total count of fewer than 100–150 million sperm in the seminal fluid) will almost never result in fertilization of the egg. Frequent ejaculation (one or more times a day for several consecutive days) will lower the sperm count; this deficiency, obviously, is easily remedied. Usually, however, the problem is more serious. Infectious diseases that involve the testes may cause sterility. The most common such disease is mumps (if it occurs after puberty). Infections of the prostate gland may also affect fertility. Direct damage to the testes through trauma or radiation may result in decreased sperm production or mechanical obstruction to the movement of the sperm.

Cryptorchism (failure of the testes to descend into the scrotum from the abdomen during development) affects about 2 percent of postpubertal boys bilaterally and results in sterility because sperm do not mature at the higher temperature to which they are exposed within the abdomen. This condition can sometimes be remedied either medically or surgically before puberty. If one testicle is present in the scrotum, fertility is usually not impaired.

Certain hormone disorders, particularly hypothyroidism and diabetes, may be associated with low sperm counts. Men with such disorders can often be successfully treated with supplemental hormones.

Another approach to infertility in men with low sperm counts is known as AIH (artificial insemination with husband's semen). This is achieved by collecting and storing a series of ejaculates (as described earlier) and inseminating the wife when sufficient sperm have accumulated. If the husband produces no sperm at all, artificial insemination with donor sperm (AID) is sometimes performed, a procedure which has led to unresolved moral and legal questions. For instance, does AID constitute adultery? In the event of divorce must a man support a child unrelated to him biologically?

The most common cause of infertility in women is failure to ovulate. This may be related to hormonal deficiencies or to other factors, such as vitamin deficiency, anemia, malnutrition, or psychological stress. If a woman does not ovulate, there are several possible solutions. One is the drug *clomiphene,* which stimulates ovulation by causing the release of gonadotrophins from the pituitary. Clomiphene has also been used successfully, on an experimental basis, to treat men with low sperm counts. If a woman does not respond to clomiphene, it is sometimes possible to stimulate ovulation by hormone injections (FSH).

Overstimulation of the reproductive system with hormones or drugs, however, can result in undesirable side effects. Complications include blood clotting and accumulation of fluid in the abdomen. Another problem is multiple births. These occur because it is not always possible to calculate the exact dosage necessary to stimulate one (and only one) follicle. One study of women treated with clomiphene found that 10 percent of them had twins or other multiple births. There also have been cases in which women treated with hormones had pregnancies with as many as 15 fetuses. In such cases the risks of fetal death, miscarriage, and birth complications are extremely high.[6] In at least one case, however, a woman has given birth to sextuplets. The six infants were born live, and the mother did well.

Infections of the vagina, cervix, uterus, tubes, or ovaries may cause infertility by inhibiting or preventing passage of sperm or

[6] Austin and Short (1972), vol. 5, chapter 4.

eggs to the site of fertilization. Treatment involves identification of the particular microorganism causing the infection and administration of the appropriate antibiotic.

There are also various congenital malformations of the female reproductive tract, as well as tumors (particularly cervical or uterine), that may prevent fertilization. Many of these conditions can be corrected surgically (some conditions are described in more detail in Chapter 7). A woman may inadvertently be preventing conception by using certain commercial douches or vaginal deodorants containing chemicals that destroy or inhibit the motility of sperm.

A physician consulted by a couple having infertility problems will take complete medical histories, and each partner will undergo a physical examination with particular emphasis on the reproductive organs. Laboratory tests to rule out infections, anemia, and hormone deficiencies will be performed. The husband will be instructed to bring in a complete ejaculation for sperm analysis. The wife will be instructed to keep a morning temperature chart during her next several menstrual cycles. The purpose of this chart is to determine if and when she is ovulating, as indicated by a rise in basal body temperature (BBT) approximately in midcycle (the use of such charts to avoid conception in the practice of the "rhythm method" is described in Chapter 6).

If these tests indicate that the male is producing adequate numbers of apparently normal and motile sperm and that the female is ovulating, then further tests to determine why conception is not occurring will be indicated. The most common site of obstruction of the egg in its journey from the ovary is the fallopian tube, and the so-called "Rubin's test" is performed to determine whether the tubes are obstructed. The test involves forcing carbon dioxide under pressure into the uterus through the cervix. If the tubes are open, there will be a drop in pressure as the gas passes through them. If there is an obstruction, the pressure will increase.

The most common site of obstruction of the sperm in their journey is the cervix; an analysis of the cervical mucus may also be in order so as to rule out an abnormality at this point. Once a correctable problem has been identified, treatment may begin. If no abnormalities can be found, couples are sometimes advised to adopt children. A previously infertile couple may sometimes succeed in having children of their own after having adopted a child. However, the incidence of pregnancy following adoption is no higher in couples who never adopt, contrary to a widely held view that adoption may "cure" infertility.

"Test-Tube Babies"

Although there certainly are couples who cannot have children, research into fertility has found solutions to many fertility problems. A method has been developed that enables women who could not become pregnant because of blocked fallopian tubes to conceive. In simplified terms, the egg is removed from the ovaries just prior to ovulation, when the mature follicle is a visible swelling on the ovary. Once removed the egg is mixed with sperm from the husband. After it has been fertilized and has divided into 8 or 16 cells, the conceptus is introduced through the cervix into the uterus. If all goes well, implantation in the endometrium occurs and pregnancy continues normally. There are numerous technical problems, and the failure rate for the procedure is high. In 1978 the first so-called "test-tube baby" was born. This was the first birth to result from a fertilization performed outside the body.

This technique raises many ethical and legal questions. If one accepts the proposition that life begins with conception, then the many experiments that have involved study of fertilized human eggs in the laboratory, in such a way that their ultimate destruction was

necessitated, constituted murderous acts; indeed, the scientists involved in this and related research have been accused of just that.

Another possible application of current knowledge in this area would be the implantation of the fertilized egg into the uterus of a surrogate or host mother who would undergo the pregnancy (presumably for a fee) and surrender it to the biological mother at birth. But what if the biological parents have changed their minds, divorced, or simply refuse to accept the child? One law professor has raised these and many other thorny issues that could arise, including such questions as:

What if the host mother refuses to relinquish the child or has intercourse with her husband following implantation . . . and gives birth to twins? Can she be forced to relinquish the child? Both children? If the host mother has an abortion because early months of nausea cause her to change her mind about carrying the fetus to term, would this amount to breach of contract? . . . If she contracted German measles during the first three months of pregnancy so that the child was born deformed, is she responsible for the care of the child or are the couple who contracted with her to produce it responsible?[7]

Pregnancy

Pregnancy today is an experience which many women look forward to and enjoy. A woman should consult a doctor early in pregnancy (preferably by the second missed period) in order to receive proper care, which can help her have a pregnancy free of complications and deliver a healthy baby. Childbirth has not always been as safe as it is today (*see* Box 5.4 near the end of the chapter).

The average length of human pregnancy is 266 days, or approximately nine cal-

[7]Schroeder (1974), pp. 542–543. For further discussion of these issues, see also Austin and Short (1972), chapters 4 and 5.

endar months.[8] It is traditional obstetrical practice to divide pregnancy into three-month periods called *trimesters*. We shall discuss each trimester from the perspectives of the expectant mother's experiences and developments within the uterus. The details of each stage in fetal development are available in textbooks on embryology. Our aim is to enable the reader to visualize more clearly the fascinating steps that intervene between conception and birth, without becoming bogged down in details and complex terminology.

The First Trimester

First Signs of Pregnancy

Many readers of this book will vividly recall a time when they themselves or acquaintances failed to menstruate as expected. The experience may have been particularly joyful if it signaled the news that mutual desire between a man and woman for a child was to be fulfilled. On the other hand, it may have been an experience of fear and guilt, the unintended consequence of sexual intercourse. Or the news may have been met with mixed feelings, as when a young couple wanted to have children "but not yet." But the knowledge that a woman has missed her period is rarely met with indifference by those concerned.

A woman may miss her period for many reasons other than pregnancy, however, as we have pointed out in Chapter 4. Various

[8]There is great variation from this mean in both directions. Premature births are well known. Extended pregnancies also occur; the length of pregnancy assumes legal importance in establishing the legitimacy of a child when the husband has been away for more than ten months. In the United States the longest pregnancy upheld by the courts as legitimate was 355 days. In England in *Preston-Jones* v. *Preston-Jones*, conducted in the House of Lords in 1949, the husband claimed adultery on the grounds that the interval of sexual abstinence between himself and his wife before birth of the child in question would have meant a pregnancy of 360 days. Although he was initially overruled, he finally won his case in the Court of Appeals.

illnesses and emotional upsets may result in failure to menstruate. In addition, women under 20 and over 40 may skip periods occasionally for no apparent reason. A woman who has recently delivered a child, particularly one who is still nursing, may not menstruate for five or six months or more. She cannot rely on the absence of menstruation as an indication of pregnancy and may indeed become pregnant without having had a menstrual period since her previous pregnancy. She need only have ovulated.

Conversely, a woman may continue to have cyclic bleeding, though in smaller quantities and for shorter durations than usual, during pregnancy. Such bleeding, often called "spotting," occurs in about 20 percent of pregnant women and is not necessarily ominous. It is particularly common among women who have had children before. But "spotting" may also be an early sign of miscarriage. Sometimes such "spotting" has led women who were in the early months of pregnancy to believe falsely that they were not pregnant.

Another early symptom of pregnancy is enlargement and tenderness of the breasts. The physiological mechanisms that lead to enlargement of the breasts have been described in Chapter 4. When hormonal stimulation of the mammary glands begins after conception, a woman will initially become aware of sensations of fullness and sometimes of tingling in her breasts. The nipples in particular become quite sensitive to tactile stimulation early in pregnancy.

Many women experience so-called "morning sickness" during the first six to eight weeks of pregnancy. Usually it consists of queasy sensations upon awakening, accompanied by an aversion to food or even to the odors of certain foods. This nausea may be accompanied by vomiting and great reluctance to be near food. Some women experience "morning sickness" in the evening, but about 25 percent of pregnant women never experience any vomiting at all. On the other hand, about one in 200 pregnant women in the United States experiences vomiting so severe that she must be hospitalized. This condition is known as *hyperemesis gravidarum* and may have serious consequences (including malnutrition) if it is not properly treated. Occasionally therapeutic abortion may be required in order to save the life of the mother, but this necessity is quite rare.

A phenomenon known as "sympathetic pregnancy" is sometimes observed in the husband of a pregnant woman. He too becomes nauseated and vomits along with his wife. The etiology of this condition is implied in its name.

More frequent urination is another symptom of early pregnancy and is related to increased pressure on the bladder from the swelling uterus. This symptom tends to disappear as the uterus enlarges and rises up into the abdomen, but frequent urination again becomes a common complaint toward the end of pregnancy when the fetal head descends into the pelvis and exerts pressure on the bladder.

Fatigue and a need for more sleep are often most striking early in pregnancy and may be quite puzzling to a woman who is usually very energetic. The sensation of drowsiness early in pregnancy may be so overwhelming as to make sleep irresistible, even in the midst of conversation.

Early Diagnosis of Pregnancy

A sexually active woman who has missed her menstrual period, is having "morning sickness," and has noticed breast enlargement and tenderness, increased frequency of urination, and extreme fatigue has reason to suppose that she is pregnant. If she is particularly anxious to verify this suspicion, she may see a physician for a "pregnancy test." Actually there are many ways in which a physician can determine whether or not a woman is pregnant, none of which is 100 percent accurate early in pregnancy.

The sixth week of pregnancy (that is, about four weeks after missing a period) is the earliest point at which a physician can by physical examination, determine with any reliability that a woman is pregnant. By this time certain changes in the cervix and uterus are apparent upon pelvic examination. Of particular usefulness to the physician is *Hegar's sign,* which refers to the soft consistency of a compressible area between the cervix and body of the uterus and becomes apparent in the sixth week of pregnancy. To an experienced clinician it is a fairly reliable indication. The examination is performed by placing one hand on the abdomen and two fingers of the other hand in the vagina.

Various laboratory tests can also be performed to detect pregnancy in its early stages. If performed correctly these tests are 95 to 98 percent accurate. The most often used such tests are based on the presence of HCG (a hormone produced only by pregnant women). These tests are relatively simple and inexpensive. The woman's blood or urine sample is put into a test tube or in a small dish with specific chemicals. If HCG is present, it can be detected within minutes, even in very small amounts. The test for HCG using the woman's urine is the most common test for determining pregnancy. It can also detect HCG as early as two weeks after conception. The blood test for HCG is used less frequently in part because it is a more expensive test. The advantage of the blood test is that it can detect HCG within six to eight days after fertilization.

A relatively inexpensive version of the HCG test is also available for home use. If used correctly, it can detect HCG in the urine of a pregnant woman as early as nine days after a missed period. Recent studies found that only 3 percent of home tests indicated pregnancy when the women were not pregnant. But, in 20 percent of tests giving negative results, the women were actually pregnant even though the tests indicated that they were not. When the women with negative results performed a second test eight days later, the accuracy of the test increased to 91 percent.[9] Thus, home tests giving positive or negative results should be confirmed by a doctor.

Once pregnancy has been reasonably established, the first question that the woman asks is usually, "When is the baby due?" The expected delivery date (EDC, or expected date of confinement) can be calculated by the following formula: Add one week to the first day of the last menstrual period, subtract three months, then add one year. For instance, if the last menstrual period began on January 8, 1980, adding one week (to January 15), subtracting three months (to October 15), and adding one year gives an expected delivery date of October 15, 1980. In fact, only about 4 percent of births occur on the dates predicted by this formula. But 60 percent occur within five days of dates predicted in this manner.

False Pregnancy (Pseudocyesis)

Occasionally a woman may become convinced that she is pregnant despite evidence to the contrary. About 0.1 percent of all women who consult obstetricians fall into this category. Usually they are young women who intensely desire children, but some are women near menopause. A certain percentage of these women are unmarried; in fact, the phenomenon was not unknown among nuns in medieval convents, who took their marriage vows with Christ literally and believed that they had been impregnated by Christ.

Women suffering false pregnancy often experience the symptoms of pregnancy, including morning sickness, breast tenderness, a sense of fullness in the pelvis, and the sensation of fetal movements in the abdomen.

[9]McQuarrie and Flanagan (1978).

They often cease to menstruate, and physicians may observe contractions of the abdominal muscles that resemble fetal movements. Even though pregnancy tests are negative, a woman suffering from a severe mental illness like schizophrenia may persist in her delusion for years.

Ectopic Pregnancy

An ectopic pregnancy occurs when a fertilized egg implants outside of the uterus. About 1 in 250 pregnancies is ectopic. Often such pregnancies spontaneously abort. The most common site of ectopic pregnancy is the fallopian tubes. If an embryo that implants in the tube continues to develop, the tube may rupture, causing hemorrhaging and in some cases death to the mother. Signs of an ectopic tubal pregnancy are lack of menstruation, abdominal pain, and nonmenstrual bleeding.

Rare sites for ectopic pregnancies include such locations as the ovary or intestines. In very rare cases the pregnancies result in the birth of a child (via surgical methods). In 1979 a New Zealand woman who previously had had her uterus removed gave birth during surgery to a baby girl after eight months of pregnancy. The fertilized egg had become attached to her bowel, where it continued to develop.

Sexual Activity during the First Trimester

There is no reason why early pregnancy or the suspicion of pregnancy should inhibit a healthy woman's sexual activities. Although occasional morning sickness may cause lack of interest during the early part of the day, and fatigue may be a deterrent in the evening, most couples are able to find mutually satisfactory occasions for continued sexual relations. Decreased sexual interest was reported by about one-fourth of women in a recent study, but the frequency of sexual activity did not change significantly when compared to frequency prior to conception (*see*

Table 5.1   Percent of Women Having Various Frequencies of Coitus at Different Stages of Pregnancy

Number of acts of coitus per week	Baseline (1 year before conception)	1st trimester	2nd trimester	7th month	8th month	9th month
None	0%	2%	2%	11%	23%	59%
1	7%	11%	16%	23%	29%	19%
2–5	81%	78%	77%	63%	46%	23%
6 or more	12%	9%	5%	2%	2%	1%

Table 5.1).[10] Factors influencing sexual interest in the first trimester include nausea, fatigue, and probably general anxiety in some women who are pregnant for the first time or who had complications with a previous pregnancy. Also, physiological changes during this period can make sexual stimulation somewhat painful. In particular, the vasocongestion of the breasts that occurs during sexual excitement may be painful to a woman who is already experiencing tenderness there.

There is no evidence to support the notion that intercourse during the early months of pregnancy can cause abortion of the fetus. Nevertheless, concern about injuring the fetus during intercourse is often reported by women during the first trimester, particularly if they are pregnant for the first time or have had previous miscarriages as has been said. It is interesting that some preliterate societies believe continued intercourse after conception essential to the continuation of pregnancy; they believe that the sperm serve to nourish the developing fetus.

Intrauterine Events of the First Trimester

After the human egg has been fertilized, it begins to divide into multiple cells as it moves down the fallopian tube (see Figure 5.5). The original egg becomes two cells, these two become four, the four become eight, and so on. There is no significant change in volume during these first few days,

[10]Wagner and Solbert (1974).

but the initial egg has become a round mass subdivided into many small cells. This round mass of cells is called a *morula* (from the Latin *morum*, ''mulberry''), and the cells of the morula arrange themselves around the outside of the sphere during the third to fifth days after ovulation, leaving a fluid-filled cavity in the center. This structure, called a *blastocyst*, floats about in the uterine cavity, and sometime between the fifth and seventh days after ovulation attaches itself to the uterine lining and begins to burrow in, aided by enzymes that digest the outer surface of the lining, permitting the developing egg to reach the blood vessels and nutrients below (see Figure 5.6). By the tenth to twelfth day after ovulation the blastocyst is firmly implanted in the uterine wall, yet the woman still cannot know that she is pregnant, for her menstrual period is not due for several more days.

The blastocyst, which has embedded itself in the lining of the uterus, will develop from a tiny ball of cells into an easily recognizable human fetus during the first trimester. In the early stages of development a disk-shaped layer of cells forms across the center of the blastocyst and from this *embryonic disk* the fetus grows. The remaining cells develop into the *placenta*, the *membranes* that will contain the fetus and the *amniotic fluid*, and the *yolk sac* (which in humans is insignificant in function).

Development of the Placenta

The placenta is the organ that exchanges nutrients and waste products with

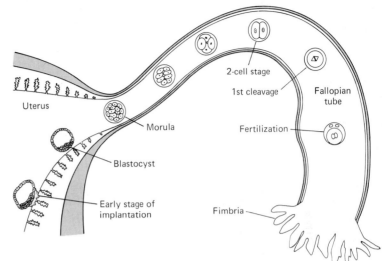

Figure 5.5 Fertilization to implantation of the human embryo. From Tuchmann-Duplessis and Haegel, *Illustrated Human Embryology.* vol. I (New York: Springer-Verlag; London: Chapman and Hall; Paris: Masson et Cie, 1971). Reprinted by permission.

the mother. It is constructed from both fetal and maternal tissue and during the first trimester develops into a bluish-red, round, flat organ about 7 inches (18 centimeters) in diameter and 1 inch (2.5 centimeters) thick. It weighs about 1 pound (0.45 kilogram) and constitutes, along with the fetal membranes, the "afterbirth." The blood vessels of the placenta are connected to the circulatory system of the mother through the blood vessels in the wall of the uterus. The circulatory system of the fetus is connected to that of the placenta by the blood vessels of the *umbilical cord*, which is attached to the placenta. Ox-

ygen and essential nutrients reach the fetus through the umbilical vein, and waste products from the fetus reach the maternal system through the two umbilical arteries.

The placenta also functions as an endocrine gland, producing hormones essential to the maintenance of pregnancy. The hormone human chorionic gonadotrophin (HCG) stimulates continued production of progesterone by the corpus luteum during the first trimester.[11] Gradually, however, the placenta

---

[11]Claims that administering additional doses of HCG by injection during pregnancy will raise a baby's IQ have no basis in fact.

Figure 5.6 Low- and high-power photographs of the surface of an early human implantation obtained on the twenty-second day of cycle, less than eight days after conception; the site was slightly elevated and measured 0.36 × 0.31 mm. (*Left*) the actual size of the embryo indicated by the white square at the lower right; the mouths of uterine glands appear as dark spots surrounded by halos. From Eastman and Hellman, *Williams Obstetrics,* 13th ed. (New York: Appleton-Century-Crofts. 1966), p. 123. Reprinted by permission.

Box 5.3   Cojoined Twins

Congenital malformations have always fascinated the human mind. In early days, malformed babies were called monsters. In a book written in 1560, Ambroise Paré wrote, "We called Monsters, what things soever are brought forth contrary to the common decree and order of nature."[1] Cojoined twins were well known at the time, even though this malformation is quite rare (approximately 1 in 50,000 births). According to Paré, the most likely cause of cojoined twins was thought to be "An abundance of Seed and overflowing of matter."

In a book titled *Cosmology*, published in 1552, Sebastian Munster described having seen two girls in Mainz who were joined at the forehead. He presented the following explanation. When the mother was pregnant with the two daughters, she had been gossiping with

Cojoined twins similar to those described by Munster. An unsigned woodcut from 1510 in the collection of the Yale Medical Historical Library.

[1]Guttmacher and Nichols (1967).

itself begins to produce large amounts of progesterone and estrogens. It also produces other hormones, like cortisol and androgens, in small amounts. There is evidence that placental production of progesterone and estrogens falls off just before delivery and that this drop plays a role in initiating labor.

Development of the Fetus

The first trimester is a period during which the rather simple structure of the embryo is transformed into the very complex organism called the *fetus*, though with relatively little change in size. The embryo becomes a fetus after the eighth week of pregnancy. (The ovum becomes an embryo one week after fertilization.)

The embryonic disk described earlier becomes somewhat elongated and ovoid by the end of the second week after fertilization. The embryo is about 1/16 inch (1.5 milli-meters) long at this point. The actual sizes of the embryo at various stages in the first seven weeks are depicted in Figure 5.7.

During the third week growth is particularly noticeable at the two ends of the embryo. Differentiation of the *cephalic* (head) end is particularly notable in comparison to that of the rest of the body. By the end of the third week or the early part of the fourth week the beginnings of eyes and ears are visible. In addition, the brain and other portions of the central nervous system are beginning to form. By the end of the fourth week two bulges are apparent on the concave (front) side of the trunk. The upper one represents the developing heart and is called the *cardiac prominence;* the lower one, the *hepatic prominence,* is caused by the protrusion of the developing liver (*see* Figure 5.8). At this point the embryo is only about four millimeters long and weighs about 1/7 of an ounce

Box 5.3 continued

another woman and unexpectedly their two heads struck together. The pregnant woman became ill with fright and the fruit within her womb suffered the consequences.

Today it is recognized that cojoined twins represent an aberration in the process that leads to the development of identical twins.[2] Cojoined twins result from a partial but incomplete splitting of a single embryo into two separate twins. The area at which they are joined can lie at any point along their bodies: the abdomen, chest, back, or top of the head.

Some of the most well known of cojoined twins in modern times are the Siamese twins, Chang and Eng, who were born in 1811 in Siam (now Thailand) of Chinese parents. They were joined by a small band of skin and were not greatly impaired in movement. They were displayed in P. T. Barnum's circus for many years.

Surgical procedures can be successful in separating cojoined twins if the twins do not share vital organs.

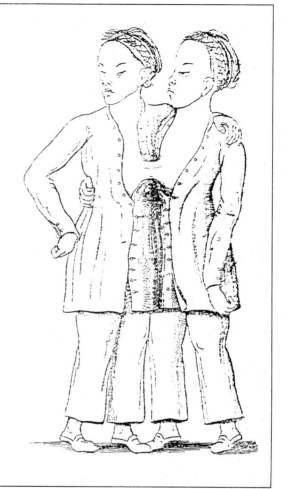

Chang and Eng Bunker. From an early description by J. C. Warren in 1929. (An account of the Siamese twin brothers united together from birth. *American Journal of Medical Science,* 1829).

[2]Zimmermann (1967).

(0.4 gram). A prominent "tail" is present in the young embryo, but it is almost gone by the eighth week.[12]

Between the fourth and eighth weeks the facial features—eyes, ears, nose, and mouth—become clearly recognizable (*see*

[12]In rare instances the tail fails to regress, and there are documented cases of human infants born with tails. The tails are usually removed surgically at an early age but in one case reported in the medical literature a 12-year-old boy had a tail 9 inches long.

Figure 5.9). Fingers and toes begin to appear between the sixth and eighth weeks (*see* Figure 5.10). Bones are beginning to ossify, and the intestines are forming. By the seventh week the gonads are present, but cannot yet be clearly distinguished as male or female. Similarly, the external genitals cannot be identified as male or female until about the third month (*see* Chapter 2).

Between the eighth and twelfth weeks the fetus increases in length from about 1.5

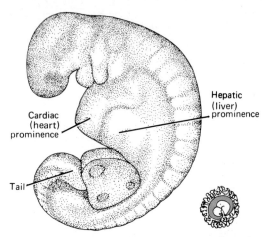

Figure 5.8 A human embryo about four weeks after fertilization (crown-rump length 3.9 mm). Retouched photograph (×20) of embryo 5923 in the Carnegie Collection. Sketch, lower right, shows actual size of embryo. As modified by Patten for *Human Embryology*, 3rd ed., p. 70, McGraw-Hill Book Company. With permission.

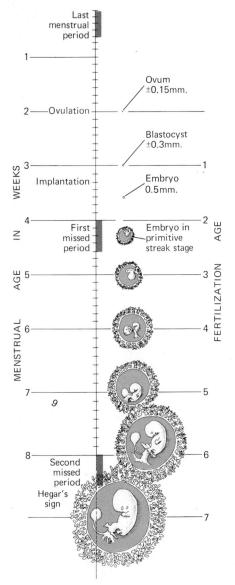

Figure 5.7 Actual sizes of embryos and their membranes in relation to a time scale based on the mother's menstrual history. From Patten, *Human Embryology*, 3rd ed., p. 145. Copyright © 1968 by McGraw-Hill, Inc. Used with permission of McGraw-Hill Book Company.

inches to about 4 inches, and in weight from about 1/15 ounce (2 grams) to approximately 2/3 ounce (about 19 grams). The skin takes

on a pinkish color and the internal genitals become recognizable as male or female. Although still very small, the fetus at 12 weeks is unmistakably human, and from this point on development consists primarily of enlargement and further differentiation of structures that are already present.

Complications during the First Trimester

Miscarriage, or *spontaneous abortion*, occurs most often during the first trimester of pregnancy. Between 10 and 15 percent of all pregnancies end in spontaneous abortion; that is, the pregnancies terminate in miscarriages before the fetuses have any chance of survival on their own. About 75 percent of spontaneous abortions occur before the sixteenth week of pregnancy, and the great majority occur before the eighth week. The first sign that a woman may miscarry is vaginal bleeding, or "spotting," which was also mentioned earlier. If the symptoms of pregnancy

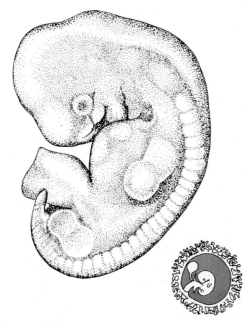

Figure 5.9 A human embryo a little more than six weeks after fertilization (crown-rump length 14 mm). Retouched photograph (×8) of embryo 1267A in the Carnegie Collection. From *Human Embryology.* 3rd ed., p. 74, Copyright © 1968 by McGraw-Hill, Inc. Used with permission of McGraw-Hill Book Company.

disappear and the woman develops cramps in the pelvic region, the fetus is usually expelled. About 50 percent of such miscarried fetuses are clearly defective in some way. About 15 percent of miscarriages are caused by illness, malnutrition, trauma, or other factors affecting the mother. In the remaining 85 percent the reasons are not apparent. A woman who has had one spontaneous abortion usually can conceive again and have a normal pregnancy.

Effects of Drugs and Diseases

It is very important to realize that substances other than nutrients may reach the developing fetus through the placental circulatory system. Various drugs taken by the mother may have harmful effects on the developing fetus, particularly during the first trimester. Therefore, a woman should avoid taking any drugs (including aspirin and vitamins) during pregnancy without first consulting her doctor.

In recent years the effects of the sedative thalidomide have been widely publicized. This drug causes abnormal development of

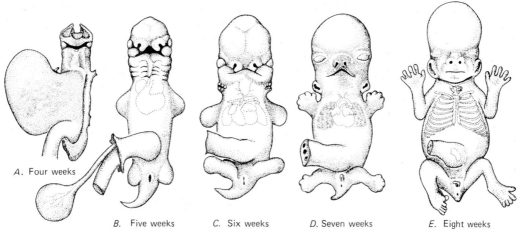

A. Four weeks B. Five weeks C. Six weeks D. Seven weeks E. Eight weeks

Figure 5.10 Frontal views of a series of human embryos, drawn as they would appear if the body curvatures had been straightened. From Patten, *Human Embryology,* 3rd ed., p. 146. Copyright © 1968 by McGraw-Hill, Inc. Used with permission of McGraw-Hill Book Company.

the arms and legs of the baby (*phocomelia*). In infants suffering from this condition the hands and feet are attached to the bodies by short stumps rather than by normal arms and legs.

In the past 20 years a number of women were treated with various combinations of sex hormones during the first trimester to prevent threatened miscarriage. Follow-up studies have shown that girls whose mothers received androgenic hormones during the first trimester may exhibit alterations in behavior as well as in anatomy. The clitoris may be enlarged at birth, and the behavior of these girls, when compared with matched controls who were not exposed to the hormones, was distinctly "tomboyish." They showed a preference for athletic activities as opposed to playing with dolls, for example.[13] Boys whose mothers received exogenous female hormones (estrogen and progesterone) have been found to rank significantly lower on scales of masculinity, assertiveness, and aggressiveness.[14]

A potent estrogen known as DES (diethylstilbestrol) has been shown to cause cancer of the vagina in some girls whose mothers took the drug while pregnant. DES is still in use as the "morning-after pill" (*see* Chapter 6).

Regular use of addictive drugs, like heroin and morphine, by the mother produces addiction in the fetus. When the infant is born, it must be given further doses of the drug to prevent withdrawal effects that may be fatal.

Alcohol is another drug that can cause birth defects. Researchers have found that facial, limb, and heart defects are more common among children of women who drink heavily during pregnancy than among those of women who do not drink. Three ounces (88.7 milliliters) of alcohol (for example, whis-

key) a day or one big binge may be enough to cause damage.

Smoking during pregnancy is harmful. Fetuses carried by women who smoke while pregnant have an increased risk of prematurity, low birth weight, and death before birth than fetuses carried by women who do not smoke. Also, newborn infants born to women who smoke during pregnancy have a greater risk of death than babies born to women who do not smoke.[15]

Certain viruses are also known to have damaging effects on the fetus during the first trimester. The most common is the virus of rubella, or German measles. If a woman has rubella during the first month of pregnancy, there is a 50 percent chance that the infant will be born with cataracts, congenital heart disease, deafness, or mental deficiency. In the third month of pregnancy the risk of such abnormalities decreases to 10 percent. Since 1969 a rubella vaccine has been available in the United States. About 85 percent of adult women have acquired immunity to rubella since they had it as children. If she is in doubt about her immunity, a woman should first be tested and, if found to be susceptible, vaccinated. However, a woman should *not* receive rubella vaccine if she is already pregnant and should avoid conception for six months after the vaccination because the vaccine contains the live rubella virus, which could cause the disease it is designed to prevent. Rubella is different from "regular measles," and being vaccinated against the latter does not protect a person from rubella.

A potentially serious and even fatal anemia of the fetus can result from the transfer across the placenta of antibodies to the red blood cells of the fetus. These antibodies occur when the mother is Rh negative and the fetus is Rh positive. The disorder is called Rh incompatibility. For the fetus to be at risk in this disease, the mother must be Rh neg-

---

[13]Erhardt and Money (1967).
[14]Yalom et al. (1973).

[15]Meyer and Tonascia (1977).

ative and the father Rh positive (as is the case in about 10 percent of U.S. marriages). Normally, Rh incompatability is not a problem in the first pregnancy. The mother develops antibodies if Rh positive fetal blood mixes with her Rh negative blood. This most commonly occurs during childbirth, miscarriage, or abortion. In the mother's next pregnancy with an Rh positive fetus her antibodies can travel across the placenta and attack the red blood cells of the fetus. This happens in about one out of every 200 pregnancies. In most cases the serious results of this disease (death or brain damage) can be avoided by early identification (parental blood-typing and, in women with a previous history of the disease, amniocentesis) and prompt treatment (blood transfusion of the fetus). The incidence of Rh incompatibility has been reduced due to the development of a vaccine, Rhogam. After an Rh negative woman miscarries, aborts, or delivers, she is given an injection of Rhogam within 72 hours, which keeps her from developing the harmful antibodies. Matings of two Rh positive or two Rh negative individuals do not lead to Rh incompatibility, nor does the mating of an Rh positive woman and an Rh negative man.

Positive Diagnosis of Pregnancy

From a medicolegal point of view, pregnancy can be positively established by one of three means: (a) verification of the fetal heartbeat, (b) photographic demonstration of the fetal skeleton, (c) observation of fetal movements. Until very recent developments in technology none of these signs of pregnancy could be verified until well into the second trimester. Using a conventional stethoscope a physician can hear the fetal heartbeat by the fifth month. The fetal heart rate is 120–140 beats per minute, and this can be differentiated from the mother's heartbeat, which is usually 70–80. A fetal pulse detector now available commercially can detect the fetal heartbeat as early as 9 weeks, and reliably

after 12 weeks. This device is based on ultrasonic technology. A sound wave of very high pitch is directed at the uterus and is reflected back to a receiver. Movements of the fetal heart cause changes in the pitch of the reflected sound, which are converted to an audible tone and amplified.[16]

Variations in the echo from an ultrasonic pulse resulting from reflection off the fetal skeleton can now be converted to a photographic image that is far more distinct than a conventional X ray. Present evidence indicates that the ultrasonic technique is safer than X rays since it does not involve the radiation hazard to the fetus inherent with X rays. Obviously, neither technique is used routinely, but each is of value in verifying suspected complications such as fetal head size larger than the pelvic opening, retarded fetal head size secondary to a malfunctioning placenta, gross malformation, and multiple fetuses.

Fetal movements can usually be felt by the end of the fifth month. Kicking movements of the fetus become outwardly visible later in the second trimester. Fetal movements not only confirm pregnancy but indicate that the fetus is alive.

The Second Trimester

Experiences of the Mother

The pregnant woman becomes much more aware of the fetus during the second trimester because of fetal movements ("quickening") just described. In addition, her waistline begins to expand (particularly in women who have borne children previously), and her abdomen begins to protrude, necessitating a change from regular to maternity clothes. Her pregnancy now becomes publicly recognizable.

The second trimester is generally the most peaceful and pleasant period of preg-

[16]Goodlin (1971).

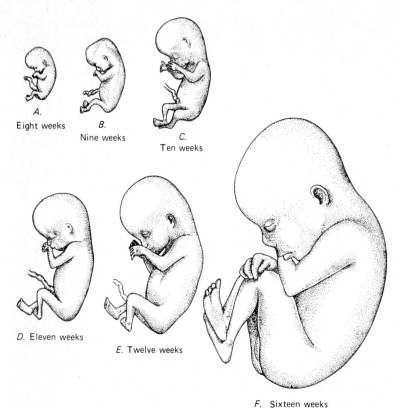

A.
Eight weeks

B.
Nine weeks

C.
Ten weeks

D. Eleven weeks

E. Twelve weeks

F. Sixteen weeks

Figure 5.11 Human fetuses between 8 and 16 weeks, about one-half actual size. *A-D* from photographs of embryos in University of Michigan Collection. *E* and *F* are redrawn, with slight modification, from DeLee. "Obstetrics." From Patten, *Human Embryology*, 3rd ed., p. 150. Copyright © by McGraw-Hill, Inc. Used with permission of McGraw-Hill Book Company.

nancy. Nausea and drowsiness present during the first trimester tend to disappear during the second. Concerns about miscarriage are generally past, and it is too early to start worrying about labor and delivery. Barring complications or illness, the pregnant woman can be quite active during the second trimester. She can continue to work if she wishes,[17] do housework, travel, and participate in recreation and sports. Rather than eliminating specific activities, most physicians nowadays urge "moderation in all things."

[17]Some employers still discharge pregnant employees or require them to take maternity leave. These practices are being challenged in the courts and will probably be eliminated as discriminatory in most instances. Yet in 1974 the U.S. Supreme Court ruled that pregnancy is not a disability, and therefore a woman who must stop working because of pregnancy is not eligible for disability benefits.

Sexual Activity during the Second Trimester

Frequency of sexual intercourse does not decrease significantly during the second trimester (*see* Table 5.1). Some women who experienced extreme nausea and fatigue during the first trimester may have renewed sexual interest as these symptoms disappear. There is usually an increase in vaginal lubrication from the second trimester on—and less breast tenderness. However, the expanded abdomen of the later stages of pregnancy produces a pronounced shift in preferred coital positions during the second and third trimester. Use of the male superior position declines significantly and the female superior, side-by-side, and rear-entry positions are used more frequently. Frequency of orgasm declines somewhat during the second trimes-

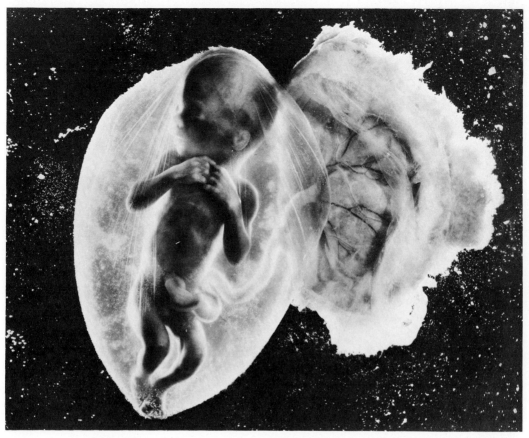

Figure 5.12   Fetus, about four months, eight inches long. From Nilsson et al., *A Child is Born* (Boston: Delacourte Press/Seymour Lawrence, Inc., 1965), pp. 116–117. Reprinted by permission.

ter, and, unlike coital frequency, is closely associated with level of sexual interest on the part of the woman.[18]

Development of the Fetus

Beyond the twelfth week the fetus is clearly recognizable as a human infant (*see* Figures 5.11 and 5.12), although it is much smaller than it will be at birth. It has a proportionately large head with eyes, ears, nose, and mouth. The arms and legs, which began as "limb buds" projecting from the trunk, now have hands and feet, fingers and toes.

[18]Wagner and Solberg, op. cit.

The digits of the hands and feet begin with the formation of four radial grooves at the ends of the limb buds, lending the initial appearance of webbed hands or feet (*see* Figure 5.13). In some children remnants of this webbing remain after birth, causing embarrassment to the parents, perhaps, but it usually is of no other significance.

Hair appears on the scalp and above the eyes in the fifth or sixth month. The first hairs, called *lanugo,* are fine, soft, and downy. The skin at the fifth and sixth month is quite red because the many small blood vessels below its surface show through. Beginning in the seventh month, however, layers of fat

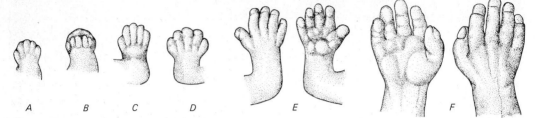

Figure 5.13 Stages in early development of the hand. (*A*) Anterior limb bud of an embryo 12 mm long; (*B*) anterior limb bud of an embryo 15 mm long; (*C*) anterior limb bud of an embryo 17 mm long; (*D*) hand and forearm of an embryo 20 mm long; (*E*) two views of the hand and forearm of an embryo 25 mm long; (*F*) two views of the hand of a fetus 52 mm long. After Retzius, from Scammon, in Morris, *Human Anatomy.* From Patten, *Human Embryology,* 3rd ed., p. 148. Copyright © 1968 by McGraw-Hill, Inc. Used with the permission of McGraw-Hill Book Company.

build up beneath the skin, and the baby develops the characteristic chubby pinkness.

Beside further maturation of the internal organ systems during the second trimester, there is a substantial increase in the size of the fetus. At the end of the third month the fetus weighs about 1 ounce and is only about 3 inches long. By the end of the sixth month it weighs about 2 pounds and is about 14 inches long. By this time the eyes can open, and the fetus moves its arms and legs spontaneously and vigorously. The fetus alternates between periods of wakefulness and sleep. The uterus is a very sheltered environment, but such stimuli as a loud noise near the uterus, a flash of high-intensity light, or a rapid change in the position of the mother can disturb the tranquility of the womb and provoke a vigorous movement by the fetus. Changes in outside temperature are not perceived by the fetus, since the intrauterine temperature is maintained by internal mechanisms at a very constant level just slighly (0.5°C) above that of the mother.[19]

If delivered at the end of six months, the fetus usually survives for a few hours to a few days. With heroic efforts on the part of the medical staff 5 to 10 percent of babies weighing about 2 pounds (800 to 1000 grams) survive. The smallest infant known to have survived weighed less than a pound at birth (it weighed 400 grams; 1 pound = 455 grams). The fetus was estimated to be 20 weeks old at the time of delivery. Since fetuses can now be legally aborted up to 24 weeks, it is possible some could survive with extraordinary medical assistance. This is only one of many facets of the ongoing abortion controversy (*see* Chapters 6 and 15).

The Third Trimester

Experiences of the Mother

During the last three months of pregnancy the expectant mother becomes more acutely aware of the child that she carries within her swelling abdomen (*see* Figure 5.14). The fetus becomes quite active, and its seemingly perpetual kicking, tossing, and turning may keep the mother awake at night. The woman's weight, if not controlled up to this point, may become a problem, as the woman realizes that she has already gained her "quota" and still has three months to go. Often working against her is an increased appetite that is partly caused by the hormonal changes of pregnancy. According to the Committee on Maternal Malnutrition of the National Research Council, the desirable

[19]Austin and Short (1972), vol. 2, chapter 3.

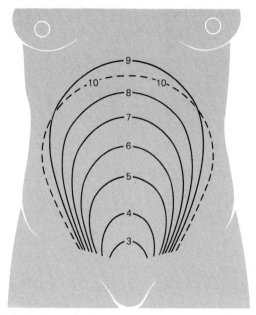

Figure 5.14 Relative height of the top of the uterus at the various months of pregnancy. From Eastman and Hellmann, *Williams Obstetrics*, 13th ed. (New York: Appleton-Century-Crofts, 1966), p. 263. Reprinted by permission.

weight gain during pregnancy is 24 pounds (10.9 kilograms). The average infant at nine months weighs only about 7.5 pounds (3.4 kg). The rest of the weight gain is accounted for as follows: the placenta, about 1 pound (0.4 kg); the amniotic fluid in the uterine cavity, 2 pounds (0.9 kg); the enlargement of the uterus, 2 pounds (0.9 kg); enlargement of the breasts, about 1.5 pounds (0.7 kg); and the retained fluid and fat accumulated by the mother, the remaining 10 pounds (4.5 kg) or more. There are several reasons why attention is paid to the mother's weight gain during pregnancy. Most important is the higher incidence of medical complications during pregnancy (for example, strain on the heart and high blood pressure) in women who gain excessively. In addition, movement becomes more awkward for the woman who has gained perhaps 40 pounds (18 kg), and she tires more easily.

By the ninth month of pregnancy a woman is usually anxious to "have it over with" and "see what it is." There is speculation about the sex of the child; prospective names are considered; and the nursery is made ready. As the delivery date approaches, a woman may also become anxious about whether or not the baby is going to be "all right"—healthy and without congenital defects.

Prematurity
A major complication during the third trimester is premature labor and delivery of the fetus. Since the date of conception is not always accurately estimated, and because the age and weight of the fetus are highly correlated, it is traditional to define prematurity by weight rather than estimated age. An infant who weighs less than 5 pounds, 8 ounces (2.5 kg) at birth is considered premature. The mortality rate among premature infants is directly related to size: The smaller the infant, the poorer are its chances for survival. Although an infant born in the seventh month or later can usually survive for a few hours without great difficulty, a smaller one, between 2 and 4 pounds (0.9 and 1.8 kg), often develops difficulty in breathing leading to severe respiratory distress and death within 48 hours.

It is estimated that about 7 percent of births in the United States are premature. Prematurity may be associated with various maternal illnesses—like high blood pressure, heart disease, and syphilis—or with factors such as heavy cigarette smoking or multiple pregnancy. At least 50 percent of the time, however, the cause of prematurity is not clearly known.

Complications during the Third Trimester
One of the most serious complications of pregnancy, if untreated, is a condition called *toxemia* (from the Latin word for "poi-

son''). In fact, much modern prenatal care has been developed as a result of research done on the cause and treatment of toxemia. The cause of toxemia is still unknown, but it seems that a toxin, or poison, produced by the body causes the symptoms—high blood pressure, protein in the urine, and the retention of fluids by the body. This disease occurs only in pregnant women, usually in the last trimester, and if it is not treated successfully the result can be death for both the mother and the child. Uncontrolled toxemia is a major cause (along with hemorrhage and infection) of maternal mortality. Between 6 and 7 percent of all pregnant women in the United States develop toxemia and a small percentage of these die.

Sexual Activity during the Third Trimester

Frequency of sexual intercourse (and orgasm) declines significantly with each successive month of the third trimester (*see* Table 5.1). The most common reasons given for this change are, in order of frequency: physical discomfort, fear of injury to the baby, loss of sexual interest, awkwardness in having sexual relations, recommendation of a physician, and feelings of loss of attractiveness (as perceived by the woman).[20]

The primary medical concern about intercourse and/or orgasm late in pregnancy is the risk of inducing premature labor. It is well known that orgasm in the third trimester is accompanied by strong contractions of the uterus, and in the ninth month the uterus may go into spasm for as long as a minute following orgasm. One study reported a 15 percent risk of premature labor or rupture of fetal membranes in women who were orgasmic after the thirty-second week.[21] (Rupture of the fetal membranes can lead to infection as

[20]Wagner and Solberg, op cit.
[21]Goodlin et al. (1971). A more recent study (Wagner and Solberg, 1974) did not find any correlation between sexual activity and prematurity.

well as prematurity.) It would appear that the women most at risk are those with a prior history of vaginal bleeding during pregnancy, ruptured membranes, or a prematurely ''ripe'' (soft) cervix. Women who do not have a history of these complications and who are otherwise healthy can probably participate in sexual activity throughout the third trimester at no risk to themselves or the fetus. Some couples prefer to practice intracrural (between the thighs) intercourse or mutual masturbation during the last month of pregnancy.

Final Development of the Fetus

The third trimester is a period of growth and maturation for the fetus, which by now has developed all the essential organ systems. By the end of the seventh month the fetus is about 16 inches (40.6 cm) long and weighs about 3 pounds, 12 ounces (1.7 kg). If delivered at this time, the baby has about a 50 percent chance for survival.

At the same time the fetus has usually assumed a head-down position in the mother's uterus. This position, called *cephalic presentation* (since the head appears at the cervix first during delivery), is the most common position for delivery and presents the fewest complications. During the seventh month, however, about 12 percent of fetuses are still upright in the mothers' uteruses (the so-called *breech presentation*), and a few are oriented with the long axis in a transverse position (called *shoulder presentation*). In addition to the baby's small size and immaturity, there is thus the added risk of a more complicated breech delivery early in the third trimester. At full term (nine months) only about 3 percent of babies are in the breech position.

By the end of the eighth month the fetus is about 18 inches (45.7 cm) long and weighs about 5 pounds, 4 ounces (2.4 kg). If delivered at this time, it has a 90–95 percent chance of survival.

During the ninth month the fetus gains more than 2 pounds (0.9 kg), and essential organs like the lungs reach a state of maturity compatible with life in the outside world. In addition, less crucial details like hair and fingernails assume a normal appearance and may even grow to such lengths as to require trimming shortly after delivery. At full term the average baby weighs 7.5 pounds (3.4 kg) and is 20 inches (50.8 cm) long.[22] Ninety-nine percent of full-term babies born alive in the United States survive, a figure that could be improved even further if all expectant mothers and newborn babies received proper medical care.

Childbirth

As the end of pregnancy approaches, the expectant mother experiences contractions of her uterus at irregular intervals. The woman who has not delivered previously may rush to the hospital in the middle of the night only to be sent home because she is experiencing *false labor.*

Three or four weeks before delivery the fetus "drops" to a lower position in the abdomen. The next major step in preparation for delivery is the softening and dilation of the cervix. The mother may be unaware of this process, but usually just before labor begins there is a small, slightly bloody discharge (*bloody show*) that represents the plug of mucus that has been occluding the cervix. In about 10 percent of pregnant women, however, the membranes encapsulating the fetus burst (*premature rupture of the membranes*), and there is a gush of amniotic fluid down the woman's legs. Usually labor begins within 24 hours after such a rupture; but if it does not, there is risk of infection and the mother should be hospitalized for observation.

Labor

The exact mechanism that initiates and sustains labor in humans is not fully understood, but a number of hormonal factors are known to be involved. Current research indicates that the fetus actually triggers labor.[23] The fetal adrenal gland is stimulated to produce hormones that act upon the placenta and uterus and cause these organs to increase the secretions of other chemicals, *prostaglandins.* Prostaglandins (*see* Chapter 6) stimulate the muscle of the uterus, thereby causing labor to begin. We have already mentioned the loss of the inhibitory effect on the uterus of placental hormones, particularly progesterone, as production drops off near term. Finally, *oxytocin,* a hormone produced by the posterior pituitary gland (*see* Figure 4.1) is released in the late stages of labor and stimulates the more powerful contractions required to finally expel the fetus.

Labor begins with regular uterine contractions ("pains"), which dilate the cervix. Labor is divided into three stages, the first of which is the longest, extending from the first regular contractions until the cervix is completely dilated—about 4 inches (10 cm) in diameter. This stage lasts about 15 hours in the first pregnancy and about 8 hours in later ones. (Deliveries after the first are generally easier in all respects.) Uterine contractions begin at intervals as far apart as 15 or 20 minutes, but they occur more frequently and with greater intensity and regularity as time passes. When the contractions are coming regularly four or five minutes apart the woman usually goes to the hospital, where she is admitted to a labor room (essentially a regular hospital room) for the remainder of the first stage. Her husband is usually allowed to remain with her during this time.

The second stage begins when the cervix is completely dilated and ends with delivery of the baby (*see* Figures 5.15, 5.16, and

[22]There is great variation in birth weights, however, ranging usually from five to nine pounds. Weights of ten or eleven pounds are not uncommon, and the largest baby known to have survived weighed 15.5 pounds at birth. Stillborn babies as heavy as twenty-five pounds have been delivered.

[23]Daly and Wilson (1978), p. 192.

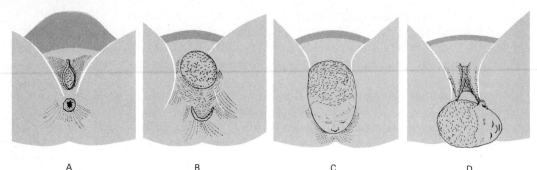

A   B   C   D

Figure 5.15 (A) The scalp is visible at the vaginal opening. (B) More of the infant's head can be seen. (C) The head of the baby has emerged. (D) The shoulders of the baby are beginning to appear. The woman's pubic hair is absent in this figure. The pubic hair is often shaved when the woman enters the hospital. Redrawn from White, *Emergency Childbirth: A Manual* (Franklin Park, Ill.: Police Training Foundation, 1958), pp. 20–21.

5.17). The woman is taken to a delivery room (similar to a surgical operating room), and the husband may or may not be allowed to be present, depending on the laws of the state, hospital regulations, the discretion of the physician, and the wishes of the couple. The second stage may last from a few minutes to a few hours. If any anesthetic is used, it is usually given before this stage begins. General anesthesia for childbirth is becoming less popular than it was earlier in this century. Its disadvantages include all the risks to the mother that general anesthesia entails under any circumstances, plus a slowing effect on labor and depression of the infant's activity (particularly respiration). Caudal or spinal anesthetic is currently popular. The anesthetic is inserted

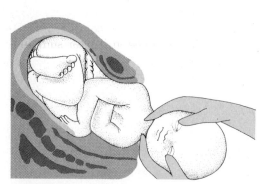

Figure 5.16 Gentle traction to bring about descent of anterior shoulder. From Eastman and Hellman, *Williams Obstetrics,* 13th ed. (New York: Appleton-Century-Crofts, 1966), p. 423. Reprinted by permission.

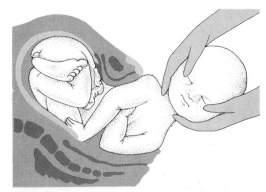

Figure 5.17 Delivery of anterior shoulder completed; gentle traction to deliver posterior shoulder. From Eastman and Hellman, *Williams Obstetrics,* 13th ed. (New York: Appleton-Century-Crofts, 1966), p. 423. Reprinted by permission.

by needle into the spinal canal, producing temporary loss of sensation (and paralysis) below the waist only. Advantages include the mother's awareness through delivery and the infant's freedom from anesthetic effects.

In some cases local anesthesia, which simply blocks nerves in the vicinity of the vagina, is sufficient for a comfortable delivery in women who desire a minimum of medical intervention at this stage.

In the third stage the placenta separates from the uterine wall and is discharged as the *afterbirth* (placenta and fetal membranes). The uterus contracts to a significantly smaller size during this stage, and there is variable bleeding. The third stage of labor lasts about an hour, during which time the physician examines the mother and baby carefully and sews up any tear that may have occurred in the *perineum* (the skin and deeper tissues between the openings of the vagina and anus). The *episiotomy* incision, if there has been one, is also sewn up at this time. An episiotomy is an incision of the perineum that is sometimes performed to ease the passage of the baby's head. These "stitches" may cause itching and discomfort for several days, but they usually heal with no complications.

Cesarean Section

Occasionally, as when the baby is too large (or the woman's pelvis is too small) to accommodate vaginal delivery, a cesarean section is performed. In this operation the baby is removed from the uterus through an incision in the abdominal and uterine walls. About 10 percent of deliveries in the United States are by cesarean section, although the figure is increasing and may be as high as 22 percent in some hospitals.

With modern surgical techniques the incidence of complications in this kind of delivery is no greater than that in vaginal delivery. It is not necessarily true that a woman who has had one cesarean section must have all her later children by this method: A cesarean

delivery may be followed by normal vaginal deliveries. On the other hand, it is possible also to have several children by cesarean section, despite the common notion that a woman can endure only one such operation. The recovery period is somewhat longer after a cesarean section, and hospitalization usually lasts seven to ten days.

It is unlikely that Julius Caesar, for whom this operation was named, was actually delivered by cesarean section. Although it is known that the operation was performed in ancient times among both civilized and primitive peoples, it was almost always performed after the mother had died, and in hopes of saving the baby. Caesar's mother lived for many years after his birth. Cesarean section was definitely being performed on living women in the seventeenth century, but the operation at that time involved *removing* the uterus with the baby still inside and then sewing up the abdomen. The current practice of removing only the baby and leaving the uterus in place dates from 1882.

Natural Childbirth

Intervention and assistance at childbirth in the form of rituals, prayers, potions, and medicines to relieve pain or dull the senses and physical extraction of the baby are as old as recorded history. In Europe childbirth usually occurred at home in familiar surroundings, and those assisting were women with special training and experience. The pattern changed significantly about 300 years ago. Male physicians and surgeons began to replace midwives; deliveries were moved from home to lying-in hospitals in large cities; and forceps (invented about 1600) became popular. While significant new knowledge in the field of obstetrics was acquired in the ensuing centuries, the clinical practice of obstetrics did not always improve the lot of women in labor. Many women died of childbed fever (*see* Box 5.4).

Box 5.4   Childbed Fever

Before the mid-1800s, there was no knowledge that childbirth should take place in a clean, antiseptic environment. One woman in ten who gave birth in hospitals or clinics was likely to die of puerperal fever—childbed fever—and sometimes epidemics of puerperal fever took the lives of 50 to 75 percent of the women in maternity wards.

The maternity wards of early hospitals and clinics were often dark and poorly ventilated. Few people took precautions to prevent new mothers from being exposed to sources of infection. Oliver Wendell Holmes was among the first to realize in the 1840s that puerperal fever was infectious in nature; but his essay on the topic was denounced by colleagues and had little effect. Most doctors attributed puerperal fever to accident or Providence—the "curse of Eve"—and were certain that nothing could be done to alter the death rates.

In Vienna in 1847 a young doctor, Ignaz Semmelweiss, observed that the death rate of women who were attended by medical students was substantially higher than it was in wards where the women were attended by midwives. The patients were aware of this difference, too; and women begged to be assisted by mid-wives. Apparently, students often came directly to the maternity wards after handling the infected and the dead, thus passing the fever to the healthy women. Semmelweiss ordered the students to wash their hands in a solution of chlorinated lime before attending women in the maternity wards. The mortality rate from puerperal fever dropped from 18 percent to 3 percent within two weeks and to 1.27 percent with a year.

Semmelweiss's work was heavily criticized by his superiors. After months of persecution, he resigned his post and moved to another city. In 1861 he published his major work on puerperal fever, but the medical profession continued to reject this theory. He died in 1865 of puerperal fever contracted through a wound on his finger. A few years later, the work of Lister and Pasteur made the importance of germs and antisepsis better understood, and the incidence of puerperal fever began to decline permanently.

[1]Guthrie (1958)
[2]Gortvay and Zoltán (1968).

Chloroform anesthesia was introduced in the nineteenth century and became quite popular in England after Queen Victoria was delivered of her eighth child under chloroform in 1853. By the twentieth century childbirth had taken on the trappings of a surgical procedure, even when routine and uncomplicated. The woman was hospitalized, sterilized (in the antiseptic sense), anesthetized, and a variety of instruments were used in the delivery, which was performed in a room resembling a surgical suite in appearance, facilities, and regulations (for example, husbands and other "nonparticipants" were excluded).

It is not surprising that given these developments there would be a reaction to one or more aspects of the procedure. To some, the exclusion of the father was most repugnant; to others, the domination of obstetrics by men (in the United States) was objectionable; and for many, the most disliked aspect of twentieth-century childbirth was the use of instruments and anesthetics. Anesthetics have a depressant effect on the mother and infant. The widespread practice of performing episiotomies was also criticized as being unnecessary in many instances and even damaging in some cases.

The term "natural childbirth" was coined

by the English physician Grantly Dick-Read in 1932. Dick-Read postulated that the pain of childbirth is primarily related to fear and subsequent muscular tension during labor. Very briefly, his still-popular method of "natural childbirth" involves eliminating fear through education about the birth process before delivery in order to break the cycle of fear, tension, and pain. The method is best described in his book *Childbirth without Fear.*

A second type of "natural childbirth" originated in Russia, but was popularized by the French physician Bernard Lamaze. The "Lamaze method" is based on Pavlov's description of conditioned-reflex responses and is sometimes called the "psychoprophylactic method" of childbirth.[24] It involves conditioning the pregnant woman mentally to dissociate uterine contractions from the experience of pain through repeated reinforcement of the notion that such contractions are not painful. Prescribed exercises requiring voluntary relaxation of the abdominal muscles are also part of the program.

Prepared Childbirth

The methods of *prepared childbirth* currently used in the United States incorporate a variety of techniques from Dick-Read, Lamaze, and other sources. The goal of prepared childbirth is to allow women to experience and to help in giving birth while feeling as little pain as possible. Although drugs are available if they are needed, the use of drugs is minimized to avoid risk of side effects to the mother and the baby. Usually, an expectant mother (and father) attend classes for 6 to 10 weeks before the birth in order to learn the birth procedures and practice techniques that will ease the birth process.

First, the classes are designed to inform prospective parents about each step of labor. This education helps answer the woman's questions and dispel her anxiety. Women

who learn the birth procedures in advance have less to fear and can help more in each stage of labor. In addition, they can be awake and aware of the remarkable experience of bringing a child into the world.

Second, the woman is taught a variety of exercises that increase her muscle control such that she can voluntarily tighten or relax specific muscles in various parts of her body. Part of the pain that women experience in childbirth results from their tightening their abdominal and perineal muscles and thereby making it harder for the baby to emerge. By learning to relax these and other muscles, women can allow the baby to pass through the birth canal more easily and thus decrease the total amount of pain. In preparation for the second stage of labor, the woman also learns the muscle contraction patterns needed to help push the baby through the birth canal while keeping the vagina and perineum relaxed.

Third, women are taught methods for distracting their attention from the experience of pain. They learn several breathing techniques that ease the birth process and keep their attention focused on systematic tasks. They learn patterns of hand movement—gently massaging the abdomen in a circular motion—that keep their hands busy, make them feel better, and help produce relaxation. They concentrate their visual attention on specified targets, and they hear their husbands counting and measuring the lengths of the contractions. These combined inputs from several sense modalities keep the woman's mind occupied with thoughts that help decrease the sensation of pain.

Finally, having the husband present during childbirth provides a source of comfort and security for the woman. The husband's reassuring words partially divert her attention from the pain. The husband learns to give gentle massages that bring comfort and help distract the woman's attention from other sensations. His concern and emotional sup-

[24]Chertok (1967), pp. 698–699.

port make the experience more positive for her. In addition, the husband makes sure that she continues her breathing exercises, keeps her abdominal muscles relaxed, and practices the other methods consistently throughout the birth process.

Although early advocates of "natural" childbirth claimed that women would feel no pain during birth, the present approach to prepared childbirth does not deny the existence of pain. Instead it helps women learn to cope with the experience in as positive a way as possible.

Leboyer Method

Another method of childbirth that has become popular in recent years was developed by the French physician Frederick Leboyer. This method concentrates on protecting the infant from the pain and trauma of childbirth. In *Birth without Violence,* Leboyer describes what he believes to be the pain infants suffer being born and then goes on to describe a method of making birth less painful and shocking to the infant. It is a slow, quiet birth in which everything is done to protect the infant's delicate senses from shock. Lights are kept low, and unnecessary noises are avoided. When the infant's head appears the birth is eased along by the doctor's fingers under each of the infant's armpits. Supported so, the infant is gently settled onto the mother's abdomen. There, for several minutes, the child is allowed to adjust to its new environment while it continues to receive warmth and comfort from its mother as it did before birth. Instead of being held up and slapped (which helps the infant start breathing), the *Leboyer method* allows the child to lie quietly on its mother's abdomen with the umbilical cord still attached. The infant continues to receive oxygen from its mother in this way until it starts breathing on its own. Then the child is gently lowered into a warm bath where it will eventually open its eyes and begin to move its limbs freely. The result of such a nonviolent birth, according to Leboyer, is not a screaming, kicking, terrified infant, but a relaxed and even smiling child.

If a woman can give birth without surgical intervention or anesthesia, one might wonder why the birth need take place in a hospital. The primary medical justification for hospital delivery is the availability of backup personnel and equipment in the event of a sudden complication (for example, hemorrhaging). However, there is a growing interest in the United States in "alternative birth centers" (clinics that are more homelike and family oriented and less expensive than hospitals), in home deliveries, and in midwives. One reason for this interest is the rising costs of hospitalization. Another reason is the impersonal atmosphere of hospitals and restrictions that separate husbands from wives during childbirth and mothers from their babies in maternity wards. Increasingly, hospitals have been modifying their regulations to allow husbands to be present throughout labor and delivery and to allow "rooming-in," that is, keeping newborn babies in the same room with their mothers rather than in a separate nursery. This allows the mother to hold and feed her new baby when she wishes, rather than according to a fixed schedule.

The Leboyer method and other so-called methods of natural childbirth are becoming increasingly popular in the United States with expectant couples as well as with some obstetricians and in some hospitals. But the term "natural" does not mean that the more traditional type of hospital delivery is wrong. Many women and children are alive today thanks only to the extraordinary hospital care they received and to the techniques of modern obstetrics.

Multiple Births

The delivery of two or more infants after one pregnancy is an event of great fascination in all cultures. Twins occur in 1 of 90 births in the United States. Triplets occur in about 1 of 9000 births, and quadruplets in about 1 of 500,000 births. Multiple births of more than four children are extremely rare. The Dionne quintuplets of Canada, born May 28, 1934, were the first quintuplets known to survive. All five were girls; and they weighed a total of 13 pounds, 6 ounces at birth. Because of their small sizes and usually premature delivery, the mortality rate among infants in a multiple birth is significantly higher than with single births. Twins are born an average of 22 days before the EDC. Their mortality rate is two to three times that of single births.

There are two types of twins, identical and fraternal. Two out of three sets of twins are fraternal, developed from two separate eggs fertilized simultaneously. It is biologically possible for twins to have different fathers. This phenomenon is called *superfecundation* and has been clearly documented in animal studies. In 1975 a German woman gave birth to fraternal twins—one fathered by a black man and the other fathered by a white man. She had had intercourse with both men at different times on the same day.

Another rare occurrence is *superfetation,* the fertilization and subsequent development of an egg when a fetus is already present in the uterus. There are a few such cases reported in the medical literature. In one instance, a woman gave birth to two normal children three months apart.

Identical twins result from subdivision of a single fertilized egg before implantation. Identical twins usually share a common placenta, whereas fraternal twins usually have separate placentas.

Twins show a slight tendency to "run in families," but the heredity of "twinning" is rather vague. Fraternal twins are more likely to reoccur than are identical twins.

The Postpartum Period

A woman nowadays usually leaves the hospital two or three days after an uncomplicated delivery, though the length of the stay varies somewhat from place to place. With a first baby the first week at home may be a bit of a turmoil for the young mother, who is trying to cope simultaneously with the needs of the baby (feeding, bathing, changing diapers) and the calls of many well-meaning friends and relatives anxious to see "the new addition." Fatigue may be a major complaint at this point, along with a general "let-down" feeling.

About two-thirds of all women experience transient episodes of sadness and crying some time during the first ten days after delivery, a phenomenon known as the "postpartum blues" syndrome. Women (and their families) are often puzzled by this reaction, for it comes when they are expected to be especially happy, celebrating the arrival of the new child. Doubts about their competence as mothers, fatigue, feelings of rejection or neglect by their husbands, and the drastic hormone changes that occur at this time are some factors involved.[25]

Breast-Feeding

Milk production (*lactation*) begins 48 to 72 hours after childbirth and is accompanied by a feeling of engorgement in the breasts. Two pituitary hormones are involved in the physiology of breast-feeding. *Prolactin* (*see* Chapter 4) stimulates the production of milk by the mammary glands, and *oxytocin* causes the ejection of the milk from the breast to the nipple in response to the stimulus of suckling by the baby. At the time of weaning, the breast is no longer subject to the stimulation of the nursing infant, with the result that secretion of prolactin and oxytocin, and therefore lactation, ceases.

Breast-feeding is currently becoming more popular in the United States than in earlier times, and organizations such as La Leche League provide information and encouragement to women who are interested

[25]Yalom et al. (1968).

Box 5.5 Mammaries

Mammals include all animals that feed their young with milk from the female mammary glands. Many mammals bear a litter of young at each birth and have several mammaries to provide milk for them. Although humans normally have only two mammaries, about 1 percent of both males and females are born with extra nipples and mammaries.[1] The extra mammaries can develop at any location along the milk lines, which extend from the armpits to the inguinal regions. Not all nipples have mammary tissue, but those with mammary tissue are capable of lactation. The presence of such extra nipples reveals the similarities in body plan between humans and the other mammals. The extra mammaries can be removed surgically without complications.

The male mammary is potentially capable of the full development seen in adult women. Transsexuals who were born male and take female hormones develop breasts with the typical female structure and shape. The male breast has the potential to produce milk. When both male and

female babies are born, they may have droplets of milklike substance (known as "witch's milk") in the nipples. Before birth, the fetus's breasts had been stimulated by the mother's hormones in the uterus, hence the fetus's breasts—whether male or female—began to develop the capacity to produce milk much the same as the mother's breasts did.

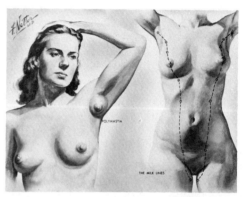

From Netter, *Reproductive System.* The Ciba Collection of Medical Illustrations, vol. 2. © Copyright 1954, 1965 CIBA Pharmaceutical Company, Division of CIBA-GEIGY Corporation. Reproduced with permission. All rights reserved.

[1]Netter (1965).

in learning more about it. The experience of nursing, from the mother's standpoint, can be emotionally satisfying, pleasurable, and even sensual. In fact, there is a positive correlation between postpartum sexual interest and nursing. There may be some discomfort at the beginning, but this can be overcome with patience. Conversely, women with an aversion to nudity and sexuality are less likely to breast-feed.[26]

From the standpoint of the baby there is no question of the superiority of human milk over cow's milk or commercial formulas. Human milk contains the ideal mixture of nutrients for human babies; it contains antibod-

ies that protect the infant from certain infectious diseases; it is free of bacteria; and it is always the right temperature.

In many countries cow's milk is neither hygienic nor cheap; and the water available for dilution of formula preparations may be contaminated. Nevertheless, the trend in many areas of the world has been to abandon the breast for the bottle. The results could be nutritionally and economically disastrous if this trend continues.

Resumption of Ovulation and Menstruation

There is wide variation in timing of the resumption of normal menstrual cycles after delivery. For about four weeks the woman

[26]Newton (1973).

has a bloody vaginal discharge called *lochia* (from Greek *lokhios*, "pertaining to childbirth"). One or two months later a mother who is not nursing may have a menstrual period. If she is nursing, however, her periods may not resume for as long as 18 months, although 5 months is more common. The first few periods after pregnancy may be somewhat irregular in length and flow, but women who have had painful periods before pregnancy often find that they suffer no such discomfort after childbirth.

It should be emphasized that ovulation can occur *before* the first postpartum menstrual cycle and that consequently a woman can become pregnant without having a menstrual period after the birth of her baby. It should also be noted that women can conceive while nursing. The notion that nursing is "nature's method of contraception" is misleading.

Sexual Activity during the Postpartum Period

There is considerable variation in patterns of sexual activity after delivery. Fatigue, physical discomfort, and the obstetrician's injunctions play an important part in determining when a woman resumes sexual relations after childbirth. Although doctors commonly advise women to refrain from intercourse for six weeks after delivery, there is no medical reason why a healthy woman cannot have vaginal intercourse as soon as the episiotomy or any lacerations of the perineum have healed and the flow of lochia has ended. The only medical concern is the possibility of infection through the vagina. Couples who practice intracrural intercourse, manual manipulation of the genitals to orgasm, or sexual activity other than vaginal intercourse early in the postpartum period are not hampered by this concern.

Studies have shown that a certain percentage of men feel driven to extramarital sexual affairs during the period of absti-

nence—"six weeks before and six weeks after"—that is rigidly adhered to by some women. That this explanation is a rationalization is certainly possible, because the imaginative couple that considers regular sexual activity desirable can find satisfying forms of gratification during periods when vaginal intercourse is inadvisable.

Pregnancy and Childbirth in Other Societies

Preliterate people have developed various beliefs and practices in connection with pregnancy and childbirth. Many tribes believed that the fetus developed from a combination of male semen and menstrual blood. The Venda tribe of East Africa believed that "red elements" like muscle and blood were derived from the mother's menses (which ceased during pregnancy because the menstrual blood was being absorbed by the developing fetus). The "white elements"—like skin, bone, and nerves—were believed to develop from the father's semen.

Some societies imposed dietary restrictions on pregnant women, often from fear that the fetus might otherwise take on undesirable characteristics of food, plants, or animals. For example, if the mother ate rabbit, the child might have weak legs; if she ate trout, he might exhibit characteristic quivering movements. In addition, Ashanti women were forbidden to look upon any deformed object or creature during pregnancy lest their children be born with similar deformities.

The majority of primitive tribes that have been studied prohibited sexual intercourse during the last month of pregnancy on the grounds that it might kill the child or cause premature delivery, an interesting observation considering the similar concern in modern societies and the absence so far of substantial medical evidence for or against this belief.

Abortions were performed in some societies, particularly if the women were un-

Box 5.6 Natural Childbirth in Other Societies

Natural childbirth is quite different from the prepared childbirth common in the United States today. Women have been giving birth the natural way all through history, and many have suffered more than the woman does in modern prepared childbirth. Women in preliterate societies have practiced many methods of natural childbirth.[1,2] Sitting, squatting or kneeling positions were very common. In addition, various forms of assistance have been given to "facilitate" birth. The following methods are among those that have been reported: suspending the woman from a limb; massaging the abdomen; sitting or standing on the abdomen; blowing smoke into the vagina; and tossing the woman with a blanket to shake the baby out of her body.

[1]Englemann (1883).
[2]Witkowski (1892).

married or were pregnant as the result of adultery. Usually the fetuses were killed *in utero* by violent beating upon the abdomen, and this was followed by mechanical extraction of the fetus or spontaneous stillbirth.

Contrary to popular opinion, childbirth was not considered a routine and painless event by most preliterate people. Among many tribes elaborate dietary and exercise regimens were practiced to prevent painful and difficult deliveries. Various rituals might be performed to ensure easy delivery, and particular attention was paid to confession of sexual indiscretions at this time, for difficult deliveries were often attributed to violations of the tribal sexual codes.

The placenta was almost always viewed as a potentially dangerous object and was carefully disposed of, usually by burying it in a special place. There was also usually a taboo on sexual intercourse for several weeks or more after delivery, another striking similarity to taboos in modern societies.

Deformed babies and multiple births were viewed with alarm in most primitive societies. Twins, triplets, and babies with congenital deformities were usually killed at birth. Twins were often believed to result from adultery or impregnation by an evil spirit. A more benign explanation was offered by the Kiwai tribesmen of New Guinea, who believed that a woman would give birth to twins if she ate bananas from a tree with two bunches!

Chapter 6

Contraception

Some of the oldest documents to mention contraception (voluntary prevention of conception) date back nearly 4000 years to ancient Egypt.[1] One method called for douching, or washing, the vagina after intercourse with a mixture of wine, garlic, and fennel. The practice of coitus interruptus is mentioned in *Genesis* 38:8–9, as well as in the Talmud. Absorbent materials, root and herb potions, pessaries, and more permanent means of sterilization were used by the Greeks and Romans and have been used subsequently by many peoples around the world.

Prior to the present era it was very rare for any society to limit population as a matter of general policy. A few primitive cultures practiced selective infanticide, usually of female infants; and some peoples living in unusually harsh environments, such as the Eskimos, allowed the very old to die of starvation. However, the historical incentives for birth control were usually personal or idiosyncratic: Slaves, harlots, and illicit lovers tried to avoid pregnancy; and other people sought to regulate the sizes of their families because of economic, medical, or psychological factors. Such personal incentives continue to be important, but there is now a mounting concern that entire nations and even humanity as a whole must urgently check galloping population expansion.

In the United States contraception has had a turbulent history. In 1873 Congress passed the Comstock law, which made it illegal to disseminate contraceptive information. Soon state laws were also passed, some of which were even more restrictive than the federal law.

Margaret Sanger was a leader in the birth control movement. She became aware of the need for contraception during her work as a nurse in the poor tenements of New York City in the early 1900s. There she saw the misery and suffering caused by a lack of contraceptive knowledge. After one particularly difficult experience (*see* Box 6.1), she vowed "to do something to change the destiny of mothers whose miseries were as vast as the sky."[2] She devoted the rest of her life to the cause of helping women gain control over their own bodies. In the face of strong opposition she worked to make birth control available to all women. Her early publications were banned and she was indicted on nine federal offenses. In 1916 she opened the first birth control clinic in the United States, only to be arrested and have the clinic closed. When released on bail she reopened the clinic; this time she was arrested and sentenced to 30 days. But she was having her impact. In 1918 the courts ruled that doctors could give contraceptive information for pre-

[1]Suitters (1967).

[2]Sanger (1938).

Box 6.1 Margaret Sanger

Then one stifling mid-July day of 1912 I was summoned to a Grand Street tenement. My patient was a small, slight Russian Jewess, about twenty-eight years old, of the special cast of feature to which suffering lends a madonna-like expression. The cramped three-room apartment was in a sorry state of turmoil. Jake Sachs, a truck driver scarcely older than his wife, had come home to find the three children crying and her unconscious from the effects of a self-induced abortion. He had called the nearest doctor, who in turn had sent for me. Jake's earnings were trifling, and most of them had gone to keep the none-too-strong children clean and properly fed. But his wife's ingenuity had helped them to save a little, and this he was glad to spend on a nurse rather than have her go to a hospital.

The doctor and I settled ourselves to the task of fighting the septicemia. Never had I worked so fast, never so concentratedly. The sultry days and nights were melted into a torpid inferno. It did not seem possible there could be such heat, and every bit of food, ice, and drugs had to be carried up three flights of stairs.

Jake was more kind and thoughtful than many of the husbands I had encountered. He loved his children, and had always helped his wife wash and dress them. He had brought water up and carried garbage down before he left in the morning, and did as much as he could for me while he anxiously watched her progress.

After a fortnight Mrs. Sachs' recovery was in sight. Neighbors, ordinarily fatalistic as to the results of abortion, were genuinely pleased that she had survived. She smiled wanly at all who came to see her and thanked them gently, but she could not respond to their hearty congratulations. She appeared to be more despondent and anxious than she should have been, and spent too much time in meditation.

At the end of three weeks, as I was preparing to leave the fragile patient to take up her difficult life once more, she finally voiced her fears, "Another baby will finish me, I suppose?"

"It's too early to talk about that," I temporized.

But when the doctor came to make his last call, I drew him aside. "Mrs. Sachs is terribly worried about having another baby."

"She well may be," replied the doctor, and then he stood before her and said, "Any more such capers, young woman, and there'll be no need to send for me."

Margaret Sanger The Sophia Smith Collection, Smith College, Northampton, Mass.

Reprinted from *Margaret Sanger: An Autobiography* (New York: Norton, 1938). By permission.

Box 6.1 Continued

"I know, doctor," she replied timidly, "but," and she hesitated as though it took all her courage to say it, "what can I do to prevent it?"

The doctor was a kindly man, and he had worked hard to save her, but such incidents had become so familiar to him that he had long since lost whatever delicacy he might once have had. He laughed good-naturedly. "You want to have your cake and eat it too, do you? Well, it can't be done."

Then picking up his hat and bag to depart he said, "Tell Jake to sleep on the roof."

I glanced quickly at Mrs. Sachs. Even through my sudden tears I could see stamped on her face an expression of absolute despair. We simply looked at each other, saying no word until the door had closed behind the doctor. Then she lifted her thin, blue-veined hands and clasped them beseechingly. "He can't understand. He's only a man. But you do, don't you? Please tell me the secret, and I'll never breathe it to a soul. *Please!*"

What was I to do? I could not speak the conventionally comforting phrases which would be of no comfort. Instead, I made her as physically easy as I could and promised to come back in a few days to talk with her again. A little later, when she slept, I tiptoed away.

Night after night the wistful image of Mrs. Sachs appeared before me. I made all sorts of excuses to myself for not going back. I was busy on other cases; I really did not know what to say to her or how to convince her of my own ignorance; I was helpless to avert such monstrous atrocities. Time rolled by and I did nothing.

The telephone rang one evening three months later, and Jake Sachs' agitated voice begged me to come at once; his wife was sick again and from the same cause. For a wild moment I thought of sending someone else, but actually, of course, I hurried into my uniform, caught up my bag, and started out. All the way I longed for a subway wreck, an explosion, anything to keep me from having to enter that home again. But nothing happened, even to delay me. I turned into the dingy doorway and climbed the familiar stairs once more. The children were there, young little things.

Mrs. Sachs was in a coma and died within ten minutes. I folded her still hands across her breast, remembering how they had pleaded with me, begging so humbly for the knowledge which was her right. I drew a sheet over her pallid face. Jake was sobbing, running his hands through his hair and pulling it out like an insane person. Over and over again he wailed, "My God! My God! My God!"

venting and curing disease. This was the beginning of many changes.

Contraception remains a controversial issue. This is not surprising when one considers the profound emotions that have come to be associated with reproduction as the result of the long history of our attempt to survive as a species. Indeed, the fact that reliable birth control has not been available and practiced throughout most of human history accounts in part for our survival. But today, the survival of *Homo sapiens* may depend on a reversal of attitudes and a change in birth control practices. Although opposition to birth control programs is gradually diminishing, it is still formidable in certain parts of the world and in certain segments of our own society. Among married people in the United States who are at risk of an unplanned pregnancy, nine out of ten couples use some form of contraception.[3]

[3]Tietze 1979(a).

Preventing Unwanted Pregnancies

The overwhelming majority of people who currently use contraceptives do so for personal and private reasons: avoiding pregnancy out of wedlock; postponing pregnancy for economic and psychological reasons (as when the future of a marriage is uncertain); preventing the birth of a deformed or seriously ill child; and limiting family size because of economic, health, and other considerations.

Moral judgments in these matters vary widely. Although some people do not use contraceptives under any circumstances, most people approve of their use for certain purposes—"Their use is legitimate if a woman's life will be otherwise endangered by pregnancy"; "Married people may use them"; "People about to be married may use them"; "All adults may use them."

The use of contraceptives is becoming progressively more legitimate, despite opposition. If moral considerations were not involved, the realistic approach would be to prescribe contraceptives to the entire postpubertal population upon demand. The common fear is that dispensing information and contraceptive devices tacitly encourages youngsters to engage in intercourse. The large number of adolescent pregnancies indicates however, that lack of contraceptive knowledge or of the willingness to use contraception is not discouraging many teenagers from engaging in sex.

There are, on the other hand, countless educated and financially secure adults who become pregnant only unintentionally or for questionable reasons: to perpetuate family names, to please the grandparents, to bolster failing relationships, to "tie a partner down," to force partners into marriage, to conform socially, and so on.

The true motivations for having children are often rationalized or unconscious. Parents may view children as extensions of themselves. Through their children parents may seek to gratify their own unfulfilled childhood needs, to replay early dramas and this time to come out the "winner." Parents may regard their offspring as a means to fill their own inner void, to give meaning to their lives, and to consolidate a faltering sense of self-worth. Pregnancy may result from conscious or unconscious hostility, as an aggressive or punitive act against the sexual partner who does not want parenthood.

A surprising number of sophisticated unmarried young men and women risk unwanted pregnancies because taking contraceptive measures implies forethought. They feel that such precautions rob sex of its spontaneity and turn it into a calculated and unemotional activity. Such "refined" considerations, however, frequently conceal confusion and guilt about premarital sex. Consider, for instance, a couple in college. They are fond of each other and would like to have intercourse, but one or the other feels that they should not. They engage in progressively heavier petting, which ultimately does culminate in intercourse without contraceptives. Although stricken with remorse, they try to alleviate their guilt by claiming that they did not plan intercourse, that they could not help it. (Occasionally alcohol is used as the scapegoat in these encounters.) Premarital sex has definite moral implications that must be faced. A person may decide for or against it for a variety of reasons, but the difficult decision-making process cannot be evaded without risks to both parties involved.

Until very recently, little was known about contraceptive behavior among those who are sexually active but wish to avoid pregnancy. Sufficient data are now available to support these observations.[4] Among sex-

[4]For further information on current contraceptive behavior in the U.S. among various age, socioeconomic, ethnic, and religious groups, see Kantner and Zelnick (1972, 1973); Miller (1973); Shah, Zelnik and Kantner (1975); Westoff and Bumpass (1973); Zelnick and Kantner (1977); and Zelnik, Kim, and Kantner (1979).

ually active teenagers, birth control pills, condoms, and withdrawal are the most common methods; but about 37 percent report using no method at last intercourse. Also, about one-fourth of sexually active teenagers say they *never* use contraception. The pregnancy rates for teens who are sexually active before marriage reflect their failure to use contraception. Thirty-five percent of these women become pregnant before they are 19. Among unmarried college students the same methods are most popular. At least 10 percent of unmarried sexually active college students report *never* using contraceptives and, not surprisingly, one recent study of college seniors found that 9.5 percent of the women had become pregnant (and had abortions) during their first 3½ years of college.

Concerning married adults a particularly striking change in contraceptive behavior has occurred among American Catholics. The proportion of Catholic women using a contraceptive method other than rhythm increased from 30 percent in 1955 to 51 percent in 1965, and between 1965 and 1970 increased to 68 percent. Of the Catholic women who were married between 1970 and 1975, 90.5 percent used methods other than rhythm.[5]

There is now a great need for safer, more reliable means of contraception, a particularly poignant need, considering that approximately one-third of the births to married women in the United States are unintended—either unwanted or mistimed.[6] This number is even larger for teenage pregnancies. A survey of teens who had had unprotected intercourse revealed that only 7 percent wanted to become pregnant and an additional 9 percent did not mind if they became pregnant.[7] One study, based on interviews of all pregnant women who came to a

university medical center obstetrics clinic during a one-month period, revealed that only one-fourth of the cases involved planned pregnancies in which both parents looked forward to the baby's arrival. The remaining three-fourths fell into three groups of about equal size, according to whether their "rejection" was rated severe, moderate, or mild.

A woman considered to show "severe rejection of pregnancy" would be extremely agitated and upset about being pregnant and would state unequivocally her objections to having a child. She would generally either have practiced a "reliable" contraceptive method that had failed or would volunteer the information that she had attempted to have an illegal abortion or would have had an abortion had it been legal. (This study was conducted in California one year before the abortion law was liberalized.)

Women in the category of "moderate rejection of pregnancy" expressed ambivalence about their pregnancies, but gave very firm reasons for not wanting children. They also had generally been using contraceptive methods that had failed them.

Women in the category of "mild rejection of pregnancy" were unhappy about being pregnant at that particular time, though they declared previous plans to have children at some later date. The women were often using methods of contraception that they knew to be somewhat unreliable, such as the rhythm method. In summary, although varying degrees of regret over pregnancy were revealed in this study, only 25 percent of the sample definitely wanted the children that they were about to deliver.[8]

Even with legalized abortion, many women give birth to unwanted children because abortions are not readily available to them or because they find abortion personally unacceptable.

[5]Westoff and Jones (1977).
[6]Tietze (1979a).
[7]Shah, Zelnick, Kantner (1975).

[8]Yalom et al. (1968), p. 18.

Contraceptive Methods

The effectiveness of contraceptive methods is measured in terms of *failure rates.* For example, the condom has a theoretical failure rate of 3 percent, which means that three women out of a hundred would become pregnant in one year if the condom were the only method of contraception used during that year. Because people do not always use contraceptives as carefully as they should, actual failure rates are higher than the theoretical rates. The average failure rate associated with the condom in actual practice is 10 percent, which means that ten women out of a hundred would become pregnant in one year if the condom were the only method of contraception used during that year. The theoretical and actual failure rates for all the contraceptive methods are summarized in Table 6.2 at the end of the chapter.

The Pill

No drug since penicillin has been as rapidly and as widely accepted as *the pill,* the popular name for a number of commonly used oral contraceptives. The pill was first put on the market in 1960, and by 1977, 54 million women around the world were using it.

History

Early in this century researchers discovered that ovulation does not occur during the luteal, or postovulatory, phase of the menstrual cycle (*see* Chapter 4) or during pregnancy. It was also discovered that those are the times at which the levels of progesterone are highest. The connection seemed obvious—progesterone prevents ovulation. This conclusion was tested after progesterone was isolated and purified in the laboratory in 1934. When administered to rabbits, progesterone was shown to inhibit ovulation and to prevent pregnancy. Estrogen, another female sex hormone, was chemically isolated at about the same time, and by 1940 it was being used to treat certain menstrual disorders.

The next step in the development of an oral contraceptive was taken in 1954 when Carl Djerassi succeeded in synthesizing in the laboratory a group of steroid chemicals called *progestogens.* The term comes from the word "gestation" and refers to the ability of these synthetic compounds to bring about "pseudopregnancy," or fake pregnancy. The progestogens produce certain changes in the lining of the uterus (endometrium) and elsewhere in the reproductive system that are similar to changes seen during pregnancy. Once these changes have taken place a woman usually will not ovulate and cannot get pregnant. The synthetic compounds were found to be much stronger than natural hormones and could therefore be used in much smaller doses to prevent pregnancy.

Margaret Sanger and Katharine McCormack supported and financed the work of Gregory Pincus (sometimes called the "father of the pill") and coworkers J. Rock and C.R. Garcia in the search for a better method of contraception. This team of researchers began testing about 200 of these new compounds on animals. Several were found to be particularly effective as antifertility agents, and the first large-scale field trials on human beings of a contraceptive pill were initiated by Pincus and his colleagues in San Juan, Puerto Rico, in 1956. The drug was highly successful in these initial trials, and within a few years the era of "the Pill" had clearly begun.

Effects

Most contraceptive pills contain synthetic compounds resembling progesterone and estrogen. Studies of animals and humans have shown that progestogens tend to inhibit secretion of LH by the pituitary, while synthetic estrogens inhibit secretion of FSH. Both LH and FSH are essential to ovulation (*see* Chapter 4), and the pill is believed to work primarily by preventing ovulation. The only sure way to find out if this is the case is by microscopic examination of the ovaries and fallopian tubes of a woman who has been taking the pill.[9] Such observations have been made during hysterectomies (surgical removal of the uterus), and so far no eggs have been found in the tubes of women using the pill. It is still possible, however, that the woman may have ovulated earlier in her period or that she would have done so later.

Even if the pill does not prevent ovulation, it brings about other changes that can prevent pregnancy. There is some evidence, for instance, that the pill has a direct effect on the ovarian follicles and prevents maturation of the ova. It is also possible that the pill increases the rate at which the egg travels to the uterus, causing it to arrive there before it is sufficiently mature or before the lining of the uterus is ready to receive it.

A delicate balance of progesterone and estrogen is necessary if the lining of the uterus is to be receptive to implantation of the egg. However, changes in the endometrium have been seen in women taking the pill, and these changes may contribute to temporary infertility. In addition, the cervical mucus is changed by the pill (it becomes thicker and has a more acidic pH), and this may act as a barrier to the sperm on their way to the uterus.

Usage

The contraceptive pills commonly available (with a physician's prescription) contain a mixture of synthetic progestogens and estrogen compounds and thus are called *combination pills*. Each pill contains from 0.3 to 10.0 milligrams of the progestogen (depending on the specific compound used and on the manufacturer) and a much smaller amount of estrogen, from 0.02 to 0.15 mg per pill. These pills are usually taken for 20 or 21 days

of the cycle, beginning on the fifth day after the start of menstruation. If the pills are not begun until the sixth day, they are still effective, but if they are not started by the seventh or eighth day, there is a risk of failure.

After three weeks the pills are stopped. "Withdrawal bleeding" (considered by some not to be "true" menstruation because ovulation presumably has not occurred) usually begins three to four days after pill taking has stopped. The first day of withdrawal bleeding is considered the first day of the next cycle, and the pills are resumed on the fifth day thereafter. Common brand names for the pill are *Enovid, Ortho-Novum, Ovulen,* and *Norinyl.*

Some manufacturers now produce and recommend a 21:7 pill program. The pills are the same as before, but the woman takes 21 pills, then stops for seven days, then repeats the series again, regardless of when menstruation begins. The main advantage of this regimen is that the woman always starts taking her pills on the same day of the week. Another way to help a woman to remember to take the pill is to have her take one every day—21 hormone pills followed by seven placebo (inert) pills packaged in such a way as to prevent her from taking the wrong pill on any given day.[10]

Many new contraceptive pills are coming onto the market, but they differ from older types mainly in the specific proportions of the progestogen and estrogen compounds. The trend has been toward smaller doses of both of these compounds in order to reduce side effects. Whereas most early birth control pills contained 10.0 mg of progestogen, later this amount was reduced to 5.0 mg and then to

---

[9]There are indirect indications like elevation of the basal body temperature (BBT) and excretion of a progesterone metabolite called "pregnanediol."

[10]As there is relatively little difference in composition among most birth control pills, competitors have tried to improve packaging as a selling point. Some pills come in fancy plastic cases rather than in paper containers. Some packages have built-in calendars or other "reminders," and some have dispensers indicating which pill is to be taken each day by date, which eliminates the worrisome question: "Did I take my pill today?"

2.5 or 1.0 mg by several manufacturers. The progestogen content is as low as 0.30 to 0.50 mg in some pills. The estrogen content was reduced from the early 0.10–0.15 mg to 0.02–0.05 mg per pill. Until 1976 a "sequential" pill was also marketed. These pills were taken on a 20-day cycle, but the first 15 pills contained only estrogen; the remaining five contained estrogen and progesterone. This was supposed to be more like the normal sequence of hormonal events during the menstrual cycle, but the sequential pills had several serious drawbacks. They were less effective and were possibly associated with a risk of blood clotting and cancer. When this was discovered, the sequential pills were removed from the market.

The Mini-Pill

In 1973 the first so-called *mini-pill* was marketed, containing only 0.35 mg of progestogen and no estrogen. The mini-pill is slightly less effective than the combination pill, with a theoretical failure of 1.5 percent. The actual failure is closer to 5 or 10 percent. The irregular menstrual cycles and spotting associated with the mini-pill make it unacceptable to some women.

The "Morning-After" Pill

The "morning-after" pill was approved by the Food and Drug Administration (FDA) in 1973 for use in emergency situations only (rape, incest, or where, in the physician's judgment, the woman's physical or mental well-being is in jeopardy). It contains a potent estrogen, diethylstilbestrol (DES), taken in a dosage of 25 mg twice a day for five days. To be effective in preventing pregnancy treatment must begin within 72 hours of unprotected intercourse, preferably within 24 hours. The most common side effect, occurring in about 16 percent of women, is nausea and vomiting.[11] The drug may also cause cancer in female offspring of women who take the

drug while pregnant (*see* Chapter 7). The *FDA Bulletin* (May 1973) states:

There is at present no positive evidence that the restricted postcoital use of DES carries a significant carcinogenic risk either to the mother or the fetus. However, because existing data support the possibility of delayed appearance of carcinoma in females whose mothers have been given DES later in pregnancy, and because teratogenic and other adverse effects on the fetus with the very early administration recommended are ill understood, failure of postcoital treatment with DES deserves serious consideration of voluntary termination of pregnancy.

Effectiveness of the Pill

There is no question that birth control pills, when properly used, are the most effective contraceptive measure available today except for surgical sterilization. Taken as directed they are virtually 100 percent effective in preventing pregnancy by the second month of usage. Effectiveness is slightly less than 100 percent during the first month. If a woman does become pregnant while using the pill, it is probably because she failed to take it regularly. Forgetting one pill is not usually significant, provided that the woman takes two the next day, but there is a fair risk of failure if pills are skipped for two days or more. In order to minimize the risk of pregnancy in such cases, a woman who has missed two or more pills should rely on another form of contraception (such as condoms) for the remainder of the cycle. The actual failure rate of about 4 to 10 percent reflects the fact that women do make mistakes in taking their pills.

Side Effects[12]

The users of oral contraceptives are probably one of the largest and most closely-watched groups in the history of medical sci-

---

[11]Kuchera (1972), p. 177.

[12]For a more comprehensive review of this topic, see Rinehart and Piotrow (1979), Potts et al., (1975), and Rudel et al. (1973), chapter 3.

ence. The reason for such close scrutiny is the large number of reports of side effects and possible side effects. The most common complaints of users of the pill are *nausea, weight gain, headaches,* and *vaginal discharge.*

Nausea is an estrogen-dependent side effect, and pills with smaller amounts of estrogen (or none at all) may be recommended if the symptom persists. In many cases nausea and other side effects diminish and then disappear after two or three months of usage.

Weight gains occur in 5 to 25 percent of women, depending on the particular preparations used. Partly these gains result from greater fluid retention caused by progestogens. They can be countered by drugs (diuretics) or sometimes by switching to different birth control preparations. Most weight gains, however, are caused by actual accumulation of fat, especially in the thighs and breasts. They occur mainly in the first month of using the pill and are partly related to increased appetite, not unlike the increased appetite that occurs in pregnancy. The additional pounds gained in the first few months often remain as long as the woman is on the pill, however. Weight gains are most common with high-dosage combination pills.

It is not clear why headaches are more frequent among pill users; but there may be a connection with some of the documented physiological side effects of the pill, which include increased blood pressure, fluid retention, and alteration of thyroid, adrenal, and blood sugar control mechanisms.

There is substantial evidence for an increase in vaginal discharge and vaginal infections with the use of oral contraceptives. The pill alters the chemical composition of the cervical secretions and the composition of the vaginal flora (microorganisms that normally inhabit the vagina and are not pathogenic). These factors make the vagina more susceptible to fungus infections (*see* Chapter 7). Unlike nausea and other gastric complaints, this side effect is more likely to be related to prolonged progesterone therapy.

Breakthrough bleeding, or minor "spotting," while taking birth control pills is annoying but can often be remedied by switching to a different preparation.

Acne sometimes improves with oral contraceptives, but pigmentation of the face (*chloasma,* the so-called "mask of pregnancy") and eczema can be undesirable skin manifestations of prolonged pill usage.

Less common side effects include tenderness of the breasts, nervousness, depression, alterations in libido patterns, menstrual irregularities, and general malaise. Women with histories of liver disease (for example, hepatitis) may find the ailments reactivated by the pill, and they must take it only under strict medical supervision.

Subsequent Fertility

Contraceptive pills do not change subsequent fertility, although a few women may experience a delay in returning to normal fertility levels.[13] There is no evidence that prolonged use of the pills either hastens or postpones menopause.

Although the pill is known to be responsible for certain side effects, there are indications that some of the side effects blamed on the pill may be due to psychological rather than to physiological factors. In one study, for instance, the frequency of such complaints as dizziness, headache, nervousness, and depression was essentially the same for IUD users as for oral contraceptive users. In another study, women who thought they were receiving oral contraceptives but who were actually receiving placebos (inactive pills) reported a higher incidence of side effects, including decreased sexual drive. And in a third study of women using oral contraceptives, the researchers changed the color of the pills every six months and found a change in libido with each new pill color. Libido would gradually return to the previous level only to drop again with each color change.

[13]Potts et al. (1975); Vessey (1978).

Certain beneficial side effects of the pill have also been found and have led to their prescription even when contraception is not the major goal. For example, the pill can help relieve premenstrual tension and eliminate menstrual irregularity and pain, as well as other menstrual disorders. Pill use has also been linked with decreased incidence of ovarian cysts, rheumatoid arthritis, and iron deficiency anemia. In addition, some women report a general sense of well-being, as well as increased pleasure in sexual intercourse, while using the pill. This last effect is probably partially due to elimination of the fear of unwanted pregnancy.

When Not To Use the Pill

Alerting people to the possible problems associated with pill usage can decrease the incidence and severity of some pill-related side effects. Recent research has shown that the pill can have serious side effects that, while rare, can be fatal. Large-scale studies clearly indicate that there is a small, though statistically significant, increase in the incidence of blood clotting with subsequent complications in women who take the pill. A blood clot (*thrombus*) may, for instance, form in one of the deep veins of the leg in association with a local inflammation (*thrombophlebitis*). The clot may then break loose (as an *embolus*) and travel toward the lungs, where it may block a major blood vessel (as a *pulmonary embolus*). The result can be fatal. There is also a slightly greater chance of a blood clot in the brain (*thrombotic stroke*) among users of the pill. The risk of death from blood clots is between 1.5 and 4 per 100,000 users versus 0.4 per 100,000 among non-users.[14] The risks are greater than this for women 35 and older, and especially for

[14]Two British studies reported higher death rates (Beral and Kay, 1977; Vessey, McPherson, and Johnson, 1977); but other researchers are critical of the applicability of these studies to the United States. For a complete discussion see Rinehart and Piotrow (1979) and Tietze (1979b).

women with certain predisposing conditions. Women with histories of difficulties with blood clots are advised not to use contraceptive pills. However, it should also be noted that the incidence of deaths associated with pregnancy and labor is about four times greater than that associated with thromboembolic disease in users of the pill.

So serious are some of the pill's side effects that the Federal Food and Drug Administration now requires that each prescription for oral contraceptives contain a leaflet that describes the possible side effects as well as be labeled with a warning about smoking.

The warning about smoking is directed particularly at women 35 years of age and older. It is based on studies showing an increased risk of heart attack and other circulatory problems, such as stroke, for women who smoke while using oral contraceptives. Healthy women who do not smoke but who do use oral contraceptives double the risk of suffering a heart attack, compared with women who do not take the pill. However, users of the pill who also smoke, especially if they smoke 15 or more cigarettes a day, are three times more likely to die of a heart attack or of other circulatory disease than are users of the pill who do not smoke, and are ten times more likely to die of a heart attack or circulatory disease than are women who neither smoke nor use oral contraceptives. The risk of heart attack for women taking the pill increases with the amount of smoking and with age, and is higher in women with other conditions that may lead to heart attack, such as high blood pressure, high serum cholesterol levels, obesity, and diabetes.

In addition to the warning about smoking, the leaflet that now comes with each prescription of contraceptive pills points out several other possible dangers associated with the pill and makes the appropriate warnings:

Women who have had blood clotting disorders, cancer of the breast or sex organs, unexplained vaginal bleeding, a stroke, heart attack, or angina pectoris, or who suspect they may be pregnant should not take oral contraceptives.

Women with scanty or irregular periods (conditions that should be determined by a physician) are strongly advised to use another method of contraception, because if they use oral contraceptives they may have difficulty becoming pregnant or may fail to have menstrual periods after discontinuing the pill.

Possibly fatal (though rare) side effects include blood clots in the legs, lungs, brain, heart or other organs, cerebral hemorrhage, liver tumors that may rupture and cause severe bleeding, birth defects (if the pill is taken during pregnancy), high blood pressure, stroke, and gallbladder disease.

Estrogen, an ingredient in many oral contraceptives, causes cancer in certain animals and it may therefore also cause cancer in humans, though studies of women using the currently marketed pill do not confirm this. There is, however, evidence that estrogen use may increase the risk of cancer of the uterine lining in postmenopausal women [see Chapter 7].

Women who wish to become pregnant should stop using oral contraceptives and use a different method of birth control for a few months before attempting to become pregnant. This will help minimize the risk of birth defects associated with the use of sex hormones during pregnancy.

A woman should consult her physician before resuming use of the pill after childbirth, especially if she intends to breast-feed the baby, because hormones in the pill may be transferred to the infant through the mother's milk or may decrease the flow of milk.

The brochure that comes with oral contraceptives concludes: "Oral contraceptives are the most effective method, except sterilization, for preventing pregnancy. Other methods, when used conscientiously, are also very effective and have fewer risks. The serious risks of oral contraceptives are uncommon [rare] and 'the Pill' is a very convenient method of preventing pregnancy."

Intrauterine Devices

Another method of contraception that has proved to be highly effective is the *intrauterine device,* or IUD. Such devices have had a long history. Ancient Greek writings mention IUDs, and for centuries Arab camel drivers have used IUDs to keep their camels from becoming pregnant on long journeys. The camel drivers inserted a round stone in the uterus of each camel before a journey, and this practice is still used in some parts of the world.

A variety of intrauterine devices for women was popular during the nineteenth century, both for contraception and in the treatment of such gynecological disorders as displacement of the uterus. These devices fell into disrepute in the early twentieth century, but in 1930 the German physician E. Gräfenberg developed a ring of coiled silver wire; he inserted duplicates in 600 women for the purpose of contraception. He reported a failure rate of only 1.6 percent. In the next few years, however, several gynecologists published articles condemning the use of intrauterine devices on the grounds that they might lead to serious infection of the pelvic organs. That some of the most vocal critics had no experience with this method did not lessen their influence, and intrauterine devices again fell into disrepute until 1959. In that year two promising reports were published, one by the Israeli W. Oppenheimer, who had worked with Gräfenberg, and one by the Japanese physician A. Ishihama. Oppenheimer reported having used the Gräfenberg device in 1500 women over a period of 30 years with no serious complications and a failure rate of only 2.4 percent. Ishihama reported on the use of a ring developed by another Japanese physician, T. Ota, which had been used in 20,000 women, with a failure rate of 2.3 percent and no serious complications. Ota was the first to use plastic instead of metal in an intrauterine device.

These reports triggered a new enthusi-

Box 6.2 Early Contraception

People have been attempting to prevent unwanted pregnancies for millennia.[1] An Egyptian papyrus from 1850 B.C. prescribed various contraceptive methods. One consisted of crocodile dung mixed with a paste for use in the vagina. A mixture of honey and sodium carbonate was used to irrigate or plug the vagina.

Four centuries before Christ, Aristotle observed that "some prevent conception

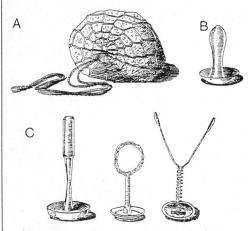

A sponge in a silk net has a string to facilitate withdrawal (above left). An intracervical pessary was used to plug the cervix (above right). Intrauterine pessaries extended into the uterus (below).

by anointing that part of the womb where the seeds fall with oil of cedar, or with ointment of lead, or with frankincense commingled with olive oil."

Many materials have been used to plug the cul de sac of the vagina and provide a barrier against sperm.[2] Some native Americans have used soft clay; and in other places leaves from various shrubs have been used. The Japanese have inserted paper; and the French, balls of silk. Various types of sponge and cotton balls have been used, sometimes in conjunction with medicated mineral oil or mild acid ointments to serve as spermicides. Many chemicals and drugs have been tried—with various levels of success—in different societies.

Intracervical pessaries made of gold, silver, or rubber have been used to plug the cervix. They were inserted by a doctor at the end of one menstrual period and removed at the onset of the next period. Intrauterine pessaries were longer and extended into the uterus to decrease the likelihood of their slipping out of place.

Needless to say, all of these methods were quite ineffective compared with modern contraceptives.

[1]Suitters (1967).
[2]Cooper (1928).

asm for intrauterine devices made of inert synthetic materials. By 1977 there were approximately 50 to 60 million IUDs in use throughout the world. China accounts for the largest number, with 40 million or more IUDs in use. Among married women in the United States of reproductive age about 6 percent use the IUD.

Effects

How the IUD prevents pregnancies in humans is unknown. Although considerable research has been devoted to it, the mechanism is unclear. Studies have shown that IUDs are effective in every species of animal tested, but the mechanism varies from species to species. In sheep, for example, the IUD has been shown to inhibit the movement of sperm, thus preventing fertilization. In cows, on the other hand, it is the functioning of the corpus luteum that is impaired; and, though fertilization may occur, implantation in the uterus is inhibited. In the rhesus monkey a fertilized ovum can be found in a tube but not in the uterus of an animal fitted with an IUD, suggesting that the site of action is the uterus rather than the fallopian tubes.

In humans, studies have shown *no systemic effects* (for example, no alteration of pituitary or sex hormones secretion) from the IUD. This finding is in marked contrast with those related to the pill, which affects the pituitary glands, ovaries, breasts, uterus, liver, and other organs. Examination of the ovaries and fallopian tubes of women fitted with IUDs shows normal morphology and functioning. Tissues and secretions of the cervix and vagina are also normal.

At present the most widely accepted theory of the contraceptive action of the IUD is that it causes cellular and biochemical changes to occur in the uterus. It seems likely that the fertilized egg and sperm are destroyed or consumed by special cells of the body's defense mechanisms. A related theory is that the IUD interferes with implantation in some way that is still unknown.

Types of IUDs

Intrauterine devices are made in various shapes and from various materials (Figure 6.1). A metal ring was the first widely used device, but it has the disadvantage that dilation of the cervix is required to insert or remove it. The same is true of the Ota ring, which is made of plastic and has been widely used in Japan and Taiwan. The Zipper ring is, however, made from coils of nylon thread and can be inserted through the cervix without prior mechanical dilation.

Most IUDs currently in use are made of plastic that is flexible and can be stretched into linear form to facilitate insertion. Once inside the uterus the device returns to its original shape. These devices all have nylon threads that hang down through the cervical opening into the vagina, enabling the wearer to check that the device is in place. The threads are small enough not to interfere with intercourse, however. These newer plastic

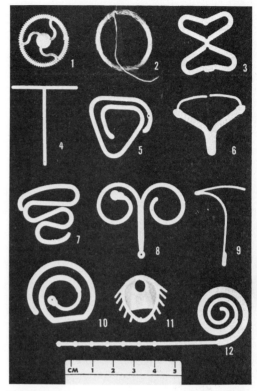

Figure 6.1 Various intrauterine devices: 1. Ota ring, 2. Zipper ring, 3. Birnberg Bow, 4. "T" device, 5. Ahmed, 6. K. S. Wing, 7. Lippes Loop, 8. Saf-T-Coil, 9. Copper "7," 10. New Margulies Spiral, 11. Dalkon-Shield, and 12. Gynecoil. From Rudel, Kincl, and Henzl. *Birth Control: Contraception and Abortion,* figure 4.1 (New York: The Macmillan Company, 1973), p. 158. Copyright © 1973 by Macmillan Publishing Co., Inc.

devices also contain small amounts of barium in the polyethylene, which allows for visualization of the device on an X-ray picture.

Very popular among the new plastic devices is the Lippes loop. It comes in four sizes, ranging from 22.5 millimeters in diameter (for women who have not had children) to 30 mm. It is easily inserted by a physician, who stretches the loop into linear form and pushes it into the uterus through a plastic tube that is inserted in the cervical opening (*see* Figure 6.2).

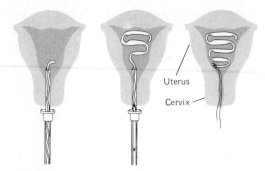

Uterus

Cervix

Figure 6.2 Insertion of the Lippes Loop.
Courtesy of Ortho Pharmaceutical Corporation.

Another relatively new device, the Copper 7, contains a small amount of copper that slowly dissolves in the uterus. (The amount of copper that dissolves daily is less than the amount recommended for a balanced diet and is therefore safe.) The Copper 7 is said to offer a higher rate of contraceptive protection than other IUDs, although how it does so is unknown. This device must be replaced every three years.

Finally, there is a recently developed IUD that contains progesterone, which is released at a slow, constant rate. The small amount of progesterone (.05 to .10 milligram per day) does not inhibit ovulation but alters the lining of the uterus in a way that prevents implantation. These progesterone-containing devices must be replaced every year.

Effectiveness

There is substantial agreement among various studies of the effectiveness of IUDs. Figures show a theoretical failure rate varying from 1 to 3 percent during the first year of use. In actuality the failure rate is approximately 5 percent. The failure rate tends to decline after the first year of use. One reason IUDs are usually more effective than some other contraceptive methods is that there is nothing either partner must remember to do to make it effective (although the woman

must check periodically to see that the device has not been expelled).

IUDs are also effective in preventing pregnancy in cases in which intercourse has taken place without any form of contraception being used.[15] Some doctors will insert IUDs under such circumstances within a few days after unprotected intercourse.

Side Effects[16]

The two most common side effects associated with IUDs are irregular bleeding and pelvic pain—seen in from 10 to 20 percent of the women using IUDs. However, as with most of the minor side effects associated with the pill, these problems tend to disappear after the first two or three months of use. Other side effects include bleeding, or "spotting," during the menstrual cycle and menstrual periods that may be heavier than usual after insertion of the IUD. Uterine cramps or general pelvic pain may also occur, and one study of 16,734 women reported that 833 had their IUDs removed for these reasons.[17] A lower incidence of cramping is reported with the progesterone containing IUD.

More serious and uncommon complications associated with the IUD are pelvic infection, perforation of the uterus, and problems during pregnancy. Normally these complications can be successfully treated, but in rare cases death can occur. The annual death rate associated with IUD usage is seven deaths per million users.

In the study mentioned above infection of the pelvic organs (uterus and tubes) was observed in 171 women, though hospital records showed that half of them had previous histories of such infections. As insertion of an IUD seems to exacerbate these conditions, women who have recently suffered pelvic infections are generally advised against using

---

[15]Lippes et al. (1978).
[16]For a more comprehensive review of this topic see Piotrow et al. (1979).
[17]Borell (1966), p. 53.

IUDs. Careful attention to antiseptic technique when inserting the IUD and careful screening for a history of prior infection can decrease the problem of infection. While it is more common for an infection to occur soon after insertion, it can occur two years or longer after insertion. The woman who has not had children appears to have a greater risk of infection than women who have had children. Perforation of the uterus is very rare (it occurs less than once in 1000 insertions). As with infection, the incidence of this complication varies with the skill and care of the physician inserting the device.

Women who accidentally become pregnant with the IUD in the uterus have an increased risk of several problems. Approximately 3 to 4 percent of these pregnancies will be ectopic. The rate for such pregnancies in nonusers is 0.4 percent. IUDs containing progesterone appear to be associated with a greater risk of ectopic pregnancy than other IUDs. If the pregnancy of the IUD user is a normal uterine pregnancy and the device is left in the uterus, approximately one-half of these pregnancies will spontaneously abort. This problem can be decreased by about 50 percent by removing the IUD. Also, if the device is left in place a rare complication, septic (infected) abortion, may occur. This problem can be avoided by removing the IUD when the pregnancy is discovered.

Spontaneous expulsion of IUDs can also be a problem, especially during the first year of use and especially with the smaller IUDs. In 1978 the FDA reported an overall expulsion rate of 4 to 18 percent during the first year after insertion.[18] Expulsion occurs most often in younger women and in women who have had no children and is more likely to occur during menstruation. When expelled into the vagina, the IUD is sometimes discarded with tampons or sanitary napkins

[18]*Second Report on Intrauterine Contraceptive Devices* (December 1978).

without the woman realizing it has been expelled. The various "tails" on IUDs enable women to check and verify that they are still in place.

There is no evidence so far that an IUD increases the risk of cancer of the cervix or uterus. Plastics of the type commonly used in IUDs have also been used extensively by surgeons for prosthetic devices in various parts of the body and have never been known to cause cancer. Some people have feared that a pregnancy that occurs with an IUD in the uterus might result in a deformed child. This is *not* true. The IUD does not cause an increased incidence of deformities.

Subsequent Fertility
IUDs appear to have no effect on subsequent fertility and can be easily removed by a doctor when a woman wishes to become pregnant. Studies have shown that after removal of IUDs 60 percent of sexually active women become pregnant within three months and 90 percent within one year. These figures are similar to those for women who have never used any form of contraception. There is some concern that future studies *might* find a slightly decreased fertility in former IUD users due to the increased incidence of pelvic infection in women that use this device. In some cases pelvic infection can cause sterility.

The Diaphragm
Until the advent of the pill and the intrauterine devices, the *diaphragm* and other mechanical devices designed to cover the cervix were widely used for contraception. Many women objected to the aesthetic or nuisance aspects involved in the repeated insertion and removal of these devices. Nevertheless, the absence of side effects related to the devices still outweigh the disadvantages as far as some women are concerned.

The diaphragm is the modern equivalent of an old idea. The history of contraception includes many examples of women in-

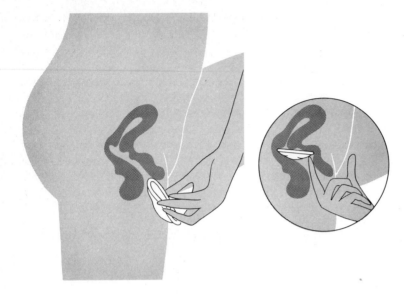

Figure 6.3   Insertion and placement of diaphragm. Courtesy of Ortho Pharmaceutical Corporation.

serting gums, leaves, fruits, seed pods, sponges, and similar items into their vaginas in attempts to block the sperm. The women of Sumatra, for example, molded opium into a cuplike shape and inserted it into the vagina. The women of Hungary used beeswax melted into round disks. The modern diaphragm was invented by a German physician in 1882.

Effects

The principle of the diaphragm is straightforward. A thin rubber dome is attached to a flexible, rubber-covered metal ring; it is inserted in the vagina so as to cover the cervix and thus to prevent passage of sperm into the cervical canal (see Figure 6.3). The inner surface of the diaphragm (that is, the surface in contact with the cervix) is coated with a layer of contraceptive jelly before insertion.[19]

Diaphragms come in various sizes and must be individually fitted by a physician. They are usually about three inches in diameter. In addition, following the birth of a

child or any other circumstance that may have altered the size and shape of her vaginal canal, a woman must be refitted.

The diaphragm and jelly must be inserted no more than six hours before intercourse in order for the jelly to be effective. Thus, unless a woman knows in advance that she is going to have intercourse on a particular occasion she may have to stop and insert the diaphragm in the midst of lovemaking or risk pregnancy. During menstruation it is unlikely that a woman will become pregnant. Nevertheless, some women use the diaphragm during menstruation to keep the lower portion of the vagina free of blood and to protect against the unlikely possibility of pregnancy.

When the diaphragm has been properly inserted, neither partner is aware of its presence during intercourse. After intercourse, the diaphragm should be left in place for six to eight hours and can be left in for as long as 24 hours. It should then be removed and washed. After drying it can be dusted with cornstarch if desired and stored in its plastic case. If it is reinserted, the contraceptive jelly must be applied.

[19]The effectiveness of the diaphragm is greatly decreased if the contraceptive jelly or cream is omitted.

Effectiveness

In theory the diaphragm and spermicide together make a very effective method of contraception, with an ideal failure rate of 3 percent. The actual failure rate for the diaphragm is closer to 17 percent. There are several reasons for this discrepancy between the failure rates. First, the diaphragm is not always used when it should be or is not inserted correctly. Second, even if it is coated with jelly and correctly in place before intercourse, it may have slipped by the time of ejaculation. The diaphragm may become dislodged during intercourse and expose the cervix, especially if it fits loosely, or if the woman participates in vigorous intercourse with multiple withdrawals of the penis in a position other than flat on her back (particularly when she is on top of the man).[20]

The diaphragm is most effective when certain guidelines are followed:

The diaphragm and jelly can be inserted six hours before sexual intercourse; however, if a woman has intercourse more than two hours after insertion of the diaphragm, she should leave the device in place and insert an applicator full of spermicidal jelly or cream.

An additional applicator of cream or jelly should be inserted every time intercourse is repeated before the diaphragm is to be removed. The diaphragm is removed six to eight hours after the *last* act of intercourse.

The diaphragm should be refitted after pregnancy, a weight change of ten or more pounds, pelvic surgery, and one year after the start of intercourse on a regular basis.

Spermicidal Substances

Contraceptive jellies, like those used with diaphragms, are among several *spermicidal,* or sperm-killing, *substances* available. Various foams, creams, jellies, and vaginal suppositories that kill sperm on contact are available in drugstores without a prescription and are simple to use. A plastic applicator is usually supplied for inserting the substance in the vagina. Vaginal foam, actually a cream packaged in an aerosol can, provides the best distribution of the spermicide in the vagina.

Effectiveness

Of the currently available products, Delfen and Emko are among the best. Vaginal foams are most effective when the following directions are followed:

Insert a *full* applicator of foam as soon before intercourse as possible, but no longer than 15 minutes before intercourse. (Some clinics recommend using two full applicators.)

Insert the spermicide while lying down and do not get up prior to intercourse.

Do not douche for at least eight hours after intercourse.

Insert another applicator full with *every* act of intercourse.

Use the preparation with a condom for a very safe method of contraception.

The least effective spermicides are the foaming vaginal tablets and suppositories that get distributed more unevenly in the vagina and depend partly on mixing with natural lubricants and dispersion during the movements of intercourse. If ejaculation occurs before sufficient lubrication, mixing, and dispersion have occurred, the spermicide will be of little benefit. Another drawback is that the foam tablets often cause temporary irritation of the vagina. The theoretical failure rate for foams is 3 percent. The actual usage failure rate is closer to 22 percent. The creams and jellies are even less effective. The tablets and suppositories are the least effective with a failure rate closer to 30 percent.

A new vaginal suppository being sold in the United States is the *Encare Oval.* It is advertised as a very effective contraceptive, claiming a failure rate of 1 percent. It is highly

---

[20]Calderone, ed. (1970), p. 234.

questionable whether or not additional studies will confirm this low failure rate. Until further studies can be done on the effectiveness of this suppository, it should be considered to have a failure rate similar to the foam—about 20 percent.

Douching

A time-honored but rather ineffective method of contraception is *douching,* that is, washing the sperm out of the vagina immediately after intercourse. This method is simple, requiring only a bidet or a douche bag and plain tap water. Various commercial products are available for douching; vinegar, lemon juice, soap, or salt may also be added to enhance the spermicidal properties of the solution. Actually these substances add little to the spermicidal properties of tap water and may irritate the vaginal tissues. The major disadvantage of douching as a contraceptive method is that within one or two minutes or *less* after ejaculation some sperm are already on their way up the cervical canal and beyond the reach of the douche. The woman must literally run from bed to bathroom if the douche is to be even mildly effective. The overall failure rate for the douche as a contraceptive method is about 40 percent.

Condoms

Another contraceptive device that has been making a comeback in recent years is the *condom* (*see* Figure 6.4). Condoms, also known as "rubbers," "prophylactics," "French letters," and "skins," are thin, flexible sheaths worn over the erect penis to prevent sperm from entering the vagina. They are the only mechanical birth control device used by men. Condoms used to be kept hidden under the pharmacist's counter and sold rather quietly; now that they have become more popular, they are produced in bright colors and can be openly displayed in drugstores in most states. Approximately 750 million are sold in the United States each year.

Condoms are cylindrical sheaths with a ring of thick rubber at the open end. The thickness of the sheath is about 0.0025 inch (0.00635 centimeter). Each is packaged, rolled, and ready for use. Some condoms also come lubricated. The sizes of the various condoms are approximately the same.

The advantages of condoms include their availability and the protection they offer against venereal diseases. One minor disadvantage is that they reduce sensation somewhat and thus may interfere with the sexual pleasure of the male or female. (To some

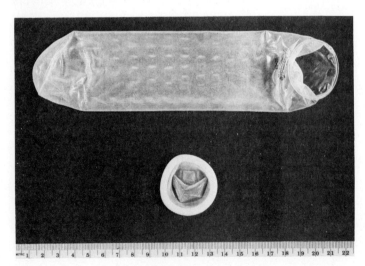

Figure 6.4 Condom, rolled and unrolled. Scale is in centimeters.

men this slight decrease in sensation might be desirable if it allows them to prolong sexual intercourse.) Putting on the condom interrupts sexual activity after erection but before the penis is placed in the vagina. This may be distracting, but many couples learn to integrate it smoothly into their sexual activity.

Effectiveness

Condoms have been known to burst under the pressure of ejaculation, to leak, or to slip off during intercourse, but they are quite effective if used consistently. Failure rates range from a theoretical 3 percent (with very consistent usage) to an actual 10 percent. Using condoms with spermicidal cream or foam increases their effectiveness. Condoms are most effective when the following precautions are taken:

The condom should be put on before the penis comes in contact with the vulva because the secretions from the Cowper's glands may contain sperm that escapes before ejaculation.

When putting the rubber on, leave about one half inch (1.3 centimeters) at the end (if no reservoir is built in already) to allow space for the ejaculate so that it does not break the condom. The air should be squeezed out of the space at the end of the condom.

To avoid leakage the male should withdraw from the vagina soon after ejaculation—before detumescence—and should hold on to the rim of the rubber while withdrawing from the vagina.

Condoms (or the diaphragm) should not be used with vaseline or any other petroleum-based product that can destroy rubber. If additional lubrication is desired, a water soluble lubricant such as K-Y jelly may be used. The use of the contraceptive foam for lubrication would have the extra advantage of increasing the safety of the condom.

Store condoms away from heat. Unopened condoms remain good for about two years if kept away from heat.

Withdrawal

Withdrawal of the penis from the vagina just before ejaculation (*coitus interruptus*) is probably the oldest known method of birth control and is still commonly used throughout the world.[21] The decline of the birthrate in western Europe from the late nineteenth century onward is believed to have been due to the popularity of this method.

The major problem with coitus interruptus is that it requires a great deal of motivation and willpower just at the moment when a man is most likely to throw caution to the winds. Nevertheless, this method costs nothing, requires no devices, and has no physiological side effects—although some people find it psychologically unacceptable.

When withdrawal is the only contraceptive measure taken, the theoretical failure rate is 9 percent. Actual failure rates range from 20 to 25 percent. This is partly because the male does not always withdraw quickly enough or far enough from the vulva and partly because small amounts of semen may escape before ejaculation.

The Rhythm Method

The *rhythm method* involves abstaining from intercourse during the presumed fertile period of the menstrual cycle. (*see* Chapter 4). This method is unreliable, particularly for women whose menstrual cycles are irregular. If a woman has kept track of her periods for 10 or 12 months she can calculate her fertile period from Table 6.1. The "safe period" for intercourse includes only those days not included in the "fertile period."

---

[21]As we mentioned at the beginning of this chapter there is reference to this method in *Genesis* 38:8–9: "Then Judah said to Onan, 'Go in to your brother's wife, and perform the duty of a brother-in-law to her, and raise up offspring for your brother.' But Onan knew that the offspring would not be his; so when he went in to his brother's wife he spilled the semen on the ground, lest he should give offspring to his brother."

Table 6.1 The Fertile Period

Shortest Cycle (Days)	Day Fertile Period Begins
22	4
23	5
24	6
25	7
26	8
27	9
28	10
29	11
30	12
31	13
32	14
33	15
34	16

Longest Cycle (Days)	Day Fertile Period Ends
22	12
23	13
24	14
25	15
26	16
27	17
28	18
29	19
30	20
31	21
32	22
33	23
34	24

The safe and unsafe days are calculated by subtracting 18 from the woman's shortest cycle and 10 from her longest cycle. Thus, for the woman with a regular 28-day cycle the fertile period extends from day 10 through day 18. For women with cycles ranging from 24 to 32 days, the periods of abstinence must extend from the sixth through the twenty-second day, an unacceptable span for many couples. Nevertheless, to have intercourse during this period is akin to playing Russian roulette, for there is no way of knowing in advance whether or not "the chamber is loaded."

There are several ways of making the rhythm method more effective. One is based on changes in a woman's body temperature, which goes up slightly at the time of ovulation. In order to pinpoint the time of ovulation and fertility by this method a woman must take her temperature immediately upon awakening every morning before arising, moving about, eating, drinking, or smoking. An increase of 0.4°F (0.2°C) above the average temperature of the preceding five days indicates ovulation if the increase is sustained for three days. Minor illnesses like colds and sore throats, however, can throw off the temperature curve. Also, some women do not have their temperature rise even though they have ovulated.[22]

A BBT (basal body temperature) chart does indicate when ovulation has occurred, but it is not helpful before ovulation. So if the BBT chart (see Figure 6.5) is to be used to determine the "safe period," a woman should abstain from intercourse from the end of her menstrual period until three days after the time of ovulation.

A device called the ovutimer has been developed by researchers at the Massachusetts Institute of Technology. It can be used to make the rhythm method more reliable and can also be used by couples who want to know when the fertile days are so they can try to conceive a child. The ovutimer is a 7-inch (17.8-centimeter) long plastic device that, when inserted into the vagina, determines the time of ovulation by measuring the stickiness of cervical mucus, which becomes thin and watery at the time of ovulation.

The ovutimer and the BBT method promise to make the rhythm method more reliable, but even when the time of ovulation is known, the success of the rhythm method depends on a couple's ability and motivation to follow directions exactly. Large-scale studies show actual failure rates ranging from 15

[22]Moghissi (1976).

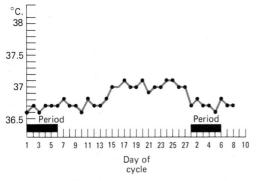

Figure 6.5   BBT chart showing ovulation about the thirteenth day (36°C = 98°F). From *International Planned Parenthood Federation Medical Handbook*, p. 62. Reprinted by permission of the International Planned Parenthood Federation, 18–20 Lower Regent Street, London SW1, England.

to 35 percent when the rhythm method is the only contraceptive method used.

Cervical Mucus

To use the *cervical mucus method* a woman must watch the changes in the cervical mucus that occur during the monthly cycle in order to determine when intercourse is safe or unsafe.[23] She can study the mucosa by checking her toilet paper and underpants or by putting a finger into her vagina. Some women insert a speculum (a device for separating the vaginal walls) into the vagina in order to judge the state of the mucus. The changes in the cervical mucus should be written down every day on a calendar. For a few days after menstruation many women have a few ''dry'' days during which no noticeable discharge is present and there is a sensation of dryness in the vagina. Some women have no dry days after menstruation. The ''dry'' days are considered relatively safe for intercourse. Within a few days after menstruation is over a mucus discharge is produced which is white or cloudy and tacky. Gradually the mucus

[23]This method has been developed by Evelyn and John Billings who have described it thoroughly in their book, *Atlas of the Ovulation Method.*

changes to be clear and stretchy—rather like the consistency of egg white. This is called the peak symptom and usually lasts for one or two days. Generally, a woman ovulates around 24 hours after the last peak symptom day. After the last peak symptom day the mucus changes to cloudy and tacky. Intercourse must not occur beginning with the first day in which mucus is present until four days after the last peak symptom day. By that time the egg will no longer be capable of fertilization and a woman can engage in intercourse without becoming pregnant. The actual failure rate for this method appears to be approximately 15 to 25 percent. At present the research on the effectiveness of this method is limited.

Sterilization

Voluntary surgical sterilization has become increasingly popular in recent years among both men and women in the United States and in countries like India, where sterilization (especially for males) has been encouraged by the government. In fact, the acceptance rate of sterilization by people in the United States in the last half of their reproductive years (older than age 29) has increased significantly in recent years. It is estimated that more than one million surgical sterilizations are now being done in the United States each year.

Male Sterilization

The operation that sterilizes the male is the *vasectomy,* a simple procedure that can be done in a doctor's office in about 15 minutes. A small amount of local anesthetic is injected into each side of the scrotum, and a small incision is made on each side in order to reach the vas deferens (*see* Chapter 2). Each vas is then tied in two places, and the segment between is removed in order to prevent the two cut ends from growing together again. After this operation sperm will no longer be able to travel through the vas from the testes. The sperm, which continue to be produced but are now trapped in the testes, are simply reabsorbed by the body as they degenerate.

No change in sexual functioning occurs as a result of vasectomy. The sex glands continue to function normally, secreting male sex hormones into the blood. Ejaculation still occurs because the seminal fluid contributed by the testes through the vas only accounts for about 10 percent of the total volume. The only difference is that the semen will be free of sperm. Sperm may still be present two or three months after a vasectomy because they are stored in the reproductive system beyond the site of the vasectomy, but these sperm can be flushed out with water or with a sperm-immobilizing agent during the vasectomy. Once these remaining sperm are gone, vasectomy is virtually 100 percent effective as a birth control measure.

Vasectomy does not interfere physiologically with a man's sexuality. His sexual response and orgasm after vasectomy are the same as before. Some men feel a new sense of freedom after being sterilized, but others experience negative psychological effects—possibly because vasectomy is usually considered a permanent form of sterilization. However, improved surgical techniques are changing this, and vasectomy may eventually become a reversible or temporary form of sterilization. The reversal procedure is not simple, but the cut ends of the vas can be reunited surgically. Using pregnancy of partner as a measure of success, some surgeons report rates of reversal of vasectomy as low as 18 percent, others as high as almost 80 percent.[24] Another method of making vasectomy reversible consists of inserting a small valve in the vas. The valve allows the flow of sperm to be turned on or off when desired. These valves are still in the experimental stage, and the truly reversible vasectomy is still in the future, but there are several reasons

[24]Silber and Cohen (1978).

why some men request that their vasectomy be undone: remarriage after divorce or death of wife, death of one or more children, improved economic condition, and removal of negative psychological effects of vasectomy.

Female Sterilization

The most common surgical procedure for sterilizing women is often called "tying the tubes" or *tubal ligation*. Tying or cutting the fallopian tubes prevents eggs from reaching the uterus and sperm from reaching the eggs in the fallopian tubes. The eggs that continue to be ovulated are simply reabsorbed by the body as they degenerate. Female sterilization used to be a major surgical procedure involving hospitalization, general anesthesia, and all the associated costs and risks. The search for simple, effective, and inexpensive sterilization procedures, however, has led to the development of more than a hundred techniques for cutting, closing, or tying the tubes.

There are still medical situations in which a major abdominal operation may be necessary for female sterilization, but the current trend is in the direction of an outpatient procedure performed under local anesthetic. It is possible to approach the fallopian tubes through the vagina rather than through the abdominal wall and to perform the sterilization with a *culdoscope*. This instrument is basically a metal tube with a self-contained optical system that allows the physician to see inside the abdominal cavity. Sterilization using the procedure called *culdoscopy* involves puncturing the closed end of the vagina and, after locating the tubes with the culdoscope, tying and cutting them.

In addition to the traditional methods of tying the tubes, a variety of clips, bands, and rings have been developed for blocking the tubes. Chemicals that solidify in the tubes, caps that cover the ends of the tubes, and lasers that heat and destroy a portion of the tubes are among the sterilization methods currently under investigation. Various plastic and ceramic plugs have also been designed

Table 6.2 Summary of Contraceptive Methods

Method	Ideal Failure Rate[1]	Actual Failure Rate[1]	Advantages	Disadvantages
Birth control pills	0.34%	4–10%	Easy and aesthetic to use	Continual cost, side effects; requires daily attention
IUD	1–3%	5%	Requires little attention; no expense after initial insertion	Side effects, particularly increased bleeding; possible expulsion
Diaphragm with cream or jelly	3%	17%	No side effects: minor continual cost of jelly and small initial cost of diaphragm	Repeated insertion and removal; possible aesthetic objections
Vaginal foam	3%	22%	Easy to use: no prescription	Continual expense
Douche	?	40%	Inexpensive	Inconvenient; possibly irritating
Condom	3%	10%	Easy to use: helps to prevent venereal disease	Continual expense; interruption of sexual activity and possible impairment of gratification
Withdrawal	9%	20–25%	No cost or preparation	Possible frustration
Rhythm	13%	21%	No cost, acceptable to Roman Catholic Church	Requires significant motivation, cooperation, and intelligence; useless with irregular cycles and during postpartum period
Cervical mucus	?	15–25%[2]	No cost	Requires careful observation, cooperation
Vasectomy	0.15%	0.15%	Permanent relief from contraceptive concerns	Possible surgical/medical/psychological complications
Tubal ligation	0.04%	0.04%	Permanent relief from contraceptive concerns	Possible surgical/medical/psychological complications

[1]Hatcher et al. (1978).
[2]Klaus, et al. (1977); Wade et al. (1979); World Health Organization (1978).

for blocking the tubes, and one still-experimental plug appears to be both effective and removable—allowing for reversibility of sterilization.

Most methods currently being used to sterilize women are almost 100 percent effective and, like vasectomy, have no physiological effect on sexual functioning. Female sterilization, like male sterilization, is considered a permanent method of birth control. But, recent advances have resulted in an increased success at reconnecting the tubes. One study reports a pregnancy rate of 80 percent after reversal.[25] Generally, the rates of pregnancy after reversal are 25 to 50 percent depending on which method of sterilization was used and the skill of the doctor.

In addition to sterilization by tying the tubes, many women have been sterilized by the surgical procedure known as *hysterectomy* (surgical removal of the uterus). It is estimated that one-third of all women in the United States have had a hysterectomy by age 65, but charges have been made that the operation is overused. The operation is performed in one of two ways: through an incision in the abdominal wall or through the vagina. The ovaries are left in place (unless there is some medical reason for their removal), so the secretion of female sex hormones remains normal. Hysterectomy is usually not performed solely as a means of sterilization, however, but is done because of some medical problem, such as tumor removal.

See Table 6.2 for a comparison of the contraceptive methods discussed in this chapter.

[25]Ibid.

Abortion

Abortion has been used as a form of birth control for thousands of years in numerous cultures, whether or not the procedure was considered legal. In the United States in the mid-1800s, for instance, abortion was relatively common: It is estimated that there was one abortion for every five or six live births. Abortionists advertised in newspapers and frequently sold drugs that were supposed to induce abortion. Laws were gradually enacted against abortion in the last century, but these laws were not always strictly enforced. Illegal abortions continued to be performed. Kinsey found that about 23 percent of the white women he sampled had an illegal abortion by the time they finished their reproductive years. Illegal abortions are much more dangerous to the woman than legal abortions are. In 1973 abortion was legalized in the United States, and by 1977 legal abortions were estimated at 1.3 million per year. Meanwhile, illegal abortions declined from an estimated 530,000 in 1970 to 10,000 per year.

Even though legal, abortion has not become a primary means of birth control. As a backup procedure when contraception fails, however, abortion is becoming increasingly popular, and although it remains a highly controversial issue on ethical and moral grounds (*see* Chapter 15), it is widely practiced in the Soviet Union, parts of eastern and central Europe, and Japan. It is less common in some of the Catholic countries of Europe and South America.

The method used for abortion in the United States is usually determined by the length of the pregnancy. During the first trimester, abortion is performed by mechanically removing the contents of the uterus through the cervix. Evacuation is sometimes used as late as the twentieth week, but during the second trimester, abortion is usually performed by stimulating the uterus to expel its contents—in effect, inducing a miscarriage.

Although abortion does present risks,

the overall death rate due to abortion is relatively low. The death rate for legal abortions performed during the first trimester is 1.7 deaths per 100,000 abortions. Almost 90 percent of abortions in the United States are performed during the first trimester. In the second trimester the figure increases to 12.2 per 100,000. This death rate is slightly higher than the death rate due to childbirth complications: 11.2 per 100,000.

Vacuum Aspiration

We have already mentioned (*see* Chapter 4) the use of suction techniques for "menstrual extraction." *Vacuum aspiration* has become very popular for first-trimester abortions for a number of reasons. It can be performed on an outpatient basis quickly and at a relatively low cost. Prior to eight weeks of pregnancy, minimal or no anesthesia may be required, and it is often unnecessary to dilate the cervix mechanically.

Following preparation similar to that for a pelvic examination a suction curette is passed through the cervical opening into the uterus. Suction curettes come in various shapes and sizes, but most are essentially a plastic tube with a hole at each end and a hole on the side. One end is inserted into the uterus (*see* Figure 6.6) and the other end is attached to a suction pump. The hole on the side can be covered and uncovered as required to increase or decrease the vacuum pressure within the uterus. The suction tip is rotated gently within the uterus until, on examination, all tissue related to conception has been eliminated. The curette is then removed and, in some clinics, a uterus-contracting drug (for example, oxytocin; *see* Chapter 5) may be administered to minimize bleeding and ensure complete evacuation of the uterus. The entire procedure (excluding examination and preparation time) can usually be performed in less than two minutes.

Complications of vacuum aspiration are relatively uncommon, but may include per-

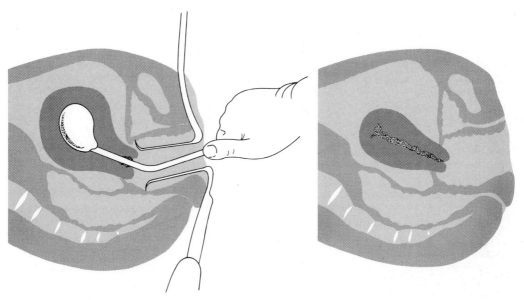

Figure 6.6 (*Left*) initial insertion of angled suction curette into the cervical canal; (*right*) uterus contracted after completion of evacuation of the uterus.

foration of the uterus, hemorrhage, uterine infection, cervical lacerations, and drug reactions, if anesthetics or other drugs are used. The specific incidence of these complications varies with the skill and experience of the physician, as well as the state of health of the woman undergoing the abortion.

Dilation and Curettage (D and C)[26]

Another method of abortion sometimes used during the first trimester is dilation of the cervix and curettage (scraping) of the uterus. The first step, *cervical dilation,* can be accomplished by passing a series of progressively larger metallic dilators (curved rods) through the cervical opening, but in recent years a less painfull (if slower) method has become popular—*laminaria sticks*. These sticks, which are made from compressed seaweed, are inserted into the cervix. As they absorb cervical secretions they expand to five times their dry

size in about 24 hours. When the cervix is enlarged sufficiently, a *curette* (a bluntly serrated metal instrument) is inserted and used to scrape the tissues off the inner walls of the uterus. In more advanced pregnancies dilation may have to be more extensive in order to allow passage of a forceps that can be used mechanically to grasp the fetal tissues for removal. The possible complications of an abortion by the D-and-C method are the same as those of vacuum aspiration.

Dilation and Evacuation (D and E)

After the twelfth week of pregnancy, abortion becomes an increasingly serious procedure, and the rate of complications increases. One abortion technique that is often used between the thirteenth and twentieth weeks of pregnancy is *dilation and evacuation.* D and E is similar to D and C and the suction method, although the fetus is larger at this stage and not as easily removed as during the first trimester. Once dilation is achieved, suction, forceps, and curettage are used. D and

---

[26]D and C is also employed for the diagnosis and treatment of a number of pelvic disorders.

Box 6.3 New Female Contraceptives

A variety of promising new contraceptive methods are being developed for use by women.

Plastic vaginal rings that are impregnated with progestins have been proved to be 98 percent effective in preventing ovulation.[1,2] The rings are slightly smaller than a regular diaphragm and are more easily inserted. They are placed in the vagina on the fifth day of the menstrual period and are left in place for the next 21 days. Menstruation begins a few days after the ring is removed. Each ring can be used up to six months. The progestins in the rings are released slowly and absorbed through the vaginal wall into the woman's bloodstream. The hormones prevent ovulation, change the endometrium, and thicken the cervical mucus. There are few side effects, and the ring does not interfere with intercourse.

Instead of taking a pill every day, it is possible that a safe, long-acting injection will be developed for contraceptive purposes. One such preparation is already being used in some parts of the world but has not been approved for use in the United States.[2] Each dose of the preparation (brand name, Depo Provera) contains 150 milligrams of progesterone, enough to prevent ovulation for 90 days.

Side effects include irregular menstrual bleeding and an unpredictable period of infertility following cessation of the shots. The FDA's primary reason for disapproval of this drug for long-term contraception is based on studies showing that it is related to an increased incidence of premalignant breast tumors in dogs. The drug's effect on humans is still being investigated.

HCG—human chorionic gonadotropin—is the hormone produced by the zygote that travels to the woman's body and signals: "You're pregnant." HCG causes the corpus luteum to continue producing estrogen and progesterone; and these two hormones prevent menstruation while preparing the endometrium for the early phases of pregnancy. Antibodies to HCG are being developed which allow the female body to be immunized to its own HCG.[1] Women with antibodies to HCG no longer respond to the HCG mechanism that signals the body to skip menstruation and to begin the hormonal developments of pregnancy. When antifertility vaccines become available, immunized women will menstruate each month, whether their ova are fertilized or not.[2]

[1]Shapiro (1977)
[2]Hatcher et al. (1978)

E is considered to be a simple, effective, and relatively inexpensive procedure, and recent studies suggest that, up to the twentieth week, D and E is as safe as or safer than some of the other procedures that are commonly used during the second trimester.

Saline Abortions

During the second trimester, abortion is commonly induced by the injection of a concentrated salt solution into the uterus. It should be noted that *saline abortion* is more complicated for the woman than is abortion in the first trimester. The fourth month of pregnancy is a particularly difficult time for an abortion. The pregnancy is too far along to allow for a safe, simple aspiration; but the uterus is not yet large enough to allow the physician to easily locate the proper place in the abdominal wall in which to insert a needle for saline injection. Because of this problem many physicians are reluctant to perform saline abortions earlier than the sixteenth week of pregnancy.

Box 6.3   Continued

Another promising new method for the future is a zinc-medicated and acidically buffered collagen sponge.[3] Collagen is a natural protein prepared from bovine skin and Achilles tendons. Collagen has a very high fluid binding capacity and the collagen sponge can easily absorb several ejaculates. The device is shaped somewhat like a diaphragm and inserted into the upper vagina where it covers and blocks the cervical opening. The acidity of the vagina and the sponge destroys the sperm which become trapped in the sponge. In addition, the sponge also has some spermicidal effects because of the zinc additives. The sponge can be removed after 8 hours from intercourse and washed. It can then be reinserted and left in place for 3 to 5 days since it does not irritate the vaginal mucosa. The collagen sponge has a beneficial side effect: the zinc appears to prevent genital herpes from replicating. For best results, it is used in conjunction with spermicides.

[3]Chvapil (1976, pers comm)

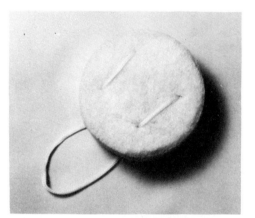

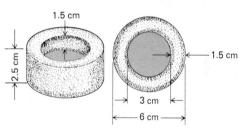

The collagen sponge and applicator. Courtesy of Dr. M. Chvapil, Section of Surgical Biology, College of Medicine, University of Arizona.

The mechanism of action of the saline abortion is not known. The method is quite straightforward. After examination (to verify exact location of the uterus) and sterile preparation of the abdominal skin, a needle is inserted through the abdominal and uterine walls using local anesthesia. About 200 cubic centimeters (less than seven ounces) of amniotic fluid is removed (compare the procedure for amniocentesis described earlier). An injection of 200 cubic centimeters of a 20 percent sodium chloride (common salt) solution is then introduced into the uterus. Some clinics send the woman home to await the onset of uterine contractions, while others keep all saline abortion patients hospitalized for observation until the abortion is complete. Contractions usually begin within 12 to 24 hours, and about 80 percent of women deliver the fetus and placenta within 48 hours of the injection. Others take longer and may require another injection of saline. Some physicians administer oxytocin to stimulate more vigorous labor contractions.

Box 6.4 New Male Contraceptives

At present males have only three methods they can use to prevent unwanted pregnancies: withdrawal, the condom, and vasectomy. What changes are likely to occur in the next decade or two? Expert opinions vary considerably. Some researchers believe that effective methods will be available within a few years. Others predict that nothing will be available until after the year 2000.[1]

There are promising leads and many researchers are working on male contraceptive methods; but the problems of controlling millions of sperm without damaging other cells, causing genetic mutations, or reducing testosterone output are considerable. The current guidelines on clinical experimentation and drug testing in the United States will probably introduce long time lags between the development and wide usage of any new male method.

The Chinese have reported very rapid progress in developing and testing a male method that they claim is 99.8 percent effective and has no serious side effects. At first it was noted that men had decreased fertility in certain areas of China in which unrefined cottonseed oil was part of the daily diet. Gossypol in the cottonseed oil appears to interfere with sperm production in the seminiferous tubules, resulting in nonviable sperm. For the past several years, thousands of Chinese men have been using gossypol for birth control, with apparent success. In addition, the men have been reported to regain fertility after they stop taking gossypol. This contraceptive method would not be so rapidly adopted in the United States because gossypol is known to have several toxic effects, hence extensive testing would be needed.

Numerous researchers have been studying other drugs. Almost every chemical that reduces sperm count has also had toxic effects on the body. However, some drugs—such as danazol—have had

[1]Djerassi (1979).

Uncommon but severe complications are known to occur with saline abortion. Most serious is *hypernatremia* ("salt poisoning"). Early symptoms of hypernatremia are abdominal pain, nausea, vomiting, and headache. More serious results, if correct treatment is not instituted promptly, can include high-blood pressure, brain damage, and death.

Other complications of saline abortion include intrauterine infection and hemorrhage. Delayed hemorrhage (days or weeks after the abortion) occurs most commonly in association with the complication of retained placenta—that is, in instances where the fetus is successfully aborted but part or all of the placenta remains behind. In such cases curettage and blood transfusion may sometimes be required.

Prostaglandin Abortions

More than 45 years ago it was reported that injections of human semen into the uterus cause vigorous contractions of uterine muscles. By 1935 it was shown that the substance responsible for this action is produced by the prostate gland and seminal vesicles, and it was thus named *prostaglandin*. Later it was discovered that there are more than a dozen chemically related prostaglandins, and some of them can now be synthesized in the laboratory.

Because prostaglandins cause uterine contractions, they can be used to induce abortion. They are usually injected directly into the uterus but can also be injected into the bloodstream or into a muscle. Laminaria sticks are sometimes used with prostaglandins

Box 6.4   Continued

promising results in reducing male fertility.[2] Danazol is a synthetic hormone with a structure similar to the progestins. It prevents the release of FSH and LH from the pituitary and it tends to have masculinizing effects on the body, rather than feminizing effects. In preliminary studies, men have been given danazol in conjunction with testosterone for 6 months at a time. The drug

A sperm coated with T-mycoplasmas (× 12,900). From Fowlkes, DM, Dooher, GB, O'Leary, WM: Evidence by scanning electron microscopy for an association between spermatozoa and T-mycoplasmas in men of infertile marriage. *Fertility and Sterility* 26:1203, 1975. [Fig. 5, p. 1207]. Reproduced with the permission of the publisher, The American Fertility Society.

caused sperm counts to drop to 0.5–5 percent of normal levels in the majority of men tested. The men did not lose sexual function, and they regained normal fertility within 5 months after the end of treatment.

A microorganism called T-mycoplasmas has been linked to infertility in some men who are naturally infertile. In contrast to normal sperm, the sperm from men with T-mycoplasmas are coated with spherical T-mycoplasmas microorganisms and have coiled tails.[3] The sperm from the men with T-mycoplasmas cannot move as fast as sperm from men without the microorganism. Men who have T-mycoplasmas can become fertile again after receiving antibiotics that destroy the microorganisms. Because T-mycoplasmas and the active chemical from it cause infertility, they may offer possible new approaches to male contraceptive methods.

[2]Shapiro (1977:289).
[3]Fowlkes et al. (1975a, b).

because by dilating the cervix they reduce the number of uterine contractions necessary to expel the fetus. This can hasten the abortion of the fetus and the placenta. Some success has also been reported in bringing about abortion after insertion of a prostaglandin suppository into the vagina. This procedure has been used to induce first- and second-trimester abortions, but suction is still the primary procedure for first-trimester abortions in the United States.

Complications with prostaglandin abortion include nausea, vomiting, and headache, with at least 50 percent of women experiencing one or more of these side effects. These effects are temporary, rarely serious, and can be easily treated. Complications such as hemorrhage, infection, and uterine rupture (possible with all types of second-trimester abortion) are infrequent with prostaglandin abortion. One major drawback is that the proportion of live births is higher with prostaglandin than with saline abortion, especially after the twentieth week (45 live births out of 607 abortions, in one recent study). For this reason some physicians do not like to perform abortions after the twentieth week. When they do, they sometimes use saline, and some have reported success in using a combination of prostaglandin and urea. Urea can also be used alone to induce abortion. It has the same effects as saline but is slightly less effective than either saline or prostaglandin.

Chapter 7

Sexual Disorders

Since everyone experiences physical ill health and mental turmoil at one time or another, it is realistic to view a certain amount of illness as a natural part of life. In addition to the ordinary wear and tear on our bodies and minds, we are all subject to certain common ailments, as well as to some less common and more serious disorders. Some knowledge of these matters is helpful in allaying worry and discomfort as well as in alerting us to the presence of danger signals.

A vast number of disorders may affect the sex organs and sexual functioning. The sex organs may also suffer secondary effects from general systemic diseases. Several medical specialties are involved in the treatment of these various disorders. *Gynecologists* deal with disorders of the female sexual or reproductive system. Most male disorders are treated by *urologists*.

We shall deal primarily with three types of sexual disorder in this chapter: first, venereal diseases and other sexually transmitted diseases; second, common bothersome conditions; and third, certain serious conditions the early recognition of which may save lives.

Sexual Hygiene

We wish to mention, in connection with disorders of the reproductive system, some general principles for the cleansing and care of the genitals and related tissues. Specific preventives of disease, if these are available, are mentioned in conjunction with specific diseases later in this chapter.

It is fair to say that any person who practices regular and thorough cleansing of the genitals and related areas is less likely to be afflicted with some of the infectious diseases we will describe. As we will discuss in Chapter 10, one's attractiveness as a sexual partner may be enhanced by specific attention to matters of sexual hygiene. It is not by any means necessary to equate hygiene with the elimination or covering up of natural odors. A large-scale advertising campaign in recent years has attempted to convince people that vaginal deodorant sprays and similar products are a necessity for sexual hygiene. Actually, these products should be avoided as some of them have been found to contain chemical irritants, and there may also be allergic reactions associated with their use in some people. There is a difference, however, from both hygienic and aesthetic viewpoints, between the causes and effects of fresh and stale odors. The fresh and often attractive odor of someone who bathes regularly is related to a combination of the secretions of various glands located on and around the genitalia and, perhaps, a slight residue of unscented or mildly scented soap. The stale and often offensive odor of someone who bathes infrequently, or does not wash the genital region carefully, is related to the action of skin bacteria and other microorganisms on accumulated body secretions and, on occasion, remnants of fecal material as well. A lengthy delay in changing tampons or externally worn absorbent pads during menstruation can produce similar results, but this is a less common occurrence.

Most of the skin is smooth, relatively hairless, and relatively devoid of glands other than sweat glands. Both the male and female genitalia, on the other hand, are wrinkled (the labia in the female, the scrotum and foreskin in the male), surrounded by hair, and rich in various glands (see Chapter 2). These three factors contribute to the likelihood of unpleasant odors in this area. (The next most likely source of strong odor is under the arms, where similar conditions exist, except that there are not as many crevices that can be overlooked.) The primary means of preventing these adverse health and aesthetic consequences is simple: regular, careful washing of the genital region with soap and water. "Regular" means several times a week or more, at least as frequently as one has sexual intercourse (and, from the partner's viewpoint, preferably before intercourse.) "Careful" means somewhat methodical coverage of the genitals with a washcloth; a simple shower is less than satisfactory for cleansing this area.

Although the vagina is a self-cleansing organ, some women do find it desirable to cleanse the vagina by douching. This is not usually necessary for hygienic purposes, but the insertion of creams, foams, gels, lubricants, and so forth results in residues that may necessitate douching for some of the women who use them. Others prefer to douche at least once a month at the end of their menstrual periods. If a woman does choose to douche, she normally should not do so more than twice a week. Aside from possibly being irritating, excessive douching can upset the vaginal environment and may lead to infection. Plain tap water or a mildly acidic solution (for example, two tablespoons of vinegar in

a quart of water) is preferable to most commercial douching preparations. Regular, alkaline (soda) douches should be avoided because they interfere with the normal chemical balance and flora of the vagina.

With these general principles in mind, let us move to a discussion of the causes, treatment, and prevention of various sexual disorders.

Venereal Diseases

The term "venereal" comes from the Latin *venereus,* "pertaining to Venus," the goddess of love. Venereal diseases are spread through intimate sexual contact. Our discussion will focus on *gonorrhea,* the most common form of "VD" in the United States, and *syphilis,* the most serious. Less common and less serious venereal diseases are mentioned later in this chapter.

Although both diseases are readily curable with penicillin or other antibiotics, the incidence of gonorrhea is rising, though at a slower rate than between 1965 and 1975 (see Figure 7.1). The incidence of syphilis has been relatively stable since the early 1960s (see Figure 7.2). The preponderance of cases occurs in the 15–29 age group (see Figure 7.3); it is currently estimated that 50 percent of American young people contract syphilis

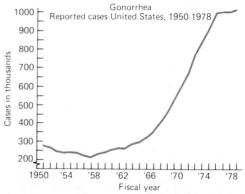

Figure 7.1 Gonorrhea, reported cases, United States, 1950–1978.

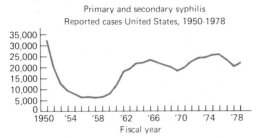

Figure 7.2 *Primary and Secondary Syphilis, Reported cases, United States, 1950–1978.*

or gonorrhea by age 25. It is not an overstatement to describe the present situation in the United States as an epidemic. In recent years gonorrhea has been the most prevalent disease of those reported to the U.S. Public Health Service, and syphilis ranks third. Gonorrhea is more common today than measles, mumps, or tuberculosis. Of all the contagious diseases, VD is second in prevalence only to the common cold. Although public health codes require physicians to report all cases of venereal disease to public health authorities, in actual practice probably less than one-third of the cases are reported.[1] For instance, there

[1]Kolata (1976).

were 1,013,436 *reported* cases of gonorrhea in 1978 (*see* Figure 7.1), but experts estimate that there were probably more than 3 million cases that year.

The purpose in reporting cases of venereal disease is to enable public health workers to locate sexual "contacts" of contagious individuals and to treat them. This method has been successful in virtually eliminating epidemics of other infectious diseases. But many people are unwilling to disclose names and addresses of sexual contacts for a variety of reasons, ranging from embarrassment to fear of more serious consequences, including self-incrimination and incrimination of past or present lovers. In many states intercourse with someone other than a spouse is a criminal offense. Homosexual acts are also crimes in most states (*see* Chapter 14). Although such information cannot legally be used as a basis for criminal prosecution, it is not difficult to understand the reluctance of someone who, by revealing the identity of a sexual partner, is revealing the identity of a partner in crime.

Gonorrhea

Gonorrhea is an infection caused by the bacterium *Neisseria gonorrhoeae,* and can affect

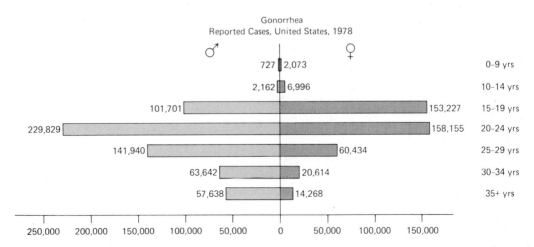

Figure 7.3 Age distribution for reported cases of gonorrhea, United States, 1978.

Box 7.1   Gonorrhea Evolving

Ever since 1958, new strains of gonorrhea have been appearing that are resistant to penicillin. Originally, 200,000 units of penicillin were needed to cure gonorrhea. Today, nearly 5 million units are needed, an increase of 25 times! As doctors utilize higher doses, the least resistant forms of gonorrhea are destroyed, while the most resistant forms survive. Over the years, this process of selection has caused the evolution of increasingly resistant forms of gonorrhea.

A new form of gonorrhea—called "supergon" or "superclap"—has now appeared that is different from the penicillin-resistant forms.[1] The new strain of gonorrhea has the ability to produce the enzyme penicillinase, which destroys penicillin and renders the drug totally ineffective in controlling the disease.

Penicillinase-producing gonorrhea appears to have originated in the Philippines, where prostitutes regularly take low doses of penicillin to keep from contracting venereal diseases. Under these conditions, any new form of gonorrhea that could destroy penicillin would have a selective advantage in the "survival of the fittest." It appears that as many as 20 to 40 percent of the Philippine prostitutes now carry the new penicillinase-producing gonorrhea. Military personnel and the merchant marine have facilitated the spread of the new disease to other countries. By early 1976, penicillinase-producing gonorrhea had been reported in 18 countries.

The first case of penicillinase-producing gonorrhea was reported in the United States in 1975. By June 1979, 685 cases had been reported in 36 states, the District of Columbia, and Guam; and the disease is continuing to spread. Penicillinase-producing gonorrhea can be cured by the antibiotic spectinomycin. However, there are two problems. First, spectinomycin costs 7 or 8 times as much as penicillin. Although people in affluent countries can afford the increased cost, it is likely that the drug will not be widely used in less-developed countries. Second, when spectinomycin is used with greater frequency in treating gonorrhea, it is likely that new forms of gonorrhea will evolve that are resistant to this drug. Drug researchers are working on new drugs to replace obsolete drugs; but scientists are concerned about staying ahead of the new forms of the various diseases that are developing resistance to current drugs.

At present people with gonorrhea are treated with penicillin. Only if a patient has proved resistant to penicillin is spectinomycin used as a treatment. If spectinomycin were used more extensively, it would only hasten the evolution of new forms of gonorrhea with resistance to that drug.

[1]Culliton (1976).

a variety of mucous-membrane tissues. This microorganism does not survive without the living conditions (temperature, moisture, and so on) provided by the human body. It is transmitted from human being to human being during contact with infected mucous membranes of the genitalia, throat, or rectum. A new strain of gonorrhea that has evolved recently is potentially more dangerous than the original forms of gonorrhea (*see* Box 7.1).

Ancient Chinese and Egyptian manuscripts refer to a contagious urethral discharge that was probably gonorrhea. The ancient Jews and Greeks thought that the discharge represented an involuntary loss of semen. The Greek physician Galen (A.D. 130–201) is credited with having coined the term "gonorrhea'' from the Greek words for ''seed'' and ''to flow.'' For centuries gonorrhea and syphilis were believed to be the same disease, but by the nineteenth century a series of experiments had demonstrated that they were two separate diseases. In 1879, A. L. S. Neisser identified the bacterium that causes gonorrhea and now bears his name (*see* above).

Symptoms in Males

In males the primary symptom of gonorrhea (known also as the ''clap'' or ''strain'') is a purulent, yellowish urethral discharge. The usual site of infection is the urethra, and the condition is called *gonorrheal urethritis*. Most infected males have symptoms, but a few males are asymptomatic. A discharge from the tip of the penis usually appears within three to ten days after contraction of the disease, and is often accompanied by burning during urination and a sensation of itching within the urethra. The inflammation may subside within two or three weeks without treatment, or it may persist in chronic form. The infection may spread up the genitourinary tract to involve the prostate gland, seminal vesicles, bladder, and kidneys. In 1 percent of cases the disease spreads to the joints of the knees, ankles, wrists, or elbows, causing gonorrheal arthritis, a very painful condition.

More than 90 percent of cases clear up immediately with prompt penicillin treatment. For persons allergic to penicillin, tetracyline or erythromycin may be used. The discharge often disappears within 12 hours after treatment, although a thin flow persists for a few days in 10–15 percent of patients.

Gonorrheal urethritis can usually be prevented by one of two methods (*see* Box 7.2): (1) use of a condom and thorough washing of the sex organs and genital area with bactericidal soap or solution after sexual exposure, or (2) a single dose of penicillin or other appropriate antibiotic within a few hours after exposure.

Symptoms in Females

In females the symptoms of gonorrhea may be mild or absent in the early stages. In fact, 80 percent of women with gonorrhea (and 10 percent of men) are essentially without symptoms, a major factor in the unwitting spread of the disease. The primary site of infection is usually the cervix, which becomes inflamed (*cervicitis*). The only early symptom may be a yellowish vaginal discharge which may be unnoticed by the female. Not all such discharges are gonorrheal, however. Microscopic examination and bacterial culture of the discharge are required for definitive diagnosis.[2] Treatment with antibiotics is usually effective if the disease is recognized and treated promptly.

If left untreated, however, the infection may spread upward through the uterus to involve the fallopian tubes and other pelvic organs. Often this spread occurs during menstruation, when the uterine cavity is more susceptible to gonorrheal invasion. Acute symptoms—severe pelvic pain, abdominal distension and tenderness, vomiting, and fever—may then appear during or just after menstruation. Again, treatment with antibiotics usually brings about a complete cure, but if the disease is not treated or is inadequately treated, a chronic inflammation of the uterine tubes (*chronic salpingitis*) ensues. This condition is accompanied by formation of scar tissue and obstruction of the tubes and constitutes a common cause of infertility in females, particularly those who frequently contract gonorrhea.

Nongenital Gonorrhea

Pharyngeal gonorrhea is an infection of the throat that is transmitted most commonly during fellatio (oral stimulation of the penis). Cunnilingus (oral stimulation of the vulva)

[2]Unfortunately, there is no routine blood test that will detect gonorrhea. This is a major reason why identification of asymptomatic gonorrhea has been much less successful than identification of asymptomatic syphilis.

Box 7.2 Controlling Gonorrhea

In the United States the number of cases of gonorrhea reported in the 1970s increased at an alarming rate. It nearly doubled between 1969 and 1976. In contrast, the number of cases reported in Sweden has been declining! It dropped by 50 percent between 1969 and 1976.[1]

Kondom

The Swedish condom symbol.

The major reason for the decline in gonorrhea in Sweden appears to be increased use of the condom. Because gonorrhea is passed between the male and female through the male's urethral meatus, covering the penis with a condom blocks the route of transmission. Condoms also provide partial protection against the transmission of syphilis, herpes, and other sexually transmitted diseases by covering the penis. The Swedish government has encouraged use of the condom through public education and by making the devices more readily available. The Swedish condom symbol (illustrated) has been displayed widely in order to heighten people's awareness of the condom's value. As condom use increased, gonorrhea rates decreased. In Denmark, Norway, and Finland—neighboring countries in which there was no program of public education about the effectiveness of condoms in controlling gonorrhea—there was no decrease in gonorrhea rates.

Condoms are rarely mentioned on television in the United States. Newspapers, magazines and even radio have been more candid about venereal diseases than TV.[2] Because many people do not want to read or hear about venereal disease, the media have been reluctant to deal with these topics.

[1]Kolata (1976).
[2]Blakeslee (1976).

---

does not usually cause pharyngeal gonorrhea. (Kissing does not provide sufficient contact to transmit gonorrhea.) The primary symptom is a sore throat, but there may also be fever and enlarged lymph nodes in the neck. In some cases there may be no symptoms.[3]

Rectal gonorrhea is an infection of the rectum usually transmitted during anal intercourse. In women with gonorrhea of the cervix the infection is sometimes spread to the rectum by exposing the rectum to the infected vaginal discharge.[4] Both rectal gonorrhea and pharyngeal gonorrhea are common in male homosexuals. The symptoms are itching associated with a rectal discharge.[5] Many cases are mild or asymptomatic, however. Treat-

[3]Fiumara (1971), p. 204, and Wiesner (1975).

[4]Rein (1975).
[5]Schroeter (1972), p. 31.

Figure 7.4 Typical organisms of *Treponema pallidum* from tissue fluid in a dark field. The length of each is about ten microns. From Jawetz et al., *Review of Medical Microbiology,* 9th ed. (Los Altos, Calif.: Lange Medical Publications, 1970), p. 220. Reprinted by permission.

ment of rectal or pharyngeal gonorrhea is the same as for gonorrheal urethritis.

Until recently a common cause of blindness in children was *ophthalmia neonatorum,*

a gonorrheal infection of the eyes acquired during passage through infected birth canals. Instilling penicillin ointment or silver nitrate drops into the eyes of all newborn babies is now compulsory and has helped to eradicate this disease.

Syphilis

It was not until 1905 that the microorganism that causes syphilis was identified. A German investigator, Fritz Richard Schaudinn, identified and named *Spirochaeta pallidum,* describing it as a "slender, very pale, corkscrew-like object" (*see* Figure 7.4). (The name *Treponema pallidum* is now the technically correct one, although "spirochete" is more commonly used.)

Symptoms

In its late stages syphilis can involve virtually any organ or tissue of the body, producing myriad symptoms similar to those of other diseases, which led the famous physician Sir William Osler to call it the "Great Imitator." The first stage or *primary stage,* is marked by a skin lesion known as a *chancre* at the site where the spirochete entered the body. The chancre (pronounced "shank-er")

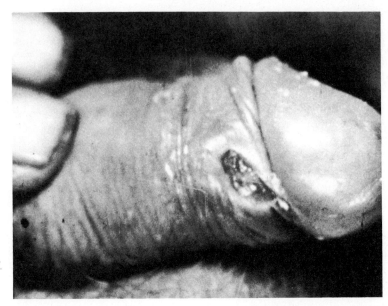

Figure 7.5 A chancre of the penis. Note the raised, hard appearance of the ulcer. From Dodson and Hill, *Synopsis of Genitourinary Disease,* 7th ed. (St. Louis: C. V. Mosby Co., 1962), p. 201. Reprinted by permission.

Box 7.3 The Spread of Syphilis

There are two theories about the origins of syphilis. Some believe that syphilis was present in the Old World since ancient times but became more virulent, perhaps because of a mutation, in the late fifteenth century.

It is more commonly believed that syphilis was brought to Europe by Columbus and his crew after their first voyage to the West Indies. It is true that, within a few years after Columbus' return in 1493 from his first voyage to the New World, epidemics of syphilis spread across Europe with devastating effects. History suggests that the Spaniards introduced the disease to the Italians while fighting beside the troops of Alfonso II of Naples. Then in 1495 an army of mercenaries fighting for Charles VIII of France conquered Naples. As they returned home through France, Germany, Switzerland, Austria, and England, they took the disease along with an excess of celebration. By 1496 syphilis was rampant in Paris, leading to the passage of strict laws banishing from the city anyone suffering from it. In 1497 all syphilitics in Edinburgh were banished to an island near Leith. In 1498 Vasco de Gama and his Portuguese crew carried the disease to India, and from there it spread to China; the first epidemic in that country was reported in 1505. Outbreaks of syphilis in Japan later followed the visits of European vessels.

The New World origin of syphilis is also suggested by the discovery of definite syphilitic lesions in the bones of Indians from the pre-Columbian period in the Americas. There are no comparable findings in the bones of ancient Egyptians, nor are there any clear descriptions of the disease in the medical literature of the Old World before Columbus. Physicians in the early sixteenth century did not have a name for the disease, but the Spaniards called it the "disease of Española" (present-day Haiti). The Italians called it "the Spanish disease"; and the French called it "the Neopolitan disease." As it spread to many countries it acquired the name *morbus Gallicus,* the "French sickness," a name that persisted for about a century. The term "syphilis" was introduced in 1530 by the Italian physician Girolamo Fracastoro, who wrote a poem in Latin about a shepherd boy named Syphilus (from the Greek *siphlos,* meaning "crippled" or "maimed"), who caught the disease as a punishment from the gods (for having insulted Apollo). As this name was ethnically neutral, it gradually became accepted as the proper term for the dread disease.

Various historical figures have been afflicted by syphilis, as is indicated by records of their physical appearances and symptoms. Columbus himself died in 1506 with symptoms typical of advanced syphilis, involving the heart, extremities, and brain. It is generally accepted that the first four children of Catherine of Aragon, first wife of Henry VIII of England, all died of congenital syphilis, leaving only one survivor, the future "Bloody Mary." (Mary died at age 42—of complications of congenital syphilis, it appears.) Henry's disappointment over not having a male heir undoubtedly played a role in his insistence on legalizing his second and subsequent marriages, which led to the break between England and Rome.

is a hard, round ulcer with raised edges, and is usually painless. In the male it commonly appears somewhere on the penis, on the scrotum, or in the pubic area (*see* Figure 7.5). In the female it usually appears on the external genitals (*see* Figure 7.6), but it may appear in the vagina or on the cervix and thus escape detection. It may also appear on the mouth, in the rectum, on the nipple, or elsewhere on the skin.

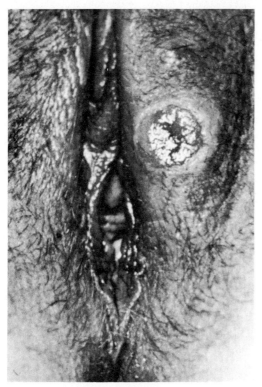

Figure 7.6 A large chancre on the labia majora. Primary syphilis in the female is not usually this obvious. From Weiss and Joseph, *Syphilis* (Baltimore: Williams & Wilkins, 1951), p. 73. Copyright © 1951 by The Williams & Wilkins Co.; reprinted by permission.

As syphilitic infections in men may begin at sites other than the penis, condoms do not necessarily provide protection against them. And, as it is usually not apparent that someone is a carrier of syphilis, the only sure way to avoid the disease is to know before sexual contact whether or not the anticipated partner has had a negative blood test for syphilis—an unlikely question to ask as a prelude to making love. The point is, however, that casual sexual contacts are more likely to expose one to syphilis (or other venereal disease), for statistically the greater the number of sexual partners, the greater the probability of encountering someone who is a carrier.

The chancre appears two to four weeks after contraction of the disease and, if not treated, usually disappears in several weeks, leading to the illusion that the individual has recovered from whatever he or she thought was the trouble. Actually this chancre is usually only the first stage in the development of a chronic illness that may ultimately be fatal. Treatment with penicillin or other antibiotics when the chancre occurs cures most cases, and relapses after proper treatment are rare.

Secondary and Tertiary Syphilis

When syphilis is untreated, the *secondary stage* becomes manifest anywhere from several weeks to several months after the healing of the chancre. There is usually a generalized skin rash, which is transient and may or may not be accompanied by such vague symptoms as headache, fever, indigestion, sore throat, and muscle or joint pain. Many people do not associate these symptoms with the primary chancre.

Syphilis (and gonorrhea) are transmitted *only* by intimate contact with another human being. The most infectious times are when a chancre is present or during the second stage of the disease when skin lesions are present (particularly lesions in moist areas of the body, such as the mouth). Thus, syphilis can be caught through kissing if the chancre is on the lips or if the lesions are on the mouth. Explanations involving contact with contaminated toilet seats, wet towels, chairs, drinking glasses, swimming pools, or domestic animals may save face but are pure myth and/or self-deception.

After the secondary stage all symptoms disappear, and the so-called *latent period* begins. During this period, which may last from 1 to 40 or more years, the spirochetes burrow into various tissues, particularly blood vessels, the central nervous system (brain and spinal cord), and bones.

About 50 percent of untreated cases reach the final, or "tertiary," stage of syphilis,

Box 7.4   Three Uncommon Venereal Diseases[1]

There are three venereal diseases that are relatively uncommon in the United States. There is a higher incidence of these diseases in tropical areas; and they are more prevalent in the southern states than in the North.

Chancroid ("soft chancre") is caused by a bacillus known as *Hemophilus ducreyi* (the bacillus of Ducrey). The primary lesion of this venereal disease is a chancre which resembles the syphilitic chancre in appearance, but, in contrast to the syphilitic lesion, is quite painful. Diagnosis is based on microscopic examination or culture of the bacillus. Treatment with sulfa drugs is quite effective. The disease has become quite rare in Western countries, although it is still common in the East and in tropical regions. In 1978, there were 521 cases reported in the United States.

Lymphogranuloma venereum ("tropical bubo," LGV) is caused by a microorganism that is neither a bacterium nor a virus but has some of the properties of each. Although the site of entry is usually the penis, vulva, or cervix, the first obvious manifestation of the disease is usually enlarged, tender lymph glands in the groin accompanied by fever, chills, and headache. Treatment consists of sulfa or broad-spectrum antibiotics such as chlortetracycline. LGV is most common in the tropics and subtropics. In the United States it is seen most frequently in the South. In 1978, 284 cases were reported in the United States.

Granuloma inguinale ("chronic venereal sore") is caused by an infectious agent known as *Donovanian granulomatis*, or the "Donovan body," after its discoverer. Like LGV, it is most common in the tropics and subtropics. It does occur in the southern U.S. states; seventy-two cases were reported in the United States in 1978. The disease is characterized by ulcerated, painless, progressively spreading skin lesions. It is not highly contagious. The most common sites of infection are the skin and mucous membranes of the genitalia, but the disease may also involve the rectum, buttocks, or mouth. The most effective antibiotics for treatment are tetracycline and streptomycin.

[1]Brown *et al.* (1970); King and Nicol (1975).

---

in which heart failure, ruptured major blood vessels, loss of muscular control and sense of balance, blindness, deafness, and severe mental disturbances can occur. Ultimately the disease can be fatal, but treatment with penicillin even at late stages may be beneficial, depending on the extent to which vital organs have already been damaged.

Syphilis can be transmitted to the fetus through the placenta; hence the mandatory blood tests to identify untreated cases of the disease before marriage and before the birth of a child. Treatment with penicillin during the first half of pregnancy can prevent congenital syphilis in the child. Nine out of ten pregnant women who have untreated syphilis either miscarry, bear stillborn children, or give birth to living children with congenital syphilis.

Children with congenital syphilis are prone to impaired vision and hearing, as well as to certain deformities of the bones and teeth. Treatment with penicillin can alleviate many of the manifestations of congenital syphilis if it is initiated early in infancy.

Other Sexually Transmitted Diseases

In recent years doctors and public health workers have become increasingly aware of the sexual transmission of other diseases besides the traditional venereal diseases. In the past these diseases were less common or the degree to which they were sexually transmitted was not realized. While many of the following diseases have become quite common, doctors and laboratories are not required to report these diseases to Public Health Service officials. Thus, there are no national figures on the incidence of these diseases although estimates are available based on limited samples.

Trichomoniasis

A common vaginal infection is *trichomoniasis,* which is caused by a protozoan called *Trichomonas vaginalis.* It is characterized by an odorous, foamy, yellowish or greenish discharge that irritates the vulva, producing itching or burning sensations. Trichomoniasis is usually a sexually transmitted disease.[6] A man may harbor this organism in the urethra or prostate gland without symptoms, or he may have a slight urethral discharge. Since both sexual partners may have the infection, it is customary to treat both partners simultaneously with a drug called metronidazole (*Flagyl*) to prevent reinfection.[7] Trichomonads are sometimes spread nonsexually. If an uninfected person's genitals come in contact with something such as a washcloth or wet bathing suit that has been contaminated with the protozoa through contact with the genitals of an infected person, the uninfected person may become infected.

Nongonococcal Urethritis

A form of urethritis that is perhaps more common than that caused by gonorrhea is *nongonococcal urethritis* (NGU). This disease is most often seen among white and affluent patients and is probably the most common form of urethritis seen in student health centers and in the offices of private physicians.

---

[6]Rein and Chapel (1975).
[7]There have been highly publicized reports that large doses of this drug may cause tumors in rats. There is no evidence of such effects in humans.

NGU is transmitted sexually (the organism involved is frequently, but not always, *Chlamydia trachomatis*), and although it causes urethritis in males (with a urethral discharge as in gonorrhea), it may be asymptomatic in females.

Because NGU was only recently identified as a sexually transmitted disease and because it is sometimes asymptomatic, many cases have gone undiagnosed and mistreated. The result is that this disease is becoming more and more widespread. NGU can be effectively treated with tetracycline and usually clears up within five days of treatment.

Nonspecific Vaginitis

Nonspecific vaginitis occurs when women have vaginitis (irritation of the vagina) but the organism responsible for the infection cannot be isolated or identified easily. As a result, many cases have been undiagnosed and mistreated. Some forms of nonspecific vaginitis are sexually transmitted. The frequency of nonspecific vaginitis is difficult to determine, but health officials believe that it is becoming more widespread.

Nonspecific vaginitis can be caused by the same organisms that cause nongonococcal urethritis in the male. As already mentioned, *Chlamydia trachomatis* can affect both sexes. *Hemophilus vaginalis* is probably a common cause of nonspecific vaginitis.[8] Because it can often be recovered from the sexual partners of infected women, it is possible that it is sexually transmitted. Ampicillin is the treatment of choice for women infected with *Hemophilus.*[9]

Herpes

One viral infection of the genitals is *Herpes Simplex Virus Type 2* (HSV-2), which is now recognized as being a very common sexually

---

[8]McCormack (1974).
[9]Rein and Chapel (1975).

transmitted disease in the United States. The Public Health Service estimates that there are 300,000 new cases of genital herpes a year. HSV-2 should not be confused with HSV-1, which causes "cold sores," eye infections, and skin conditions above the waist. Some cases of genital herpes (perhaps 10 percent) are caused by HSV-1, however. Likewise, some herpes infections above the waist are caused by HSV-2.

The HSV-2 infection results in the appearance of small vesicles (fluid-filled pockets or blisters) surrounded by inflamed tissue, which usually appear three to seven days after exposure to the virus. The most common sites of herpes infections in females include the surface of the cervix, the clitoral prepuce, and the major and minor lips; in males, the foreskin and glans. When the blisters are internal, such as on the cervix, the condition may go undetected because the cervix is insensitive to pain. In some instances, males may also be asymptomatic. Herpes causes burning and itching sensations in most cases. When the blisters break open, they may become infected with bacteria from the skin.

The usual mode of transmission of HSV-2 is intimate sexual contact; therefore sex should be avoided when herpes blisters or ulcers are present. Even though the blisters usually clear up after a few weeks, the virus may remain in the body for years, and the infection can recur cyclically. Although some people never have another active outbreak, others have recurring outbreaks for years.

There are special problems associated with herpes. A pregnant woman who has an active outbreak at the time of birth runs a risk (one in four) that her newborn child will be seriously damaged or die of the virus. To avoid this problem many doctors will perform cesarean sections in this situation. In rare cases the fetus has become infected while still in the uterus.[10] There is also the possibility that HSV-2 can cause cancer. Approximately 6 percent of women who have HSV-2 develop cervical cancer, so it is recommended that women who have had herpes get Pap smear tests every six months to check for cancer.

One reason that the disease has spread so rapidly is that people often do not recognize it or know that they have it. Also, in some instances the sores associated with recurring outbreaks may not be noticed during a casual inspection.

People with active herpes are advised to take hot sitz baths and to keep sores clean and dry. Other treatments for herpes have not been found to be effective. But in 1979 a new method for treating herpes was developed that appears promising.[11] The drug used in this treatment, 2-deoxy-D-glucose, is an antiviral agent that interferes with the multiplication of herpes virus. In a study on 36 women with active genital herpes, 89 percent of the cases were cured within four days (see Figure 7.7). Of course, further studies are needed to guarantee its efficacy.

Genital Warts

Genital warts (also known as *condylomata acuminata*) are most commonly transmitted by sexual contact, although this is not their only mode of transmission. The symptoms include obvious bumps and possible itching or irritation. They usually appear from one to three months after contact. Genital warts are similar to common plantar warts and both are caused by a virus. They appear most often in women on the vulva, vagina, and, less frequently, the cervix; in males, on the surface of the glans and below the rim of the corona. They have also been known to develop in and around the anus, particularly in male homosexuals. Traditionally, physicians have treated genital, or "venereal," warts in several ways: surgically, with electrodes, with cryosurgery (freezing), or with the direct ap-

---

[10]Kaufman and Rawls (1974).

[11]Blough and Giuntoli (1979).

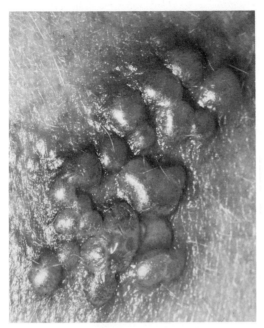

Figure 7.7 Typical herpes virus lesions before treatment (*left*) and four days afterward, after cure (*right*). From Blough and Giuntoli, Successful treatment of human genital herpes infections with 2-deoxy-D-glucose, *Journal of the American Medical Association,* 241 (© 1979), 2798–2801. Courtesy of Dr. H. A. Blough and the American Medical Association.

plication of various drugs. A vaccine made from the patient's own wart tissue has also been shown to be effective in fighting the virus and in getting rid of the warts.

Pubic Lice

Pediculosis pubis (pubic lice, "crabs") is an infestation of the pubic hair and is usually transmitted sexually. However, it is occasionally acquired from contact with infested bedding, towels, or toilet seats. The primary symptom of pubic lice is intense itching, which results from bites (the lice feed on blood like mosquitoes). Adult lice are visible to the naked eye, but just barely. They are bluish-gray and about the size of a pinhead. Cream, lotion, or shampoo preparations of gamma benzene hexachloride (*Kwell*) are very effective in eliminating both adult lice and their eggs ("nits").

Scabies

Scabies is a contagious skin infection that is caused by an itch mite (*Sarcoptes scabiei*). The mites provoke intense itching and can be spread by close personal contact, including sexual contact and contact with infested objects such as clothing or bedding. Scabies is commonly found in the genital areas, buttocks, and elsewhere on the body. The female itch mite burrows into the skin and lays eggs along the burrow. The larvae hatch within a few days. The mites are more active and cause the most itching at night. Once the person begins to scratch the infected areas, the scratching usually opens the skin to bacterial infection which causes secondary inflammation. This parasitic infestation can be eliminated by washing with *Kwell,* the same preparation used in treating lice.

Other Common Problems

Leukorrhea

Some amount of vaginal mucus is normal. Women have varying amounts of discharge during their monthly cycle and during sexual excitement. When the discharge becomes excessive or abnormal it is called *leukorrhea*. Almost every woman experiences leukorrhea at some time in her life. It is not a discrete disease entity but rather a condition that can be caused by infections, chemicals, and physical changes. We have already mentioned several infections such as trichomoniasis that can cause leukorrhea. Irritating chemicals in commerical douche preparations may also cause vaginal discharges. In fact, frequent douching of any sort is likely to increase the production of vaginal mucus. Leukorrhea may result from irritation by foreign bodies (such as a contraceptive device). Leukorrhea may also be related to alterations in hormone balance (during pregnancy or menopause).

Candidiasis

A common vaginal infection that causes irritation and a discharge is *candidiasis* (also known as moniliasis, monilia, or yeast). It is caused by a yeastlike organism called *Candida albicans.* The thick white discharge causes itching and discomfort, which may be severe. This organism is normally present in the vagina, but it produces an infection only when it multiplies excessively. Candidiasis is most commonly seen in women using oral contraceptives, in diabetic women, and during the course of pregnancy or prolonged antibiotic therapy for some other condition. Candidiasis can be very annoying, especially when it involves itching skin on the thighs. Usually this condition responds to treatment with nystatin (*Mycostatin*) suppositories. Though much less common in males, this fungus infection does occur, particularly under the foreskin of an uncircumcised male. Often these males have no symptoms, but there may be a white discharge and irritation. An infected male is also treated with nystatin, but in cream form.

Prostatitis

Prostatitis, or inflammation of the prostate gland, is a relatively common problem in men who have passed the age of 40.[12] Chronic prostatitis is much more common than acute prostatitis. The acute form of the disease may result from complications of either nonspecific urethritis, gonorrhea, or other infections.[13] Although most cases of the acute form can be resolved with antibiotic treatment, some cases become subacute or chronic.

Chronic prostatitis can be caused by infections, prolonged congestion of the posterior urethra due to excessive intake of alcohol, prolonged sexual excitement without ejaculation, or long periods of abstinence after times of frequent ejaculation.[14] Among the symptoms of chronic prostatitis are lower back pain, perineal pain, incomplete erection, urinary problems, and premature, painful, or bloody ejaculation. In the past, physicians often recommended that men with prostatitis should abstain from sexual activity and ejaculation. Today, it is more often recommended that men should continue their normal rate of sexual activity, although they should avoid prolonged foreplay without ejaculation in order to minimize congestion of the gland. Massage of the prostate has been used to help drain the ducts of the gland, but sexual release may be more effective. Antibiotics may be of use in some cases; but complete cure is often not possible. Warm sitz baths may reduce the symptoms.

Cystitis

Cystitis is an infection or inflammation of the bladder. It is not a sexually transmitted disease, but its occurrence in women is sometimes associated with sexual activity. (It is so

[12]Barnes et al. (1967).
[13]Sturdy and Lyth (1974).
[14]Davis and Mininberg (1976).

common among newlywed women, for instance, that the term "honeymoon cystitis" has been used to describe it.)

The bacteria that invade the bladder through the urethra are not usually caught from the sexual partner, but are normally present on the genital skin of the infected person. Women are more prone to cystitis because their urethras are significantly shorter than those of males. The primary symptom of cystitis is frequent and painful ("burning") urination. It may subside spontaneously in a few days, but it is advisable to receive proper antibiotic treatment because untreated infections may spread from the bladder to the kidneys, causing a much more serious condition called *pyelonephritis*.

Cancer of the Sex Organs

Common cancers in both sexes involve organs of the reproductive system.

Of the Breast

Cancer of the breast[15] is the most common form of cancer in women. It is extremely rare in women under age 25, but increases steadily in each decade thereafter. For women in the 40–44 age group, cancer of the breast is the most common cause of death. Ultimately, almost 1 in 13 women will develop breast cancer. Males too can develop breast cancer, although this condition is rare, accounting for less than 1 percent of all breast cancers. The cause of this disease is unknown, but it is clear that blows to the breast do not cause breast cancer. Many breast cancers respond to sex hormones. The spread of these cancers may be accelerated by increased hormone secretion during pregnancy. Some investigators feel that the long-term ingestion of hormones in birth control pills may stimulate the growth of breast cancer. Thus far the available re-

search does not support this hypothesis. Studies dealing with the effects of the pill on breast cancer have not found an increase in breast cancer among women who use oral contraceptives. More research is being conducted in this area.

Removal of the ovaries is often beneficial in the treatment of breast cancer, as is treatment with the male sex hormone testosterone. The primary treatment is surgical removal of the breast (*mastectomy*) and related tissue.

When breast cancer is detected and breast removal recommended, one of the most difficult problems the woman faces is the disfigurement caused by the mastectomy. But this situation is changing. Breast reconstruction techniques have become so sophisticated in recent years that women no longer need fear loss of self-image and confidence as a result of the operation. Plastic surgeons not only can reconstruct the breast contours (using silicone gel implants), they can also reconstruct the nipple and areola from the intact nipple.

Cancer of the breast can be fatal, but with early diagnosis and treatment the prognosis is much more favorable. About 65 percent of patients with cancer of the breast are still alive five years after the initial diagnosis. Early diagnosis and treatment are often missed because cancer of the breast begins with a painless lump in the breast, which may go unnoticed for a long time, in part because approximately three-fourths of women do not regularly perform a breast self-examination. This is unfortunate since the best way to reduce the mortality rate for breast cancer is to detect the disease early before it spreads to other parts of the body. Over 90 percent of all breast cancers are discovered by the women themselves. Thus, every woman beginning in her teens should do a breast self-exam once a month about one week after the end of her period or on one set day a month after menopause (*see* Box 7.5).

[15]Although not technically sex organs, the breasts are part of the reproductive system and are highly sensitive to sex hormones, as was noted in Chapter 4.

Box 7.5 How To Do a Breast Self-Exam[1]

1. In the Shower. Examine your breasts during your bath or shower, since hands glide more easily over wet skin. Hold your fingers flat and move them gently over every part of each breast. Use the right hand to examine the left breast and the left hand for the right breast. Check for any lump, hard knot, or thickening.

2. Before a mirror. Inspect your breasts with arms at your sides. Next, raise your arms high overhead. Look for any changes in the contour of each breast: a swelling, dimpling of skin, or changes in the nipple.

Then rest your palms on your hips and press down firmly to flex your chest muscles. Left and right breast will not exactly match—few women's breasts do. Again, look for changes and irregularities. Regular inspection shows what is normal for

Not all women are at equal risk for developing breast cancer. Women who are known to be at higher risk include women over 50, women who have a family history of breast cancer, women who experience a late menopause, and women who have never had children. Women with a somewhat higher risk include women who have their first child after 30 and women who began menstruating early.

Women should consult a doctor immediately if they notice a lump or other changes in their breasts, such as a discharge from the nipple. Approximately 80 percent of breast lumps are noncancerous, but the lump needs to be examined by a doctor in order to rule out the possibility of cancer.

Techniques for diagnosis of breast can-

cers include mammography and xerography (both of which involve special X-ray pictures of the breast) and thermography (which uses an infrared scanning device to detect a slight increase in heat that is usually produced by cancer tissue). Mammography is not generally recommended for women under 50, unless they are in certain high-risk groups, because X rays may actually cause breast cancer. Future methods that are being developed for early detection include the T-antigen test, nipple aspiration, and microwave radio signal detection.

Of the Cervix

Cancer of the cervix is the second most common type of cancer in women. About 2 percent of all women ultimately develop it. It is

Box 7.5 Continued

you and will give you confidence in your examination.

    3. Lying down. To examine your right breast, put a pillow or folded towel under your right shoulder. Place your right hand behind your head; this distributes breast tissue more evenly on the chest. With the left hand, fingers flat, press gently in small circular motions around an imaginary clock face. Begin at outermost top of your right breast for 12 o'clock, then move to 1 o'clock, and so on around the circle back to 12. (A ridge of firm tissue in the lower curve of each breast is normal.)

Then move 1 inch inward, toward the nipple and keep circling to examine every part of your breast, including the nipple. This requires at least three more circles. Now slowly repeat the procedure on your left breast with a pillow under your left shoulder and left hand behind your head. Notice how your breast structure feels.

    Finally, squeeze the nipple of each breast gently between the thumb and index finger. Any discharge, clear or bloody, should be reported to your doctor immediately.

[1]From the American Cancer Society. Used by permission.

very rare before age 20, but the incidence rises over the next several decades. The average age of women with cancer of the cervix is 45. This disease is more common in women who have had large numbers of sexual contacts and who have borne children.[16] The disease is very rare among Jewish women, which has given rise to the theory that smegma, which tends to collect under the foreskins of uncircumcised males (Jewish males are usually circumcised) may play a part in the development of cancer of the cervix. However, there is no difference in the incidence of cervical cancer among Muslims (males circumcised) and Hindus (males uncircumcised), so the association of cervical cancer and uncircumcised sexual partners is far from established.[17]

    Cancer of the cervix may present no symptoms for five or ten years, and during this period treatment is extremely successful. The well-publicized Pap smear test is the best means now available for identifying cancer of the cervix in the early stages (when it is most susceptible to treatment). This test should be done annually beginning when a woman is 20 (or earlier if a woman is sexually active). From the patient's point of view the Pap smear is an extremely simple test to perform. The physician simply takes a specimen of

[16]One study of 13,000 Canadian nuns failed to reveal a single case of cervical cancer. See Novak et al., (1970), p. 212.

[17]Ibid., p. 211.

cervical mucus with a cotton-tipped swab and makes a "smear" of this material on a glass slide. The procedure is quick, simple, and painless. The smear is then stained and examined under a laboratory microscope for the presence of cancerous cells.

As cancer of the cervix begins to invade surrounding tissues, irregular vaginal bleeding or a chronic bloody vaginal discharge develops. Treatment is less successful when the cancer has reached this stage. If treatment (surgery, radiation, or both) is instituted before the cancer spreads beyond the cervix, the five-year survival rate is about 80 percent, but it drops precipitously as the disease reaches other organs in the pelvis. The overall five-year survival rate for cancer of the cervix (including all stages of the disease) is about 58 percent.

One possible cause of cancer of the cervix is the drug DES (diethylstilbestrol, a synthetic estrogen). Between 1940 and 1970, DES was given to many pregnant women who had a history of bleeding, repeated miscarriage, or long periods of infertility. DES was of dubious value in preventing miscarriages, and a greater than usual risk of cancer of the cervix or vagina (a rare cancer) has been found in daughters of women who took the drug while pregnant. It is recommended that women find out whether their mothers took DES and, if so, inform their doctors so that they can be checked for vaginal cancer.

Of the Endometrium

Cancer of the endometrium (the lining of the uterus) is less common than cancer of the cervix, eventually affecting about 1 percent of women. It usually occurs in women over 35, most commonly in women 50 to 64. Many cases of this cancer are detected by the Pap test, but not all. Thus, in addition to having a regular Pap test each year, women over 35 should report any abnormal bleeding to their doctor in order to rule out the possibility of cancer of the endometrium. The five-year survival rate for endometrial cancer is 77 percent.

Cancer of the endometrium has also been linked to the use of estrogens. Estrogens have proved to be effective in treating certain symptoms of menopause (*see* Chapter 4), but some evidence suggests that the risks of this treatment may outweigh the benefits, especially in postmenopausal women who were given estrogens over a prolonged period of time. The Food and Drug Administration now suggests that if estrogen therapy is employed, it be used cyclically in the lowest effective dose for the shortest possible time with appropriate monitoring for endometrial cancer. There is some recent evidence that the addition of progesterone to the estrogen therapy may decrease the risk of endometrial cancer.

Of the Prostate

Cancer of the prostate is the second most common form of cancer in men. Nevertheless, cancer of the prostate has never been a significant cause of death, although the mortality rate is rising as the life expectancy has risen. Historically, cancer of the prostate has had a low mortality rate for two reasons: First, it is rare before age 40 and uncommon before age 50. Most cases of prostate cancer occur in males 55 and older. About 25 percent of men in the ninth decade of life have cancer of the prostate. By that time they are likely to die of other causes, such as heart disease, rather than of cancer. Second, most cancers of the prostate are relatively small and grow very slowly. Only a minority spread rapidly to other organs.

Cancer of the prostate, like cancer of the breast, is responsive to sex hormones. Androgens stimulate its growth, and surgical castration (removal of the testicles) is sometimes part of the treatment for this disease. Also, estrogens slow the growth of prostatic cancer and are often given as part of the treatment, again highlighting the physiological antagonism between estrogen and androgen

Box 7.6   Chromosomal Abnormalities

In the past decades a series of disorders associated with abnormal sex-chromosome patterns has been identified. A normal female has two X chromosomes (one from the mother and one from the father); and a normal male has one X chromosome (from the mother) and one Y chromosome (from the father) (*see* Chapter 5). But occasionally an individual ends up with an unusual combination of sex chromosomes because of errors that occur before fertilization or immediately after the zygote begins its earliest cell divisions. The most common such anomalies are the XXX (*triple-X syndrome*), XXY (*Klinefelter's syndrome*), XO (*Turner's syndrome*), and XYY patterns.[1]

Triple-X females have been called "superfemales," but are not unusually feminine (or masculine). Because XXX women have been found during chromosome surveys in mental institutions, some people initially concluded that the triple-X syndrome was associated with mental retardation. However, there are many perfectly normal XXX women in the population, and it may be incorrect to assume that XXX women are any more prone to mental problems than other women.

People with Klinefelter's syndrome (XXY) have a relatively normal male body appearance. However, the masculinization is incomplete; and the XXY man has a small penis, small testes, low testosterone production, and therefore incomplete development of secondary sex traits. Some have partial breast development at puberty. XXY men are infertile. These men may have problems with their gender identity, and some exhibit mental retardation.

Females with Turner's syndrome have only one X chromosome (the XO pattern). Ovaries are absent or present only in

[1]Money (1968), Money and Ehrhardt (1972).

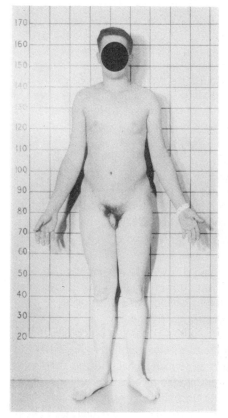

Breast development and small genitals can be seen in this 19-year-old boy with Klinefelter's (XXY) syndrome. From Money, *Sex Errors of the Body* (Baltimore: Johns Hopkins University Press, © 1968), p. 105. Reprinted by permission.

rudimentary form, and if present they do not produce eggs or female hormones. Therefore, the XO female is infertile and does not undergo puberty unless treated with female sex hormones. XO females have short stature. They may have congenital organ defects, webbing between the fingers and toes or between the neck and shoulders. Despite incomplete development of the female organs, XO females are completely feminine in their psychosexual development.

Box 7.6 Continued

The XYY syndrome originally received a great deal of publicity because a high percentage of such men were found among prisoners who had committed crimes involving violence or sex. XYY individuals are thoroughly masculine in appearance, tend to be more than six feet tall, and show a normal range of intelligence. Does the presence of XYY males in prisons demonstrate a relationship between XYY and aggression? Not if the rate of violent crime of XYY males is no higher than the rate for XY males. A well-designed and well-executed study in Denmark analyzed the sex chromosomes of 4139 men from an unbiased sample and found no higher rate of violent crime among XYY men than among XY men.[2] Thus, the early notion that XYY men are overly aggressive does not appear to be valid.

[2]Witkin et al. (1976).

(compare the use of testosterone in treatment of cancer of the breast). Whereas administration of androgen to women causes beard growth, deepening of the voice, enlargement of the clitoris and may increase sex drive, administration of estrogen to men may cause enlargement of the breasts, impotence, and decreased sexual interest.

The initial symptoms of prostatic cancer are similar to those in benign enlargement of the prostate (which is common in men over 50). They include frequent urination, particularly at night; difficulties initiating urination; and difficulties emptying the bladder. These symptoms largely result from partial obstruction of the urethra by the malignant growth. Early in the course of the disease sexual interest may increase, and frequent erections may occur. Later on, however, there is usually a loss of sexual functioning. A tentative diagnosis of cancer of the prostate can usually be made on the basis of a rectal examination (palpation of the prostate through the rectum), the history of symptoms, and certain laboratory tests. A prostate examination should certainly be part of an annual physical checkup for any man over 50, for, as with other cancers, the prognosis is much more optimistic when it is diagnosed and treated early. The cause of prostatic cancer remains unknown despite efforts to link it with hormonal factors, infectious agents, excessive sexual activity, and sexual frustration.[18]

Of the Testes

Unlike most other cancers, which strike later in life, cancer of the testes affects young men in the 20–35 age group. In fact, it is the most common cancer in males 29–35. It accounts for only about 1 percent of all cancers in males. Males who have undescended testes or whose testes descended after age 6 are at greater risk for developing testicular cancer. Between 11 and 15 percent of these males will develop cancer of the testes.

If testicular cancer is detected early, it is a very curable cancer. If it is not detected early, it can spread to other parts of the body and cause death. To check for possible symptoms of testicular cancer a male should examine his testes once a month after a warm bath or shower. Using both hands, each testicle is rolled between the thumbs (placed on the top of the testicle) and the index and middle fingers (on the underside). If a hard lump is found it may not be cancerous, but a doctor should be consulted immediately for proper diagnosis. Treatment involves the removal of the affected testicle. A man's sexual activity and fertility are not harmed by removing one

[18]Mostofi (1970), pp. 232–233.

testicle. An implant that is similar to the original testis in size, shape, and feel is inserted into the scrotum.

Of the Penis

Cancer of the penis is rare in the United States, accounting for about 2 percent of all cancer in males. It is interesting, however, because of its apparent relation to circumcision. Cancer of the penis almost never occurs among Jews, who undergo ritual circumcision within the first two weeks of life, as do most Christians in this country. This disease is also rare, though somewhat less so, among Muslim men, who usually undergo circumcision before puberty. Yet in areas of the world where circumcision is not common, cancer of the penis is much more prevalent. It accounts for about 18 percent of all malignancies in Far Eastern countries, for instance. The usual explanation, though it has not been confirmed, is that circumcision prevents accumulation of potentially carcinogenic secretions, or possibly a virus, around the tip of the penis (the usual site of this type of tumor).

Part Two
Behavior

Chapter 8

Sexual Behavior through the Life Span

In dealing with the structure and functions of the sex organs, we have been, as it were, investigating the house but disregarding its inhabitants. Now we must turn to people themselves to see how and why they behave sexually.

The problem of assessing sexual behavior is bewildering. What is normal? Healthy? Moral?

Thorough understanding of any behavior requires some knowledge of its genesis. This chapter therefore begins with the genesis of sexual behavior during human development. But it is equally important to view sexuality in a life cycle perspective. Thus we shall follow psychosexual development through childhood and adolescence and then turn to sexual behavior in adulthood and old age. But first we need to consider briefly the nature of sexual behavior.

What Sexual Behavior Is

Just as the physiology of sex can be understood only within the context of total body functioning, sexual activity must be viewed within the framework of human behavior in general.

In the ordinary sense, "behavior" is how we act—what can be witnessed by others, in contrast to inner feelings and thoughts. This dichotomy between "inner" and "outer" is arbitrary, for we seldom act without thinking or feeling, and we rarely fail to reflect thought and emotion in our actions. Behavior is, therefore, better viewed as the integrated whole of these inner and outer aspects.

All behavior, including sexual behavior, has several main characteristics.[1] First, it is integrated and indivisible. When we describe it as conscious, unconscious, or innately or socially determined, we refer simply to different components of behavior, not to different behaviors. Second, all behavior expresses the total organism, the personality as a whole. Third, all behavior is part of a lifelong developmental sequence and can be understood only as links in a chain of events. Finally, all behavior is determined by multiple forces. Each act has biological, psychological, and social determinants, which are themselves quite complex. We do not think, feel, or do anything for one single reason.

Range of Sexual Behavior

The question "What is sexual behavior?" is deceptively simple; it is actually impossible to

[1]See Engel (1962), p. 4.

217

answer. Most people would agree that it involves more than just coitus, but how much more is another matter. A physiological definition based on tumescence of sex organs or orgasm, though not without merit, leaves out vast areas of activity that are commonly recognized as sexual. Furthermore, it would include certain behavior, like erections in very young boys, the sexual nature of which can be questioned.

Closer scrutiny of human behavior reveals that any and all objects and activities may have sexual significance. The concept then becomes so nearly global that it cannot possibly be quantified for comparison and analysis. Confronted with these alternatives we must resort to working definitions that, though deficient in some respects, are at least operationally useful. For example, although we are aware of the many varieties of sexual expression, we shall deal primarily with those that culminate in orgasm, especially when we discuss adult sexuality. Just as with the physiology of sex, orgasm will serve as our unit of behavioral measurement.

In a sense this approach is most regrettable, for it obscures the myriad nuances and the subtlety of sexuality in favor of a "mechanical" definition. Unfortunately, we have no other alternative to chaos. If we are to discuss what people do, we must have a unit of measurement. We shall not stop there, however, but shall attempt also to capture some of the less quantifiable, more ephemeral, but no less important manifestations of human sexuality.

There is still no definitive information on the sexual behavior of large communities anywhere in the world (see Boxes 8.13, 8.14, and 8.15, on pages 258, 260, 262). We shall refer often later to the distribution and frequencies of various types of sexual behavior. The presentation of such data in percentages and other mathematical forms tends to lend a certain scientific dignity and to imply accu-

racy. There is nothing in these pages, however, that can be taken to reflect accurately the behavior of whole nations or all of mankind. What we do have are fragments of information on some facets of sexual activity in some groups. The resulting picture is like the image in a broken mirror with many missing pieces. It is to be hoped that enough is reflected to suggest broader outlines.

Everything we know indicates that sexual behavior is extremely varied. Like the stars, individual patterns of activity are countless, but they cluster in definite constellations, some of which are apparent to anyone's eye and others only to trained observers.

This extreme variability is another reason for caution in drawing conclusions from information obtained from groups. Even when careful study has uncovered the patterns of behavior in a given community, this information cannot be automatically applied to any one member of that community. Averages tell us about groups but not individuals. Understanding each person requires a special study of each: There are no shortcuts. But such studies can yield more meaning if we know the averages and variations for the group.

Prepubescent Sexuality

It is reasonable to assume that in all cultures at all times there have always been some people who have been aware of the sexual potential in infants and children. There have indeed existed cultures that have not had the kinds of barriers that we do against sexual interaction among children or between children and adults. In the Western world as childhood came to be recognized as a vulnerable period of life, the protection of the rights and welfare of children led to strict prohibitions against their use as sexual objects combined with attempts at inhibition of most forms of sexual expression in childhood.

Modern recognition and acceptance of

childhood sexuality is to a significant extent due to the influence of Freud[2] (*see* Box 8.6, page 236). Unfortunately, his views were not substantiated by systematic empirical data on sexual behavior in childhood. Almost a full century later such empirical data are still largely lacking. The various reasons for this are in large part due to social constraints but also include the fact that childhood sexual behavior tends to be a sporadic thing and therefore unlikely to be encountered over the periods of time when children are usually observed in research settings. On the other hand, a more direct approach of eliciting sexual responses from children has been and continues to be considered quite unacceptable. Even if we could elicit sexual information and behavior from children, their interpretation would continue to be problematic. Since so much of sexual experience is subjective, young children are limited by their inability to express these thoughts and feelings in intelligible form. Adults are tempted then to impose on the child's sexual behavior labels and interpretations derived from adult sexual experience. It is thus easy to refer to the self-manipulation of infants as "masturbation." It may well be that what the infant is doing in such cases is in fact a prototype of adult masturbation. But it is also possible that so far as the meaning of the act is concerned, this is not the case. The situation is in a way comparable to observing monkeys pressing their lips together and calling it "kissing."

Sexual arousal in childhood is easier to detect among boys than among girls, for it takes the visible form of penile erections. Such physiological proof is not always necessary, however, and activities that are seem-

ingly of a sexual nature may be observed in both sexes before puberty. Many of these sexual interactions take the form of play. Although adults are apt to dismiss play as merely amusement, it is in many ways a serious activity for the child. In the sexual sphere, too, the behavior of children takes the form of play. When we refer to "heterosexual" and other forms of sexual activity among children, we really mean sexual play in these various forms.

Another dilemma involves various types of interaction, such as kissing, hugging, caressing, and other forms of endearment. Such interactions between adults, infants, and children are universal in one form or another and, from all that we know, vital to proper development.

Are such activities sexual? On the one hand, the very thought of ascribing erotic motives to such innocent behavior might seem repulsive. On the other hand, such acts are difficult to distinguish at times from those that occur in sexual foreplay. Is the primary difference, then, one of conscious motivation? If the intent is to arouse or to become aroused, then is the activity sexual, whereas otherwise it is not? But then what if the participants are stimulated inadvertently, or the erotic motives are unconscious?

We do not have ready answers to such questions. Yet despite the sparse and fragmentary nature of information in this area and the many pitfalls in interpretation, there is enough of value in what we do know to consider some of the salient issues concerning childhood sexuality.

Responsive Capacity

When considering prepubescent sexuality one of the fundamental questions pertains to the physiological capacity of children to be sexually aroused. Given the fact that they are reproductively immature, what exactly are their sexual capabilities in biological terms?

---

[2]There have been others of course who have contributed to attracting attention to childhood sexuality. For instance in 1912, Moll wrote, "When we see a child lying with moist, widely-opened eyes, and exhibiting all the other signs of sexual excitement as we are accustomed to observe in adults, we are justified in assuming that the child is experiencing a voluptuous sensation."

The capacity for erection is present virtually right after birth. It has been shown to be very common between the ages of 3 weeks and 20 weeks. Among children under the age of 6 years, some 20 percent of boys and 14 percent of girls are reported as capable of sexual responses.[3]

During erections, infants show a greater tendency for thumb-sucking and restless behavior, including stretching and limb rigidity, fretting, and crying. Erections in 2- and 3-day-old males have also been noted to be more common during periods of crying. There is also an apparent association between alimentary functions and the incidence of erections. Feeding, sucking, fullness of the bladder and bowels, urination, and defecation are all activities that often seem to prompt erections.[4] Infants also experience erections during sleep even more commonly than adults.[5]

Given these contexts in which such erections are common, it is difficult to ascribe as complex a reaction as sexual arousal to infants. It is therefore assumed that such erections are reflexive. But this is not to say that they are erotically "neutral" events like a knee jerk, since there is some expression of pleasure that often accompanies them. Stimulation of the genital area of children of both sexes aged 3 to 4 months elicits smiles and cooing sounds (frequently accompanied by erection in males). Thus while erections may start as reflexive response to stimulation in the genital region, they are soon endowed with pleasurable potential, and erections become the primary expression of male sexual arousal, even though we do not know when and how this reflexive response becomes "eroticized."

[3]Ellis (1938).
[4]Halverson (1940); Sears, Maccoby, and Levin (1957).
[5]Karacan, Marens, and Barnet (1968); Korner (1969).

The progressive eroticization of genital responses notwithstanding, sexual arousal in childhood and early adolescence is often part of a more generalized state of emotional excitement. As shown in Box 8.1, a wide variety of nonsexual as well as sexual sources of stimulation elicit erotic responses among younger boys. Unfortunately no comparable data are available for girls.

Over time such indiscriminate erotic responses gradually give way to more selective patterns. By the late teens sexual response is by and large limited to direct stimulation of the genitals or to obviously erotic stimulations.

Prepubescent Orgasm

It is one thing to concede that children experience sexual arousal and another to accept the observation that they can also actually experience orgasm, sometimes even before the age of 6 months. In attempting to test this observation we run into two difficulties: First, since infants cannot talk, we have no way of knowing their subjective experiences. Second, females at any age do not ejaculate with orgasm, and prepubescent orgasm in males is not accompanied by ejaculation (for the prostate is still not fully developed). We thus have only other limited evidence we can observe. But, as we shall illustrate, the similarities between the observable indications and those of adult orgasm are so striking that there can be little doubt of their sexual nature.

Kinsey reported orgasm having been observed in boys of every age from 5 months and on. The manifestation consisted of "a series of gradual physiologic changes, the development of rhythmic body movements with distinct penis throbs and pelvic thrusts, an obvious change in sensory capacities, a final tension of muscles, especially of the abdomen, hips, and back, a sudden release of convulsions, including rhythmic anal contractions—followed by the disappearance of all

Box 8.1   Sources of Erotic Stimulation in Youth

NONSEXUAL SOURCES OF EROTIC RESPONSE AMONG PREADOLESCENT AND YOUNGER ADOLESCENT BOYS

Chiefly Physical

Sitting in class	Airplane rides
Friction with clothing	A sudden change in environment
Taking a shower	Sitting in church
Punishment	Motion of car or bus
Accidents	A skidding car
Electric Shock	Sitting in warm sand
Fast elevator rides	Urinating
Carnival rides, Ferris wheel	Boxing and wrestling
Fast sled riding	High dives
Fast bicycle riding	Riding horseback
Fast car driving	Swimming
Skiing	

Chiefly Emotional

Being scared	Big fires
Fear of a house intruder	Setting a field afire
Near accidents	Hearing revolver shot
Being late to school	Anger
Reciting before a class	Watching exciting games
Asked to go front in class	Playing in exciting games
Tests at school	Marching soldiers
Seeing a policeman	War motion pictures
Cops chasing him	Other movies
Getting home late	Band music
Receiving grade card	Hearing "extra paper" called
Harsh words	Adventure stories
Fear of punishment	National anthem
Being yelled at	Watching a stunting airplane
Being alone at night	Finding money
Fear of a big boy	Seeing name in print
Playing musical solo	Detective stories
Losing balance on heights	Running away from home
Loking over edge of building	Entering an empty house
Falling from garage, etc.	Nocturnal dreams of fighting, accidents, wild animals, falling from
Long flight of stairs	high places, giants, being chased, or frightened.

SEXUAL SOURCES OF EROTIC RESPONSE AMONG 212 PREADOLESCENT BOYS

Seeing females	107	Physical contact with females	34
Thinking about females	104	Love stories in books	32
Sex jokes	104	Seeing genitalia of other males	29
Sex pictures	89	Burlesque shows	23
Pictures of females	76	Seeing animals in coitus	21
Females in moving pictures	55	Dancing with females	13
Seeing self nude in mirror	47		

From A. C. Kinsey, W. B. Pomeroy, and C. E. Martin, *Sexual Behavior in the Human Male*. Philadelphia, Saunders, 1948, pp. 164–165. By permission.

Box 8.2   Orgasm in Infancy

The following description is by a mother who watched her three-year-old daughter go through the experience (from A. C. Kinsey, W. B. Pomeroy, C. E. Martin, and P. H. Gebhard, *Sexual Behavior in the Human Female*. Philadelphia: Saunders, 1953, pp. 104–105):

Lying face down on the bed, with her knees drawn up, she started rhythmic pelvic thrusts, about one second or less apart. The thrusts were primarily pelvic, with the legs tensed in a fixed position. The forward components of the thrusts were in a smooth and perfect rhythm which was unbroken except for momentary pauses during which the genitalia were readjusted against the doll on which they were pressed; the return from each thrust was convulsive, jerky. There were 44 thrusts in unbroken rhythm, a slight momentary pause, 87 thrusts followed by a slight momentary pause, then 10 thrusts, and then a cessation of all movement. There was marked concentration and intense breathing with abrupt jerks as orgasm approached. She was completely oblivious to everything during these later stages of the activity. Her eyes were glassy and fixed in a vacant stare. There was noticeable relief and relaxation after orgasm. A second series of reactions began two minutes later with series of 48, 18, and 57 thrusts, with slight momentary pauses between each series. With the mounting tensions, there were audible gasps, but immediately following the cessation of

pelvic thrusts there was complete relaxation and only desultory movements thereafter.

The following case is reported by a pediatrician (from H. Bakwin, Erotic feelings in infants and young children, *American Journal of Diseases of Children* 126 (July 1973):52):

At about 7 months of age . . . the daughter of a physician . . . took great fancy to dolls. She would press her body against a large rag doll to which she was very attached and make rhythmic movements. The movements at first took place only in the evening at bedtime. At 1 year of age she and the doll became inseparable. She carried it about with her all day and from time to time would throw the doll on the floor, lie down on top of it, and rhythmically press her body against it "as in the sexual act," according to her parents. Attempts to distract her during these episodes caused screaming. She would cling to the doll until she "felt satisfied." The parents thought that she "completed an orgasm in her own way." By about 15 months of age the episodes had decreased in frequency and were of shorter duration and by 17 months the masturbation took place only at bedtime.

When heard from at 4½ years, she was to all appearances a normal child. Her mother described her as alert, bright, and vivacious. She practiced her habit occasionally, perhaps three or four times during the preceding two years. At present she is a medical student.

symptoms."[6] Similar behavior has been observed among female infants (*see* Box 8.2).

Another interesting aspect of the sexual capabilities of childhood is the capacity for multiple orgasm. Kinsey reported one boy of 11 months who could reach 10 orgasms in an hour and another who experienced it 14 times in 38 minutes.

It is impossible to say how many infants and children have such experiences or how often. Although such activity is probably not

an everyday occurrence, much of it happens unobserved. Adults tend to ignore it or at least to fail to recognize its sexual significance. Although sexual responsiveness develops at different rates, Kinsey estimated that more than half of all boys could achieve orgasm at 3 to 4 years of age and almost all boys could do so three to five years before reaching puberty. (No comparable data exist for girls).

Autoerotic Play

Self-exploration and self-manipulation are the most common forms of sex play in the

[6]Kinsey et al. (1948), p. 177. The Kinsey survey is described in Box 8.14.

Figure 8.1 Infantile masturbation. From *The Erotic Drawings of Mihály Zichy*. New York: Grove Press, 1969, plate #24. Copyright © 1969 by Grove Press, Inc.; reprinted by permission.

child. As already noted, such activity has been observed in infants and children of all ages. Among infants observed from birth to the age of one year, self-stimulation of the genitals has been observed in more than 60 percent of cases.[7]

It is generally assumed that such masturbatory activity is discovered accidentally. As the infant shows an active interest in exploring his own body, he initially explores in a random and indiscriminate manner. But since contact with the genitals proves pleasurable, it tends to be repeated. As the child grows, self-exploration becomes more thorough and the sexual intent more obvious (*see* Figure 8.1).

Occasionally, an individual may actually remember masturbating, sometimes to the point of orgasm, as early as at 3 years of age. Particularly among girls (more than 85 percent), orgasm is first experienced through self-stimulation. Although boys indulge in considerable handling of their own genitals, fewer boys seem to carry it to climax: Under

70 percent reach their first orgasms this way.

Fondling the penis and manual stimulation of the clitoris are the most common autoerotic techniques.[8] Children easily discover the erotic potentials of thigh friction by rubbing against beds, other furniture, toys, and the like. Girls in particular are apt to stimulate themselves by rhythmic movements of the buttocks while lying down. A child may, however, learn to masturbate from seeing someone else do it, or from actually being taught by someone more experienced. Such experiences are more common among boys than girls.

Autoerotic activities in general seem more prevalent among boys. During the first year of life, males have been noted to engage in autoerotic activity about twice as frequently as female infants.[9] A higher prevalence for this activity among males has also been re-

[8]Autoerotic activities during the first year of life have been subsumed under three categories: self-stimulatory rocking, stimulation of the genital area, and manipulation of the penis (Spitz, 1949).

[9]Spitz (1949). But another investigation of the same age group has found no sex differences in this regard (Galenson, 1975).

[7]Spitz (1949).

ported for ages 1 and 2 years[10] and 4 through 14 years.[11]

Infantile masturbation may or may not be continuous with childhood masturbation. Most boys seem to learn to masturbate from one another. In the Kinsey sample nearly all males reported having heard about the practice before trying it themselves, and quite a few had watched companions doing it. (Three out of four boys were led to masturbating by hearing or reading about it. About 40 percent mentioned observing others as their primary inspiration.) Pubescent boys thus appear to be much more communicative about their sexual activities than are girls and are also bolder in seeking information. Fewer than one in three boys reported discovering this outlet by himself, and fewer than one in ten was led to it through homosexual contact.

Females learn to masturbate primarily through accidental discovery of the possibility (two out of three in the Kinsey sample), and they may begin as late as their thirties. Apparently females do not discuss their own sexual behavior as openly as males do; some women who know of male masturbation are startled to discover that the practice also occurs among females. Occasionally a woman may masturbate for years before she realizes the nature of her act, though such innocence was perhaps more common in the past. Furthermore, slightly more than 10 percent of girls in the Kinsey sample were initiated into masturbation through petting, which was true for very few males. After a girl experiences orgasm through petting (usually as a result of manipulation by the male) she may then use the same methods autoerotically.

It has also been theorized that the psychological significance of infantile and childhood masturbation is different. For example, Freud found childhood masturbation of critical importance as a potential cause of neurosis. He believed that its effects "leave behind the deepest (unconscious) impressions in the subject's memory, determine the development of his character, if he is to remain healthy, and the symptomatology of his neurosis, if he is to fall ill after puberty."[12]

His reasoning was that early infantile masturbation is no more than innocent self-exploration, that the infant obtains pleasure from it but is too young to be blamed or even to comprehend blame, and that masturbation is therefore conflict-free. During the next phase boys (at about 3 years old) go through the critical oedipal state; they are now capable of fantasies, and when masturbation is resumed, incestuous wishes become linked to it so that guilt and fear of punishment emerge.

In addition to these inner changes, the environment also now treats children differently: A boy of 4 is expected to behave properly, and masturbation is considered improper. He is told to stop, is threatened, and perhaps is ultimately punished. Parents may actually imply that harm will come to his genitals if he persists. He is bewildered. Are the threats directed at the act or at the fantasies (of which most parents are quite oblivious)? What will happen to him? What should he do? From this welter of unconscious conflicts under a façade of childhood innocence his psychological future takes shape.

Sociosexual Play

A child who is 2 or 3 years old interacts with other children with sufficient intimacy to carry his or her sexual explorations over into these relations. The child investigates playmates' genitals as well as exhibiting his or her own.

Next to autoerotic activities, the most common forms of prepubescent sex play are exhibiting and handling one's genitals in the presence of companions. These types of sex play are the precursors of future sociosexual

---

[10]Kleeman (1975).
[11]Gebhard and Elias (1969).

[12]Freud, *Three Essays on the Theory of Sexuality* (1905), in Freud (1957%1964), Vol. VII, p. 189.

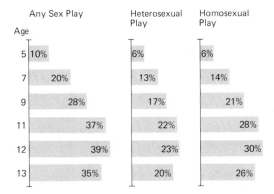

Figure 8.2 Percentages of prepubescent boys who had engaged in sociosexual play. From Kinsey et al., *Sexual Behavior in the Human Male.* Philadelphia: Saunders, 1948, p. 162. Courtesy of the Institute for Sex Research.

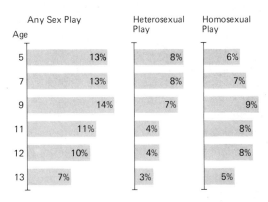

Figure 8.3 Percentages of prepubescent girls who had engaged in sociosexual play. From Kinsey et al., *Sexual Behavior in the Human Female.* Philadelphia: Saunders, 1953, p. 129. Courtesy of the Institute for Sex Research.

encounters. Figures 8.2 and 8.3 show the extent to which such sex play occurred at various ages and the sexes of the companions involved in the Kinsey data.

Although some people claim to remember specific instances of sexual arousal and orgasm from as early as the age of 3, it is only around the age of 5 that substantial numbers of children (about one in ten) appear to have their first sexual experiences beyond autoerotic exploration, thus qualifying as "sociosexual" behavior.

Comparison of Figures 8.2 and 8.3 also shows that boys became considerably more active in sex play than girls as age increased. Approximately 10–14 percent of girls were engaged in some form of sex play between the ages of five and twelve years (Figure 8.3). By contrast, there was an almost fourfold increase in the prevalence of sex play among boys between the same ages (Figure 8.2). The peak age for girls was 9, when 14 percent engaged in some form of sex play; boys attained their peak at age 12, when 39 percent were similarly involved.

In the Kinsey study, "sex play" meant actual genital play. This definition was not as stringent as that of "sexual outlet," which re-

quired culmination in orgasm (*see* Chapter 7), but it certainly excluded casual physical contact between children with uncertain erotic intent. Much prepubescent sex play is motivated by curiosity and influenced by the availability and sex of companions. To the extent that a child's companions are of the same sex, his sex play will likely be "homosexual." When a boy lies on top of a girl, it is viewed as coital play.

These actual or estimated percentages should not be taken to mean that children are constantly involved in sex play. For most children it is a sporadic activity. For example, one out of four boys who had engaged in sex play had done so only during one year, and some had participated in such play just once before puberty. Only one in three boys had persisted in such play on and off over five or more years. These limitations applied even more strongly to prepubescent girls. Nevertheless, Kinsey thought that his reported percentages were altogether too low and that probably nearly all boys (but only about a fifth of all girls) had engaged in sex play sometime before reaching puberty.

Finally, in both sexes prepubescent sexual activity did not increase with the approach of puberty. In fact, there was a slight but noticeable decline in sex play once the peak ages were passed. There is evidence that in some cultures the development of sexual behavior does not manifest such a "break" between childhood and the attainment of sexual maturity. Among other anthropoids also the sexual activity of the young animal merges imperceptibly with adult behavior. These observations suggest that the pattern shown in the Kinsey data may have been culturally determined.

Among prepubescent girls, in one out of three instances the activity did not go beyond genital exhibition and superficial exploration. Interestingly, girls were more likely to engage in mutual genital examination among themselves than with boys, and the same was true for vaginal insertions. Also only 5 percent of girls with prepubescent homosexual experience continued it into adolescence.

Adults must be careful about how they perceive and react to homosexual sex play among children. Since children are often quite unaware of the significance of such acts, we should refrain from ascribing adult sexual motives to them. These activities are largely experimental, imitative, exploratory play, sexual only in a general sense—unless an older, more experienced person stimulates the child and initiates him into a more frankly erotic response. It is particularly important not to label the sex play of children as deviant or perverse, no matter what it entails. To do so would be like calling a child who believes in ghosts and fairies "delusional" or "mentally ill."

Preteenaged boys are generally group- or gang-oriented. Sexual activities, as well as other behavior, thus tend to occur in these contexts; genital exhibition, demonstration of masturbation, group masturbation, and similar activities are quite common (*see* Figure 8.4). They satisfy social needs that are far broader than the mere release of sexual tension. Occasionally sex play with companions

becomes more like adult homosexual behavior, with oral-genital contacts and attempts at anal intercourse.

What is the relation of preadolescent homosexual play to adult homosexual behavior? According to the Kinsey data, fewer than half of all males continued homosexual play before puberty into adolescent and adult activity. At lower educational levels the likelihood of such continuation was greater (one out of two) than among college-educated men (a little more than one in four). Because the socioeconomically lower-class male youngster has relatively free access to coitus, his preference for homosexual contacts nonetheless may indicate stronger homosexual inclinations. Although prepubescent homosexual play more often than not stops at puberty, most adult homosexuals do trace their sexual preference to prepuberty; that is, whereas prepubescent homosexual acts do not necessarily lead to adult homosexuality, an adult homosexual is likely to have started homosexual practices before reaching puberty.

It has also been reported that more homosexuals than heterosexuals recall having had strong erotic attractions during childhood for members of their own sex. In addition, more homosexuals have never dated and have begun masturbating before the age of 13.[13]

The first heterosexual play experiences occur somewhat earlier for most boys than do their initial homosexual encounters, which usually occur at about age 9. Boys, rather than girls, are usually the instigators of heterosexual play, which 40 percent of men and 30 percent of women recall having experienced before puberty. Again, genital exhibition and handling are the most common activities.

Activities beyond these are difficult to evaluate. Finger insertions, for instance, are more apt to be part of an exploratory sequence and do not go farther in than the girl's

[13]Manoswitz (1972).

Figure 8.4 Boys masturbating. From *The Erotic Drawings of Mihály Zichy*. New York: Grove Press, 1969, plate #30. Copyright © 1969 by Grove Press, Inc.; reprinted by permission.

introitus. Children also have well-known games like "playing house," "papa and mamma," and "doctor." The titles vary, but the scripts are the same. During such play there is usually a good deal of lying on top of one another, but even when children occasionally undress, the activity does not proceed beyond mere genital apposition. In the Kinsey sample more than 10 percent of boys, but only a small proportion of girls, were reported to have engaged in such "coital play."

Adult types of sexual activity during preadolescence are much more likely to occur when one partner is older and more ex-

perienced. In the hands of an experienced partner, a child can be trained to engage in practically all forms of sexual activity, including oral-genital contact and coitus. Even where children are not directly instructed in such activities, they are more likely to engage in them if they have had occasion to observe adults in such behaviors.

Prepubescent Sexual Contacts with Adults

Sexual interactions between adults and children can be viewed in two broad contexts: In the first, adults act as the socializing agents in the sexual development of the child; in the second, adults themselves become the actual partners in the sexual activity involving children.

Adults as Socializing Agents

In developmental terms, socialization is the process whereby children learn the norms of their society and acquire their own values, beliefs and personality characteristics.[14] Children are socialized in regard to most forms of behavior through such institutions as the family and schools. A good deal of socialization also occurs of course informally. Currently sexuality is by and large left out of the formal process of educating children be it in schools or at home.

Why sexuality should be singled out for such neglect or active suppression is hard to understand and even harder to justify. The prevailing view indeed seems to regard the best sexual teaching as that which teaches without provoking further questions or sexual behavior.

Parents have been described as exercising three main types of information control concerning sexual matters. First, through "unambiguous labeling," parents point out and label certain behaviors as wrong but with no explanation as to why they are wrong. Second, through "nonlabeling," they avoid the issue by attempting to distract the child when he manifests sexual interests. Finally, through "mislabeling," a sexual activity is condemned not for what it is but for spurious reasons. Thus, the child may be told not to play with his sex organs to avoid "getting germs."[15] This last maneuver has also been described as the use of "borrowed sanctions." Parents may also avoid labeling sex altogether or give the genitalia and sexual acts amorphous names.

It is often suggested that children should be educated sexually at home. Many parents find the prospect bewildering since they often lack adequate information themselves. But even if well informed, when is one to begin such instruction? What does one say? How far does one go beyond stories of "birds and bees"? Now that many adults have by and large abandoned their traditionally restrictive attitudes, even sophisticated parents may feel paralyzed by uncertainty at what to encourage and what to discourage in their children.[16] Professional advice tends to be fragmentary and more often based on the adviser's "common sense" and convictions than on tested evidence. Not that such advice cannot be quite useful.[17] As a result, even enlightened parents tend to fall back on steering a moderate course whereby they neither give coital demonstrations to their children nor punish the children when they touch their genitals. Instead, the parents try to respond to the children's questions as they arise. But this often entails considerable uncertainty and discomfort for all involved.[18]

The sexual activities of children and their often unused sexual potential raise important developmental, as well as social, questions. In the West there is no general agreement on how we should regulate the sex lives of children. The dominant traditional values have generally been restrictive: Sexual contact with adults has been strictly prohibited and sex play among children discouraged. Often even didactic sexual instruction in any form has been opposed as potentially stimulating and therefore harmful. There is

---

[14]Wrightsman (1977). Also see Brim (1966). For a comprehensive review of socialization theory and research, see Goslin (1969).

[15]Gagnon (1968); Sears et al. (1957).

[16]It is reported that toilet training, masturbation, sex play, and concerns about homosexuality are the more common problems that prompt parents to seek professional guidance regarding their children's behavior (Heagarly, Glas, and Ming, 1974).

[17]For examples of current professional opinion in this regard, see Spock (1970), pp. 372–383, and Fraiberg (1959), pp. 210–241.

[18]For an overview of sex education and its potential in preventing sexual disorders, see Calderone (1978).

Box 8.3   Cross-Species Comparisons in Childhood Sexuality

Comparison of human sexual development patterns with those of subhuman species is particularly instructive in clarifying the biological and cultural components of preadolescent sexuality. Subhuman primates and lower mammals show a great deal of sexual activity before puberty. Clearly, sexuality precedes fertility, and the rudiments of adult sexual behavior are easily discernible in the sex play of the young of many animal species.

Lower mammals show juvenile sexual behavior more clearly among males than among females. Before the first period of heat the female animal is sexually unresponsive. Males, however, show mounting behavior long before reproductive maturity has been achieved.

Young monkey masturbating. From Harlow, "Lust, Latency and Love: Simian Secrets of Successful Sex." in D. Byrne, and L. Byrne, (Eds.) *Exploring Human Sexuality.* New York: Crowell, 1977, p. 166. Reproduced by permission.

Infant and adolescent chimpanzees are well known for their active involvement in autoerotic (solitary masturbation is more common in males), heterosexual, and homosexual sex play. Long before reproductive maturity is reached, they attempt copulation and experiment with various positions. Males may orally stimulate females, who may, in turn, manually arouse the males.

Young monkeys imitate practically all adult sexual behavior.[1] A seven-month-old pigtail monkey (equivalent in development to a 2-year-old child) was observed mounting his mother, having an erection, and making copulatory thrusts. Similar manifestations of early sexual activity have been observed among baboons and other subhuman primates of both sexes.

Adult sexual activity among chimpanzees often takes place in full view of infants and juveniles, who seem to take an active interest, as is reported in this account:

On six occasions in the wild, late infant-twos watched carefully when their mothers were copulating. On one occasion an infant went close, peered intently underneath its mother, reached out one hand and felt in the region where the penis was inserted into the vagina. This behavior was also observed by Kortlandt (personal communication). An adolescent male, which had probably just attained puberty, had no difficulty in performing the sexual act.[2]

[1]Zuckerman (1932). Beach also See (1947).
[2]Jane Goodall, in DeVore (1965), p. 450. This source also has other accounts of juvenile primate behavior.

now, however, growing concern that this area may be one of the most neglected in the upbringing of children and that a great deal of confusion and damage result when the children are left to "sink or swim" in their sex lives. In certain countries (for example, Swe-den) there are already extensive sex education programs in schools. Attitudes in the United States are still ambivalent, and the issue has caused sharp disagreement among various segments of the population.

It may well be that the opposition to sex

Box 8.4 Cross-Cultural Comparisons in Childhood Sexuality

Cross-cultural comparisons of child-rearing practices offer opportunities to learn from what are, in fact, "natural experiments." We may, for instance, learn about the effects of sexual contacts between children and adults, which we would be loath to experiment with among ourselves. Unfortunately, because of the limited and fragmentary nature of cross-cultural data, only some of our questions can be answered.

Ford and Beach[1] have thus categorized cultures according to levels of adult permisiveness: restrictive, semi-restrictive, and permissive.

Restrictive primitive societies vary in the severity of their control of preadolescent sexuality, but as a rule they attempt to keep children from learning about sexual matters and to check their spontaneous sexual activities. For instance, both the Apinaye (a primitive, peaceful, monogamous people in Brazil) and the Ashanti (a complex polygynous society in Guinea) expressly forbade children to masturbate from an early age. In New Guinea a Kwoma woman who saw a boy with an

erection would strike his penis with a stick. Kwoma boys soon learned not to touch their penises even while urinating.

The secrecy that surrounded sex also often extended to reproductive functions. Humans or even animals giving birth might not be watched by children, and fictitious explanations of where babies come from were offered. Special precautions were taken to keep children from surprising adults while they were engaged in coitus; children might even be placed in separate sleeping quarters at an early age.

It is interesting that even in these more restrictive societies the expression of sexuality in childhood could not be entirely checked. Children still engaged in sex play when they could, even though they may have done so in fear or shame.

Messenger has provided a detailed account of an unusually repressive island folk community in Ireland, which he calls Inis Beag:

The seeds of repression are planted early in childhood by parents and kin through instruction supplemented by rewards and punishments, conscious imitation, and unconscious internalization. Although mothers bestow considerable affection and attention on their

[1]Ford and Beach (1951).

---

education in schools is not broadly based but comes from a highly vociferous minority. In support of this are the findings of a 1977 Gallup poll showing that 77 percent of the respondents (as against 65 percent in 1970) approved of sex education in schools. Similarly, the percentage who supported the discussion of contraceptives in sex education courses went up from 36 percent in 1970 to 69 percent.[19]

When confronted with the issue of sex-

[19]Family Planning Perspectives (1978).

ual socialization of children, cross-cultural and cross-species comparisons can prove quite useful (*see* Boxes 8.3 and 8.4).

Incestuous relations with parents are of particular concern. Though admittedly quite rare, current work shows that actual incestuous involvement is far more common than previously assumed. Also, traditionally, incest has been viewed as an overwhelming and frightening experience for the child. While this model may well hold true in many cases, there are also situations when the incestuous interaction occurs in a gentle, affectionate

Box 8.4 Continued

offspring, especially on their sons, physical love as manifested in intimate handling and kissing is rare in Inis Beag. Even breast feeding is uncommon because of its sexual connotation, and verbal affection comes to replace contact affection by late infancy. Any form of direct or indirect sexual expression—such as masturbation, mutual exploration of bodies, use of either standard or slang words relating to sex, and open urination and defecation—is severely punished by word or deed. Care is taken to cover the bodies of infants in the presence of siblings and outsiders, and sex is never discussed before children.[2]

Permissiveness toward sexual behavior during the developing years does not mean complete absence of rules and regulations. All societies have prohibitions on certain sexual activities in childhood and later. Relative to the cultures already discussed, however, permissive societies showed remarkable laxity toward youngsters' sexual activity.

Among various Pacific islanders and other permissive cultures, children of both sexes freely and openly engaged in

[2]John C. Messenger, "Sex and Repression in an Irish Folk Community," in D. S. Marshall, and R. C. Suggs, eds. Englewood Cliffs, N.J.: Prentice–Hall, Inc., 1971, p. 29. Reproduced by permission.

autoerotic activities and sex play, including oral-genital contacts and imitative coitus. These children were either instructed in sex or allowed to observe adult sexual activity. In a few societies adults actually initiated children sexually. Siriono (polygynous nomads of Bolivia) and Hopi parents masturbated their youngsters. Mangaian women orally stimulated the penises of little boys.

In these permissive cultures sex play became progressively more sophisticated and gradually merged with adult forms of sexual activity. With the exception of incest, youngsters were generally free to gratify their growing and changing sexual needs. Sexual activity was actually encouraged early in life. The Chewa (polygynous advanced agriculturists of central Africa) believed that children should be sexually active if they wished to ensure fertility in the future. The Lepcha (monogamous agriculturalists of the Himalayas) believed that sexual activity was necessary if girls are to grow up: At 11 or 12 years most girls were engaging in coitus, often with adult males. Trobriand boys of 10–12 years and girls of 6–8 years were initiated into coitus under adult tutelage.

manner, aberrant as the broader context may be.[20]

Children of both sexes have been sexually exploited by adults probably in all cultures. Regardless of criminal sanctions (*see* Chapter 14) some adults continue to approach children sexually. We do not know exactly how prevalent this problem is. In the Kinsey female sample about one out of four women had been sexually approached by

[20]Rosenfeld et al. (1979); Rosenfeld (1979). For an extensive discussion of incest see Meiselman (1978).

someone five or more years older than herself when she was preadolescent. Most women (80 percent) had experienced such contacts only once each, about 5 percent had had such encounters nine or more times before adulthood. About half the time the adult was a stranger, but one-third of the approaches involved friends and acquaintances; and about one in five involved relatives (uncles, fathers, brothers, and grandfathers in order of decreasing frequency).

In about half the instances the approaches consisted of exhibition of the adult male genitals. Next came fondling the children without genital contact (31 percent) and genital manipulation (22 percent). Other forms of activity were rare. Coitus, for instance, was reported in only three out of one hundred instances of adult sexual approach (0.7 percent of the entire female sample). A few of the girls were as young as 4 or 5 years old when these incidents occurred, but most were 10 years old or older (though still prepubescent).

In a Playboy Foundation survey,[21] 14 percent of males had had sexual contact with a "relative" (13 percent heterosexual; 0.5 percent homosexual). The corresponding figure for females was 9 percent (8 percent heterosexual and 1 percent homosexual). Most of these contacts fell short of incest as the term is commonly used: Two-thirds of the male and two-fifths of the female experiences were with cousins; over a quarter of the males and over half the females went no further than "light petting" and so on. Sexual contacts within the nuclear family mainly involved siblings: 3.8 percent of the males reported contact with sister; of the female subjects 3.6 percent reported contact with brothers and 0.7 percent with sisters. Contact with parents were restricted to fathers with daughters (0.5 percent).

Adults as Sexual Partners

Many forms of socialization entail the direct interaction of adults with children whereby they become partners in work and play. In the sexual realm such interaction between adult and child is highly restricted. Children are to various degrees exposed to nudity at home and in the public media. Even several decades ago 90 percent of the women in the Kinsey sample reported having seen male genitals (most often those of their fathers) by adolescence. It is also not uncommon to hear, if not see, parents or other adults

engaged in amorous activities. But beyond such distant involvements actual sexual contact between adults and children is mainly restricted currently to secret, guilt-ridden, and variously pathological interactions. At least it is these sorts of interactions that come to social or medical attention.

The impact of precocious sexual stimulation on young children is generally believed to be quite detrimental. Clinicians have traced serious psychological disturbances in adults to such childhood experiences. The Kinsey survey, though admittedly superficial from a clinical point of view, did not seem to substantiate the notion that childhood sexual experience with adults necessarily results in serious damage. There is also some cross-cultural evidence that in societies where the handling of children's genitals by adults is socially acceptable, there seem to be no resultant psychological problems.[22]

Perhaps the most cogent argument against the sexual association of adults and children is that such partnerships work out best among equals. Children are dependent on adults and therefore vulnerable to exploitation. They cannot reasonably be assumed to enter such a relationship with a comparable understanding of what it entails and are not equally experienced to manage their end of the relationship.

It is also important to bear in mind that when children are subjected to such experiences, it is not just the nature of the act but the manner in which they have been dealt with that may determine the psychological impact. The attitudes of the parents are also crucial when the activity comes to light. Much of the meaning the child may attach to what happened will be colored by the parents' handling of the situation.[23]

---

[21]This survey is described in Box 8.15.

[22]Stephens (1963), pp. 376–377; see also Box 8.4.

[23]We shall discuss further the issue of sex between adults and children when we deal with pedophilia and incest (*see* Chapter 11).

Theories of Psychosexual Development

Theories of psychosexual development are attempts to explain the evolution of sexual functioning in the context of general development. As the term "psychosexual" indicates, sexual and psychic processes are intimately interrelated, and it is not possible to understand one apart from the other.

Currently there is no generally accepted theory of psychosexual development. Nevertheless, there are many areas of general agreement. Also certain aspects of sexual development are best explained by one theory and other aspects by some other theory.

The main contributions to our concepts of sexual development come from biology, psychoanalysis and learning, and sociological theories. We cannot discuss these approaches here adequately at any length and the usual brief synopses tend to oversimplify and distort these complicated notions (Boxes 8.5, 8.6, and 8.7 provide a few highlights).[24]

What we shall discuss at some length is an interesting approach to psychosexual development through the study of monkeys.

The Development of Affectional Systems

During the past two decades psychologists have been studying the development of affectional systems in monkeys, with fascinating results. Although this research is still in progress, enough has been learned to postulate certain general principles that appear to be quite pertinent to understanding human sexual behavior.[25] Monkeys, of course, are not the same as people, and their interactions lack the enormous complexity of human relations. Yet the relative simplicity of their behavior patterns, coupled with the opportunities to manipulate them experimentally, make them excellent subjects for study.

Perhaps the most important result of this research so far is the confirmation of the notion that sex, even among nonhuman primates, involves complex behavior that can emerge effectively only when related developmental tasks have been properly met. Monkeys do not "automatically" copulate. Their ability to do so is dependent on a long sequence of antecedent interactions with caretaker adults, as well as with peers.

In this context "love" refers to affectional feelings for others (thus excluding narcissism or self-love). It consists of five basic kinds: maternal love, paternal love, infant-mother love, peer or age-mate love, and heterosexual love. These love systems, though discrete, are not necessarily temporally distinct. Each love system prepares the individual for the next phase, with which it overlaps, and problems in one are reflected in having difficulties in the others.

These integrated and interdependent affectional systems have their "sexual" components. The infant monkey clings to its mother without an overt desire for coitus; but it is nevertheless manifesting a form of behavior that is a necessary precursor for more specifically sexual activities in the future. In this sense, the following discussions of love are not a digression from but an integral part of our discussion of sexuality.

Maternal Love

The love of the mother for the infant is as nearly universal an emotion as we could hope to find. We generally assume that maternal love is innate in females. Girls respond to babies differently than do boys long before they reach puberty. Although such differences between the sexes could reflect cultural influences, the coexistence of innate propensities is not ruled out. For example, similar differences in attitudes toward rhesus monkey

---

[24]The general principles of psychoanalytic theory and theories of learning are covered in most introductory psychology texts. See, for instance, Hilgard et al. (1979), McConnell (1977), or Zimbardo (1979).

[25]The leader in this research is Harry F. Harlow. For a general discussion of his work see Harlow et al. (1971).

Box 8.5 Biological Approaches to Sexual Development

For many years the biological basis of sexual behavior was tied to the concept of a "sexual instinct." Although there is no agreement on what constitutes an "instinct," many students of behavior still find this concept useful in explaining activities that appear to be universal in members of a species, that have demonstrable physiological bases, and that are adaptive.[1] But "instinctive" must not be equated with "innate" in efforts to reduce behavior to its "learned" and "unlearned" components. Attempts at drawing such dichotomies in behavior have generally proven fruitless. For example, it is often impossible to differentiate between behavior that is learned and genetically determined behavior that does not appear until maturation.

Despite the ambiguities, however, the biological basis of sexual behavior and the influence of biological factors in the development of such behavior can hardly be denied. In humans, as in the vertebrates as a whole, adult sexual behavior is the product of the interaction of biological (genetic, hormonal, and so on) and experimental (psychological, social) factors throughout the life cycle. During intrauterine life, development is predominantly under the influence of genetically determined factors. But adult humans, in contrast to very young human beings and to lower animals, appear relatively emancipated from the control of these biological forces, though to exactly what extent we do not know.

Nevertheless, as Beach has pointed out:

To interpret the sexual behavior of men and women in any society it is necessary first to recognize the nature of any *fundamental*

[1]Tinbergen (1951) has defined "instinct" as, ". . . a hierarchically organized nervous mechanism which is susceptible to certain priming, releasing, and directing impulses of the internal as well as external origin, and which responds to these impulses by coordinated movements that contribute to the maintenance of the individual and species."

There is extensive literature on this topic. For a general discussion of instincts see Curtis (1968), pp. 614–624. See also Young, ed. (1961), Vol. II, Chapter 23, for a discussion of the ontogenesis of sexual behavior in man by Hampson and Hampson;

---

babies have been demonstrated among prepubescent male and female macaque monkeys, even though the latter had not been raised by monkey mothers and had never before seen infants younger than themselves.[26]

The maternal-love system appears in several stages. First is the stage of care and

comfort. As the very survival of the infant monkey depends on the feeding, care, and protection afforded by its mother, it spends a great deal of time being physically cradled or clinging to the mother and thus obtaining vital "contact comfort." It is in this early and intimate relationship that the infant establishes the basis for all its future associations, sexual and otherwise.

Maternal love is initially elicited by the mere presence of the baby, but if it is to be sustained, the baby in turn must respond. A monkey mother can even "adopt" a kitten as her own, but because the kitten cannot reciprocate by clinging as a monkey baby can, she will ultimately abandon it.

[26]Chamove et al. (1967), pp. 329–335. Such findings are particularly interesting, for they appear to provide some biological basis for the nearly universal cultural attitude that the care of the infant is the mother's privilege and obligation. From this premise follow additional conclusions about the place and role of women in society and so on, conclusions that are currently being challenged in some quarters. Incidentally, though it is true that the female animal is *usually* the primary caretaker of the young, this is not always the case.

Box 8.5 Continued

mammalian pattern and then to discover the ways in which some of its parts have been suppressed or modified as a result of social pressures brought to bear upon the individual [emphasis added].[2]

The abstract arguments over the concept of instinct that preoccupied scientists in the past have now been replaced by the experimental approaches of ethologists—Konrad Lorenz and Niko Tinbergen being the two best known. Although the applicability of their findings to the study of man is often unclear, much has been learned from their work about the interaction of innate patterns of behavior and environmental factors that elicit such behavior.

It has been demonstrated that some animals respond to very specific cues from the environment. For example, a mother hen responds to the peeping of a chick. She will ignore a chick that she cannot hear (if the chick is under a glass jar, for example), but will come to the rescue of any object that peeps as if it were a chick.

[2]Quoted in Diamond (1965), p. 167.

The mating behavior of the stickleback progresses quite predictably. The male fish displays his red underbelly, in response to which the female turns to him her swollen abdomen and follows him to the nest that he has built. The pair go through a number of additional moves and countermoves, and the sequence culminates when the male fertilizes the eggs laid by the female in the nest.

In these and numerous other examples the animals exhibit specific, stereotyped behavior that is innate and believed to be mediated through neurophysiological mechanisms called "Innate Releasing Mechanisms" (IRM). The external cues that stimulate these mechanisms are specific ("cue stimuli" or "social releasers"). Systematic study and demonstration of similar phenomena among humans remain to be accomplished, but the presence of such mechanisms among animals is itself of great interest, for it permits the experimental, rather than the speculative, study of innately determined patterns of behavior.

Among humans the life-sustaining functions of the mother can be adequately replaced with bottle feeding and so on. But close, physical, comforting contact with affectionate adult caretakers remains imperative.

The second, or transitional, stage in maternal love is characterized by ambivalence. As the infant must ultimately survive on its own, the monkey mother begins to encourage the development of independence by becoming less protective and even by rejecting and punishing at times.[27] In sexual

terms this emotional "weaning" is essential if the infant is going to be able to go out as an adult and relate to mates.

The third and final stage of maternal love is that of relative separation, which among monkeys gradually leads to the severance of the affectional bond between the mother and the maturing offspring. The arrival of a younger sibling accelerates this process.

Older infants who have established peer relations are able to forgo the need for close maternal contact during the day, but at nightfall they make persistent efforts to reestablish maternal contact; as a last resort they may even seek physical comfort from adult males.

[27]Chimpanzees, unlike monkeys, are less likely to resort to physical punishment. A chimpanzee mother who is trying to wean her infant will resort to tickling and other playful techniques to distract it from the nipple (Van Lawick-Goodall, 1967).

Box 8.6   Psychoanalytic Stages of Psychosexual Development

Freud viewed the "sexual instinct" as a psychophysiological process (like hunger) with both physical and mental manifestations. By "libido" (Latin for "lust") he meant the psychological manifestations, the erotic longing aspect of the sexual instinct. The libido theory was a conceptual scheme that purported to explain the nature and manifestations of the sex drive throughout development.

Psychoanalytic formulations of psychosexual development start with the assumption that the newborn child is endowed with a certain libidinal "capital." Psychosexual development is then the process by which this diffuse and labile sexual energy is "invested" in certain pleasurable zones of the body (mouth, anus, genitals) at successive stages of childhood. The vicissitudes of the libido during psychosexual development determine not only the sexual functioning of the individual but also the entire personality structure and psychological (and at times physical) health.

The oral zone is thus the first site of libidinal investment and the mode of its gratification is through "taking in," or incorporation. The erogenous zone invested with libido during the second stage of development is the anus. The general modes of gratification at this stage are two:

retention and elimination (counterparts of incorporation). The oral and anal stages generally extend through the first three years of a child's life. As the genitals have not yet been invested with libido, these stages together are designated "pregenital"; they are identical for males and females.

At the age of about 3 years the child becomes keenly aware of his or her genitals and of the pleasures of manipulating them. The zones now invested with libido are the penis in the male and the clitoris in the female. Behavior is dominated by the "intrusive mode."

The main psychoanalytic issue related to this stage is the development of the Oedipus complex. The child develops an erotic attachment to the parent of the opposite sex and feelings of aggressive rivalry toward the parent of the same sex. This development places the child in a dilemma: First, he or she does not have the capacity to gratify the genital impulse; second, he or she still loves (and fears) the "rival" parent, and thus suffers guilt. A boy imagines that he deserves punishment involving genital damage or "castration" (actual loss of the penis, rather than the testes). The "reasoning" behind this fear is that he expects punishment of the offending part. He has discovered that girls

Incidentally, there are interesting differences among monkey species in this regard. For example, among pigtail monkeys the infant interacts socially primarily with the mother and close relatives. Yet bonnet monkeys appear to interact with kin and others with equal frequency.[28] Since pigtail and bonnet monkeys are all part of the macaque group, it is clear that such "cultural" differences exist even among closely related groups in primitive animal societies.

[28]Kaufman and Rosenblum (1969).

Infant Love

The love of the infant for the mother is closely related to and reciprocal with maternal love. The two affectional systems are nevertheless distinct and can be studied separately. Unlike the mother, who develops emotional ties to the baby even while she is still pregnant, the newborn is at first quite indiscriminate in his feelings toward others. Among both humans and other primates, the infant's earliest responses are reflexively determined. They include sucking responses, the rooting reflex (stimulation of the cheek elicits explor-

Box 8.6   Continued

have no penises, and his fear that the penis can be lost is substantiated. A girl's reaction to the discovery that boys have penises may be to conclude that she has lost her own and to envy the male's apparent advantage ("penis envy").[1] The child resolves the oedipal conflict by giving up the parent as an erotic object (while continuing to love this parent) because of the child's own fear of disapproval and retaliation and the obvious hopelessness of the desires. Instead, the child identifies with the parent of the same sex, hoping one day to acquire comparable prerogatives. To ensure that unacceptable wishes will not be fulfilled or continue to torment the person, the entire conflict is buried in the unconscious. The oedipal wishes never-theless do not simply fade, and their deriv-atives occasionally seep into consciousness.

The successful resolution of the Oedipus complex signals the end of the phallic stage and makes it possible for "genital maturity" to emerge—not that the 3- or 4-year-old child is sexually adult. The next phase of development (latency) is for

most youngsters a period of intellectual growth, social maturation, and fairly limited sexual activity.

At the beginning of adolescence sexuality reawakens. To the extent that past conflicts have been satisfactorily resolved, the young person is free to initiate sexual interaction along adult lines. But such conflicts may not all have been resolved. Pregenital fixations may make it difficult, if not impossible, to invest the libido in "normal" sexual objects.

Gradually, however, "genitality" should manifest itself. The young man should cease to be preoccupied with his penis and should react sexually with his whole self. The young woman should go beyond the intrusive mode and incorporate the "inceptive" and "inclusive" modes into her psychosexual structure.

The psychoanalytic ideal of "gen-itality" encompasses the integration of pregenital stages to permit the recon-ciliation of genital orgasm with love and to facilitate establishment of satisfactory life patterns of sex, procreation, and work. Freud's response to the question of what ought to be the central purpose of life was "work and love."

[1]Psychoanalysts now concede that Freud developed his sexual theories from a male perspective; using the male as his prototype, he superimposed his model on his description of women also. See Salzman in Marmor, ed. (1968), p. 127.

atory head movements that help to locate the nipple), groping, grasping, clinging, and so on. Such unlearned, species-specific behavior patterns among human infants have been called "instinctual response systems."[29]

As these interactions between infant and mother are reflexive, the first stage in the development of the infant's affectional sys-tem is that of "organic affection." This stage is practically concurrent with the stage of comfort and attachment that, among mon-

keys, consists of actual bodily contact be-tween infant and mother soon after birth. This stage includes both the cradling of a passive infant and active clinging by the infant to the mother. Such "contact comfort" seems to be more important than even nursing in the de-velopment of the monkey infant's attachment to the mother.

Next comes the stage of solace and se-curity, in which the presence of the mother or mother surrogate enables the infant mon-key (and the older human child) to wander beyond the mother's immediate vicinity to

[29]Bowlby (1969).

Box 8.7   Theories of Learning

"Learning" is readily understood in an everyday sense, yet it defies a formal definition that would be generally acceptable. A simple way to approach it is to consider as learned all behavior that would not appear unless it was either specifically taught by someone else or learned by the individual through trial and error, imitation, and so on. Innate responses (like nest-building by birds), new behavior that reflects maturation (like flying of birds when they are of age), and changes in performance resulting from fatigue are thus excluded. Reasoning, imagination, inventiveness, and insight are mental functions that also differ from learning in a strict sense, but are dependent on and closely related to it.

We are interested here in the learning of human sexual behavior. Unfortunately, little of the literature on learning theory treats sexual behavior specifically. We shall therefore assume that learning sexual behavior proceeds along the same general lines as does all other learning.

Although learning theory may seem to offer a unified approach or a single conceptual scheme, actually there is no single widely accepted learning theory. Instead there are many theories of learning, including those of Thorndike (connectionism), Guthrie (contiguous conditioning), Skinner (operant conditioning), Hull (systematic behavior), Tolman (sign learning), and Lewin (field theory), as well as those of the classical Gestalt school, the more eclectic approach known as "functionalism," and various approaches using mathematical learning models.

The original experiments on conditioning were conducted by Pavlov.[1] His paradigm is now called "classical conditioning" to differentiate it from later-developed techniques of "operant conditioning."

In Pavlov's experiment the salivation of the dog always occurs in response to a specific external stimulus (food or bell). But in actual life most animal behavior is spontaneous. Dogs do not sit around waiting for food, but actively look for it. To differentiate such spontaneous behavior from activity that involves actions elicited by specific external stimuli, the term "operant behavior" is used, and the acquisition or modification of spontaneous behavior is called "operant conditioning."[2] The concept of operant behavior provides a much more versatile and comprehensive framework than does classical conditioning for understanding both animal and human behavior, sexual and otherwise.

[1]Pavlov (1927).
[2]Skinner (1938).

explore the environment. This initial effort is followed by greater detachment and environmental exploration, culminating in a stage of relative independence.

The parallels between the development of the maternal and infant love systems are quite clear. First, there is a phase of close and intense attachment, followed by progressive independence. When the infant's personal and social security are established, he can move out. Without this basic security the infant is socially paralyzed. On the other hand, when the attachment to the mother persists in full force, the infant remains helplessly dependent on her. The primary function of the maternal and infant love systems is, then, to prepare the infant for the demands and satisfactions of the peer relations that must be developed next.

Paternal Love

Manifestations of paternal love among monkeys and apes are infrequent and inadequately studied. It has been hypothesized

Box 8.7 Continued

Although in Pavlovian and related theories there is the general notion of a drive that activates the organism, in Skinnerian and related theories the notion is less of a push from within than of a pull from without (exerted through the mechanism of reinforcement) which shapes the learning behavior. Without dwelling on these differences, let us now examine some specific examples of how the mechanism of conditioning may explain the learning of sexual behavior.

A little girl becomes sexually aroused while climbing a rope, riding a bicycle, or pressing herself against her mattress. She does not understand the significance of this novel feeling, but since it is pleasant, she tries to elicit it again, and this time she uses her hands. One day she carries the activity far enough to experience orgasm; she has now learned to masturbate. The pleasure thus obtained positively reinforces the activity, and it may become habitual.

A boy who has already experienced the pleasurable effects of orgasm finds himself one evening in bed fretting over the events of the day or anxious about some forthcoming activity. He gets sexually aroused and masturbates. In addition to pleasure (positive reinforcement) his troublesome thoughts and anxious feeling disappear as sexual excitement increases (negative reinforcement). From then on

masturbation holds for him a dual reward, and he may resort to it to obtain pleasure or to be rid of unpleasant feelings.

Bandura and Walters[3] have proposed a social learning theory that focuses attention on modeling, whereby the person learns from someone else's experience rather than through spontaneous personal trial (hence referred to as "no-trial learning").

How much of such research can be generalized to the learning of sexual behavior? One would think that the general principles would apply, and in specific instances this can be seen to operate, such as when youngsters learn to masturbate from each other or older peers. This type of imitative behavior has also been reported among nonhuman primates.

Probably the major reason why so little psychological research pertains directly to sexual behavior is because of its emphasis on experimental work. Since psychologists are subject to the same internal and external inhibitions and pressures of their cultures as others are, such experimental work remains unfeasible at this time.

[3]Bandura and Walters (1963).

that innate, biologically determined affection for the infant is much less strong in the nonhuman primate male than in the female. Male monkeys do, however, learn to love and protect infants through imitation of the mother. Conversely, the infant's affectional ties to the male are far less apparent than are its attachment to the mother, although infants will occasionally seek out adult males for comfort when no females are available.

Among humans paternal love can be just as intense as maternal love, and, though

in most cultures mothers perform the primary child-rearing functions, fathers can and occasionally do fulfill the same role. It is generally assumed that, ideally, maternal and paternal love must supplement each other in providing the infant with full complement of love and emotional nurture during growth and development.

Age-Mate or Peer Love

Research with monkeys indicates that the peer affectional system is probably the most important of all affectional systems in sociosexual development. The rudiments of peer love appear in early infancy and expand progressively throughout childhood, adolescence, and adulthood. The primary vehicle for the development and expression of peer love is play, through which earlier affectional systems are integrated and the love systems to follow are anticipated.[30]

Attachment to peers begins as the infant becomes capable of wandering away from the mother briefly and is permitted and encouraged to do so. In humans, affectional relations with peers are usually established at about age 3 years (4 months for monkeys) but do not reach their peak until the ages of 9 to 11 years. They gradually decline during adolescence as the heterosexual affectional system emerges.

The transfer to peers of at least part of the infant's love for the mother has been explained according to different theories. In the psychoanalytic scheme the shift involves an unconscious reorganization of libidinal attachments ("cathexes") through the use of such "defense mechanisms" as displacement. Learning theorists account for it through "stimulus generalization" from mothers to peers. It has also been suggested that "contact comfort" is transferred from mother to peers. If the child is to develop normal sexual responses, he or she must have been provided with and must have accepted a certain degree of physical contact very early. Such contact must have been pleasurable and comforting for the child to seek it in play with peers. Contact comfort does not necessarily refer to specifically genital contact, but is based on general body contact. At the psychological level the child must also be able to transfer to peers the "basic trust" that he or she has developed toward the adult caretaker. We shall discuss this important notion of "basic trust" later.

Heterosexual Love

The heterosexual affectional system has its roots in the earlier love systems, but it emerges as a distinct entity at the time of puberty, matures during adolescence, and operates as the primary sociosexual affectional system for most adults.[31]

The heterosexual love system in primates, including humans, develops through three subsystems: mechanical, hormonal, romantic. The mechanical subsystem depends on the anatomical and physiological properties of the sexual organs, physiological reflexes, appropriate body postures and movements, and so on. As discussed in earlier chapters, some of these mechanical functions, like penile erection, are present at birth. Others, like ejaculation, develop at puberty. Some features of this mechanical subsystem (for example, sexually differentiated genitals or pelvic thrusting) are common to all primates. Others are peculiar to some. Monkeys, for example, have a basic adult sexual posture (*see* Figure 8.5), whereas man is far more versatile in this respect (*see* Figures 10.5 and 10.7). This basic adult monkey posture has been shown to arise out of three discrete responses during infant play: threat by the male and passivity (turning her back) and rigidity (supporting the male) by the female.

In Figure 8.6 we see the basic presexual play position adopted by a juvenile pair and

---

[30]Play is a complex activity that serves different functions at different ages. Presocial play (play with inanimate objects), for example, precedes social play. Presocial play may in turn be exploratory, parallel (playing beside other children rather than with them), or instigative. Social play may be free, creative, or formal. For a discussion of these various forms of play as they relate to sexual development, see Harlow et al. (1971), pp. 76–85.

[31]Throughout this discussion we assume that heterosexuality is a normative affectional system in adults, which is the point of view expressed in Harlow et al. (1971). As we discussed in Chapter 7, neither the bases of judgments in these matters nor the issue of "normality" will be considered here.

Figure 8.5 Basic adult sexual posture. Courtesy of Wisconsin Regional Primate Research Center.

Figure 8.6 Basic presexual position. Courtesy of Wisconsin Regional Primate Research Center.

in Figure 8.7 the first attempts at mounting. These monkeys are engaged in play, not in coitus, yet the female's passive position and willingness to support the male and the latter's grasping of her hindquarters and efforts at mounting have an unmistakable resemblance to the basic adult sexual posture (*see* Figure 8.5).

The second, or hormonal, subsystem has also been discussed as it operates in humans (*see* Chapter 4). The sexual behavior of nonhuman primates and of lower animals is much more firmly under hormonal control. Although much remains to be learned about the precise roles of sex hormones in human physiology, their importance cannot be underestimated, particularly in relation to sexual growth and maturation.

The third component of the heterosexual love system is the romantic subsystem— among monkeys the subsystem of transient heterosexual attachments. Although we cannot attempt to do justice here to human ro-

mantic love, we should point out that in a general sense comparable attachments also characterize the relations of nonhuman primates, with due allowance for their cognitive limitations. Nonhuman primates are not indiscriminately promiscuous. Rather, their associations are characterized by the formation of pairs of compatible individuals. Relations between lower animals show no such selectivity, with some notable exceptions: Beavers, one species of deer, and wolves are known to form long-lasting relationships.

Although each of these three subsystems can operate independently to some extent, full heterosexual expression requires their integrated and complementary functioning. These subsystems also vary in their vulnerability to disruption. For example, social isolation early in life does not disturb hor-

Figure 8.7 The first attempts at mounting. Courtesy of Wisconsin Regional Primate Research Center.

monal functioning but seriously disrupts some mechanical functions and has a disastrous effect upon the transient affectional, or romantic, subsystem. Inasmuch as studies of social isolation in infant monkeys conducted by Harlow and his associates have provided highly pertinent insights into sexual behavior, we shall briefly describe them here.

In these experiments male and female monkeys were reared in isolated wire-mesh cages and thus denied the opportunity to develop infant- and peer-love affectional systems. At puberty the socially deprived males showed every evidence of normal physical development. They also achieved erection and masturbated, sometimes to orgasm, at rates comparable to those of undeprived monkeys. Socially deprived females also be-

Figure 8.8 Inappropriate response by socially deprived male to receptive female. Courtesy of Wisconsin Regional Primate Research Center.

Figure 8.9 Inadequate sexual presentation by socially deprived female. Courtesy of Wisconsin Regional Primate Research Center.

haved essentially in a fashion comparable to that of undeprived females, as far as hormonal functioning and autoerotic activities were concerned.

But the effect of social isolation in infancy on adult sociosexual behavior was calamitous. Deprived males would be visibly aroused in the presence of females, but would stand puzzled, not knowing what to do (*see* Figure 8.8). They would grop aimlessly and act clumsily with receptive females, or they would brutally assault them. The impact of social isolation on females was somewhat less damaging. Although they mistrusted physical contact and would flee or attack males, they could be induced in time to endure at least partial sexual contact with undeprived males. Figure 8.9 shows the inadequate sexual posturing of a socially deprived female and the sexual disinterest of a normal male in response to it.

These experiments leave no doubt that heterosexual activity cannot develop adequately in an affectional vacuum and that even the coital postures have to develop in the context of infantile and peer interactions. Although we obviously cannot and should

not attempt to replicate these findings in humans, there is much in them that seems familiar to faulty human sexual development. Human interactions are infinitely more complex, and the transition from peer love to the romantic subsystem involves transitional mechanisms of great intricacy, involving trust, acceptance of physical contact, and motivation for physical proximity and behavioral sex role differentiation. As Harlow has put it: "Sex secretions may create sex sensations, but it is social sensitivity that produces sensational sex."[32]

Adolescent Sexuality

Despite the importance of prepubescent sexuality, puberty and adolescence are the periods when adult sexuality emerges. The discovery of the importance of infantile sexuality so fascinated early psychoanalysts that adolescence for a while attracted only secondary interest, but it has more recently been restored to its position as a crucial phase for the study of sexual development.

[32]Harlow et al. (1971), p. 86.

Biological Aspects

Biologically the key features of puberty are accelerated growth, development of secondary sex characteristics, and initiation of reproductive capacity. These changes have already been discussed (*see* Chapter 4), and we shall not examine them again here. Certain features will, however, have to be reiterated because of their bearing on the development of sexual behavior.

First, puberty and adolescence are not points in time but periods of time. Puberty extends over three or four years in females and longer in males. Adolescence is even more protracted.[33] As puberty generally begins one or two years later in males, pubescent girls are clearly ahead of boys in reproductive development. But, as we shall see, reproductive capacity is not the same as sexual responsiveness.

Second, puberty begins at different times for different members of each sex. There is also some variation in which of the many body changes appear first. Convention and convenience dictate adoption of menarche in the female and first ejaculation in the male as the primary points of reference, but they are not entirely satisfactory because a number of changes, like growth of pubic hair, generally precede them. In fact, some young men and women may be fully developed sexually for several years before having their first ejaculations or their menarches. Nor does the appearance of these physiological processes necessarily indicate the beginnings of the psychological changes of puberty. Despite the intimate association between reproduction and sex, the two are separate functions and develop on separate schedules.

There is no doubt that the bodily changes

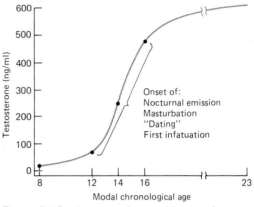

Figure 8.10 *Amount of testosterone in the plasma of human males at different ages.* From Beach, in *Reproductive Behavior*, ed. W. Montagna and W. A. Sadler. New York: Plenum, 1974.

of puberty are the result of hormonal influences. But what about the concomitant changes in sexual behavior? The intensification of sexual interest and activity during adolescence has been traditionally ascribed to an upsurge of "sexual drive," and this in turn has been assumed to be another reflection of endocrine influences. This is a plausible hypothesis. As shown in Figure 8.10, the increase in the level of testosterone certainly does seem to correlate with a number of significant events, but we are far from understanding the more precise relationship of increased levels of steroid and other hormones and the marked changes in sexual behavior. The likelihood is that such behavioral change is not a simple outcome of higher hormone levels. For instance, in precocious puberty increased hormonal levels and their somatic manifestations are not generally accompanied by a concomitant increase in sexual motivation in precocious children who continue to act their age. Thus all we can say at this point is that the profound changes in hormonal balance at puberty can be presumed somehow to influence the sexual motivation of the growing individual.

---

[33]Adolescence is often divided into "early adolescence," which encompasses most of the high-school years, and "late adolescence," which may extend into the twenties. These age ranges are subject to great individual and cultural variation.

Sex Differences

During prepubescence the male and female orgasmic experiences are physiologically similar, if not identical. But following puberty, when males begin to ejaculate during orgasm, a distinct sex difference is established—with physiological and psychological repercussions.

Although the adolescent boy may have already experienced orgasm, his first ejaculation is an impressive and long-remembered event. Among physiologically normal males in the Kinsey sample the earliest ejaculation remembered was at about 8 years of age and the latest, again among apparently healthy men, at 21 years of age. About 90 percent of all males had had this experience between the ages of 11 and 15 years (the mean age was 13 years and 10.5 months).[34] Ejaculation could occur outside these limits in pathological conditions. Even this apparently purely biological phenomenon reflected socioeconomic influences: In the lowest educational group the mean age for first ejaculation was 14.6 years, almost a year later than in the most educated group. The differences among individuals were very great: Some boys in elementary school were sexually more mature than other boys in high school.

The first ejaculation resulted most often from masturbation (in two out of three instances), nocturnal emissions (one out of eight instances), and homosexual contacts (one out of 20 instances). It may rarely have occurred "spontaneously" (through fantasy alone, without direct genital stimulation). Contrary to popular belief, nocturnal emissions were not the most frequent harbingers of puberty. Usually they occurred a full year after the first ejaculation had been (or could have been) experienced. First ejaculations through nocturnal emissions were more common in higher socioeconomic groups.

[34]Kinsey et al. (1948), pp. 185–187.

"Spontaneous" ejaculations, though rare, are of special interest. As the ability to have them is almost always lost after puberty, it, too, attests to the high and indiscriminate level of excitability in younger males. "Spontaneous" ejaculations reportedly occurred in response to various physical (but not genital) activities (chinning on bars, vibrations of a boat) and psychological provocations (watching couples petting, milking a cow, reciting in front of a class). Some ejaculations that appear to be spontaneous (as when climbing a tree) may in fact be caused by genital friction, even though the boy may be, at least initially, quite innocent of sexual intent.

The second sex difference of some consequence is the discrepancy in the rate of maturation of sexual functions. As reported by Kinsey and as illustrated in Figure 8.11, the development of puberty as manifested by the appearance of pubic hair starts in girls a year or two earlier than in boys. But while there is a close developmental association between this event and the experience of the first ejaculation, the curve for female orgasm is widely set apart from that of pubic hair de-

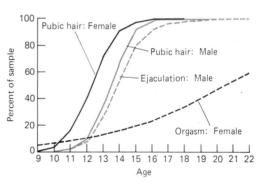

Figure 8.11 Cumulated percents, comparing female and male: onset of adolescence and sexual response. Appearance of pubic hair is taken as first adolescent development, and orgasm or ejaculation as specific evidence of erotic response. From Kinsey et al., *Sexual Behavior in the Human Female*. Philadelphia: Saunders, 1953, p. 126. Reproduced by permission.

velopment. It is quite possible that this apparent sex difference merely reflects social factors that retard the maturation of the female sexuality during puberty. Since attitudes in this regard have changed since Kinsey's time more current information will help clarify the existence and nature of this sex difference.

Behavioral Aspects

The psychosocial transition to adulthood through adolescence is as complex and crucial an event as the physical passage through puberty. It is indeed far more confused and problematic for many persons in contemporary society.

Sexual behavior in adolescence is in many ways continuous with its childhood antecedents. But the transition is by no means a simple progression from sexual play to the "real thing" or an inexorable turning up of the volume of desire and activity as the person enters adolescence. For one thing, there seems to be a definite reduction in sexual experience during preadolescence (Figures 8.2 and 8.3). Furthermore, the meaning of various sexual acts in childhood may be quite different later on. In this sense sexual experiences through the life cycle can be considered somewhat discontinuous.

To recapitulate our earlier discussion, boys and girls seem to reach peaks of prepubescent sexual activity and then, in our culture, to manifest gradual declines. The subsequent course of events differs for the two sexes. Partly because prepubescent sex play is more prevalent among boys, despite its relative decline before puberty more of it actually continues into adolescence. In this regard, in the Kinsey sample petting to orgasm was found to be more likely to persist during the transition into puberty and adolescence (among 65 percent of boys) than were other sexual outlets. Homosexual contacts were most likely to be interrupted. A year or so before the onset of puberty this relative qui-

escence apparently comes to an end, and boys show an upsurge of sexual activity that accelerates during the period of puberty: Sporadic prepubescent sex play is replaced by steady levels of sexual activity. In a few years most boys reach the sexual acmes of their lives. As a group they will never again attain higher levels of total sexual outlet.

The sexual development of females contrasts with that of males in a number of ways. First, as prepubescent sex play was less prevalent among females, the interruption in sexual activity before puberty appeared much more marked. The pubescent girl had to begin all over, as it were. Furthermore, during female puberty there was no sudden upsurge in sexual activity comparable to that of males. Instead, women showed slow but steady increases in sexual responsiveness that reached peaks in the middle 20 and early 30 years of age (Figure 8.11).

There have been many studies of adolescent dating behavior, but few specific investigations of adolescent sexual activities. Much of this information is scattered in various reports.[35] Sorensen's survey would have filled a major gap in our knowledge of adolescent sexuality, but regrettably its findings are not generalizable to the U.S. population (see Box 8.8 for an evaluation of his work). They are nevertheless of some interest, given their currency.

A better study of the sexual behavior of young people was carried out in Britain in the early 1960s by Schofield (Box 8.8). Its findings too cannot be generalized to the U.S. population, but we shall refer to some of them nevertheless.

In Sorensen's sample of youth of both sexes between the ages of 13–19, 48 percent were virgins (girls 55 percent, boys 41 percent), and 52 percent had had sexual intercourse one or more times (girls 45 percent,

---

[35]For a review of the literature in adolescent sexuality, see Schofield (1965) and Katchadourian (in press).

Box 8.8 Surveys of Adolescent Sexual Behavior

There have been quite a few studies of the sexual behavior of college students in this country, but few investigations of teenage sex. One of these was conducted by Robert C. Sorensen, a social psychologist and marketing and research executive.[1] The objective was to collect a comprehensive set of data on various forms of sexual behavior that would be generalizable to the population at large. The task of data collection was delegated to a commercial survey research organization. The instrument used to gather the data was a self-administered questionnaire. The sample was restricted to those between the ages of 13 and 19.

Of the original randomly selected 839 adolescents eligible for the survey, less than half were actual respondents. We are confronted, therefore, with a serious problem of self-selection. The problem of self-selection was further compounded by the process of obtaining parental consent. As one would suspect, the more conservative parents would be more likely to deny their consent, and the examples of parental refusals that Sorensen duly reports confirm this. In other words, the sample used has a high probability of being weighted in favor of the sexually more permissive adolescents of sexually more liberal parents, rather than being a true national portrait.[2]

By contrast, studies of premarital sex by John Kantner and Melvin Zelnik have utilized excellent samples and rigorous research methods. In the first phase of this work a national probability sample of 4611 never-married women aged 15 to 19 were studied in 1971.[3] The focus was on contraceptive use and frequency. The study

was repeated in 1976 (with a sample of 15- to 19-year-old women including the never-married and the ever-married).[4]

Both the 1971 and 1976 data were derived from national probability sample surveys of women in the specified categories living in households in the continental United States. Samples were stratified by race to ensure substantial numbers of black respondents. The 1971 study yielded 4392 and the 1976 study 2193 completed interviews.

This research provides good comparisons on coital behavior at a five-year interval between whites and blacks and relative to a number of other social variables.

An interesting study of teenage sexual behavior in Britain was conducted by Schofield in the early 1960s.[5] The subjects were 1873 unmarried persons of both sexes, aged 15 to 19, and drawn from seven districts in England, three of which were in London. The subjects were interviewed by members of the research team of the same sex. The refusal rate was 15 percent.

During the interview, subjects were first asked for answers to simple questions on background and leisure activities following which more questions on sexual behavior were introduced. The interview schedule consisted of 261 items of which 234 were direct questions. Following these questions, the teenagers were given an attitude inventory of 50 statements. The interviewers were also expected to rate the subjects under ten headings. Schofield's report is instructive in showing how careful work in this area is done and what pitfalls remain nevertheless. Part of this research population was restudied seven years later.[6]

[1]Sorensen (1973).
[2]For a more detailed critique of the Sorensen report, see Kantner (spring 1973).
[3]Kantner and Zelnik (1972) and (1973). See also the chapter by these authors in Westoff and Parke (1972), pp. 359–374.

[4]Zelnik and Kantner (1977).
[5]Schofield (1965).
[6]Schofield (1973).

boys 59 percent). About one in five persons in the total sample was "sexually inexperienced," not having engaged even in petting (girls 25 percent, boys 20 percent). An almost equal ratio (17 percent) had engaged in petting, but not coitus (girls 19 percent, boys 14 percent). The balance of the virginal group was not classifiable in the above groups.

The nonvirgins were also separable into various categories. About one in five (girls 28 percent, boys 15 percent) had had a sexual relationship with one person ("serial monogamist"). Fifteen percent of all adolescents were "sexual adventurers," who freely moved from one partner to another (boys 24 percent, girls 6 percent). The balance of nonvirgins were "inactive" (no coitus for more than a year) or classified in still different ways. Sorensen provides additional information on the background characteristics of these adolescents and their correlation with sexual activity.[36]

The sexual behaviors reported by Schofield among 15- to 19-year-olds could be fitted into five stages:

I. *Little or no contact with the opposite sex:* may have been out on a date but has never kissed.
II. *Limited experience of sexual activities:* has experience of kissing as defined in this research and may have experience of breast stimulation over clothes, but has never experienced this under clothes.
III. *Sexual intimacies which fall short of intercourse:* has experience of breast stimulation under clothes and may have experienced genital stimulation or genital apposition, but has no experience of sexual intercourse.
IV. *Sexual intercourse with only one partner.*
V. *Sexual intercourse with more than one partner.*[37]

Figure 8.12 shows percentages of boys and girls who have engaged in the various

[36]Sorensen (1973), p. 122.
[37]Schofield (1965) p. 41.

sexual activities listed above. Most individuals who engage in sex would seem to follow a fairly predictable sequence. What kinds of sexual liberties one takes and when are largely determined of course by the particular cultural context. In this regard, not only the adult world but the youth subculture in particular is very influential. But we must resist lumping all youth together in this or in any other regard. Despite superficial similarities, young people can act in quite individualistic ways. Nor should one conclude that the behavioral sequences described above are necessarily the best way in which adolescent sexuality could be manifested. We shall deal in more detail with specific sexual behaviors in adolescence, such as masturbation, coitus, and homosexual contacts in subsequent chapters.

Psychosocial Aspects

Puberty and adolescence are among the most important landmarks in the life cycle. It is through the biological and psychological changes experienced during the second decade that the transition to adulthood is accomplished on many fronts, particularly in the sexual realm. The most crucial change from the perspective of the survival of the human species is the development of reproductive maturity. But from an individual's perspective the psychosocial tasks of becoming a sexual adult are just as significant (*see* Box 8.9). Sexuality is important to the psychosocial tasks of adolescence at three major levels: As part of the process of identity formation; as vehicle for developing interpersonal relationships; and as part of the socialization process into adulthood.

From the point of view of psychosexual development the primary significance of petting is its role in initiating heterosexual psychosocial encounters. Although petting in adolescence progresses concurrently with masturbation and less often with homosexual

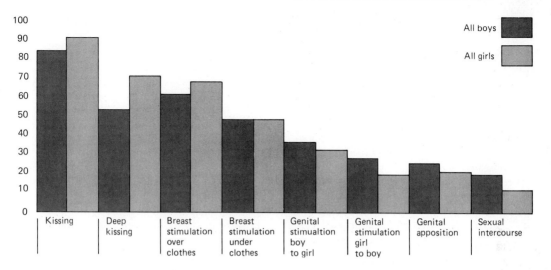

Note: Passive genital stimulation for girls is placed with active genital stimulation for boys in the fifth category. In the following category active genital stimulation for girls is placed with passive genital stimulation for boys. In general girls take the passive role in most sexual activities; thus when the activities are put in this order, the overall pattern of sexual development for both sexes is followed.

Figure 8.12 The incidence of eight sexual activities shown in percentages for boys and girls. From Schofield, *The Sexual Behaviour of Young People*. Boston: Little, Brown, 1965, p. 31. Reproduced by permission.

contacts, it gradually gains in primacy; for most people it provides the bridge to adult heterosexual intercourse. Adolescents learn much about each other's bodies, sexual responses, and so on while petting. Through these encounters they also learn the social rules and customs of sexual behavior.

These tentative and often tremulous encounters frequently go beyond the specifically sexual and involve feelings of intimacy, tenderness, and love. Through these interactions adolescents learn about each other's emotions and thoughts. It is during this period that concepts of sex roles, notions of masculinity and femininity, and the other components of sexual identity begin to be consolidated.

Our remarks here are intended only to be illustrative. We do not pretend to offer a universal model of sexual development during adolescence. The same tasks may be accomplished with minimal or no physical sexual contact at all. Or adolescents may proceed directly to full-fledged sexual activity without

benefit of these "trials." The outcome in the nature and quality of adult sexual life is thus not a simple function of how much sex or what sort of sex a person has during adolescence. Rather, a host of factors, sexual as well as other kinds, interact to shape sexuality in the context of overall development.

From a social perspective adolescent sexuality is of enormous significance. It may be relatively easy for parents and society to dismiss or deny the manifestations of sexuality in childhood. But with adolescence it becomes impossible to continue to do so. Adolescents in Western societies currently engage in a good deal of sexual activity amidst considerable ambiguity as to the desirability of such behavior. Without becoming judgmental over the issue of teenage sex, it is necessary to confront two very serious outcomes of sexual behavior in adolescence. The first is venereal disease, and the second is pregnancy. About half the cases of venereal disease reported in the United States occur among per-

Box 8.9   The Eriksonian Approach to Psychosexual Development

In Erikson's scheme the life cycle—the entire life span from birth to death—is characterized by eight phases of psychosocial development. Each phase is defined by the primary accomplishment of a phase-specific task, even though the resolutions are generally prepared in preceding phases and worked out further in subsequent ones.[1]

Erikson views development as proceeding according to the epigenetic principle "that anything that grows has a ground plan, and that out of this ground plan the parts arise, each part having its time of special ascendency, until all parts have arisen to form a functioning whole."[2] This view is a reformulation of the fundamental principle that embryological development progresses from the simpler to the more complex through the building units or cells. Viewed in this light, the child is not simply a miniature adult, just as the sperm is not a tiny fetus. Sexuality is a

potential that will develop if permitted and assisted throughout the individual's life span but particularly during the formative years.

Sexuality is an important factor in the task of identity formation, the concept for which Erikson is best known. Part of the process of identity formation is the formation of its sexual aspect. Biological features are the primary "givens," but they do not necessarily determine the individual's own self-perceptions as masculine or feminine or the way that he or she is perceived by others. The components of such definitions and the sex-role expectations implied vary markedly from culture to culture, even though the basic biological givens remain constant. It is thus up to each individual to clarify and consolidate his or her own sexual character as part of the larger task of identity formation. Cultures that provide clear and consistent models and guidelines facilitate this task for their members.

Despite the upsurge in sexual activity during adolescence, only after identity formation has been fairly well consolidated does true intimacy with the opposite sex (or with anyone else) become possible. Adolescent sexuality is often experimental, part of the search for identity. People may

[1]For Erikson's reformulation of psychosexual development see *Childhood and Society* (1963), chapter 2. His scheme of psychosocial development is briefly stated in chapter 7 of the same work, but it is more fully elaborated in *Identity and the Life Cycle* (1959), Part II, and in *Identity: Youth and Crisis* (1968), chapter 3.

[2]Erikson (1968), p. 92.

---

sons who are younger than 25; about one in ten in this group contracts venereal disease in a given year. There are an estimated 200,000 teenagers who contract venereal disease (usually gonorrhea) each year, making these infections less common only than the common cold. The highest rates of gonorrhea among women are at age 18. Since many cases of venereal disease go unreported, such official figures as quoted here do not even indicate the actual number of cases.

The statistics on teenage pregnancy are equally startling. An estimated million teenage girls, constituting one in ten between the

ages of 15 and 19, get pregnant every year. Of this group, about 600,000 actually bear children, sometimes with serious consequences both to the mother and to the child.[38] Even marriage does not always help, since three out of five teenagers who marry after getting pregnant will get divorced within six years.

These are sobering statistics, which must be understood and dealt with without casting a pall on the marvelous process of the blos-

[38]For further discussion of gynecological problems that result from teenage sexual activity see Raub and Burket (1979).

Box 8.9 Continued

marry in the hope of finding themselves through each other, but the need to fulfill defined roles as mates or parents often actually hampers this effort.

The task of intimacy versus isolation is specific to young adulthood (Phase 6). On the strength of the accomplishments of earlier phases, the young adult develops the capacity to establish a workable ratio between these two extremes. Intimacy requires expressing (and exposing) oneself, giving and sharing, and both sexual and more general union.

Isolation and loneliness ("distantiation") in appropriate amounts are also necessary. No matter how satisfying a relationship, both partners need some solitude. A certain distance in this sense helps them to keep each other in proper focus. When intimacy fails or is exploited, self-preservation is reliant on the ability and readiness to repudiate it, to isolate oneself, and, if necessary, to annul such destructive ties.

The similarities in the general conclusions we can draw from Harlow's experimental work and Erikson's clinical research are quite clear. Monkeys or humans cannot grow and function in isolation. Even though each individual is unique, he or she can be understood only in the context of relations with fellow beings. Sex is a complex and pervasive force that has a biological basis but can function properly (or be understood adequately) only in the context of affectional networks and life as a whole.

Erikson has said:

As an animal, man is nothing. It is meaningless to speak of a human child as if it were an animal in the process of domestication; or of his instincts as set patterns encroached upon or molded by the autocratic environment. Man's "inborn instincts" are drive fragments to be assembled, given meaning, and organized during a prolonged childhood by methods of child training and schooling which vary from culture to culture and are determined by tradition. In this lies his chance as an organism, as a member of a society, as an individual. In this also lies his limitation. For while the animal survives where his segment of nature remains predictable enough to fit his inborn patterns of instinctive response or where these responses contain the elements for necessary mutation, man survives only where traditional child training provides him with a conscience which will guide him without crushing him and which is firm and flexible enough to fit the vicissitudes of his historical era.[3]

[3]Erikson (1963), p. 95.

soming of sexuality during adolescence. How to become a full-fledged sexual adult is thus among the most important issues facing us personally and as a society. Unfortunately, we seem to be still quite far from being able to deal with it collectively in a satisfactory way.

Sexual Identity

The term "identity" (from the Latin for "sameness") refers to the persistent individuality and sameness of a person or thing over time and under different circumstances. Sexual identity is the component of a person's identity that pertains to his or her sex. Two key components of sexual identity are gender identity and sex roles.

Among the most important determinants of sexual behavior are the gender identity of the individual and the sex roles defined by society. To be genetically, hormonally, and anatomically male or female lays the groundwork for sexual behavior. The resultant maleness and femaleness is the "sex" of the person. But on this biological bedrock must be constructed the psychosocial structure of the sexual identity of that person. The fact of being a biological female or male must be given cultural meaning. Thus, beyond

Box 8.10 The Concept of Gender Identity

The origin of the term *gender identity* is recent, yet preoccupation with masculinity and femininity long antedates contemporary scientific interest in it. In Chinese philosophy and religion, the masculine principle called *Yang* and the feminine principle called *Yin* are attributed not only to men and women, but to everything in existence, including inanimate objects, spirits, and events. [1]

Although the Yang and Yin cannot be simply equated with facets of sexual identity, some contemporary writers have used the Yang and Yin or some similar idea to represent the male and female points of view, which are present in different proportions in every individual of either sex. The Jungian concept of the animus and anima is a case in point.

Jung conceived the anima and the animus as archetypal figures that are rooted in the collective unconscious. The *anima* represents the feminine personality components of the male and at the same time the image that he has of feminine nature in general—in other words, the "archetype" of feminine. Likewise, the *animus* represents the masculine personality components of the female and also her concept of masculine nature. Normally, both masculine and feminine characteristics are present in every individual, but the person expresses outwardly the set of characteristics that are considered socially appropriate to his or her sex, and are therefore not disturbing to the ideal self-image. [2]

The word *gender* is derived from the Latin *genus* meaning birth or origin, and hence representing a certain type. It is primarily a grammatical term representing the subclassification of certain words, usually nouns and pronouns, as masculine, feminine, or neuter. The term "gender identity" was introduced only a few decades ago because of the concern that the use of the word "sexual" in sexual identity was ambiguous since it also could refer to sexual activities.

As expressed by Robert Stoller, who introduced the term *gender identity*, ". . . the word *sexual* will have connotations of anatomy and physiology. This obviously leaves tremendous areas of behavior, feelings, thoughts, and fantasies that are related to the sexes and yet do not have primarily biological connotation. It is for some of these psychological phenomena that the term *gender* will be used: One can speak of the male sex or the female sex, but one can also talk about masculinity and femininity and not necessarily be implying anything about anatomy or physiology. Thus, while *sex* and *gender* seem to common sense to be practically synonymous, and in everyday life to be inextricably bound together, the realms (sex and gender) are not at all inevitably bound in anything like a one-to-one relationship, but each may go in its quite independent way. [3] The concept of gender identity has proved useful in emphasizing the psychosocial components in sexuality. The contrast between maleness and femaleness as reflections of biological sex, and masculinity and femininity for its nonbiological aspects, has indeed helped refine discussions.

[1] Thompson (1969).
[2] Jung (1969).
[3] Stoller (1968), pp. vii–ix.

being male or female, the person develops a sense of being masculine or feminine. These characteristics of the personality are referred to as gender identity (*see* Boxes 8.10 and 8.11).

Currently, there is a good deal of confusion over what terms like gender identity and sex roles mean. [39] For our purposes here,

[39] For further discussion of the terminological problems of sex and gender see Katchadourian (1979).

Box 8.11   The Concept of Sex Roles

A closely related concept to gender identity is that of sex role, alternately referred to as gender role. The term as well as the notion of *role* originated in the theater. The Latin word *rotula* means a small wooden roller. The parchment containing the actor's script was rolled around this rod and hence was referred to as the *roll* (or *rowle*). The actor's role is thus defined by the script to be reenacted in the play.

Sociologists define *role* in terms of an individual's "position," by which they mean the "location" of an "actor" or class of actors in a system of social relationships. Such a position is independent of any particular person and entails a more or less explicit set of responsibilities and prerogatives. A *role* is then the set of social expectations as to how someone in a given position should behave towards others in other positions. Roles are in this sense another variety of norms or shared rules about behavior.

Sex roles are those roles determined by sex. They pertain to many aspects of our lives. Some of these define societal expectations of, for instance, what women and men are supposed to do vocationally. Other sex roles pertain more directly to how males and females are supposed to behave sexually. Such social expectations are enormously influential in how we behave sexually. Thus, in addition to determining for instance whether or not a man or a woman or both should take the initiative in sexual encounters, the differential functions and status to which the two sexes are relegated even in ostensibly totally nonsexual contexts may significantly affect their sexual lives.

---

we will rely on the definitions of Money and Ehrhardt whose integration model of psychosexual differentiation will be discussed shortly. These definitions are as follows:

Gender Identity: The sameness, unity, and persistence of one's individuality as male, female, or ambivalent, in greater or lesser degree, especially as it is experienced in self-awareness and behavior; gender identity is the private experience of gender role, and gender role is the public expression of gender identity.

Gender Role: Everything that a person says and does, to indicate to others or to the self the degree that one is either male, or female, or ambivalent; it includes but is not restricted to sexual arousal and response; gender role is the public expression of gender identity, and gender identity is the private experience of gender role.[40]

The genesis of gender identity and sex roles long antedate adolescence. But for most persons these tasks of sexual definition reach their culmination during adolescence, hence

[40]Money and Ehrhardt (1972), p. 4.

the justification of our discussing them at this juncture.

An Integrative Model of Psychosexual Differentiation

No serious investigator of psychosexual development now argues against the proposition that human gender identity can best be understood as the end product of the interaction between biological and social variables. But such an agreement, in the abstract, has not prevented serious controversy about the relative influences exerted by various factors in shaping sexual identity.

Traditionally, it was assumed that genetic sex determined at conception inexorably guided sexual development throughout the prenatal and postnatal life eventuating into full-fledged sexual adulthood. The effects of learning as well as deviations from the norm were recognized, but the major underlying differentiating force was assumed to be biological.

During the past two decades this model

was challenged by a number of investigators who studied a group of hermaphrodites and showed that, in the majority of cases, these children grew up according to their assigned sex rather than genetic sex (*see* Chapter 4 and Box 8.12). Their conclusion was:

. . . in place of a theory of instinctive masculinity or femininity which is innate, the evidence of hermaphroditism lends support to a conception that psychologically, sexuality is undifferentiated at birth and that it becomes differentiated as masculine or feminine in the course of various experiences of growing up.[41]

This hypothesis of sexual neutrality at birth was quite influential, but did not go unchallenged. The major criticisms were that data from hermaphrodites may not be generalizable to the general population, and also that this approach failed to take into account other evidence that pointed to the existence of a distinct sexual orientation rather than sexual neutrality at birth.[42]

More recently, Money and Ehrhardt have brought together a vast amount of information from numerous fields and have proposed an interactional model of psychosexual differentiation that is integrative and attempts to avoid outmoded dichotomies between, " . . . nature versus nurture, the genetic versus the environmental, the innate versus the acquired, and biological versus the psychological, or the instinctive versus the learned.[43]

Money and Ehrhardt refer to their proposed scheme as a model of psychosexual or gender identity differentiation (rather than psychosexual development), and consider

[41]Money, Hampson, and Hampson (1955).
[42]For an exposition of this viewpoint and a critique of the sexual neutrality at birth theory, see Diamond (1965).
[43]Money and Ehrhardt (1972), p. 1. In the following discussion we will rely primarily on this source, but will be unable to do more than briefly outline the salient aspects of the work. For those interested in further study of this topic, the Money and Ehrhardt book provides the best overview currently available.

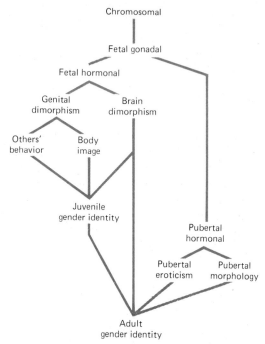

Figure 8.13 *The sequential and interactional components of gender-identity differentiation. Money and Ehrhardt, Man and Woman, Boy and Girl, Baltimore. The Johns Hopkins University Press, 1972, p. 3. Reproduced by permission.*

the process as a continuous one starting with conception and culminating in the emergence of adult gender identity (*see* Figure 8.13).[44]

We have already discussed many of the component events that constitute this model. Therefore, our primary purpose here will be to emphasize how all these diverse events fit together and interact.

The succesive stages in sexual differentiation in this scheme are compared to a relay race, in the sense that the "program" of instructions of sexual differentiation is initially carried by the chromosomes and handed

[44]The reason Money and Ehrhardt prefer the term "differentiation" to "development" is because the reproductive system in dimorphic (Greek for "two-shaped"), namely female or male, and the process of sexual development is normally a process of differentiation into primarily one or another of these two alternatives.

Box 8.12   The Critical Period for Gender Definition

A significant advance in our understanding of the learning of behavior has to do with the concept of "critical periods." It has been established that during the early life of an animal there are limited and often highly specific critical periods during which the learning that largely determines the subsequent behavior of the animal occurs. A well-known example is Lorenz' experiment with the graylag goose. Shortly after birth the gosling begins to follow its mother. If immediately after hatching it is taken into human care it will follow the human caretaker (or wooden models of the mother). Once this pattern has been established—that is, once the gosling has been "imprinted"—it will continue to follow the initial object rather than its own mother or members of its own species.

There is some evidence of an analogy between the establishment of gender role in early childhood and the phenomenon of imprinting in lower animals. Based on research involving cases that were matched biologically but sex-assigned and reared differently and drawing from clinical experience with gender reassignment, it has been proposed that a critical period exists for the formation of

gender identity. This period was placed at about 18 to 36 months (which also coincides with language development). The further one moved from this critical period the more difficult and problematic was the attempt to reassign gender in cases that had been brought up contrary to their biological sex because of ambiguous-looking genitals at birth.[1] (Money and Ehrhardt, 1972).

Yet, a curious finding seems to contradict the rule that after age 3 gender identity cannot be shifted readily. In 1974, a medical team found 24 girls who had "turned" into boys at puberty in a remote village in the Dominican Republic. These persons were genetic males but because of a genetic defect failed to produce adequate amounts of active embryonal androgen (dihydrotestosterone). As a result their genitalia were insufficiently masculinized and they were thought to be girls at birth and reared as such. At puberty, under the influence of testosterone their bodies were masculinized and apparently their gender identity followed suit.[2]

[1]Money and Ehrhardt (1972).
[2]Imperato-McGinley et al. (1974).

on to the undifferentiated gonad, which in turn "passes it on" to the hormonal secretion of its own cells, and so on. (It is not a relay race in the sense that one team is trying to outrun the other.) Another parallel is to the programing of language development, which is the outcome of our "phyletic" capacity to use language as human beings, and the learning or "social-biographic" process whereby each of us as an individual learns a given language.

The original developmental message is carried by the X or the Y sex chromosome of the sperm that joins with the X chromosome

of the ovum (*see* Chapters 4 and 5). The female (XX) or male (XY) chromosomal combination then transmits the program of instructions to the undifferentiated gonad. Depending on the message, the gonad will evolve either into a testis (starting about the sixth week of gestation) or into an ovary (beginning about another six weeks later).

The chromosomes, having passed on the genetic message, have apparently no further effect on the course of events. For example, if the embryonal gonads are removed before the critical period when the rest of the reproductive anatomy is formed, the embryo will go on to differentiate anatomically into a female regardless of genetic sex. Evidently, the ovaries are not essential at this stage for female development. For masculine differentiation to occur, the fetal testis must take over (*see* Chapter 2).

Testosterone is essential for the differentiation of the external genitalia. In a normal genetic male, fetal androgen will travel through the bloodstream and at a later stage masculinize the external sex organs into the male pattern. In abnormal conditions high levels of testosterone in the genetic female embryo will masculinize her external genitalia, resulting in a grossly hypertrophied clitoris or even a normal-looking penis and scrotal sac (but no testes). This may occur, for instance, in the adrenogenital syndrome where excess androgen is produced by the hyperactive adrenocortical glands of the female embryo herself. Or the source of androgen may be "external," such as androgen-producing tumors in the pregnant mother or the ingestion of certain drugs that pass through the placenta and masculinize the female fetus.

The normal development of the testis does not insure that all will necessarily go well. The levels of fetal testosterone may be normal, but if the target tissues are unresponsive then it is of no avail. In cases of such androgen-insensitivity syndromes a genetic male is born with incompletely masculinized and ambiguous-looking genitals. In practice this is more often due to inadequate production of testosterone, sometimes caused by metabolic errors that block its process of production.

These are all rare conditions. Normally, the sequence of events leads to genital dimorphism whereby genetic males and females are born with internal and external sex organs congruent with their chromosomal sex. To follow the left part of Figure 8.13 first, we next encounter the effects of "other's behavior" and "body image."

Up to this point social factors have had

no direct bearing in sexual dimorphism. But the moment the baby's sex is identified at birth, social influences become enormously important. Cultures undoubtedly differ in this respect, but the infant's perceived or assigned sex will from here on constitute one of the key factors defining the person. The choice of pink or blue clothing is the first step of sartorial identification. Choice of name, pronominal use, legal statutes, social conventions, and a myriad other distinctions relentlessly remind and reinforce in the child's mind that he is a boy or she is a girl, and with a varying degree of clarity and consistency define what that means in behavioral terms.

Differential attitudes based on the sex of the child are pervasive and often barely conscious. But such attitudes are not all externally imposed. There are sex differences in behavior that appear very early and presumably spontaneously, which themselves elicit differences in response.[45] The presence of cultural forces does not necessarily mean the absence of biologically determined influences in gender differentiation. These two sets of variables mutually reinforce each other, often creating "chicken-and-egg" sequences that cannot be readily disentangled.

Body image refers to the concept of our physical self or the way in which we visualize our bodies. Sexuality is an important component of body image and includes at the most concrete level the knowledge of our gender, of which we become aware early in childhood. More involved are our notions of masculinity, femininity, and "sex appeal," which are far more ambiguously defined. All of these factors contribute to our eventual sexual definition of ourselves.

The impact of fetal hormones on brain dimorphism presents a far more complicated situation than the more obvious changes of genital dimorphism. As indicated earlier (*see*

[45]There is an extensive literature on this topic. See, for example, Maccoby (1966) and Stone et al. (1973).

Chapter 3) there is as yet no direct evidence for sex differences in the human brain. But there is a wealth of positive information in this regard among animals and some inferential data on humans, which allow the tentative assumption that the brain (particularly the hypothalamus) is prenatally influenced by fetal hormones and that it continues to exert a subtle influence on subsequent behavior.

Some of the indirect evidence of brain dimorphism is that genetic females who had been subjected to high levels of androgen before birth but who were treated early with corrective surgery and who looked and were reared as girls have been reported to show "tomboyish" behavior compared to a control group. These girls were more self-assertive, athletic, functional in dress, more interested in boys' games than doll play, more achievement-oriented than romance- or marriage-oriented. Likewise, boys with the androgen-insensitivity syndrome revealed a picture the obverse of the above. But because of their female-looking genitalia, these boys had been reared as girls, so that in their cases the possible effects of prenatal hormones (or their lack) could not be separated from socially imposed role expectations.[46]

These findings raise interesting conceptual and political problems. Who decides what is "tomboyish"? Have these traits naturally evolved or for various reasons been monopolized by males? Are we using a biological or a cultural yardstick?

The factors of the behavior of others, body image, and brain dimorphism lead to juvenile gender identity, which is further differentiated through identification and all of the learning devices that are theorized to be operative in shaping human behavior.

The last major developmental event in Figure 8.13 is puberty. The effects of pubertal hormones and their impact on sexual mor-

phology and eroticism (discussed in detail in Chapter 4) combine with the gains of juvenile gender identity and culminate in adult gender identity.

The model of psychosexual differentiation just outlined is unlikely to be the last word on this complex issue. Many pieces of the puzzle are still missing. Many of the conclusions are inferences and extrapolations from animal research or clinical work that need to be substantiated as to their applicability to normal human development. But this model adequately underscores the multifaceted complexity of the issues and provides a fitting departure point for our subsequent considerations of the varieties of human sexual behavior.[47]

Sexuality in Adulthood

Sex in childhood is play and in adolescence it is experimentation and searching. It is with adulthood that sexuality comes unto its own. There are important biological and psychosocial reasons why this is the case. At the physiological level many adolescents are capable of conception but full reproductive maturity does not usually get established for most people until adulthood. Whatever hormonal and other biological factors that underlie such reproductive maturation may concurrently also influence behavioral patterns, even though we do not as yet fully understand these processes.

At the societal level sexuality is fully legitimized, at least in this culture, in adulthood even though our tolerance of sexual behavior during adolescence has greatly increased during recent decades. Social institutions such as marriage enable adults to establish the kinds of stable bonds that allow ready access to a sexual partner. Whatever its biological roots, a good deal of sexual behavior needs to be

[46]For a more detailed discussion of this research see Money and Ehrhardt (1972), Chapters 6 and 7; Green (1979); Davidson (1979); Ehrhardt (1979).

[47]There is a large and rapidly growing literature, both polemical and scholarly, on gender identity and sex roles. For current views on this issue from multidisciplinary perspectives see Katchadourian (1979).

Box 8.13 The Study of Sexual Behavior

The vast store of presently available information and misinformation on sex has been gathered largely through informal observation and inference. Only a small part of it is the result of careful, systematic study. Because even the latter often has serious shortcomings, and because the notion of sex research itself raises certain pertinent questions, we shall briefly review those studies we have cited most often in this book.

Research on sexual behavior has had a short though checkered history,[1] but is now less controversial than it has been in the past. Although the origins of behavioral sex research go back to the nineteenth century, it is largely a twentieth-century phenomenon.

Henry Havelock Ellis (1859–1939) is probably the most widely recognized pioneer in sex research. He was a physician in Victorian England, but his contributions went beyond clinical study, and his major work evolved over several decades into a vast compendium of sexual knowledge—

from anthropological and medical literature to clinical case histories, life histories, and so on.[2] Ellis was subjected to considerable public vilification, but eventually his contributions were duly recognized. There are several biographies of him,[3] in addition to his autobiography.[4] Other pioneers around the turn of the century include August Forel, Iwan Bloc, A. Moll, Magnus Hirshfeld, and Richard von Krafft-Ebing. We shall make further reference to Krafft-Ebing's work in Chapter 11.

Sigmund Freud was born three years earlier than Ellis; they died in the same year. Freud was not a sex researcher, in the sense that he did not deliberately initiate the investigation of sexual behavior; rather he developed his theories of human sexuality from his clinical work in psychoanalysis.[5] Nevertheless, his influence, both directly and through his followers, in making sexuality a focus of attention probably has outweighed that of any other person or group. Freud's multivolume col-

[1]See A. Ellis, and Abarbanel, eds. (1967), pp. 25–33; Diamond, ed. (1968), chapter 23; Brecher (1969).

[2]H. Ellis (1942).
[3]For example, Peterson (1928), Goldberg (1926), Collis (1959), Calder-Marshall (1959).
[4]H. Ellis (1939).
[5]E. Jones (1953).

learned particularly as it pertains to patterns of courtship. Sexual negotiation in human interactions is not an easy matter for most people. Even within a marital context sex is not always available just for the asking. It takes considerable effort and experience for individuals to be able to identify others who are not only sexually desirable partners, but who are likely to reciprocate their sentiments and be able to interact with them in a manner that will not be damaging to either party.

Sexuality in adulthood fulfills a variety of functions. Some of these are direct and self-evident, such as reproduction and the attainment of sexual pleasure. But sex also fulfills many other aims that could be considered nonsexual in nature. For example, sex is used as a vehicle for expressing and obtaining love or satisfy dependency needs. It may be a defense against loneliness or a means of bolstering self-esteem. Thus, sexuality is not only a major component of human relationships in its direct form; it also significantly influences many other aspects of our dealings with each other, even though we may not be conscious of that fact. Sex is one of the major currencies of interpersonal exchange, and it may be variously inflated, debased, or overvalued. Sexual malfunction will often interfere with other functions and in

Box 8.13 Continued

lected works[6] include countless discussions of sexuality in human development and its "normal," as well as pathological, manifestations. The same is true of the writings of other psychoanalysts, though some have dealt with sexual issues more extensively than have others. We shall make further references to psychoanalytic theory in Chapters 7–12.

Some sex research has also been conducted by anthropologists. With some notable exceptions (like Bronislaw Malinowski[7]), most early anthropologists paid less attention to (or at least reported less material on) the sexual practices of the cultures they studied than to other features of those cultures. A considerable body of anthropological data on sexual behavior has nevertheless accumulated over the years. Much of this information (pertaining to 190 societies) has been abstracted and made more accessible by Ford and Beach in a volume that also includes extensive material on sexual behavior among animals.[8]

[6]Freud (1957–1964).
[7]Malinowski (1929).
[8]Ford and Beach (1951). Another excellent and more current source of comparative data on sexual behavior is Marshall and Suggs (1971).

Of all contemporary anthropologists Margaret Mead has probably done most to attract the attention of the general public to differences in norms of sexual behavior (particularly relating to premarital sex) in other cultures.[9] Through her work, as well as that of other anthropologists, many more people have become willing to view cross-cultural alternatives as potentially valuable models, rather than as merely exotic oddities.

All the sex research mentioned so far has been clinical or descriptive in nature. Indispensable as such work is, it fails to provide a comprehensive view of the sexual behavior of large populations (as opposed to that of special groups and individuals). Also, since such findings are usually not presented in quantitative terms, they do not lend themselves to systematic statistical analysis, which in turn seriously hampers investigation of correlations and possible casual relations between component variables. Attempts at more quantitative study of sexual behavior are discussed in Boxes 8.14 and 8.15.

[9]Mead (1929, 1935, 1949).

turn is highly vulnerable to conflicts in other areas. In short, sexuality in adulthood permeates many aspects of our lives and becomes one of the major motivating forces that directly and indirectly guides our actions.

The ubiquity of sex in human interactions can hardly be denied. Yet this is not to say that sex is necessarily a dominant influence in each and every life. Like many other human functions such as friendship, parenthood, the quest for power, altruism, and so on, sex defines people in variable degrees. For some it may be the guiding principle of their lives, whereby much of their time and energy are devoted to seeking sexual experiences. For others it may play an unsignificant role, either by choice or by virtue of circumstances. For most of us its attractions wax and wane, depending on a host of internal needs and the dictates of external circumstances.

Since most of this book deals with adult sexuality, we will leave the more detailed discussions of its various manifestations to the appropriate chapters. Our aim here will be mainly to review the statistical information available on the frequency and types of sexual behavior. We must do this mindful of the fact that we know very little in this regard (*see* Box 8.13). The one major study of sexual

Box 8.14 The Kinsey Survey

The investigations of Alfred C. Kinsey (1894–1956) and his collaborators have so far been the one major attempt at the taxonomic study of human sexual behavior. The primary goal of this approach is to make understanding of individuals possible through the examination of their behavior in relation to that of the group as a whole. Basically, that is the purpose of the statistical approach in any field. It is one tool—though by no means the only or always the best tool—for the study of a given problem, and it is indispensable to any systematic study of behavior.

Some taxonomic studies were conducted before the Kinsey survey (*see* Box 8.15), but none has come close to matching the scope of Kinsey's work.

Kinsey left no autobiography. There are, however, many brief accounts of his career,[1] and detailed biographies have recently been published by two of his associates.[2]

Kinsey was an entomologist (specializing in the gall wasp) at the University of Indiana, but his interest in sex research was aroused when he discovered in mid-career the inadequacy of our knowledge of human sexual behavior. His method of study was taxonomic, and his main research tool was the detailed personal interview. He and his associates collected more than 16,000 histories from people in all walks of life across the United States. Kinsey alone collected 7000 such histories—an average of two a day for ten years.[3] He died, however, long before he could fulfill his goal of interviewing 100,000 individuals.

In discussing the Kinsey data we shall refer often to the "Kinsey sample." This sample was comprised of 5940 female and 5300 male residents of the United States whose sexual histories were gathered by the Kinsey staff. This population of 11,240 people included individuals of a wide variety of age, marital status, educational level, occupation, geographical location, religious denomination, and so on. Since all these groups were represented in the sample population in sufficient numbers to permit comparison, the Kinsey sample was properly "stratified." But it was not "representative," in that each group in the sample population was not

[1]For example, see Brecher (1969), chapter 5.
[2]Christenson (1971), Pomeroy (1972).

[3]Brecher (1969), p. 116.

behavior conducted by Kinsey and his collaborators was flawed and by now is quite out of date (*see* Box 8.14). Yet not a single study following it has come close to it in scope and seriousness. Sexual research on large populations seems to have recently become the province of magazine editors, market researchers and assorted self-appointed experts (*see* Box 8.15). For lack of nothing better, we will occasionally refer to their findings to give at least a semblance of currency to what we describe. Fortunately, there are some good studies in more specific aspects of sexual behavior, such as premarital sex within limited age groups, to which we shall refer in more detail.[48] Because of the historical importance of the Kinsey survey and the fact that it provides a comprehensive baseline, we shall deal with it in considerable detail. But the figures we quote must be taken by way of illustrative

[48]The more reliable surveys have been conducted by serious population researchers concerned with contraceptive practices. See, for example, Westoff (1974) and Kantner and Zelnick (1977). See also Box 8.8.

Box 8.14 Continued

proportionate to the size of that group in the American population at large. For example, lower educational levels and rural groups were underrepresented. Some sectors were, in fact, not represented at all: All the subjects whose histories were used were white. Kinsey collected many histories from nonwhites, but not enough to permit statistical analysis. Kinsey was quite aware of this fact and made no claims to the contrary: "This is a study of sexual behavior in (within) certain groups of the human species. . . not a study of the sexual behavior of all cultures and of all races of man."[4]

The second objection to the Kinsey study is more obvious. Do average people talk freely to a relative stranger about the intimate details of their sex life? This question cannot be answered with any certainty, and Kinsey was well aware of the possibility of distortion. But, although it is true that in an interview of several hours much may be omitted or fabricated, this risk would exist even if the subjects could be interviewed over periods of years. The critical issue is to know whether the magnitude of distortion totally invalidates

[4]Kinsey et al. (1953), p. 4. For other critiques of the Kinsey survey see Chall (1955) and Cochran et al. (1954).

the data or can be approximately corrected.

Since the Kinsey data were gathered more than two decades ago, their applicability to current behavior becomes increasingly problematic with the passage of time. Information becomes obsolete at different rates, however, and it is not necessary to reject all data categorically simply because they were gathered some time ago.

In the furor raised by some of Kinsey's findings (especially those on premarital sex and homosexuality) his important contributions on sexual physiology and other aspects of sexuality have been overlooked by the general public. Even if Kinsey and his associates had collected not one single item of new information they would still have rendered an invaluable service through their meticulous research into existing sources of sexual data. The Institute for Sex Research (usually called the Kinsey Institute) at the University of Indiana, presently headed by one of Kinsey's collaborators, Paul H. Gebhard, has probably the most extensive library and film collection in this field. Over the years the Institute has served a major educational function, while continuing to conduct research on sexuality.

approximations rather than reliable data on current sexual behavior in the population at large.

Frequency of Sexual Activity

How much sex should a person have? Although each culture apparently assumes a range of permissible sexual activity for those with access to legitimate sources, that range is rarely, if ever, spelled out.

The frequency of sexual behavior has health implications in the minds of many peo-

ple. Occasionally there are differences between husband and wife over how often they will make love. These conflicts are inevitably assessed against hypothetical standards of what is "reasonable" and "healthy."

To estimate how much sex a person was having Kinsey combined all sexual activities over a period of time and viewed them as the person's "total sexual outlet." To speak of "sexual outlets" conveys a certain view of the nature of sexuality. It implies a pressure from within that needs release, a

Box 8.15   Recent General Surveys of Sexual Behavior

In view of the extraordinary interest created by the Kinsey survey, one would have expected that during the following three decades additional investigations would have taken place in an effort to verify, challenge, or otherwise complement Kinsey's findings concerning sexual behavior. This has not been the case. The few studies that have been reported are either restricted in focus, such as investigating premarital sexual behavior only, or disappointing in the manner they have been carried out.

The Playboy Foundation Survey

One relatively recent investigation was sponsored by the Playboy Foundation and carried out by The Research Guild, Inc., an independent market survey and behavioral research organization. The sample investigated in the Playboy survey consisted of 2026 persons residing in 24 cities in the United States. This sample, 982 males and 1044 females, reportedly paralleled closely the U.S. population of persons 18 years old and older. The data were gathered by means of an extensive self-administered questionnaire.

An additional sample of 200 individuals similar in characteristics to the survey sample was selected for more intensive investigation. This group of 100 men and 100 women was interviewed by Morton Hunt and Bernice Kohn, both professional writers. Preliminary reports from this survey appeared in five installments in *Playboy* magazine, and a more comprehensive presentation was offered in a book.[1]

Despite attempts to be comprehensive and representational, this survey has a number of apparently serious shortcomings, including the lack of specific demographic details concerning the survey respondents. One does not know, for example, the exact age distribution of the sample. To be told that the "sample closely parallels the American population of persons 18 years old and over" is not sufficient. The same criticism applies to all of the other variables in question. Aside from these and other shortcomings, Hunt's analyses and interpretations are sensible. In subsequent chapters we will present some of these data while maintaining our reservations.

Magazine Surveys

Two extensive sex surveys have been conducted by magazines. In July 1969 a questionnaire on sex consisting of 101 items was published in *Psychology Today* and

[1]Hunt (1974).

---

blind urge that demands gratification in one way or another. Sexuality in a way becomes like hunger and elimination. Unfortunately, the riddle of sex is not to be solved through analogy.

Frequency must be measured over specific periods of time. As our lives are generally organized around weekly schedules, Kinsey found the week a useful unit of measure. Furthermore, sexual activities change over the years, and Kinsey therefore examined them over five-year periods. In the following pages

"total outlet" refers to the total number of orgasms achieved during an average week through masturbation, sex dreams, petting, coitus, homosexual activities, and animal contacts; the "average week" is based on given five-year periods of a person's lifetime.

Frequency of Total Outlet among Males

The mean frequency of total sexual outlet for white males between adolescence and 85 years of age was calculated by Kinsey to be

Box 8.15   Continued

readers were invited to respond by anonymously returning the completed questionnaires.[2]

. The Redbook Report[3] on female sexuality was compiled from responses to a questionnaire published in the October 1974 issue of *Redbook* magazine. Reportedly, 100,000 women responded, which is indeed an impressive number. But given the claim that approximately 10 million women read the magazine, the response rate is a minuscule 1 percent. Furthermore, the readers of any magazine obviously tend to be of a selected background rather than representative of the women in the country at large.

The Hite Report

The *Hite Report* was also primarily based on questionnaires that were initially distributed through "women's groups, including chapters of the National Organization of Women, abortion rights groups, university women's centers, and women's newsletters." Subsequently, attempts were made to broaden the study's representatives by placing notices in various magazines and church newsletters, but the women who responded cannot be

viewed as representative of the general population or even of some definable part of it. After all was said and done, only 3000 persons responded of the 100,000 who had received the questionnaires—a response rate of only 3 percent.[4]

Beyond the Male Myth

The last of these "nation-wide surveys" focused on men. As reported in *Beyond the Male Myth* by Pietropinto and Simenauer, some 4066 men responded to the survey questionnaire administered by the staff of a private marketing research firm. The subjects were "approached primarily in shopping centers and malls, as well as office building complexes, tennis clubs, college campuses, airports, and bus depots." In attempting to get to the average person, the investigators seem to have literally gone to the proverbial "man in the street." The interviewers "estimated" that half of the men approached agreed to respond.[5]

As scientific studies of sexual behavior, such studies are of no real value. But they are not totally worthless because they produce interesting revelations about individual lives.

[2]Athanasiou (1972).
[3]Tavris and Sadd (1978).

[4]Hite (1976).
[5]Pietropinto and Simenauer (1977).

nearly three orgasms in an average week.[49] To reiterate earlier cautions, this figure should not be taken to mean that the "average man" necessarily had this many weekly orgasms, and it certainly does not mean that such frequencies are standards of normality, health, virility, and so on.

Before we go on to the more common levels and averages, we must emphasize the

[49]In these and subsequent examples the figures cited are approximations based on the more specific data in the Kinsey surveys.

extreme variation among apparently healthy people living under reasonably similar conditions. Some men in this group had experienced very few orgasms over long periods: One man in apparently good physical health had had only one orgasm in 30 years. Others reported many orgasms each week, week after week. One man, also apparently in good physical health, claimed to have averaged 30 orgasms a week for 30 years.

Much more significant than such single figures is the frequency pattern of the number

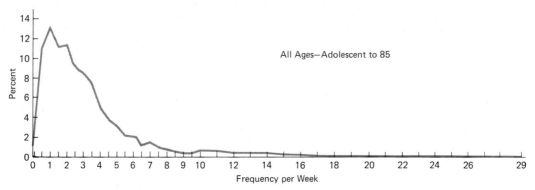

Figure 8.14 Individual variation in frequency of total sexual outlet among males. From Kinsey et al., *Sexual Behavior in the Human Male.* Philadelphia: Saunders, 1948, p. 198. Courtesy of the Institute for Sex Research.

of orgasms per week for the same population (*see* Figure 8.14). It is important to note that a higher percentage of men attained about one orgasm a week than any other single frequency. The weekly mean of three orgasms was thus inflated by the more active rates.

The asymmetrical nature of the curve indicates that men cannot be readily grouped as typical, or average, on the basis of frequency of orgasm, and that high-frequency and low-frequency individuals cannot be clearly distinguished as deviating from the norm. In this group, whereas three-quarters of the men had one to six orgasms a week, almost a quarter fell outside this range. It is apparent that weekly rates of male orgasm fall on a continuum: Some men are a little more active than the others, who are in turn more active than the rest, and so on. Although the range between the two extremes may be tremendous, there are intermediate frequencies all along.

The frequency of total outlet was related to a variety of factors, of which age was the most important. In Figure 8.15 we see how the average number of orgasms experienced each week was related to the age group of the individual. The first group consisted of boys 15 years old and younger (but past puberty), the next group of those be-

tween 16 and 20 years of age, and so on in five-year spans.

The most active groups appear to have been those below the age of 30. After 30 the frequency of orgasms steadily declined with advancing age. It is startling to realize that the level of activity did not gradually rise to a peak, but was already close to its maximum in the youngest age group. This trend runs contrary to the popular notion that sexuality is awakened during adolescence, gradually reaches its peak during the "prime of life," and then wanes.

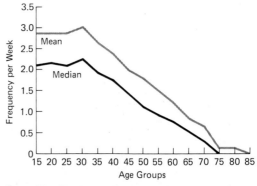

Figure 8.15 Frequency of total sexual outlet for males, by age groups. From Kinsey et al., *Sexual Behavior in the Human Male.* Philadelphia: Saunders, 1948, p. 220. Courtesy of the Institute for Sex Research.

The curve for the mean is higher than that for the median at every point. The peak mean (for the group between 26 and 30 years old) was three orgasms a week, whereas the median was only a little more than two (2.24). This disparity means that an average week for this age group included three orgasms per person, but that the average person had only about two orgasms each week.

Frequency of Total Outlet among Females

Comparisons of sexual behavior in the two sexes must be undertaken with care so that differences are neither exaggerated nor minimized. Also the significance of female sexuality must be recognized in its own right rather than just in relation to that of the male.

Because of certain important differences in male and female sexual behavior, comparisons can be carried out only up to a point. For example, orgasm is a less satisfactory measure of female than of male sexuality. Less of what is obviously sexual behavior culminates in orgasm for women; even when orgasm does occur, it is more difficult to recognize and count because of the absence of ejaculation. Also, as the sexual behavior of women is in general more stringently controlled than that of men, behavioral criteria alone yield a less accurate picture of true female sexual potential. To counteract these distortions it is therefore necessary to consider all female sexual behavior, even that which does not culminate in orgasm. It is also necessary to look at the data on certain subgroups, like married women, with particular care, for social constraints on these women are fewer, and thus their behavior probably more closely reflects natural tendencies.

The range of individual variation in frequency of total sexual outlet among females is so much greater than among males that questions about "average number of orgasms per week" cannot be answered meaningfully. The Kinsey volume on the female does not have a counterpart to Figure 8.14, nor does it report data that would permit the construction of such a graph for females.

Figure 8.16 shows the mean and median frequencies of total sexual outlet among various age groups. This figure is the female counterpart of Figure 8.15. Comparison of the two figures reveals several differences. First, the frequencies of total sexual outlet for females were lower than were those for males in all comparable age groups. This finding confirms the common notion that women as a group are orgasimically less active than men, but it also seems to contradict earlier references (see Chapter 3) that showed women to be more capable of multiple orgasm than men are. The apparent confusion arises from the fact that Masters and Johnson were actually counting the number of orgasms during an episode of sexual activity, whereas Kinsey obviously could not have expected his subjects to recall accurately how many orgasms they had reached during past sexual acts and thus had to be content with their memories of the number of sexual acts that culminated in orgasm. This contradiction illustrates the ambiguities in sweeping generalizations about whether men or women are more "highly sexed." Females revealed themselves as having higher total outlets than most people would have expected, however. The differences between the two sexes are, after all, not that striking: Whereas the most active

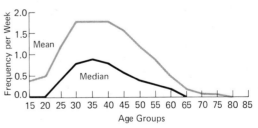

Figure 8.16 Frequency of total sexual outlet for females, by age groups. From Kinsey et al., *Sexual Behavior in the Human Female.* Philadelphia: Saunders, 1953, p. 548. Courtesy of the Institute for Sex Research.

male group achieved an average (mean) of three orgasms a week, its female counterpart experienced almost two orgasms (1.8) during the same period of time.

The disparity in medians is somewhat more marked: The average male in the peak group experienced somewhat more than two (2.2) weekly climaxes, whereas the average female had almost one (0.9).

Among females the wider disparity between the means and medians indicates wider individual variability. There must have been some women whose levels of activity were so much higher than the rest that their performances unduly inflated the mean values for the group as a whole. More detailed study of the female sample shows that this assumption is valid.

The second, and more intriguing, sex difference is revealed by the shapes of these curves, which indicate quite different patterns of relation between age and frequency of sexual outlet among males and females. Whereas men achieved high levels of sexual activity right after puberty and by the age of 15, the youngest female group was quite inactive sexually. Its weekly mean was 0.3 orgasm a week (one orgasm in about every three weeks). The median was zero, which does not mean that the average girl had no orgasms at all, but that more than half the girls in this age group did not experience weekly orgasms.

Between the ages of 16 and 20, males attained their highest rates of sexual outlet and maintained them for a full decade. For females the period between 16 and 30 years was one of gradually increasing activities culminating in orgasm. But they maintained this peak frequency for a full decade, whereas in males it steadily declined. The fall in female frequencies was thus preceded by reductions in male frequencies by about ten years. Because of the overall higher male weekly rates, at no time was a given group of females having more orgasms a week than were the males in the corresponding age group. The mean curve for females is closest to the mean curve for males in the age group of 41–45 years.

Many female groups were more active than were certain male groups. For instance, female groups in their peak decade (31–40 years old) had more frequent outlets than did all male age groups beyond 45 years put together (note the portions of the male mean curve that fall below the high point of 1.8 sustained on the female curve).

Once the decline had begun, increasing age brought the two sexes progressively together. Although men maintained a slightly higher frequency than women, in advanced old age the rates for both sexes were very low.

The progress of the median was quite similar. The average female between puberty and age 15 was, unlike the male, sexually quite inactive in terms of achieving orgasm. Her rates increased steadily, but she did not attain her peak until she was almost 30 years old. Even then she averaged only about one orgasm a week, whereas males between adolescence and the same age had more than twice that many. She sustained this weekly rate until she was almost 40 and then had progressively fewer orgasms. By the age of 65, whereas the average man attained an orgasm about every other week, the average woman achieved very few.

The notable variability among individuals (especially women) makes the application of group rates to given individuals hazardous if not meaningless. In the Kinsey sample, within each age group of either sex there were individuals whose weekly rates of sexual outlet were totally out of keeping with the group mean or median. People in the least active groups—perhaps an adolescent girl or an old woman—may have regularly experienced more orgasms during an average week than did some men in the most active years (ages 15–30). Such deviation from group averages is in itself no indication of pathology.

Varieties of Sexual Experience

If variety is, in fact, the spice of life, then sexual behavior is spicy indeed. Throughout history people have resorted to every imaginable type of activity in pursuit of sexual gratification. They have copulated with each other, with members of their own sexes, and with animals. They have used their bodies in solitude, in pairs, in triads, and in greater numbers. Every orifice that can possibly be penetrated has been penetrated; and every inch of skin has been caressed, scratched, tickled, pinched, licked, and bitten for love. Orgasms have come amid murmurs of tender affection and screams of pain, in total awareness and while fast asleep. An important aspect of this diversity is also the fact that some members of the population lead very restricted sex lives and that there are some apparently healthy people who go through life without ever experiencing orgasm.

How do we explain these vast differences? Do we not all share the same biological heritage? Are our cultures so diverse as to permit such a bewildering range of behavior?

Some of the observed differences are undoubtedly real. Variation is a cardinial rule of all biological phenomena, and cultures are by definition diverse. Other apparent differences in sexual behavior are based on ignorance and willful concealment. If we could be quite open about what we do with our sex lives, a great many apparent differences in sexual behavior might be revealed as considerably less sharp.

Finally, to an important extent, the magnitude of these apparent differences is a function of the particular methods of observation and interpretation used. Among psychoanalysts, for example, the definition of sexual behavior is incomparably broader than among most psychologists or anthropologists. When investigators use different yardsticks for different settings, obviously considerable disparities will emerge independent of whatever actual variation may exist in the groups under study.

The six components of total sexual outlet that were found by Kinsey to account for practically all orgasms experienced by men and women were coitus, masturbation, homosexual relations, orgasm during sleep, petting, and animal contacts.

Correlates of Sexual Behavior

If two events or characteristics occur together more frequently than chance would indicate, we have a positive correlation. If they occur together less often than chance would indicate, then we have a negative correlation. Correlations do not necessarily reflect causal relations, but they may provide leads to common causes. They are thus useful as predictors. A child, for instance, will soon learn that snow and cold go together, even though he may not know which comes first. Usually it is only this type of elementary insight to which we can currently aspire in studying the correlates of sexual behavior.

The conditions and characteristics that coexist with various types and frequencies of sexual activity are so many that we need some means of sorting them out. Many daily events distract or stimulate erotic interest, and external circumstances facilitate or hamper sexual expression.

Possible influences on sexual behavior are legion. What we are primarily concerned with here are not the obvious, transient, or externally imposed conditions but rather the biological and social characteristics that may be consistently related to rates and patterns of sexual outlet: gender, age, marital status, age at puberty, social class, religion, and urban or rural background.

Components of Total Sexual Outlet among Females

Figures 8.17 and 8.18 show how marital status was correlated with sources of orgasm in the female sample.[50] These patterns of sexual

[50]These three figures are based on an "active sample" defined earlier: All subjects in this group had experienced orgasm through one means or another.

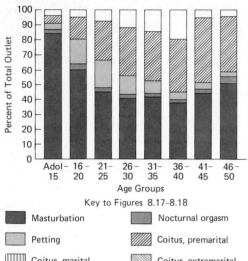

Key to Figures 8.17–8.18

- ▉ Masturbation
- ▥ Petting
- ⦀ Coitus, marital
- ≣ Coitus, postmarital
- ▦ Nocturnal orgasm
- ▨ Coitus, premarital
- ▧ Coitus, extramarital
- ☐ Homosexual

Figure 8.17 *Percentages of total outlet: sources of orgasm among single females. From Kinsey et al., Sexual Behavior in the Human Female. Philadelphia: Saunders, 1953, p. 562. Courtesy of the Institute for Sex Research.*

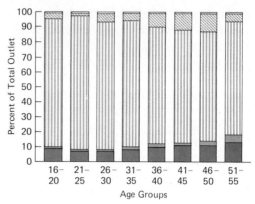

Figure 8.18 *Percentage of total outlet: sources of orgasm among married females. From Kinsey et al., Sexual Behavior in the Human Female. Philadelphia: Saunders, 1953, p. 562. Courtesy of the Institute for Sex Research.*

behavior show striking though in some ways expected differences, as well as certain similarities.

For single women (*see* Figure 8.17) in the youngest age group masturbation was the primary orgasmic outlet (84 percent of total outlet). In successive age groups this proportion declined, so that between ages 36 and 40 coitus and masturbation provided equal proportions of orgasms (37 percent of total outlet each). In the next two age brackets masturbation moved ahead, but only enough to account for slightly more than half of all orgasms in the group between 46 and 50.

Coitus was the second most important source of orgasm for single women. Beginning with the youngest age group, in which premarital coitus accounted for 6 percent of orgasms, this outlet reached its peak between the ages of 41 and 45 years, when it provided 43 percent of total outlets.

Homosexual contacts provided a stead-

ily increasing proportion of the orgasms of single women up to the age span of 36 to 40 years, when almost one out of five orgasms was reached by this means.

In comparison to single women, married women showed much more uniform sex lives (*see* Figure 8.18). Through all the age levels examined they registered an overwhelming reliance on coitus as a source of no fewer than four out of five orgasms. It will be noted, however, that some of these orgasms occurred during extramarital intercourse at all age levels. Between the age of 41 and 50, when the rates of extramarital orgasm are highest, they accounted for somewhat more than 10 percent of total outlet.

Although coitus was the primary source of orgasm for married women in the Kinsey sample, it was not the only source. Masturbation provided a fairly steady proportion (about 10 percent) of total sexual outlet, and there was a slight increase with age. The same was true of nocturnal orgasms, but to a much lesser extent. Homosexual contacts were either absent or a negligible source of orgasm for married women.

Previously married women (that is, women who were separated, divorced, or widowed) would be expected to show a pattern intermediate between that of single and married women, for previously married women share some of the characteristics of all married women, as well as many of the life circumstances of single women. Actually previously married women appeared to be closer in their sexual behavior to married than to single women: Coitus was the predominant source of orgasms, even though these women did rely more heavily on masturbation, nocturnal orgasms, and homosexual contacts than married women did.

These data do not permit full elucidation of the relation of marriage to sexual outlet. To what extent is there preselection of women primairly attached to coitus (and attractive to men similarly inclined)? To what extent is the preeminence of coitus in marriage a function of readily available partners, social and moral approval of marital sex, and so on? The pattern for previously married females indicates that both sets of factors were at work. If the differences in sexual behavior between the single and married reflected only the external consideration of marital status itself, then the pattern of the previously married would be similar to that for singles. If, on the other hand, the differences reflected only preselection, then the pattern would be the same as that of married women. In this regard comparison with widows alone would be preferable; the separated and divorced can be thought of as having rejected marriage (assuming that such choices are freely available, which often they are not).

No mention has been made so far of orgasm through animal contacts, for in none of the female groups do they constitute a frequent enough outlet to allow representation on the graphs.

Components of Total Sexual Outlet among Males

We shall next examine the data from the male Kinsey sample to highlight the effect of education. For our purposes it suffices to examine two groups only: men with elementary-school educations and men with some college education. To simplify matters further, we shall deal only with single men.

The Kinsey study demonstrated important associations between educational level and the components of total sexual outlet. Among single males with elementary-school educations (*see* Figure 8.19) masturbation accounted for little more than half the total sexual outlets even at the youngest age levels. It became less significant with increasing age; between 21 and 35 it accounted for only about a quarter of orgasms. Starting at age 16, coitus was the primary outlet for this group. Note that these single men showed increasing reliance with age on prostitutes as sexual partners. Homosexual contacts also increased so that between 31 and 35 they accounted for one-fourth of all orgasms. Nocturnal orgasms provided a modest but steady

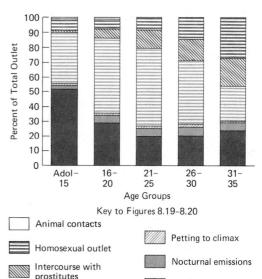

Figure 8.19 Sources of orgasm for single males with elementary-school educations, by age groups. From Kinsey et al., *Sexual Behavior in the Human Male.* Philadelphia: Saunders, 1948, p. 490. Courtesy of the Institute for Sex Research.

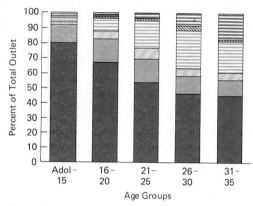

Figure 8.20 Sources of orgasm for single males with some college education, by age groups. From Kinsey et al., *Sexual Behavior in the Human Male.* Philadelphia: Saunders, 1948, p. 491. Courtesy of the Institute for Sex Research.

outlet for these men, but petting contributed only very slightly to total outlets.

In contrast, single males with some college education relied heavily on masturbation (*see* Figure 8.20). In the youngest age group it accounted for four out of five orgasms. In successively higher age groups the ratio declined, but not much below 50 percent. The better educated single male's reliance on masturbation was at the expense of coitus, particularly with prostitutes. Petting and nocturnal emissions were more substantial outlets in this group, but homosexual contacts were less important than for less-educated males. There was, however, a similar increase in reliance on such contacts with age.

These data on males further illustrate the important associations of sexual behavior with various biosocial variables. For example, as there are no demonstrable biological differences between less- and more-educated males in general, the important differences between these two groups must be explained on psychological and social grounds. It must be emphasized, however, that education itself was not the key factor. These men were not behaving differently because of what they were taught in school. The pertinence of ed-

ucation was primarily as an index of "social class." It was social class that determined the styles of life, values, and so on of these men. Similar associations could be shown, for instance, between occupational choice and patterns of sexual behavior.

These observations are but a few of many that have emerged from the Kinsey data. Some of them were obvious and expected, others paradoxical and questionable. Some of these same observations are probably equally applicable today, but others are not. What is more important for our purposes is the realization that sexual behavior is highly varied and profoundly influenced by a host of biological and social variables, even though we remain ignorant of the precise nature and magnitude of these influences. The cross-cultural comparisons in Box 8.16 are intended to highlight these points further.

Sexuality and Aging

Traditionally, just as individuals in the early years of life have been seen as being sexually unripened, those in the later part of life have been viewed as sexually depleted. Having performed their reproductive function and obtained whatever fun they could out of sex, older individuals have been expected to have no further interest in sex or, if they should, not to act on it. Whenever older people, especially women, have behaved differently, society has tended to view their persistent sexuality as unnatural and undignified.[51]

Such attitudes have undergone considerable change recently. This is in part due to a broader shift in societal perceptions of the elderly who now live longer, are in better health, and engage in athletic and other ac-

[51]Such attitudes are not exclusively Western or modern. The following is from the Kama Sutra: "As to coitus with old women, it acts like a fatal poison. . . . Do not rummage old women. . . . Beware of mounting old women [even] if they cover you with favours. . . . The coitus of old women is a venomous meal" (Vatsyayana, 1964 ed., p. 149).

Box 8.16   Cross-Cultural Comparisons of Sexual Behavior

Anthropologists have gathered large volumes of data from primitive cultures, some of which pertain to sexual behavior. The term "primitive" is misleading, but hallowed through usage. It refers to preliterate cultures that have evolved along lines different from ours. They do not necessarily represent early stages already passed through by literate societies, nor are they always simple in social organization. The sexual behavior of such groups is widely assumed to be free and unlimited. It would be useful to see whether or not the available data support this notion.

In their review of anthropological studies of almost 200 primitive societies Ford and Beach found the quantitative data on sexual outlets to be quite limited.[1] Observation, rather than measurement, has been the traditional anthropological approach. Fragments of information have nevertheless revealed three aspects of these cultures that are quite relevant to our immediate concerns.

First, there seemed to be tremendous variation among various primitive peoples in the frequency of sexual activity. Males of the Keraki (seminomads of New Guinea) generally had coitus once a week, of the Lesu (hunters, fishers, and primitive agriculturists of New Ireland) once or twice a week, of the Chiricahua (Arizona Indians who hunted, gathered, and carried on some agriculture) two or three times a week, of the Hopi (farmers) three or four times a week, of the Crow (seminomadic hunters) every night, of the Aranda (Australian hunters and gatherers) three to five times a night, and of the Chagga (advanced agriculturists of Tanganyika) up to ten times a night.

Second, every society had some restrictions on sexual activity. There is no human society anywhere that permits a man or a woman to engage in sex at absolutely any time and place. The human erotic potential is, therefore, never given free rein in any organized social group.

Third, at least some primitive groups seemed to share Western notions about the effects of frequency of sexual activity on health. Crow Indians, active as they were, believed that too frequent intercourse weakened the participants. The Seviang (cultivators of New Hebrides) recommended that a man with a single wife should have coitus for three nights, then rest for two; one who had two wives should copulate for two nights and rest on the third.

All attempts at using anthropological data must view each feature of a culture in its total context. The point in learning about other cultures is not to search for better models or to congratulate ourselves on how much more "civilized" we are. It is neither meaningful nor possible to import or export wholesale a given set of sexual practices. Such behavior only makes sense in its larger context, but if viewed in this manner, it does provide insights into the workings of other cultures thereby hopefully enhancing the understanding of our own. Ultimately our aim is to better comprehend the universals as well as the diversities in human behavior of which the sexual is only one component.

[1]Ford and Beach (1951). It must be emphasized that this survey dealt with different cultures and not with separate geographical or political units. The cultures surveyed were selected from several thousand described by anthropologists. For example, of Western cultures only that of the United States was included. Furthermore, the book is now several decades old, and the original reports from which the data were drawn are even older. Most of these cultures have undoubtedly undergone profound changes, and some may even be extinct. Nevertheless, these changes do not detract from the value of the original data for our purposes. For a more current account of comparative sexual behaviors see Marshall and Suggs (1971).

tivities traditionally considered inconsistent with late adulthood. Concurrently, more accepting and positive social attitudes concerning sexuality have also come to be extended to them. Of particular importance has been the realization that older individuals actually have more active sexual lives than generally realized.

Vicissitudes in social attitudes notwithstanding, sexual functions undergo significant changes in the later years of adulthood. The evidence consistently points out that when individuals are considered in large groups, there is distinct decline in the frequency of orgasm with aging. But if the Kinsey statistics are valid in this regard, this decline does not begin with what we commonly think of middle age or old age but is already in progress by the end of the third decade (*see* Figures 8.15 and 8.16).

More current evidence confirms these earlier Kinsey findings. In a study of 628 men between the ages of 20 and 90 coital activity was found to decrease after the thirties. Weekly frequencies declined from 2.2 at ages 30–34 to 0.7 at ages 60–64, 0.4 at 65–74, and 0.3 at 75–79.[52]

It is important to bear in mind that although such statistical trends may be valid for large groups, they need not apply to everyone within it. Thus getting older does not necessarily mean that there will be an inexorable decline in sexual activity. Even when there is actual decline in frequency, it need not necessarily reflect a failure of sexual functions or satisfaction.

When one examines such statistics, there is a strong temptation to presume that the decline in sexual function is due to the aging process as such and to further assume that it has a biological basis. Neither of these two assumptions is safe. First, it is important to differentiate the effects of aging as such from the effects of illness, which tend to affect

[52]Martin (1977).

increasingly higher proportions of people as they grow older. Thus, sexual malfunction should not be necessarily attributed to the aging process simply because it happens to seemingly correlate with it. As to the biological basis of declining functions, one must bear in mind that important as these may be, psychosocial considerations may independently or in conjunction with biological changes also affect behavior and function in profound ways. Anxiety about sexual performance is a very common cause of malfunction at all ages, particularly in older years when one is expected to show sexual decline and when altered physiological responses are misinterpreted as evidence of such decline. For this reason we shall attempt to deal with the biological and psychosocial components of this issue separately while bearing in mind that they are inextricably interrelated in actual life.

Physiological Aspects

Aging affects the sexual functioning of men and women in various ways, some of which are common to both and some specific to each. Information on this problem is scarce and still incomplete, for obtaining it has so far proved difficult even for investigators who have otherwise been successful pioneers in sex research.

The impact of aging on sexual physiology seems to be fairly consistent and predictable in general terms, but these observations are not necessarily applicable to every individual. Some men and women function in old age as if they were many decades younger. In addition to many important biological and psychological factors, there seems to be some correlation with the intensity and regularity of sexual activity: Individuals who lead active sex lives in their youth and throughout adulthood appear to carry this pattern into their old age.

Changes in the sexual physiology of older people are the result partly of visible anatomical alterations involved in aging and partly of less obvious causes. In general there is slowing and attenuation of body responses in both sexes. The older person does not react in a novel or abnormal manner; some of the reactions of the sexual response cycle continue uninterrupted, whereas others are modified and a few cease altogether. Basically the older man and woman respond as before and continue to be capable of orgasm. In considering departures from earlier functioning, this central fact must not be forgotten.

In the Male

For the older male the key concern is potency: the ability to initiate and sustain penile erection. The physiological changes that influence the erectile response are as follows. First, the reaction to erotic stimulation is slower. Instead of a matter of seconds, all that is required in the prime of youth, the older man needs more time to achieve erection, no matter how exciting the stimulation is. Second, after age 50 or so, psychological stimulation is often not enough in itself and the male requires direct physical stimulation in the appropriate psychological context to achieve erection. Once erection has been achieved by the older male, it can be maintained longer, perhaps because of better control based on experience or because of changes in physiological functioning. But should the older person lose his erection before orgasm, he will encounter greater difficulty in reviving it. Although erection can be maintained throughout the excitement and plateau phases, it is not sustained at its maximum, which is achieved just before orgasm only. During orgasm contractions start at the same intervals of 0.08 second, but they die out after very few throbs. But this does not mean orgasm becomes less pleasurable. Ejaculation is no longer so vigorous, and in very old age the semen may simply seep out. Older men also have a reduction in volume of ejaculate, which probably accounts for the lessened pressure to ejaculate.

The response of other male organs is similarly attenuated: Scrotal changes may not occur at all; testicular elevation is limited; and after 55 years of age the testicles may not increase in size during the sexual response cycle.

During the resolution phase whatever physical changes have occurred disappear with greater speed; in fact, some bodily responses disappear before they can be detected. Penile detumescence occurs in a matter of seconds after orgasm, rather than in a lingering two-stage process.

Few older men seek multiple orgasms, and even fewer can achieve them; but, given a chance to recharge during a longer refractory period, some men can and do go on to have additional orgasms.

In the Female

The impact of age on the female sex organs is more severe. The postmenopausal woman exhibits progressive and marked anatomical changes. The vaginal walls lose their thick, corrugated texture, purplish complexion, and elasticity, and appear thin and pale. The vagina is less responsive. Lubrication takes longer (several minutes) and is less profuse; the tenting effect is limited and delayed; the orgasmic platform develops but not fully. The size of the lumen of the older woman's vagina is nevertheless comparable to that of a younger woman, for, as the introitus has become narrower, even the less-developed orgasmic platform sufficiently obstructs it. This point is of some interest in view of the importance attached to the grip of the excited vagina on the penis.

In the orgasmic and resolution phases the older vagina is comparable to the older penis: Orgasmic contractions are fewer and less intense, and resolution is prompt and precipitate.

Thinner vaginal walls, delayed or inadequate lubrication, and the loss of tissue flexibility may lead to painful coitus. But these problems can often be remedied medically and by the use of lubricants.

Older women develop a tendency toward burning during urination following intercourse. The underlying mechanism is similar to that of "honeymoon cystitis" and results from irritation of the bladder and urethra by the penis. Whereas in newlyweds frequency or novelty of intercourse may be responsible, the cause in older women is the thinner, partly atrophied vaginal wall, which gives inadequate protection to the bladder. Discomfort may persist for several days following coitus. It does not follow orgasm through masturbation.

The uterus is another organ that undergoes marked changes. Within a decade after its procreative functions have ceased, its body is reduced in size. Uterine elevation during the sexual response cycle is less marked and occurs later, and no vasocongestive enlargement can be detected in the postmenopausal uterus. Uterine contractions have not been measured during orgasm, but older women report spasms that can at times be quite painful, comparable to labor pains. Sometimes they are sufficiently distressing to prevent an older woman from seeking sexual gratification.

The responses of the labia alter considerably with advancing age. Again actual anatomical changes occur during menopause: The major lips lose their subcutaneous fatty deposits and appear thin. They show no visible response to sexual stimulation (particularly if they are nulliparous). The minor lips do produce vasocongestive response, but swelling is less and the striking preorgasmic color change is attenuated or absent. Clitoral response seems to remain largely unchanged even in very old age. Resolution is unusually rapid.

Extragenital responses in both sexes decline in variable degrees. The heart and respiratory reactions persist and are more taxing. The breasts continue to respond with nipple erection, but vasocongestion in the female breast is greatly reduced. The responses of the anal sphincter and urethra are also attenuated.

Despite these pervasive changes, there is even less physiological cause for cessation of female sexual activity than for male activity during late adulthood. Paradoxically, as the sex organs become seemingly less adaptive to sexual intercourse, sexual desire need not decline during the menopause; in some cases it seems to be enhanced. This may be due to the erotogenic effects of adrenal androgen that is now freer of the dampening effect of estrogen. Estrogen therapy (which must be used with caution) can retard or reverse many of the anatomical changes.[53] The use of simple vaginal lubricants alone will fully compensate for the lack of natural lubrication. Most important, an active sexual life itself seems to significantly counteract the effects of aging and maintain the aging woman in sexual fitness.

In summary, we find that men and women of advanced age are handicapped to some extent by inevitable physical changes. Men are less virile and must husband their strength. Women are more sensitive to pain and discomfort. None of these obstacles is so great that it cannot be remedied, however. Physiologically, the older man and woman remain sexually capable. As they adjust to other physical limitations, they can adjust to sexual ones. Time takes its toll, but it need not quench sexual desire or cripple its fulfillment. Furthermore, as in other aspects of life, age brings its own rewards that contribute to sexual contentment.

Psychosocial Aspects

To some of us at least, there is still something startling in the idea that people in their older years may be interested in and capable of

---

[53]The concerns with estrogen therapy relate to its possible linkage to endometrial and breast cancer as well as the side effects of estrogen therapy. (see Chapter 4).

engaging in sex. We assume that old people lack sexual desires and that they are incapable of fulfilling such desires even if they happen to have them. Should they act sexually, there are concerns about the effects on their fragile body. Besides, the whole notion of sex in old age somehow sound odd and shameful.[54]

These and similar attitudes probably have a more devastating impact on sexuality among the elderly than all of the physiological changes due to aging. Societally imposed and internalized expectations influence sexual behavior at all ages, but this is particularly true in older years. Especially for those in nursing homes the available sexual options can be severely limited.

From a psychosocial perspective, the sexual behavior of older persons is further handicapped for a number of reasons. Probably most important is the self-fulfilling prophecy of gradual decline in sexual interest and function. Especially given the anatomical alterations and changes in physiological response and ignorance of what these mean, the aging individual is inclined to conclude that he or she is on the road to join the ranks of the sexually inert. Even in cases where the person does not experience such a change of heart, society does not facilitate sexual expression in the elderly especially for women who face a particular problem due to their relative longevity and larger numbers. Added to the 7 percent of women who never marry are those who are widowed and others whose older husbands are sickly. As a result, there simply are not that many available older men as sexual partners.

Were it not for the existence of strong age barriers for sexual interaction, there would of course be many more sexual partners available to the elderly. Yet older individuals are generally considered to be sexually less attractive, especially in the case of women. If

the elderly do consort with younger partners, women are once again more likely to meet social disapproval than is the case with older males who attract more envy than resentment when they manage to win the favors of a younger woman.

Another impediment to sex in the older years comes from health considerations. As people age, they become increasingly likely to be concerned with their health. In many instances, general failing in health or more specific ailments will seriously interfere with sexual function. But many older individuals are also under the impression that sexual activity is itself debilitating. This is particularly the case for individuals who have suffered heart attacks.[55] There are indeed certain illnesses during which sexual activity, like many other kinds of activity, must be refrained from or indulged in with caution, but by and large sex helps maintain older individuals in better health rather than act as a detriment to good health.

All of these obstacles notwithstanding, older individuals are reported to nevertheless engage in considerable sexual activity. In one study of 101 men between 56 and 86 years who were free of ailments likely to interfere with potency, 65 percent between 56 and 69 and 34 percent over age 70 were still sexually active.[56]

In a more extensive investigation of 261 men and 241 women between 45 and 71 years, more than 75 percent of the men aged 61 to 71 were engaging in coitus at least once a month; 37 percent of those 61 to 65 years old and 28 percent of those 66 to 71 years old had coitus at least once a week. Among the women, only 39 percent of those between 61 and 65 and 27 percent of those between 66 and 71 were still engaging in intercourse. A similar disparity was apparent in sexual interest: Only 6 percent of the men but

---

[54]Butler and Lewis (1973), p. 99.

[55]For a discussion of sex and heart disease see Brenton (1968).
[56]Finkle (1959).

33 percent of the women claimed to have no sexual desire; in the 66 to 71 year group those percentages rose to 50 percent and 10 percent respectively. When men gave up coitus, 40 percent did so because of impotence, 17 percent due to illness, and 14 percent due to loss of interest. Yet when women stopped engaging in sex, the main reasons given related to their husbands: 36 percent had died; 12 percent were no longer with them; 22 percent had become impotent; and 20 percent were ill.[57]

Finally, one of the most critical variables in the maintenance of good sexual function in the older years is the level of sexual activity in younger years and the sustenance of such activity during old age. Thus there is a positive correlation between the sexual activity between age 20 and 40 and that of later years. Furthermore sexual inactivity in old age results in further atrophy both anatomically and functionally. The aging woman who is sexually inactive experiences greater vaginal shrinkage. Likewise, the aging male has greater difficulty in resuming sexual activity after a long period of abstinence. Thus to retain sexual function in the older years it is important that one remain active sexually.[58]

It is all to the good that there is currently a strong impetus to recognize and encourage sex among the elderly.[59] But with our greater acceptance there is also a danger that a new set of sexual expectations will develop that while freeing up some people will become new burdens for others. Just as it is unfortunate to inhibit people from expressing their sexual urge in older years, it is equally pointless to push people into such activity if they are not so inclined. After all, the fact that sex is a good thing does not mean that one is not entitled to have had enough of it. Or, if an individual has made the choice of sharing sex exclusively with a particular partner, that person may legitimately wish to give up sex rather than turn to others if the regular partner is no longer available through illness or death. In short, it should be possible to spend the latter years of one's life in a happy and satisfying manner with or without sex.

[57]Pfeiffer et al. (1968), (1969), (1972); Pfeiffer and Davis (1972).

[58]Kolodny et al. (1979).
[59]Comfort (1976).

Chapter 9

Autoeroticism

The term "autoeroticism" was coined by Havelock Ellis at the turn of the twentieth century to describe certain solitary sexual activities such as masturbation, nocturnal orgasms, and sexual fantasies. To distinguish such activities from those that involve interaction between people (sociosexual) is useful if we do not forget that hard and fast distinctions are impossible. For example, when boys masturbate together in a group are they not in fact engaging in a form of sociosexual behavior? Is such group masturbation still to be considered an autoerotic activity simply because there is no physical contact between members of the group?

These problems of definition notwithstanding, we shall discuss in this chapter three types of sexual behavior that are commonly acknowledged to be autoerotic: erotic fantasies, sexual dreams, and masturbation.

Erotic Fantasies

There is a whole world of sexual activity that is confined to the mind, including fleeting erotic images, intricately woven fantasies, fading sexual memories, and fresh hopes—all of which are moving in and out of consciousness a good deal of the time. Erotic fantasies must be the most ubiquitous of all sexual phenomena. It is difficult to imagine any human who does not have them.[1] Fantasies are frequent preludes to other outlets, but more often they exist on their own. They also frequently coexist with other sexual activities such as masturbation and sexual intercourse. Theologians called sexual reveries *delectatio morosa* and differentiated such dallying with erotic images from simple sexual desire or intent to engage in coitus.

Although erotic daydreams are exceedingly common, only a few individuals, usually women, claim to be able to reach orgasm through fantasy alone ("psychic masturbation"). Some women are reportedly able to reach orgasm even in public simply by being in sexually exciting situations. One wonders, however, to what extent activity is purely "abstract" and whether or not in fact subtle and hard-to-detect muscular tension is not accompanying the fantasies.

The propensity of adolescents to daydream is well known, especially when they are in love. In the private and safe theaters of their minds, they endlessly rehearse their favorite fantasies—sometimes in the form of continuing stories, but more often as variations on the same theme.

[1]A medieval penitential assigned the following penances for this offense: for a deacon 25 days, for a monk 30 days, for a priest 40 days, for a bishop 50 days. Haddon and Stubbs, *Councils and Ecclesiastical Documents*, vol. 3; quoted in H. Ellis (1942), vol. II, part one, p. 184.

Figure 9.1 René Magritte, *Ready-made Bouquet.* Courtesy of Alexander Iolas Gallery.

Sexual reveries, though more common in adolescence, actually continue through the entire life span, as does all autoerotic activity. Even happily married people with satisfactory sex lives occasionally ruminate about past experiences (particularly missed opportunities). Such memories sometimes acquire a persistent, haunting quality (*see* Figure 9.1). These thoughts are often sustained by unconscious associations with ungratified childhood wishes that have been repressed and long forgotten.

The intensity of feeling accompanying such fantasies also varies. Most often images and thoughts are relatively inert, even though they may involve patently sexual themes. At the other extreme their intensity may demand sexual release.

The dramatis personae in daydreams often vary, but the individual dreamer usually remains the central character. The objects of these fantasies may be actual acquaintances or people that the dreamer knows only from afar (*see* Figure 9.2). Often they are fictitious figures with somewhat vague and occasionally changing features. The imaginary activities are countless and are determined by the dreamer's unconscious wishes, the extent to which the wishes are permitted into consciousness, and his or her imaginative gifts, which may conjure up extraordinary images.

The Nature of Sexual Fantasies

Despite their infinite variability in terms of content, fantasies can be subsumed under two major categories. The first and more common are "free-floating" erotic daydreams generated by sexual feelings and needs. Much of what has been said above about fantasies pertains to this group. The second category consists of "short-term" sexual images, which are used as stimulation mechanisms either in anticipation or during sexual experiences. These are more likely to be repetitive erotic themes that the person invokes to enhance a given sexual experience or as a supportive device to bolster performance. These standby fantasies are said to act as "old friends" that come to one's aid to heighten arousal and attain orgasm during masturbation, coitus, or homosexual encounters.[2]

There have been many attempts to classify the common themes of erotic fantasies. Given the fertility of human imagination, this would seem to be a hopeless task, yet surprisingly enough a number of common themes do in fact seem to emerge when people reveal their innermost thoughts in this regard. This appears to be true for jounalistic attempts to elucidate such themes as well as more systematic investigative approaches.[3]

Fantasies are a useful tool in studying differences in the sexual proclivities of males and females as well as between persons of different sexual orientation.

[2]Masters and Johnson (1979), p. 176.
[3]As an example of the former, see for instance Friday (1973). Selected excerpts are given in Box 9.1.

Figure 9.2 *Young man fantasizing* (artist unknown).

Masturbatory Fantasy

Unlike pure erotic fantasy, masturbatory fantasies are accompanied by various forms of self-stimulation frequently leading to orgasm. Although it is difficult to conceive that one could masturbate with a blank mind, as it were, not everyone does in fact fantasize during masturbation. Some for instance focus on the bodily sensations elicited by sexual arousal.

During masturbation, most commonly the person evokes past memories, but not infrequently, especially among better-educated people, erotic photographs or literature may also be used as sources of stimulation. In the Playboy Foundation survey sample (*see* Box 8.15), about half of the men and a third of the women indicated that exposure to erotic

pictures or movies increased their desire to masturbate, and this was true for married as well as single persons. Reading erotic literature was found to be even more potent than visual material, especially among women among whom over half reported such responses.

Kinsey reported an interesting sex discrepancy in regard to the role of fantasy in masturbation. Among Kinsey males, 72 percent almost always fantasized while masturbating, 17 percent did so sometimes, and 11 percent did not fantasize at all. The corresponding percentages for females were 50, 14, and 36. This pattern seemed to run counter to the general notion that it is women rather than men who are more inclined to be involved in the psychological aspects of sexual activities. The current data cited above indicate that the sex discrepancy noted by Kinsey was most probably culturally determined. Modern women are clearly far more responsive to erotic materials and fantasies than those of a generation earlier.

Fantasy is an important component of the masturbatory experience. In the Playboy Foundation survey sample the most commonly mentioned type of fantasy involved sexual intercourse with a loved person (reported by three-quarters of all men and four-fifths of all women). But in the case of nearly half of the males and more than a fifth of the females, masturbatory fantasies involved various acquaintances and individuals in a variety of sexual encounters. Masturbatory fantasies clearly provide "safe" expression for a variety of sexual interests whose implementation would be impossible or unacceptable to the individual. Table 9.1 presents further comparisons between male and female fantasies during masturbation.

Sorensen's results indicate rather similar patterns of masturbatory fantasy among adolescents. In this group of 13- to 19-year-olds, 57 percent of boys versus 46 percent of girls reported fantasizing most of the time

Box 9.1 Female Fantasies

The following are parts of fantasies reported by a self-selected non-representative sample of women:

"In the first sexual fantasy that I can remember, I thought of myself undressing while a boy I liked watched me. That became one of my most common fantasies when I was a teen-age girl."

"I am speeding on the New Jersey Turnpike. Two policemen stop me. I tell them I will 'do anything not to get a ticket.' They make me get in the back seat and spread my legs very wide (one of them is in the front seat, the other in the back seat). While one of them drives, the other one has me. They take turns. And then they meet a friend and he gets in on it too."

" . . . I imagine I am secretary to the headmistress of some school for girls between the ages of fifteen and nineteen. One of my jobs, being a big strong girl, is to cane girls who have been sentenced to be caned by the headmistress. . . . Then I change the fantasy and imagine that I am one of the senior girls, aged about eighteen, caught smoking. . . . We stand outside the door of the secretary's room and listen to the sounds of the caning going on inside. Then it is my turn. I go in, get out of my gym tunic, and stand there feeling tense in my tight knickers. The secretary points to the flogging block, says 'Bend over, girl,' and I get across it, ready for my thrashing with the cane on my knickers. While I am pretending that I am getting caned, I masturbate."

"I'm at this hair store. . . . I've just had a facial, so I've got this mask on, and there are cool cotton pads on my eyes. I can't see a thing. Not that I could see what's going on anyway, because there's a white silk curtain that falls from the ceiling down to my waist, then on down to the floor. No one can see me from the waist down. Neither can I. . . . Over there, on the other side, is a young man—actually, lots of them, a row of young, big, strapping types, half nude. . . . They are there to service us. . . . My particular guy is dark, good-looking in a hard,

From N. Friday, *My Secret Garden*. New York: Pocket Books, 1975. By permission.

impersonal sort of way. . . . He crouches there between my legs, and with the greatest expertise in the world, he goes down on me."

"In my lesbian fantasies, I can never put an identity to my partner. She is no one I know and has no face or personality. In my dreams she is just a female body who takes most of the initiative, while I am merely passive and just lie there as she makes love to me. I fantasize that she plays with my breasts and sucks them while masturbating herself. Then she performs cunnilingus on me. We do not kiss, and I do not touch her genitals in these fantasies; however, I do play with her breasts. I often engage in this fantasy while making it with my husband, particularly when he performs cunnilingus on me."

"I especially enjoy the thought of being watched by someone who is not aware that I know he is watching me. Or I imagine that I am making love to someone, perhaps a close friend of the family, and my husband comes in and watches us, as prearranged between my husband and myself without the knowledge of the other man. It would be equally intriguing to walk in and catch my husband with another woman, also by prearrangement."

"The doorbell rings and it is this father and his son. The father has been a lover of mine. . . . comes in and says, 'This is my fourteen-year-old son, and I want him to be as adept as I am, as I think I am, and I want you to teach him everything you know. . . . So the son and I begin, the father sitting there watching as I undress the boy, caress him, totally initiate him. But it's not the boy that excites me in this fantasy, it isn't the idea of having a young boy, it's the idea of being watched by the father."

"During the last phase of intercourse is when I fantasize. I pretend I have changed into a very beautiful and glamorous woman (in real life I know I'm somewhat plain), and that my husband and I are in bed in very luxurious surroundings, usually in a hotel, far away from where we live. I can see the bottle of wine in a silver bucket waiting for us when we finish. I think of the people walking along outside our room in the corridor who are unaware of what we are doing only a few feet away from them, and how they'd envy us if they did know."

Table 9.1 Comparative Masturbation Fantasies of Males and Females

	Percentage of Sample Reporting Each Type of Fantasy	
	Males	Females
Reported equally by males and females:		
Intercourse with a loved person	75	80
Reported more frequently by males than by females:		
Intercourse with strangers	47	21
Group sex with multiple partners of the opposite sex	33	18
Forcing someone to have sex	13	3
Reported more frequently by females than by males:		
Doing sexual things you would never do in reality	19	28
Being forced to have sex	10	19
Homosexual activities	7	11

From D. Bryne, "The Imagery of Sex," in *Handbook of Sexology*, Money, J., and Musaph, H. (Eds.), *Excerpta Medica* (1977), p. 340. Data from Hunt, 1974. Reprinted with permission.

while masturbating, but almost twice as many girls as boys said they combined masturbation with fantasy "some of the time," and 20 percent of boys but only 10 percent of girls rarely or never fantasized while masturbating.

Masturbatory fantasies varied somewhat between boys and girls. The former indicated fantasies involving sex with someone who was forced to submit, sex with more than one female, oral and anal sex, and group sex. In addition to the use of force on others, the boys also imagined themselves being forced to submit. The girls reported fantasies of sex with someone they liked, being forced to submit to several males, and also inflicting mild violence on the other person.

The nature of these fantasies among ordinary boys and girls indicates once again the feelings and inclinations expressed through a wide range of sexual activities. These youngsters were allowing themselves to be conscious of hidden wishes they would generally not want to implement into action. Among the many purposes served, masturbatory fantasy was also used to test one's own inclinations. For example, a 17-year-old girl who had fears about hidden lesbian tendencies was reassured by the fact that she could not reach orgasm while visualizing naked females.[4]

Coital Fantasy

As with masturbation, fantasy seems to be an integral part of the coital experience of many. One encounters in this regard some commonality in the erotic themes as well as considerable disagreement between various lists of erotic imagery. In one study, for example, the most common themes imagined by women during coitus were reported to involve a person other than the partner: being forced into sex; some forbidden activity; being in a different place while having sex; recalling a previous sexual experience; multiple partners; scenes of oneself or others having sex.[5] Yet, another group of women during coitus imagined a former sexual encounter (79 percent); a different sexual partner (79 percent); scene from sexually exciting movie (71 percent); embracing male genitals (64 percent); man embraces her genitals (64 percent); a romantic scene (61 percent); being excited by a seducer (54 percent); being the

[4]Sorensen (1973), p. 138.
[5]Hariton (1973); Hariton and Singer (1974).

sex object of several men (5 percent); watching others having sex (5 percent); being tied up while being stimulated (5 percent). The least frequent themes involved initiating a boy sexually (18 percent); forbidden acts (18 percent); being humiliated (15 percent); being beaten (14 percent); sex with an animal (10 percent).[6]

In a study on a male sample, in response to "What sort of thoughts do you have during intercourse or masturbation?" the majority (64 percent) reportedly claimed to fantasize about the partner they were currently involved with. This finding contradicts the results of virtually all other similar studies. Since these men gave far fewer details about their fantasies than other respondents, the investigators themselves state that these were "rarely true fantasies and focused on actual events that were happening."[7] The rest of the responses from this survey are more consistent with those of others: 11 percent fantasize about another person than the partner; 11 percent recall a past experience, and smaller percentages pertain to group sex, sadomasochistic ideas and "no thoughts" (9 percent). For examples of male coital fantasies from this study, see Box 9.2.

In another approach, when male and female college students were asked to create their own fantasies, the stories that the men wrote typically sounded like "hard-core" pornography while the themes developed by women had stronger emotional and romantic components.[8]

An intriguing comparison of the fantasies of heterosexual and homosexual men and women has been reported as part of the broader investigation of homosexuality by Masters and Johnson.[9] The specific content of these fantasies has not yet been released.

Yet even the general themes reported are of considerable interest (see Table 9.2). The female subjects in this study reported more fantasies than males in both heterosexual and homosexual groups. Lesbians in particular had the highest incidence of the four study groups. "Ambisexual" subjects showed the lowest frequencies of fantasizing.

Especially noteworthy is the high incidence of fantasies of "cross-preference," in which heterosexual men and women contemplated homosexual activities, and vice versa. These revelations did not come easily, and there were many instances where the initial reaction was one of denial. But once these subjects were willing to reveal their innermost thoughts, the most commonly expressed attitudes by both heterosexual and homosexuals toward interaction with the others was one of curiosity rather than rejection. Thus, whatever one's sexual orientation, the alternative seems to at least intrigue a substantial proportion of these subjects.

Two other trends worth noting are the fantasy substitutions of someone other than the sexual partner and the use of coercion. In the case of heterosexual males, the fantasized alternative to the actual partner was most frequently identified as a specific woman. Heterosexual women most often thought of another man they could identify but did not know personally. Homosexual males likewise tended to favor a fantasy substitute. Only lesbians brought their current partners into their fantasies with any significant frequency and they did so by invoking idealized situations.

The use of force, while common to all four subgroups, also showed some differences. This was the most common theme for lesbians and the second most common for homosexual males and heterosexuals of both sexes. Homosexual male fantasies were more violent than those of heterosexual males. Their victims were of either sex and of about equal frequency, with the homosexual male usually playing the role of rapist. Lesbians

---

[6]Crepault et al. (1977).
[7]Pietropinto and Simenauer (1977), p. 308 (see Box 8.15 for information on this study).
[8]Barclay (1973).
[9]Masters and Johnson (1979), chapter 9.

Box 9.2   Male Fantasies

The following fantasies are from a list of thoughts men report to have had during intercourse or masturbation. The subjects are a nonrepresentative sample of the population.

"Pretty blondes with shapely rears, spread apart with all sex organs exposed. Never any fantasies about my usual sex partner. Yes [during intercourse], more often about someone that I know or have seen recently."

"I think about sexy, very pretty women, nude. I fantasize about my sexual partner's nude body during intercourse."

"My favorite fantasy is making love with women I know on a daily basis who I would never have a chance to enjoy. Oral sex is a thing with me—an ego trip of another woman who one would never suspect to enjoy such things. During intercourse with my wife, I have thought of past relationships or someone else I would enjoy making love with."

"I just keep repeating the name of the woman I used to go with. I fantasize about her all the time."

"Making love to sisters-in-law. Yes [during intercourse], fantasize about different partners and positions."

"Making it with a Farrah Fawcett or some other sex symbol. [During intercourse], once in a while. When I'm not with my usual partner."

Extracts pp. 50, 185, copyright © 1977 by Anthony Pietropinto. Reprinted by permission of Times Books, a division of Quadrangle/The New York Times Book Co., Inc. from *Beyond the Male Myth* by Anthony Pietropinto and Jacqueline Simenauer.

"A past experience which was outstanding. [Think about] far-out sexy things. I fantasize about one of my ex-lovers who is the best sex partner I ever had and who is also in my heart."

"Pin-ups in girlie magazines or women that have encouraged me but I didn't pursue."

"I think about my usual sexual partner and some about past partners. I sometimes fantasize about my past partners being all together at once and exciting me."

"I sometimes think about sex with two women at the same time or about two women having sex together."

"Making a woman have an orgasm she can't handle and hold me like never before, and during orgasm having oral sex with me."

"Boobs, famous sex symbols or less famous sex symbols. Having a bigger penis."

"I have sadomasochistic fantasies."

"Having a beautiful woman with me. I think about sex symbols or my sex partner. I have fantasized about being in a different environment with my partner."

"Having sex with another partner, male/female. More times male than female. Do not fantasize during intercourse, because it is happening!"

"Yes. I enjoy dog style. Fantasize I'm a big black dog."

"I fantasize about how great the relationship is with my partner and what I can do to make her happy. I concentrate my thoughts on the fabulous feelings we are experiencing."

"Never fantasize. I believe in total reality."

more typically relied on psychological coercion than physical force and frequently switched between the roles of forcing sexual compliance and being forced with it. Less frequently, lesbian fantasies were more frankly sadistic and involved females and males as victims with about equal frequency.

For the heterosexual male, the fantasy of being forced into sex is somewhat more frequent than his using force. In the former case he was usually set upon by a group of unidentified women. When he took the active role there would usually be just one identified woman involved.

Heterosexual females usually thought of unidentified males singly or in groups in forced sexual encounters. The woman most often was in the role of victim and rarely in

Table 9.2 *Fantasy and Sexual Orientation: Comparative Content of Fantasies by Frequency of Occurrence (1957–1968)*

Homosexual male (N = 30)	Heterosexual male (N = 30)
1. Imagery of sexual anatomy	1. Replacement of established partner
2. Forced sexual encounters	2. Forced sexual encounter
3. Cross-preference encounters	3. Observation of sexual activity
4. Idyllic encounters with unknown men	4. Cross-preference encounters
5. Group sex experiences	5. Group sex experiences
	Heterosexual female (N = 30)
Homosexual female (N = 30)	
	1. Replacement of established partner
1. Forced sexual encounters	2. Forced sexual encounter
2. Idyllic encounter with established partner	3. Observation of sexual activity
3. Cross-preference encounters	4. Idyllic encounters with unknown men
4. Recall of past sexual experience	5. Cross-preference encounters
5. Sadistic imagery	

From W. Masters and V. Johnson, *Homosexuality in Perspective.* Boston: Little, Brown, 1979, p. 178. Reproduced with permission.

the role of rapist, but there was usually little violence entailed beyond her being rendered helpless.

At the turn of the century, Freud claimed that most men are driven to debase their sexual partners. This admixture of sex and aggression has been since then a frequent theme in the psychoanalytic literature. Stoller has further expanded on this association and says that hostility, the overt or covert desire to harm another is central to generating sexual excitement. In reenacting childhood hurts and fears in an effort to master them, the adult retaliates in his sexual relations and this colors the process of arousal: "Triumph, rage, revenge, fear, anxiety, risk and all condensed into one complex buzz called 'sexual excitement.' "[10]

[10]Stoller (1979).

The Functions of Sexual Fantasies

Erotic fantasies fulfill many functions. First, they are a source of pleasure to which everyone has ready access. Second, they are often substitutes for action: as temporary satisfactions while awaiting more concrete ones (tonight's date, a honeymoon in the distant future) or as compensations for unattainable goals. Despite this apparent function as wish fulfillment, an individual may not want his or her fantasies to come true, no matter how much he or she yearns for them. Such unrealizable daydreams are probably disguised replays of infantile (possibly oedipal) wishes.

Sexual fantasies that deal with real or imagined past events therefore fulfill a compensatory function. They allow partial, tolerable expression of forbidden wishes and to some degree relieve sexual frustrations. Fantasies cannot yield full gratification of sexual desires, but by easing the pain and pressure of past traumas and unfulfilled wishes they help to make them more bearable.

Third, some fantasies revolve around future events and can sometimes be of very definite help in real-life situations. As an individual anticipates problems, plans for contingencies, and mentally rehearses alternative modes of action, such a person lessens anxiety and prepares to cope with novel situations. There is thus an important difference between fantasies that substitute for action and those that prepare for it.[11]

In addition to these uses of fantasy in its free-floating form, a fourth and especially important function of fantasy involves its use as a stimulation mechanism. In this sense fantasies are psychological "aphrodisiacs" that heighten sexual arousal. Thus they function for many individuals as an integral component of other forms of autoerotic and sociosexual activities.

The practice of using fantasies during sexual encounters such as coitus elicits mixed reactions. Some individuals and therapists see it as beneficial and others as detrimental to the relationship.

The first consideration in this regard is whether or not the fantasies should be shared. If they are not, having one's mind somewhere else will be distracting the person from interacting directly with the sexual partner. One usually hopes for the undivided attention of the other during such intimate moments. But then, what if the person can switch back and forth between reality and fantasy or keep the fantasy as background to the primary interaction? If such "balancing" can be maintained and the net effect is intensification of the sexual relationship itself, then one could presumably argue in favor of the practice.

If the fantasy is shared, it could have

the beneficial effect of enhancing mutual arousal. The ability to reveal one's thoughts, however idiosyncratic, presupposes true intimacy and may further strengthen willingness and capacity to be open with others. But the counterargument is that the revelation of the fantasy can have an intensive and disruptive influence. Since the fantasy is likely to involve extraneous characters and practices, the exclusivity of the relationship is diluted.

It is unclear to what extent the forms and frequency of fantasy use differentiate those with good sexual function from others who are dysfunctional. Fantasy is currently used in some forms of sex therapy, and we shall discuss their further use in that context.

Pathological Fantasies

Given the universality of sexual fantasizing, it must be assumed to be part of normal mental life. But does it have pathological, as well as healthy, forms? Judging quantitatively, fantasizing beyond a certain point about sex or anything else is wasteful and maladaptive. Particularly during adolescence, erotic fantasies may become excessively absorbing. If they interfere with work or if they regularly take the place of satisfying interaction with others, they may interfere with normal psychosocial development.

Can fantasies be evaluated by content? If we had a commonly accepted set of qualitative criteria to separate healthy from unhealthy forms of sexual behavior, then it would probably also apply to fantasies. But we have no such reliable yardstick of "normality." Furthermore, the individual's subjective reaction cannot be taken as the sole criterion, for some people are disturbed by thoughts of very common activities whereas others may be unaffected by very bizarre fantazies. Even though there are no simple answers to these questions, several observations are pertinent.

Thinking about socially unacceptable behavior is very common. Sometimes it is

---

[11]For further consideration of the role of fantasy in sex, see Sullivan (1969), pp. 79–89, and Goleman and Bush (1978). See Singer (1968) for a more general discussion of daydreaming.

merely silly and apparently senseless (like thinking about urinating on someone), but it may also center on highly disturbing, guilt-provoking behavior.

What do such thoughts mean, and how does one deal with them? First, it may be comforting to realize that most of these fantasies are never acted upon. We all have reservoirs of repressed wishes that occasionally surface in thinly disguised forms, residues of our earlier undifferentiated sexuality. They do not "define" us as adults. Thus, the fact that a person fantasizes about forced sex does not mean that he or she would actually want to go through the experience even if the opportunity presented itself.

There is no easy way to deal with unpleasant or disturbing fantasies. Conscious attempts to dispel them often simply cause us to focus on them more strongly. It is better to take them for what they are: isolated thoughts that do not mean very much. We can, of course, minimize opportunities for lengthy reveries. We are not as helpless in these matters as we sometimes think.

Since fantasies reflect our thoughts and feelings, they can certainly mirror problems that may exist regarding sex. Some women, for instance, have fantasies that during intercourse their vaginas will be torn apart. some men fear that vaginas are full of razor blades, ground glass, or armed with teeth (*vagina dentata*) to mutilate the penises that venture in. Such perceived threats to the integrity of the genitals bespeak of an admixture of aggressive and sexual impulses. Fleeting thoughts of this type are nevertheless quite common and should not always be taken seriously.

There are also cases when a fantasy may be the prelude to action. In rare instances a person may correctly realize that he or she is losing control and is likely to commit a seriously antisocial act. The individual must then seek help. It is better to find psychiatric or other professional assistance rather than turning to family or friends.

The issue of undesirable aspects of fantasy has important societal components: One of these is moral. If one believes that "one can sin in one's heart" just as effectively as through overt behavior then of course sexual fantasy becomes the object of moral scrutiny.

Another social concern is based on the presumption that erotic mental stimulation leads to sexual action. This is the basis of much of the concern over the deleterious effects of "pornography." Considerable work was done in this regard through the Commission on Obscenity and Pornography.[12] The general conclusion was that sexual books, pictures and movies have little effect on subsequent behavior. If there is an increase in sexual activity, it is apparently limited to the brief period following such exposure. The issue is far from settled, however, given evidence from research on nonsexual behavior showing how specific behavior may be demonstrably initiated by observers[13] and other work that shows how manipulation of the content of fantasies are followed by alterations in relevant behavior.[14] Another possibility that remains open is that the stimulation of sexual fantasy has long-range effects in sexual attitudes and behavior that do not emerge in the sort of studies generally conducted in this regard.[15]

Sexual Dreams

Man has sought in his dreams a key to his future and a window into his past. Freud called dreams "the royal road to the unconscious." Within the last decade or so inquiries into the neurophysiology of sleep and dreaming have yielded new and intriguing findings, some of which are particularly relevant to the study of sexuality.

Like all other dreams, sexual dreams

[12]Commission on Obscenity and Pornography (1970).
[13]Bandura et al. (1963).
[14]McClelland (1965).
[15]Byrne (1977).

Box 9.3 Freudian Dream Interpretation

Freud's monumental *The Interpretation of Dreams,* is a psychoanalytic classic. The following is a small sample of his method of dream analysis.

In this instance the dreamer was a young woman suffering from a phobia of open spaces (agoraphobia) based on her unconscious fears of seduction.

"I was walking in the street in the summer, wearing a straw hat of peculiar shape; its middle-piece was bent upwards and its side-pieces hung downwards" (the description became hesitant at this point) "in such a way that one side was lower than the other. I was cheerful and in a self-confident frame of mind; and, as I passed a group of young officers, I thought: 'None of you can do me any harm!' "

Freud's comments in response to the dream were:

Since nothing occurred to her in connection with the hat in the dream, I said: "No doubt the hat was a male genital organ, with its middle-piece sticking up and its two side-pieces hanging down." . . . I intentionally gave her no inter-pretation of the detail about the two side-pieces hanging down unevenly; though it is precisely

details of this kind that must point the way in determining an interpretation. I went on to say that as she had a husband with such fine genitals there was no need for her to be afraid of the officers—no need, that is, for her to wish for anything from them, since as a rule she was prevented from going for a walk un-protected and unaccompanied owing to her phantasies of being seduced. I had already been able to give her this last explanation of her anxiety on several occasions upon the basis of other material.

The way in which the dreamer reacted to this material was most remarkable. She withdrew her description of the hat and maintained that she had never said that the two side-pieces hung down. I was too certain of what I had heard to be led astray, and stuck to my guns. She was silent for a while and then found enough courage to ask what was meant by one of her husband's testes hanging down lower than the other and whether it was the same in all men. In this way the remarkable detail of the hat was explained and the interpretation accepted by her.[1]

[1]Freud, *The Interpretation of Dreams* (1900), in Freud (1957–1964), vol. IV–V, pp. 360–361.

are also usually fragmentary and difficult to describe. Sometimes their sexual content is accompanied by appropriately erotic emotions. Quite often, however, imagery and affect seem contradictory: A person may dream of a flagrantly sexual activity without feeling aroused; or he may feel intense excitement while dreaming of an apparently nonsexual, even improbable, situation like climbing a pole, flying, and so on. Psychoanalysts explain such dreams in terms of their symbolic rather than their manifest content.

Psychoanalytic Concepts of Dreaming

Freud thought that the function of dreams was to protect sleep. During sleep, when the vigilance of the ego relaxes, somewhat, unacceptable (often sexual) wishes threaten to break through into consciousness and thus to disrupt sleep. These wishes are permitted partial expression in disguised form and are experienced as dreams. The process of transforming unconscious wishes into dream imagery is known as "dream work." A dream therefore has two components: the manifest content (usually woven around some actual experience, "the day residue") and the latent content (which carries the real message in disguised and symbolic form); see Box 9.3.

Symbolism is a major component of dreams, though it is by no means restricted to dreaming. It is also present in art, literature, myths, legends, proverbs, jokes, and so on.

In dreams symbols may be highly individual—tailored to the occasion, as it were. More frequently we use symbols that have common or universal meanings. The meaning of a dream symbol may be transparent or highly camouflaged and distorted. To complicate matters further, a given symbol may have several meanings, and the correct interpretation in any given instance must be arrived at from its context and associations.

In psychoanalytic reckoning a great many (but not all) symbols have sexual meanings. For example, long objects like sticks or tree trunks may stand for penis. The opening of an umbrella may represent an erection. Knives, daggers, and nail files (possibly because they rub back and forth) also symbolize penis. On the other hand, boxes, chests, cupboards, ovens, rooms, ships—in fact any enclosed space or hollow object— usually represent the female genitals. The significance of actions involving such objects or places is not hard to surmise: Going in and out of a room would signify intercourse, and whether or not the door is locked thus has special meaning. Walking up and down steps, ladders, and staircases also stands for coitus, for in both climbing and orgasm we reach the apex through rhythmic movements and with loss of breath, after which we can go down again rather quickly.

Sexual dreams, particularly those culminating in orgasms, are intensely pleasurable but can also be quite bewildering. It has been suggested that nightmares have a sexual basis or component. The feeling of agonized dread, the oppressive sensation in the chest, and the feeling of helpless paralysis that characterize nightmares are suggestive of the experience of being raped.[16]

Fantasies and dreams are closely related. In both there is transient relaxation of conscious restraints and repressed wishes are permitted partial expression. Daydreams generally remain relatively more subject to the dictates of logic and reality ("secondary-process thinking"), however. In dreams the vigilance of the ego is lessened to the point at which deeply buried material emerges—without much regard for ordinary logical processes and the restraints of reality. Nevertheless, although in dreams anything becomes possible ("primary-process thinking") unconscious material rarely surfaces in a stark and undisguised form.

The intelligibility of fantasies and dreams varies from obvious to enigmatic. They may represent patent or thinly veiled wish fulfillments or deeply concealed fears. Most dreams make no overt sense at all and can be given meaning only through detailed analysis of their symbolic content.

The psychoanalytic literature on dream interpretation is extensive. Among numerous contributors to this field we should mention C. G. Jung, whose best-known work on dreams is his "General Aspects of Dream Analysis."[17]

The Neurophysiology of Sleep and Dreaming

Sleep is not the uniform state that it appears to be, nor are dreams erratic events that punctuate it unpredictably. Rather, there is a definite sleep-dream cycle that recurs nightly. Brain waves (electroencephalogram, or EEG, tracings) show four distinct sleep patterns. One of these is characterized by a fast rhythm and bursts of rapid eye movements (REM). A person who is awakened during this phase will almost inevitably report that he or she has been experiencing vivid dreams. During the other sleep phases dreaming has been found to be more erratic and less vivid.

During an ordinary night's sleep there are four or five active dream periods, accounting for almost a quarter of total sleeping time: The first occurs 60–90 minutes after fall-

---

[16]E. Jones, (1949).

[17]In Jung (1960), pp. 237–281.

ing asleep, and the rest at approximately 90-minute intervals. These dream periods are generally quite constant, which means that everyone dreams every night, regardless of whether or not the dreams are remembered in the morning.[18]

These periods of active dreaming (called REM periods because of their association with rapid eye movements), furthermore, appear to be times of intense physiological activity, with rapid and irregular pulse and respiration. Also in a remarkably high number of instances (85–95 percent) partial or full erections have been observed during REM states among males, even among infants and elderly men. These erections are not necessarily accompanied by sexual dreams, and their full significance remains unclear.[19]

Evidence of sexual arousal during sleep is more difficult to detect among women than it is among men. Therefore to date the association of REM sleep with female sexual response has not been as convincingly demonstrated.[20] There is no known physiological reason as to why females should react differently from males in this regard.

Nocturnal Orgasms

Visitations by "the angel of the night" (which is what the pioneer sexologist Paolo Mantegazza called nocturnal emissions) have left many a young man in an awkward situation in the morning. Although orgasms during sleep (nocturnal or daytime) do not constitute an important proportion of total sexual outlets (2–3 percent for females, 2–8 percent for males, depending upon the population subgroup), they are nevertheless of considerable interest. Substantial numbers of people experience them (by age 45 almost 40 percent of females and more than 90 percent of males have had such experiences at least once). As involuntary acts nocturnal orgasms are less subject to moral censure, and as a "natural" outlet they supposedly act as a safety valve for accumulated sexual tensions.

The universality of the experience is well documented. Babylonians believed in a "maid of the night" who visited men in their sleep and a "little night man" that slept with women.[21] Such imaginary beings became more prominent in medieval times in the form of demons (see Figure 9.3) who would lie upon women (incubus) and under men (succubus). The West African Yoruba tribe believed in a single versatile being who could act either as male or female and visit members of either sex in their sleep.[22]

Nocturnal orgasms occur more often in males than females. They are, therefore, generally called "nocturnal emissions" or "wet dreams," designations that are applicable only to males. For the same reason the experience is more difficult for males to conceal.

Nocturnal orgasms are almost always accompanied by dreams, but the dreamer often awakens in the process.[23] The manifest content of such a dream may or may not be clearly erotic, but there is always a subjective sensation of sexual excitement. Pleasure may, however, be tinged with apprehension and remorse. As in all dreams, there is usually a succession of apparently discrete images, rather than a coherent scenario. These images may be purely heterosexual, or they may have homosexual or other elements.

---

[18]For a concise, authoritative, and not overly technical presentation on current research on sleep and dreams, see Dement (1972).

[19]See Fisher et al. (1965), Gulevich and Zarcone (1969), Kleitman (1963), Dement (1965), and Karacan et al. (1976, 1977).

[20]William Dement, personal communication.

[21]Jastrow, Religion of Babylonia, and Ploss, Das Weib; quoted in H. Ellis (1942), vol. I, part one, p. 198.

[22]H. Ellis (1942), vol. I, part one, p. 188

[23]The dreamer's awareness of what is happening may be hazy. In some instances orgasm is completed, and he goes back to sleep without having fully awakened. At other times he may wake up startled; and if orgasm has not started, it may be possible to avert it. Medieval theologians mercifully permitted believers to complete nocturnal orgasms on awakening, provided that they did not willfully enjoy them.

Figure 9.3 Illustration by Frédéric Bouchot in *Diabolico Foutromanie.*

Occasionally the dreamer will sleep right through the experience and will have only vague recollections of the dream in the morning.

It is also possible for orgasm to occur without dreams. For instance, a man with a completely severed spinal cord (but with intact ejaculatory spinal centers) can have nocturnal orgasms. Because of the interruption of the spinal tracks, the brain can no longer communicate with the portions of the spinal cord below the lesion, and dreaming (which occurs in the brain) cannot possibly influence the ejaculatory center in the lower spinal cord. In these instances erection and ejaculation may result from tactile stimulation caused by friction in the bed or from some other reflexive source.

Information on nocturnal orgasm among primitive groups is scarce. Male nocturnal orgasm is widely recognized, but there are few references to female experiences.

Males of several species of mammals are known to have erections and orgasms during sleep. There is also accumulating evidence of REM sleep periods in animals.

Prevalence, Frequency, and Correlates

Orgasms during sex dreams constituted a minor outlet for both sexes in the Kinsey sample. They accounted for only 2–3 percent of the female and 2–8 percent of the male total sexual outlets, depending on age, marital status, and other characteristics (see Chapter 7). Almost 50 percent of males, but fewer than 10 percent of females, reported experiencing orgasm during sleep more than five times a year. Approximately 5 percent of men and 1 percent of women averaged weekly orgasms through this means. This experience is one in which the range of variation among males was greater than among females.

Despite the low frequencies of orgasm, sex dreams are experienced by a wide segment of the population. In the Kinsey sample two of three women and practically all the males reported having had erotic dreams sometime in their lives. Yet by the age of 45 only about 40 percent of women and 80 percent of men had actually reached orgasm during such dreams.

Frequencies of nocturnal emission in males are highest among the college-educated and progressively lower in lower educational groups. There is an almost sevenfold difference between the averages of the two extremes. At all social levels frequencies are higher before marriage. Otherwise there are no differences between rurual and urban groups, among various religious groups, or between those practicing and not practicing their religions. Such correlations with female nocturnal orgasms are even less impressive.

Health Aspects

The attitude toward nocturnal orgasm in our society is generally benevolent, though the phenomenon has not entirely escaped concern and opprobrium. Adolescents used to be advised to empty their bladders at bedtime, not to sleep in one position or another, not to wear tight nightclothes, and so on in order to minimize the chances of nighttime "pollutions." More commonly, however, this outlet is regarded as nature's way of taking care of sexual needs in the absence of other legitimate outlets.

Do nocturnal orgasms actually fulfill such a compensatory function? This possibility was tested on Kinsey's female sample. A compensatory correlation with other outlets was found in about 14 percent of respondents; as these women refrained from other forms of sexual expression, nocturnal orgasms became more frequent. This compensatory function appeared most often when other outlets had been drastically reduced or completely eliminated, as during the imprisonment or after loss of a spouse. Nocturnal orgasms seemed to increase more when sociosexual outlets, rather than masturbation, were reduced.

When the compensatory increase in nocturnal orgasms occurred, it was nowhere commensurate with the magnitude of the reduction in other outlets: A woman who lost the chance for several coital orgasms a week might have only a few more nocturnal orgasms a year. Besides, in about 7 percent of the sample there was even a positive correlation: As other outlets became more frequent, so did nocturnal orgasms. In 10 percent of the sample this outlet was first experienced only after one or more of the other outlets had been experienced.

The evidence, at least for females, is far from supporting the idea of nocturnal orgasms as a "natural" safety valve. It is ironic that the one outlet (aside from marital coitus) that has some legitimacy among large numbers of people turns out to be one of the least effective.

Masturbation

Masturbation was probably practiced long before mankind appeared in the world. The practice is prevalent among mammals and must have continued while man was evolving

---

Box 9.4 Masturbation among Animals

Self-stimulation is quite prevalent among animals.[1] Among males of many species masturbation to the point of orgasm has been documented. It is less certain for females, where capacity to attain orgasm appears to be less developed so far as can be determined, and such determination is more difficult among female animals.

It must also be emphasized that much of the available information on sexual behavior among animals, including masturbation, has been based on observations of animals in captivity. Such data are useful in the same sense that observations on human behavior in prisons is useful. But it cannot be generalized. Thus, if animals in captivity engage in nonreproductive sexual behavior, it does not follow that such behavior is necessarily "natural." It merely indicates that animals are capable of this kind of behavior and engage in it under certain circumstances.

More recent studies of primates in the wild indicate that sex in general is less important than for animals in captivity. Beyond that, information on

nonreproductive sexual behavior among animals in the wild is at this point insufficient to allow further theorizing. The more crucial data are going to come from observations of animals in their natural habitats. Otherwise it will be impossible to separate spontaneous behavior from artificially generated oddities. For example, male baboons in one African park have reportedly developed erotic responses to automobiles and are in the habit of jumping on the hoods of cars and ejaculating at the windshield.[2]

Self-stimulation can be observed among subprimates. A sexually aroused porcupine, for instance, holds one forepaw to its genitals while walking about on the other three paws. It may also rub its sex organs against various objects; one captive male was observed hopping about with a stick between its legs, showing obvious signs of arousal.

Dogs and cats lick their penises before and after coitus; elephants use their trunks; captive dolphins rub their erect penises against the floor of the tank, and one male has been observed stimulating itself by

[1]The data presented in this section are from Ford and Beach (1951), pp. 159–161.

[2]Bates (1967), p. 70.

(*see* Box 9.4). Since historical and anthropological records also attest to its universality (*see* Box 9.5), certainly whether it is harmful or harmless should be known by now. Yet the voluminous literature and even more voluminous folklore on masturbation did not settle the question until relatively recently. The harmlessness of masturbation is now established, however, and there is no need to belabor the issue, even though there may be lingering doubts in some minds.

The vulgar Latin verb *masturbari* dates from the first century A.D. It is believed to have been derived from the Latin for "hand"

(*manu-s*) and "to defile" (*stuprare*) or "to disturb" (*turbare*). An alternative explanation is that "mas" is derived from *mas* ("male seed," or semen). In view of other than manual methods of achieving the same ends, "self-stimulation" seems more accurate.[24]

What actually constitutes masturbation

[24]The term "onanism" is a misnomer, for the biblical event to which it refers had no connection with masturbation (Genesis 38:8–11). Pejorative terms like "self-abuse" and "self-pollution" have also been dropped in serious discussions. The vernacular expressions for masturbation are many: "jerking off," "whacking off," and so on. Most of these terms are obviously more descriptive of male masturbation than of its female counterpart.

Box 9.4 Continued

holding its penis in the jet of the water intake. Comparable activities have been noted among rats, rabbits, horses, bulls, and other animals.

A curious practice has been observed among red deer, whose antlers apparently become erotically sensitive during rutting season.

This act is accomplished by lowering the head and gently drawing the tips of the antlers to and fro through the herbage. Erection and extrusion of the penis from the sheath follow in five to seven seconds. There is but little protrusion and retraction of the penis and no oscillating movements of the pelvis. Ejaculation follows about five seconds after the penis is erected, so that the whole act takes ten to fifteen seconds. These antlers, used now so delicately, may within a few minutes be used with all the body's force behind them to clash with the antlers of another stag. These mysterious organs are a paradox; at one moment exquisitely sensitive, they can be apparently without feeling the next.[3]

Self-stimulation is quite common among primates in captivity. Male apes and monkeys manipulate their penises by hand or foot and also take them into their

[3]Darling (1937), quoted in Ford and Beach (1951), p. 161.

mouths or rub them against the floor. Masturbation does not occur only in captivity; free spider monkeys manipulate their genitals with their tails, and adult male rhesus monkeys have been observed masturbating to the point of orgasm in the presence of receptive females. But this does not apply, for example, to wild gorillas.

Female mammals of subprimate species apparently masturbate only rarely. During the breeding season some may manipulate their vulvas, rub them against various objects, walk about astride sticks, and so on; the types of activity are quite similar to those of the males. Self-stimulation, furthermore, appears to serve more than merely autoerotic functions, for the genital secretions left on objects or even on the ground by a female in heat attract and excite males.

Masturbation is definitely less frequent among female primates than among males, both in the wild and in captivity. Females can be seen fingering or rubbing their genitals but often only perfunctorily. Even when such activity is clearly autoerotic, it does not lead to definitely observable orgasms.

---

is as uncertain as its etymology. It is easy to agree that it involves more than simply manipulating one's own genitals. What about the woman who achieves orgasms by fondling her breasts or through erotic fantasy alone? What about infants who seem to enjoy pulling and tugging at their genitals? What about indulgence in such tactile stimulation as thumb-sucking and back-scratching for sensual pleasure? Are all these and countless other acts masturbatory activities in disguise? An all-inclusive conception of masturbation would have little heuristic value: We could not possibly count all episodes of thumb-sucking,

back-scratching, and the like for study. The alternative is to restrict our definition to those deliberate acts of self-arousal that culminate in orgasm without direct physical interaction with others. Unfortunately, this definition leaves out activities that are generally accepted as forms of masturbation, to say nothing of the myriad types of behavior that psychoanalysts believe to be ''masturbatory equivalents.''

When we refer here to the findings of the Kinsey study we shall consider only masturbation that leads to orgasm. Otherwise we mean by ''masturbation'' any erotic activity

Box 9.5 Masturbation in Cross-Cultural Perspective

Masturbation is as nearly universal a phenomenon as is coitus but, like all human behavior, is subject to cultural variation. European masturbation patterns seem very similar to those of the United States. Is masturbation a predominantly Western practice? The anthropologist Mantegazza (whose writings were prominent in the 1930s) called Europeans a "race of masturbators." He reasoned that Western civilization simultaneously stimulates and represses sexuality and that restrictions on nonmarital coitus compel people to masturbate instead. Let us see what the historical and anthropological records show.

Masturbation has been documented for many ancient cultures, including the Babylonian, Egyptian, Hebrew, Indian, and Greco-Roman. Greeks and Romans believed that Mercury had invented the act to console Pan after he had lost his mistress Echo.[1] Zeus himself was known to indulge

occasionally.[2] Aristophanes, Aristotle, Herondas, and Petronius refer to masturbation.[3] Classical attitudes, nevertheless, seem to have been ambivalent: Demosthenes was condemned for the practice, whereas Diogenes was praised for doing it openly in the marketplace.[4]

Masturbation is reported by Ford and Beach for about forty primitive cultures[5] and is thought to be less prevalent in societies that are permissive toward nonmarital coitus and rare in many preliterate groups.[6] Most groups seemed to disapprove of it for adults. For instance, Trukese men (monogamous fishermen of the Caroline Islands) were said to masturbate in secret while watching women bathe. Men of Tikopia (Pacific island agriculturists) and of

[1]Parke (1906), p. 373.

[2]Frazer, trans. (1898).
[3]Aristophanes finds it unmanly but acceptable for women, children, slaves, and feeble old men.
[4]H. Ellis, (1942), vol. I, part one, p. 277.
[5]Ford and Beach (1951).
[6]P. Gebhard, in Marshall and Suggs (1971), p. 208.

that involves voluntary self-stimulation. Most often it occurs in private, but two or more people may masturbate together; mutual stimulation, however, is not masturbation but either petting or homosexual play. Masturbation thus involves a variety of sexual behaviors that overlap with other forms of sexual expression. The techniques of masturbation can be viewed more generally as techniques of stimulation. The same acts are also performed during petting or coital foreplay.

Techniques

Similarities in human physiological makeup impose certain general characteristics on all forms of masturbation in both sexes. There is, nevertheless, considerable variation owing to anatomical differences, diverse life experiences, and different cultural patterns of sexual behavior.

It is impossible, and hardly necessary, to catalog each and every method of masturbation used. Instead we shall restrict ourselves to the more common forms, plus a few of the more exotic variants that illustrate how far some people go in their autoeroticism.

Predictably, the external genitals, which are most sensitive, are the primary targets of stimulation. But, as we noted earlier, individuals may be differently conditioned. The physiological mechanisms underlying all sexual responses are vasocongestion and in-

Box 9.5   Continued

Dahomey (West African agriculturists and fishermen) masturbated occasionally, even though both cultures permitted polygamy.

Female masturbation also occurred, but infrequently; it was generally disapproved. Vaginal insertions seemed more common than clitoral stimulation among some primitive people: African Azande women used wooden dildos (and were severely beaten if caught by their husbands); the Chukchee of Siberia used the calf muscles of reindeer; Tikopia women relied on roots and bananas; Crow women used their fingers, and so did the Azanda of Australia.

Among the Lesu (polygamous tribesmen of New Ireland) female masturbation was condoned. Powdermaker reported:

Masturbation . . . is practiced frequently at Lesu and regarded as normal behavior. A woman will masturbate if she is sexually excited and there is no man to satisfy her. A couple may be having intercourse in the same house, or near enough for her to see them, and she may thus become

aroused. She then sits down and bends her right leg so that her heel presses against her genitalia. Even young girls of about six years may do this quite casually as they sit on the ground. The women and men talk about it freely, and there is no shame attached to it. It is a customary position for women to take, and they learn it in childhood. They never use their hands for manipulation.[7]

Anthropological reports also indicate that, even where masturbation occurs, it does not seem to be very frequent. The fact that adults of both sexes masturbate in primitive cultures is, however, more relevant than is the purported frequency of the practice in any of them. Information from anthropological field notes is nevertheless hardly comparable to the results of thorough and systematic population surveys. Until such rigorous surveys are conducted cross-culturally, we cannot discuss comparative rates with any certainty.

[7]Powdermaker (1933), quoted in Ford and Beach (1951), p. 158.

---

creased muscular tension. The first is beyond voluntary control, but the second can be deliberately used to heighten sexual tension.

Genital Manipulation

Manual techniques are the most common for both sexes. The most frequent form of male masturbation involves simply manipulating the penis by hand. This technique usually consists of gripping the shaft and moving the hand over it firmly to and fro or in a "milking" motion. The glans and frenulum may be lightly stroked in the earlier stages, but as tensions mount and movements become more vigorous direct contact with these areas is generally avoided because

of their extreme sensitivity. It is possible, however, to continue stimulation of these parts by moving the prepuce over them.

Women also rely primarily on genital manipulation.[25] The clitoris and the labia minora are the structures most commonly involved (see Figure 9.4) They are stroked, pressed, and rhythmically stimulated. Since they are the most sensitive parts of the female genitals, the motions are usually quite gentle and deliberate. Just as men avoid direct friction of the penile glans, many women avoid

[25]In the Hite sample almost 80 percent of the women exclusively relied on manual stimulation of the "clitoral/vulval area." The majority did this while lying on their back and directing stimulation to the clitoris.

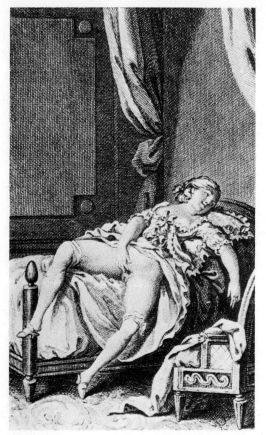

Figure 9.4   Illustration by Caylus in *Thérèse Philosophe.*

The inner surfaces of the labia minora are also quite sensitive and are frequently stimulated during masturbation. The motions involved are similar: gentle stroking, steady or rhythmic pressure, and so on. Actually these movements merge into one another, and the fingers of one or both hands move from one structure to the other, perhaps pulling on the labia and stimulating the clitoris alternately with circular strokes to excite the introitus. The outer labia are less often involved and are only incidentally stimulated.

In both male and female masturbation the buildup to orgasm follows the description given earlier (Chapter 3). Slow and deliberate initial movements become progressively more intense.

Friction against Objects

It is physiologically immaterial whether the genitals are excited by the hand, the heels, or the back of a chair. But behaviorally such distinctions are significant. When a person resorts to manual handling of the organs, there can be no mistake about the nature of the act. This may be one reason why some prefer nonmanual self-stimulation. Others use this approach simply because they find it more exciting.[26]

The possibilities are many, for any reasonable object will do: a pillow, a towel, nightclothes tucked between the legs, a bed cover, or the mattress itself may provide a convenient surface to rub and press against, and one can often achieve orgasm without ever touching one's genitals (*see* Figure 9.5).

Many an adolescent may actually discover the potential of self-stimulation through some innocent activity like climbing a pole or riding a bicycle . The health manuals of some years ago devoted considerable thought to the proper design of bicycle seats (especially for girls) in order to minimize such an event.

the glans of the clitoris. Instead, they concentrate on the clitoral shaft, which they can stimulate on either side. If too much pressure is applied or manipulation is prolonged over an area, the site may become less sensitive. Switching hands or moving the fingers about is therefore quite common.

Although the clitoris is often cited as the primary erotic target, Masters and Johnson have discovered that women usually manipulate the mons area as a whole. In this way they can prolong the buildup of tension and avoid potentially painful contact with the clitoral glans. Sometimes rhythmic or steady pressure over the mons is all that is necessary to elicit orgasm.

---

[26]Among the Hite subjects 4 percent relied on ''pressing and thrusting'' the ''clitoral/vulval area'' against a soft object.

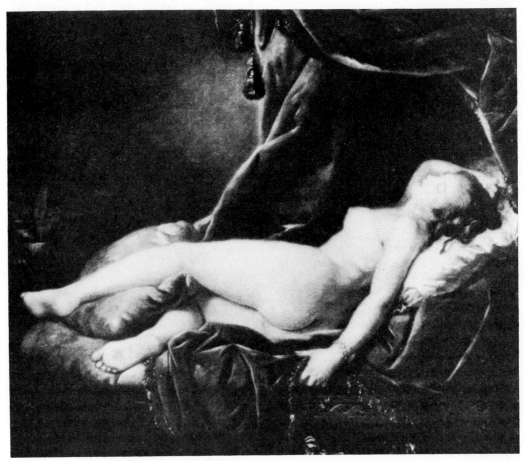

Figure 9.5 Jean Honoré Fragonard, *Sleeping Girl.*

Apart from its usefulness in camouflaging masturbation, using friction against objects also may seem more akin to sexual intercourse and may facilitate coital fantasies.

Muscular Tensions

Even when the first two techniques of masturbation are used, muscular tension is also used to heighten sexual excitement. Occasionally, however, a person will attain orgasm by relying exclusively on tension. The use of thigh pressure to reach orgasm is probably an exclusively female method.[27] When

a woman's legs are crossed or pressed together, steady and rhythmic pressure can be applied to the whole genital area. This method combines the advantages of direct stimulation and muscular tension. It can be indulged in practically anywhere the woman may be and can be detected only the the particularly observant. Havelock Ellis described one such episode:

. . . A few years ago, while waiting for a train at a station on the outskirts of a provincial town, I became aware of the presence of a young woman, sitting alone on a seat at a little distance, whom I could observe unnoticed. She was leaning back with legs crossed, swinging the

[27]Among the Hite subjects 3 percent reported masturbating through rhythmic thigh pressure.

crossed foot vigorously and continuously; this continued without interruption for some ten minutes after I first observed her; then the swinging movement reached a climax; she leant still further back, thus bringing the sexual region still more closely on contact with the edge of the bench and straightened and stiffened her body and legs in what appeared to be a momentary spasm; there could be little doubt as to what had taken place. A few moments later she slowly walked from her solitary seat into the waiting-room and sat down among the other waiting passengers, quite still now and with uncrossed legs, a pale quiet woman, possibly a farmer's daughter, serenely unconscious that her manoeuvre had been detected, and very possibly herself ignorant of its true nature.[28]

Years ago, when people were more preoccupied with the effects of masturbation than they are today, they went to some trouble to uncover it. There are descriptions, for instance, of how in large French dress factories (equipped with treadle-operated sewing machines) shop stewards would listen for the occasional uncontrollable acceleration of a machine as its female operator went through mounting excitement and orgasm.[29]

Vaginal Insertions

Men commonly think that females often insert their fingers or objects into their vaginas when they masturbate, but only one in five women in the Kinsey sample reported such insertions, and often they may have meant merely slight penetrations of the sensitive introitus.[30] The vagina itself is poorly supplied with nerves, which explains why penetration is not used more often in masturbation. Some women, however, clearly derive additional pleasure from deep penetration, perhaps because it stimulates coitus.

When insertions do occur, fingers are

most often used. Insertion is not usually an isolated activity but is accompanied by manipulation of adjoining parts. The use of various objects is quite rare and often resorted to for the purpose of entertaining males.

The majority of objects used in auto-erotic activities are household items. Conveniently shaped vegetables and objects like bananas,[31] cucumbers, pencils, and candles have no doubt been pressed into service from time to time.

There also are special devices that are used as aids to masturbation. The most common are artificial penises. Although the frequency with which these objects are used is often exaggerated, there is simple evidence that they are available in many parts of the globe.

Artificial penises have been fashioned from gold, silver, ivory, ebony, horn, glass, wax, wood, and stuffed leather; they range from crude specimens to products of fine craftsmanship. Their most common name in English is "dildo" (from the Italian *diletto*), though the French form *godemiche* is also used. Dildos are easily identified in works of antiquity and are mentioned by Aristophanes (*Lysistrata,* v. 105). Herondas wrote an entire play (*The Private Conversation*) around an *olisbos.* These devices have sometimes been modified to permit the passage of warm liquid (usually milk) to stimulate ejaculation. Contemporary versions have been further refined to befit an industrialized world and can vibrate on battery power.

Dildos are also used by male homosexuals. Artificial penises are not always merely gadgets, but may have ritualistic and symbolic relevance. The human penis, real and coun-

---

[28]H. Ellis (1942), vol. I, part one, p. 180.
[29]Pouillet (1897).
[30]Among the Hite subjects only 1.5 percent said they used this method exclusively. But vaginal entry was also used by a higher proportion of women in conjunction with other techniques such as clitoral stimulation.

[31]"O bananas, of soft and smooth skins, which dilate the eyes of young girls . . . you alone among fruits are endowed with a pitying heart, o consolers of widows and divorced women." (From a poem in *The Arabian Nights,* quoted in H. Ellis [1942], vol. I, part one, p. 171.) In the mythology of Hawaii, goddesses were impregnated by bananas placed under their garments. (H. Ellis [1942], vol. I, part one, p. 171.)

terfeit, has much more meaning than simply as a sexual organ (*see* Chapter 2).

There are other ingenious devices. One is the Japanese *rin-no-tama*, two hollow metal balls, one of which is empty and is introduced first into the vagina. The other contains a smaller metal ball, lead pellets, or mercury, and is inserted next. Both are held in place by a tampon. The slightest movement then makes the metals vibrate and sends shocks of voluptuous sensations through the vagina; some geishas reportedly swing in hammocks and rocking chairs while thus equipped.

There are also vibrators of various shapes and designs. Some are cylindrical dildos; others have vibrating rubber tips or can be attached to the back of the hand, through which they transmit their vibrations. Many of these gadgets are sold as instruments for massage, or they are advertised as devices that "soothe the nerves" yet are "harmless to delicate tissues," and so on.

There are no reliable statistics pertaining to the use of these devices. Among the *Redbook* survey respondents 21 percent of women reported having used some form of gadget ("vibrators, oils, feathers, and dildos").[32] This figure is probably quite inflated relative to the general population. Vibrators are sometimes used in the treatment of orgasmic dysfunction. We shall discuss their use in this regard further on (*see* Chapter 12).

The use of vibrators is not restricted to female masturbation. They are also used by males autoerotically as well as by heterosexual and homosexual couples. Some men also rely on other mechanical devices ("penis milkers") and "masturbatory dolls" made of inflatable, life-size rubber or vinyl material which may come equipped with an artificial vagina. There is no reason to believe that such artificial "masturbatory aids" play a significant part in the autoerotic activities of many.

[32]Tavris and Sadd (1978), p. 76.

Other Methods

Occasionally masturbation revolves around organs other than the genitals or involves an unusual method of stimulation. Breast stimulation is confined essentially to females. About one in ten women in the Kinsey sample manipulated her own breasts (often just the nipples) as part of her autoerotic activities. On rare occasions such manipulation alone may lead to orgasm. Some women find that running a strong stream of water over the genitals is very exciting. Wearing very tight clothing or any other practice that either creates friction or induces muscular tension may have the same effect.

In anal masturbation objects are inserted in the rectum, either in conjunction with or independently of genital manipulation. Homosexuals are probably more likely to resort to this method. Curiosity, however, or the search for novel sensations, may prompt others to try it also.

Urethral insertions are rare. Women and children are more likely to attempt them, and for those to whom pain is erotically arousing this approach may be tempting. Surgeons not infrequently recover hairpins and other foreign bodies from the urinary bladders of children or mentally incompetent women who often feign ignorance of how the objects came there. Some women are able to suck on their own nipples, and occasionally a man may be able to put his penis in his mouth (many try).

Masturbation is clearly a versatile procedure. Combined with fantasy it can be put to any use that the person may wish. We have discussed the association of fantasy with masturbation and we shall return to its social implications further on.

Prevalence and Frequency

Even those who decry the practice concede that masturbation is very prevalent among males and much more common among females than is widely recognized. Prevalence figures from various studies differ somewhat, but all have been high.

Sources of information on masturbation are quite inadequate. The Kinsey survey, despite its serious shortcomings, still provides the relatively best informational base and therefore will be discussed in more detail. Our primary purpose in this regard is to use the Kinsey findings more by way of illustration rather than as reflections of current behavior. We shall simultaneously refer to other more recent, but otherwise variously inadequate, studies for additional perspective.

In the Kinsey sample, 92 percent of males and 58 percent of females were found to have masturbated to orgasm at some time in their lives. An additional 4 percent of women had masturbated without reaching orgasm. If we try also to include those who have the experience while oblivious of its "true nature," about two of three women may be supposed to have masturbated. Males rarely masturbate without ejaculating, and when they ejaculate there is no mistake about it. The male percentages do not therefore really change much when those with experiences stopping short of orgasm are also included.

Figures 9.6 and 9.7 shows the percentages of people in the Kinsey samples who masturbated to orgasm at some time in their lives. Such graphs (known as "accumulative incidence curves") plot answers to the question: "How many people ever have such experiences by a given age?" The curves do not differentiate among behavior of individuals: A person who masturbates only once in his life and one who does so many times are counted in the same way.

In Figure 9.6 we note that only a negligible percentage of men had masturbated to orgasm by age 10 (even though the majority had attempted self-stimulation, stopping short of orgasm). Between ages 10 and 15 the incidence curve climbed dramatically and then leveled off as it approached age 20. Practi-

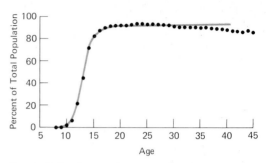

Figure 9.6 Accumulative incidence curve for masturbation by males (data corrected for U. S. population). From Kinsey et al., *Sexual Behavior in the Human Male*. Philadelphia: Saunders, 1948, p. 502. Courtesy of the Institute for Sex Research.

cally every man who was ever going to masturbate had already done so by this age. The curve did not go beyond 92 percent; 8 of every 100 males never masturbated to orgasm.

The female pattern was quite different (*see* Figure 9.7). First, the curve never rose beyond 62 percent—a graphic restatement of what we have already discussed. Second, the curve climbed only gradually to this high point. Up to the age of 45 years, more and more women were still discovering this outlet by experiencing orgasm through masturbation for the first time.[33]

What was the weekly frequency of masturbation among men? As we noted in connection with total outlet, age and marital status made a great deal of difference. In boys from puberty to 15 years old, among whom this practice reached a peak, the mean frequency of masturbation was twice a week. If we consider the "active population" only— that is, only those who actually had masturbated sometime or other—then the weekly mean was 2.4 times. These figures decreased

[33]At age twelve about 12 percent of females and 21 percent of males had experienced orgasm; by age fifteen 20 percent of females and 82 percent of males; and by age twenty, 33 percent of females and 92 percent of males had done so.

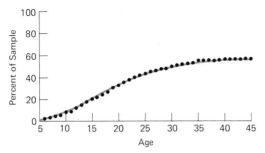

Figure 9.7 Accumulative incidence curve for masturbation to orgasm by females (curve for masturbation short of orgasm omitted). From Kinsey et al., *Sexual Behavior in the Human Female.* Philadelphia: Saunders, 1953, p. 141. Courtesy of the Institute for Sex Research.

steadily with age: In the total unmarried population, the 45–60-year-old group averaged fewer than one orgasm every two weeks; in the active population the mean was 1.2. Frequencies for married men were very small. There was no mean higher than once every two or three weeks.

How often did the average male masturbate? In the active unmarried population frequencies ranged from almost twice a week (in the postpubertal group up to 15 years) to about once every two weeks (in the 45–50-year-old-group). In "active" married groups the rates were much lower. In no age group did an average married male masturbate more than once a month. Medians were consistently lower than were means, and both averages declined with age.

These frequencies must be understood within the context of the wide range of variation. There were men (apparently healthy) who never masturbated or did so only once or twice in their lives. Others may have averaged 20 or more such orgasms a week over many years.

The average (mean and median) frequencies for the active female sample were quite uniform at various age levels (up to the mid-fifties) and did not show the steady de-

cline with age that was characteristic of males. The average unmarried woman, if she masturbated at all, did so about once every two or three weeks; the median for her married counterpart was about once a month.

The range of variation in frequency of female masturbation was very wide. In addition to many who never masturbated, some masturbated yearly, monthly, weekly, or daily; and some occasionally reached staggering numbers of orgasms in a single hour. These few individuals inflated the female means to two or three times the corresponding medians.

It is interesting to compare these frequencies with those of recent college students. In a study conducted by Simon and Gagnon, the occurrence of masturbating ranged from daily (males: 1 percent of freshmen, 4 percent of sophomores, 2 percent of juniors, 4 percent of seniors; females: 0 percent in all groups) to less than once a month (males: 17 percent of freshmen, sophomores, and juniors, 18 percent of seniors; females: 25 percent of freshmen, 28 percent of sophomores, 41 percent of juniors, and 47 percent of seniors).[34]

In the Hunt married sample, every other male and one out of three females reported having masturbated during the preceding year. For both sexes there was a distinct and similar correlation between age and prevalence of the practice. The highest rates were in the 25–34-year group (about 70 percent for males, 45 percent for females). The prevalence among 18–24-year-olds was almost as high (about 65 and 35 percent respectively), but the rates for both sexes steadily declined among older persons. By age 55 and over, only about 20 percent of males and 10 percent of females were engaging in the practice.

[34]Gagnon (1977), p. 157. For more information on the masturbatory practices of college students, see Arafat and Cotton (1979).

The prevalence rates for singles were higher than for marrieds for both sexes. The overall rate for single males was almost 85 percent. The rate for 18–24-year-olds was slightly lower; that for 25–34-year-olds somewhat higher. The overall female rate was about 45 percent; that for 18–24-year-olds a bit lower, but the rate for the 25–34-year group was almost 70 percent. Unlike Figures 9.6 and 9.7, which deal with the occurrence of masturbation during the person's lifetime, the Hunt figures indicate the prevalence of the practice during the preceding year only. The cumulative totals otherwise come very close to the Kinsey percentages and show that 94 percent of modern males and 63 percent of females have masturbated at some time in their lives.

The prevalence figures from the Hite report are even higher and most probably inflated because of the nature of the sample. Of the women in this group, 82 percent said they masturbated, 15 percent said they did not, and 3 percent failed to respond. Most of the women who did masturbate did so to the point of orgasm.[35]

Additional changes in masturbatory behavior since the time of Kinsey are moderately impressive. Attitudes have become more liberalized but remain ambivalent. There is a distinct change in that boys and girls appear to start masturbating earlier. In the Kinsey sample the incidence of masturbation among boys of 13 years of age was about 45 percent. In the *Playboy* survey sample the corresponding percentage figure had increased to 65 percent. The rates for girls were lower than those for boys in both the Kinsey and Hunt studies. But the same pattern described for boys was also present among girls. Thus, while in the Kinsey sample the incidence of masturbation by age 13 was about 15 percent, in the Hunt sample the corresponding

percentage had increased to close to 40 percent.

This increase in prevalence rates in masturbation since the Kinsey survey was not restricted to adolescents. Prevalence rates for single young males have gone up moderately, and for single females more markedly. Currently, 60 percent of women between the ages of 18 and 24 report some masturbatory experience as opposed to a quarter of single girls in their upper teens and a third in their early twenties among the Kinsey females. There is also an increase in the frequency rates: Kinsey males between 16–25 averaged 49 times a year against 52 times among modern 18–24-year-olds. The corresponding rise for females is from 21–37 times a year.[36]

Additional current information has been reported from the Sorensen survey pertaining to masturbation.[37] In this sample 58 percent of boys and 39 percent of girls between 13 and 19 years of age reported having masturbated one or more times in their lives. Girls generally had had their first experience a year or so earlier than boys, and for most girls this occurred before they were 13.

While quite prevalent masturbation was not very frequent. Only 28 percent reported having masturbated during the preceding month. Of these, 30 percent had done so only once or twice, 18 percent at least 11 times, and 7 percent 20 or more times during the past month. Boys were generally more active in this regard than girls.

Masturbation and Social Class

The better-educated person in the Kinsey sample (especially if female) was more likely to masturbate. Only 89 percent of males with only grade-school educations masturbated some time in their lives. In the group with no education beyond high school

---

[35]Hite (1976), pp. 410–411.

[36]Hunt (February, 1974), pp. 54–55.
[37]Sorensen (1973), pp. 129–145.

95 percent masturbated; for those with college educations the figure was 96 percent. The corresponding figures for females were 34, 59, and 60 percent.

The frequency of masturbation showed definite correlation with education among males and was highest among college-educated groups. Females did not show this correlation. Although a woman's social background (as measured by education) may have influenced her decision whether or not to masturbate, it did not affect the frequency.

Masturbation was clearly a very important outlet for the better educated. It was used by almost all college-educated males and nearly two-thirds of the females. It constituted not only the chief source (60 percent) of male orgasms before marriage but also almost 10 percent of orgasms following marriage. More than two-thirds of college-educated men masturbated at least some time after marriage.

These differences in frequency of masturbation can be explained by several factors. First, better-educated people are less fearful of masturbation as a health hazard. In their social circles masturbation may be openly condoned or at least not seriously condemned. At less-educated levels there are strong taboos against masturbation and for that matter against all sexual practices other than coitus. To many in this group masturbation seems not only unhealthy but also unnatural and unseemly. They find it difficult to understand, for instance, why a married man with ready access to a woman would ever want to masturbate.

An additional factor is the difference in class attitudes toward premarital coitus. Although better-educated people have gradually relaxed restrictions against premarital relations, they are probably still less permissive than are their counterparts in the lower classes. The greater reliance on masturbation may then arise partly from aversion to its alternatives rather than from direct preference for it.

Currently these class-related differences (as measured by occupational and educational status) appear less significant, although they still persist even among the younger generation.

Adult masturbation is sometimes viewed as a product of "hypocritical" attitudes and sexual inhibitions characteristic of Western (particularly Anglo-Saxon) societies. The less educated among these groups are assumed to be less handicapped by such cultural distortions and closer to living under more "primitive" and therefore more "natural" conditions. The data from other cultures (and from behavioral studies of animals) do not substantiate these allegations.

Masturbation and Marriage

We noted in Chapter 7 that masturbation accounted for far greater shares of total outlet for single people than for those who were married—as would be expected. In fact, we may ask why married people masturbate at all.

Current data indicate that there is an apparent increase in the prevalence of masturbation among young married men and women compared to the Kinsey sample: Whereas about 40 percent of husbands in their late twenties and early thirties masturbated in the past (median rate 6 times a year), now about 70 percent do so (median rate 24 times a year). For wives of corresponding ages the percentages have gone up from 30 percent to 70 percent, but the median rate has not changed (10 times a year). These data when viewed in the larger context of the study do not suggest that increased masturbation is in compensation for frustrations in marital coitus. As we shall see in the next chapter, this is far from the case. Rather, modern married persons, especially those who are younger, appear relatively freer to rely on masturbation as an auxillary outlet for sexual and related needs.[38]

Masturbation and Religion

As most interpreters of Jewish and Christian moral codes have condemned masturbation, let us see what effect this condemnation has had on actual behavior. Interestingly, men and women seem to have been influenced differently. The very high prevalence of masturbation among males indicates that religious belief has not had a significant effect. A man may feel less or more guilty about masturbating, but sooner or later more than nine out of ten men indulge in the practice. There is a difference, however, in how often they do so. The more religious men (particularly Orthodox Jews and practicing Roman Catholics) in the Kinsey sample did masturbate somewhat less often. The highest frequencies were among religiously inactive Protestants.

Among women, masturbation was definitely less widespread among the more devout (41 percent) than among the nondevout (67 percent). The degree of devotion seemed more important than the particular denomination. In contrast to men, once a woman had engaged in this practice she did not seem influenced by her religious beliefs in how often she used it.

Even though the devout female was less likely to masturbate, this practice accounted for a higher proportion of her total sexual outlet than it did for her nondevout counterpart. Masturbation still apparently provided a "lesser evil" in comparison with alternatives like premarital coitus.

Hunt reports that religious devoutness continues to have a significant influence on the practice of masturbation today: The nonreligious are more likely to masturbate, start doing so at a younger age, and are more likely to continue it into adult life and also into marriage.[39] But these differences between the devout and the nondevout are operating less effectively among the young. The effect of religion is generally much more marked among women than men.

Miscellaneous Factors

Boys who reached puberty at a younger age were more likely to masturbate and to do so more frequently than were boys who reached puberty later. The same did not apply to girls.

Women born after 1920 were more likely (by about 10 percent) to masturbate than those born before 1900. Among males there was a slight increase in the lower-educational groups in these two age categories. Otherwise, no substantial changes seem to have occurred in the masturbatory activities of successive generations.

Differences in background seemed to make some difference for women, but not for men: Urban women were more likely to masturbate, but there were no differences in how often they did so. The practice also accounted for a smaller percentage of the total outlet of urban women.

The Functions of Masturbation

The primary functions of masturbation are similar to those of sexual fantasy, which we discussed and need not repeat at length: Like fantasy, masturbation is an activity that is indulged in for its own sake or as a substitute. The role of masturbation in psychosexual development has also been dealt with in that context as an important means of learning about one's own sexual responses.

In adulthood, the relief of sexual tension is the most frequently verbalized motivation for masturbation (claimed by four out of five men and two out of three women in the Hunt survey sample). The need for such a release

---

[38]Hunt (February 1974), pp. 176–177.

[39]For denominational differences in this regard see Hunt (1974), pp. 87–88.

is often to compensate for the lack of a sexual partner or temporary unavailability of one because of illness, absence, or some other reason. But masturbation is also relied on as an auxilliary source of gratification, even by the happily married. The predominant reason for both sexes is the temporary unavailability of the spouse—through absence, illness, pregnancy, disinclination, and so on. Of all the alternatives to marital coitus (other than abstinence and nocturnal orgasm) masturbation is the least threatening to the marital relationship.

There are other instances in which masturbation may actually be preferable to coitus. A man may then be able to give freer reign to his fantasies, whereby, if he is simply after sexual release, he may circumvent lengthy and tedious courting of a demanding and exacting wife. If he has potency problems it saves him repeated humiliation. A woman, on the other hand, may find coitus unsatisfying and may attend to her own sexual needs through self-stimulation. As an autoerotic activity masturbation provides a person with full and complete control without the obligations and restraints necessary in dealing with another person.

The fantasy gratification functions of masturbation were discussed earlier. Other motivations behind the practice are nonsexual. In the Hunt sample over a quarter of males and a third of females reported that they masturbated to combat feelings of loneliness. People also resort to the practice to release tensions caused by occupational or personal problems or to simply relax in order to go to sleep.[40]

Masturbation, Health, and Society

"There is really no end to the list of real or supposed symptoms and results of mastur-

bation," according to Havelock Ellis, who was himself ambivalent about the practice.[41] Insanity; epilepsy; various forms of headaches (in addition to "strange sensations at the top of the head"); numerous eye diseases (including dilated pupils, dark rings around the eyes, "eyes directed upward and sideways"); intermittent deafness; redness of nose and nosebleeds; hallucinations of smell and hearing; "morbid changes in the nose"; hypertrophy and tenderness of the breasts; afflictions of the ovaries, uterus, and vagina (including painful menstruation and "acidity of the vagina"); pains of various kinds, specifically "tenderness of the skin in the lower dorsal region"; asthma; heart murmurs ("masturbator's heart"); and skin ailments ranging from acne to wounds, pale and discolored skin, and "an undesirable odor of the skin in women" are all supposed consequences of masturbation.

There is no evidence to support any of these or any other claims of physical harm resulting from masturbation. Yet for more than 200 years (from the dawn of the Age of Enlightenment) and until recently these dire effects have held an unshakable place in the beliefs of the medical elite in the Western world. The historical emergence of these notions is worth reviewing.

From the time of Hippocrates physicians have voiced their concern that overindulgence in sex is detrimental to health. Only in the last 250 years, however, has masturbation been singled out as a particularly harmful activity. Before the eighteenth century we can find only occasional references to masturbation in medical texts. Early in the eighteenth century a book entitled *Onania, or the Heinous Sin of Self-Pollution* appeared in Europe. The author was probably a clergyman turned quack who peddled a remedy along with the book. Although the work became very popular throughout Europe (and

[40]These are but some of the reasons why people masturbate. Ellis (1979) lists some 50 "advantages" and claims the list could easily be doubled.

[41]H. Ellis (1942), vol. I, part one, p. 249.

Box 9.6 Combating Masturbation in the Nineteenth Century

Medical authorities were quite eclectic in their proposed treatments for masturbation. These included hydrotherapy, special diets, drugs, surgery (including cliterodectomy), and the use of restraints. Especially curious were appliances such as those illustrated.

40132.   40133.

Godet argent.   Godet métal argenté.

40132.   Ceinture contre l'onanisme, pour garçon.... depuis   120 »   depuis
40133.   —   —   —   — fillette.....   —   120 »   —
        Ces appareils se font également en forme de caleçons hermétiquement fermés.

40134.   Mouffles en métal formant râpe, pour les mains................... depuis
40135.   Entraves pour les bras.. —
40136.   —   —   — jambes... —

Appliances for the treatment of masturbation illustrated in the Maison Mathieu catalog for 1904.

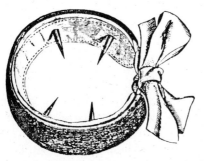

A four-pointed penile ring and a toothed penile ring, as illustrated in J. C. Milton's *Pathology and Treatment of Spermatorrhea* (1887).
From Alex Comfort, *The Anxiety Makers.* New York: Dell Publishing Co., 1967.

is referred to in Voltaire's *Dictionnaire Philosophique*), it appears to have had no immediate impact upon medical opinion.

Then in 1758 *Onania, or a Treatise upon the Disorders Produced by Masturbation* by the distinguished Swiss physician Tissot appeared. It reiterated and amplified the claims of the former work. Tissot's views, coming from an unimpeachable authority, seem to have found ready acceptance. Despite rebuttals and accusations that he was exploiting his medical reputation to further his private moral points of view, the book became a standard reference. By the end of the eighteenth century the "masturbatory hypothesis" of mental disease and assorted ills was well entrenched, and drastic cures were proposed (*see* Box 9.6). The further progress and eventual discrediting of these notions have been described by Hare.[42]

What about the psychological aspects of masturbation? As current medical views have been strongly influenced by psychoanalytic concepts, it may be best to examine first the reasoning behind some answers to questions about what masturbation means and what its consequences are.

Masturbation has received a great deal of attention in psychoanalytic theory. There are references to it in almost every one of the 23 volumes of Freud's collected works. The same is true of the writings of other analysts, and W. Stekel has devoted an entire volume to this topic.[43]

Masturbation, viewed within the framework of psychoanalytic theory, is seen as a universal normal activity of childhood and adolescence and a legitimate adult outlet when coitus is not possible (*see* Chapter 8). It is considered harmful, however, when it engenders guilt and anxiety—and symptomatic of sexual immaturity when it is preferred to heterosexual intercourse.

Currently no informed person should have any real concern about the deleterious effects of masturbation in a physical sense.[44] Whatever concerns exist pertain to psychological and moral issues. Psychological judgments in this regard are based on the motivations behind the practice, the degree of dependency on this outlet, and the extent to which the practice excludes sociosexual relationships.

A proper evaluation of masturbatory behavior, as with any other type of behavior, eventually has to be made in the context of the individual's overall life. In this regard it is conceivable that masturbation can become a liability if it is compulsively relied on at the expense of ultimately more rewarding interpersonal encounters. It is a convenient shortcut that carries the potential of shortchanging oneself. The problem in these cases is not primarily the result of masturbation but rather other, more fundamental psychological conflicts. In these cases masturbation becomes one more facet of the general picture of maladaptation. It must be recognized, however, that even in these pathological conditions it may provide one of the few readily available forms of sexual release and psychological comfort to the disturbed individual.

From a moral perspective, current attitudes towards masturbation may seem to be quite liberal in substantial segments of society. Yet the matter remains clearly problematic for at least some. For instance, as recently as 1975, the Vatican formally reiterated its position that masturbation is "an intrinsically and seriously disordered act."[45] We shall consider this issue further when dealing with sexual morality (Chapter 15).

Masturbation is still not quite "respectable." Ambivalence in this regard appears to

---

[42]Hare (1962). See also Comfort (1967) and Schwarz (1973).
[43]Stekel (1950).

[44]Some physicians may be nevertheless ambivalent about the practice and its being carried "to excess." For a range of medical opinions see *Medical Aspects of Human Sexuality* (April 1973), pp. 12–24.
[45]Vatican Declaration on Sexual Ethics (1975).

characterize even modern youths who have been generally spared the horror stories of former times. Sorensen reports that of all the sexual practices queried, masturbation elicited the most reticence and defensiveness.[46]

The problem was partly one of guilt. Among the adolescents currently masturbating, only 19 percent claimed never to have felt guilty (32 percent did so rarely, 32 percent sometimes, and 17 percent often). There was also an element of shame, since masturbation implied that one is not mature enough, attractive enough, or sophisticated enough to have a sexual partner. Yet, paradoxically, masturbation was found to be more common among those also engaging in coitus than in those who were not.

Similar attitudes have been reported from the Playboy Foundation survey. People generally seem to feel ashamed and secretive about the practice and "... almost no adults, not even the very liberated can bring themselves to tell friends, lovers, or mates that they still occasionally masturbate.[47]

Though a remarkable percentage of people still feel that masturbation is wrong, there is a clear association between the prevalence of such attitudes and age. In the 55 and older age group, 29 percent of males and 36 percent of females agree that, "masturbation is wrong." These percentages steadily decrease so that in the 18–24-year-old bracket only 15 percent of males and 14 percent of females still agree with this statement. These figures indicate not only a relative change in attitude but the disappearance of sex discrepancy in such attitudes.[48]

The general social acceptability of the practice is thus clearly on the rise, as can also be judged by the explicit discussions of masturbation in popular and literary works (notably *Portnoy's Complaint*).[49] The polite tolerance of earlier marriage manuals toward the practice has also given way to unabashed endorsement by writers of some of the currently popular sex manuals.[50]

Masturbation has currently attained particular importance for those women who see it as a means toward female sexual autonomy. Given that women generally learn about their own sexuality through male initiative, masturbation allows them to become free of such dependence. In this manner women are able to discover their own eroticism and their own sexual responses without male dominance.[51]

As times change, so do our societal concerns about this seemingly simple sexual practice. Since masturbation usually affects no one but oneself, one wonders why it is not viewed as one more physiological function that should concern no one but oneself. Yet, as any other sexual activity, masturbation can only be understood currently in its conflictual and complex psychosocial context.

[46]Sorensen (1973), p. 143.
[47]Hunt (February 1974), p. 54.

[48]Hunt (February 1974), p. 55.
[49]Roth (1967).
[50]"J" (1969), pp. 38–52; "M" (1971), pp. 60–68. For additional positive views on masturbation, see DeMartino (1979).
[51]Dodson (1974).

Chapter 10

Sexual Intercourse

For many adults, sexual intercourse is generally what sex is all about. Sexual intercourse is not the only sexual outlet, of course, and substantial numbers of people obtain their sexual pleasures through other means. Some do this out of preference and others because coitus is not available to them.

Lower animals copulate in accordance with their physiological drives, and so do humans. Yet millennia of evolutionary development have endowed the sex act with profound psychological and moral significance for humans. Intercourse is a complex interaction between two individuals that can be understood only within the overall context of their relationship.

Sexual intercourse is not just orgasm. It is a union between two people acting in a social context in accordance with their physiological and psychological needs. This is implied in the terms "coitus" and "intercourse."[1] It is also significant that the more common English vernaculars for sexual intercourse (fuck, screw) also mean to cheat, trick, take advantage of, and to treat unfairly. In its

various forms they also stand for inferior, unpleasant, difficult, confusing, blundering, wasteful, disorganized, in trouble, "neurotic." The same word that expresses our desire to make love also expresses dismay, annoyance, or anger. Our very language thus betrays our ambivalence and the fact that sexual encounters involve far more than the gratification of our erotic needs.

In this chapter we shall primarily focus on coitus as the paradigm of sociosexual relations. But much of what we have to say could be equally applicable to other forms of sexual relationships including the homosexual. Furthermore, when sex is engaged in for nonreproductive purposes, coitus is not necessarily the crucial component. For example, some handicapped persons who cannot engage in coitus can still have highly meaningful sexual relationships. Thus there is more to sociosexual sex than coitus.

Foreplay

Foreplay, in one form or another, is a universal prelude to coitus. Even lower animals engage in some courting before intercourse. In the West foreplay usually consists of more or less the same activities engaged in during petting, except that in this case they lead to sexual intercourse.

Despite its standard association with coitus, foreplay is best thought of as sexual

---

[1] "Coitus" or *coition* (Latin for "going together") is the specific term for heterosexual intercourse. "Sexual relations" and "sexual intercourse" are less specific since homosexual pairs may also be said to be having sexual relations and there can be nonvaginal forms of heterosexual intercourse. However, common usage has made these terms (as well as "making love" and numerous colloquial expressions) synonymous.

play, which may or may not lead to coitus or eventuate in orgasm. Even though high degrees of sexual arousal generally demand orgasm, there are many pleasurable erotic encounters that need not lead to such release.

Marriage and sex manuals are replete with instructions on techniques of sexual arousal, apparently on the assumption that people do not know what to do beyond the most rudimentary kiss and caress. Even if this assumption were correct (which it is not), to give erotic advice without belaboring the obvious or sounding silly is very difficult. Actually, most of us do seem to manage our sexual activities without benefit of formal instruction. Given fundamentally healthy and accepting attitudes, a couple innocent of sexual experience will learn fast enough.[2]

Instruction in erotic techniques may nevertheless be useful for those of us who are anxious about sex and unsure of ourselves. Even when nothing new is said, the written text inspires confidence actually to do what we already know about. Those who wish to go beyond ordinary levels of sexual competence may also want to learn from the experiences of others who are more imaginative and resourceful.[3]

Because of the wide range of preferences and differences in levels of responsiveness, we shall deal here primarily with general principles of effective sexual arousal and shall restrict our description of specific techniques to only a few examples.

[2]There is an extensive literature of sexual instruction in the form of "marriage manuals." Some of these are translations of ancient erotic works, but mostly they have been written in the West during the past hundred years or so, usually by physicians or other professionals. Since these books number in the thousands and some have sold millions of copies, they obviously have been responsive to a wide public need even though many of them tend to be inaccurate in various ways. For current professional views concerning their usefulness, see "Do Marriage Manuals Do More Harm than Good?" (1970).
[3]For a good example of a book with such sophisticated appeal, see Comfort (1972).

Psychological Context

Excluding relations in which sex serves aggressive purposes, most people require certain minimums of affection and trust before they can engage in satisfactory sexual encounters. Many profess and some actually believe that unless they are "in love" they cannot engage in sex without cheapening the act.

Discussions of sexual arousal and coitus must be understood within this larger emotional context. For a person who is deeply in love, the mere presence or the slightest touch of the beloved can be unbearably stimulating; in other cases intense love may be consciously devoid of erotic content. Still others may achieve high levels of sexual gratification without benefit of such intense emotions. But even then there is usually some reaction to the partner as a person beyond physical sexual interest.

Nothing could be more appropriate than expressions of affection during foreplay, and few measures are more effective in arousing a partner. Such sentiments, however, sometimes become feigned prepayment for sexual favors rather than manifestations of genuine feeling.

Even though expressions of affection are more meaningful when they are spontaneous, some people cannot help trying to extract such assurances at every turn; others are guilty of mouthing passionate endearments for pragmatic ends. There are many ways of expressing affection and all (not just the verbal forms) should be recognized.

The prelude to coitus may be as pleasurable as coitus itself. A certain mix of seriousness (but not heavy drama) and lightheartedness (but not comedy) is often the most effective mood. There is no absolute standard, and different occasions require different attitudes. Some couples enjoy chasing each other around, wrestling on the floor, tickling each other, and jumping into each other's arms amid screams and giggles. Others prefer a more subdued mood, with voices gentle and hushed and movements restrained. Although a certain element of romance may be cherished at these moments, it is also notable that some couples can proceed right to coitus after only a few perfunctory caresses.

There are various ways of approaching sex, but it is perhaps best simply to "be oneself," though emphasizing one's assets. Yet it is difficult to drop all pretense without a feeling of mutual trust. To "be oneself" and to accept the other person as he or she is, however, is only the beginning. As incompatibilities and differences are unavoidable, both partners must also be willing and able to accommodate to each other's idiosyncratic needs—but only up to a point. Some relationships may be incompatible and are best abandoned. People may be so hopelessly dominated by neurotic conflicts that they need to mature or change before they can engage in sexual intercourse responsibly and satisfactorily.

Another way of looking at it is to consider one of the functions of sex as a form of adult play. Play is of crucial importance during childhood and ought to retain some of its usefulness in adulthood as well. In order for adults to play, it is necessary that we regress to some extent to regain the carefree ability to pretend and play-act without losing touch with reality or becoming deceitful. Such play-acting revitalizes and makes sex more fun and allows our fantasies safe and partial fulfillment.

In order for such games to be fun, safe, and meaningful, they must be private. Some people engage in "baby talk." Others pretend to be strangers, fictitious characters, or even antagonists in a "rape" scene. Whatever the scenario, the two partners must find it comfortably tolerable. There is no justification for forcing such activity on an unwilling or uninterested partner. And as with children's games, it ought to stop when the game becomes nasty or hurtful.

In sexual matters it is tempting to look for simple physical means to ecstacy, and we are annoyed when instead we are offered psychological generalities. Nevertheless, if one aspires to become an accomplished lover, the simpleminded search for buttons and levers will have to be abandoned. There is no denying the importance of knowing where the nerve centers are, but the current that feeds those circuits is emotion.

Sex does not operate within a psychological vacuum, and the range of possible emotional reactions varies tremendously, depending on circumstances and the relations of the individuals. As we cannot possibly deal here with even a fraction of these variations, we shall assume in this chapter that we are dealing with physically healty and affectionate couples engaging in sexual intercourse without conflict and with a clear conscience.

A very important component of the psychological context of sexual encounters are the gender-related expectations of who does what to whom. Traditional models for such behavior are now increasingly recognized as having been less than optimal. For mature people, making love is an interaction between equals. It is irrevelant who takes the initiative and who is the more active stimulator at any given time. These pleasures and burdens are best shared. Sex calls for honesty and mutual concern, not stereotypes.

Techniques of Arousal

A clear understanding of which parts of the body respond to which types of stimulation is a prerequisite for becoming a competent lover. The information on "erogenous zones" and the body's responses to sexual stimulation offered earlier (Chapter 3) is relevant here. Of the innumerable activities that may be included in foreplay, we shall single out a few that are generally found to be quite effective and are acceptable to most people.

Kissing

Erotic kissing is a ubiquitous component of sex play in many, but not all, cultures.[4] It is both an expression of sexual desire and an effective erotic stimulant. Although it takes several forms, it generally involves the tongue and the inside of the mouth. "A humid kiss," says an ancient Arabic proverb, "is better than a hurried coitus." Erotic kissing, like coitus, builds up gradually and requires sensitivity and timing.

Initially kissing involves mostly lip contact. A light, stroking motion (*effleurage*) may be used in alternation with tentative tongue caresses and gentle nibbling of the more accessible lower lip. Gradually, as the tongue becomes bolder, it can range freely in the mouth of the partner, who may suck on it (*maraichinage*). The use of the tongue in erotic kissing is sometimes referred to as "French kissing," but as Figure 10.1 illustrates, this is a common form of foreplay and unlikely to have originated in a single culture.

This type of voluptuous kissing not only serves as a prelude to coitus but may also continue right through it. Occasionally an ardent couple may start with a deep kiss and not break oral contact until coitus is over.

Kissing need not be restricted to the sexual partner's lips. Any part of the body may be similarly stimulated although the neck, ear lobes, breasts, inside of the thighs, fingertips, palms of the hands, and so on, as well as the genitals, have a higher erotic potential, as discussed earlier (Chapter 3).

[4]There are important differences even within the various social classes in a given culture. In the Kinsey sample, for instance, 77 percent of the college-educated males but only 40 percent of those with only grade-school educations reported practicing the erotic, or deep, kiss. Simple lip kissing is much more frequent and was reported by almost all (99.4 percent) of the married male Kinsey respondents.

Figure 10.1 Mochica pottery. Courtesy of William Dellenback and the Institute for Sex Research.

Kissing is practiced in many cultures other than in the West, but in some societies it is unknown, at least in a form familiar to us.[5] Tinquians (monogamous Philippine agriculturists and headhunters) and Balinese used to bring their faces together and smell each other ("rubbing noses"). The Thonga of Mozambique (primitive agriculturists), on the other hand, seemed to be revolted by the Western kiss: "Look at them—they eat each other's saliva and dirt."[6]

Behavior resembling human kissing can also be observed in primates. Immature chimpanzees, for instance, occasionally press their lips together as a prelude to further sexual exploration. Bingham has also reported that

[5]For a discussion of crosscultural aspects of kissing see Opler (1969).
[6]Ford and Beach (1951), p. 49.

during coitus a male chimpanzee would occasionally suck vigorously on the female's lower lip.[7] Oral contact during sexual activity also occurs in other animals; for example, mice (males lick the females' mouths), sea lions (they rub mouths), and elephants (males insert the tips of their trunks into their partners' mouths).

Caressing

Caressing, like kissing, is a means of expressing affection which may or may not be erotic in intent or effect. Such activity is perceived as erotic usually because the "erogenous zones" are being stimulated or because of the manner in which it is done and the context in which it occurs.

Caressing is a form of tactile stimulation, as are fondling and scratching. Physiologically, the principle is the same as in kissing, namely, stimulation of surface sensory receptors. The evolutionary roots of skin stimulation long antedate humans as evidenced by the grooming activities of nonhuman primates.

Tactile stimulation can be greatly enhanced if surfaces are moist. The mouth has a natural advantage over the hands in this regard, but saliva can also be used quite effectively to moisten the area to be caressed. Even more effective is the use of lotions. Any hand lotion that has a pleasant scent for both partners will do. Apart from their physical effects, lotions provide additonal advantages. Whereas ordinary caresses may be cursory and fleeting, when lotions are used, foreplay is prolonged, becomes more deliberate, and helps the participants to stimulate each other unabashedly rather than furtively. Even its "messiness" may have an arousing quality, possibly because of its association with the genital fluids.

Breast Stimulation

The practice of fondling female breasts is well known in many cultures. In the Kinsey sample 98 percent of respondents reported manual stimulation and 93 percent oral stimulation of female breasts by males. Despite the widespread prevalence and acceptance of the practice, one should not assume that women necessarily find it enjoyable: Almost one-third of heterosexual women queried by Masters and Johnson reported that their breasts were not especially enjoyable erogenous zones.[8] Even women who generally do enjoy such stimulation may find the experience uncomfortable during certain phases of the menstrual cycle. It has been observed under laboratory conditions that wives sometimes find breast stimulation uncomfortable yet do not inform their husbands of this fact because "he likes to play with my breasts so much I didn't want to distract him."[9] Breast stimulation can be enhanced by using both the mouth and hands. The nipples, though the most responsive parts, need not be the exclusive focus of attention. Women may also enjoy more general fondling, mouthing, and caressing of their breasts. The size of the breast has no relation to its sensitivity, and a small-breasted women should not be assumed to be less sensitive in this area.

Techniques of breast stimulation among lesbians appear more effective than in heterosexual encounters. At least under laboratory conditions, women turn to breast stimulation only after preliminary holding, kissing, and caressing of the body: Men usually spent a minute or less before focusing on the breasts. Furthermore, lesbians spent a good deal more time on stimulating both breasts during sexual play and more carefully monitor their partner's reactions: Men are more

---

[7]Bingham (1926), in Ford and Beach (1951), p. 49.

[8]Masters and Johnson (1979), p. 67.

[9]Masters and Johnson (1979), p. 68. When the husbands were informed about this by the researchers they were surprised and inevitably asked, "Why didn't she tell me?"

perfunctory in this regard and frequently they become so absorbed in their own erotic response to the female breast that they seem less aware of their partner's reaction.

Stimulation of the male breast is mainly centered on the nipple and is mainly observed in homosexual encounters. Masters and Johnson observed nipple stimulation in almost three-quarters of "committed homosexual male couples," whereas no more than three or four among 100 married men were similarly stimulated by their wives.

Genital Play

Tactile stimulation of the genitals is particularly exciting for most people. In the Kinsey sample 95 percent of males and 91 percent of females reported manually stimulating the genitals of their sexual partners. Males tended to be more active in this regard.

The techniques of genital stimulation during foreplay would be expected to be similar to those employed in autoerotic activities. But this is not always or even often the case. People presumably know how to please themselves, but their partners may or may not know what is required. There is thus much that can be learned from autoerotic activities that would be useful in foreplay. These can then be modified and supplemented with additional techniques of stimulation that become possible with the presence of a partner. For instance tactile stimulation of the inner thighs, buttocks, and genitals can be most effectively combined with oral stimulation of these parts.

It is also instructive for heterosexuals to know how homosexuals stimulate each other, since they have the gender advantage of knowing about the other's body through knowing about their own.

For instance, in lesbian genital play, the labia, mons pubis, inner thighs, and the vaginal opening are usually approached prior to direct clitoral stimulation. Likewise homosexual males dwell on the thighs, lower abdomen, scrotum, and the anal region before turning to the penis.

These more deliberate approaches are effective ways of leading to more direct stimulation of the genitals. To reach truly high levels of arousal such direct genital stimulation is usually necessary—especially in the case of clitoral stimulation, which many women need to experience orgasm.

Oral-Genital Stimulation

An exceedingly effective but somewhat controversial erotic stimulant is the "genital kiss."[10] It involves oral stimulation of the genitals and is a fairly widespread though unevenly distributed practice. In the Kinsey samples almost half the college-educated males, but fewer than 5 percent of those with grade-school educations, reported having stimulated their wives in this manner.

Women reciprocated much less frequently. Almost 60 percent had never attempted it, and the rest had done so only infrequently. Female reluctance may have resulted from shyness, ignorance of what to do, or fears of indecency or perversion. The possibility that a man might ejaculate in the process may have been a further deterrent, although some women have no hesitation in deliberately bringing a man to orgasm in this fashion.

Current data indicate that the practice has become considerably more prevalent since the Kinsey survey was conducted. The Playboy Foundation–sponsored survey found 80 percent of single males and females between the ages of 25–34 years, and about 90 percent of married persons under 25 years, had engaged in mouth-genital stimulation

---

[10]The Dutch gynecologist Van de Velde boldly (for his time in 1926) favored this practice. It was he who coined the term "genital kiss" in preference to the technical terms "cunnilingus" ("to lick the vulva") and "fellatio" ("to suck") for the oral stimulation of female and male genitals respectively (Van de Velde, 1965, pp. 154–156).

during the past year. It is interesting to examine additional details from these data.[11]

Let us first consider the relationship between educational level and the prevalence of the practice. In the Kinsey sample about 15 percent only of high-school-educated males reported having used cunnilingus at least sometimes during sexual encounters with their wives. The corresponding figure from the Hunt survey has risen to 56 percent. High-school-educated married women also showed an increase in the prevalence of the practice, but the discrepancy was nowhere as striking: In the Kinsey sample 50 percent had had the experience at least sometimes; the current percentage is 58 percent.

Among college-educated married males in the Kinsey sample 45 percent reported having orally stimulated the genitals of their wives. The corresponding percentage figure in the Hunt sample was 66 percent. College-educated married women in the Kinsey sample reported such experiences in 58 percent of cases. Currently, 72 percent of married women have had their genitalia orally stimulated by their husbands. The increase in prevalence of cunnilingus among married couples is thus present in all four subgroups, but the most impressive change is among lesser-educated males, where the practice appears to have lost some of its former unacceptability.

It is of further interest to compare the practice of mouth-genital contact where a given sex is alternately stimulating the partner and being stimulated by the partner. Such behavior must be examined as reported by each sex. That is, we need to know what percentage of men report performing cunnilingus and what percentage of women report being the passive partners in such activity. The same is true where the oral stimulation of male genitalia is involved. We are concerned here exclusively with the heterosexual form of these practices.

In the Hunt sample well over three-quarters of married males between the ages of 18–34 reported having engaged in cunnilingus during the past year. The percentage of married women who concurred corresponded quite closely with the male figures. The prevalence of the practice declined with age. In the 35–44-year-age group less than two-thirds, and among the 45–54-year-olds less than half indulged in the practice as reported by either sex. By age 55 years and older, cunnilingus was reported by only about one in four persons.

The overall prevalence rate of cunnilingus for singles was similar to the married. The same was true for the 25–34-year-age group. But the rate for single 18–24-year-olds was considerably lower (about 60 percent) than that for married persons in the same age group (about 80 percent).

The prevalence pattern of oral stimulation of male genitalia by females was generally similar to those of cunnilingus, although one would have expected markedly lower rates for heterosexual fellatio.

Evidence from the *Redbook* and Hite surveys further attest to the growing prevalence and wider acceptance of these practices as well as the ambivalence and negative reactions people have in this regard (*see* Box 10.1). Among the *Redbook* wives, about 40 percent had ''often'' practiced cunnilingus and 40 percent fellatio. Another 48 percent and 45 percent, respectively, had ''occasionally engaged'' in these activities. Only 7 percent of the women had never had their genitalia orally stimulated and 9 percent have never stimulated a male in similar fashion. Not surprisingly, although women engaged in these two types of erotic play with about equal frequency, they found cunnilingus ''very enjoyable'' in 62 percent of cases as against 34 percent for fellatio. Only a small percentage found these activities unpleasant or re-

[11]Hunt (October 1973), p. 88. For an evaluation of these data, *see* Chapter 7.

Box 10.1 Female Attitudes about Cunnilingus

"I lie on my back with my partner between my legs, flicking his tongue very gently over the same area, over and over. I like not doing anything else except concentrating on the sensation until I orgasm."

"I dislike it when my partner's tongue digs too close to the clitoral nerve inside the hood— it really hurts."

"Orally, he vibrates his tongue very fast (great!) and/or sucks. He also blows air into my vagina, which is strange, yet exciting."[1]

"I like a slow, steady rhythm, very gentle and circular in motion, right at the front part of my private parts, then moving down to my opening, with a deep penetration of his tongue just before I come."

"Nibbling and nuzzling on the clitoris, like simulated chewing is good—but gently and tenderly."

"My husband asks me to let him frequently but I shudder at the thought. This is an issue that causes arguments. My husband says that all women do it and like it. I say he's crazy."

"If my partner will apply clitoral stimulation with

his tongue, and at the same time gently rub my nipples, I can achieve an orgasm within a few seconds. Some men try to stimulate my *vagina*, but that really does very little for me."

"A tongue is much gentler than a finger usually and also involves a bigger area."

"The tongue is warmer, wetter, and softer than a penis or finger and makes more delicate motions."[2]

"I've gotten to dislike cunnilingus because I've gotten so aroused without coming. Men seem to think that once they've done that for a while that's all, they can just climb back on and come, having done their best for the good of the cause. I guess it's this feeling I have that they are doing it in a mechanical way because they read that it's a nice thing to do to women and that all women really like it, and that they are good guys to do it."

"It is all very distasteful. You sound like you approve of oral sex. If it is what I think it is! It's the most filthy, obscene, and unnatural. It can only be associated with a corrupt and decadent mind."[3]

[1]This practice can be dangerous especially if the woman is pregnant. If air is forced into the circulation, the resultant air embolism may produce injury or death.

[2]From Shere Hite, *The Hite Report*, pp. 233 and 245. Copyright © 1976 by Shere Hite. Reprinted by permission of The Macmillan Company.
[3]C. Tavris and S. Sadd, *The Redbook Report on Female Sexuality*, New York: Dell, 1975, p. 128.

---

pulsive (6 percent for cunnilingus, 15 percent for fellatio).[12]

The data from these recent surveys, such as they are, make a plausible case that mouth-genital stimulation is now fairly prevalent but it is probably less so than they would lead one to believe.

There are no "standard procedures" for oral-genital contacts. Usually a man gently caresses the minor lips, the area of the introitus, and the clitoris with his tongue, occasionally sucking and nibbling at them. The

saliva produced in this process serves as an additional lubricant. In the male the glans is the primary focus of excitement; gentle stroking of the frenulum with the tongue and lips mouthing and sucking the glans while firmly holding the penis, and grasping and pulling gently at the scrotal sac with the other hand are some of the means of stimulation. These activities must be conducted with tact and tenderness, since few people appreciate a tooth-and-nail assault.[13]

[12]Tavris and Sadd (1978). Hite's data in this regard are confusing. Reportedly 42 percent of women had orgasm during oral sex and a very small number said they had never had the experience.

[13]Currently popular books on sex provide explicit instructions on oral-genital stimulation. *See*, for example, "J" (1969), pp. 119–123; "M" (1971), pp. 110–116; Comfort (1972), pp. 137–140. Also see Hite (1976), pp. 244–245.

A couple may engage in mutual oral-genital contact ("sixty-nine") as a prelude to coitus or for its own sake (*see* Figure 10.2). Some couples appreciate the mutuality involved in such simultaneous stimulation. Others find this distracting and prefer either to devote their full attention to the needs of their partner or to focus on their sensation and enjoyment.

Oral-genital stimulation is repulsive to some people. If the genitals are clean, objections are difficult to support on hygienic grounds. A person is not obliged to perform or submit to such activity, of course, if it does not appeal to him or her, but to carry judgments beyond personal preference and to make legal or moral issues out of them is another matter.

Oral-genital contact is also reported in other societies. Among the Aranda, Ponapeans, and Trukese, for instance, both men and women have been reported to stimulate their partners in this way. In other groups only one or the other sex is permitted to do so.

Oral stimulation of female genitals is quite common among primates, and females reportedly respond with obvious pleasure. Stimulation of the male organ, however, is less well documented. Quadrupeds rely on their mouths quite frequently during sexual activity. Their activities include smelling, licking, mouthing, and so on.

Other Means

Stroking the anal orifice and inserting fingers into the rectum are appreciated by some and rejected by others on esthetic and other grounds. To suspect underlying homosexual motives in all such anal insertions is questionable.

The erotic potential of pain is well known. Even ordinary versions of foreplay and coitus involve enough physical activity to result in some strain. Within limits and with certain partners mild pain from bites and scratches can be quite stimulating. It will be recalled from Chapter 3 that the threshold of

Figure 10.2   *Fantasy,* attributed to P. Breughel.

pain is higher during sexual excitement, and this type of stimulation is usually attempted during advanced stages of lovemaking.

There are wide cultural variations in the sexual use of pain. In some primitive groups sex is a violent affair in which either the male or the female may be the active party. Animal studies clearly demonstrate the deep phylogenetic roots of the erotic functions of pain. The mating behavior of most animals has a definite aggressive component. The males are the ones who invariably bite, paw, and sometimes injure their partners. The females do not reciprocate.

There are many additional techniques of stimulation. Indian manuals have lengthy discourses on bites, nail marks, slaps, and blows that may prove baffling to most of us. Tickling is another activity to which people react differently.[14]

---

[14]For a discussion of the sexual significance of tickling see Kepecs (1969).

A person may use many of the means described to stimulate himself or herself during foreplay or even coitus. The impact of this on the partner varies. If the person becomes preoccupied with oneself to the exclusion of the other, then the activity will look like masturbation (which may or may not be exciting for the partner). However, if self-stimulation is artfully incorporated in sexual play then it can greatly enhance arousal without proving distracting or disrupting to the relationship. Much of the outcome has to do with the meaning that the behavior conveys.

Additional Considerations

Several additional considerations are important. First is the matter of timing. The correct technique applied to the right place at the wrong time will fail to arouse. The same stimulus may be experienced as unpleasant or painful at one stage yet catapult a person to peak excitement at another. Correct timing in turn requires the ability to gauge excitement.

Most people find it best to start slowly and with the less sensitive areas. Some do crave rough handling, but many others do not. As no one objects to tenderness, it would seem preferable to start gently and to become more forceful as appropriate, rather than to startle and offend at the beginning. Particularly effective is a carefully timed "teasing" approach, whereby the partner is helped to reach peak excitement in successive waves before culminating in orgastic release.

Sensitive surfaces respond best to gentle stimulation, whereas larger muscle masses require firmer handling. Once an area has been singled out for stimulation, it should be attended to long enough to elicit arousal. Frantic shifting from one part of the body to another can be as ineffective as monotonous and endless perseverance. If stimulation is to be effective, it must be steady and persistent. Its tempo and intensity may be modulated, but sexual tension must not be permitted to dissipate. Erotic arousal requires patience and is not always free of tedium. Yet effective lovers manage to sustain a sense of novelty and a feeling of excitement.

When natural lubrication is inadequate, it is necessary that the couple use saliva or a coital lubricant (for example, "K-Y jelly"). In these cases the jelly need not be applied just prior to intromission. Preferably it should be used much earlier during coital foreplay when it not only lubricates the introitus but greatly enhances tactile stimulation of the clitoris and the adjoining structures.

The necessity for effective communication is obvious to most people, but it is often difficult to achieve. Almost everyone will complain when in pain, but most of us are much more reluctant to ask for enhancement of pleasure for fear of seeming forward, lascivious, or perverted. Wishes are sometimes more easily communicated simply by guiding the partner's hand or otherwise indirectly.

Expression of emotion during lovemaking should cause no feeling of shame. It is a time to let oneself go. Furthermore, a person who wishes to enhance the partner's excitement and pleasure can most effectively do so by letting the partner know how he or she feels. The sighs and moans, squeaks and squeals, grunts and groans of sex are also songs of love.

How long does foreplay usually last? Preferences seem to vary widely among individuals and cultures. The Lepcha and Kwoma, for instance, proceed to coitus without much ado. Trobrianders may spend hours in foreplay. Western sex manuals devote much attention to the necessity of foreplay in preparing the woman for intercourse. Some even specify various time periods as irreducible minimums.[15] Among married couples in the Kinsey sample the lengths of time involved in foreplay were three minutes or

[15]For a range of opinions see Kroop and Schneidman (1977).

less in 11 percent, four to ten minutes in 36 percent, 11 to 20 minutes in 31 percent, and beyond 20 minutes in 22 percent. Some couples spent several hours each day in erotic play.[16]

It is also of interest that in cases where coitus was preceded by 20 minutes or more of foreplay only 7.7 percent of the wives did not experience orgasm. Where penile intromission lasted 16 minutes and longer, only 5.1 percent of the wives failed to reach orgasm.[17]

In the Hunt sample, single people under 25 typically spent about 15 minutes in foreplay; those 25 to 34 years of age, about 20 minutes.[18]

It seems best to leave the length of foreplay to each couple to decide. Aside from preferences, different circumstances require different amounts of preparation. Physiologically, full erection and adequate vaginal lubrication indicate readiness. Emotionally, a couple is ready when both members feel a mutual urge for sexual union.

In attaining physiological and emotional readiness for sexual intercourse the importance of psychological factors cannot be emphasized enough. All of the foreplay techniques in the world will lead nowhere if the person is not in the right frame of mind. The mental set that is conducive to making love is in turn influenced by a host of factors including a reasonable conviction that one is doing the right thing, warmth and affection for the other, and a basic acceptance of one's own sexuality.

In view of these possibilities the techniques for erotic arousal and those to be described for sexual intercourse must be understood in their psychological contexts. A few tender words felt and expressed convincingly and a gentle caress executed with flair are

[16]Kinsey et al. (1953), p. 364.
[17]Gebhard (1968).
[18]Hunt (1974), p. 160.

likely to be far more effective stimulants than furious friction of some erogenous zone. A basic acceptance of oneself and one's partner as individuals, unabashed pride in the body and its sexual functions, the conviction that sex is moral and honorable, and some knowledge of the basic (rather than the exotic) sexual functions are what generally count most in sex.

Intercourse

Making love has been compared to a game of chess: The moves are many, but the ending is the same. Coitus proper starts with the introduction of the penis into the vagina. It can be achieved from a variety of postures, and intercourse involves various types of movements. Even though there is more to making love than coital mechanics, understanding the physical basis of the act is helpful. The relationship between male and female sexual organs during face-to-face intercourse is illustrated in Figure 10.3; the theme was also treated by Leonardo da Vinci five centuries ago (*see* Figure 10.4).

Although discussions of the mechanics of coitus suggest that their main contribution is to enhance the physical aspects of intercourse, the benefits are in fact mostly psychological. Some of us approach sex with uncertainty and a tendency to hurry. In experimenting with various approaches, we become more deliberate, controlled and purposeful. This effort implies care and concern for the partner, so that intercourse literally fits the meaning of the term: an interaction between two people. Involving the female partner more actively often increases her enjoyment. Knowledge of and experimentation with sexual techniques can thus greatly enrich a sexual relationship.

A second advantage is obtained from the variety of possible postures. Married couples especially, sooner or later, begin to find sex a bit monotonous. "Marriage," Honoré de Balzac wrote, "must continually vanquish

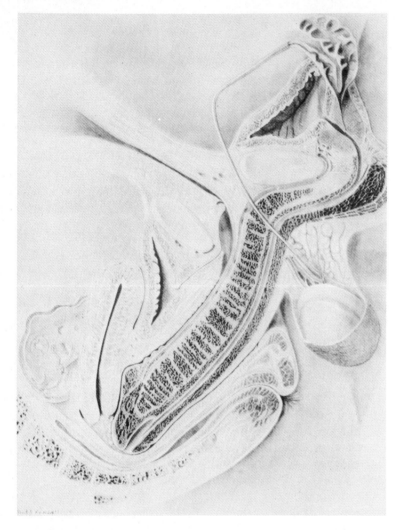

Figure 10.3 Male and female genitals in face-to-face coitus. From Dickinson, *Atlas of Human Sex Anatomy,* 2nd ed. Baltimore: Williams & Wilkins, 1949, figure 142. Copyright © 1949 by The Williams & Wilkins Co., and reprinted by permission.

a monster that devours everything: the monster of habit.[19] The imaginative use of different positions can be an antidote to habit, though sustaining real variety year after year is difficult to do.

Various coital positions also yield different physical sensations, and, though most of us are able to improvise, some of us need the inspiration and information that come from knowing about the experiences of others. Finally, it is important to know how conducive

to impregnation a given position is likely to be. Such knowledge is helpful to a couple that is trying to conceive a child, but no posture is reliable as a contraceptive measure.

It is important to recognize that simply trying different coital positions offers no sexual panacea. But it is difficult to imagine any actual harm that might result from it. After all, most people have enough sense not to proceed in the face of pain or discomfort, no matter how elegant or exotic their embrace.

There is nothing mysterious or magical about coital positions. Experimentation shows

[19]Quoted in Van de Velde (1965), p. 45.

Figure 10.4 Leonardo da Vinci, figures in coition.

one approach to be more exciting at one time and others under other circumstances. There is no "position to end all positions," and the search for mechanical perfection is endless and pointless.

A certain agility is indispensable to both partners if they wish to explore the limits of coital gratification, but sex should not become a series of gymnastic feats. There is a story of an Oriental courtesan who had attained such perfect control that she could engage in coitus while holding a cup of tea on one uplifted foot.

Another potential drawback is that reading about coital techniques can result in a "cookbook" approach to lovemaking, which robs the act of the spontaneity that ought to be its hallmark.

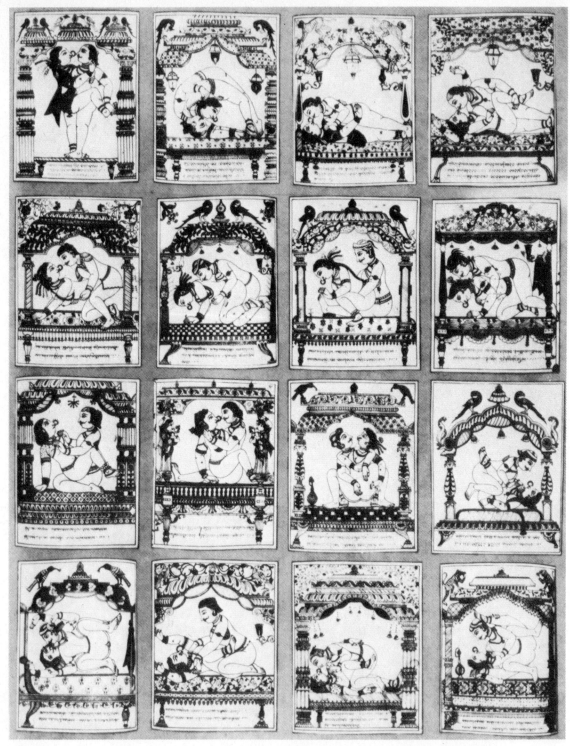

Figure 10.5 Pages from a nineteenth-century Orissan posture-book. Reprinted by permission of G. P. Putnam's Sons and Weidenfeld & Nicholson Ltd., from *Erotic Art of the East*, Philip Rawson, ed., p. 43. Copyright © 1969 by Philip Rawson.

Many marriage manuals, both ancient and contemporary, give such detailed instructions that the reader becomes overwhelmed by the apparent complexity of the act and cannot help but wonder how millions of people ever manage to accomplish it all by themselves. Illustrations of coital postures are no less bewildering, particularly some of those from the Far East (*see* Figure 10.5). The complexity of Indian sexual practices prompted the sixteenth-century Arab sage, Sheikh Nefzawi, to comment: "This position, as you can perceive, is very fatiguing and very difficult to attain. I even believe that the only realization of it consists in words and designs.[20] Representations of coital positions can be found in many other cultures (*see* Figure 10.6).

To speak of coital positions is thus misleading, for we are actually dealing with general approaches rather than specific postures. During face-to-face intercourse, for instance, a woman lying on her back will stretch her legs out, then pull them up halfway or bring her knees close to her chest for a while, then strech them out again, and so on. Even when more marked shifts in posture occur, one position flows into another, and sexual activity never loses its fluid quality.

Approaches

Despite the innumerable erotic postures described in love manuals, the basic approaches to coitus are relatively few. The couple may stand, sit, or lie down; the two may face each other, or the woman can turn her back to the man; one person can be on top, or both can lie side by side.

Figure 10.7 illustrates some of the more common coital approaches and obviates the need for detailed descriptions.[21] (*See also* il-

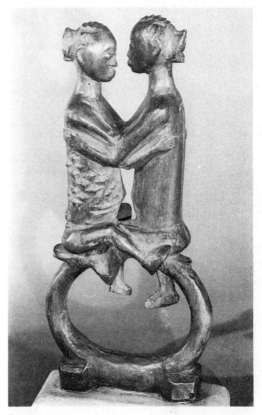

Figure 10.6 A carved wooden figure from the Luba (or BaLuba) tribe of Central Africa. The sculpture shows the two figures in a coital position. Courtesy of the Musée Royal de L'Afrique Centrale, Tervuren, Belgium.

lustrations in Chapter 13.) Instead, we shall examine the relative advantages of these various alternatives.

Face to Face

The primary advantage of face-to-face approaches is the opportunity for direct interaction. The partners can kiss and gaze into each other's eyes, fully communicating their feelings through speech and facial expressions.

In the traditional and most commonly used approach in the Western world (but not necessarily the most enjoyable), the woman

---

[20]Nefzawi (1964 ed.), p. 132.

[21]Sex manuals are replete with such description. See, for instance, Van de Velde (1965), chapter 11; Nefzawi (1964 ed.), chapter 6; Harkel (1969); and Comfort (1972).

Figure 10.7 Four variations in coital position (*top*) the so-called "missionary" position; (*middle left*) rear entry, which can be used with the couple either sitting or standing; (*middle right*) with the woman in the superior position, sitting; and (*bottom*) side entry.

lies on her back with the man on top of her.[22] But, Figure 10.7 shows that considerable variety can be achieved within this basic arrangement.

The man-above position is useful when erection is relatively weak. Its advantage is that penetration is not deep.

When the woman flexes her legs the effect is the opposite, and deep penetration is possible. Placing a pillow under her lower back makes this alternative more comfortable. Once the couple is established in this position, the woman's legs may be placed in a number of ways: She may simply hold her legs up, or she may place them on the man's shoulders. He may hold them under his arms. Or she may entwine her legs around his back and lock her feet together, which gives her excellent leverage for moving her pelvis to meet his thrusts or simply for sustaining muscular tension.

Another advantage of the man-above position is that it is the most likely to lead to pregnancy. The optimal pooling of the ejaculate in this approach has been described earlier (*see* Chapter 5). In order to maximize the chance of conception, the woman must maintain this posture for a while after coitus, and the man should not withdraw abruptly.

There are also several drawbacks to these positions. If they are used exclusively, sexual interest may eventually diminish. The man's weight can also be a problem: He can support himself, but a really heavy man will still be a considerable burden on the woman. Furthermore, in this position the man's hands will not be free to stimulate his partner.

A more serious problem is the restriction that such positions impose on the woman's movements. Although she can move her legs, her pelvis remains largely immbolized or can be moved only with considerable effort.

Just as many variations are possible if the woman lies or sits on top of the man, an alternative that currently is widely used.[23] Her weight is usually less of a problem, and she has the opportunity to express herself fully by regulating the speed and vigor of her movements and the depth of penetration. Many women find it easier to achieve orgasm in this manner. Furthermore, a man is less likely to be immobilized by her weight and is therefore less handicapped than she would be underneath.

A host of other alternatives is available to the partners when they lie on their sides. Penetration is somewhat more difficult in these positions and requires that the woman lift her upper leg. Partners may effect union in one of the other positions and then roll onto their sides.

This lateral position was recommended by Masters and Johnson in their treatment of certain forms of sexual dysfunction and subsequently adopted by three-quarters of the couples who tried it. More than half of Hunt's sample also reported using it.

The primary advantage of this approach is the comfort it provides by eliminating weight on either partner. The participants lie side by side, with their legs intertwined in one of several ways. Penetration is, however, shallow and movements are restricted. Coitus tends to be prolonged and leisurely. Ovid commended this approach above others: "Of love's thousand ways, a simple way and with least labor, this is: to lie on the right side, and half supine."[24]

The prone face-to-face approaches provide a rich variety of alternatives, allowing either partner to take the active role. Depending on excitement, fatigue, body build, and agility, each partner has the opportunity of give and obtain pleasure. An important

---

[22]This approach is sometimes referred to as the "missionary position." The term was coined by natives who had noted the consistent preference of Western missionaires for this coital posture.

[23]Among the Hunt sample three-quarters of married couples used it at least occasionally (Hunt, 1974, p. 202).

[24]Ovid, quoted in Van de Velde (1965), p. 227.

advantage of all prone postures is that the postorgasmic lassitude can be accommodated effortlessly.

Sitting and kneeling positions involve deliberate attempts at variety, for couples cannot simply "roll" into these positions but must set them up.

In seated intercourse the man sits in a chair or on the edge of the bed. The woman stands in front of him and lowers herself onto his erect penis. By keeping her feet on the ground she can control her pelvic movements up and down. Or she may achieve deeper penetration by straddling him and perhaps locking her feet behind the chair. His pelvic movements are restricted, but his hands are entirely free.

In the kneeling position (the man on the floor beside the bed) he controls the pelvic thrusts. Being on solid ground gives him excellent leverage, which he cannot achieve lying down unless he pushes against the frame of the bed. Pushing the toes down into the bed is not very effective. The kneeling position is often recommended for a woman's first coitus. The superior control of the man, the angle of penetration, and the exposed position of the woman in combination are said to make the rupture of the hymen least painful for her and easier for him.

There is another, famous approach in this category: The woman straddles the man lying on his back and lowers herself onto the erect penis. She can then lean forward and backward. His legs may be extended or flexed enough to provide support for her back. As her feet rest firmly on the bed, her control of movement is excellent. The ancient Romans were reportedly fond of this position and women boasted of how they "rode" their partners (some writers still call this position the "attitude of equitation"). Many experts consider it, of all possible approaches, to have the maximum voluptuous potential.

Penetration, when the couple is standing face to face, is difficult. If, however, the woman can lift one leg high enough, it is pos-

sible. She may then wrap her legs around his waist while he supports her buttocks. Ancient manuals call this position "climbing the tree."

A very satisfactory variant of the kneeling position involves an arrangement in which the man stands. His partner must be higher up, as on top of a table. As he is squarely on his feet, with both hands free, he has maximum control of his movements and is able to engage in protracted coitus. Ejaculating while standing constitutes no problem for most men, but the postcoital phase is not very comfortable.

Rear Vaginal Entry

The dominant form of coitus among animals is from the rear but not for many people. In the Kinsey sample, only about 15 percent reported having tried it but in the Hunt sample 20 percent in the 18–24 age group reported using this position often. In addition to the variety that they provide, the rear-entry positions make it easy for the man to fondle the woman's breasts and stimulate her genitals manually. In all other positions, though manipulation of the clitoris is possible, it tends to be more awkward and interferes with full contact between the partners.

Rear-entry positions have no serious disadvantages. It is true that they somewhat isolate the partners, who cannot conveniently see each other. On the other hand, close and comfortable body contact is easy to achieve— no other position will allow a woman to curl up as snugly in a man's lap.

Rear entry is possible while lying down, sitting, or standing up. When a woman is lying on her face, penetration is not deep. Coitus in this manner may be impossible for obese people. If the two lie on their sides (usually on the left), however, intromission is easy even with a relatively weak erection. This method is very restful and is suitable for coitus during pregnancy or ill health, when exertion is better avoided. In the sitting versions the man is astride the woman's buttocks. Or the chair position already described may be modified so that she has her back turned to him.

The rear approach allows many other variations in the woman's position. She can go down on all fours or even put her head down ("knee-chest position"). Penetration is easy, and the man's hands are free to roam over her buttocks, inside her thighs, on her genitals, over her breasts, and so on.

Movements

In contrast to emphasis on sexual approaches, the importance of coital movements has been generally neglected. Pelvic thrusts during coitus are a mammalian characteristic. Typically such thrusts start with penetration, build up momentum, and culminate in orgasm.

Coital movements, like positions, have an almost infinite variety, often shading into one another. Generally the initial thrusts are slow, deliberate, and progressively deeper. Thrusts and counterthrusts may then follow various patterns. The man can thrust and withdraw; then the woman does the same. Or they may thrust and withdraw simultaneously. These movements may be rhythmic or not, fast or slow, with shallow or deep penetration, and so on. It is possible for a movement to be executed by only one person while the other remains relatively passive. Some recommend a nine-stroke rhythm: nine shallow thrusts, then one full lunge, or nine full lunges followed by a shallow thrust.

In all these movements, variation and steady work must be artfully combined with an element of surprise. Frantically rushing through pattern after pattern is as bad as monotonous concentration on one, unless both of the partners prefer it that way, in which case their choice should supersede the combined advice of all experts. As coitus progresses, the penis may be thrust completely into the vagina and be rotated inside with a circular motion.

The motions described are merely illustrations. These and other movements must be coordinated with the various approaches. Some movements are quite versatile; others can be used only with particular approaches. Perhaps the most important dictum in this connection is that control of coital movements should be as much a prerogative of the female as of the male. During sexual intercourse the genitals must cease to be the exclusive possessions of the male or female and must become instead shared organs.

Enhancement of Pleasure

Are some orgasms "better" than others? Even in physiological terms, orgasm is not a uniform experience, particularly among females (*see* Chapter 3). The subjective perception of orgasm also varies between individuals and in the same person at different times. Although we have no objective criteria with which to assess the psychological intensity of orgasm, experience would indicate that some orgasms are perceived as more pleasurable and gratifying than others. It is safe to assume that a host of psychophysiological factors determine this. The identity of the partner and the circumstances under which coitus is taking place all contribute to the mood of the individual, which greatly colors his perceptions. But in addition, physical factors evidently play a role. These may include the time interval since the preceding orgasm, level of fatigue, length and nature of foreplay, and so on. While it is reasonable to assume that these factors are significant, we do not know as yet with sufficient certainty how and why they are important. On this matter every person is his or her own expert.

Probably the most important factor in the enhancement of coital pleasure is the attitude of the sexual partners toward each other. In this regard gender roles play an important part. Traditionally the male has taken the initiative in determining the course and pace of coitus. Especially when women silently submit to this male approach their chances of obtaining optimal sexual gratification are likely to be diminished. Men tend

Box 10.2 Primate Coital Behavior

Although the sexual behavior of any animal has potentially some bearing on our understanding of humans, the relevance of such comparisons is much more obvious where it involves man and the nonhuman primates.[1] Once again, one must be alert to the danger of lumping many diverse species as if they were one homogeneous group. There are over 200 living species of nonhuman primates, and one encounters among them wide differences of social structure and behavioral patterns. Since chimpanzees most resemble man, our subsequent remarks will primarily refer to them. When the female is ovulating, she is in estrus (Greek for "mad desire") or "in heat." The sexual excitation and receptiveness of the female through physiological and behavioral cues elicits sexual interest in the male, which leads to attempts at copulation.

The female chimpanzee is in estrus for about six days during the mid-portion of her 35-day menstrual cycle. Among other physiological changes the female manifests

at this time a swelling and redness of the anal and genital region ("sex skin"). During this interval the female is both receptive and attractive to males.

Chimpanzees show some courtship behavior, but about half the time the male simply seems to approach the female and proceed to copulate. This is often preceded, however, by the male inspecting the female genitalia, including inserting a finger into the vagina and smelling it.

In about half the time, where there is a discernible courtship display, it is the male that usually takes the initiative. Jensen describes the more common forms of chimpanzee courtship:

Chimpanzees show relatively little courtship behavior. There are two courtship display behaviors used only in the sexual contexts, beckoning and tree-leaping. The beckoning male stands upright facing the female, extends his arm out in front and draws it swiftly down to his body. The tree-leaping display is a series of leaps and swings through the branches in an upright position while he faces in the general direction of the female. Two displays are used in both aggressive and sexual contexts. One is called the swagger. The male with hair erect stands upright on his two feet as he swaggers in a rather confident, aggressive way toward

[1]For a concise introduction to primate sexual behavior, see chapter 2 by Jensen in Zubin and Money (1973). More detailed accounts of primate sexual behavior can be found in DeVore (1965) and Jay (1968). Also see Lancaster (1979) and Beach (1947).

to be more genitally oriented and, if left to their own proclivities, they go through foreplay in a hurry to culminate the act in coital orgasm. This approach often proves unsatisfactory to the woman. It also robs the man himself of the greater pleasures of having a sexually active partner who shares in the joys and burdens of the erotic encounter.[25]

The way in which penetration is performed sets the tone for the act. If it is being done by the man, this initial step calls for gentle firmness and confident deliberateness. Even when the vagina is properly lubricated,

the introitus may still be tense. The glans must first be placed firmly against the introitus, and a little patience may be required before the orifice relaxes. A skilled lover may not penetrate even then but may keep moving his

[25]There is also considerable variation in who takes the more active role. Some primitive peoples are quite similar to those of the West in this respect. The Chiricahua Apaches, for instance, even shared the Victorian notion that a woman, besides being passive, should display no emotion during coitus. On the other hand, the Hopi, Trukese, and Trobrianders considered an inactive female apathetic and a poor sexual partner. For a cross-species perspective see Box 10.2.

Box 10.2   Continued

the female. This behavior is a threat in agonistic situations. A glaring look is another display. Occasionally a high-ranking male induces a female to approach and present for copulation by simply glaring at her. All of these displays work very well. Females respond to 82 percent of approaches or courtship displays of mature males by presenting for copulation. They either remain crouched while the male approaches or actually run toward him and present.[2]

Female chimpanzees, however, are not always passive under these circumstances. Out of a series of 32 copulations observed by Goodall, in four instances the initiative was taken entirely by the female.:

The soliciting female approached to within six feet and flattened herself in front of him in the "crouch position," looking back at him, and on three occasions copulation took place immediately. Once the female was ignored; she backed toward the male, who got up and moved a few yards away, at which the female backed after him, looking over her shoulder, until she was almost touching him, when copulation took place.[3]

Sexual encounters among chimpanzees do not always operate so smoothly. A soliciting female may be ignored by a male. Or the female may scream when approached by a male at the end of a courtship display.

The sexual behavior of the male chimpanzee appears to be subject to social situations. For example, copulation is more likely to occur during periods of excitement when two groups meet, or when the animals who are hungry arrive at a favorite food source. At these times the males make vigorous charging displays accompanied by penile erection, and if there happens to be a receptive female around, copulations frequently follow. In cases where several chimpanzee males copulate with the same female, the higher-ranking males generally have first choice.

A female in heat may be followed by half a dozen or more adult males with whom she will copulate freely. Such promiscuity is actually characteristic of most species of nonhuman primates. But some chimpanzee couples may also stay together for days or weeks, even when the female is not in heat. Similar relationships that have been observed among baboons and macaque monkeys are referred to as "consort relationships."

[2]Zubin and Money (1973), p. 19.
[3]DeVore (1965), p. 449.

glans in the introitus as well as in the clitoral region until the woman shows through her own pelvic thrusts the unmistakable signs of wanting deeper penetration.

If the vagina is insufficiently lubricated, intromission must not be attempted. But the fact that there is adequate lubrication does not necessarily mean the woman is ready for coitus. The final criterion is psychological readiness.

It is equally appropriate and sometimes preferable that the female partner herself introduce the penis into the vagina. This helps remove doubts about her readiness. In doing this she must in turn be sensitive of course to his level of arousal. If the penis has not attained a certain firmness when intromission is attempted, a sense of failure may cause some men to lose their erection.

The majority of writers in this field and an increasing proportion of the population at large also believe that in striving for sexual enhancement an adult couple need not feel inhibited in doing anything so long as it is by mutual consent, pleasurable to both, injurious to neither, and out of sight and earshot of unwilling observers. One encounters a range of opinion whereby these interactions are viewed as legitimate only between loving married couples at one end or any consenting pair at the other with no further questions asked.

Enhancement of coital pleasure as such is a rather global and often ill-defined aim that comes to mean different things to different people. But there are also some aspects that are commonly held to be desirable, including, for instance, prolongation of coitus and mutual orgasm.

A number of techniques have been evolved to extend the period of sexual intercourse on the premise that if sex that lasts half an hour is fun then that which lasts an hour should be twice as much fun. This is sound common sense in general, but nonsense as a blanket rule. There are brief but intense sexual encounters that will take your breath away, while protracted episodes may drag on tediously.

Ejaculation may be delayed through mental distraction (thinking of something else or looking the other way) or through deliberate checks on the build up of muscular tension (slowing coital movements, pausing entirely, consciously relaxing). It is also helpful to minimize friction, particularly on the glans. In short, when excitement seems to be mounting out of control, one follows the opposite of what we have described as effective methods of erotic stimulation. How long to sustain coitus is a matter of individual judgment. Sexual intercourse is not an endurance contest. The only criterion is optimal gratification.

Another lauded accomplishment is mutual orgasm. There may be something to be said for the occasional joint experience of orgasm, as long as it does not become the overriding criterion of a successful sexual encounter. Such preoccupations mar sexual enjoyment. Actually there is much advantage to entering the climax separately. If the woman wishes to experience orgasm several times, the last may be made to coincide with the male's ejaculation.

The enjoyment of coitus is in part dependent on the circumstances under which it takes place. There is a general human preference for privacy during coitus. It is not clear why. It is true that man is vulnerable to attack at such a time, but animals generally do not seem to mind copulating in front of one another. When two partners are bothered by a third animal, they will, of course, try to elude it.

In various cultures coitus occurs in or out of doors, depending on which affords more privacy. For the sake of novelty and additional excitement, some venturesome couples in Western society occasionally make love on the beach or in other natural settings. Sometimes simply using a room other than the bedroom fulfills the same function.

Bedrooms are usually furnished with some thought to romantic atmosphere. Most often, provisions are made for soft lighting; less often, mirrors are positioned strategically so that the partners can observe themselves. Only rarely is a couple bold enough, however, to place a mirror on the ceiling or in some other place where its exclusively sexual function would be obvious. Besides, not everyone finds the prospect of viewing themselves stimulating. There is no end to the refinements that can be added—sound systems, erotic art, and so on.

Animals also prefer certain settings. In fact, many fishes and birds can mate only under certain environmental conditions. Some male mammals may restrict their contacts with females to their own territories. There is a general tendency to seek sex where it has been enjoyed before. In novel situations animals as well as humans are apprehensive and easily distracted from sexual aims.

The preferred times for coitus vary in different cultures. Practical, as well as psychological, considerations play a role. Most couples in our culture make love at night because it is convenient within the routine of everyday life. But it is unwise always to relegate coitus to the very last waking moments of the day, for a certain amount of stamina and alertness are essential for real pleasure. It is thus advisable occasionally to change the time for coitus to the morning or the middle of the day, simply for variety.

In the animal world copulation occurs during the active period of the day. Subhuman primates, for instance, and diurnal animals, and both sex and eating occur in broad daylight. Man's shift to a nocturnal sexual pattern is probably the result of cultural influences.

Nudity during coitus is also subject to cultural and individual preferences. Men generally have been thought to obtain more excitement from looking at female bodies than women do from looking at males. But this may not be the case generally. It certainly is not for some women. Women may also, however, prefer to make love naked because it enhances intimacy.

Should intercourse be planned or spontaneous? Some people claim that coitus requires preparation, as does any other activity. Apart from practical considerations they believe that anticipation heightens excitement. Others cannot even bring themselves to take contraceptive measures because they imply forethought.

Some of the most exciting sexual encounters may well occur at the spur of the moment and in the least likely of places. Nevertheless, the realities usually require some advance planning if the act is to have more than ordinary significance. As in almost everything else in life, virtuosity in sex requires that natural gifts be supplemented by preparation and practice.

Preparation usually is not a matter involving elaborate arrangements and fine-tuning of exotic machinery. Sometimes it is simply a matter of brushing your teeth or taking

a shower. A recurrent whiff of unpleasant odor is all it may take to ruin things for some. These are highly idiosyncratic matters culturally and individually.

In the United States one encounters a wide variety of attitudes, but the general emphasis is on cleanliness and being odor-free. This can be carried to phobic lengths where people prepare for lovemaking as if they were to undergo aseptic surgery. At the other extreme, being "natural" and "earthy" seem to be confused at times with smelling like an open sewer.

Body odors can be stimulating if fresh. The smell of perspiration, semen, or vaginal fluid can be highly erotic, but not after bacteria have worked on them for a while. It is usually not very effective to try to mask these odors by artificial scents. But the use of perfumes, colognes, aftershave lotions, or burning incense can also be quite pleasant and provide an interesting variety of olfactory sensations which in turn impart novelty to the overall coital experience.

The issue of sexual hygiene is discussed further in Chapter 7.[26] So much of these considerations is plain common sense. When combined with an unabashed acceptance of one's own body, warts and all, the physical aspects of sex become so much more easily manageable. Even coitus during menstruation can be taken in stride and grace and comfort, as many couples already know.

Other physical aspects that may cause discomfort are the unexplained sounds and smells that occasionally emanate from the digestive tract. Persistent rumbling or gurgling noises from the abdomen can be further distracting if one is tense. Passing flatus is potentially quite embarrassing (others hardly seem to mind belching in the partner's face). It is also not unusual for air to get sucked into the vagina during genital foreplay and then

[26]See also Pierson and D'Antonio (1974), pp. 84–87.

come out audibly. One can ignore these noises or laugh at them together, but if handled clumsily, they become more than mere nuisances.

Other Forms and Variations

More esoteric forms of lovemaking often rely on special equipment. These may be no more complicated than condoms of different colors, with attachments, or they may involve specially constructed chairs, vibrators, or water beds, which owe at least part of their popularity to their contribution of novelty to lovemaking.

Combining sex and bathing is an ancient device. Soaping each other and making love while showering together can be quite pleasurable. Doing it in the bath tub is another variant, but this is harder on the man since erections are difficult to maintain in warm or cold water. This often necessitates that intromission precede submersion.

Erotic massage, especially with the use of lotions and scented ointments, adds many dimensions to coitus, as was indicated earlier in connection with foreplay.[27] Unlike some of the mechanical devices, erotic massage blends far more naturally with the tender, caring aspects of making love while simultaneously stimulating the body.

There are other techniques that tend to strike most people as wild or hardly believable (and some as more idiotic than erotic). One marriage manual recommends jamming a cold towel or ice pack into the groin at the moment of orgasm.[28] Illustrations of Eastern erotic art show aristocratic men shooting arrows at tigers while coupling with complacently smiling maidens. One portrays a couple precariously balancing upside down on a galloping pony. Much of this is probably pure fantasy or to be understood in some symbolic sense only.

Combining motion and sex offers other possibilities. One can use rocking chairs or swings. For intercourse, train berths speeding along with rhythmic noises and jerks are much recommended and so are ship cabins. Airplane bathrooms provide more cramped and hectic shelter. Where life comes cheap, cars and motorcycles may intrigue some people as sexual arenas.

Many of these devices operate in part by modifying the mood of the sexual partners. In this regard drugs can be highly effective. The question of true aphrodisiacs is as yet unresolved, but there is no question that a wide variety of substances that alter consciousness also influence the perception of sexual experience, and this influence can be for better or worse.

Finally, some coital variants involve ejaculation at a point other than intravaginally. While hardly anyone practices withdrawal for fun, some do prefer a body orifice or the surface over the vagina as part of foreplay or as the end point of coitus. Any and all body surfaces and orifices that can be used have probably been used in this way at one time or another.

Anal intercourse is the most common choice in this category. According to the Playboy Foundation survey, almost half of married men and more than a quarter of married women between the ages of 18 and 34 have tried anal intercourse at least once. Rates for singles and older married couples are lower. Doubtless, many more persons have thought about it but have never done it.[29]

For most people anal intercourse is an experimental or occasional variant rather than a mainstay of their sexual lives. It is enthusiastically endorsed by some and thought to be unspeakably vulgar and offensive by others. Apart from matters of personal preference and legality (''sodomy'' penalties are

---

[27]See, for example, Inkeles and Todris (1972).
[28]Eichenlaub (1961), pp. 107–108.

[29]Hunt (October 1973), p. 86. Also see Masters and Johnson (1979), pp. 83–86.

horrendous, as described in Chapter 14), anal intercourse entails certain health considerations. First, it often entails some discomfort even when adequate lubricants are used. Second, there is a serious risk of infection if vaginal intercourse follows without washing first. Finally, repeated experience may result in a variety of chronic ailments.[30]

It is neither possible nor necessary for our purposes here to continue to catalog the countless additional variations and refinements that have been proposed to heighten sexual gratification. (In Chapter 12 we will discuss further issue of sexual performance in the context of sexual malfunction.) All sex manuals have something to say in this regard, though much of it is redundant. A sophisticated source is Comfort's *Joy of Sex* (fashioned after the *Joy of Cooking*), which lists 63 entries under "Sauces and Pickels" (as opposed to "Starters" and "Main Courses"), ranging from "anal intercourse" and "armpit" to "vibrators," "Viennese oysters," "voyeurs," and "wetlook."[31]

To persevere with the culinary metaphor, lovemaking, like eating, offers more potential pleasure with more variety. It is a matter of personal preference as to what one chooses from a menu. Granting to each the freedom of such personal choice does not invalidate the distinction between the glutton and the person with a discriminating palate. Eventually sex must fit in and make sense in the larger context of our everyday lives. Relatively few of us have the energy, the need, or the means to stage a major production each time we engage in sex. On the other hand, far too many people reduce making love to the level of routine, as regular and uninspiring as brushing their teeth and going to the bathroom.

The Aftermath

If the proof of the pudding is in the eating, then the quality of intercourse is best judged by the figurative taste it leaves in the mouth. This is why the postorgasmic phase or aftermath of coitus requires separate consideration here. Coitus does not end with orgasm. The final phase is one in which the physiological effects of excitement recede and the individual regathers his or her wits. The physical manifestations during this stage of detumescence and its behavioral components have been described earlier (*see* Chapter 3).

Laboratory observation seems to confirm gender differences in postcoital behavior. Irrespective of sexual orientation or the manner of reaching orgasm, males tend to rest briefly and are soon ready to leave the bed. Women usually desire to remain quiet longer and more frequently fall asleep in the postorgasmic phase.[32]

Even before such documentation was present, marriage manuals devoted considerable attention to this phase. Men were warned not to dismount abruptly and turn their backs or to go to sleep; rather they were told to disengage themselves gradually with endearments and tender caresses, and remain attentive to their partner's needs for quiet intimacy.

There is a good deal to be said for these admonitions, although the presumably gender-linked differences should not be exaggerated. A man needs and will want as much tenderness as a woman, unless he is made to feel "unmasculine" or "weak" if he should reveal such inclinations.

The aftermath of coitus is a time of reflection. Thoughts meander, earlier experiences, sexual or otherwise, float into consciousness. There must be room for parallel solitude. But the partners should not drift away emotionally.

One may share feelings and thoughts at

---

[30]These include hemorrhoids, fissures, and anal incontinence with involuntary loss of feces (Rowan and Gilette, 1978).

[31]Comfort (1972, 1974).

[32]Masters and Johnson (1979), p. 82.

this time with some discretion. If coitus was not all that it could have been, tenderness restores confidence and makes amends. But this is no time for clinical postmortems or statistical tallies. Even if orgasm has been highly pleasurable, the experience may be partially ruined if the feeling is conveyed that another notch was added to one's belt or that one came out "on top" and is gleefully chuckling over the victory. Likewise, a sinking feeling that one was seduced or manipulated against one's own interests can be quite disturbing.[33]

These remarks presuppose that both partners have reached orgasm. But sometimes one partner, more often the woman, lags behind. Until she is able to catch up, no matter what happens during afterplay the outcome may be relatively unsatisfactory. Because the male is less frequently able to have multiple orgasms, it is generally preferable that the woman's climax comes first or simultaneously with his. When occasionally the man's climax precedes the woman's, and he feels unable or disinclined to have a second erection, the woman should be brought to climax by noncoital stimulation if that is what she wishes.

The aftermath of coitus may signify the end of an episode of sexual activity or it may simply be an interlude between two acts of intercourse, where afterplay imperceptibly merges into foreplay again. Even nonconsecutive acts of coitus are to some extent linked together through memory. In a letter to her husband, Abelard, after years of enforced separation, Heloise writes:

Truly, those joys of love, which we experienced together, were so dear to my soul that I can never lose delight in them, nor can they vanish from the mirror of my remembrance.
Wheresoe'er I turn, they arise before me and old desires awake.[34]

---

[33]What transpires following coitus is said to reveal more about the relationship than the preceding sexual activity (Crain, 1978).
[34]Quoted by Van de Velde (1965), p. 251.

Intercourse and Marriage

Of all the social correlates of sexual intercourse, marriage is undoubtedly the most important. Coitus is the predominant sexual outlet for married persons. Sex is universally approved with marriage; in most Western societies marriage is the only context where it is permissible at least in principle. Although there certainly is much more to marriage than sex, the adequacy of conjugal sex has tremendous bearing on the quality and permanence of the marital relationship.

The family is the basic unit in most societies. Its form and nature may vary across cultures, but it serves the same fundamental needs. One of its major functions is making readily available sexual intercourse in a setting of mutual affection and trust and to provide for the care of offspring that may result from such union.

The institution of marriage is timeless, complex, and taxing. There have been efforts, both voluntary and forced, to alter or even to eradicate it. They have failed in the past, but experiments continue.[35]

There has been much speculation about the origins of the human family, and there have been many attempts to trace its evolution. Particularly interesting are recent studies of subhuman primate groups in their natural habitats. In all this research the role of sex in the formation of family bonds has been duly noted, but its exact nature is a matter for debate. One thing is clear: Animals engage in sex because it is enjoyable or reduces tension. They do not do so in order to procreate; they can hardly be expected to associate coitus with pregnancy causally.

Important as the institution of marriage

---

[35]Sparta, Nazi Germany, the Soviet Union, and Communist China tried unsuccessfully to abolish marriage on a national scale. Various American communal groups, like the Oneida colony of a century ago, have done so on a smaller scale (Bishop, 1969). There are also, of course, people who live together in a stable relationship without being formally married. Much of what is discussed in this chapter is applicable to them.

may be, it is not the object of our immediate interest here. Nor are we primarily concerned at this point with the critical moral and legal issues involved in sex outside of marriage, which we shall deal with in Chapters 14 and 15. Instead, we shall examine here the available information on contemporary sexual behavior. Since marital coitus is of such vital concern, we shall begin with it and examine its characteristics in greater detail; then we shall turn to coitus outside of marriage.

Marital Intercourse

As we would expect, the majority of married people have sex with their spouses. Some do so rather infrequently, however, and a few never have coitus in years of marriage—often because of inability or lack of interest.

Important as coitus is for most married people, it frequently does not seem to fulfill all their sexual needs. We have already examined (*see* Chapter 8) to what extent marital coitus was supplemented by other sexual outlets in various age groups in the Kinsey samples. Coitus accounted for 90 percent of the total sexual outlets of married males, but only about 85 percent of total outlets involved coitus with their wives. The remaining 15 percent of total sexual outlets involved extramarital coitus, homosexual contacts, masturbation, nocturnal emissions, and animal contacts. Obviously, each individual male did not divide his sexual activities in just this way. Some had only marital coitus, others only one additional outlet, and so on.

The relative insufficiency of marital coitus became more apparent when all males, regardless of marital status, were considered as a group. Although about two-thirds of the adult male population is married at any given time, marital coitus accounted for fewer than half the orgasms (46 percent) experienced by all males.

Nor did marital coitus account for the total sexual outlets for women. Up to the mid-thirties in age, the proportion of female or-

gasms resulting from conjugal sex was similar to that of the married male group (85 percent). Other outlets then seemed to become more prominent, so that by the late forties only slightly more than 70 percent of total sexual outlets resulted from marital coitus. Males did not show a comparable change with age.

For the vast majority of married people whose primary outlet is conjugal sex, how often to engage in it is a pertinent question.

Marital intercourse does not occur with clockwork regularity, nor is it entirely erratic. After allowances for periods of illness, pregnancy, menstruation, and so on, most couples settle into some form of sexual routine after a few years of marriage. Although most couples resolve this issue in a mutually satisfactory manner, for some it remains a matter of conflict. The average (median) frequency of coitus for younger married people in the Kinsey samples was somewhat less than three times a week. By the age of 30 this figure had dropped to about twice a week, by the age of 40 to once every four days, by the age of 50 to once a week, and by the age of 60 to once every 12 days (couples who abstained from marital coitus were excluded from the sample). These averages conceal the wide differences among people's sexual activities. Some couples make love sporadically, others every night, and a few several times a day.[36]

The more recent findings of the Hunt survey, sponsored by the Playboy Foundation, indicate that during the few decades following the Kinsey survey important changes seem to have come about involving marital intercourse. The overall conclusion is that married people are currently engaging in intercourse more frequently, spend more time during it, rely on more variations, and obtain greater satisfaction from it.

---

[36]For a general discussion of factors affecting coital frequency, see Burgoyne (1974), pp. 143–156; and for the issue of conflicting estimates between spouses of coital frequency see Levinger (1970).

When the male and female estimates of the weekly frequency of marital coitus are combined, comparisons become possible between nearly corresponding age groups within the Kinsey and Hunt samples. In both populations there is a steady decline in coital frequency with increasing age. But the rates are nevertheless higher for each age subgroup in the current sample.

In the Kinsey sample the weekly median of marital coitus was 2.45 for the 16–25-year age group; it is 3.25 (18–24-year-olds) in the Hunt sample. Likewise, the weekly medians for 26–35-year-olds have increased from 1.95 to 2.55 (25–34-year-olds) in the Hunt sample. For the 36–45-year group it was 1.40; more recently it is twice a week (35–44-year group); for the 46–55-year group it was 0.85, and for the 55–60-year group it was once every two weeks (0.50). More cur-

rently, 45–54-year-olds and those 55 years of age or older have on the average (median) marital coitus once a week. Apart from the significance of the increases in coital frequency as such, it is equally impressive that this increase seems to involve all age groups and, in particular, middle-aged and older persons.

More reliable data on marital coitus come from studies by Westoff. Like the Kantner and Zelnik studies on premarital sex, these were two fertility studies conducted by Westoff—the first in 1965 and the second in 1970, utilizing national probability samples.

Figure 10.8 shows the mean frequency of coitus among currently married women under age 45 living with their husbands. The two salient features of this figure are the decline of monthly coital frequency with increasing age and the apparent increase in coital

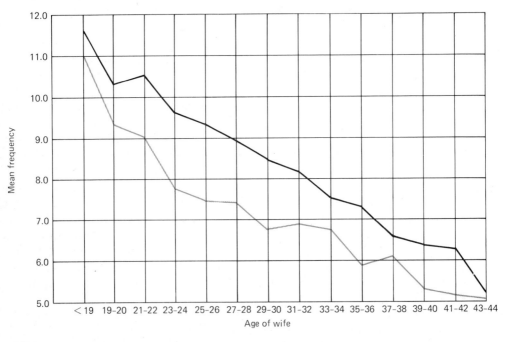

1965 ——— 1970 ———

Figure 10.8 Mean frequency of marital coitus in four weeks prior to interview, by age, 1965 and 1970. From Westoff, *Family Planning Perspectives* 6:3 (1974), p. 137. By permission.

frequency between the 1965 and 1970 samples at all ages. Although a number of factors could be confounding the picture, the evidence is suggestive of a real increase in this regard. This increase amounts to 21 percent (from an average of 6.8 to 8.2 times during the four weeks preceding the interview).

This increase in the frequency of marital coitus is probably explained by a combination of factors including reduced anxiety about pregnancy because of better contraceptive means and the availability of legal abortions. Also pertinent have been the increased sexual permissiveness and wider acceptance of a woman's right to personal fulfillment. Within these groups of women, the average coital frequency is higher among those with more "modern" outlooks, among the more highly educated, and among those who work mainly for reasons other than money.[37]

Comparison of the Kinsey and Hunt data also reflects differences in the prolongation of the period of intercourse involving both foreplay and coitus. Kinsey's female data showed a median duration of 12 minutes for foreplay, which has now increased to 15 minutes in the Hunt sample. A comparably modest increase is apparent among college-educated husbands, but more striking changes have occurred among the less-educated males, who in the Kinsey survey reported engaging only in very brief and perfunctory foreplay.

The prolongation of the duration of coitus itself is more impressive. Kinsey estimated that three-quarters of married males ejaculated within two minutes following intromission. The median duration of marital coitus has now increased to ten minutes beyond

Evidence for increased reliance on variations comes from several aspects of intercourse. We discussed earlier the greater prevalence of mouth-genital stimulation. A similar change has occurred in the use of coital pos-

tures. In the Kinsey sample a little more than a third used the female-above position—now three-quarters of married couples do so ranging from occasionally to very often. A little more than one in ten in the Kinsey sample used the rear-entry approach—now two out of five married couples use it at least occasionally. There is also an interesting age discrepancy in this regard: 20 percent of those under 25 years use this approach against less than 1 percent for those who are 55 years or older.

Increased experimentation has also extended to more controversial activities. Over half of the married males and females in the younger (under 35) half of the current survey sample have engaged in manual anal foreplay, and about one out of four has engaged in anal intercourse at least once with the spouse.

In terms of increased satisfaction, 90 percent of the wives currently surveyed report that marital coitus within the past year has been pleasurable or very pleasurable.[38] Only 10 percent found it unpleasant or were indifferent to it. The reactions of the husbands are even more affirmative.

These statistical data are interesting but must be supplemented by less readily quantifiable information and insights into the nature of the marital sexual bond. Unfortunately, the matter is so intertwined with many other facets of the complex conjugal relationship that one can hardly do justice to it by examining a few select aspects.

Marital intercourse offers special joys as well as special problems. Ideally, a husband and wife form a compatible pair, and their

---

[37]Westoff (1974).

[38]Pleasurable in this context does not necessarily mean attaining orgasm. Among this same sample of women only slightly over half reached orgasm during marital intercourse almost all the time (Hunt, December 1973, p.90). For a more detailed presentation of the above data, see pp. 90–91 and p. 256 of that article. The full discussion of marital sex in the Playboy Foundation survey is in Hunt (1974), pp. 174–232.

sexual life meshes harmoniously with their overall relationship. In reality, marriages fall short of this ideal for large numbers of people, as divorce rates and conflict-ridden households attest.

It is impossible to arrive at a consensus on the relative importance of the sexual and other aspects of marriage. People admit to having married for predominantly romantic or sexual motives, but soon enough their interactions come to revolve around the more prosaic business of everyday living. The arrival of children further drains any reserves of energy and interest that the couple may have and marital sex takes on the attributes of uninspired home cooking: It is wholesome and available and, since one is paying for it, one may as well eat it.

We are all acquainted with the endless caricatures of marital boredom: the man with the shrewish or ugly wife who yearns for the joys of bachelorhood, and the woman with the dull-witted and wilted husband who dreams of romance. If these fates await us, why marry? One cynical reason is that the available alternatives are hardly more cheerful: the lonely bachelor nursing stale drinks at a bar, the white-haired Casanova making a fool of himself, the aging seductress still being passed around from man to man, and so on.

More affirmatively, people marry because these fates are by no means inevitable. There are married couples who sustain the excitement and romance of their youth into old age. True, their sexual relations change along with other circumstances and aspects of their lives; but, after all, that is to be expected. Familiarity for them does not breed contempt, but a fuller respect and deeper affection. Repetition does not lead to boredom, but a better understanding of the other's needs and desires and hence a more harmonious match. Such couples do not tire of each other because they are not static personalities mired in unresolved conflicts; they grow and change together. Children do not

detract from but rather further cement their relationship. Finally, while such couples count on each other, they do not take each other for granted, and they persist in a state of ongoing courtship.

These characterizations are deliberately overdrawn. Most married people are neither bored to death nor blissfully happy in their sex lives, but rather vacillate somewhere in between.

Even when we take a less gloomy and more realistic approach, there is no escaping the fact that sex within marriage is no guaranteed source of unbounded joy. Nor, for that matter, is sex outside marriage necessarily an endless lark. What intensifies sexual problems within marriage is that the couple is bound together by profound social ties and expectations. When a man fails sexually with a casual acquaintance, he need not see her again; the husband must face his wife at the breakfast table. If a single woman finds coitus unsatisfactory, she can change partners or forget about sex for a while. A wife cannot exercise these options without serious risk to her marriage and, in some cultures, to her economic survival.

In view of such problems, traditional approaches to improving marital sex have been handicapped by the fact that one is dealing at least in principle with a "fixed capital," namely, the couple and no one else. Currently, there is considerable ferment in looking at alternatives to marital sexual exclusiveness as a solution—in other words, nonmarital sex.

In this regard premarital sex can be viewed as an alternative to marriage, if sex is the primary motivation for getting married. Or it can be thought of as necessary in the choice of a compatible sexual partner and as practice in preparation for marital sex. Extramarital sex may also be seen as fulfilling a variety of compensatory or complementary functions to marital sex, as we shall discuss further on.

Nonmarital Intercourse

The primary importance of coitus outside of marriage lies in its social and psychological implications. In strictly physiological terms it is immaterial whether or not the sexual partners are married to each other. But in individual cases sexual performance can be very much influenced by social and moral considerations.

A detailed discussion of the moral issues involved in sex outside of marriage will not be attempted here (Chapters 1 and 15 treat them at some length). Instead, we shall briefly outline a few of the more salient psychological and social considerations and discuss the figures reported by Kinsey and more recent studies on the prevalence and correlates of nonmarital intercourse.[39]

Sex outside of marriage can be discussed as a whole for certain purposes. But there are important distinctions between premarital, extramarital, and postmarital sex. For example, in the first and last instances, where the person has never married or is separated, divorced, or widowed, there is no third party to consider. Extramarital relations are usually complicated by concern about the spouse.

Despite important historical and cultural differences, sex outside of marriage seems to have always coexisted with sex within marriage for some or perhaps many people, and sex as such is, of course, older than marriage. The pertinent questions refer to variations in the prevalence of these practices and in our attitudes toward them.

Premarital Intercourse

Premarital coitus has posed one of the thornier social problems in the West, particularly regarding women. (For cross-cultural comparisons see Box 10.3.) Since the individuals involved are usually young, parents and society have assumed protective attitudes to prevent mistakes by young people that would wreak harm to personality, career, marital prospects, and so on. However, social attitudes appear to be changing rapidly and the increased availability of contraceptives is significant in this regard, since the effective separation of sexual from reproductive functions is bound to have repercussions on public attitudes.

On some college campuses, at least, the prevalent attitudes toward premarital sex appear to be much more open and flexible than were those of the past. For many, premarital coitus no longer carries its former stigma, although promiscuity seems to be neither common nor generally approved. Some students seem concerned if they do not feel ready for intercourse while in college, even though they engage in considerable sexual activity short of it.[40]

Several decades ago the Kinsey survey revealed what was for many Americans a staggering fact—that half of all the women in the sample had had sexual intercourse before marriage. Most often (46 percent of respondents), premarital intercourse involved only engaged people who subsequently married. Among males the rates of premarital coitus was even higher, but less surprising. In the group with only elementary-school educations, practically every male (98 percent) had had coitus before marriage; in the more-educated groups, the percentages were lower (85 percent for high-school graduates and 68 percent for those with college educations).

Premarital coitus usually occurred irregularly and rather infrequently. Males had intercourse, on the average, once every two weeks; females once a month or so. Premarital intercourse accounted for a third of the male outlets in the early-twenties age group but a somewhat smaller proportion of the female outlets. The proportion remained the

---

[39]For considerations related to premarital sexual standards, see Reiss (1960, 1967, 1977).

[40]Student Committee on Human Sexuality (1970), p. 11.

Box 10.3   Cross-Cultural Perspectives on Premarital Sex

In preliterate societies, in about two-fifth to one-half of cases, females are allowed to have premarital coitus. If societies that overtly condemn but covertly condone such behavior are included, then the figure rises to 70 percent. Where they have free access to each other, young men and women appear to engage in sex almost daily. But the choice of partners is not indiscriminate.

Marshall has provided a detailed account of a sexually permissive society of Polynesians living on the island of Mangaia (one of the Cook Islands in the South Pacific).[1] These people seem to have mastered the art of "looking the other way" where sexual matters are concerned.

Mangaian boys may experiment with coitus prior to being formally initiated into manhood, but these contacts usually involve promiscuous older women or widows. To have access to their peers or the more desirable "good girls," a boy must first undergo the initiation rite of superincision, whereby the skin at the upper surface of the penis is cut along the midline.

The standard pattern for premarital

[1] In Marshall and Suggs (1971), pp. 103–162.

sex is "sleep crawling," which appears to be a general Polynesian cultural practice. As the following description indicates, for youth to get together in Mangaia is not that easy, which again shows that even sexual permissiveness does not imply free and indiscriminate access to sex.

A youth bent on courting must first slip out of his own home and then avoid village policemen who are out searching for violators of the nine o'clock curfew. He must then get to the girl's house before other suitors. His effort may be made at sometime between ten o'clock in the evening and midnight; if successful, he may remain until three o'clock in the morning. If the girl has invited him to visit her, or if he is a regular visitor, his task is much easier. If not, he is faced with the alternative of "sweet talking" her (with the risk of waking the family) or of smiting her or gagging her mouth with his hand or a towel until he has made his penetration. Mangaian boys believe that most girls will not call the family if the suitor talks to her but that many a girl will call out to her father if the boy tries force. In any event, once penetration is made, most resistance is gone— "She has no voice to call." Less aggressive boys or the darker skinned and other less sociably desirable youths may take up to a year of "sweet talk" to win the girl they desire; others

---

same for males in their mid-forties, but rose to more than 40 percent for women in that age group.

The prevalence of premarital intercourse was markedly related to educational level and age at marriage (the older the person, the more likely he was to have already had coitus) for males, but much less so for females. There was little relation to parental occupational class for either sex.

Of women born before 1900 only 14 percent had had premarital sex; among those born later than 1900 this figure had almost quadrupled. Men did not show this genera-

tional difference. Premarital sex was more common among both sexes in urban areas. It was also distinctly less common among the more devout.

Intercourse between unmarried people most often occurred in the woman's home. Each act generally lasted longer than marital intercourse did, although the couple was less likely than were married people to experiment with coital positions.

Current studies show that important changes have been taking place in this area, and general observations can now be documented by more formal data. We shall con-

Box 10.3   Continued

may speed their suit by serenades. Most of them simply take what they want, when they want it.[2]

The majority of cultures surveyed by Ford and Beach have been placed in the semirestrictive category.[3] They were characterized less by differences in sexual codes for juveniles than by the lack of vigor in enforcing existing prohibitions.

For example, the Alorese (polygynous agriculturalists of Indonesia), the Andamanese (monogamous semi-nomadic gatherers, hunters, and fishers), and the Huichol (monogamous Mexican people who live by animal husbandry and agriculture) all formally disapproved of premarital intercourse, but made little effort to check it. As long as the practice was not flaunted and did not result in pregnancy, it was generally tolerated. When pregnancy occurred the couple was pressured into marriage. Contraceptive measures were therefore frequently used by youngsters in these cultures. Methods include coitus interruptus, ejaculation

between the girl's legs, placing a pad in the vagina, and washing the vagina after coitus. A pregnant girl might also have resorted to abortion. Restrictive societies constitute the minority in Ford and Beach's survey.

Female virginity at the time of marriage was highly valued in these cultures. The ancient custom of parading bloodstained bed sheets on the wedding night is well known. Yungar (Australian aborigine) brides were deflowered by pairs of old women. In either culture, should the hymen have been tampered with earlier, a girl would be in serious difficulty.

Restrictive societies may go to great pains to enforce prohibitions on preadolescent sexual behavior. Warnings, chaperoning, and segregation are some preventive measures. Disgrace, punishment, and even death are invoked when prevention fails. Among the Chagga (advanced polygynous agriculturalists of Tanganyika, now Tanzania), for instance, if a boy who had not been initiated was caught in the sex act, he and his partner were placed on top of each other and staked to the ground.

[2]Donald Marshall, "Sexual behavior in Mangaia," in Marshall and Suggs (1971), p. 129. Reproduced by permission.
[3]Ford and Beach (1951).

---

sider briefly some salient findings from several studies whose scope and methodology have been already discussed (*see* Chapter 8).

The prevalence of premarital intercourse reported from the Hunt survey is quite striking. The percentage of married persons who have had sexual intercourse prior to getting married was 95 percent for males and 81 percent for females between the ages of 18 and 24. These percentages steadily declined among older persons, especially for females. Thus, in the 25–34-age group the percentage who had premarital coitus was 92 percent for males, 65 percent for females; in the 35–44-

age group, 86 percent for males and 41 percent for females; among the 45–54-year olds, 89 percent for males and 36 percent for females; for the oldest age group of 55 and over, 84 percent of males, but only 31 percent of married females reported having had premarital coitus.

The remarkable increase in prevalence in the younger age groups amply illustrates the marked changes that have taken place since Kinsey's survey. But at the same time there is an equally remarkable consistency in that the major portion of premarital intercourse currently occurs between people who hope to marry, as was the case at the time of the Kinsey survey. Thus, despite the increase in premarital sex among modern youth, they generally seem to retain the relational requirement and have not abandoned the romantic for the more purely recreational aspects of sex.

Married women in the Kinsey sample born before 1900 who had had premarital coitus had done so with their fiancés only in 40 percent of cases, with other men in 20 percent; and the balance of 40 percent had had coitus with their fiancés as well as others. Those born between 1910 and 1919 (which would make them 56–65 years old in 1975) reported a similar percentage for premarital coitus with the fiancé (42 percent), a lower percentage for coitus with others (12 percent); and a balance of 46 percent of those who had premarital coitus had done so with the fiancé and other men.

The later figures from the Hunt survey are remarkably similar. Married women born during 1938–1947 (28–37 years old in 1975) who had engaged in premarital coitus had done so with their fiancés only in 49 percent of cases, with others in 8 percent, and with both fiancé and others in 43 percent of cases. Finally, for those born between 1948 and 1955 (20–27 years old in 1975), the corresponding percentages were 54, 3, and 43 percent. Thus, although young women now are more likely to engage in premarital coitus than their mothers and grandmothers, their choice of partners are even more likely to be someone they expect to marry.

Within this general framework premarital sex is not only more prevalent but more frequent, more varied, and less inhibited. In the Kinsey sample single males between the ages of 16 and 25 who were coitally active had a median frequency of 23 times a year. In the Hunt sample it is 33 times a year. Single women 16–20 years of age in the Kinsey sample had intercourse once every five weeks and those 21–25 years of age had it once

every three weeks. Currently, 18–24-year-olds who have intercourse do so once a week. The female-above position is now used twice as frequently as before, and rear-entry approaches six times as often. Whereas half of the Kinsey survey women reached orgasm in premarital coitus, now three-quarters are able to.

Despite increased liberalization of attitudes, the first coital experience remains problematic for some. Only four out of ten young males and two out of ten young females find the first experience "very pleasurable." More than a third of young males and close to two-thirds of young females feel regret and worry afterward, even after repeated experiences. The concerns are generally related to emotional and moral conflicts, fear of VD and pregnancy, and worry about adequacy of performance. Some of these problems are due to liberalization of attitudes, which sometimes create considerable peer pressure to engage in coitus before one is psychologically ready or morally at peace about it.[41]

In Sorensen's sample (ages 13–19) 52 percent of the adolescents surveyed have had sexual intercourse (59 percent of boys, 45 percent of girls). Within this group 13 percent (17 percent of boys, 7 percent of girls) had their first experience at age 12 or younger. By age 15, 71 percent of boys and 56 percent of girls in the nonvirgin group had engaged in coitus.

This sample of adolescents is further divided by Sorensen into "serial monogamists" and "sexual adventurers." The former constitute 21 percent of the sample population, and consist of adolescents in sexual attachments of uncertain duration but where partners intend and generally remain faithful to each other while the relationship lasts. These couples do not live together and move

[41]Hunt (November 1973), pp. 74–75. The more complete discussion of premarital sex is in Hunt (1974), pp. 106–171.

on to successive relationships over years. In a sense they are like adults who have a succession of marriages.

The sexual adventurers (15 percent of adolescents in the sample: 25 percent of boys, 6 percent of girls) have no monogamous links, but are interested in having many sexual partners simultaneously or in rapid succession (an average of 2.3 in the past month).

In terms of the relationships among the partners the following findings emerge. Sixty percent of the nonvirgins had first partners who were older, 14 percent younger, and 26 percent the same age. A quarter of the boys and almost 60 percent of the girls were going steady with their first partners, and about a third of the girls but less than 10 percent of the boys said they planned to marry at the time. In 40 percent of cases intercourse took place in the home of the boy or girl (only 2 percent had it in a hotel or motel).[42]

The most reliable statistics to date on premarital coitus come from the two studies by Kantner and Zelnik (*see* Box 8.8). As shown in Figure 10.9, their findings clearly confirm other evidences that the level of sexual activity among American youth has been increasing.

This trend, which for white females has been traced to the late 1960s, is clearly in evidence when the figures for 1976 are compared with those of 1971. For all ages between 15 and 19 the more recent percentages are higher: Whereas 27 percent of this age group had engaged in premarital sex, 35 percent had done so in the group studies in 1976—an increase in prevalence of 30 percent. The median age at first intercourse has also declined by about four months (from 16.5 to 16.2 years).

These data also show significant racial differences. The rates for black women between 15 and 19 years of age is much higher:

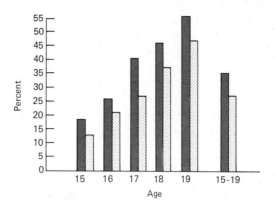

Figure 10.9 *Percent of never-married women aged 15–19 who have never had intercourse, by age, 1976 and 1971. From Zelnik and Kantner,* Family Planning Perspectives, *9:2 (1977), p. 56. By permission.*

51.2 percent versus 21.4 percent for whites in 1971 and 62.7 percent versus 30.8 percent for whites in 1976. The higher ratio for blacks is true for each age group for both studies, but the relative differences are smaller in 1976, showing that the rates are rising more steeply for whites.

Sexual intercourse for these women is a one-time experience only in 15 percent of cases: 85 percent have engaged in sex more than once. But the frequency with which they engage in sex is quite low. In 1971 only three in five and in 1976 only half reported coitus during the preceding month.

Most of the time premarital sex takes place not in a parked car or behind a bush but in someone's home. More than three out of four of these young women said they engaged in sex in their own homes, the partner's home, or that of a friend or relative: Especially favored was the partner's home. Girls who are initiated into sex before 13 have the experience most often in their own home.

The fact that young women are now sexually more active does not mean that they

[42]For further details see Sorensen (1973).

are also generally promiscuous. Most confine themselves to one partner, and this is true for both blacks and whites. Only about 6 percent in 1971 and 10 percent in 1976 reported having had six or more partners (whites were considerably overrepresented in this group). There is however some tendency more recently for involvement with a larger number of partners, especially among blacks. Thus in 1971 some 60 percent of blacks and whites reported only one partner: Five years later this was only true for 53 percent of whites and 40 percent of blacks.

The male partners at first intercourse are usually teenagers themselves (85 percent among blacks, 73 percent among whites). But they tend to be two or three years older than the young woman. The partner at the most recent intercourse is older than the first partner: More than half of recent partners are at least 20 years old.[43]

What is the effect of premarital sex on subsequent marital life? Numerous answers have been offered, mostly based on commonsense expectations. Predictably they range from the traditional conservative view—that it is best to enter marriage in sexual purity—to the opposite viewpoint—that the more experience one has had premaritally, the better one will do in marriage.

Available research evidence so far has failed to indicate definitively a significant effect of premarital sex on marriage one way or the other. Premarital sex and marital adjustment are each complex variables, and it will probably remain impossible to show meaningful links between the two in some simple, straightforward way.[44]

Extramarital Intercourse

Moral considerations aside, premarital relations have a certain self-evident justifica-tion. Single people need sex just as the married do, and lacking a spouse they have no choice but to make love to others. But why would a married person with ready sexual access to a spouse wish to sleep with someone else? The question has tormented moralists as well as spouses for a long time.

Extramarital relations have been condemned in the West and numerous other cultures but have never been suppressed successfully. People seek sexual partners outside of marriage for a host of reasons, often in combination. Some considerations are practical: lengthy separations, chronic debilitating illness in the spouse, lack of interest or sexual dysfunction, and so on. In short, any situation where sex is no longer available within marriage.

In a second set of conditions marital sex is available but unsatisfactory. This may result from the effects of aging, the monotony of habit, or mismatches in intensity of desire or willingness to experiment. In these and countless other similar circumstances the apparent motivation is to compensate for and supplement what is lacking within the marriage.

But then there are also those who neither lack sex nor profess to be dissatisfied with their marital partners, yet feel that their sexual lives will be further enriched with extramarital liaisons. In sexual, as well as other matters, the objective is to relinquish the traditional expectation that spouses be all things to one another. These more flexible marital relationships have been called by a variety of names, a popular term being "open marriage."[45]

One can make other and parallel classifications listing motivations for extramarital sex according to mental-health considerations, moral criteria, and the consequences of the act. Quietly supplementing one's marital sex life with due regard to the sensibilities of the spouse and society is different from aggressively flaunting nonmarital affairs to hurt,

[43]Zelnik and Kantner (1977); Kantner and Zelnick (1972).

[44]For a range of opinions see *Medical Aspects of Human Sexuality* (November 1968 and April 1973).

[45]O'Neill and O'Neill (1972).

offend, or humiliate.[46] A person who gets involved after due thought and understanding of what he or she is doing differs from the uncontrollably driven individual who gets embroiled in senseless liaisons. Even in moral terms people are more inclined to "understand" some forms of "going astray" more readily than others. This issue of permissible relativism is one of the central concerns in sexual ethics (*see* Chapter 15).

All of these issues are complicated by the fact that there is far more than sex involved in such interactions. As we discussed in Chapter 8, the significance of sex in the life cycle varies considerably, and the incentive for extramarital intercourse may be linked to the psychological events of a given life phase or time interval in the marriage. Phrases such as "the seven-year itch" attest to general awareness of this problem. A common observation is that there may be an increased tendency for extramarital sex in the transition into middle age, as the person tries to fulfill unresolved yearnings of youth "before it is too late," or hope to magically avert the onslaught of age by clinging or regressing to youthful activities epitomized by sexual adventurism.[47]

Despite endless speculation and moralization, there has been relatively little reliable information on extramarital behavior. In the Kinsey sample, about half the men and a quarter of the women admitted that by age 40 they had had at least one extramarital affair each. Like premarital coitus, this outlet was generally irregular, occurring only once every one to three months; it accounted for fewer than 10 percent of total outlets.

Extramarital coitus was somewhat more prevalent among less-educated males, particularly before age 25. It was higher among better-educated women after the age of 25. (These figures do not mean that these two groups were having affairs with each other.) There was no relation to parental occupational class. As would be expected, the more devout were less likely to be unfaithful to their spouses. The length of involvement in extramarital affairs and the number of partners involved varied. About 41 percent of women with this experience reported one partner, but about an equal percentage had had affairs with two to five men.

More current findings, contrary to popular belief, show no evidence of major changes in attitude or behavior regarding extramarital behavior, in sharp contrast to the changes described in premarital behavior. Between 80 and 90 percent of the couples in the Hunt survey found the prospect of infidelity by the spouse unacceptable (and this applied to younger as well as older couples). Behavior in this regard was by and large consistent with stated attitudes, and most of these couples refrained from extramarital sex because it was "sinful," "wrong," and "dishonest" (as well as out of fear of V.D. and pregnancy).

Even though there has been no substantial increase in the practice since the Kinsey survey, the amount of extramarital sex remains considerable. Half of married men in the Hunt sample eventually had affairs and so do about one in five married women by the time they reach 45 years. There was an important change, however, in that among the younger women rates approached male rates, which is one more evidence of the dissolution of the double standard.

Extramarital sex continued to be a predominantly secret (only one in five spouses know about it), conflicted, and often guilt-ridden activity. It was also generally less gratifying than marital sex: 53 percent of women reached orgasm almost always with their husbands, but only 39 percent did so in extramarital coitus; only 7 percent of women never reached orgasm with their husbands against

---

[46]For examples, see Masters and Johnson (1976).

[47]For examples of contemporary medical opinions about causes of marital infidelity, see *Medical Aspects of Human Sexuality* (January 1974), pp. 90–110, Salzman (1972), pp. 118–136, and Livsey (1979).

35 percent in extramarital affairs. Two-thirds of married males rated coitus in the past year with their wives as "very pleasurable," but fewer than half of the men who had extramarital coitus during the past year rated it as highly. Yet, despite all this, extramarital sex continues to tempt, and the excitement, rediscovery of passion, and other psychological rewards make it highly gratifying for many, even though the experience may be marred for some by fear and guilt.[48]

One form of extramarital relations that seems to command considerable fascination involves arrangements variously known as "wife swapping," "mate swapping," "group marriage," "swinging,' and so on. Available information indicates that there is far more talk than activity in this area.[49] In the Hunt survey only about 2 percent of the men and fewer women had ever participated in such exchanges and even then had usually done so only once.

Popular images of carefree orgies to the contrary, "swingers" frequently appear to be plagued by jealousy, conflict, fear of disease, disgrace, and loss of love. Quite understandably sexual malfunction is also reported to be common at these times.[50] One could argue that the problem is not in the nature of the activity but the background and "hang-ups" of the participants. And there certainly are some who appear to have no difficulties as a result of such activities.

Many different criteria are used to assess extramarital intercourse. Some consider the element of honesty to be the paramount factor. Others maintain that what the spouse does not know cannot hurt. It has been generally believed that extramarital relations reflect weaknesses in the marital relations and are detrimental to the institution of marriage. Currently there are counterclaims that some extramarital relations can actually enrich and strengthen a marriage. As a result, some writers now differentiate between healthy and disturbed reasons for having extramarital relations.[51]

Rational analyses of the social aspects of extramarital behaviors do not necessarily satisfy the moral questions on these issues. Regulations governing extramarital relations are complicated by a wide diversity of qualification in various societies. Such coitus may be permissible with some but not others, during special periods but not generally. Almost universally, men are allowed a freer rein. Still, in two-fifths to three-fifths of preliterate societies wives are also allowed at least some degree of freedom in this regard. The concerns with extramarital sex seem to be predominantly social and revolve around issues such as the impact on the spouse and society, resultant failure in marital duties and obligations, complications arising from pregnancy, the effects on kinship loyalties, and the like.

Postmarital Intercourse

Sexual relations involving the separated, divorced, or widowed are in general less socially controversial than premarital or extramarital coitus. These individuals tend to be emancipated from parental control, and society tends to extend them some special consideration. And there is no uninvolved spouse to be considered. These social attitudes permit the widowed or divorced more freedom, but also place them in special situations. The women in this group in particular resent being viewed as easy sexual prey. In the Kinsey sample the statistical characteris-

---

[48]Hunt (January 1974), pp. 60–61, 286–287. See also Hunt (1974), pp. 233–290.

[49]For a general study of group sex and an evaluation of its positive and negative aspects, see Bartell (1971). Also see Gilmartin (1975) and Masters and Johnson (1976).

[50]Hunt (January 1974), pp. 286, 287.

[51]For discussions of the distinction between "healthy" and "unhealthy" reasons for extramarital relations, see A. Ellis (1969). Neubeck (1969) also includes other essays on extramarital relations. For a range of professional opinions about the significance of extramarital relations, see "The Significance of Extramarital Sex Relations" (1969).

tics of sexual behavior in this group generally fell somewhere between the patterns of married and single persons.

The divorce rates have greatly increased since Kinsey's survey and the onus of being divorced has by and large disappeared. Current data indicate that divorced people, women in particular, are now far freer in their sexual behavior. As a group, the divorced are sexually as free as the population of under-25 married couples who constitute the more sexually active and uninhibited sector.

In the Hunt survey no divorced man of any age was found to have been coitally inactive during the past year, and the same was true for 90 percent of the women. Median frequency of coitus for both sexes was twice a week (four times greater than reported by Kinsey). Men had a median of eight coital partners a year, women 3.5.[52]

The divorced are not on a perpetual spree of promiscuity, but they appear to have quite satisfactory sexual lives. Ninety percent of divorced women and even more divorced men report that their sex lives are pleasurable or very pleasurable. Yet, interestingly enough, about four in five remarry—hopefully having become wiser for the experience.

[52]Hunt (January 1974), pp. 60–61.

Chapter 11

Homosexuality and Other Sexual Behaviors

Human sexual life has many facets. Even though heterosexual intercourse is the preferred mode of sexual expression for most adults, many people also engage in other forms of sexual behavior at one time or another; some do so exclusively.

Such departures from standard coital practices have generally been known as *sexual deviations*. Those who object to implications of pathology in this phrase prefer the term *sexual variations*. This conflict over terminology reflects current uncertainties in the evaluation of such behavior. There is no serious disagreement when the activity is flagrantly bizarre or demonstrably harmful. The conflict does not center on necrophilia or sex murder but rather on such behavior as homosexual contacts in private between consenting adults. Ironically, the majority of Americans (71 percent in one public-opinion poll) view homosexuality as an illness, yet the American Psychiatric Association deleted the term from its authoritative *Diagnostic and Statistical Manual of Mental Disorders* in 1973 and no longer supports the view that homosexuality as such is a psychiatric disorder.[1]

Aberrant sexual behavior has interested people for a long time. There are references to such practices in the oldest historical records. More recently an extensive sexual behavior literature has developed, particularly around the theme of homosexuality. Unfortunately, most such works abound in stereotypes and speculations although there are exceptions, such as a study of homosexuals recently published under the auspices of the Institute for Sex Research at Indiana University.[2]

Our approach in this chapter will be predominantly descriptive, and, in view of the many types of behavior possible, it will have to be cursory. We have already dealt with some of these topics in earlier chapters, and shall return to them in subsequent ones.

There is a common tendency to conduct discussions of sexual deviations in the manner of a tour through the zoo, pointing out individuals with one peculiar characteristic or another. The following considerations must therefore be emphasized.

First, although it is convenient to call individuals "homosexuals," "voyeurs," and so on, it is much more useful to speak of homosexual or voyeuristic *behavior* and of people who have had various degrees of such

[1]Weinberg and Williams (1974), pp. 6, 20.

[2]Bell and Weinberg (1978).

experiences. The sex life of humans consists not of "pure" types of behavior but of combinations of various activities at various times. Furthermore, even when some individuals are oriented predominantly in one of these aberrant directions, to label them accordingly is to exaggerate their differences from other people to the point of caricature.

Second, many types of aberrant behavior exist in all shades and gradations and are exceedingly common (even though we may not be conscious of them). Again, we are not mainly interested in the bizarre: Although few of us are necrophiliacs or child molesters, there is a range of voyeuristic–exhibitionistic and sadomasochistic activity, for instance, that is part of common heterosexual experience, and that we do not—and have no reason to—label as "deviant" or "pathological."

Judgments of sexual behavior are just as appropriate as are judgments of other forms of human activity. Not all sexual behavior is equally adaptive, healthy, socially desirable, moral, and so on. Such judgments, however, ought to be made with great care. Experience shows how arbitrary they can be and how easy it is to inflict unnecessary hardship on people whose main offenses may consist in being different. Our objective at this point is primarily to describe rather than to condone or condemn.

Classification of Sexual Variations and Deviations

The first attempt at a comprehensive review of sexual aberrations was undertaken by the Viennese psychiatrist Richard von Krafft-Ebing, who published his classic *Psychopathia Sexualis* in 1886. Freud's own formulations, to be discussed here, appeared in 1905 in his *Three Essays on the Theory of Sexuality* (*see* Chapter 8).

Freud based his classification of sexual aberrations on the assumption that among adults any form of sexual behavior that *takes precedence* over heterosexual intercourse represents a defect in psychosexual development. Freud labeled the person from whom sexual attraction emanates the "sexual object" and what one wishes to do with the object the "sexual aim." In a healthy, or mature, sexual relationship an adult of the opposite sex would thus be the sexual object and the wish for coitus the sexual aim.[3]

It then follows that deviations from this pattern can take one of two forms: deviations in the *choice of sexual object* and deviations in the *choice of sexual aim*. In the first instance the alternative object could be an adult of the same sex (as in homosexuality),[4] a child (as in pedophilia), a close relative (as in incest), an animal (as in zoophilia), an inanimate object (as in fetishism), or even a dead body (as in necrophilia). In the second instance, instead of seeking (and when permissible engaging in) coitus, the individual would prefer to watch others having coitus (voyeurism), to expose his own genitals (exhibitionism), to inflict pain (sadism), or to suffer pain (masochism). When deviation involves both choice of object and sexual aim, it is usually designated by the choice of object.

This classification is not primarily concerned with the social significance of these various aberrations, and it would label as deviations certain widely accepted practices such as oral-genital contacts and even kissing if practiced as ends in themselves when legitimate access to coitus is available. Freud's primary interest was not in these deviations as such but in their theoretical significance for his conceptions of infantile sexuality and psychosexual development. Our use of Freud's

---

[3]The use of the term "object" in this context is not intended to imply that people are or should be used as inanimate objects. Applied to persons, "objects" means individuals who fulfill essential functions in the gratification of others. For further discussion of this concept, *see* Engel (1962), p. 17.

[4]As noted earlier, homosexuality has been deleted from the category of deviations in the current psychiatric nomenclature. In all other respects the classification described here is still widely accepted in psychiatry and in law.

classification system is primarily pragmatic; the system is convenient and widely used, and adoption of it does not necessarily imply acceptance of Freud's related theories.

Homosexuality[5]

Of all the possible variations and deviations, homosexuality is the most common. There is considerably more information about it as well, and for these reasons we shall discuss it in greater detail.

Perhaps no single sexual behavior has been as widely misunderstood as homosexuality. It has only been in the past two or three decades that reliable scientific information has become available about the behavior and life-style of homosexuals with which to evaluate the psychological adjustment, social adjustment, and social acceptability of homosexuality. Kinsey discovered that 37 percent of the males and 13 percent of the females in his sample had engaged in at least one homosexual interaction to the extent of having orgasm.[6] Subsequent research established that homosexuals were, for the most part, not distinguishable from their heterosexual counterparts in psychological or social adjustment.[7] More recently, Masters and Johnson's extensive laboratory studies[8] have demonstrated that the sexual responses of homosexuals and heterosexuals are virtually identical in every way. In addition, they found that homosexuals are more sensitive and more effective lovers than their heterosexual counterparts. Bell and Weinberg have carried on the research of the Kinsey Institute and demonstrated that "relatively few homosexual men and women conform to the hideous stereotype most people have of them."[9] There is an enormous range of behavioral and social variations among homosexuals, just as there is among heterosexuals. Naturally, a certain portion of the homosexual population has sexual dysfunctions and psychological or social problems, but the same is true of the heterosexual population.

What Is Homosexuality?

Homosexuality is typically defined as sexuality that is directed toward individuals of the same sex. Because the definition is made in terms of a person's preference for sexual partner, the definition puts a great deal of emphasis on sexuality; and indeed many early myths about homosexuals portrayed them as hypersexed, constantly obsessed with sex, and therefore sexually perverted.

The studies done on homosexuality during the past three decades have given a much clearer picture of the complexity of homosexual behavior and the enormous variability within the homosexual population. This research indicates the importance of defining homosexuality more in terms of *lifestyles* than in terms of *sexual performance.* The title of Bell and Weinberg's book, *Homosexualities,* captures a main finding of their study—that homosexuals do not fit in one single mold; there are many forms of homosexual life patterns. Bell and Weinberg's study revealed the following general patterns. Many homosexuals (28 percent of the men and 45 percent of the women) formed stable relationships with one partner and lived normal home lives much the same as married couples. Others (27 percent of the men and 15 percent of the women) preferred to have multiple partners and were very socially ac-

---

[5]The term "homosexual" is derived from the Greek *hom,* "the same," rather than from the Latin root *homo* "man." The term has numerous synonyms, both in the vernacular and technical. Some, like "homophile" and "gay," reflect attempts to eliminate pejorative connotations. Others like "bisexuality" and "inversion," reflect particular etiological points of view. All these terms are corrrectly applicable to either sex, but current scientific usage tends to differentiate between the two sexes by using the terms "male homosexual" for men and "lesbian" for women.

[6]Kinsey et al. (1948, 1953).

[7]Hooker (1957), Chang and Block (1960), Freedman (1967), Wilson and Greene (1971), Saghir and Robins (1973), and Riess et al. (1974).

[8]Masters and Johnson (1979).

[9]Bell and Weinberg (1978).

tive, often cruising bars and other places where they were likely to meet new people. Approximately 16 percent of males and 11 percent of females were relatively asexual and led lives indistinguishable from many other singles in society. The remaining individuals (29 percent of males and 29 percent of females) had life-styles that did not fit into any easily labeled categories.

The data gathered by Bell and Weinberg indicate that homosexuals are not any more sexually active than their heterosexual counterparts. On the average, homosexual men had sex about 2 or 3 times per week, and lesbians about 1 or 2 times per week. There was, of course, variation within the homosexual population: 11 percent of homosexuals had sex less than once a month; 24 percent had sex 1 to 3 times a month; 49 percent had sex 1 to 3 times a week; and 16 percent had sex 4 or more times a week. This type of variability is also typical of the heterosexual population. Most homosexuals report that they do not think about sex a great deal during their daily lives; and again this corresponds closely to the habits of heterosexuals. These data certainly indicate that homosexuals are not hypersexed or obsessed with frequent sexual activity. Many homosexuals object to being labeled with a term that stresses only one aspect of their behavior. If the label distorts people's perception of their actual life styles, it can make it difficult for many heterosexuals to understand them. It is for this reason that many prefer to call themselves "gay," "lesbians," or "homophiles."

Cross-Cultural Comparisons

Whether one focuses on the life-styles or the nature of sexual interactions, it is quite clear that no single stereotype suffices to explain more than a small percentage of the variability in homosexual behavior. Cross-cultural data underscore this conclusion. Ford and Beach analyzed the data on 190 preliterate societies and found 76 societies for which data on homosexuality were available.[10] In one form or another, homosexuality was permitted and considered normal in 64 percent of the 76 societies. Even though the remaining 36 percent did not condone homosexual activity (and some punished it severely), the data indicate that clandestine homosexual activity probably did occur in many of these societies.

There was significant variability in homosexual expression across the cultures. Male homosexuality was more commonly reported than female homosexuality. In some societies, homosexuality among males was used as a rite of passage to adulthood: Young men and boys were the recipients of homosexual interactions (often anal intercourse) during the initiation to adulthood because (as the adults would say) "the juices of manhood are necessary for the growing boy."[11] In other societies, such as the Kukukuku of New Guinea, young men formed homosexual relationships with each other for the express purpose of ingesting semen during oral sex.[12] Semen, the masculine essence, was presumed to have magical powers as a source of virility, strength, and masculinity; thus the homosexual experiences were an important aspect of becoming a man. Several societies allowed men to have homosexual interactions before marriage, during those periods when their wives were pregnant, when intercourse was taboo, or when the wife was not interested in sex as much as the husband was.

Little is known about lesbian sexuality in preliterate societies, in part because the anthropologists were primarily male and had limited access to information about the private lives of women (or were less interested in women's activities). However, lesbian practices were reported in 17 of the 76 societies analyzed by Ford and Beach, although details on lesbian activities were limited.

[10]Ford and Beach (1951).
[11]Williams (1936).
[12]Money and Ehrhardt (1972), p. 126.

In classical Greece, homosexual relationships were quite common and highly praised during certain periods.[13] In general, the Greek men held women in low esteem and developed a very male-oriented social life. Male homosexual lovers were thought to be especially brave and fierce warriors because nothing could make a man want to fight more valiantly than to be fighting side by side with his lover. In some states young men from prominent families were trained in the art of manhood by an older man with whom they formed a homosexual relationship. One of the best-documented historical accounts of lesbian love comes from the work of Sappho, who lived on the Greek island of Lesbos (from which comes the term "lesbianism") in the sixth century B.C. Sappho's poems extolled the virtues of the love of women for each other. Sappho was also a proponent of women's rights and had a school for young women in which poetry, dancing, music, and art were taught.

The Romans were quite tolerant of many forms of sexual expression in both men and women, and homosexual relationships were common.

Cross-cultural data, fragmentary as they may be, generally contradict simple explanations of homosexual behavior as arising only when heterosexual outlets are unavailable or blocked by inhibitions and restrictions. The historical emergence and functional explanations of homosexual behavior remain generally obscure.

Homosexuality in Western Culture

The Judeo-Christian tradition has consistently held homosexuality to be an unnatural and sinful act, and homosexuality has been forcefully repressed throughout much of the Christian era in the West.[14] In early Christian Rome, laws were passed that punished homosexual behavior with death by burning at the stake. By the Middle Ages, it was believed that the sins of homosexuality could only be atoned for by a painful death; and torture was used in the Inquisition to extract confessions from people who were believed to have practiced homosexuality. Homosexuals were burned to death as late as the second half of the eighteenth century. Under the influence of the Judeo-Christian tradition, the laws of most Western countries have made homosexual behavior a crime, and homosexuals could be punished by imprisonment or even death, depending on the country and the historical era.

Given this strong negative sanctioning of homosexual behavior, it is understandable that in the past most homosexuals have tried to keep their sexual orientation secret. As a result, historians have little concrete data with which to evaluate the form or frequency of homosexual practices during the past centuries in the West. Some very famous people appear to have been homosexual, however. These include Leonardo da Vinci, Michelangelo, Francis Bacon, Tchaikovsky, Oscar Wilde, Somerset Maugham, Lawrence of Arabia, John M. Keynes, D. H. Lawrence, Walt Whitman, Herman Melville, Nathaniel Hawthorne, Henry James, George Santayana, and W. H. Auden (*see* Box 11.1)[15] Again, much less is known about lesbians than about male homosexuals. Women have apparently been more secretive about their private lives, and historians have focused less attention on women than on men.

It has only been in the past decade or two that the laws and religious teachings about homosexuality have begun to change in the United States and other Western countries. As of 1977, homosexual behavior in private between consenting adults was a criminal offense in 31 states (*see* Chapter 14).[16] Police harassment of homosexuals

---

[13]West (1977), p. 117f.
[14]See Genesis 19, Judges 19, Leviticus 20, Romans 1:27.

[15]Rowse (1977).
[16]Bell and Weinberg (1978), p. 187.

Box 11.1   Homosexuals in History

Some prominent figures in history have been homosexuals.

Leonardo da Vinci (1452–1519), one of the best examples of "the Renaissance man," was an outstanding painter, sculptor, architect, engineer, scientist, and musician. From childhood he loved nature and was an avid student of all natural phenomena. Leonardo's art had a pervasive influence on the European art of the sixteenth century and subsequent periods. The Mona Lisa—among the best known of his works—is one of the most sensitive and mysterious portraits of a woman ever to be painted. Leonardo was fascinated by everything and created voluminous notebooks full of pictures and theories in the fields of mathematics, engineering, science, and military strategy. No aspect of life escaped his sensitive eye. The notebooks reveal the mind of a genius far ahead of his time. Leonardo did extensive anatomical studies of plants, animals, and people; designed flying machines; and conducted scientific studies of geology, botany, mechanics, and hydraulics. Leonardo was a gentle, reserved person who remained aloof from most of society. His work made him famous throughout Europe and his personal charm and creativity "won all hearts," yet he led a withdrawn, secretive life.

Walt Whitman (1819–1892) was one of America's finest poets. His poetry was an affirmation of individual freedom and a tribute to the brotherhood of man. Because his homosexuality and unconventional moral values were not deeply hidden, his work was strongly criticized, he was fired from his job in the Department of the Interior, and his publishers dropped his publications. Whitman's empathy for working-class people and his refusal to be fettered by the constraints of middle-class life led him to keep his roots in the lives of the common people and be their spokesman. During the Civil War, Whitman worked as a volunteer nurse in a Washington hospital

Leonardo da Vinci, self-portrait

where he dedicated himself to helping the wounded. For three years he unflaggingly devoted long hours to sustaining the body and spirit of men who had borne the brunt of the most tragic war of the century. Whitman wrote: "Sometimes I took up my quarters in the hospital, and slept or watched there several nights in succession. Those three years I consider the greatest privilege and satisfaction . . . and, of course, the most profound lesson of my life." Whitman cared for men of both the North and the South, and eventually found a lifelong friendship with a captured Southerner, Pete Doyle, who later was invaluable in describing Whitman's life after he gained posthumous fame.

Herman Melville (1819–1891) is among the great American writers and is

[1]Rowse (1977).

Walt Whitman

Herman Melville

well known in world literature. Melville grew up in a poor family and was 12 when his father died. At 15 he quit school and at 20 he went to sea—to a man's world— where he gained the experiences that would shape much of his later writing. Among his adventures were intolerable hardships on a whaler, escape from the ship, capture by cannibals (who treated him well), rescue, and sojourns in Tahiti and other Pacific islands. His early books captured the excitement of his experiences and brought him success and prosperity. As his style matured, he wrote *Moby Dick,* which is a highly symbolic philosophical treatise on good and evil. The increasing complexity and obscurity of this and subsequent works was beyond his audience, and his contemporaries ignored the works that have best stood the test of time. At the age of 31, Melville met Nathaniel Hawthorne, who was 15 years older. Although both men were extremely

withdrawn and private people, Melville wrote enthusiastically of Hawthorne's work. The affair itself did not last long. Hawthorne was married and the two men's personalities differed too much for a lasting relationship. Homoerotic themes are present in much of Melville's work, and they became more pronounced after the end of the relationship with Hawthorne. Mrs. Hawthorne described Melville as follows: "As for external polish, or mere courtesy of manner, he never possessed more than a tolerably educated bear. In his gentler moods, there was a tenderness in his voice, eyes, mouth, in his gesture, which few men could resist, and no women." As Melville lost readers, he was forced to sell his property and take a low-paying job as a customs inspector in New York City. When he died he was poor and unknown. Thirty years after his death he was "rediscovered," and his works were truly appreciated for the first time.

sometimes continues even in those states without laws against homosexual behavior, as police use loitering, disorderly conduct, and other charges to arrest homosexuals. Male homosexuals are much more likely to be arrested than lesbians. The law and police activity have caused a great deal of problems and anguish for homosexuals. In Bell and Weinberg's study in 1970, 27 percent of male homosexuals and 4 percent of lesbians in the legally liberal San Francisco area had been picked up or arrested in connection with homosexuality.[17] For a long time the medical profession and psychiatry supported the theory that homosexuality was a perversion and illness. Theories that develop the view that homosexuality is an illness are presented on pages 367 to 369.

During the 1970s several of the Protestant denominations liberalized their views on homosexuality, welcoming homosexuals as fully approved members and in some cases allowing them to become ministers. Others have established study groups to reconsider the historical position that condemns homosexuality. The Roman Catholic Church—along with the United Methodist Church and several other Protestant denominations—continues to hold that homosexuality is an unnatural and unacceptable act (see Chapter 15). In a 1966 poll only 9 percent of Americans thought that homosexuality was a sin.[18] A 1977 U.S. poll revealed that even though the majority of Americans did not approve of homosexuality, 56 percent would vote in favor of legislation that guaranteed civil rights for homosexuals.[19]

The gradual acceptance of homosexuality in some sectors of American society has resulted from several types of social influences. The gay community has become better organized and more outspoken in demanding equal rights and legal protection for homosexuals. Although far from completely successful, Gay Liberation has furthered the cause of homosexuals. The "sexual revolution" of the 1960s and 1970s made many Americans more tolerant of variations in sexual behavior and variations in life-style (see Chapter 13), and these more liberal attitudes have benefited the homosexuals. Studies such as those by Kinsey, Hooker, Freedman, and more recently by Bell and Weinberg, Masters and Johnson, Jay and Young, and others have made available scientific information that dispels many of the myths about homosexuality.

Nevertheless, society changes slowly and modifying the laws does not change people's thoughts and feelings over night. Most homosexuals continue to feel the repressive attitudes of society. The uneasiness, and even hatred, that some people show toward homosexuals can cause homosexuals to feel paranoid, cut off, lonely, or depressed. As a group, homosexuals report lower self-acceptance than heterosexuals probably because of the stigma, social pressure, and hostile feelings they experience. However, homosexuals who have close, supportive relationships with other homosexuals score the same as heterosexuals in self-acceptance.[20] Because of the increasing societal tolerance of homosexual behavior and greater support from the gay community, many homosexuals are finding it easier to accept their life-style and sexual orientation than was possible in the past. A decade or two ago, many homosexuals remained "in the closet"; that is, they kept their homosexuality concealed and avoided public activities that would expose their secret. As a consequence, many were cut off from contacts and stable relationships. Many homosexuals are discovering that homosexuality need not be viewed as an illness or a perversion and hence are escaping the self-

---

[17]Ibid., p. 189.
[18]Weinberg and Williams (1974), pp. 19–20.
[19]Yankelovich et al. (1977).

[20]Bell and Weinberg (1978), pp. 200, 209 and 216.

doubts and guilt that were more commonly felt a decade or two ago.

As society becomes more tolerant of homosexuality, the homosexual life-style can also change. When homosexuality is treated as a perversion, homosexuals are forced into secrecy, may be forced to frequent bars for picking up contacts, and may feel forced to engage in fleeting, anonymous sex. In areas where homosexuality is now more openly accepted, homosexual men and women can live more open and unrestricted lives, and their life-styles begin to look more and more like those of heterosexuals. In general, homosexuals are more accepted in urban areas than in rural areas and more accepted in liberal than in conservative areas.[21] However, even today few homosexuals feel completely free of social pressure. Masters and Johnson found that most homosexual couples valued their partners as a "port in the storm," where they could escape oppressive social attitudes.

The Kinsey Continuum

There is another dimension of variability to homosexual behavior that we have not yet mentioned. Not all homosexuals are exclusively homosexual in partner preference. There is a continuum that extends from exclusive homosexuality to exclusive heterosexuality, and people's sexual practices can be located at various points along this continuum. As Kinsey stated:

Not all things are black nor all things white. It is a fundamental of taxonomy that nature rarely deals with discrete categories. The living world is a continuum in each and every one of its aspects. The sooner we learn this concerning human sexual behavior the sooner we shall reach a sound understanding of the realities of sex.[22]

Kinsey devised a seven-point scale (from 0 to 6) to categorize a person's degree of homosexual preference (see Figure 11.1). A

[21]Masters and Johnson (1979), p. 229.
[22]Kinsey et al. (1948), p. 639.

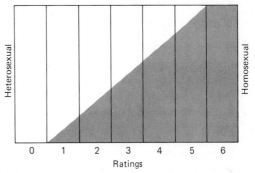

FIGURE 11.1   Heterosexual-homosexual rating scale. From Kinsey et al., *Sexual Behavior in the Human Female* (Philadelphia: Saunders, 1953), p. 470. Courtesy of the Institute for Sex Research.

person who is categorized as a 6 on the scale is exclusively homosexual, with no heterosexual inclinations. At the other end of the continuum is the person who is categorized as a 0 on the scale, who is exclusvely heterosexual with no homosexual inclinations. The bisexual, with equal interest in homosexual and heterosexual activity, is at the midpoint of the continuum, in category 3 (see Box 11.2). People in categories 1 and 5 have predominantly heterosexual (1) or homosexual (5) orientations, with only incidental interest in the other sex. Categories 2 and 4 include those in whom a clear preference for one sex coexists with a lesser but still active interest in the other.

This rating scale indicates not the amount of sexual activity but only the ratio between two sexual orientations. A person with 100 heterosexual and 10 homosexual experiences would be placed close to the heterosexual end of the scale, whereas a person with 10 homosexual and no heterosexual experiences would be at the other end of the continuum.

Table 11.1 summarizes Kinsey's findings about people's degrees of homosexual experience. The top category (0) contains people who have never had any homosexual experiences. The next line (categories 1–6)

Box 11.2   Bisexuals and Ambisexuals

Bisexuals are people who engage in both homosexual and heterosexual activities. They would be classified in the middle range of Kinsey's homosexual-heterosexual scale. These people claim that they are not "basically" one way or the other and that they do not simply alternate sexual objects occasionally. Rather, they claim a permanent need for relations with both sexes—to enjoy the best of two worlds, as it were. Other people may view them as standard homosexuals who are simply rationalizing their activities. Because of their dual orientations they are sometimes called "AC-DC" (for "alternating" and "direct" current). While some may exhibit conflicts over their ambivalent sexuality, others do not.

During their research on homosexuals, Masters and Johnson studied 12 people who carried bisexuality to an extreme.[1] These people were designated as "ambisexuals," which Masters and Johnson defined as people of either sex who truly enjoy sexual activities with partners of either sex to an equal degree and have no interest in establishing a continuing relationship with partners of either sex. The ambisexuals showed an equal interest and sexual involvement in sexual activities with either men or women. They clearly enjoyed sexual interactions with both heterosexuals and homosexuals, and they expressed no value judgements about homosexuality or heterosexuality. They played either role equally well and neither defended nor berated either sexual orientation. They saw sexuality as part of the human birthright, to be directed in any way a person chooses.

Given the pervasive nature of sexual bias in American society, these people were remarkably free of sexual prejudice. The ambisexuals had a great deal of sexual appeal that resulted from their ability to express sexual interest free of prejudice and bias and from their high level of confidence in sexual performance.

However, the fact that ambisexuals had no lingering attraction to either sex and no interest in settling down with any specific individual meant that they ended up with a lonely life-style. They were attracted to people sexually but felt little interest in or affection for them. Lacking any psychosexual identification with any of their partners, the ambisexuals adopted a "man-is-an-island" philosophy. Such complete neutrality between the heterosexual and homosexual ends of the Kinsey continuum makes ambisexuality quite rare in society.

[1]Masters and Johnson (1979), pp. 144ff and 221ff.

shows the number of people who have had any degree of homosexual contact (from 1 to 6). Each step down the table focuses on people who are more exclusively homosexual. It is clear that in the 1940s, when society was sexually more restrictive and harsh on homosexuals than it is today, a large number of people had "at least some homosexual experience" (1–6), while as many as 3–8 percent of women and 7–26 percent of men had "mostly homosexual experience" (4–6). In most categories the proportion of female homosexuals is only about a third as great as that of the male group. (See Chapter 8 for limitations of this information.)

Adolescent Homosexuality

About 9 percent of young people in the United States have one or more homosexual experiences between the ages of 13 and 19. As with adults, the incidence is higher among males (11 percent) than females (6 percent). The likelihood of homosexual activities in adolescence is significantly greater among those

Table 11.1 Heterosexual-Homosexual Ratings (ages 20–35)

	Category	In Females (percent)	In Males (percent)
0	Entirely heterosexual experience		
	Single	61–72	53–78
	Married	89–90	90–92
	Previously married	75–80	
1–6	At least some homosexual experience	11–20	18–42
2–6	More than incidental homosexual experience	6–14	13–38
3–6	As much or more homosexual experience than heterosexual experience	4–11	9–32
4–6	Mostly homosexual experience	3–8	7–26
5–6	Almost exclusively homosexual experience	2–6	5–22
6	Exclusively homosexual experience	1–3	3–16

Data are from Kinsey et al. (1953), p. 488.

who have had homosexual experiences prior to adolescence.

Contrary to popular myths that portray adult homosexuals as preying on the young and innocent, most adolescents who have homosexual experiences share their first such experience with another adolescent. There are no data to support the idea that a homosexual teacher is any more likely than a heterosexual teacher to molest a child. Thirty-seven percent of boys and 14 percent of girls report someone making homosexual advances to them on at least one occasion, but most adolescents apparently turn away such approaches without trauma or serious emotional upset. Among the minority who have homosexual experiences during adolescence, the frequency of such activity appears to be low, and in many instances it is motivated by curiosity or factors other than a love relationship.

Change

Some people change in their level of homosexual or heterosexual commitment during life. In some cases, a person may spend the first 25 or 30 years of life as a heterosexual (0 on the scale), then discover homosexual relationships and adopt a new position on the scale with a stronger homo-

sexual orientation. Likewise, some people who originally had a strong homosexual orientation may change to a more heterosexual orientation. Some of these changes occur spontaneously and others are made with therapeutic assistance.

Doubtlessly, some people can change to become more heterosexual or more homosexual with relatively little effort. If they want to change and find a cooperative partner who will help and support them during the transition, they can probably make the change without major problems. Generally, people do not change to another preference against their will. In cases where homosexuals have been coerced into therapy by relatives or legal authorities, only a very small percentage have been changed to be exclusively heterosexual.[23] In contrast, when people want to change but do not know how, therapy can be quite effective. For example, Masters and Johnson have developed a therapeutic procedure in which about 80 percent of the homosexuals treated became heterosexual within two weeks.[24] (During a five-year follow-up period, several reverted to homosexuality and some could no longer be con-

[23]Bandura (1969), p. 519.
[24]Masters and Johnson (1979).

tacted, lowering the known long-term success rate to about 60 percent.[25] Masters and Johnson observed, much as others had before, that the therapeutic change depended on the cooperation of the homosexual and the support of a heterosexual partner who can help make the transition to a heterosexual orientation more rewarding and positive for the homosexual.

It must be pointed out that most homosexuals are quite satisfied with their homosexual orientation and very few want to become heterosexual. Bell and Weinberg asked homosexuals whether they would want to use a "magic heterosexual pill" if such a device allowed them to make an effortless change to heterosexuality. Only 5 percent of the lesbians and 14 percent of the male homosexuals said that they would want the pill.[26] It used to be thought that heterosexual or homosexual fantasies and dreams represented a subconscious wish to change to a hetero- or homosexual orientation. Bell and Weinberg found that 24 percent of homosexual males and 35 percent of lesbians do have heterosexual fantasies, and 34 percent of male homosexuals and 52 percent of lesbians have heterosexual sex dreams.[27] In the past, therapists have often used heterosexual dreams and fantasies as evidence that a homosexual should undergo therapy. Masters and Johnson's study revealed, however, that both homosexuals and heterosexuals commonly have cross-preference fantasies, and that none felt the need or desire to act out the fantasy. Masters and Johnson recommend a rethinking of the notion that fantasies reveal hidden needs for a change in sexual orientation.[28]

[25]Since some people did not maintain contact with Masters and Johnson during the five-year follow-up period, the actual success rate cannot be determined precisely; but it lies between 43 and 72 percent. The success rate stated in the text is based on only those people who maintained contact during the entire five-year follow-up period.

[26]Bell and Weinberg (1978), pp. 124 and 129.

[27]Ibid., p. 289.

[28]Masters and Johnson (1979), chap. 17.

Laboratory Studies

In 1979 Masters and Johnson published a book that summarized a decade of laboratory research with homosexuals and provided a comparison with heterosexuals of the same general age, socioeconomic status, and educational background.[29] Careful laboratory observations on the sexual activities of homosexuals and heterosexuals revealed virtually no differences in the biological sexual responses of homosexuals and heterosexuals. The physiological responses of homosexual and heterosexual females were almost identical. The same was true for males.

There were differences, however, in the way that homosexuals and heterosexuals treated their partners during sexual interactions. In general, the homosexuals were less rushed during sexual interactions than were the heterosexuals. The homosexuals lingered over the various stages of increasing sexual excitement in order to allow their partner to enjoy the pleasure. Heterosexuals, on the other hand, were much more rushed, goal-oriented, working for the end point of orgasm. The homosexuals were more communicative than the heterosexuals, often asking their partners whether this felt good, or that would be preferable, or any changes should be made. This extra level of communication allowed the homosexuals to be more sensitive to each other's needs than were the heterosexuals, and it facilitated their pleasure-oriented—as opposed to orgasm-oriented—sexual interactions. In addition, the homosexuals had better empathy for their partner's sexual needs, and this "same-sex empathy" helped the homosexuals to be more sensitive lovers. Since females are likely to know what kind of stimulation females like and males are likely to know what males like, homosexuals have a significant advantage over heterosexuals in being able to predict their partner's needs.

[29]Ibid.

Some people wonder what homosexuals do during sexual interactions. Basically homosexuals engage in all the sexual activities that heterosexuals do, except for vaginal intercourse.[30] This includes manual and oral stimulation of the breasts and genitals and, for male homosexuals, anal intercourse. There is no "homosexual act" that cannot be performed by a heterosexual couple. What characterizes an act as homosexual is not the act itself but the fact that the partners are of the same sex. Anal intercourse carries some of the same risks as does vaginal intercourse. Venereal disease, for instance, is readily transmitted in this way, and promiscuous homosexuals have some of the highest rates of such disease in the country (see Chapter 7).

Multiple Etiologies

Why do people become homosexuals? That is a classic question which many heterosexuals have asked. The answer is no easier than the answer to the question, "Why do people become heterosexuals?" There is an enormous amount of learning involved in developing any sexual orientation, and a multitude of experiences influence the particular balance of homosexual and heterosexual interests and behaviors that a person acquires.

For many years psychiatrists searched for one single theory that would explain homosexual behavior. This resulted in part from the mistaken idea that homosexuality was a single entity and therefore it would have one etiology or one set of causes. In the past when homosexuality was considered to be a disease or a mental illness, it was only logical for the medical profession to assume that they might find one underlying cause and one developmental pattern. Current research suggests that homosexuality is not an illness but may be a learned preference.[31]

Now that it is realized that there are many forms of homosexual behavior, it is easy to understand why recent studies on the development of homosexuals from childhood through adulthood reveal no single pattern of causal events, no single etiology. Instead, the data indicate that there are multiple experiential routes that may result in a homosexual preference.

Homosexual Life-Styles

The first criterion for differentiating among homosexual life-styles is whether a man or woman is a covert or an overt homosexual. Covert homosexuals are to be found in all sectors of our society. They "pass" for heterosexuals in most of their business and social relationships. They may even be married, be parents, and in most other respects remain indistinguishable from the rest of the population. They may lead "double lives," or restrict their homosexual behavior to periods when they are away from home. Overt homosexuals constitute a smaller group than covert homosexuals. They have given up all pretense and openly rely on the homosexual community for gratification of their sexual needs. Because of certain important differences, we shall discuss the life-styles of female and male homosexuals separately.

Lesbians

Lesbians share a great deal in common with heterosexual women. They are generally more interested in love and fidelity than are either homosexual or heterosexual males.[32] Lesbians tend to have only a small number of sexual partners during their lives. In Bell and Weinberg's study, 57 percent of lesbians had had fewer than 10 partners in their lives (whereas 57 percent of the male homosexuals had had more than 250 partners).[33] In addition, sex plays a less important role in lesbian relationships than in the relationships

[30]Bell and Weinberg (1978), pp. 55ff; Masters and Johnson (1979).
[31]Gagnon and Simon (1973), and Masters and Johnson (1979), pp. 271–273.

[32]Gagnon and Simon (1973), pp. 176ff.
[33]Bell and Weinberg (1978), p. 308.

Table 11.2 Percent of Homosexuals Living Various Life-Styles in San Francisco in 1970

	Lesbians	Male Homosexuals
Close couples	28	10
Open couples	17	18
Functionals	10	15
Dysfunctionals	5	12
Asexuals	11	16
Other	29	29

Data are from Bell and Weinberg (1978), pp. 346–347.

of male homosexuals (and male heterosexuals). Again, this seems to reflect the general socialization of females in our culture: Females are socialized to value love more than sex (while males are more likely to be socialized to place a greater importance on sex).[34]

In Bell and Weinberg's study, 45 percent of lesbians were currently living with one partner as a couple, compared with 28 percent of the male homosexuals (*see* Table 11.2). In fact, the most preferred life-style among lesbians was that of living as a close couple. Although they did go to the movies, the theater, restaurants, and other public places, they were less likely to do so than male homosexuals. The picture that emerges is one of women who value close, monogamous relationships and, when possible, develop them to the fullest.

Although the stereotype of lesbian relationships is that some women play a male role while others play a female role, studies find that most lesbians do not show this type of role specialization. Most lesbians prefer partners with the more feminine characteristics that they have been socialized to value: gentleness, affection, fidelity, and nonaggressiveness. Bell and Weinberg found that 92 percent of close lesbian couples shared their roles equally.[35]

[34]Safilios-Rothschild (1977).
[35]Bell and Weinberg (1978), p. 324.

The majority of lesbians, like their male counterparts, are indistinguishable from the general population in physique, dress, and mannerisms. Two women may live together for ten years or more and never arouse the suspicions of their neighbors or families, much less of casual acquaintances, which is not true for men in a similar situation. Consequently the lesbian is subject to relatively little harassment or social pressure, except for the occasional well-meaning friend or relative who insists on arranging heterosexual dates for her. (Of course, women friends may also live together without being lesbians.)

Some lesbians do visit gay bars, but even in the lesbian bars differences in atmosphere and activities can be detected. The lesbian rarely goes to a gay bar looking for a pickup. She usually goes with a friend to socialize, exchange gossip, have a few drinks, and dance. (Dancing and petting are often restricted to private back rooms, where only customers known to the management are admitted.)

Male Homosexuals

There is a greater diversity among male homosexuals than among lesbians. Some male homosexuals are conventionally married men, others live with another man in a close relationship, and others cruise the bars looking for "action." Most studies show that male homosexuals are more interested than lesbians in having sex with a variety of partners. Male homosexuals share much of the typical male socialization that heterosexual males receive in our culture, which orients them to wanting more sex than females want. They also tend to want more variety in partners and prefer sex without commitment more than lesbians do. Of the homosexual males in Bell and Weinberg's study (with an average age in the early thirties), 26 percent had had 1000 or more partners and 74 percent said that more than half of their partners were strangers (while in contrast only 6 percent of lesbians said that more than half of their partners were strangers).[36] Male homosexuals also tend to engage in sex more frequently than lesbians do: 70 percent of the male homosexuals in Bell and Weinberg's study reported having sex once a week or more, whereas only 54 percent of females reported this. The male homosexuals tended to "cruise" for possible new partners much more than lesbians did. Only 3 percent of lesbians cruised once a week or more, but 42 percent of male homosexuals did. Most homosexual males strongly prefer masculine partners to effeminate partners. Similar to the lesbians, male homosexuals do not have as many role differences as heterosexuals. When two male homosexuals interact they usually play relatively equal, and generally masculine, roles.

Male homosexuals tend to be more visible in society than lesbians. It is true that many "pass" as heterosexuals much of the time, but those who seek multiple partners, frequent bars, and get involved in the gay culture become significantly more visible than lesbians usually do. As a consequence, male homosexuals are more likely to be the target of social pressures, to be arrested for homosexually related activities, and to suffer blackmail, extortion, or beatings.[37]

If a man does not blatantly display his homosexual way of life, can he be identified through physique, dress, mannerisms, and so on? The answer is generally "no." Probably the most common misunderstanding of male homosexuals is reflected in stereotypes that portray them as "effeminate," "swishy," "faggots," or "fairies." There are individuals who fit these stereotypes, to be sure, and within the homosexual community they are known as "queens." But these men represent only a very small proportion of the homosexual population and are by no means appreciated by the rest. Some gay bars will actually refuse admission to "queens in drag"—that is, men dressed in flagrantly effeminate fashion.

At the other extreme, there are homosexuals who make a point of looking and acting extremely "masculine." Some are bodybuilding enthusiasts, with formidable muscular development. Others may be military career officers with all the trappings of power and authority. (There were reportedly high proportions of homosexuals in the Nazi *Wehrmacht* and among cowboys in the old American West.)

Most homosexuals look and act much the same as everyone else; they do not stand out from the heterosexual population. However, homosexuals can usually identify each other by subtle cues.

Types of Life-Styles

Given the fact that there are many types of homosexual life-styles and that no single description can capture the variability seen in the homosexual population, it is not easy to present a simple portrayal of the homosexual way of life. Yet there are some features of the homosexual patterns that can be alluded to at a general level. In Bell and Weinberg's study 71 percent of the homosexuals could be categorized as belonging to one of five general types of life-styles (*see* Table 11.2). The remaining 29 percent were too diverse to be easily categorized.

Close Couples

About 28 percent of lesbians and 10 percent of male homosexuals lived as close couples, much as if they were happily married. Some 30 percent of these lesbians had been living together for four or more years, as had 38 percent of the closely coupled men. The closely coupled homosexuals rarely cruised for new sexual contacts. They had the fewest sexual, social, or psychological problems. They were unlikely to regret being

[36]Ibid., pp. 229 and 308.
[37]Ibid., pp. 187–194.

homosexual. They were happy with their partners and enjoyed spending their leisure time at home. These people were exuberant about life and had warm and caring relationships. They were the happiest of all the homosexuals interviewed.

Open Couples

About 17 percent of lesbians and 18 percent of male homosexuals lived as open couples. These people were less happy with their partners, less deeply committed to them, and more likely to look for social and sexual gratification outside their relationship. The openly coupled men cruised more than average and the openly coupled lesbians did more cruising than any other lesbians. The openly coupled homosexuals worried that their partners would find out about the cruising. They had a variety of social and sexual problems with their partners. On the whole, the psychological adjustment of the openly coupled homosexuals was quite normal, although they were less happy, less self-accepting and more lonely than the closely coupled homosexuals. Lesbians found the open-couple relationship more unacceptable than male homosexuals did.

Functionals

People who were well adjusted, had few if any sexual problems, did not live with another regular roommate, and followed a "swinging singles" life-style were designated as functionals. Some 15 percent of the homosexual males and 10 percent of the lesbians were in this group. These people had a very high level of sexual activity and a large number of partners; and they centered much of their lives around their sexual activities. They were highly involved in the gay community and cruised a great deal. They had the least amount of regrets about being homosexual. They thought of themselves as very sexually attractive and were much more interested in having multiple partners than in finding someone with whom to establish a close relationship. They had many friends and were energetic, exuberant, friendly, self-reliant, and almost as happy as the close couples. Their overall social and psychological adjustment was second only to the closely coupled homosexuals.

Dysfunctionals

Homosexuals who had many partners, were not living in couples, and had psychological and sexual problems were designated as dysfunctionals. About 12 percent of male homosexuals and 5 percent of lesbians were in this group. These people were prone to worry, find little gratification in life, and show a poorer overall adjustment than the previous three types. They were most likely to regret being homosexual. They worried about their sexual inadequacies, their inability to form an affectionate relationship, and their lack of fulfillment. If any group of people came close to fitting the stereotype of the "tormented homosexual," it was the dysfunctionals.

Asexuals

Some homosexuals have a low level of sexual activity, few partners, and no close relationships. These people, designated as asexuals, were characterized by their lack of involvement with others. Some 16 percent of male homosexuals and 11 percent of lesbians followed this solitary life-style. They tended to be older than the people in the other categories and they tended to spend much time alone. Although they described themselves as lonely, their general psychological adjustment was about the same as the general homosexual population.

The Gay Community

Although many homosexuals used to remain "in the closet," many are now "coming out" and joining with others to create a gay community. The gay community provides social and emotional support for members who are having troubles, and it provides an easy way for homosexuals to meet others having similar interests.

In addition, many homosexuals have organized various groups designed to defend gay rights and to counteract the distorted images of homosexuals held in many parts of society. The Mattachine Society was the first major U.S. homophile organization. Founded in 1950 in Los Angeles, it was at first a secret organization, although the secrecy was dropped after a few years. The Mattachine Society (named after medieval court jesters, who were fearlessly outspoken) is now a national organization with chapters in many major cities and a predominantly but not exclusively homosexual membership. The purpose of such groups is to promote fair and equal treatment for homosexuals and to protest the oppression and abuse to which they have been subjected, as have other minorities. The Mattachine Society holds meetings, arranges lectures, and issues several publications (for example, *Homosexual Citizen* and *Mattachine Newsletter*).

The best known of the lesbian organizations is The Daughters of Bilitis (founded in 1956), which draws its name from a book of prose poems by Pierre Louys, which appeared in 1894 and purported to be a translation from the Greek of Sappho's love poems to a courtesan named Bilitis. The general aims and functions of this society are comparable to those of male homosexual organizations. These women, however, claim double social disadvantages, being both female and homosexual. *The Ladder: A Lesbian Review* is the society's official publication.

Since the organization of these original groups, important changes have been taking place in the homosexual world as part of the "gay liberation movement." Organizations like the Gay Liberation Front and the Gay Activist Alliance are much more open and forcible in their efforts to acquaint the public with their cause.[38]

The beginnings of gay liberation as a movement go back to June 1969, when there was a riot by homosexuals at a gay bar in Greenwich Village that was reportedly precipitated by police harassment. Immediately following that riot the first Gay Liberation Front was organized in New York City. There are currently an estimated 50 or so such groups, but no national Gay Liberation Front as yet. Despite the common name, these organizations vary widely, from moderately conservative to extremely radical in orientation.[39]

Despite these differences there is generally far greater readiness among homosexuals in these groups to come out into the open. On a number of college campuses, for example, there are semiformal homosexual organizations that make no effort or pretense at concealing their identities. At least among younger homosexuals there is now a tendency to shun gay bars and other traditional hangouts in favor of dances and a variety of social and political functions. There are also gay communes, "consciousness-raising groups," and various alliances with other "liberation movements" in pursuit of common goals.

These often dramatic changes in attitudes both inside and outside the homosexual community are not uniform throughout the country. In some cities police officers participate in encounter sessions with homosexuals in an effort to further mutual understanding. In others, homosexuals continue to live in constant fear of the police. In view of these disparities it is impossible to describe general patterns of homosexual life. Much of what is said in this chapter, for example, may be applicable to some parts of the country but out

[38]This new attitude is partly reflected in the proliferation of such homosexual publications as *Gay, Come Out, The Advocate, Gay Power, Gay Flames, Gay Sunshine, San Francisco Free Press, Vector,* and so on.

[39]Kameny (1971).

of date in others, or true of some subgroups but not at all of others.

Homosexuality in Prisons

It is well known that homosexuality is common in men's prisons, but it exists in women's prisons too. Most of the people who engage in prison homosexuality are heterosexual by choice.

Homosexuality in prison is a complex topic that cannot usefully be discussed separately from prison society as a whole, including its internal organization and codes of conduct. For some people homosexual contacts become the only way to counteract desperate loneliness behind bars. For others it is a means of establishing their positions in the prison pecking order. Given the rough environment typical of men's prisons, homosexual acts often become imbued with a ferocity of which many a man with no homosexual leanings becomes the helpless victim. Although female homosexuality is common among heterosexual women in prison, it often exists in the form of quiet relationships, without the violence prevalent in men's prisons.

Homosexuality as an Illness

Although the American Psychiatric Association has rejected the "homosexuality as illness" concept, as we have seen, many professionals, particularly Freudian psychoanalysts, maintain a different viewpoint. Their judgment is based on both theoretical grounds and clinical experience. Homosexuals are viewed as having suffered stunted psychosexual development, or as having been conditioned to respond to inappropriate sexual objects. They are considered unhappy; immature; and neurotic; unable to achieve satisfying sex lives; and missing the rewards of mature heterosexual relationships, parenthood, and family life.

A comparison of self-ratings for general unhappiness and mistrust of others did show a higher incidence of these feelings among male homosexuals than among the general male population. However, there was no significant difference between the two groups in reported psychosomatic complaints.[40]

It is reasonable to assume that homosexuals who seek psychiatric help are neurotic and unhappy people. Why else would they seek such help? But the same reasoning applies to heterosexuals who seek psychiatric treatment. What is less clear is whether or not homosexuals who express no need for clinical assistance are as badly off; that is, whether their claims of contentment (provided that they are not harassed) are justified or simply pretense.[41] At any rate, homosexuality in the West, as in most of the rest of the world, creates formidable problems of adjustment for the individual, especially in authoritarian countries.

If one accepts the notion that homosexuality is an illness (apart from the problem of social reactions to it), then one can legitimately ask what causes it. As for other forms of deviant behavior, there are many theories of causation, but none that is generally accepted. At present we simply do not know with any certainty what factors are the critical determinants in homosexual (or heterosexual) behavior.

The situation is akin to our understanding of handedness. We know that most people are right-handed, but a minority are left-handed and another minority are ambidextrous. Is handedness an inherited trait or a behavior pattern acquired during early development? Is there any advantage to species survival in being right-handed?

Until recently there was an obvious advantage for heterosexuals in terms of species survival. But does an orientation which pre-

[40]Weinberg and Williams, *op. cit.*, p. 152.

[41]For a challenge to definitions of homosexuality as a clinical entity, *see* Hooker in Ruitenbeek, ed. (1963), pp. 141–161; Kameny (1971); and Masters and Johnson (1979).

cludes reproduction of the species constitute an illness? The theories to be discussed here have been chosen primarily to reflect current thinking on this problem, rather than final answers.

Biological Causes

Physical examinations, chromosome studies, and endocrine studies have so far failed to identify any particular biological difference between homosexuals and heterosexuals. There is thus no evidence to date that biological factors determine object choice. The author of one large-scale study of identical twins has claimed a genetic basis for homosexuality.[42] He has shown that all the identical twins studied were concordant for homosexuality (that is, if one twin was homosexual, so was the other). Among fraternal twins the degree of concordance for homosexuality was not statistically significant. This study has been criticized on the grounds that similarities in environment were not taken into consideration, and other investigators have failed to replicate its findings.

The lack of evidence does not, however, mean that none will be forthcoming. Many researchers remain convinced (as Freud was) that there is a genetic or constitutional predisposition toward homosexuality, and that the life experiences of the individual serve either to reinforce or to extinguish it.

One theory involves the concept of *infantile bisexuality*, in which elements of both masculinity and femininity are assumed to be present at birth and the balance between them to be determined by genetic and hormone factors. In Chapters 4 and 5 we discussed the different proportions in which male and female sex hormones are present in both sexes. There is a steadily growing body of evidence indicating that behavior and anatomy are both influenced by the relative amounts of sex hormones present.

[42]Kallman (1952).

A few investigators have reported male hormone deficiencies among male homosexuals, but one recent study found testosterone levels in a group of young, exclusively homosexual males to be significantly higher than in a control group of heterosexuals.[43]

Psychological Causes

Psychoanalytic studies have focused on the family relations of young boys who become homosexuals. A study by Bieber and his colleagues compared 106 male homosexuals with 100 male heterosexuals.[44] Although the fact that all the subjects were undergoing psychoanalytic treatment renders generalization from these data questionable, the findings are consistent with general observations about the families of many (but not all) homosexuals. Essentially the pattern found was that of a dominant mother and a passive father. The mother has further been described as overprotective and unusually intimate with her son. (Gebhard and his colleagues, among others, have shown that homosexuals are usually only children, youngest children, or youngest sons.)[45] The father, when present, has been described as detached, unaffectionate, and hostile toward his son. Psychoanalysts hypothesized that such parents tend to inhibit the expression of masculine behavior in their boys. The domineering mother is said to prohibit the expression of heterosexual impulses except when directed toward herself, as she is jealous of any interest that her son shows in any other female. The boy whose father is aloof or openly hostile lacks a masculine figure with whom he can identify and whose behavior he can use as a model. In later life the boy retains a fear of heterosexual relationships

[43]Brodie, et al. (1974)
[44]Bieber et al. (1962). The psychoanalytic literature on homosexuality is quite extensive. A classic reference work is Fenichel (1945). Other reviews can be found in Bieber et al. (1962), and Marmor, ed. (1965).
[45]Gebhard et al. (1965).

and a frustrated need for the masculine (paternal) love that he failed to receive as a child.

Psychoanalytic attempts to unravel the dynamics of homosexuality start with the assumption that all children are "polymorphously perverse," and that for various reasons some do not outgrow and repress these infantile perverse tendencies (see Chapter 8). The reasons may include, for instance, unresolved oedipal ties (to avoid conflict, the child may have become sexually attached to the parent of the same sex and may carry this pattern into his adult life) or castration anxiety (in which males consort with males because the sight of female genitals evokes earlier fears that they too may lose their penises; and in which females may prefer relations with each other to avoid being reminded that they lack penises). These conflicts, though simply stated here, are quite complex and submerged in the unconscious.

Critics of the theory that homosexuals harbor unconscious fears of women claim that it makes just as much sense to say that heterosexuals are plagued by unconscious fears of men. Furthermore, the pattern of intense involvement with the mother and a poor relationship with the father is not always present in a homosexual's background.

Explanations based on learning theories use the same concepts of conditioning and so on that we discussed in Chapter 8: that pleasant and painful experiences shape sexual orientations, which then remain subject to continuing modification. For instance, orgasm is a pleasurable and therefore reinforcing experience. If a person discovers that homosexually-produced orgasm is pleasant, there will be a tendency to repeat the experience, just as the person who finds heterosexually-produced orgasm reinforcing tends to repeat heterosexual activities. Although superficially quite plausible, these explanations are also by no means clearly supported by objective studies. Furthermore, they leave important questions unanswered. If, as Masters and Johnson imply, an orgasm by whatever means produces

the same sensation, why do most people (particularly males) shift from masturbation to heterosexual or homosexual outlets as they get older? It may be true in the animal world that "an orgasm is an orgasm is an orgasm." But for humans, psychological and cultural factors may well override physical pleasure, or perhaps we are creatures of instinct after all.

That childhood experiences are important is beyond doubt, but what specifically is relevant is more difficult to pinpoint. The notion that boys who are forced into homosexual activities by older men ("homosexual child molesters") necessarily become homosexuals when they grow up is difficult to evaluate. Some follow-up studies seem to show that it is unfounded. However, in the Gebhard sample a quarter of the homosexual adults in prison had had, as children, sexual contacts with adult males.[46] "Tomboyishness" and preference for sports or "being one of the boys" in young girls are not correlated with a woman's choice of women as sexual partners in adulthood. (But adolescent girls who become involved in frequent or prolonged "crushes" on other girls or older women may be exhibiting early homosexual tendencies.)

Treatment

For those who view homosexuality as a pathological condition, improvement or "cure" means changing the individual's orientation to a heterosexual one. Relatively few such "cures" have been reported. There are several reasons why.

First, most homosexuals do not consider themselves abnormal or sick and thus do not seek treatment. When they come to psychiatrists for problems of anxiety or depression, they may pay lip service to the need to resolve their "sexual problems" with-

[46]Gebhard et al. (1965), p. 356. For additional information on the effects of early homosexual experiences, see Westwood (1960), pp. 24–39; and Doshay (1969).

out any real intention of changing their orientations. What they want is relief of their symptoms.

A small percentage of homosexuals are apprehended and forced to undergo treatment by court order, either in state institutions or as a condition of probation. As we might suspect, such individuals are little motivated to change.

There are, finally, some individuals who seek psychiatric treatment of their own volition, who are genuinely eager to change their sexual orientations. The results of treatment in such situations is determined by several variables; for example, how long the patients have been homosexual and whether or not they have had heterosexual experiences. Some psychiatrists believe that changing the sexual orientation of homosexuals is either unnecessary or unrealistic, and consequently gear their treatment to helping individuals become "better adjusted" homosexuals so that they will no longer be dissatisfied with their orientations. "Cures" in this sense are more likely than those involving personality reorientation, but there are also reports of homosexuals who have been "cured" in the latter sense.

Even though some psychiatrists are openly hostile to homosexuals, the more general attitude is one of tolerance. This attitude is expressed in a famous letter from Freud to a mother who had requested treatment for her son:

April 9, 1935

Dear Mrs. X

I gather from your letter that your son is a homosexual. I am most impressed by the fact that you do not mention this term yourself in your information about him. May I question you, why do you avoid it? Homosexuality is assuredly no advantage, but it is nothing to be ashamed of, no vice, no degradation, it cannot be classified as an illness; we consider it to be a variation of sexual function produced by a certain arrest of sexual development. Many

highly respectable individuals of ancient and modern times have been homosexuals, several of the greatest men among them (Plato, Michelangelo, Leonardo da Vinci, etc.). It is a great injustice to persecute homosexuality as a crime, and cruelty too. If you do not believe me, read the books of Havelock Ellis.

By asking me if I can help, you mean, I suppose, if I can abolish homosexuality and make normal heterosexuality take its place. The answer is, in a general way, we cannot promise to achieve it. In a certain number of cases we succeed in developing the blighted germs of heterosexual tendencies which are present in every homosexual, in the majority of cases it is no more possible. It is a question of the quality and the age of the individual. The result of the treatment cannot be predicted.

What analysis can do for your son runs in a different line. If he is unhappy, neurotic, torn by conflicts, inhibited in his social life, analysis may bring him harmony, peace of mind, full efficiency, whether he remains a homosexual or gets changed. If you make up your mind he should have analysis with me (I don't expect you will!!) he has to come over to Vienna. I have no intention of leaving here. However, don't neglect to give me your answer.

Sincerely yours with kind wishes.

Freud

P.S. I did not find it difficult to read your handwriting. Hope you will not find my writing and my English a harder task.

Other Sexual Behaviors

Transsexualism

The transsexual is a person (usually a male) who wishes to be, or sincerely believes that he is, a member of the opposite sex. Some males say that they have always felt themselves to be "women in male bodies" and trace such feelings to their childhoods. Although the transsexual may engage in homosexual (as well as heterosexual) relations, these activities are not homosexual in their view. After all, if a man feels himself to be a

FIGURE 11.2   Dr. Richard Raskin (left), eye surgeon and championship tennis player, who became Dr. Renee Richards (right) after a sex-change operation. Wide World Photos.

woman, he will view sex with a man from a different perspective.

The transsexual male likes women and would prefer to be a full-fledged woman himself. He does everything possible to attain this end, with occasionally astounding results. The ultimate aim for many of these biological males is a "sex change" operation, in which the penis and the testes are removed and an artificial vagina is created through reconstruction of pelvic tissues. The individual thus altered can have vaginal coitus. Contrary to occasional newspaper reports, however, pregnancy is absolutely impossible. A full transplant of ovaries and uterus has never been attempted, although it is not beyond the realm of possibility.

A few people who have undergone sex change operations are relatively well known. Wendy Carlos (previously Walter Carlos) is probably best known for her development of and compositions for the Moog synthesizer. At the age of 5 or 6 Carlos became aware of a desire to be a female. Carlos states, "And I remember being convinced I was a little girl, much preferring long hair and girls' clothes,

and not knowing why my parents didn't see it clearly. I didn't understand why they insisted on treating me like a little boy."[46] In 1972 at the age of 32, Walter underwent a sex-change operation to become Wendy. Sex-change operations are now performed in a few medical centers in this country. Applicants are carefully screened to eliminate those with serious mental problems and those who might have second thoughts after the surgery. If the applicant has not already had hormone treatments, he must undergo them first. The resulting changes are marked but reversible, so that the patient's reactions can be further evaluated before the irrevocable step of surgery is taken.

Female transsexuals also feel they are in the wrong body and desire to be a male. About one female wants to change her body to that of a male for every four males desiring the opposite change. A female must undergo hormone therapy with androgens. A penis and scrotum are created from tissues in the genital area (see Box 2.5).

[46]Bell (1979).

Swinging

Swinging usually involves one married couple exchanging partners with another married couple in order to engage in sexual activity without commitment.[47] In some cases a married couple swings by adding one other person to their sexual interaction. There are also occasions when four or more people engage in group sex. Typically it is the husband who draws his wife into swinging. Usually swingers have sex with people they basically do not know or plan to become intimate with. After engaging in sexual activity with a couple on one occasion or sometimes two, the relationship usually ends: It is time to find another couple. Swingers generally do not want to become emotionally involved with their new partners. However, there are some couples who swing with friends over a long period of time. Swingers are predominantly middle class, white, and married. Studies indicate that in their normal, everyday lives, swingers are conventional people. It is estimated that about 2 percent of married couples have tried swinging on one occasion.[48] Many never repeat the experience. Only a minority of these couples continue to swing occasionally. The 1974 *Redbook* survey on female sexuality found that almost 4 percent of their sample had tried swinging, but half of these had done so only once.[49]

Swingers use several methods to locate other couples. Couples meet other swingers at swinging bars or clubs, through personal referral, and by actively recruiting new couples. They also contact fellow swingers by advertising in underground papers and swinger magazines. The following is an example of such an ad:

Washington, D.C.; 50 miles radius, early thirties; she, lovely, 37-26-38, sensuous; he, handsome,

athletic, but tender; like French culture, etc. Exchange pictures, phone, and address. Write Box #007.

After an exchange of pictures and letters, the two couples may meet for coffee or drinks and arrange a future place to engage in sex if all goes well. Usually the sexual encounter occurs at a motel or the home of one of the couples. The couples switch partners and go to separate rooms for the sexual interaction. Sometimes the sexual encounter occurs with both couples in the same room or with all people engaging in group sex together. There are also occasions for group sex during parties for swingers. Overt homosexual contact among males is rare during group sex, but it is common among females. Swingers often conceal their true identities from the couple with whom they are swinging because they do not want their swinging activities to become public knowledge for fear that it would damage their everyday life.

Fetishism

In fetishism usually an inanimate object takes on special sexual significance.[50] Most often it is a piece of clothing or footwear. Parts of the body may also take on fetishistic significance, however. The boundary between normally erotogenic objects or parts of the body and fetishes is frequently quite nebulous. Many heterosexual males, for instance, are aroused by the sight of female underwear. Many males and females are also partial to particular parts of the anatomy of the opposite sex besides the genitals. Such attractions are a common part of sexual behavior.

There is a group of people in whom such partiality becomes quite pronounced.

---

[47]For a discussion of swinging see Denfield and Gordon (1970), Bartell (1971), and Gilmartin (1977).
[48]Hunt (1974).
[49]Tavris and Sadd (1977).

[50]The word "fetish" means an artificial, or fake, object. Anthropologists apply it to objects that are believed by primitive peoples to have magical power. In a more general sense it includes any article that is valued beyond its intrinsic worth because of superstitious or other meanings ascribed to it.

Box 11.3 Aphrodisiacs and Variations in Sexual Experiences

The search for substances that may vary the sexual experience by increasing sexual drive or enjoyment is as old and, so far, as unsuccessful as is the search for the fountain of youth. "Erotic potions" are described in medical writings from ancient Egypt (c. 2000 B.C.). Among various societies since that time all the following and many more preparations have been recommended: pine nuts, the blood of bats mixed with donkey's milk, root of the valerian plant, dried salamander, cyclamen, menstrual fluid, tulip bulbs, fat of camel's hump, parsnips, salted crocodile, pollen of date palm, the powdered tooth of a corpse, wings of bees, jasmine, turtles' eggs, henna (externally applied), ground crickets, spiders or ants, the genitals of hedgehogs, rhinoceros horn, the blood of executed criminals, artichokes, honey compounded with camel's milk, swallows' hearts, vineyard snails, certain bones of the toad, sulfurous waters, and powdered stag's horn. We have already mentioned the role of androgens in human sexual arousal (see Chapter 4). When taken in excess of normal physiological doses, androgens have a number of side effects, particularly in women where beard growth, clitoral enlargement, and other indications of virilization will occur.

From time to time aphrodisiac properties are noted as side effects of drugs that have been developed for other medical purposes. One such drug is levodihydroxyphenylalanine (L-dopa).

L-dopa has been widely used in human subjects as a treatment for Parkinson's disease, a neurological disorder, and a number of investigators have reported apparent sexual rejuvenation in male patients in their sixties and seventies as a result of taking the drug. Although informal reports of renewed sexual vigor in males have had wide publicity, studies have not consistently found this to be true.

Marijuana is reported by some users to enhance sexual pleasure and decrease inhibitions. However, it is not an aphrodisiac because it is actually not a sexual stimulant. Its effects on sexual enjoyment appear to be related to suggestibility and to changes in perception rather than to actual changes in sexual desire and response. Males who smoke four or more marijuana cigarettes per week have significant decreases in testosterone production. The decrease in testosterone is related to the amount smoked; that is, heavier usage produces even lower levels of hormone production. Sperm production is similarly affected.[1] Since the active ingredient in marijuana (tetrahydrocannabinal) is known to cross the placental barrier, the depression of fetal testosterone production during critical periods of sexual differentiation is a possibility if a woman uses marijuana heavily during the first trimester of pregnancy.

Alcohol, barbiturates, and various sedative drugs have an indirect effect on sexual activity by decreasing inhibition and producing a state of relaxation when used in moderate amounts. In large doses these drugs have a negative effect on sexual desire and performance, and in males often produce impotence.

Among the more potent illicit drugs, heroin is known to decrease sexual desire and activity temporarily. Amphetamines and cocaine are claimed by some users to increase sexual desire initially. Continued usage significantly reduces the pleasure of intercourse because of the side effects of these drugs (dryness and inflammation of the vagina, feelings of nervousness, exhaustion, and paranoia). Psychedelic drugs, such as LSD, are not aphrodisiacs, but obviously alter the sensory experience of sex in ways that are often idiosyncratic to the user, the partner, and the setting in which the "trip" takes place. Sexual

[1]Kolodny et al. (1974).

Box 11.3   Continued

relations under the influence of LSD usually are not highly erotic.[2]

Amyl nitrite ("poppers") is a highly volatile drug, which—when inhaled from a small glass vial that is "popped" open for use—causes rapid dilation of the blood vessels. This pharmacologic action of amyl nitrite causes a drop in blood pressure and a feeling of giddiness. Historically, the drug has been used to relieve chest pains associated with heart conditions (*angina pectoris*), but in recent years it has been used in conjunction with sexual activity. Reports indicate that amyl nitrite is used much more frequently by men than women. It is claimed that inhaling a "popper" just prior to orgasm intensifies and prolongs the experience of orgasm although there are no solid data to confirm this. In rare cases death has occurred after the use of this drug during sexual relations. The most common side effect is a severe but usually brief headache.[3]

Cantharides (Spanish fly) is a powder made from certain dried beetles (*Cantharis vesicatoria*) found in southern Europe. When taken internally it causes acute inflammation and irritation of the urinary tract and dilation of the blood vessels of the penis, producing, in some instances, prolonged erections. Spanish fly is a dan-

gerous drug and can produce severe systemic illness. Legend has it that in sixteenth-century Provence cantharides was used to cure fever. One woman reported that after she gave the drug to her husband he had intercourse with her 40 times in 48 hours and then died.

Yohimbine is an alkaloid chemical derived from the bark of the African yohimbe tree (*Pausinystalia yohimbe*). Its use was first observed by Europeans among natives in the nineteenth century. Samples were brought back to Germany for analysis. The drug stimulates the nervous system and is dangerous in large doses. It is available (by prescription) in the United States in capsule form in combination with *nux vomica* (also a nervous system stimulant) and testosterone.

A drug commonly thought to have antiaphrodisiac properties is saltpeter (potassium nitrate). Rumors occasionally circulate among boys in boarding school or men in prison that saltpeter is added to the food to eliminate the sex drive and sexual activity. Saltpeter tends to increase urine flow, but it has no particular effect on sexual interest or potency.

[2]Kaplan (1974).
[3]Hollister (1974).

This group, at least in the sense in which the term fetishism is generally used, is almost exclusively male. It is only when a man becomes clearly focused on paraphernalia or body parts to the exclusion of everything else, however, that we can speak with confidence of fetishism. For example, a man may become so preoccupied with the shape of a woman's legs or her provocative stockings and garters that he loses sight of the woman as a whole. In fetishism the object or body part becomes the source of sexual enjoyment rather than merely enhancing a sexual situa-

tion. A man may masturbate with female underwear because he has no access to a woman and the feminine garment helps him in his fantasies. In this sense the underwear is more a masturbation aid than a fetish.[52]

[52]There is a sizable industry that caters to the market for such masturbation aids, the most sophisticated of which is a life-size and presumably lifelike doll of inflatable rubber or plastic. The simpler models are sold openly as "party gags." More sophisticated ones are advertised as "hard-to-get items"; they come equipped with "pubic fur," "vagina," "clitoris," and so on (*see* Thompson, 1967, p. 142). The use of dolls, conventional or otherwise, in fetishism is sometimes called *puppetophilia*.

The key criterion is whether the choice of object is "voluntary" or resorted to only in the absence of feminine company.

In principle, any article or body part can become endowed with fetishistic meaning, but some objects are more commonly chosen than others. The attraction may arise from the shape, texture, color, or smell of the article, or from a combination of these features. Most fetishes fall into two categories: "feminine" objects that are soft, furry, lacy, pastel-colored (like pink panties with frilly edges); and "masculine" objects that are smooth, harsh, or black (like chains and leather garments). The latter category is more often associated with sadomasochistic fantasies and practices.

What do fetishists do with these objects? Most incorporate them into masturbation sequences. Some may actually ejaculate into or over their fetishes. A fetish can also become associated with some other practice. For example, a masochist may require that he be whipped by a woman wearing spike-heeled shoes, black garters, and so on.

Transvestism

Transvestism, though a separate category, is closely linked to fetishism, for the transvestite (also usually a man) achieves sexual gratification through wearing the clothing of the opposite sex. Again, appearances can be quite misleading. Some "transvestites" are actually transsexuals. As far as they are concerned, they are wearing the clothes of their own sex. Others are homosexuals using female clothing, not to achieve sexual gratification but to attract other homosexuals. Then there are socially accepted instances in which men dress as women, as in amateur burlesque skits or Japanese Kabuki plays.

Only a small proportion of transvestites in the Kinsey data were overt homosexuals or even consciously inclined toward homosexuality. Most of these transvestites were heterosexual men who claimed simply to enjoy wearing women's clothing, and it was not unusual for their mothers to have dressed them as girls in childhood.

Others

A number of additional categories related to fetishism should be mentioned. A few men become highly aroused by filth ("mysophilia"), feces ("coprophilia"), and urine ("urophilia"). Some may be exclusively preoccupied with such elimination functions.

Necrophilia is the sexual use of corpses. It is exceedingly rare and usually involves psychotic men. Literary and artistic references to love and death are sometimes interpreted as suggestions of necrophiliac fantasies.

Voyeurism

Leofric, Lord of Coventry in the eleventh century, agreed to remit an oppressive tax if his wife, the Lady Godiva, would ride through the town naked on a white horse. The lady, a benefactress of monasteries and a friend of the poor, consented. Out of respect and gratitude everyone in town stayed behind closed doors and shuttered windows during her ride—everyone, that is, except Tom the tailor, who peeped and went blind. That is the legend from which comes the name "peeping Tom."

Men commonly enjoy looking at unclothed females and sometimes become erotically aroused. Although females traditionally have been characterized as not enjoying viewing uncovered males, more females are beginning to report that they like to look at bare or partially clad male bodies. In fact, there are now a few male strip shows in the United States that are attended mainly by females. Male interests have been widely indulged through "girl watching," attending "topless" shows and so on. This type of behavior is not considered to be the same as true voyeurism.

Voyeurism occurs when a person, usu-

FIGURE 11.3 Chinese bathing scene (eighteenth century?). Artist unknown.

ally a male, prefers to obtain sexual gratification by viewing others nude or during sexual activity rather than by engaging in coitus. While some voyeurs prefer observing people engaging in sexual behavior, many are content just to watch solitary females undress. They frequently masturbate while watching or immediately thereafter. Voyeurism is socially unacceptable when the woman is observed without her knowledge and would be offended if she became aware of it.

The typical voyeur is not interested in ogling his own wife or female friend. In 95 percent of incidents he observes strangers. What draws him to peep through their windows is in large measure the danger and excitement this entails. The practice is culturally widespread (*see* Figure 11.3).

Voyeurs tend to be young men (the average age at first conviction is 23.8 years).[53] Two-thirds of them are unmarried; one-fourth are married; and the rest are either divorced,

[53]Gebhard et al. (1965). All statistical references in the remainder of this chapter are from this work, unless otherwise specified.

widowed, or separated. Very few show evidence of serious mental disorders, and alcohol or drugs are usually not involved in their deviant behavior (only 16 percent of the sample of Gebhard and his associates was drunk at the time of offense, and none was under the influence of drugs). The voyeur usually takes great care not to be seen by the object of his attentions, and most voyeurs are reported to the police by passersby or neighbors rather than by the women being looked at. Voyeurs are also known to have fallen off window ledges or been shot as burglars.

In intelligence, occupational choice, and family background, "peepers" tend to be a heterogeneous group. They are, however, more likely to be the youngest children in their families. The single most common characteristic of this group of sex offenders is a history of very deficient (both in quantity and in quality) heterosexual relationships. Most voyeurs do not have serious criminal records, but many have histories of minor offenses (misdemeanors). As a rule they do not molest their victims physically.

Exhibitionism

An exhibitionist is a male who obtains sexual gratification from exposing his genitals to women or children who are involuntary observers, usually complete strangers. In a typical sequence the exhibitionist drives or walks in front of a woman with his genitals exposed. He usually, but not always, has an erection. Most often, as soon as she has seen him, he flees. Sometimes he wears a coat and exposes himself periodically while riding on a subway or bus. Or he may stand in a park and pretend that he is urinating.

The exhibitionist, in common with the voyeur, does not usually attack or molest his "victim." His gratification comes from observing her reaction, which is predictably surprise, fear, disgust, and so on. Women who keep calm foil his attempt. Some men ejaculate at the scene of exposure; others merely enjoy the experience; and still others become highly aroused and masturbate right afterward.

The average age of the exhibitionist ("the flag-waver" in prison slang; "the flasher" is another term) at conviction is 30 years. About 30 percent of arrested exhibitionists are married; another 30 percent are separated, divorced, or widowed; and 40 percent have never been married. The exhibitionist often describes a compulsive quality in his own behavior, triggered by feelings of excitement, fear, restlessness, and sexual arousal. Once in this state he feels "driven" to find relief. Despite previous arrests and convictions, he tends to repeat his behavior. One-third of the offenders in this category in the Gebhard study had had four to six previous convictions, and 10 percent had been convicted seven or more times.[54]

The exhibitionist seems to need to display and reaffirm his masculinity, and sometimes an element of sexual solicitation (rarely realized) is present as well. Exhibitionists do not usually show signs of severe mental disorder, and alcohol and drugs are involved only in rare instances.

The word "exhibitionist" is a good example of the arbitrariness and confusion with which certain terms, and the concepts that they embody, have come to be used. The drunken man who fleetingly exposes his genitals to a woman passing by while he is urinating in a dark alley is sometimes called an exhibitionist (for practical purposes, only if she takes offense). A woman who spends hours on end undressing herself to musical accompaniment or displays herself naked on a stage in front of a paying audience is "exhibitionistic" in her behavior but is not an "exhibitionist" (*see* Figure 11.4)

Although this type of behavior by a man carries a prison sentence, a woman is permitted to make her living this way. However

[54]Ibid., p. 394.

FIGURE 11.4 Thomas Rowlandson, *Untitled.*

badly females may fare in other areas of sexual behavior, where voyeurism and exhibitionism are concerned, the law is on their side. A woman undresses in front of an open window, and a man looks up at her: He is a voyeur. The roles are reversed: Now he is an exhibitionist.

Although usually not classified with exhibitionism, the practice of making obscene telephone calls is similar in some ways. The caller is usually a sexually inadequate person, who can have sexual interchanges with the opposite sex through this apparently safe method (though progressively less safe as detection mechanisms are improved). His pleasure is also derived from eliciting embarrassment and intense emotion. Telephone companies recommend that the recipient of an obscene call remain calm and either hang up immediately or alert the operator by means of a second telephone to trace the call to its source and have the caller arrested.

In a similar category are men who try to shock women by using obscenities or telling off-color jokes. There is no absolute criterion for determining what is obscene. The important factor is not the word used or the content of the story but its intended impact on others.

Sadomasochism

Although the term is often used loosely, sadism refers to instances in which the individual achieves sexual satisfaction by inflicting pain. Masochism, also frequently used loosely, is applied to instances in which the individual achieves satisfaction through being subjected to pain.[55] These two behaviors will be discussed jointly, for they are mirror images of the same phenomenon. Although innocent people occasionally are harmed by sadists or inadvertently satisfy the masochistic needs of others, sadists and masochists in general use each other as partners.

Sadism and masochism tend to be discrete. That is to say, a sadist does not wish alternatively to whip someone and then to be whipped himself (see Figure 11.5). It is neither possible nor necessary to catalog the infinite variety of obvious, as well as startling, devices that have been imagined and sometimes (though very rarely) actually used in sadomasochistic sexual encounters.

The majority of sadomasochistically oriented people tend to restrict their activities to reading special magazines that feature either cartoons or photographs of women dressed in leather and spike-heeled shoes trying to look menacing as they gag, bind, chain, whip, and variously "torture" their vic-

FIGURE 11.5 Mauron, *The Cully Flaug'd* (eighteenth century illustration for *Fanny Hill*).

tims. Sadomasochistic sexual practices may include "bondage," which consists of tying down the sexual partner prior to sexual stimulation, but they stop short of physical harm to the partner.

Sadists who are more apt to act out their impulses are another matter. At their mildest, sadistic men soil women ("saliromania") or cut their hair off. At their worst they may rape, mutilate, and kill. In general, however, the masochist poses no serious threat to society and is rarely arrested. Sadists and masochists are usually male.

Animal Contacts

Sexual contacts with animals (*zoophilia*, or *bestiality*) were by far the least prevalent of the six components of total sexual outlet studied by Kinsey. Even though 8 percent of adult males and 3 percent of females reported such contacts with animals, their activities accounted for a fraction of 1 percent of the total sexual outlets. In some groups, however,

[55]These terms are derived from the names of two historical figures who wrote on these respective themes. The first was the eighteenth-century French nobleman Donatien-Alphonse-François, Marquis de Sade; the second was the Austrian Leopold von Sacher-Masoch (1836–1905), also a nobleman. The works, as well as the biographies, of both men are widely known. For a summary of both lives, see Ellis, H. (1942), vol. 1, part 2, pp. 116–119.

such behavior was relatively common: Among boys reared on farms, as many as 17 percent had had at least one orgasm through animal contact after puberty.

Humans have a long history of intimate associations with animals in many aspects of life, including sexual ones (*see* Figure 11.6). This theme has been an important source of fantasy and an inspiration for many works of art. Classical mythology abounds with tales of sexual contacts between the gods disguised as beasts and apparently unsuspecting goddesses and mortals. Zeus, for instance, approached Europa as a bull, Leda as a swan (*see* Figure 11.7), and Persephone as a serpent. From such unions issued the many half-man, half-beast denizens of the mythological

FIGURE 11.6   Petroglyph in a cave in northern Italy. From Anati, *Camonica Valley* (New York: Alfred A. Knopf, 1961), p. 128. Reprinted by permission.

FIGURE 11.7   *Leda and the Swan* (after Michelangelo). Courtesy of The National Gallery, London.

woods: satyrs (half-goats), centaurs (half-horses), and minotaurs (half-bulls), to name only the most familiar.

Historical references are also plentiful. The historian Herodotus mentions the goats of the Egyptian temple at Mendes, which were specially trained for copulating with human beings. More often, we find references to animals as sexual objects framed as prohibitions. The Hittite code, the Old Testament, and the Talmud specifically prohibit such contacts for males; and the Talmud extends the prohibition to females. The prescribed penalties for animal sexual contacts tended to be severe (death for both human and animal participants; *see* Leviticus 20). Such sanctions remained in effect in Europe throughout the Middle Ages and, indeed, until fairly recently. In 1468 one Jean Beisse was convicted of copulating with a cow and a goat. Jean, the cow, and the goat were all burned at the stake. Sixteen-year-old Claudine de Culam was convicted of copulating with a dog in 1601. Both were hanged, and their bodies burned. In 1944 an American soldier was convicted at a general court-martial of sodomy with a cow and sentenced to a dishonorable discharge and three years at hard labor.

The animals and the specific activities involved in these sexual encounters vary widely. Copulation with dogs is well documented. Common sense suggests that the animals most often used would be those found on farms and in homes, and that the most common activity would be some form of masturbation or intercourse.

In the Kinsey sample general body contact with animals was more often reported by women, whereas men were more likely to have masturbated the animals. Oral-genital contacts involving the animals' mouths and the human genitals were reported by both sexes, but coitus with animals was more common among men and very rare among women.

Pedophilia

The pedophile (from the Greek, "lover of children") is someone who uses children for his sexual gratification.[56] This offense is more common than many people recognize. Kinsey found that almost one-fourth of the females in his sample reported that before adolesence they had been approached or contacted sexually by an adult male at least five years older than themselves. Pedophilia is a serious legal offense; almost all pedophiles who are arrested are male. They are more commonly interested in prepubescent females than in prepubescent males.

The heterosexual pedophile is often pictured as a stranger who lurks about the school playground, abducts an unsuspecting little girl, takes her by force to some secret place, and ravishes her. The facts rarely fit this stereotype. Studies have shown that in about 85 percent of such incidents the pedophile is either a relative, a family friend, a neighbor, or an acquaintance. He makes advances to the child either in her home, where he is visiting or living (as an uncle, stepfather, grandfather, or boarder), or in his own home, where she is used to visiting or is enticed by promises of candy or other treats. (Seventy-nine percent of such contacts occur in homes, 13 percent in public places, and 8 percent in cars.) Physical damage to the child occurs in about 2 percent of the instances, although threats of force or some degree of physical restraint is present in about one-third of in-

[56]The definition of a pedophile depends on the definition of a child. The laws of many states define "child molesting" and related offenses like "statutory rape" to include victims up to the ages of 16, 18, or even 21. Sexual involvement with even a postpubescent 15-year-old girl, however, is usually a different sort of activity from what we describe here as pedophilia. In the former the "victim" may actually have been the seducer, and the "offender" may have misjudged the age of his sexual partner because of her physical appearance or because she lied about her age. Gebhard et al. (1965) define a child as younger than 12 years old, a minor as between 13 and 15 years old, and an adult as more than 16 years old. These age limits correspond well with stages in biological maturation.

stances in which arrests and convictions follow.

The entire pedophiliac episode is often quite brief, and, though there may be a series of such episodes before the child reports them to her parents, it is unusual for a prolonged or intimate relationship to develop. If a child experiences such contact, the parents should be careful not to overreact. A very alarmed reaction on their part may do more psychological harm to the child than the actual experience did. At least one session with a counselor or therapist is probably advisable, for both the child and the parent or parents.

Actual sexual contact most often consists of the man's taking the child on his lap and fondling her external genitals. Intercourse is rarely attempted because, among other factors, these men are often impotent. (Coitus is attempted in about 6 percent of instances, but intromission is achieved in only about 2 percent.)

Individuals involved with little girls (heterosexual offenders against children) tend to be older than any other group of sex offenders, with the exception of those involved in incest. The average age at conviction is 35, and 25 percent of these offenders are over 45. About 5 percent are actually senile individuals whose judgment is impaired through mental deterioration; 15–20 percent of offenders are mentally retarded.

The majority of heterosexual offenders with children are, however, neither senile nor mentally defective; 70–80 percent have been married at some time in their lives. They tend to be conservative and moralistic, and some require alcohol before they can commit their offenses. They usually do not have criminal records, with the exception of possible previous convictions for molesting children.

The homosexual pedophile obtains sexual gratification through the use of young boys as sexual objects. Although this activity is viewed by some people as a variation of adult homosexuality, it is uncommon and

scorned by the vast majority of homosexuals. Most homosexuals confine their sexual activities to other adults.

Homosexual pedophiles also do not usually molest strangers, and the boys with whom they become involved are most often relatives or the sons of acquaintances. In addition, contacts are sometimes made through youth organizations. The popular notion that better police surveillance will prevent such crimes is thus difficult to justify.

Sexual activities with a young boy may include fondling and masturbation of the boy, mutual masturbation, fellatio and *pederasty* (anal intercourse with a child).

Homosexual offenders against children generally show deficiencies in socialization and interpersonal relationships. They often say that they prefer the company of boys because they feel uneasy around adults. Their average age when they commit their offenses is 30.6 years, and only 16 percent are married at this time. Their sexual experiences have usually been predominantly, but not exclusively, homosexual. The child molester, especially when he uses force, arouses strong aversion and anger in the community. Even in jail he is so poorly tolerated that he must be isolated from other inmates.

Incest

Incest is one sexual offense that is universally condemned, but it does occasionally occur, and historical and literary records include some well-known examples.[57]

The term "incest" (from the Latin for "impure," or "soiled") is commonly used for

---

[57]The story of Lot and his daughters is told in Genesis 19 and that of Oedipus in the Greek tragedy *Oedipus Rex* by Sophocles. The circumstances in both stories are extraordinary. Lot and his daughters are the only survivors of the cataclysmic destruction of Sodom and Gomorrah, and the apparent motivation of Lot's daughters in intoxicating and seducing their father is to ensure the continuity of their family line. Oedipus (*see* Chapter 8) is not even aware that the queen whom he has married is his own mother.

sexual relations between parents and off-spring. In this sense it is much more common between fathers and daughters than between mothers and sons. Actually incest includes all sexual relations between a person and his close relatives (for example, siblings, grand-parents, uncles, and aunts). The taboo is extended to cousins in some but not in all groups. (The Roman Catholic and Greek Orthodox churches prohibit marriage between first cousins, but such marriages are permitted by many Protestant churches, as well as by Judaism and Islam.) In a study of court cases of incest 90 percent of the cases involved fathers and daughters, stepfathers and step-daughters, grandfathers and granddaughters, and 5 percent involved fathers and sons.[58]

While reported cases of incest are rare, the actual incidence of incestual abuse is unknown since incest is often not reported to authorities. Although incest used to be considered a lower-class phenomenon because people of this class reported more cases to authorities than other classes, researchers are becoming increasingly aware that incestual abuse also occurs (but is less often reported) in middle- and upper-class families.[59]

The only data on offenders of incest laws available from the Gebhard study is on father-daughter relationships. The ages of the daughters at the time of the offense were correlated with some characteristics of the fathers. Fathers who became sexually involved with prepubertal daughters tended to be passive, ineffectual men who drank excessively. The sexual contacts involved either fondling the external genitals or oral-genital contacts.

Offenders against maturer daughters tended to be religious, moralistic, and often active in fundamentalist sects. (They were rated as the most religious of all the groups of sex offenders studied by Gebhard and his colleagues.) They were poorly educated and

had a median age of 46 at the time of the offense. Activity culminated in coitus in 91 percent of instances. Charges of incest are usually pressed by wives, but sometimes the daughters go directly to the police. Often an incestuous relationship has been continuing for some time and then is suddenly discovered by the wife or is reported by the daughter. Recent studies have found increased incidences of prostitution, sexual problems and drug abuse among women with incestual backgrounds, especially father-daughter incest.[60] Some researchers suggest that incest abuse by close relatives increases the child's likelihood of being sexually exploited by others, especially if the child runs away from home.[61]

The incest taboo is generally assumed to have appeared early in human evolution in an attempt to safeguard the integrity of the family unit, for sexual competition within the family would be highly disruptive (as it is when incest does occur). Furthermore, mating outside the family has been important in the formation of larger social units held together by kinship ties. The proposition that the incest taboo arose from recognition of the genetic dangers of inbreeding (through concentration of disease-carrying recessive genes) is much less plausible.[62]

Whatever its precise origins, prohibitions against incest are now universal. Ford and Beach came to the conlusion that:

Among all peoples both partners in a mateship are forbidden to form sexual liaison with their own offspring. This prohibition characterizes every human culture. This generalization excludes instances in which mothers or fathers are permitted to masturbate or in some other sexual manner to stimulate their very young children. A second exception is represented by

[58]Maisch (1973).
[59]Hunt (1974), Butler (1978).

[60]Giarretto (1976).
[61]James and Meyerding (1977).
[62]For an analysis of the functional significance of the incest taboo see Murdock (1949). For a sociological review see Weinberg (1963).

Box 11.4 Preventing Rape

Some rapes are avoidable. This does not mean that women are provoking rapes (for example, by enticing the rapist or dressing too sexily), but rather that some rape victims could have taken certain precautions. Unfortunately, to decrease the risk of being raped a woman must be on the defensive.[1]

Since many rapes occur in the victim's home, there should be locks on the doors and windows. Doors to the outside should be equipped with a dead-bolt lock and a chain lock. These doors should always be kept locked when a woman is alone. A woman must avoid allowing strangers into the home; hence, doors should not be opened to unknown people. Requesting identification from service people may deter a potential rapist.

When away from home, it is best to avoid deserted, enclosed stairwells. Car keys should be out and ready before arriving at the car to minimize the vulnerable time needed to open the door. The back seat should be checked to make sure no unexpected passenger is present. It is important to keep the car doors locked while driving. Picking up strangers is very dangerous, as is hitchhiking. At her job, a woman should refuse to work alone or in a deserted building. When outside it is wise to avoid walking alone at night especially in dark deserted streets or open areas. If a woman has to walk outside at night, she should stay close to the curb on well lighted streets and walk quickly. Dressing in clothes that do not restrict movement will allow her to run if necessary. A woman should not stop and give instructions to men driving in a car at night. If a woman does walk alone at night, she should consider carrying something in her hand that could be used to disable an attacker temporarily. A handbag, umbrella, books, keys, and other objects can be used effectively as weapons. Some women purchase a freon horn that creates a loud noise when activated. In addition, taking a course or reading books on self-defense may prove to be invaluable to a woman if she is attacked.

What should a woman do in an actual rape encounter? Unfortunately there is no single right answer that applies to all rape encounters. Every woman must judge for herself what the best course of action is in each particular rape situation. In some cases it is possible to talk a rapist out of committing a rape. An assertive tone of voice and defiant posture will dissuade some rapists, since some potential rapists do not want to become involved with a woman who resists. If the rapist attacks, fighting back will increase the woman's chances of escaping in some circumstances, but resisting may cause the rapist to become more violent and hurt the victim more. A woman should scream and run if possible. Sometimes shouting "Fire" is more effective than screaming.

A woman who is raped should contact the police and receive medical attention immediately before doing anything else, such as washing, douching, changing clothes, or cleaning up the rape scene. Contacting a Rape Crisis Center can be very helpful to the woman. Most centers have personnel who provide emotional support, transportation, clothes, information, and numerous other services. Having a close friend present can also be helpful.

[1]For an elaboration of these suggestions and others on rape prevention see Horos (1974) and Conroy (1975).

the very rare cases in which a society expects a few individuals of special social rank to cohabit with their immediate descendants. The Azande of Africa, for example, insist that the highest chiefs enter into sexual partnership with their own daughters. In no society, however, are such matings permitted to the general populations.[63]

Similar exceptions for intermarriage between siblings were also made among the Incas and the ancient Egyptian pharaohs (Cleopatra was the offspring of and herself a partner in such matings). Incidentally, 72 percent of the societies surveyed by Ford and Beach were found to have more extensive incest prohibitions than are common in the West. Sometimes they were broad enough to exclude half the population as potential sex mates for a given individual.

Rape

Rape is an act of aggression in which a person is forced to participate in a sexual act against her or his will (or for various reasons is not able to give consent). The victim is usually a female, but men are sometimes raped by other men in prison. To the woman being raped, the experience can be extremely frightening and traumatic. Not only is she forced to engage in a sexual act, she has no way of knowing how much force the rapist would actually use if she did not submit. She cannot judge whether his intent is to rape her or to rape, beat, and murder her.

Rape is the most rapidly increasing violent crime in the United States. The FBI reported 63,020 cases of rape for 1977.[64] In 1960 there were 17,190 reported cases. The exact incidence of this crime is actually unknown since most women do not report rapes to the authorities (*see* Chapter 14). It is estimated that only one in 5 to 10 rapes is reported. Nine percent of the 40,000 males responding to a 1977 *Redbook* questionnaire on male sexuality reported that they had used

force or the threat of force to make a woman engage in sex.[65]

Rapists are generally young men in the 15–24 age group.[66] About half of the rapists have been arrested before, mainly for crimes against property or another person, or for public disorder. The victims of rape are usually between 10 and 29 years of age, but a victim of any age can be raped.[67] Females 6 months old and 93 years old have been raped.

Rapists use force or the threat of force to make the female submit to their sexual demands. In one large study by Amir 85 percent of the rapes involved actual physical force and in one fifth of these cases the victims were brutally beaten. The rapist sometimes has a weapon such as a knife or a gun.[68] Although some rapes are done on impulse because the opportunity is present or because judgment is impaired (usually by alcohol), 71 percent of rapes are planned. Many rapists have a low regard for women. From her study on rape Hursch concludes that a common attitude among rapists "is that it is important to dehumanize the woman, to keep her anonymous and to see her as an object rather than as a person."[69]

In the United States rapes occur most often in homes and apartments. Other common sites include public buildings, automobiles, and outdoors. Rape occurs more frequently at night, especially on weekend nights. A slight increase in rape occurs during the

[63]Ford and Beach (1951), p. 112.

[64]Federal Bureau of Investigation (1977).

[65]In addition, 8 percent of the males reported using less direct forms of force, such as threatening a woman with loss of job or monetary assistance (Tavris, 1978).

[66]Amir (1971). All statistical references in the remainder of this section are to this work, unless otherwise specified.

[67]Brownmiller (1975).

[68]Hursch (1977, p. 53–54) found that 59 percent of rape victims reported the presence of a weapon, whereas Amir (1971, p. 153) noted intimidation with a weapon occurred in 21 percent of cases.

[69]Hursch (1977).

summer months. Although the majority of rape offenses occur between strangers, in at least 40 percent of cases the rapist is a casual acquaintance, friend, relative, employer, or is otherwise known to the victim.[70] In some cases the woman is raped by more than one man. The incidence of group or "gang" rapes varies in different studies. Forty-three percent of Amir's sample involved group rapes. A woman may be walking along a fairly empty street when a car full of several men stops by her and she is forced to join them. Sometimes a woman is forced to a deserted place by one man where other men then participate in raping her. The following description was given as a representative example of many of the women rape victims in Hursch's 1973 study conducted in Denver, Colorado:

She is about twenty years old. . . . She lives in a small, neat one-bedroom or buffet apartment near the downtown area, and she works as a secretary, telephone operator, nurse, paramedic, or [at some] other semiprofessional job nearby. She has moved here to take advantage of the job opportunities of a big city. This is her first job after college or business school, or she has taken time out from college to earn money with which to continue her education. This is the first time she has lived away from her parents' home, except during her college life. She is raped in her own bedroom after access is gained by a man who removed the screen, and forced her window open. As far as she could tell, she has never seen him before, and may have "seen" little of him during the rape since the entire episode took place in the dark. He held a weapon on her while he forced her to comply.

I met her again and again and again, each time with a different face. She was a very nice girl.[71]

About 1 in 500 rapists also kill their victims.[72] The sex murderer is a dangerous and terrifying person (*see* Figure 11.8). He usually

FIGURE 11.8 Franz Masareel. *Sex Murder.* Book illustration, *Ginzberg L'Enfer*, p. 185.

tortures and sexually assaults his victim before killing her. Such men, who are very seriously deranged (often psychotic) may also mutilate the corpses or have further sexual contact with them. Every decade brings a few of these murderers, who keep entire cities in terror until apprehended.

What is it that drives people to violent sexual activities with unwilling partners? Unfortunately most answers are only conjectural. The personality and family profiles drawn by Gebhard and his associates are revealing but do not permit conclusions about causation. For instance, heterosexual aggressors against children tend to be intellectually dull and the victims of broken and unhappy homes. They have few and poor relationships with adult females and rely heavily on prostitutes for sexual partners. They tend to use alcohol excessively. Offenders against minors

---

[70]Macdonald (1971), pp. 77–78.
[71]Hursch (1977), p. 76.
[72]Brownmiller (1975).

Box 11.5 The Aftermath of Rape: The Victim's Experience

The obvious possible aftereffects of rape include emotional trauma, physical injury, pregnancy, and venereal disease. If the victim suspects that she is at high risk for becoming pregnant, the drug DES is often given to her (*see* Chapter 6). One of the few studies on the experience of rape victims found that all of the 92 women studied underwent an acute "disorganization" phase.[1] Immediately after the rape most women displayed either (1) feelings of fear, anxiety, and anger or (2) a controlled external appearance such that their true emotions were not obvious. Many women reported various problems in the first weeks after the rape, including physical pain from injury during the rape, tension and tiredness, upset stomach, and gynecological problems. The most common emotion mentioned during this time was fear of death and physical violence. Generally, about two to three weeks after the rape the women began the second phase, the "reorganization phase." At this time almost half the victims moved to a new location. Others took a trip. Most women turned to family or friends during this period. Many changed their telephone numbers. Some of the women reported nightmares and fears of such situations as being outdoors, indoors, alone, or in crowds. The rape caused sexual problems for some women.

From their clinical experience Masters and Johnson have identified several problems that occur in some women after they have been raped.[2] Most rape victims do not experience these problems, but a few do. The exact frequency is unknown since Masters and Johnson made their observations on a limited clinical sample of people who had come to them for help with sexual problems. The most common complication noted after rape was the development of a dislike for sexual activity

and a diminishing interest in sex. This was more common when the rape had become public knowledge. This aversion to sex most commonly developed in women who were made to participate in a number of sexual acts with one or more men over an extended period of time. An aversion to sex was also more likely to develop if a woman was forced to perform a sexual act that she had never done before, such as anal intercourse.

Second, vaginismus sometimes developed, particularly in those women who had been raped a number of times by one or more males. This condition was more common among rape victims who experienced severe physical injury, especially in the genital areas.

Third, some rape victims lost their ability to have orgasms. The women most likely to lose ogasmic function were the ones who were most committed to the double standard, being totally dependent on men and viewing their sexual role as one of service.

Fourth, Masters and Johnson noted that some women experienced a number of personal problems. The most common one involved a married woman's relationship with her husband. Some husbands were unable to deal with the rape, especially if the rape was public knowledge. Sometimes the male felt that everyone now knew that his wife had been "dirtied." Some husbands wanted to seek revenge on the rapist. This male reaction added greatly to the wife's distress and increased the likelihood that she would develop sexual problems. In some cases the husbands of rape victims developed sexual dysfunctions. However, most husbands were very understanding and helpful with their wives.

[1]Burgess and Holmstrom (1974).
[2]Masters and Johnson (1976).

(12–15 years old) have equally unfortunate home backgrounds, and many have criminal records. They are usually amoral, aggressive young men who seek whatever immediate gratification they can find, regardless of the ultimate consequences. The aggressor against adults is similar in his unconcern about the welfare and rights of others. Most such men have generally sociopathic orientations. They violate women in the same way that they help themselves to other people's property, and they use whatever force is necessary to do so. The rapist appears to have a need to feel dominant over his victim by placing her in an inferior, degrading position.

To understand sexual violence, we must therefore understand the overall problem of antisocial behavior and criminality, and the mixture of sex and aggression is but one facet of this problem.

Chapter 12

Sexual Malfunction and Therapy

No human function works flawlessly all of the time, and sex is no exception. Yet how to define a given physiological sexual function or form of behavior malfunctional is highly problematic. In this chapter we are concerned with problems that relate to the desire for sexual activity, the physical ability to carry out such activity, and the psychological satisfaction that emanates from it.

In this sense sexual malfunction is distinguished from diseases of the sexual organs, such as VD (unless they interfere with sexual function), and problems of fertility or those related to pregnancy. Behavioral variations involving different sexual orientations (see Chapter 11) are also not viewed as "malfunctions" even though such behaviors may be considered problematic on other grounds. Thus, a homosexual would be considered sexually malfunctioning only if he or she had problems getting aroused, reaching orgasm, and so on. Malfunction is thus mainly a problem of failure of the sexual "machinery" and not an issue of what one wants to do with it.

There is as yet no generally accepted terminology in this area. Currently, the term most commonly used is "dysfunction" (the prefix "dys" meaning bad or difficult) to describe these conditions. We shall adhere to this practice but restrict the term to include conditions that specifically entail failure of genital function. The broader term of "malfunction" will thus also include problems with sexual desire and lack of satisfaction in the absence of any specific dysfunction such as impotence or inability to reach orgasm.

Most of the research and literature dealing with sexual malfunction relates to heterosexual intercourse. We have been so preoccupied with the social concerns involved in other sexual orientation that whether or not these persons are properly functional or not has been of little concern. These attitudes are now changing and much of what we can do to be helpful to heterosexuals who are dysfunctional can be applied as well to homosexuals.

Traditionally, sexually dysfunctional people have been viewed as individuals with discrete entities such as "impotence" or "frigidity." Presently sex therapists focus more on the dysfunctional couple rather than on one or the other person exclusively. This is not to say that every problem reflects an equal amount of disturbance. Rather, it highlights the benefit of making sexual dysfunction the couple's problem instead of the "fault" of one or the other person.

Prevalence of Sexual Malfunction

Competence in sexual intercourse is not an all-or-none phenomenon, and there is no absolute scale on which to evaluate it. No one is expected to be able to copulate at will with anyone, anywhere, anytime. Normal functioning entails considerable fluctuation in sexual desire, and it is expected that performance will occasionally falter. Beyond a certain ill-defined boundary, however, the extent or frequency of failure—whether at the level of desire, performance, or gratification—must be considered malfunction.

Probably no other human disturbance entails more silent suffering than sexual malfunctioning. Even when a person marshals enough courage to seek help, it is difficult to know where to turn. Since no one dies of sexual distress (though impotence does drive some people to suicide) and fertility may not be disturbed, the main and apparently tolerable loss seems to be erotic gratification. Actually the toll in unhappy marriages and unfulfilled lives is incalculable.

Currently there are no accurate figures about the prevalence of sexual dysfunction, let alone information about more nebulous entities such as sexual desire or satisfaction. But the consensus seems to be that there is indeed a good deal of sexual distress. Masters and Johnson about a decade ago estimated that, even by a conservative count, half of all marriages were either presently or imminently sexually dysfunctional.[1]

Statistics on sexual dysfunction often come from clinical studies. But what is more interesting is to know about disordered sexual functions among "normal" couples who are not in sex therapy. The results of one such study are presented in Box 12.1. They tend to substantiate the high rates estimated by Masters and Johnson. In this group, where 80 percent claim to have happy and satisfying sexual relations, 40 percent of the men report problems with erection and ejaculation and 63 percent of the women have trouble getting aroused or reaching orgasm. In addition, 50 percent of the men and 77 percent of the women with no dysfunction still complain of some difficulty in finding sexual satisfaction.[2]

Types of Sexual Malfunctioning

Difficulties in sexual function are not discrete disease entities, even though the specific labels attached to some of them may give that impression. Sexual malfunction can be divided into three broadly descriptive categories: disinterest, dysfunction, and dissatisfaction.

Disinterest refers to sexual apathy or the lack of interest in sex. Dysfunction, as stated earlier, more narrowly delineates failure in sexual performance. Dissatisfaction consists of varying levels of lack of sexual gratification; in this case persons get aroused and reach orgasm but feel sexually unfulfilled.

Sexual Apathy

It is expected of men and women that they will wish to engage in sexual intercourse with someone, sometime, someplace, even though they may elect not to carry out this wish or may be prevented from doing so. Beyond this stipulation, judgments of the intensity of sexual desire are arbitrary.

A most important factor in sustaining sexual desire is the satisfaction gained from coitus itself. If, for whatever reason, a person finds the experience distasteful, painful, or merely tedious, the incentive to join in it is much weakened.

In its mildest form sexual apathy is simple indifference. A person forgoes sexual intercourse for extended periods because he or she does not feel like having it, despite propitious circumstances and willing partners. Sometimes the person is so preoccupied with other events and activities that sex is under-

---

[1]Masters and Johnson (1971).

[2]Frank et al. (1978).

Box 12.1 Prevalence of Sexual Dysfunction in "Normal" Couples

The following tables are from a study of 100 couples who were predominantly white, well educated, and middle class. Eighty percent claimed to have happy or satisfying marriages. The information was gathered through a 15-page self-report questionnaire, only part of which dealt with sex. None of these couples were at the time in marital therapy or counseling, although 12 percent had had such help in the past.

Frequency of Self-Reported Sexual Problems

Problem	Women (%)	Men (%)	P*
Sexual dysfunctions—women:			
Difficulty getting excited	48		
Difficulty maintaining excitement	33		
Reaching orgasm too quickly	11		
Difficulty in reaching orgasm	46		
Inability to have an orgasm	15		
Sexual dysfunctions—men:			
Difficulty getting an erection		7	
Difficulty maintaining an erection		9	
Ejaculating too quickly		36	
Difficulty in ejaculating		4	
Inability to ejaculate		0	
Comparison of sexual difficulties reported by men and women:			
Partner chooses inconvenient time	31	16	0.05
Inability to relax	47	12	0.001
Attraction to person(s) other than mate	14	21	NS
Disinterest	35	16	0.01
Attraction to person(s) of same sex	1	0	NS
Different sexual practices or habits	10	12	NS
"Turned off"	28	10	0.01
Too little foreplay before intercourse	38	21	0.05
Too little "tenderness" after intercourse	25	17	NS

*Significance of t-test comparing men and women. NS: not significant.

Ratings of Sexual Satisfaction.

Question	Women (%)	Men (%)
How satisfying are your sexual relations?		
Very satisfying	40	42
Moderately satisfying	46	43
Not very satisfying	12	13
Not satisfying at all	2	2
How satisfactory have your sexual relations with your spouse been in comparison to other aspects of your marital life?		
Better than the rest	19	24
About the same	63	60
Worse than the rest	18	16
Do you have any of the following specific complaints about your marriage? Sexual dissatisfaction:		
Yes	21	33
No	79	67

From E. Frank, C. Anderson, and D. Rubinstein, *New England Journal of Medicine,* 299 (1978), 111–115. By permission.

Figure 12.1 William Hogarth, *Before* (left) *and After* (opposite). Courtesy of the Metropolitan Museum of Art, Harris Brisbane Dick Fund, 1932.

standably set aside for a while. But it is also possible that these other activities are at least unconsciously aimed at avoiding sex. In treating marital difficulties it is necessary to determine when a person is making unreasonable demands on a harassed marital partner and when a sexually apathetic partner is deliberately becoming exhausted before bedtime.

More often, sexual apathy is part of a general listlessness, perhaps resulting from concrete external causes or from a general depression reflecting internal conflicts. Sexual apathy is not restricted to mere listlessness, however. A person may feel consciously uneasy about coitus and may actively seek to avoid it. Perhaps the experience has been uncomfortable and dissatisfying, or feelings of guilt and shame may have overbalanced the pleasure and joy in the act. Some people actually dread coitus, out of disgust or fear.

One may rightly wonder why sexual apathy should necessarily be considered a malfunction if the person is not complaining of it. The answer is that it should not be since after all one has no obligation to engage in sex, unless of course there is a marital partner to consider or some other form of sexual obligation entailed that is not being fulfilled.

Sexual apathy is thus in fact not some abstract entity but usually a discrepancy in

sexual desire between two partners. One person may simply want more sex than the other, and if some sort of accommodation and compromise is not possible then there are grounds for conflict. In other cases there is no issue of apathy but a difference in the rhythm of arousal. Figure 12.1 illustrates Hogarth's view that although women may he "hard to start," they may be even "harder to stop."

The opposite of sexual apathy is "hypersexuality," which has been considered by some a gift and by others a curse (see Box 12.2). Currently, most clinicians do not either attempt to classify or to treat whatever be-

havior that could be hypothesized as being hypersexual, unless of course such activity is the direct manifestation of some physical or psychological pathology.[3]

Sexual Dysfunction

The most logical classification of sexual dysfunction is based on the fundamental physiological processes that underlie the sexual response cycle. As discussed earlier (see Chapter 3), these processes are vasocongestion and myotonia, or increased muscular tension.

[3]See Friedman (1977).

Box 12.2 High Levels of Sexuality Activity

Men and women considered to have exceptionally active sex lives are a source of wonder and preoccupation in many cultures. Are they specially endowed beings, or are they sick? Is one born with a higher sexual capacity, or does one develop it? If the latter, what is the secret?

The satyrs of Greek mythology were part-human, part-animal beings who lived in forests and mountains and formed part of the entourage of Dionysus, the god of wine and fertility. They were jovial, lusty creatures and have become symbolic of the sexually active male. Such "extreme" activity, with pathological overtones, has come to be known as "satyriasis."

The nymphs of Greek mythology were a more varied lot and less single-mindedly dedicated to sexual pursuits. They were young and beautiful maidens, mostly amorous and gentle. Some, however, were quite wild and behaved more as satyrs did. The sexually hyperactive woman is therefore known as a "nymphomaniac" ("inflicted with nymph madness").

Although each historical period seems to have had its sexual prodigies, some have been more celebrated than others.

Usually the exploits of the socially prominent or the flamboyant become more widely known; no one hears of the staggering "records" that otherwise ordinary husbands and wives may set.

In the folklore of sexual prowess fact and legend are intermingled and elaborated. The Roman Empress Valeria Messalina (A.D. first century) and her husband's son-in-law, the Emperor Nero, both have reputations for prolific sexual activity. Catherine II of Russia (1729–1796) seems to have been as enterprising in her sexual life as she was politically. The names of Casanova and Don Juan have, of course, come to represent the hyperactive male perpetually in search of sexual conquest.

Giovanni Giacomo Casanova de Seingalt (1725–1798), a Venetian, was expelled from school as a boy for immorality. He became an adventurer and traveled widely around Europe. After a lifetime of intrigue he retired to the castle of a prominent friend to write and study. His multivolume memoirs (originally written in French) are regarded as an important historical document.

Disturbances of vasocongestion reflect a failure in sexual arousal and are manifested in the male by *erectile dysfunction* or *impotence*. The female counterpart of failure in arousal has been called *general sexual dysfunction*.[4]

Disturbances in myotonic response are manifested by orgasmic problems. In the male these may take the form of either *premature ejaculation* or *retarded ejaculation* (also known as *ejaculatory incompetence*). In the female "premature" orgasm is usually of no negative consequence. If the woman is multiorgasmic, she can have additional orgasms if she so wishes. But even if she is content with one orgasm, the woman who reaches her climax before her partner can still continue having coitus until he reaches orgasm, which is of course not the case should he climax first.

When the problem is retarded ejaculation, the male is unable to reach orgasm during coitus (but usually has no difficulty in doing so extravaginally). The female counterpart is *orgasmic dysfunction*, wherein a woman fails to reach orgasm. The term *frigidity* was commonly used for this condition as well as a variety of other forms of female

[4]Kaplan (1974).

Box 12.2   Continued

Don Juan is not a historical character but is the literary prototype of the profligate. Although his counterparts can be found in the legends of many peoples, the Spanish version is most widely known. In this story Don Juan seduces the daughter of the commander of Seville and kills him in a duel. The Don eventually meets his own end when a statue of the commander comes to life and drags him to hell. The theme of Don Juan has been the inspiration for many artistic works. The earliest known dramatization is attributed to Gabriel Téllez (*El burlador de Sevilla*), written in 1630. Perhaps most famous are Molière's *Le Festin de Pierre* (1665) and Wolfgang Amadeus Mozart's opera *Don Giovanni* (1787). Other works include George Gordon Lord Byron's *Don Juan* (1819–1824), Juan Ignacio de Esproneeda's *Estudiante de Salamanca* (1840–1842?), Richard Strauss' *Don Juan* (1888), and George Bernard Shaw's *Man and Superman* (1903).

Study of large segments of the population reveals that frequent sexual outlet is neither rare nor legendary. More than 7 percent of males in the Kinsey sample (more than one in 15) averaged seven orgasms a week. One in four of these men was less than 30 years old.

Women with high frequencies of sexual outlet were fewer in the Kinsey sample, but certainly many were as active as the most active males. Conventions and social expectations are more inhibiting of expressions of female sexuality. Yet women are physiologically better equipped to achieve multiple orgasms during a single sexual episode (*see* Chapter 3). Some women attain multiple climaxes every time that they have intercourse throughout long and active sexual lives; occasionally such a woman may reach a dozen or more climaxes in an hour, which probably no man is capable of doing.

In view of the available data, the range of variation in sexual outlets in a large population makes it clear that individuals cannot be arbitrarily defined as abnormal or unhealthy simply by the frequency of their sexual activities. They may be happy or unhappy about these activities, but their feelings are often determined by social considerations.

---

sexual malfunction. Because of its lack of precision and pejorative connotations, this term is now shunned by many therapists.[5]

Further refinements allow for more specific designations of the disorder. Masters and Johnson call *primary orgasmic dysfunction* cases where a woman has never attained orgasm under any circumstance (the same would be true for "primary impotence").

When a woman is orgasmic under some circumstances (such as masturbation) but not others (such as coitus or coitus with a specific partner) then it is a case of *situational orgasmic dysfunction*. If the failure to orgasm is restricted to coitus then the condition is one of *coital orgasmic inadequacy*. Women who were orgasmic once but no longer are have *secondary orgasmic dysfunction*.[6]

Two other conditions, which fall somewhat outside this classification, are *dyspareunia* and *vaginismus*. The first term refers to painful coitus in women. Painful coitus does

[5]The implication in calling a woman "frigid" is that she is a cold and rejecting sort of person. Many women who are sexually dysfunctional simply do not show such traits. If the term means "sexually cold," it again is misleading since some women are not lacking in sexual passion yet still fail to reach coital orgasm.

[6]Kolodny et al. (1979).

occur in men but is relatively much more rare. Vaginismus is a condition of involuntary spasm of the musculature surrounding the vaginal opening. The result ranges from painful coitus to absolute resistance to all penetration.

Male Sexual Dysfunction

Impotence ("lacking in power") was indiscriminately invoked in the past to explain most forms of male sexual failure. More precisely defined, it consists of the inability to attain and maintain an erection of sufficient firmness to permit coitus. *Primary impotence* exists when the man has never been able to have coitus; *secondary impotence* refers to failure in a previously functional person.

Occasional inability to have an erection is exceedingly common, especially as a person gets older. Such transient failure is not pathological. In this regard there is no absolute scale against which to evaluate male performance. Obviously a man must keep his erection long enough to penetrate and reach a climax. Beyond such minimal criteria, judgments can be only relative. A penis that is powerless in one instance may perform adequately in a better-lubricated vagina, a relaxed atmosphere, with a more supportive partner, and so on.[7]

In view of these ambiguities, accurate assessment of the prevalence of impotence is very difficult. Most figures quoted in surveys include only individuals with long-standing and nearly complete impotence.

Erectile impotence affected about one of every hundred males under 35 years of age in the Kinsey sample, but the inadequacy was chronic and totally incapacitating in only some of them. At 70 years of age about one in four males was impotent. The progressive decline of potency with age is fairly general, though some men retain their potency into old age.

Among the 790 cases of both sexes reported in *Human Sexual Inadequacy* there were 245 cases of impotence (31 percent), of which 13 percent were of the primary and 87 percent of the secondary type.[8]

Erectile potency and sexual desire usually go together. The problem is worse when desire persists despite physical failure. In the rare pathological condition known as "priapism" the opposite is true—erections do not reflect sexual desire and may actually be painful.

It is difficult for many men to imagine a more humiliating and despairing problem than impotence. The damage is far more serious than loss of sexual pleasure. Male notions of masculinity and even personal worth are so closely linked to potency that any malfunctioning is likely to shatter self-esteem. The impotent man has been derided in the literature of many lands:

When such a man has a bout with a woman, he does not do his business with vigor and in a manner to give her enjoyment. . . . He gets upon her before she has begun to long for pleasure, and then he introduces with infinite trouble a member soft and nerveless. Scarcely has he commenced when he is already done for; he makes one or two movements, and then sinks upon the woman's breast to spend his sperm; and that is the most he can do. This done he withdraws his affair, and makes all haste to get down again from her. . . . Qualities like these are no recommendation with women.[9]

A more rational and compassionate view of impotence would be possible if sexual performance were to be decoupled from all the extraneous associations that it is usually encumbered with. Loss of sexual potency should be no reflection on any other aspect

---

[7]For clinical purposes a man may be considered secondarily impotent if his attempts at coitus fail in one out of four instances (Masters and Johnson, 1970, p. 157). For overviews of male dysfunction see Friedman (1977) and Kolodny et al. (1979).

[8]Masters and Johnson (1970), p. 358.
[9]Nefzawi (1964 ed.), p. 110.

of the person. Furthermore, a less genital focus would foster a broader perception of sex. There are many physically handicapped persons, for instance, who are incapable of coitus yet are able to maintain other pleasurable forms of sexual relations with their partners.

Of ejaculatory disturbances by far the most prevalent is premature ejaculation, which may or may not be associated with failures of erection. Armed with the finding that three out of four men reach orgasm within two minutes of intromission, and that most male animals do so even sooner, Kinsey made light of premature ejaculation as a form of sexual malfunctioning.

Although it may be impossible to set exact time limits to define normal functioning, there is no mistaking the fact that a significant number of men (and their partners) complain of inability to delay ejaculation until some measure of deliberate mutual enjoyment has been obtained. It is small comfort to them to realize that subhuman primates ejaculate even sooner. Especially when their own orgasms may even precede penetration, the whole point of sexual intercourse may seem lost.

For clinical purposes, premature ejaculation has been defined as the inability to control ejaculation long enough to satisfy a normally functional female partner in at least 50 percent of coital encounters.[10] On the other hand, one can exclude this as a problem if a couple agrees that the quality of their sexual relations is not influenced by efforts to delay ejaculation.[11]

The length of intercourse preceding orgasm is not always directly related to the gratification obtained by either partner. Generally, the longer a man can delay ejaculation, the greater is the opportunity for the woman to achieve orgasm. But, again, some women may be gratified by practically any potent man, whereas others would not respond, no matter how long the man could continue.[12] Some 25 percent of women seem capable of reaching orgasm during coitus in less than a minute, but another 10 percent fail to do so even if coitus lasts longer than 15 minutes. The median duration of coitus is somewhere between four and seven minutes, and the ability to persist beyond the higher limit does not significantly increase the incidence of coital orgasms for women.[13]

The opposite of premature ejaculation is retarded ejaculation. This is the least frequent of all male sexual dysfunctions and has been recognized widely as a discrete dysfunctional entity relatively recently. Unlike impotence, its primary form is more common than the secondary, which would mean loss of ability to ejaculate intravaginally in a previously normal ejaculator. Some men with ejaculatory incompetence are unable to reach orgasm extravaginally as well. In these cases arousal subsides without the climactic release of orgasm.

It should be noted that many males normally may experience occasionally a temporary inability to ejaculate during coitus. This is usually resolved by more vigorous thrusting or some other form of heightening arousal to the point of orgasm.

Another ejaculatory disturbance, which is not related to timing but the direction of semen flow, is *retrograde ejaculation*. In this case semen instead of flowing out normally empties into the urinary bladder. The sensa-

---

[10]Masters and Johnson (1970).
[11]Lo Piccolo (1977).

[12]The ultimate in control of ejaculation is required for the performance of *karezza*, or *coitus reservatus*, which has enjoyed sporadic popularity in various parts of the world, including the nineteenth-century Oneida colony in upstate New York. In *karezza* intercourse proceeds as usual, but actual ejaculation is delayed indefinitely. Those who have mastered this technique claim that they can reach a dozen or more sexual climaxes without ejaculation. It has also been suggested that such males actually experience retrograde ejaculation (*see* Chapter 3) during the act. Incidentally, coitus reservatus is not to be confused with coitus interruptus, where the male simply withdraws prior to ejaculation (*see* Chapter 6 and Lehfeld, 1968).
[13]Gebhard (1966).

tion of orgasm in this condition is unchanged, but the man is usually alarmed by the absence of semen. This condition occurs in certain illnesses and occasionally after the use of some common tranquilizers. In the latter instance the problem is transitory. When use of the drug is discontinued, the usual flow of semen is reestablished.[14]

Some men have reportedly developed the ability to produce retrograde ejaculation as a means of birth control. The physiological explanation of this phenomenon involves the functioning of the two urethral sphincters. Normally the internal sphincter (which guards the entrance to the bladder) closes during ejaculation, and the external sphincter (which is located below the point of entry of the ejaculatory ducts) opens. In retrograde ejaculation the external urethral sphincter closes and the internal sphincter opens, thus permitting the semen to back up into the bladder.

Female Sexual Dysfunction

Serious attention to female sexual dysfunction is a relatively recent phenomenon. The biological reason for this neglect is due to the fact that female sexual responsiveness is not essential to procreation. The culturally based explanation is that female sexual needs have been considered either unimportant, nonexistent, or necessary to be suppressed. Currently these attitudes have been by and large discredited at least among those more enlightened sexually.

Various studies have reported different percentages of orgasmic responsiveness in women, but these are not too inconsistent. In addition to the statistics already cited, we should note that in a study of 3705 married British women 10 percent rarely experienced orgasm and 5 percent never had.[15] Other studies have found inorgasmic women to

constitute 6 percent[16] and 5 percent[17] of study populations.[18] Even though definitive current data are lacking, the available evidence indicates that the problem of female coital inadequacy may be significantly receding. In the Hunt survey 53 percent of women who had been married for 15 years reported that they always or nearly always reached orgasm in coitus. The corresponding figure in the Kinsey survey was 45 percent. Likewise, the proportion of wives who never reached orgasm had gone down from 28 percent in the Kinsey sample to 15 percent in the Hunt sample.[19]

As discussed in Chapter 3, there is still some confusion about the nature of female orgasm.[20] Besides, orgasm and sexual gratification are not synonymous. Despite the substantial numbers of women who are not regularly orgasmic, nine out of ten of the wives in the Hunt sample reported that their marital coitus in the past year had been "generally pleasurable or very pleasurable." Likewise, in over 4 percent of "extremely happy marriages" the wives reportedly never experienced orgasm in marital coitus.[21] The inference to be drawn from these findings is not that since women can be happy without orgasm they should forget about orgasm if they cannot attain it. Rather, these data point out the greater complexity in evaluating female sexual malfunction than that of the male.[22]

In the more usual cases of orgasmic unresponsiveness a woman may become aroused sexually yet not attain orgasm. Or she may go through the motions of sexual intercourse

---

[14]Clinical aspects of retrograde ejaculation are discussed in Green, et al. (1970).
[15]Chesser (1956).
[16]Fisher (1973).
[17]Levine and Yost (1976).
[18]For an overview of female dysfunction see Musaph and Abraham (1977) and Kolodny et al. (1979).
[19]Hunt (December 1973) p. 91.
[20]For an extensive review of the determinants of female orgasm see Morokoff (1978).
[21]Gebhard (1968).
[22]For a discussion of the subjective components of various types of female orgasm, see Bardwick (1971) pp. 62-69.

but "feel nothing." To placate and satisfy her partner, she may actually be quite active sexually, and she may attain considerable gratification from his expressions of affection, from body contact, and from other aspects of lovemaking, even though erotic pleasure as such is absent. More likely, the experience leaves her frustrated and angry.

Pelvic pain is a fairly common complaint among women, and sometimes it causes problems in coitus. Pain may be experienced at penetration, during intercourse, or afterward. Pain and fear of pain may be indistinguishable, particularly in the first instance. When pain occurs only during intercourse, it is less likely to be confused with fear of pain. Pain after coitus usually takes the form of a dull ache associated with irritability. When pain is felt or anticipated, a certain amount of muscular tension is inevitable. As the pelvic muscles surrounding the introitus become spastic, penetration becomes difficult and sometimes (as in vaginismus) impossible.[23]

Vaginismus is not necessarily associated with pain. As an involuntary spasm it occurs in response to physical or psychological causes. Generally these women have no difficulty in sexual arousal. Vaginal lubrication occurs normally and they may have no difficulty attaining orgasm through noncoital means. The problem is specific to vaginal penetration.[24]

Failure in Coital Gratification

How do we determine whether or not an act of intercourse with orgasm has been satisfactory? The question is not rhetorical, even though it may be impossible to answer. Any experienced person can testify that not all coital orgasms are the same; and some may complain that, though they are potent or responsive, they are not enjoying sexual intercourse enough.

Enhancing coital gratification is an ancient quest, and we have described some ways in which it can be accomplished. As the only criterion is subjective experience, however, complaints cannot easily be evaluated as symptoms of sexual malfunctioning. Sometimes the problem is one of unrealistic expectations.

In the current preoccupation with sex and its exploitation for commercial purposes, some men and women have come to expect of every orgasm an earth-shaking experience. Ordinary and otherwise perfectly acceptable levels of gratification leave them disappointed. The only cure for this problem is to recognize that the body cannot necessarily deliver everything that the imagination calls for.

Sometimes orgasm is experienced with markedly diminished pleasure. The problem may be fear of experiencing strong emotion and resulting loss of emotional control. It is also possible that genuine neurophysiological disturbances may be present, even though we are as yet unable to identify them.

Causes of Sexual Malfunctioning

Sexual functioning is vulnerable to disruption from biological, psychological, and cultural causes. At least in theory the interaction of forces from all three areas is present. In practice, however, we identify the disorder according to the dominant cause only. The causes of sexual malfunctioning can thus be subsumed under several categories: organic, psychogenic (intrapsychic or interpersonal), and cultural.

In most cases specific correlation between cause and effect is not possible, especially where causes are psychogenic. Thus the same psychological conflict may result in impotence in one man and premature ejaculation in another. Or resentment at the partner will make one woman experience pain and another fail to reach orgasm. Where organic

---

[23]For more detailed discussion of coital pain, see de Senarclens (1977).

[24]Kolodny (1979).

causes are present, more specific linkage may be possible: A drug that disrupts parasympathetic function will cause impotence; another drug that interferes with sympathetic function will interfere with orgasm.

Organic Causes

Sexual inadequacy is known to arise from demonstrable physical causes. In these instances psychological factors may contribute or be present as secondary reactions to the malfunction itself, but they are not the primary causes.

So far as we know, the majority of cases of sexual malfunction result from psychogenic, not organic, causes. However, in a significant number of persons there may well be a physical basis underlying the sexual disorder.[25] It is therefore essential that all cases of sexual malfunction (especially where pain is present) be seriously evaluated for the presence of organic illness.

There are a large number of medical conditions with a concomitant sexual disturbance. A detailed consideration of these conditions would be inappropriate in the present context. We will, however, briefly consider some illustrative examples.[26]

Sexual functions in both sexes can suffer as a result of chronic debilitating illnesses such as cancer, degenerative diseases, severe infections, or systemic disorders involving the renal, cardiovascular, and pulmonary systems. Certain liver diseases (for example, hepatitis, cirrhosis) and endocrine disorders (for example, hypothyroidism, hypopituitarism, diabetes) are also likely to interfere with sexual performance.

Diseases specifically affecting the genitalia will obviously cause problems. Among males there are conditions that cause pain during intercourse (for example, inflammations, Peyronie's disease), interfere with intromission (for example, congenital anomalies), or affect testicular function (for example, estrogen-producing tumors). Among females there are even more common causes for pain during coitus (for example, inflammations, clitoral adhesions, deep pelvic infections, various forms of vaginitis, allergic reactions to deodorants).

Various surgical conditions that can be at fault include procedures that damage the genitals and their nerve supply (for example, some types of prostatectomy, lumbar sympathectomy). Castration will often (but not always immediately) result in loss of libido and impotence. Likewise, surgical procedures among women which damage the sexual organs (for example, obstetrical trauma, poorly repaired episiotomies) will often cause pain during coitus. Conditions that interfere with the blood supply to the genitals (for example, thrombosis) will also cause difficulty, among males in particular.

Finally, there are neurological disorders that may seriously influence sexual functions in both sexes. These include diseases of the frontal and temporal lobes of the brain (for example, tumor, epilepsy, vascular damage, trauma) or disturbances of the spinal cord (for example, congenital anomalies, degenerative conditions, trauma).[27]

Drugs are another important source of sexual difficulty that could be subsumed under organic causes. One category of drugs with deleterious effects act on the brain. These include sedatives, like alcohol, and barbiturates and narcotics, such as heroin, morphine, codeine, and methadone. The effects of these drugs are usually confined to

---

[25]It is estimated, for instance, that about 10 to 15 percent of cases of impotence have a primarily organic basis (Kolodny, 1979, p. 375).

[26]A related consideration is the effect of sex on health (see Box 12.3).

[27]For more detailed discussion, see Kaplan (1974), chapter 4. Organic causes for painful coitus in women are discussed in Fink (1972), pp. 28–47; and organic causes in impotence are dealt with in Belt (1973). A great deal of the original research in this area is in Masters and Johnson (1970). Also see Kolodny et al (1979).

Box 12.3 The Effects of Sex on Health

The beliefs that one has about the effects of sex on health often exert an important influence on one's sexual functioning. Although many of these notions have been formally discarded, the same basic concerns influence current thinking.

Man seems always to have attributed peculiar significance to semen; and Hippocrates, among other authorities, commented on its "precious" character. Pythagoras called it "the flower of the blood." It has also been considered an emanation of the brain, and even a product of the soul rather than of the body (Epicurus). As late as the turn of the twentieth century, medical textbooks, though disavowing these notions, seriously declared that loss of an ounce of semen equaled a loss of 40 ounces of blood.[1]

From such premises it would be easy to conclude that masturbation is a wasteful and debilitating practice and that "excessive" intercourse leads to ill health. Criteria for "excessiveness" and "ill effects" have varied. The following excerpt is from a medieval document by Moses ben Maimon (Maimonides; 1135–1204), but we need not search long to find similar notions even in current medical circles:

Effusion of semen represents the strength of the body and its life, and the light of the eyes. Whenever it (semen) is emitted to excess, the body becomes consumed, its strength terminates, and its life perishes. . . . He who immerses himself in sexual intercourse will be assailed by (premature) aging. His strength will wane, his eyes will weaken, and a bad odor will emit from his mouth and his armpits. . . . His teeth will fall out and many maladies other than these will afflict him. The wise physicians have stated that one in a thousand dies from other illnesses and the remaining (999 in the thousand) from excessive sexual intercourse.

Therefore, a man must be cautious in this matter if he wishes to live wholesomely. He should not cohabit unless his body is healthy and very strong and he experiences many involuntary erections. . . . Such a person requires coitus and it is therapeutic for him to have sexual intercourse.[2]

There is no evidence that in a person of average health sexual activity leads to either debility, premature aging, or ill health. Furthermore, for all practical purposes "excessive" sexual experience is impossible. Sooner or later the person will be sated; his body will respond less readily; and his activity will come to an end. Debauchery may involve a great deal of sex; but it also involves excessive drinking, eating, fatigue, and insomnia. No one questions that these factors undermine health.

Interestingly, the very opposite view— that regular sexual outlets are essential to good health—has also been popular. There may be much to be said for regular sexual outlets, but their indispensability to physical health remains to be demonstrated.

The problem is different for sick people. Orgasm places considerable strain on the cardiovascular system. People who would react adversely to any kind of exertion would also suffer from the physiological strain of sexual activity. Occasionally, increased blood pressure may cause a stroke. Death as a result of heart attack or rupture of a cerebral vessel during coitus also occurs, but rarely. With caution and common sense, people in less than perfect health can enjoy sex without adverse effects. Even heart-transplant patients have resumed sexual activity only months after surgery.

[1]Parke (1906), p. 379.
[2]Maimon, in Rosner (1965), p. 372.

the period of their use, but more permanent effects on sexual function are also possible.

A second category of drugs that may impair libido and sexual responses through the brain are the "antiandrogens," which include estrogen (as used in replacement therapy in postmenopausal women and in the treatment of prostatic cancer), adrenal steroids such as cortisone, and ACTH (often used to counteract allergies and inflammatory reactions).[28] There is also an experimental drug (cyproterone acetate) that has been employed in the treatment of certain compulsive sexual behaviors.

Other drugs act peripherally—for example, by blocking the nervous impulses controlling the blood vessels and nerves of the genitalia. Anticholinergic drugs, such as atropine, may cause impotence by their effects on the parasympathetic nervous system, and antiadrenergic drugs interfere with the sympathetic system and cause ejaculatory problems.

The main thing to remember in this connection is that whenever a person is using a drug—any drug—and develops sexual problems, the drug must be evaluated as a possible cause of the problem. This is especially true for tranquilizers and all other compounds that act on the central nervous system.

Psychogenic Causes

Psychological factors are the more common causes of sexual dysfunction, yet they are more difficult to identify and classify than organic causes, especially as they pertain to deeper rooted intrapsychic or interpersonal conflicts. For ways of distinguishing the two, see Box 12.4

Traditionally the focus in study and treatment of sexual dysfunction used to be on fundamental personality problems and patterns of conflict in the dyad or couple involved. One of the main contributions of more recent approaches to sex therapy (the so-called "new sex therapy") has been the identification of more immediate and more easily identified psychological factors in sexual dysfunction. We shall therefore first deal briefly with these factors through illustrative examples.

Immediate Causes

Psychological factors that qualify as immediate causes can be thought of in a sense as the tip of the iceberg. Although they have deeper roots, for purposes of therapy it is often not necessary to either understand or deal with these deeper roots.

An example of immediate cause for dysfunction is the failure to engage in effective sexual behavior because of sexual ignorance. A middle-aged man who does not know that it is normal that he should require more direct physical stimulation to get an erection may develop impotence by interpreting as failure his inability to respond to erotic psychological stimuli.

Sexual anxiety based on the fear of failure is notorious and possibly the most common immediate cause of psychogenic impotence. Other sources of sexual anxiety are the demand for sexual performance and the excessive need to please the partner. Such conditions elicit resentment and the anger is readily transferred into failure to perform sexually.

Another important cause is "spectatoring," whereby a person anxiously and obsessively watches over his or her reactions during sex. Because satisfactory sex requires that one be able to "lose oneself" in the erotic interaction, such spectatoring will distract the person and prevent the appropriate sexual responses building up to orgasm.[29]

Finally, the failure to communicate often forces a couple to guess what is desired and

---

[28]For the effects of birth control pills on sexual function see Chapter 6.

[29]For a range of viewpoints on how to overcome "spectatoring," see *Medical Aspects of Human Sexuality* (1977).

Box 12.4   Differential Diagnosis of Impotence

One of the key determinations to be made in cases of impotence, as with other dysfunctions, is whether the cause is primarily organic or psychogenic. Until recently, the clinician had recourse to two means to make this distinction: the first was to determine whether the patient had any of the organic conditions, such as diabetes, that are known to cause impotence; the second was to look for clues in the history of the symptom. Thus the cause would likely be psychogenic if the impotence had appeared suddenly in an otherwise healthy man or if it was transient or selective in occurrence (i.e., during coitus but not masturbation, with one partner but not another).

This approach has a number of limitations. If a condition such as diabetes is present, it is tempting to accept it as the cause without documenting the fact that it is indeed the cause in a particular case. Similarly, the conclusion that the problem is psychogenic often rests on the exclusion of organic causes and therefore at best is an inference rather than a direct determination of causality.

During the past decade the penile tumescence (NPT) has become a helpful diagnostic device in cases of impotence. The procedure is based on the finding that virtually all healthy males have erections in their sleep that occur every 90 to 100 minutes and last an average of 20 to 40 minutes. These erections are closely associated with REM sleep, as we discussed earlier (see Chapter 9).

The diagnostic procedure is carried out in a sleep laboratory where the pattern of sleep can be followed with an electroencephalogram and simultaneous observation of eye movements. Penile erections occurring during sleep are measured by strain gauges placed about the penis that accurately record the magnitude, duration, and pattern of the erection and whether it coincides with REM sleep. Complete absence or seriously deficient nocturnal penile tumescence suggests an organic cause. If NPT is normal, psychogenic factors are much more likely to be the underlying problem of the impotency.[1]

[1]Karacan (1978); Karacan et al. (1977); Fisher et al. (1975).

---

what is ineffective or objectionable in the sexual interaction. Communication that is clear and appropriate to the occasion is necessary to provide information as well as reassurance. Even when failure to communicate is not the primary cause of the dysfunction, it helps to perpetuate other existing pathological sexual interactional patterns.[30]

Intrapsychic Causes

The vast majority of the deeper roots of sexual malfunction in both sexes result from internal conflicts primarily related to past experiences. When these conflicts dominate a person's sex life to the extent that inadequate performance is the rule, then the causes can be considered primarily intrapsychic. On the other hand, when the sexual problem seems to be part of a larger conflict between two specific people, it is more convenient to label it "interpersonal." This distinction, though arbitrary, has practical merit in treatment. Intrapsychic causes must be dealt with as such. As veterans of successive divorces discover, when marital partners change, the conflicts may remain the same. Interpersonal conflicts also ultimately result from intrapsychic problems, but the latter may be more circumscribed and require no special attention.

[30]Kaplan (1974). See Chapter 7 for further discussion of immediate causes. Fay (1977) considers sexual problems related to poor communication.

Treatment may then be focused on the relationship between two individuals rather than on the individuals themselves.

In most established patterns of malfunctioning, specific external causes are difficult to identify (and there are also many instances in which such circumstances cause no sexual disturbance). We ascribe these disorders to the influence of forgotten events from the past operating as repressed conflicts or as faulty learning.

Learning theorists have proposed a variety of models to explain the genesis of sexual malfunctions. Central to many is the mechanism of conditioning, in which the affect associated with an experience determines one's future reaction to a similar situation. Sometimes the antecedents of the experience are easy to trace. A sexually adequate man suffers a mild heart attach during coitus; thereafter the very thought of sex makes him anxious. Another man develops a prostate infection, and sexual intercourse becomes painful; gradually his potency declines, even though his infection is cured and he experiences no further pain.[31]

More often, malfunctioning results from a complex series of learning experiences. The transmission of certain sexual attitudes and values to children—like teaching that sex is dirty or dangerous—is one example. A man may have forgotten specific or implied parental admonitions and punishments, but their damaging effects on his sexual performance persist.

Psychoanalysts offer extensive explanations of the intricate intrapsychic conflicts behind sexual malfunctioning. In contrast to the view that the key lies in faulty learning, psychoanalytic interpretations emphasize unconscious conflicts that influence behavior. For instance, conflicts arising from unresolved oedipal wishes may be major causes of difficulties in both sexes. Castration anxiety is a common explanation for failures of potency among males. The person who retains repressed and unresolved incestuous wishes from the oedipal period may unconsciously reexperience these forbidden and threatening desires when he attempts to engage in coitus. He feels tremendous guilt and primitive childhood fear of punishment in the form of genital mutilation. Under these circumstances he cannot perform—by losing his potency he obviates the necessity for engaging in the incestuous (symbolic but very real for him) act and its dire consequences for him.

When a man's impotence applies to coitus with his wife but not with a prostitute, he may unconsciously be equating the former with his mother and therefore failing. Men who distinguish between "respectable" women (to be loved and respected) and "degraded" women (to be enjoyed sexually) are said to have a "madonna-prostitute complex."

The female counterpart to this conflict, according to psychoanalytic theory, involves the father. As all men or certain types of men (defined by marital status, body build, or any of innumerable other characteristics) may be unconsciously identified with the father, the result may be to avoid coitus with any man, or at least to feel no pleasure in it. When no emotional involvement occurs, the woman is less likely to feel guilty about her incestuous conflict.

Some sexual difficulties result from fundamentally nonsexual conflicts. Some people experience primitive fears, for instance, of being engulfed, or losing their boundaries as individuals. Sexual penetration and the feeling of dissolution during orgasm may evoke such fears and can therefore be exceedingly threatening.

Finally, there is the threat of loss of control. As orgasm implies a certain abandonment of self-control, some men and women fear that other dangerous impulses will also be released. At times this fear is experienced consciously as a fear that the vagina will be

---

[31]Wolpe and Lazarus (1966), p. 102.

torn or that the penis will be "trapped" by the vagina (*penis captivus*).[32] Usually the apprehension is vague, not even consciously felt; the man simply fails to have an erection; and the woman fails to reach orgasm.

Interpersonal Conflict

It takes two to make love just as it takes two to quarrel. Apart from moral considerations, an irreducible minimum of affection and intimacy is required if any mutual gratification is to emanate from intercourse. Some people insist that anything short of deep love cheapens the act; others find this view utopian or naïve.

Interpersonal conflicts are extensions of intrapsychic problems, but sometimes the pathology takes the form of a particular type of relationship. There is no end to the kinds of interpersonal conflicts that interfere with sex. Some people even claim that the quality of sexual intercourse is the best indicator of the nature of the overall relationship.

Intense disappointment, muted hostility, or overt anger will obviously poison sexual interaction. Subtle insults are just as detrimental. Women, for instance, are quite sensitive about being "used." If a man seems to be interested predominantly in a woman's body and neglects her thoughts and feelings, she will feel that she is being degraded to the level of an inanimate object.

Some women associate coitus with being exploited, subjugated, and degraded. It is natural for a woman who feels this way to rebel by failing to respond.

Men and women have deeply ingrained needs for love and security that are often obtained through sex. But traditionally women have had much more at risk because of pregnancy in fulfilling these needs. Consequently, any male behavior before or during intercourse that even remotely implies unconcern and insensitivity may make a woman reluctant to respond, even though she deprives herself of pleasure as well.

The attitudes most detrimental to the male's enjoyment are those that threaten his masculinity. Lack of feminine response, nagging criticism, and open or covert derision rarely fail to have an impact on male enjoyment. A man who feels overburdened by a dependent wife may also react negatively if her sexual requirements appear to be endless as well. Women have sometimes used sexual apathy vindictively, or have used it to obtain what they want. These weapons, though effective, are double-edged swords.

The human mind is subject to such twists and turns that individual sexual responses may seem paradoxical and unpredictable. Some people respond sexually only when they are humiliated or hurt, and what would be inimical to an ordinary relationship becomes for them a prerequisite for potency and responsiveness. Often these people have such harsh consciences that enjoyment is only possible for them after punishment and pain.

Other dyadic causes include contractual disappointments. When people establish friendships or get married, their sexual expectations are rarely clearly communicated or negotiated. There is thus room for misunderstanding and anger over the person's not living up to what was expected. Or, as people change, new needs and new dislikes alter the nature of the original relationship.

In the power struggles that use sex many forms of sabotage can be seen to operate. One partner will pressure the other into sex at inopportune moments. Sex is withheld as punishment. People make themselves undesirable or even repulsive through neglect of their bodies, or cultivating the wrong image, or behaving in ways that are irritating

---

[32]Among dogs certain anatomical features make it possible that a male is unable to withdraw its fully erect penis from the vagina. It is generally held that such "locking" cannot occur in humans under any circumstances, but occasional sources claim the contrary (*see* Oliven, 1974, p. 240; Melody, 1977, p. 111).

and embarrassing to the other. The intended and sometimes unintended victim of all this is the sexual life of the couple.[33]

Cultural Causes

Even though the blessings and burdens of a culture are unevenly distributed among its people, no one is entirely exempt from cultural influences. But, although it would be foolish to deny the impact of prevalent sexual mores on individual functioning, particularly on the development of sexual attitudes in childhood, sweeping indictments of the mores of particular cultures are difficult to substantiate and reflect the absence of a true cross-cultural perspective.

In this country, for instance, a great deal has been made of the damaging effects of Victorian attitudes, especially on female sexuality. And the demands and anxieties of the modern world, the hectic pace of living, and the increasing assertiveness of women are blamed for sapping men's virility.

There is currently a growing literature linking sexual problems among males to the more radical attitudes and demands of feminists. Although one encounters terms like "the new impotence"[34] and "sexual suicide,"[35] referring to this phenomenon, these are as yet speculative notions.

Although the detrimental effects of such forces on sexual functioning may seem obvious enough to some people, it is nevertheless preferable to have more evidence before stating the causal relations categorically. What is most misleading is the common implication that at other times or in other places conditions have been better. Eastern cultures in particular are held up sometimes as models of sexual good sense. It is perhaps helpful to realize that the average Indian has never heard of the *Kama Sutra* and that knowledge of Persian love manuals is restricted primarily

to scholars of Islamic literature (many of whom happen to be Westerners). Nor have the Eastern peoples simply lost the precepts embodied in these works, for only an aristocratic minority ever had the opportunity to enjoy them.

Not that various doctrines have not warped Western sexual attitudes in the past and do not continue to do so at present. Our public attitudes toward sex are indeed often ignorant, bigoted, and hypocritical. Some people think that we have recently become tasteless and shameless as well.[36]

Guilt certainly interferes with sexual functioning, but is guilt always and necessarily bad? Goethe at least did not think so. Once, when he attempted to make love to a willing maid at an inn, his potency failed him, and he wrote and told his wife about it, apparently grateful that he had been prevented from being unfaithful.

Nevertheless, those who mistake their sexual weaknesses for strength of moral fiber ought to be aware that neurotic conflicts may lurk behind their scruples. Religions may be sexually restrictive, but no serious religion frowns on sexual enjoyment under the proper circumstances. What sometimes appears as fear of God is simply plain old fear of sex.

In our progressively secular society it is claimed that shame is replacing guilt as the primary social inhibitor.[37] Some people argue that in Western society the premium on competence and success, combined with an overemphasis on sex, creates a formidable hurdle to enjoyment. Orgasm becomes a challenge, rather than the natural climax of coitus. Inability to achieve it or failure to reach a certain intensity becomes not only a signal of sexual incompetence but also a reflection of personal inadequacy.

Ironically, as we become freer about sex, new problems are beginning to arise related to excessive demands for performance

---

[33]For further discussion see Kaplan (1974), chapter 9.

[34]Ginsberg (1972).

[35]Gilder (1973).

[36]Tyrmand (1970).

[37]Ellis and Abarbanel, eds. (1967), p. 451.

and wholly unrealistic expectations of what sex can be and do in one's life.

The first effort at developing a major treatment program for dealing with sexual inadequacy was initiated by Masters and Johnson at the Reproductive Biology Research Foundation.[38] Their approach combines well-tried methods with certain novelties. It has the outstanding merits of brevity (two weeks) and generally good rates of success. The results have ranged from the spectacular (100 percent cure for vaginismus) to the somewhat disappointing (40 percent failure for primary impotence, which is most difficult to treat). This program is based on the conviction that there is no such thing as an uninvolved sexual partner. Treatment therefore always and necessarily involves a pair and never a single individual. Furthermore, a therapeutic team composed of a man and a woman conducts the treatment. The procedure requires that the problem couple move from home to live near the treatment center for the duration of the treatment under as pleasant and relaxed circumstances as possible.

The first step is to take a detailed history from each partner. Then the partners are instructed (never commanded) to explore a little at a time their latent erotic capabilities: to disrobe in the privacy of their bedroom, to caress and explore each other's bodies in a gentle and pleasurable manner ("pleasuring"). Gradually, over the two-week period, these "sensate focus" exercises become more intimate, and eventually they culminate in intercourse. These physical activities in private alternate with detailed discussion with the therapist team. Successes and failures are analyzed with candor, in a nonthreatening, nonjudgmental manner. Ultimate success comes when it does. There is no fixed schedule, no pressure to perform.

The key tasks are to convince the couple that sex is a natural function that requires no heroic effort, but only a relaxed, accepting attitude. No one is at fault, and there is no uninvolved partner. Each must learn to give, as well as to receive, to involve himself or herself in sex rather than to remain an observer. Orgasm will come in time; there is no need to seek it anxiously. These and similar attitudes are conveyed, along with an objective, factual approach to the sex organs and their functions.

Treatment of Sexual Malfunctioning

Sexual malfunctioning may be mild and transient or may present formidable challenges to treatment. The remedies for sexual inadequacies that can be treated range from fairly simple short-term programs to highly specialized, intensive, lengthy therapy.

Until as recently as about a decade or so ago the treatment of sexual dysfunction was in the hands of generalists; that is, physicians, psychologists, marriage counselors and others who treated physical and psychological problems and marital conflicts also dealt with sexual dysfunction. Only a few professionals specialized in the treatment of these disorders. Although numerous people no doubt were helped through such care, the results generally tended to be unimpressive. Even when the outcome was successful, the procedures were rather lengthy and tedious.

Following the work of Masters and Johnson new methods of treating sexual dysfunctions have developed that appear to be more efficacious and efficient. The focus in this "new sex therapy" is on the elimination of the dysfunctional symptoms without attempting either to change the personality structures of the people involved or to alter in some basic way the interactional patterns of the couple in the nonsexual realm.[39] More intensive interventions become necessary, of course, when the more direct attempts at

---

[38]Masters and Johnson (1970). For a summary of this work see Belliveau and Richter (1970).

[39]For an overview of the effectiveness of sex therapy see Hogan (1977).

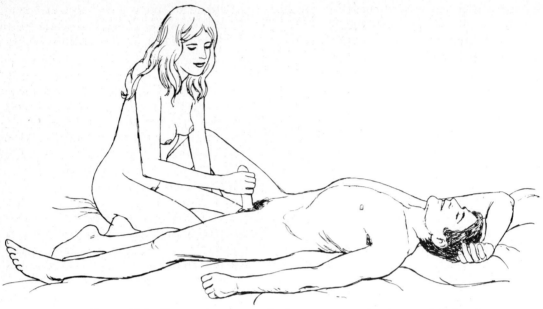

Figure 12.2   The training position for the treatment of male sexual dysfunction.

symptom alleviation fail. Another characteristic of sex therapy is that it combines therapeutic sessions in an office setting with specific tasks that the couple is expected to carry out on its own.[40]

Within this general framework more specific techniques are applied to the treatment of particular dysfunctions. For instance, when the presenting problem is premature ejaculation, it is recommended that the woman sit comfortably and that the man lie on his back facing her. This position provides her with easy and full access to his genitals (see Figure 12.2). After appropriate stimulation, when the man achieves full erection and is about to ejaculate, the woman holds the glans between her thumb and two fingers and squeezes it firmly for several seconds (see Figure 12.3) or she simply stops stimulating the penis (the "stop" rather than the "squeeze" technique). The woman then resumes genital

[40]Bereft of a conceptual base and clinical tradition, the new sex therapy can also easily deteriorate to "push-button panaceas." (Offit, 1977).

stimulation, and the procedure is repeated. Gradually the man is able to maintain increasingly longer periods of erection. Next the woman straddles him and gently lowers herself onto his erect penis (see Figure 12.4). After intromission she remains motionless in order to minimize stimulation. If the man nevertheless feels the urge to ejaculate she

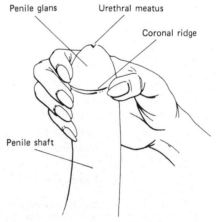

Figure 12.3   The "squeeze technique."

Figure 12.4   Coital position for the treatment of sexual dysfunction in both sexes.

withdraws and averts orgasm by the squeeze technique; then she reinserts the penis. By this method the man is able to maintain his erection intravaginally without premature ejaculation.[41]

The treatment for impotence follows the same general pattern. The first task is to bring the man to erection. He is encouraged to communicate to the woman specifically what he finds arousing. When he has achieved erection the couple is discouraged from attempting coitus at first; instead, they continue to engage in relaxed and pleasurable foreplay. Only after sufficient confidence has been attained is intromission attempted in the same position described for treating premature ejaculation.

When the presenting symptom is orgasmic dysfunction in the woman, the couple goes through the same preliminaries, but then the male becomes more active in stimulating his partner. A suitable position is with the man comfortably seated on the bed and the woman between his legs with her back turned to him, thus providing him with ready access to both her breasts and her genitals (*see* Figure 12.5). During coitus, however, the partners resume exactly the same approach as for male inadequacy. In both instances the woman takes the initiative and the more "active" role in coitus.

Starting with this basic approach various modifications have been introduced.[42] Special problems such as vaginismus have other special approaches, including progressive dilation of the vaginal orifice.[43]

In summary form, the central tasks in treating various dysfunctions are as follows: In erectile dysfunction the basic aim is to reduce anxiety so that physiological responses

[41]The basic procedure in this approach was reported by Semans (1955). For further uses of this approach see Levay and Kagle (1977).

[42]See for example Kaplan (1974); and Lo Piccolo and Lo Piccolo (1978).
[43]Kolodny *et al* (1979) chapter 17.

Figure 12.5 The training position for the treatment of female sexual dysfunction.

can take their course. In premature ejaculation the aim is to train the man to focus on his sensations so that he can learn to anticipate orgasm and modulate his level of arousal accordingly. In case of retarded ejaculation, the basic aim is the extinction of the inhibition that prevents orgasm.

When the problem is failure of arousal in women, the task is to help the person learn how to "let go." In orgasmic failure the inhibition that prevents orgasm needs to be extinguished, and in vaginismus the aim is the elimination of vaginal spasm reaction. These seemingly simple tasks are of course far from being so. Their successful attainment requires motivation on the part of the patient and partner and the necessary skills on the part of the therapist.[44]

Most qualified sex therapists have a particular theoretical orientation and basic treatment skills that they bring into such work. For instance, psychiatrists may rely on psychoanalytic theory and psychotherapeutic approaches. Psychologists will use behavior modification techniques based on learning theory. Marriage counselors are more likely to draw from various interactional theories.

Thus the competent sex therapist works out of a particular theoretical context and a therapeutic tradition. Since none of these approaches are specific to the treatment of sexual dysfunction, we shall not deal with them here.[45]

Physical and Chemical Therapies

The treatment of physical defects and other organic causes of sexual malfunction is primarily a medical matter. Some of these problems (such as pain from infections) are simple to treat, whereas others are incurable.

Tranquilizers may be helpful in allaying overt anxiety, but they do nothing for calm individuals. If the underlying cause of the sexual problem is depression, appropriate antidepressant drug therapy can be very helpful.

"Aphrodisiacs" are of no reliable use (*see* Chapter 4) but testosterone can be quite

[44]For further information on sex therapy see Kaplan (1974), Lo Piccolo and Lo Piccolo (1977), and Offit (1977).

[45]There is a vast literature on psychoanalytic technique and the methods of treatment derived from it. Succinct presentation of this material can be found in Colby (1951) and DeWald (1964). Also see Rosen (1977). Introductions to the principles of behavior modification can be found in most general psychology texts. See, for example, McConnell (1974), pp. 405–409, and Ruch and Zimbardo (1971), pp. 630–640. For more specialized presentations that include references to the treatment of sexual disorders, see Eysenck (1960), Wolpe and Lazarus (1966), Paul (1969), Yates (1970), Kaplan (1974), Lazarus (1977), and Bancroft (1977).

Box 12.5 Penile Prostheses

A prosthesis (from Greek for "addition") is an artificial substitute for a missing part of the body. The term is also applied to devices that are incorporated in the penis to help make it erect. These devices do not cure impotence; they are simple splints that make intercourse possible. Currently their use is more often for those cases of impotence that are due to irreversible organic cause. They are also a last resort for cases that do not respond to sex therapy and otherwise would have no hope of coital function.

One type of penile prosthesis consists of fixed rods made of synthetic materials that, when implanted in the penis, provide it with enough rigidity to allow coitus. These devices are relatively simple to install surgically but have the obvious disadvantage of providing the man with a permanently erect penis.

A more sophisticated prosthesis is the inflatable variety (as shown in the accompanying figure). This device consists of a circular reservoir, filled with a special fluid, that is implanted in the abdomen. It is connected by tubes to a small pump lodged in the scrotal sac, which in turn has tubes leading to the inflatable cylinders implanted in the penis. To attain erection, the man pumps the fluids into the cylinders. To return the penis to a flaccid state, a

From Robert C. Kolodny, W. H. Masters, V. E. Johnson, and Mae A. Biggs, *Textbook of Human Sexuality for Nurses.* Boston: Little, Brown, 1979.

valve in the pump is released, and thus the fluid in the penile cylinders returns to the reservoir.

The disadvantages of the inflatable device include the greater technical difficulty entailed in its installation but the complications that occasionally arise are about equal in the two types of devices. (The cost of surgery for the inflatable device, which can go as high as $9000, is about twice that of having a fixed rod implanted.)

Such devices are less than perfect substitutes for normal erections. But they do provide select cases of males a chance to enjoy coitus, which otherwise would be impossible.

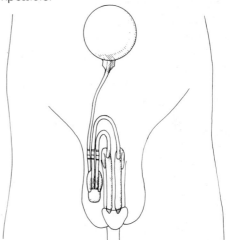

An inflatable penile prosthesis. Courtesy of American Medical Systems.

effective in select cases of male dysfunction. Finally, there are extreme measures that provide men with mechanical supports so that they can achieve penetration: Splints can be attached to the penis to carry the flaccid organ into the vagina, or silicone prostheses can actually be implanted in the penis.[46] These

permit a couple to carry on a semblance of intercourse, and sometimes, after using splints, a man gains enough confidence and potency to dispense with artificial aids (they are therefore sometimes called "coitus-training apparatus"). Currently more sophisticated mechanical devices are under development and are finding increasing use (Box 12.5).

A man who has lost his penis through

[46]Grabstald (1973).

trauma or surgery may have recourse to a penile prosthesis—actually a dildo—which he attaches. Before cringing at the thought of such devices, it is well to contemplate the despair of men in this type of predicament.

Orgasmically unresponsive women may be brought to orgasm with mechanical vibrators. Again, the hope is that once they become conditioned to experiencing orgasm, they will be able to transfer this ability to sexual intercourse.[47] Unfortunately, such transfer of orgasmic responsiveness does not seem to occur predictably, and at present the use of vibrators in therapy seems to be on the decline.

Some years ago, the gynecologist A. H. Kegel devised a set of pelvic exercises to help patients control leakage of urine that sometimes follows childbirth ("stress incontinence"). His patients spontaneously reported that their sexual functioning had also improved. These Kegel exercises are quite effective in strengthening the muscles around the vaginal orifice (the *pubococcygeus*), thus facilitating orgasm. The simplest way for a woman to learn the exercises is first to identify the main muscle involved, by voluntarily interrupting the flow of urine a few times. The exercises consist simply of flexing the same muscle ten times in a row six times a day at the beginning, and working up to longer periods. The objective, as in all other forms of exercise, is to strengthen the muscles through repeated use.

A timeless remedy that combines many aspects of these various therapies is to put the sexually inadequate person in the hands of an experienced lover. Moral considerations aside, some men and women are driven to this alternative, first to find out whether or not the failures are really their own, and then perhaps to learn from the experience. The knowing woman who seduces the tremulous young man, and the older man who initiates the virgin are well-known literary and folk figures. Some sex specialists hire women who assist in the treatment of impotent men in this way. But the practice is not free from complications and criticism.

Perhaps one of the key functions of successful sex therapy is helping individuals to place sexual fulfillment in a realistic perspective, which makes good sense for a given person at a certain stage of life. Sexual satisfaction perhaps should not be chased constantly like a never to be fully attained rainbow. Yet people with normal or somewhat faltering sexual lives also need to bear in mind that fulfillment is possible even under dire handicaps. The following guidelines intended for the physically handicapped may thus have a larger lesson for all of us:

A stiff penis does not make a solid relationship, nor does a wet vagina.

Absence of sensation does not mean absence of feeling.

Inability to move does not mean inability to learn.

The presence of deformities does not mean the absence of desire.

Inability to perform does not mean inability to enjoy.

Loss of genitals does not mean loss of sexuality.[48]

---

[47]Dengrove (1971).

[48]Anderson and Cole (1975).

Part Three
Culture

Chapter 13

Sex and Society

The social environment in which people grow up and live out their lives plays a major role in molding their social and sexual behavior. In this chapter we will examine various social and cultural factors that influence people's *sexual behavior* and their *gender roles*. Sexual behavior consists of all activities involved with masturbation and either heterosexual or homosexual sexual interactions. Gender roles consist of all the activities involved in being "masculine" or "feminine," and are not restricted to sexual activities alone (*see* Chapter 8). A person's masculine or feminine gender roles influence virtually all aspects of the person's life, affecting his or her approach to work, play, child rearing, and so forth. As a person begins to learn and feel comfortable with his or her gender roles, the person gains a sense of *gender identity,* as a male or a female.

Variability in Behavior

Anthropologists have observed a great deal of variability in sexual behavior and gender roles in their cross-cultural analyses of social patterns.[1] In some cultures sex is very important; in others it plays a minimal role. Children growing up in restrictive societies learn very different things about sexuality than children growing up in permissive societies. In Inis Beag (a restrictive Irish community) chil-

dren are never allowed to see adults in any state of undress, and sexual activities are never discussed or displayed in public.[2] Most people grow up knowing very little and feeling very guilty about sex. Misinformation is more common than correct information and it causes these people a great deal of anguish. In contrast, young people in Mangaia (a permissive society in the South Pacific) are explicitly tutored in the arts of lovemaking.[3] After the rites of passage to adulthood, young men are given formal instruction by an expert. Next, the young men are given "practical exercise" in coital techniques from an experienced woman in order that the young men can master the skills needed to be skillful lovers. At puberty the young women also receive instructions in lovemaking. Sexual activity can begin quite early in permissive societies. In the Trobriand Islands, girls may begin sexual activity at 6 or 8 years of age and boys at 10 or 12.[4] This often takes place in the context of play, in which the children are not restricted from sexual exploration (*see* Box 13.1).

Thus societal values about sex can vary considerably and have a profound influence on the way people learn to interact sexually. In addition, the social definition of gender roles—what is desirable and acceptable

[1]Davenport (1976).

[2]Messenger (1971).
[3]Marshall (1971).
[4]Malinowski (1929), p. 57.

413

Box 13.1   The Trobriand Islands

In the Trobriand Islands young children are given a great deal of freedom and independence in all areas, including their sexual explorations.[1] Not only can the children investigate the sexual responses of their own bodies and of other children, they are allowed to observe their parents engaging in sexual activities. Living with their parents in simple houses that provide little privacy, the children have ample opportunity to watch their parents and see their sexual enjoyment. All that is expected of the children is that they pretend not to be paying attention. The children hear the adults swearing and they learn to use off-color language too. Adults usually laugh when they hear children making risqué jokes.

Children are allowed to explore sexual activities during play with their peers, and they clearly obtain pleasure from doing so. They imitate adult copulatory patterns, investigate oral stimulation of the genitals, and try anything else they wish. The adults show indifference or complacency about these activities: They are tolerant and often amused but never inclined to interfere with the children's play. Naturally, not all of the children's play is sexual, but much of it has sexual overtones. The children often go into the jungle or to the beach and play at adult roles, including imitations of adult intercourse.

After puberty the children, especially the boys, leave the parents' house so as not to hamper the parents' sexual lives. The boys move to a special house, called the *bukumatula*, where young boys can bring their girl friends for sex and older boys have girls move in with them. As the period of childhood play comes to an end, more serious sexual and romantic relations develop. The adolescents have a variety of partners without any implication of settling down into an exclusive relationship. (The boys and girls also begin to take a greater role in the adult activities of the community, although they still have a great amount of freedom to leave the adults whenever they want.) The young adolescents have relatively short and casual sexual relationships, but these gradually become more serious, and eventually girls begin to cohabit with the boys in the *bukumatula*. In the *bukumatula*, discretion is practiced and couples do not break in on each other if one couple is inside making love. Nor is there group sex or swapping of partners.

As the boys and girls grow older, their relationships tend to last longer as individuals find partners with whom they get along well and form strong ties. Relationships during the period of premarital cohabitation are based on personal attraction only, and both individuals are free of any obligation to make the relationship permanent. Only after a couple has cohabited for a relatively long period of time and had considerable sexual experience would it become appropriate for the lovers and their families to consider their marriage. Only when two people are approaching the time of marriage does a sense of mutual obligation begin to require greater sexual fidelity. But even then, a partner might still have clandestine sexual relations with another person. These affairs are done with discretion, however, because too many outside relationships could endanger the plans for marriage. Before marriage, a young man and woman never eat together: Sharing a meal in common is morally unacceptable until after marriage.

[1]Malinowski (1929).

"masculine" and "feminine" behavior—also varies a great deal from society to society, and this influences the gender socialization of males and females. For example, some societies socialize males and females to have quite similar gender roles (*see* Box 13.2).[5] Among the Arapesh in New Guinea, both males and females learn gender roles in which cooperation, nurturance, and gentleness are central features. In other words, both men and women learn roles that would be identified as "feminine" by current American standards. At the other extreme, both males and females of the Mundugumor of New Guinea learn gender roles that are assertive, aggressive, and—by American standards— quite "masculine."

Although some societies socialize males and females to have similar gender roles, other societies socialize the two sexes into very different kinds of roles. We are, of course, familiar with the standard stereotypes of masculine and feminine roles in Western societies, in which males are supposed to be assertive and dominant and females are supposed to be nonassertive and nurturant. There are other possibilities. For example, role patterns almost the opposite from ours have been found in the Tchambuli of New Guinea.[5] In the Tchambuli society, males learn roles of dependence and nonassertiveness while the females learn to be dominant and self-assured (*see* Box 13.3).

The broad range of variability in sexual behavior and gender roles seen in different societies demonstrates the high level of behavioral flexibility typical of human beings. Whereas sexual behavior and gender roles of "lower" species are under strong control of genetic, hormonal and "prewired" neural mechanisms, human sexual behavior and gender roles are largely dependent on learning in a complex social environment.[6] Natu-

rally, certain aspects of human behavior are more influenced by biological factors than others. In general, patterns of foreplay and coitus are more strongly constrained by biological factors than are gender roles.[7] However, even sexual practices vary considerably across cultures.

Human learning is very much influenced by the social environment in which people live. Humans are among the most social of mammals, and virtually every aspect of an individual's behavior reflects the social patterns of the culture in which the individual lives. Even masturbation—which is usually a private behavior that children can learn without any social guidance—does not remain outside the domain of social influence. At an early age children begin to learn the social values and definitions attached to masturbation by their society. As they learn that masturbation is good or bad, natural or "sinful," these societal values will affect their thoughts, feelings, and behavior, even when they are alone.

Cultural precepts define for the individual when and where it is proper to behave in a certain manner, and they even specify the types of activities in which he may engage. In a word, the culture provides, through the habits of its members, the major learning conditions for the maturing individual.[8]

Each society structures and molds the sexual and gender behavior of its members from infancy through adulthood. The social environment provides a large number of models, rules, norms, taboos, and sanctions that guide the social development of the individual's behavior. Sexual behavior and gender role behavior are embedded in a social matrix that defines them as good or bad, regulates their occurrence, and shapes people's feelings about them. If sexuality is defined as base and sinful in one society, yet in

---

[5]Mead (1935).
[6]Ford and Beach (1951), Mischel (1966), Money (1976), and Davenport (1976).

[7]Davenport (1976).
[8]Ford and Beach (1951), p. 268.

Box 13.2 Similar Gender Roles

In some societies, men and women learn quite similar temperaments and gender roles.[1] The Arapesh, for example, live in the mountains of New Guinea. Their land is not fertile and their primary concern is with growing things: growing food and growing babies. Both men and women share the concern for making things grow; and they have similar temperaments and roles oriented toward nurturance. The people work in a very cooperative manner. Aggression and warfare are unknown. Men are not made to feel that they must be brave and aggressive in order to be masculine. From birth to death, both males and females are enmeshed in a society where everyone is cared for, and the people develop a profound sense of comfort and trust in others. The people are gentle, friendly, placid, and non-competitive. Both father and mother devote a great deal of time and energy to raising the children, and the children benefit from the security they feel at all times. Little difference is made between the rearing of boys and girls, and gender distinctions are not nearly as important as in many other societies. Children are allowed to play in any way they want, provided that they do not quarrel. Aggression is disapproved of among these peaceful

people, and from childhood the people learn not to be aggressive to each other. The children's play is not competitive or hostile. They do not play games with "sides" or "winners," but rather play at imitating the animals or the various adult activities they see around them. Raised in a world without aggression, the boys, girls, men, and women are totally un-accustomed to hostility. Even grown men cry if someone makes an unfair accusa-tion or unfriendly comment. Because the people are always surrounded by supportive family and kin, they learn to trust that everything will work out, that others will always be there to help, no matter what. Thus they come to feel that the world is a safe place. The people have a deep sense of emotional security. Free of fears, both men and women are cheer-ful, enthusiastic, and mutually supportive.

One hundred miles away is a tribe in which the gender roles show virtually the opposite extreme. Both the men and the women are hardened, arrogant, ag-gressive and intensely individualistic. The Mundugumor live in a fertile environment where they can catch fish in abundance and grow tobacco, coconuts, and other products without much effort. Since tobacco is highly valued by neighboring people, the Mundugumor are paid generously for their crops. The Mundugumor are not forced

[1]Mead (1935).

---

another it is defined as beautiful, the people in these different cultures will internalize quite different feelings and attitudes about their sexuality and related aspects of their gender roles.

Cultures are not static, unchanging structures. Modern industrial societies have changed considerably in the past several cen-turies and will doubtlessly continue to change in the future. Attitudes about sexuality and gender roles are among the cultural patterns

that change with time. Sexual behavior and gender roles in the United States in the 1980s are considerably different from the patterns of the 1940s and 1950s. Current concerns about sex and gender roles will doubtlessly help shape future changes in societal values and practices. In the remainder of this chapter we will examine the sexual and gender role behavior prevalent in American society today and describe the types of changes that have been taking place.

Box 13.2   Continued

to cooperate in order to reap the bounty of their land, and a complex set of kinship relationships tends to set the people in constant conflict such that they live in distrust of each other's motives. An air of suspicion, distrust, and hostility pervades most of their social relationships. Both men and women become hardened and defensive. Both sexes freely express anger; and frequent betrayals of trust make it such that anger is a common emotion. Men quarrel over women, since a primary concern is to attain several wives who can work to bring wealth to a man. Women quarrel with men and to some degree with other women due to the constant conspiracies and selfish rivalries that divide the entire family structure. Even children are not treated with much affection by either the mother or the father. A competitive kinship structure pits father against son, mother against daughter, such that the entire family is constantly stressed by misunderstanding, quarrels, jealousy, and even physical violence. Although women are not physically quite as strong as the men, they are just as jealous and aggressive. Before a husband picks a fight with his wife, he arms himself and makes certain that his wife is unarmed. Women are regarded as serious adversaries, and not as fragile or dainty. Many a marriage is dominated by an aggressive wife.

Box 13.3   Opposite Gender Roles[1]

Among the Tchambuli of New Guinea it is the women who have the economic and social power. By fishing and weaving, the women create goods and food for the community. The fish and woven products are traded for food and *talibun,* a currency consisting of green snail shells. The men preoccupy themselves with the arts of dancing, playing music, carving, painting, and so forth. Rarely do they contribute to the economy. The men are permitted to go to the markets, but they are trading products made by the women and the profits are controlled by the women. All through life, the only real property that a man has comes from women. In return, the men decorate their bodies, curl their hair, stage elaborate ceremonies, play music, use soft words and give pining looks to win the attention of the women.

The women value the friendship and comradeship of other women as they work together in an atmosphere of cheerful banter and jesting. "Solid, preoccupied, powerful, with shaven unadorned heads, they sit in groups and laugh together." The men vie for the eye of the women and for gifts from the women, and jealousies arise among the men as each fears that another is gaining favor with influential women. The men are temperamental. Their relationships are delicate since today's ally may be a rival tomorrow. The men are concerned with their appearance, their costumes, their skill at flute playing—and they are constantly watchful of other men, alert to catty comments and sensitive to the merest slight. Caught up in petty jealousies, the men seldom form strong, stable relationships with each other. Cast in emotionally subservient roles without stable ties with other men, each man is basically alone. In contrast, the women are joined by solid bonds of friendship that are not marred by petty bickering and jealous quarreling.

[1]Mead (1935).

Current Trends in the United States

Attitudes and values about sexuality and gender roles have been changing rapidly in the United States over the past two decades. Whereas the American society used to be quite restrictive in its attitudes about sexuality, many sectors of society have become progressively more accepting of sexuality. In general, the society has become more diversified in its values about sex. Although some sectors continue to be restrictive, the majority have become semirestrictive, and some sectors have become permissive. There has also been increasing diversity in people's conceptions of gender roles. Many retain very traditional views of masculine and feminine behavior, but others are exploring new variations. Because of this diversity, it is difficult to make sweeping generalizations that hold for all parts of the society. The following sections point to the central trends in sexual practices and gender roles in American society.

Sexual Behavior

In the 1960s it was often said that America was undergoing a "sexual revolution." Several societal changes allowed people to explore sexual activities that had previously been taboo. The development of more effective contraceptives allowed people greater freedom to enjoy sex without fear of unwanted pregnancy. Masters and Johnson's work added to the impetus originating from Kinsey's work in demystifying sex and showing a greater sexual potential in the female than had been previously presumed in American society. Sex was portrayed more openly in the media. Many religious denominations became more liberal in their views about acceptable personal behavior. The importance of virginity was de-emphasized, and many people began to accept sexual exploration before marriage. There was a greater willingness to experiment and to tolerate the experiments of others. It was a period of increasing permissiveness which paralleled rapid changes in sexual practices and values, especially among the youth.

In one sense the changes of the "sexual revolution" may actually be exaggerated. Sex is more visible now, and people can talk about it more openly. However, social values and practices tend to change slowly, since they are embedded in a vast number of habitual social practices that are resistant to change. In spite of visible signs of a new openness, many Americans remain conservative. In a 1970 representative sample of the U.S. population, 55 percent rated themselves as conservative.[9] The young were the least conservative: 41 percent of the people 21–29 years old were conservative versus 64 percent of the people 60 and older. The "fun morality" of sex (that the main reason for sex should be fun), which was advocated by Albert Ellis in 1963, was disapproved of by 65 percent of the men and 70 percent of the women.

During the next seven years the sexual attitudes of the society continued changing in the liberal direction. In a 1977 survey of a representative sample by Yankelovich, Skelly, and White, 41 percent of the Americans queried said that their views about sexual morality had become more liberal in the past few years.[10] Only 15 percent said that they had become more conservative, and 42 percent reported no change. In spite of the liberalizing trend, about 20 to 40 percent of Americans believe that all liberal values about sexuality are wrong. Again, young people tend to be most liberal.

The attitudes of the young have changed before those of the rest of the population. Several studies on college campuses between 1940 and 1971 reflect some of the early changes in values among college students.[11] The number of college women who said that premarital sex should be acceptable for both

---

[9]Wilson (1975).
[10]Yankelovich et al. (1977).
[11]Landis and Landis (1973), pp. 143–146.

Table 13.1 Attitudes about premarital sex.*

	Cornell 1940	11 colleges 1952–1955	18 colleges 1967	2 colleges 1971
The percent of women who approved of premarital sex for both men and women.	6	5	21	59
The percent of men who approved of premarital sex for both men and women.	15	20	47	70
The percent of women who approved of premarital sex for engaged people only.	6	7	23	19
The percent of men who approved of premarital sex for engaged people only.	11	16	22	16

*Landis and Landis (1973), p. 145.

men and women increased from 6 percent in 1940 to 59 percent in 1971 (see Table 13.1). College men were more likely to approve of this value than college women, with 15 percent approving in 1940 and 70 percent agreeing in 1971. As the values became liberalized, there was at first an increase in the number of students approving of premarital sex for engaged people only; but after 1967, there was a decrease in the number stating that one should wait until after being engaged.

The double standard has long prevailed in the United States. Virginity was expected of the "good" girl, but males were not expected to remain chaste until marriage.[12] At the early part of the century, young men frequently went to prostitutes to gain sexual experience. A 1976 study of 20 representative colleges and universities found that only 16 percent of men had been to a prostitute (30 percent in the South).[13] As recently as 1970 the differences between the sexes were still considerable: Approximately 49 percent of female college students were virgins, whereas approximately 18 percent of males were virgins. By 1976 many of the differences had

disappeared. At that time 26 percent of female college students were virgins and 26 percent of males were virgins. However, 14 percent of the women believed that sex should be postponed until after marriage, whereas only 8 percent of men believed the same. In a 1939 survey college students ranked 18 characteristics they would use to evaluate a potential mate, and virginity was rated tenth in importance out of the 18 characteristics. In a comparable 1978 survey, virginity was rated eighteenth by women, seventeenth by males.[14]

The frequency of premarital virginity appears to be decreasing in several segments of the population, not only among college students. The 1974 *Redbook* survey with 100,000 respondents found that while 80 percent of all women had premarital sex, 90 percent of women under 25 had had premarital sex.[15] In the 1977 *Redbook* survey on male sexuality 90 percent of the 40,000 responding males had engaged in premarital sex.[16] Interestingly, the 1974 survey on women found that the double standard is not dead: 14 percent of women would object to premarital sex for their sons, but 25 percent would object for their daughters. Even though many people are engaging in premarital sex,

[12]Approximately 40–50 percent of preliterate societies allow females to have premarital sex, and female premarital sex probably is common in 70 percent of these societies. The percentages are higher for male premarital sex (Gebhard, 1971).
[13]*Playboy* (1976).

[14]Hudson and Hoyt (in prep.).
[15]Tavris (1978).
[16]Ibid.

it does not mean that this is approved of by all. In the 1977 Yankelovich study, 60 percent of the people under 25 years of age believed that it was not morally wrong for teenagers to have sexual relations; but the majority of older people over 25 said that it was wrong.[17]

Thus the following picture emerges. Although there had been gradual social changes in sexual values and attitudes before the 1960s, there has been an acceleration of change during the past two decades. Many traditional values have not changed, however. The morality of "sex for fun" or "sex for its own sake" never appealed to even the majority of the young. The romantic ideals of marriage, fidelity, and a stable home life for rearing children are still very much alive and influential in American life. A new synthesis of values is arising. Many of the changes in sexual attitudes of the 1960s have been retained, but the more radical beliefs have been found to be unacceptable by most people. Many individuals are willing to approve of premarital exploration, but they want to be certain that no one gets hurt. Many have found that "sex for its own sake" was not as gratifying as it looked when it first became popular; and others have seen so many people hurt by irresponsible sex that they are asking for a new morality of responsible sex.

Societal Values in the Bedroom

In most societies sexual intercourse is treated as a very private, often almost secretive, interaction. In the United States most people go to great lengths to guarantee that others will not hear or see them making love. Most people continue to believe that men need sex more than women do and that it follows that men will be the natural initiators of sexual activity. Females are presumed to have less interest in sex, a lower sex drive, and a sense of discretion that would prevent

them from initiating sexual activities or directing the progress of the interaction.

It is interesting to contrast the sexual practices of Americans with the general pattern seen in most other societies and ask how much it differs.

In most of the societies for which there are data, it is reported that men take the initiative and, without extended foreplay, proceed vigorously toward climax without much regard for achieving synchrony with the woman's orgasm. Coitus is primarily completed in terms of the man's passions and pleasures, with scant attention to the woman's response. If women do experience orgasm, they do so passively.[18]

Based on his interviews in the 1940s, Kinsey noted that three fourths of married men ejaculated within 2 minutes of intromission.[19] Things changed as the "sexual revolution" made Americans aware of more gratifying modes of sexual interaction. Recent data indicate that people are spending more time in foreplay and about 10 minutes in sexual intercourse.[20] Since Kinsey discovered and Masters and Johnson documented the nature of women's multiorgasmic potential, there has been much increased interest in women's orgasm, and many women and men are attempting to develop practices that allow greater sexual satisfaction for women. Almost all of the men responding to the 1977 *Redbook* survey on male sexuality reported that it was important to them for a woman to reach orgasm—perhaps not all the time, but frequently enough to know that she was finding sex pleasurable.[21]

Caring that both partners have orgasms probably helps people have better sexual experiences than was possible in Kinsey's time,

---

[17]Yankelovich et al. (1977).

[18]Davenport (1976), p. 149. It must be noted that not all societies fit the stereotype presented in this quote. In several societies—such as pre-Christian Tahiti, Mangaia, East Bay—men have been concerned with making sex more gratifying for their partners.
[19]Kinsey et al. (1948), p. 580.
[20]Hunt (1974), p. 205.
[21]Tavris (1978).

but caring is not always enough. There is evidence that close, caring heterosexual partners still have not escaped the male dominant mode of sexual interaction. Masters and Johnson's recent comparison of homosexual and heterosexual sexual practices suggests that males still initiate and determine most of the activities in heterosexual coitus and that communication between the two partners is minimal.[22] This is especially true when a man and a woman do not know each other well; but even close married couples revealed a surprising amount of male dominance.

In virtually all the coital interactions observed between married people (who had no sexual dysfunctions and who had regular orgasmic expression), the male decided when to initiate intromission after he became sufficiently aroused himself. Without asking his wife for information, the male unilaterally decided when she was ready for intromission. Most males stated that they knew when a woman was ready for penetration by the presence of vaginal lubrication, although this physical sign has not been shown to correlate well with women's actual psychological readiness for intromission. When the male was ready to mount, he hunted for the vaginal opening and attempted to gain intromission without asking for cooperation from his wife. The fact that men often do not succeed in orienting the penis into the vagina by themselves frequently introduces moments of fumbling and distraction into the process of intromission. In spite of the distractions and frustration, women rarely offered to help their husbands and rarely initiated communication that could have facilitated better coordination.

After intromission had been accomplished, the males continued to dominate. Over 90 percent of the time the male took control of the direction of the interaction, setting the pattern of thrusting—that is, the depth, force, and frequency of thrusting.

Women were left with the role of trying to accommodate the best they could to the man's movements. This clearly created distractions for the women who frequently had to readjust their movements to suit their partner's activities. Many of the women were not optimally stimulated by coital contact, and in cases where the male ejaculated shortly after intromission the women were unlikely to overcome the problems created by their partners' behavior. In more than 80 percent of the cases observed, the man assumed the male superior position, although this position is among the least gratifying for the woman and the position makes men less likely to postpone ejaculation as long as they otherwise could. The greatest problems resulted from the male's control of the thrusting pattern. In those few cases where the man and woman showed mutual cooperation and communication, the woman attained much greater levels of excitement and more intense orgasms.

Thus, in married couples where both partners regularly attained orgasms, there was consistent evidence of male domination and control in intercourse. The female rarely assumed an equal role in determining the course of the coital events, and she usually attained her orgasms in spite of the male's suboptimal activities.

Masters and Johnson also studied coitus among males and females who were not married but who agreed to be paired with a person of the opposite sex for purposes of seeing how people engage in sex with unfamiliar partners. The picture was even more extreme than among married couples. The males assumed total control. They initiated the interaction, decided on the moment of intromission, established the pace of thrusting. "Coital activity simply became a mutual masturbational exercise, with each partner concentrating predominantly on his or her own needs."[23]

---

[22]Masters and Johnson (1979).

[23]Masters and Johnson (1979), p. 82.

Masters and Johnson freely admit that these patterns that they observed in the laboratory may not be identical with those that people experience in everyday life. Their sample was not a true cross section of the American population since it was selected from people who had no sexual dysfunctions and were regularly orgasmic. The sample was also biased by including a larger number of well-educated people than are found in the general population. Making love in the laboratory environment may have introduced some stresses even though every precaution was taken to familiarize the people with the laboratory, to make them feel comfortable there, and not to rush them to have sexual intercourse before they felt at ease. To the degree that the data from this study do reflect coital patterns in the United States, heterosexuals tend to be very goal-oriented—toward the goal of orgasm rather than that of mutual pleasure—and both men and women accept patterns of male dominance in intercourse.

In most cultures throughout history, sex has been considered to be a man's right—in fact, a man's need—and a woman's duty.[24] The man played the dominant role in initiating and determining the pattern of sexual interactions. The man was presumed to be the "sex expert" who knew what to do in coitus. Apparently, this cultural tradition has not ceased to have its influence in the West, although Masters and Johnson's research makes it clear that this "cultural influence . . . simply cannot be destroyed fast enough, for adherence to the concept of inherent male expertise in matters sexual is an anathema to effective heterosexual interaction."[25]

Between 1972 and 1975 Hite collected questionnaire data from 3019 American women about their sexual experiences.[26] Many of the women reported difficulties in reaching

orgasm, especially during intercourse. Only 26 percent of the women experienced orgasms regularly during coitus (although the number increases to 30 percent if we exclude women who have never had orgasms in any context). The women who answered Hite's questionnaires revealed that many men did not know how to provide adequate stimulation for women to orgasm and few men tried to learn. In many cases the sexual revolution has meant *more* sex, but not *better* sex. Some women indicated to Hite that the sexual revolution has left them worse off than before in some ways, since it is harder now to say no when men foist unwanted sexual attention on them.

Many males continue to be unaware of the nature of the sexual inequality in their relationships. Most studies show that men are more satisfied than women with their sexual experiences. Men not only report fewer sexual problems than women do; they say that these problems do not interfere much with their overall happiness. For example, in a questionnaire study of 52,000 predominantly young adults in 1976, the two most common male problems were the following: 19 percent of the men reported problems with premature ejaculation and 8 percent had problems in reaching orgasm.[27] In contrast, 38 percent of women reported trouble reaching orgasm and 20 percent reported slowness or inability to become aroused (these being the most commonly stated female problems). The men's problems were less likely to detract from their overall happiness than the women's problems did from their happiness. The men's problems did not prevent them from having sex or having orgasms, but the women were likely to be deprived of orgasm or they had to work to become sexually aroused. Perhaps a man's ejaculation came too soon, but at least it came. A woman, on the other hand, was less likely to receive enough effective

---

[24]Rainwater (1971), Davenport (1976).
[25]Masters and Johnson (1979), p. 219
[26]Hite (1976).

[27]Shaver and Freedman (1976).

stimulation to find sexual relations fully satisfying.

Communication

Since many men report that they care about providing sexual enjoyment for their partner, why do so many women, though liking sex, find it to be not completely satisfying? The answer lies, in part, in the lack of communication. In their research, Masters and Johnson noted that women often did not tell men what they did or did not enjoy during foreplay and coitus.[28] Women often reported that they remained silent because their partner seemed to be enjoying what he was doing so much that they hated to correct him. Although Masters and Johnson observed a few cases in which women told their partner what they would prefer, some of the men seemed to forget.

A study on 100 "normal" married couples provides another source of data about the lack of communication between men and women (*see* Chapter 12).[29] Women almost always correctly perceived and reported their husband's sexual problems, while men in contrast were less likely to note the problems their wives experienced. For example, one third of wives reported difficulty in staying excited, but only 15 percent of their husbands realized this. Other common problems reported by the 100 couples also reflect a lack of communication. These problems included: the partner chooses the wrong time for intercourse, engages in too little foreplay, or gives too little affection after the sexual interaction. Interestingly, the *Redbook* report on female sexuality found that the women who were more satisfied with their sexual and marital relations discussed their sexual feelings and needs with their partner more frequently than women who were less satisfied with their sexual and marital relations.[30]

The lack of communication between the sexes reflects in part our society's traditional restrictive treatment of sexuality. The taboos of the past continue to influence the people of today. Each person may feel uncomfortable talking with his or her partner about the intimate and personal subject of sex. Often one or both partners has limited sexual knowledge and is hesitant to speak up for fear of seeming sexually naive or inexperienced. Few people have seen models for open and considerate communication about such private topics as sexuality. The traditional folklore has been that everything will work out with time. As the people say in Inis Beag, "after marriage nature takes its course."[31] Although it does appear that many people do find their sexual interactions improving naturally with experience, studies indicate that the sexual interactions could be much more rewarding for both sexes if men and women were more knowledgeable and communicative about sex.[32]

All too often, a woman does not know that the problems which she is having are not unique to her.[33] Women often blame themselves for not being more sexual or responsive. They often fail to realize that they might ask their partner for more effective stimulation. One of the important changes of the past few years is that women are beginning to realize that it is not uncommon for other women to have difficulties in attaining a gratifying sexual response. Once a woman begins to hear or read that many women have difficulties, she is likely to realize that she is not alone and that the difficulties may not be her fault. The cultural myth that men are sex experts has not been substantiated by either laboratory research or questionnaire studies. Both women and men need to communicate more and learn about the other sex in order to make sex mutually fulfilling.

[28]Masters and Johnson (1979).
[29]Frank et al. (1978).
[30]Tavris and Sadd (1977).

[31]Messenger (1971), p. 15.
[32]Masters and Johnson (1979).
[33]Hite (1976).

Gender Roles

The activities involved in sexual interaction represent only a small fraction of the behavior that is influenced by a person's being male or female, homosexual or heterosexual. Whereas sexual activities usually occupy only a few hours of the week (at most), a person's gender identity influences his or her behavior during almost every hour of the waking day. Being male or female instantly casts one into various social roles that are to a large degree structured by society's views about the appropriate behavior for each sex. Each society molds its young for the specialized roles they will take. In the United States everyone knows that little girls are supposed to be "cute" or "ladylike" and little boys are expected to be "rowdy" and "obstreperous." Traditionally men have been expected to be assertive and success-oriented, whereas women are supposed to be more concerned with socioemotional interests.

The social roles of males and females are highly influenced by people's perceptions of and beliefs about the natural intelligence and talents of the two sexes. The belief that males are naturally more talented, competent, and assertive than women is quite common in many societies. This view used to be more strongly held in the United States than it is today, and our society is slowly changing toward a more egalitarian view. Women were not granted the right to vote until 1917 in Canada, 1920 in the United States, 1928 in England, 1945 in Japan and France, 1946 in Mexico and Argentina, and 1947 in China. More recent changes can be seen in a comparison of data from 1952 and 1976.[34] A 1952 Gallup survey revealed that most men thought society would be worse off if more females were in office. In 1976 only 17 percent of men felt the country would be worse off if more females were in office. In 1952 only 8 percent of men thought that the

women could run the country as well as men, but 43 percent of men believed this in 1976. By 1976 most men thought women were as logical as men, and 75 percent of men also felt that women are as capable as men of making scientific discoveries. But old beliefs die slowly, and even people who overtly state that men and women are equal often do not behave as if this were actually the case. Thus, even among those people who proclaim a conscious ideology of equality, there are often nonconscious biases that are carryovers from their cultural past.

Nonconscious Ideology

Although people are conscious of many of the social values and beliefs of their society, not all perceptions, beliefs, and prejudices operate at a conscious level. People can in fact express one conscious belief but behave in a way that reflects an opposite position. For example, an employer might consciously believe that men and women are equally intelligent and competent, yet give more promotions to men than to equally deserving women.

Sandra and Daryl Bem have described those beliefs and attitudes that are outside a person's awareness as a nonconscious ideology.[35] The Bems and other social psychologists have demonstrated that the nonconscious belief that women are inferior to men is still quite strong in our society. Both women and men act in ways which show that the old conscious ideology of male superiority, though now consciously denied by the majority, seems to be quite alive at the nonconscious level. (Nonconscious ideologies are difficult to combat since people are not consciously aware of their presence.)

Various studies reveal the nature of the nonconscious ideology. In one study, women were asked to evaluate a series of scholarly articles on architecture, law, city planning,

---

[34]Hunt (1976).

[35]Bem and Bem (1970).

dietetics, and so forth.[36] The articles had been prepared in duplicate. In each pair of duplicates, one copy was identified as if written by a male and the other as if written by a female. The evaluators received some articles attributed to males and some to females (but never both the male and female versions of the same article). When all the ratings were tabulated, the women ranked *every* one of the articles attributed to a male as superior to the identical article attributed to a female. Because each pair of articles was the same, except for the male or female name of the fictitious writer, the only factor that accounts for the different ratings is that the women believed that work done by men was better than work done by women. Replications of the study have generally found that both men and women judge articles attributed to men as better than identical articles attributed to women.[37]

Similar studies have been done using artwork.[38] Various pieces of artwork were prepared in duplicate and signed as if they were done by either a male or a female. Generally, both men and women who evaluated the work gave higher ranking to the art that was attributed to a male artist.

If anyone should be free of these biases against women, it should be educated people who have dedicated their lives to the study of psychology. A study was done in which job applications were sent to 228 psychology departments around the United States asking the departments to evaluate the applicants' chances of being hired and the academic rank at which they would most likely be hired.[39] Again, bogus job forms were constructed in duplicate and half were given male names while the other half were assigned female names. Thus, one application might have

[36]Goldberg (1968).
[37]Bem and Bem (1970). Some replications in Israel and parts of the U.S. have not always shown the bias in favor of men (Mischel, 1974).
[38]Pheterson et al. (1971).
[39]Fidell (1975).

"Janet Ross" written at the top while the duplicate was marked "James Ross." One hundred fifty-five universities returned their evaluations. Of the eight job applications, the male versions were preferred to the female versions in six out of the eight cases. In addition, the males were ranked as deserving more highly paid jobs with higher academic status. Since everything about the applications forms was identical except for the first name of the applicant, it is clear that sex alone can create enormous biases in the mind of the beholder. (The odds that this level of bias could occur by chance alone are less than 1 in 100.)

The nonconscious ideology of male superiority shows up in countless subtle ways in everyday life. The behavior of both men and women indicates that the cultural biases against women have a pervasive influence. For example, in conversations between males and females, males tend to dominate.[40] Males interrupt females much more frequently than females interrupt males. Males take the lead in determining changes in conversational topics; and when women start a new topic, males are less likely to follow the woman's lead than women are to follow the male's lead. When people talk with others of the same sex and social status, a typical pattern of conversation is that one person supports the other by frequently interjecting a leading question, polite "Um hmm," or exclamation of interest. Then they switch roles so the first person can have the lead. When men and women talk together, men do not relinquish the lead role. Women are forced to play support roles much more than men and to demonstrate much more interest in the males' topics than males show for female topics. Some women appear to think that men are experts, more knowledgeable, more likely to be right than they, and they rarely challenge the male's right to dominate a conversation. When

[40]Zimmerman and West (1975), Henley (1975).

Box 13.4 Who Does What?

Is there a relationship between biological sex differences and divisions of labor? G. P. Murdock compared the anthropological data on 224 preindustrial societies and found that there were very few tasks that were always done exclusively by males or exclusively by females in all societies.[1] Social tasks can be divided into subsistence activities and the manufacture of objects. Of 22 subsistence activities, only two were performed exclusively by males—hunting and the pursuit of sea mammals. In all of the remaining 20 activities—herding, fishing, cooking, carrying water, and so forth—there was considerable variation among the societies: In some societies these tasks were exclusively male, in others they were exclusively female, and in other societies they were shared by both. Turning to the 20 types of manufacturing activities reported in the 224 societies, only two were performed exclusively by men—metalworking and weapon making. In all the other 18 manufacturing activities—boat building, house building, net making, basket making, weaving, and so forth—there was variation among societies in the degree to which the task was exclusively male, exclusively female, or shared by both sexes. The inescapable conclusion is that the nature of the task is less important than cultural values in determining whether the task will be done by men or women. Almost all tasks that are performed exclusively by males in one culture are performed exclusively by females in another culture.

Barry, Bacon, and Child examined the socialization practices of 110 societies to evaluate differences in the rearing of girls and boys.[2] In the majority of cultures females received a stronger socialization in the areas of nurturance and responsibility than males did. In most societies males received a stronger socialization for achievement and self-reliance. However,

[1]Murdock (1935).
[2]Barry et al. (1957).

women do challenge males by saying, "Would you please stop interrupting me," or "Please do not change the topic yet because I'm not through," they often find that men do not know how to cope with such assertive responses from women.[41]

A number of studies indicate that women do not evaluate themselves as highly as men do themselves. Being treated as the less competent, less intelligent sex has its effects on many women. Women tend to approach situations with less self-confidence than men do.[42] They fear that they will not succeed while males predict success for themselves.

For example, in a study that asked college men and women to predict their future grades, men predicted that their grades would rise whereas women predicted that theirs would decline.[43] Males predicted larger increases than women predicted decreases. The fact that neither sex earned different grades at the end of the term reveals that women were more accurate judges, even though they lacked self-confidence. Be it grades, games, problem solving, intelligence tests, or other tasks, men regularly show a higher self-evaluation. Women come closest to male self-confidence in tasks that are explicitly labeled feminine, but even in these areas they do not surpass the males in self-confidence.[44]

[41]It is interesting that the unequal roles in male-female conversations have a parallel in parent-child conversation (West and Zimmerman, 1977).
[42]Brim et al. (1969), Crandall (1969), Feather (1969), Montanelli and Hill (1969).

[43]Crandall (1969).
[44]Stein et al. (1971).

Box 13.4 Continued

not all societies accentuated the differences between male and female gender roles. In those cultures where subsistence and survival depended on someone developing superior strength and motor skills requiring strength, males were raised to fill the roles related to strength and there were large sex differences in socialization. In cultures where strength was not crucial for survival, the two sexes were socialized more equally and gender roles were less divergent. The study also revealed a minor correlation between family structure and sex differences in socialization. Societies that have large, cooperative family groups were likely to socialize their children with large sex differences, and this was especially true of societies that practiced polygyny (having more than one wife per husband).

These findings may help explain the decrease in sex role specialization seen in Western societies in recent times. In a technological society, few jobs have any special characteristics that make it possible for the jobs to be performed only by men or only by women. Few jobs require exceptional muscular development. Thus there is little need for extreme differences in male and female socialization patterns, and technological societies theoretically can allow gender role differences to diminish. In addition, technological societies have moved away from large family sizes and polygyny, both of which accentuate sex differences in socialization. The small independent family structure of technological societies often forces family members to switch roles when one spouse or the other is busy, sick, or away. In the small family, it is not possible to call upon another wife or close relative to take over an unfilled role. Thus both sexes are sometimes called upon to perform tasks usually assigned to the other sex, and there is an increased likelihood that both men and women will learn both kinds of gender roles.

Once men and women have clearly succeeded at a task, women are more likely to attribute their successes to luck than men are. In contrast, men attribute their own successes to skill, talent, or ability. When women and men fail at a task, women are more likely than men to assume that they personally were responsible.[45] These biases in self-evaluation parallel the gender role stereotypes quite closely. Men are supposed to be competent, skillful, and confident, whereas women are presumed to be nonassertive and dependent. A brief overview of the gender role socialization process in the next section reveals many ways that males and females are socialized differently in our society.

[45]Deaux (1976), p. 41.

Gender Role Socialization

By looking at the ways in which males and females are socialized in our society it is possible to trace the development of male and female gender roles and to see the roots of the nonconscious ideology. In order to provide a brief overview of the socialization process, we will examine several important age periods in gender role acquisition. Naturally the socialization of gender roles can take place differently in different cultures or subcultures (see Box 13.4), and there is even a considerable amount of variation within any given homogeneous community.

Early Childhood

In the first months of life baby girls and boys behave so much alike that inborn differences in masculine or feminine behavior appear to be exceedingly small.[46] (Some studies have found that newborn males are *slightly* more active than females, but the differences are very small—and most studies have not found these differences.) Up until puberty, boys and girls have similar hormone balances and body size. They are basically similar in their biological potential for physical strength and general activity level. Thus, there do not appear to be any strong biological causes for gender role differences in childhood.[47]

In fact, it appears that the young child has the behavioral flexibility to be socialized into either masculine or feminine gender roles (*see* Chapter 8). The clearest example is that of a boy who lost his penis at the age of 7 months during an accident at circumcision and was raised as a girl (*see* Box 13.5). The child has learned completely feminine gender roles, though she was born and raised as a boy until 17 months of age. From data such as these it appears that the young child has the potential to internalize either masculine or feminine gender roles and identities, at least during the early years, depending on which sex the child is reared as. Given the cross-cultural data, it also is obvious that the exact nature of masculine or feminine roles can vary considerably between cultures (*see* Boxes 13.2 and 13.3).

Although the young child shows a considerable amount of behavioral flexibility in potential gender development, there is usually a decline in role flexibility with increasing age, as a person more completely internalizes one gender role or the other.[48]

Childhood

By the age of 5 or 6 years, most children have internalized a relatively consistent gender identity and a rather clear set of stereotypes about male and female gender roles.[49] In fact, children have a more dichotomous, stereotyped perception of masculine and feminine behavior than teens and adults.[50] By puberty, children have learned that there is considerable variability in both masculine and feminine roles: that women can be airline pilots and men can be flight attendants. However, the 5-year-old child tends to have a stereotyped image of male and female gender roles in which men are strong and women are weak. Men are dominant and aggressive; women are submissive and frail. Women are sensitive and emotional; men are tough and unemotional. Women think intuitively; men are rational.[51] The number of stereotyped male and female categories is quite large, and most children can cite a lengthy list of them. This oversimplified stereotype of the two roles is given to the child by society's multiple socializing agents (parents, neighbors, television, and others) in order to help the young child learn quickly which behavior is appropriate for which sex.[52] Also the cognitive development of young children appears to predispose them to seeing things in simplified terms. Only after they have learned the early basic differences between two clearly different categories can they go further to acquire finer discriminations about the subtle variations that make the stereotypes merely illusions.

Society provides numerous sources of stereotypes for the young child. Most parents make it clear for their children that different behavior is appropriate for a little boy than for a little girl. The two sexes are usually dressed differently, given different kinds of toys, and encouraged into different kinds of games, hobbies, and sports. Part of this differential treatment can be seen in a study of

---

[46]Mischel (1966).

[47]After puberty, males often put on more upper body muscle and acquire greater strength. Because this allows them to do heavier work, these biological differences can serve as a reason for gender role differentiation (Barry, Bacon, and Child, 1957). (*See* Box 13.4.)

[48]Hampson (1965).

[49]Kohlberg (1966), pp. 95–102.

[50]Gagnon and Simon (1973), p. 33.

[51]For a summary of several studies on the stereotypes found in our society see Chafetz (1978), pp. 37–55.

[52]Gagnon and Simon (1973), pp. 31–32.

Box 13.5   Raising a Male as a Female

Normally a male would not be raised as a female, nor would a female be raised as a male. However, certain circumstances may necessitate raising a child to have a gender identity other than that of its genetic sex.

One such circumstance occurred after a little boy lost his penis during circumcision at 7 months of age.[1] The child had an identical twin brother who was raised as a boy. When one of the boys was undergoing circumcision, there was too much electricity in the instrument being used for circumcision and the boy's penis was burned to such a degree that it sloughed off. The parents, of course, did not know what to do. They wanted very much to do the best thing for their little boy, and consulted several doctors. Although the child was a normal XY boy and had been reared as a boy for the first months of life, a physician suggested that it would be best to switch the child to the female role. Finally, after months of deliberation, the parents decided to raise their boy, who was now 17 months old, as a girl.

The parents gave their child a girl's name, girl's clothes, and a new hairstyle appropriate for a little girl. When the child was 21 months old, the first surgery was done to make the child's genitals look like those of a normal girl. (Additional surgery to construct a vagina will be done after the child stops growing. Female hormones will be given to her after the age of puberty to develop the feminine secondary sex traits.)

After the gender change the mother began raising her new daughter to be feminine. The child accommodated very quickly to being a girl and developed both feminine behavior and feminine gender identity. By the time she was 4½ years old, the daughter was very fond of dresses, neatness, cleanliness and having her hair set. At this time the mother stated that "One thing that really amazes me is that she is so feminine. I've never seen a little girl so neat and tidy as she can be when she wants to be. . . . She is very proud of herself when she puts on a new dress or I set her hair. She just loves to have her hair set; she could sit under the dryer all day to have her hair set. She just loves it."[2] The mother pointed out that the daughter liked to imitate her, while in contrast her brother imitated the father. The daughter would do kitchen cleaning while the son did not care about such activities. The daughter wanted traditional female toys such as a doll house, while the son wanted male toys such as a garage and cars.

At 9 years of age the little girl was an energetic child whose behavior was obviously different from the male behavior of her twin brother. There were no signs that her XY genetic inheritance or the first 17 months of being reared as a boy had any lingering effects that might detract from her femininity. A trained observer concluded that "Her behavior is so normally that of an active little girl, and so clearly different by contrast from the boyish ways of her twin brother, that it offers nothing to stimulate one's conjectures."[3]

[1]Money and Ehrhart (1972).
[2]*Ibid.*, pp. 119–120.
[3]Money (1975).

48 boys' rooms and 48 girls' rooms done in a middle-class university community.[53] The children were between the ages of 1 and 6. The rooms of boys contained many more spatial-temporal toys, educational art materials, sports equipment, and animal toys than did the rooms of girls. For example, the boys' rooms contained 375 vehicles and the girls rooms' contained 17 vehicles. On the other hand, the girls' rooms contained 26 baby

[53]Rheingold and Cook (1975).

dolls while the boys' rooms had only 3 baby dolls. The boys' rooms contained slightly more books and musical instruments, but this small difference could have occurred by chance. The furnishings of the rooms were also different. Boys' rooms were more likely to have an animal theme while girls' rooms were more likely to have a floral theme and some type of "ruffles." In addition, parents encourage boys to become independent and girls to be dependent. Several studies show that little boys are permitted greater freedom than girls to wander away from the home and explore the neighborhood.[54] Boys receive more rewards than girls for signs of independence, autonomy, and venturesomeness. Little girls, on the other hand, are shepherded indoors to be near mother and are rewarded for dependency and femininity.[55]

Many parents are aware that teaching gender stereotypes is undesirable, but few can escape the social pressure to make certain that their children "fit in" with their peers. A study of parents from many social levels in Cleveland revealed that almost half of the parents wanted to give their children—especially their daughters—more gender role flexibility than was permitted within the stereotyped roles.[56] However, when it came to actual gender role socialization, few parents risked allowing their children—especially the boys—to deviate from the stereotyped role expectations.

The socialization of males generally includes cultural conditioning for not adopting "feminine" roles.[57] During the first years of a child's life mother is the closest and warmest source of affection; hence the little child draws its early sense of identity from her. Girls can continue loving and identifying with their mothers all through life and thus internalize the female role. Little boys are forced to

Figure 13.1 These little girls are playing at their future roles. Billy Barnes; Black Star. Reprinted by permission.

abandon their early identification with their mother and to acquire a new masculine identity. In our culture, the process involves punishing boys for imitating feminine behavior

Figure 13.2 Boys, like girls, learn early what it means to be a male. John Rees; Black Star. Reprinted by permission.

[54]Saegert and Hart (1978).
[55]Hart (1979).
[56]Roberts et al. (1978).
[57]Lynn (1966), Stein et al. (1971).

and rewarding them for being tough, independent, assertive, and "masculine." Little girls do not receive much punishment if they play the tomboy role, but little boys are quite strongly punished for being "sissies" or "Mama's boys." As a result boys are conditioned to fear being called—or even thought of as—"sissies" or feminine. Even years later, males are less likely to deviate from their role stereotypes than females are.[58]

When the child begins to enter school, teachers continue exposing boys and girls to differential treatment. Boys are assigned tasks that require leaving the classroom and running errands. Boys receive much more attention from their teachers for signs of independence. Boys receive more attention for being aggressive and assertive.[59] This extra attention for obstreperous behavior puts boys at a disadvantage during their early education. Since boys are being rewarded for being active, independent, and assertive, they learn role behavior that interferes with their being serious, attentive, disciplined students. As a consequence, boys do not do as well as girls in elementary school. They have about twice as many general learning problems and reading problems as girls.[60]

The books used by elementary schools further reinforce the gender role stereotypes. One study of 2750 stories in children's readers revealed that boys were the center of the story 2.5 times more than girls, that there were three times as many men as women in the stories, that male biographies were six times more common than female, and so forth.[61] In addition, girls were portrayed as fearful and incompetent; girls were onlookers while boys did the interesting activities. Children in the United States tend to watch television for three or more hours a day, often averaging more hours per week in front of

Figure 13.3 This young girl is enjoying learning from her mother how to be the well dressed female. Abigail Heyman; Magnum. Reprinted by permission.

the television than they spend in the classroom. An analysis of TV programming revealed that three-fourths of all main characters on prime time are male.[62] Female characters tend to play passive roles or support roles in which they help the leading males. Women are portrayed as interested in romance and family, whereas males are portrayed as thinkers, planners, initiators of action, and skillful in carrying out their plans.

All of these sources of cultural information about gender roles provide the child

[58]David and Brannon (1976).
[59]Serbin and O'Leary (1975).
[60]Sexton (1969).
[61]*Women on Words and Images* (1972).

[62]*Women on Words and Images* (1975).

with rather consistent ideas about the meaning of masculinity and femininity, and these ideas affect the child's own gender identity, aspirations, and behavior. Children who are raised in environments where few stereotypes are available do not develop nearly as many gender role differences in behavior.[63]

Early Puberty

By the age of 10 or 11, at the onset of puberty, girls and boys have become well segregated into two separate socialization groups.[64] They spend most of their time with peers of the same sex and are well on the way to developing gender roles that have little overlap. They are developing skills and personality traits that will eventually create a considerable gap between the masculine and feminine personality. Although some societies segregate boys and girls more than our society does, even the level of sex separation seen in the United States creates a communication gap that few males and females completely overcome later in life.

A study on the leisure activities of 10- and 11-year-old children illustrates a great deal about the socialization experiences of boys and girls in this age group.[65] The most common pastime for boys and girls was watching television, which they did for 15–20 hours a week. Each sex preferred different shows: Boys liked adventure shows, girls liked family-oriented comedies. When the children were playing, boys played outdoors much more than girls did. Being outdoors, boys were less confined. The boys frequently played vigorous games that involved chasing and high levels of activity, whereas girls playing inside were restricted from such high-activity games. Boys tended to play in larger groups than girls. Girls often stayed inside with one or two close friends while the boys were outside, perhaps playing baseball with

five boys on each team. While girls were specializing in the learning of skills for small scale social interactions, boys were learning to interact in larger more complex groups, with people who may not be their friends. Girls selected their friends from a close circle of same-age peers with similar skills and interests, and they developed close, intimate relationships. Boys played in groups with a wider range of ages. In order to organize a baseball game the boys often had to let some of the little boys play, too; and the little boys learned how to get along, be tough, not cry, and stand up for their own rights. They learned to stifle frustrations and keep going in the face of adversity. Girls' games were usually cooperative, whereas boys mostly played competitive games. Girls' games often had no "winner" or "loser"; on the other hand, boys' games make winning and losing salient ideas. Since boys' games involved more rules than girls' games, these games helped train boys in the art of negotiating rules, handling debates, and resolving squabbles. Because the girls were deprived of these experiences, they did not have as much chance to learn negotiation skills and often were at a disadvantage in coping with social situations that involved formal rule structures. The males, more than the females, were also learning coordination and athletic skills.

Studies such as this on male and female socialization indicate that girls and boys are assimilating quite different social roles and that *both* are missing out on important learning experiences. Girls are learning to be concerned with close friendships—almost miniature versions of monogamous relationships.[66] Girls cherish their closest girl friends and suffer great emotional loss if their closest friend leaves town or jilts them to become best friends with some other girl. Boys learn how to interact with larger numbers of peers, including people they might not select as friends.

[63]Minuchin (1965), Hamer and Missakian (1978).
[64]Roberts et al. (1978), p. 20.
[65]Lever (1976).

[66]Gagnon and Simon (1973), pp. 52–73.

They learn to get along, to take their hard knocks, and to stand up for themselves in both physical and verbal conflicts. The girls miss out on learning the negotiation skills that the boys learn; and the boys miss out on learning the skills of intimacy that the girls learn. The girls are learning social skills that prepare them to expect a warm, loving relationship, and to be good at cooperating in such a relationship. Boys are not being prepared for the monogamous role, although they may be able to learn the role later in their socialization. The boys' socialization gives them skills that will help them stand on their own in the competitive world of jobs, professional advancement, and getting along with fellow workers (even those whom they do not particularly like). Girls are not being prepared for job-related skills, even though many will have to learn these skills later in life.

Figure 13.4   These young children have already internalized the typical sex role stereotypes. Alice Kandell, Photo Researchers, Inc.

Adolescence and Young Adulthood

By the time Americans reach the early or mid teens, the two sexes are beginning to terminate the long period of sex segregation that keeps boys and girls apart for many of the early years. The premarital social relationships that young men and women form cause new changes in gender roles.

When young women and men begin serious dating and other close relationships, they begin socializing each other to hold some of the values of the other sex.[67] Young women are socializing their male partners to value romantic commitment and nurturance. Young men are socializing their female partners toward increased sexuality. Both sexes change to some degree under the socializing influence of the other sex, but rarely is the effect of years of prior sex separation completely neutralized. Even though the resocialization may only partially counteract other social forces that pull males and females in different directions, premarital social relationships do help young men and women come closer together. In the past two decades young men and women have been free to explore more intimate relationships—including premarital sex and cohabiting—than was possible in previous generations, and the extra level of contact has helped decrease many gender differences.

In spite of the fact that young men and women resocialize each other to some degree, there are still significant differences in the ways males and females approach intimate relationships. When a 1976 survey of college students asked how close two people should be for sexual relationships, the largest group of women (45 percent of the women surveyed) responded that they should be lovers, while only 24 percent of the men made that reply.[68] The men's first two choices of answers were "friend" (at 39 percent) and

---

[67]Ibid., pp. 73–109.

[68]*Playboy* (1976).

"casual acquaintance" (at 27 percent). Still today, when many young men find an acquaintance they like and enjoy sexual relations with, they call it love; but when they are ready to move on, their partner realizes that the man's protestations of love were not meant as seriously as the woman had thought. When having their first sexual relationships, women are more likely to believe that they are in a close relationship than men are. Responses made by college students to a questionnaire on sexual behavior revealed that 83 percent of women had their first sexual relations with a close partner (steady, fiancé, or spouse), while only 55 percent of men had their first sexual relationship with a close partner (see Figure 13.5).

Many women are still looking for relationships with a commitment to love and affection. According to sociologist Safilios-Rothschild, the old cultural pattern still lingers: Men pursue sex, whereas women pursue love.[69] A survey of 52,000 young adults (mostly in their twenties) found that only half the people who were currently in love felt that there was equal love given by the male and the female.[70] In the remaining half, it was mostly the women who felt that they were giving more love than they were receiving. It should be added that those people who felt that they were in equal relationships expressed the greatest happiness. Thus those who overcome the gender role differences and create a balanced relationship do benefit. There seems to be some truth in the romantic ideal that equal, reciprocated love leads to the greatest happiness.

Cohabitation

An increasing number of young people are exploring cohabitation as a living arrangement and social experience to be tried before embarking into marriage. Cohabiting occurs in all sectors of society—not only among col-

[69]Safilios-Rothschild (1977).
[70]Shaver and Freedman (1976).

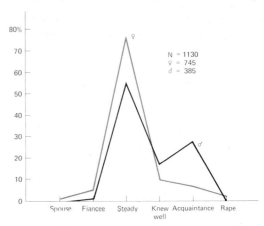

Figure 13.5   The responses of 1130 nonvirgin college juniors and seniors (745 females and 385 males) to the question: "How close was the first person with whom you had sexual intercourse?" Data from Southern California, 1977–1979.

lege students. One study found that nearly 5 percent of unmarried young adults were living with someone of the opposite sex.[71] Another study reported that 25 percent of college students had tried it.[72] If one includes all age groups, a total of 2.2 million unmarried men and women live together, although not all of these are in sexual relationships.[73] One-fourth of these couples have one or more children living with them. For many young people, cohabiting means "going very steady" and it offers a period of practice for close monogamous relations without the permanent commitment of marriage.[74]

Cohabitation does not appear to be threatening the institution of marriage. Many cohabitors eventually move on to marriage (though not necessarily to a person with whom they cohabited). Cohabitation is more common in urban areas than in rural areas

[71]Clayton and Voss (1977).
[72]Bower and Christopherson (1977).
[73]U.S. Bureau of the Census (1979).
[74]Macklin (1974).

and among people with liberal values than with conservative values. Most cohabiting couples report an equalitarian attitude and more equal sharing of household chores than married couples. Theoretically, cohabitation with equalitarian roles should help decrease the gender role separation that is established in early socialization, but data are not yet available with which to evaluate this proposition. Sex is only one facet of cohabitation, and thus most couples seek to develop total relationships rather than sexual relationships only. Most believe that their cohabiting has led to personal growth and social maturity. People cohabiting usually do not think of themselves as in a trial marriage. Many are very emotionally attached to each other, but they are not ready for a commitment to marriage. At present there are too little data available to know to what degree cohabiting helps or hinders future relationships. Society is becoming more accepting of cohabitation. In the Yankelovich survey 52 percent of people believed that it was not wrong for couples to live together before marriage.

Marriage

Although there has been a slight decrease in the number of people who are marrying, marriage is still an extremely popular institution. In the past about 95 percent of Americans have married; this figure will probably decrease by 2 or 3 percent in the next decade, judging from current trends. Most people want to marry. Eighty-nine percent of college women and eight-six percent of college men answering questionnaires in the late 1970s planned to get married.[75] The current changes that are appearing in American marriages are related more to changes in marriage age, gender roles, family size, and divorce than to a decrease in the appeal of marriage.

Males and females are marrying at a later age. In 1960 the median age at first marriage was 20.3 years for women and 22.8 years for men.[76] In 1978 the median age had increased to 21.8 for women and 24.2 for men. Another figure that shows the increasing age at marriage is the percent of women who have never been married. In 1960, 28 percent of women in the 20–24 age group were unmarried while in 1978 almost 48 percent were. However, by the time women enter the 25–29 age group, only 18 percent remained unmarried in 1978.

After marriage the gender roles of men and women continue to change. In some marriages, the man and woman continue to learn about each other's interests, values, and attitudes, and grow closer together. Those husbands and wives who attain a fair amount of role similarity are usually more satisfied with their relationships than husbands and wives who retain the more stereotyped roles that stress the differences between men and women.[77] Unfortunately, the increased financial obligations of marriage—especially after a couple begins to have children—force many couples apart, as the husband specializes in earning an income and the wife specializes in child rearing and perhaps in a job of her own. The arrival of children is the single largest stressor on marital relations and marital happiness.[78] In those couples in which the husband specializes on a job or career while the wife specializes on child rearing and domestic duties, there is often a shift back toward the stereotyped gender role differences that separate males and females and decrease the intimacy and happiness they can give each other.

As society has changed over the past decades, the stereotyped roles of husband

---

[75]Data collected in 1977–1979 on 1,222 students in Southern California. There was no difference between virgins and nonvirgins in plans for marriage.

[76]U.S. Bureau of the Census (1979).
[77]Chilman and Meyer (1966), Navran (1967), Laws (1971).
[78]Peck (1971), Bernard (1972), Scanzoni and Scanzoni (1976).

and wife have become a little less different and less separated. In the past, the male was expected to be the sole provider for the family and the woman was supposed to remain at home with the children. The 1976 Gallup poll of males found that 40 percent of men felt less pressure to provide for a family than they did in the past.[79] For males under 30, this figure is 50 percent. Corresponding to the decreased pressure some males feel to support a family, there has been an increased acceptance of women in the labor force. In 1938 a Gallup poll found that almost 80 percent of males thought it was wrong for a woman to work outside the home if the husband could provide for her.[80] In 1976 about 30 percent of males felt this way. In 1960 almost 35 percent of married females worked outside the home. Today more than 47 percent of married women work outside the home. For women in the 16–34 age group without children, the number working is approximately 80 percent. Although married women are working more outside the home, their jobs are not considered by males to be as important as the males' jobs. According to the 1976 Gallup poll 60 percent of husbands would be unwilling to resign from their jobs and find new employment if their wives' jobs required a move.

Men still appear to control the family pocketbook more than women. The 1976 Gallup poll found that over 50 percent of men said that they had more control over major purchases (for example, a refrigerator or car) than their wives. Only about one-third of men reported equal control. A small number (10 percent of men) said that the wife had more control. It may come as a surprise that males under 30 reported more control over the finances than males over 30.

Another important area in which marriage is changing is family size. In the 1950s most women had three or four children. Today most people want and have about two children. In addition, many are having children at a later age than before. The decrease in family size, coupled with an increase in number of women who work, is having an effect on gender roles. There is more pressure for husbands of working women to do housework. Almost 50 percent of men reported in a 1976 Gallup survey that they should share in the housework equally if the woman works; however, almost the same number of men said that the husband should do little or none of the housework. These responses were about the same whether the couple had children or not. In actuality, studies have found men do much less housework than their wives, even when the wife works.[81] A study of families in Cleveland found that 90 percent of mothers and 85 percent of fathers reported that the wife does all or nearly all the housework.[82]

Divorce

Divorce is now a common phenomenon in American society. The U.S. divorce rate is higher than that of any other industrialized country.[83] Over 40 percent of new marriages will end in divorce. One-half of first divorces occur within the first seven years after marriage.

Of course, not everyone has the same risk for divorce.[84] People with lower than average risk for divorce include women who marry while they are in their mid-twenties and males who marry while they are 25 to 29. Education level is also important. Males with 16 or more years of education have lower divorce rates than males with less education. Women who have completed 16 years of education have lower divorce rates than women with any other level of education.

---

[79]Hunt (1976).
[80]Ibid.

[81]Vanek (1974), Barrett (1976), Kahne (1976).
[82]Roberts et al. (1978).
[83]Glick and Norton (1977).
[84]Ibid.

Several factors can increase a person's chances of divorce. For example, teen-age marriages have a divorce rate about two times that of marriages occurring in the twenties. Couples who become premaritally pregnant or pregnant soon after marriage have a greater risk of divorce than couples who wait before having the first child. When examining education levels, men who begin a college education but do not complete it have a higher divorce rate than men of any other educational level.

Approximately 60 percent of divorced people have dependent children under 18. Most divorced people will eventually marry again: Five out of six divorced men and three out of four divorced women remarry.

The Next Generation

Once people have passed through two or three decades of socialization, many become parents and thus become the primary socializing agents for the next generation. At least while their children are young, the parents have a great deal of influence on the children's gender role development and early perceptions of sexuality.

Unfortunately, many parents feel very uncomfortable in dealing with their own children's sexual education and gender role development. In a 1976–1977 Yankelovich study, two-thirds of parents said that they have trouble communicating with their children about sex.[85] The data from a thorough study of parental socialization practices in Cleveland between 1975 and 1978 indicate that only 8 percent of fathers and 15 percent of mothers had *ever* (even once) mentioned intercourse to their children.[86] Less than 2 percent of fathers and 8 percent of mothers had ever mentioned contraception. Many of these parents said that their own parents had never told them about sex and had made

them feel uncomfortable about the topic. Now, their own lack of knowledge and uncomfortable feelings prevented them from talking with their own children, even though the parents wanted the children to have the information! The majority of parents want the school system and public services to take care of sexual education. However, a vociferous minority which opposes sex education in the schools has successfully limited open discussion of sexuality and even the evaluation of traditional gender roles in many school systems. By default, the peer group and the media continue to be the primary sources of information—often crude and inaccurate information—in the socialization of many young people.[87]

Even though most parents say little or nothing about sex to their children, there is no way that parents can avoid communicating *something* about sexuality to their offspring. If they are visibly uncomfortable or silent about sexuality, the parents are conveying the message that there is something "wrong," "embarrassing," or "indecent" about sexuality, and they are also conditioning their children to be uncomfortable about discussing the topic. True, the peer group may reverse this conditioning in part with its open talk about sex among same-sex friends, but the code of silence often remains intact when talking in public, or communicating with the other sex, or teaching one's own children.

The Cleveland study also revealed that parents have difficulty in providing their children with the gender role socialization that they want to give them. Almost half of the parents believe that males and females should not have different roles in life; yet most parents continued teaching the traditional values and gender role stereotypes to their children. Few parents could actually sit down and talk with their children about desirable gender

[85]Yankelovich (1977).
[86]Roberts et al. (1978).

[87]Gagnon and Simon (1973), pp. 110–128.

roles, and most of the parents could not provide models of the desirable roles they wanted their children to learn. In addition, most parents were afraid to allow their children to explore nonstereotyped roles for fear that the children might encounter social difficulties or become homosexuals. In the final analysis, the desire to give the children more flexible roles was sacrificed in order to follow the safer, tried-and-true, traditional route of stereotyped roles. The reluctance of even "liberal" young parents to discuss sex and nonstereotyped gender roles with their children indicates that the influence of sexual restrictiveness is still present in our society.

There are two main reasons for parents' failure to talk openly with their children about sexuality and gender roles: first, they often feel uncomfortable discussing these topics themselves; second, they fear that they do not have enough knowledge in the area. There are several ways parents can avoid being paralyzed by these problems.[88] If parents begin talking about sexuality and gender roles when their children are young and the children's questions are simple, the parents are less likely to feel uncomfortable or to fear a lack of knowledge. As the years go by, both the parents and the children will learn the habits of open, honest communication about personal topics. If a husband and wife rehearse with each other the things they want to tell their children, they will gain confidence and feel more comfortable about discussing these topics with the children. Most parents discover that they do have enough experience and knowledge to answer most of their children's questions because children are usually not asking for rigorous scientific information as much as they are asking for their parents' opinions and attitudes about sex, their gender role, ways to relate to the other sex, and so forth. Even if children do ask a difficult question, the parents can be honest, say that they do not know, and then try to find the answer from a book or a doctor.

Parents can use two additional strategies to open and maintain the lines of communication with their children: first, by being an askable parent; second, by looking for teachable moments.[89] Askable parents do not blow up, become angry, or get critical when children ask questions. Parents who show a sincere, loving concern when children come with difficult or personal questions will find that the children will continue to return with more questions about both sexuality and gender roles. The parents may not approve of a child's current values or actions, but showing anger is not the solution. Anger will cut off the communication channels and reduce the chances that the parents will be able to influence the child's views, whereas a serious, loving and concerned discussion of the problems, the risks the parents see, and positive suggestions about alternative values both keeps the communication channels open and clarifies the parents' beliefs and attitudes for the child.

What if a child never asks questions (and they often do not)? Parents can look for teachable moments, for times when information can be given comfortably, and in a relevant context. When a neighbor friend is pregnant, the adults can begin a conversation about pregnancy for the benefit of the child and set the scene for teaching the child about pregnancy and childbirth. When parents and children are in the bathroom together, there are many teachable moments when parents can breach a topic even if the children do not. When mother gets a raise or a promotion, father can tell the children how proud he is that their mother is a competent, skillful woman. After the father does a kind deed for a friend, mother can point out to the children

---

[88]Gordon and Dickman (1977).

[89]Ibid., pp. 11–13.

that she loves him for his kind, gentle ways. A central theme of this chapter is that attitudes about sexuality and gender roles are passed on to individuals by their society. People living in different societies learn different values and behaviors. However, society is not some distant, amorphous, abstract entity. Society consists of people. As people grow up, they become the socializing agents who pass on the values and beliefs of their society to the next generation. The American society is in a period of transition concerning attitudes and behavior in the areas of sexuality and gender roles; thus this is a time in which people have to face uncertainties and deal with inconsistencies in these areas. At present most scholars are reluctant to predict how attitudes about sexuality and gender roles will develop in the future in America.[90] However, in these fast moving times it is certain that the nature of sexuality and gender roles will change—for better or for worse.

[90]Gagnon and Simon (1973), 283–307.

Chapter 14

Sex and the Law

It is a fair assumption that many readers of this book are guilty of having broken one or more of the many laws governing sexual behavior in our society. Consider the following data from the Kinsey study of male sexual behavior: At some time 85 percent of men had engaged in premarital intercourse, 59 percent had participated in oral-genital contacts, 70 percent had had intercourse with prostitutes, 30–45 percent had been involved in one or more extramarital affairs, 37 percent had participated in homosexual activities, an additional 10–15 percent had been exclusively homosexual for prolonged periods (three years or more), and 17 percent of those raised on farms had had intercourse with animals.[1] All this behavior is prohibited by criminal laws in many states.

Many people are unaware of the existence of laws that define everyday sexual experiences as crimes. One of the purposes of this chapter is simply to point out the existence of these statutes, for potentially they affect almost everyone in the population. Perhaps this effort seems hardly worthwhile, for these laws are largely "dead"; they are so rarely enforced as to be inconsequential. But, as we shall demonstrate later, their very existence "on the books" allows for their occasional capricious application, which ill serves

[1]Kinsey et al. (1948), pp. 391–392.

the interests of society, the individual, and the law.

Let us consider briefly how and why these laws came to be written in the first place. We cannot begin to understand the precepts embodied in the sex laws of our society without understanding something of the Judeo-Christian tradition of sexual ethics described in Chapter 15. It will become apparent as we quote from specific statutes in a typical American penal code that the laws pertaining to sexual behavior are, for the most part, not directed toward "the preservation of public order" as most criminal laws are. Rather, they embody a particular ethical point of view of sexual behavior: that the sole purpose of sexual activity is reproduction. When we recognize that a majority of legislators held this point of view when these laws were written, it is not difficult to understand how such activities as masturbation and homosexuality came to be designated as criminal offenses. Other notions arising from the particular ethical and religious backgrounds of the founders of Anglo-American society are also embodied in law, including the opinion that sex in general is evil and the belief that having more than one spouse at a time is wrong.

Some lawyers and legislators have questioned the constitutionality of laws directed toward enforcement of the views of a particular religion in light of provisions in the U.S. Constitution for separation of church and state.

There are several other grounds on which many existing sex laws might be found unconstitutional if challenged appropriately. These include *vagueness* (many laws do not define the prohibited act, but simply prohibit "crimes against nature"), the *right of privacy* (most violations of sex laws occur in the home of the participants), *equal protection* guarantees ("lewd conduct" laws are applied in a discriminatory fashion against homosexuals despite the high incidence ot this activity among heterosexuals), and *cruel and unusual punishment* (penalties in many instances greatly exceed the penalties for violent crimes).[2]

Until recently very few people were willing to raise such issues openly because of the risk to their reputations and careers. When a legislator seeks to overturn a law that makes intercourse between an unmarried couple a crime, it is far too easy for a political opponent to say that he must also favor free love, sin, and thus "corruption" in general. Few people are willing to subject themselves to such charges, particularly if they must run for elective office periodically. An example of this phenomenon was seen in Pennsylvania, where a completely revised criminal code that deleted the laws against fornication and adultery was adopted in 1972. United Press ran a nationwide story which began: "The [Pennsylvania] State House of Representatives voted Tuesday to legalize premarital and extramarital sex" (*San Francisco Chronicle,* November 23, 1972, p. 14). Within a matter of months the legislature reinstated the sex laws. One legislator was quoted as saying, "If we don't set standards, everybody will be going around doing what they want." A similar legislative reversal occurred in Idaho for apparently similar reasons in 1971.

But, aside from the question of the constitutionality of laws governing sexual behavior, several other objections can be raised. Packer has stated them:

1 Rarity of enforcement creates a problem of arbitrary police and prosecutorial discretion.
2 The extreme difficulty of detecting such conduct leads to undesirable police practices.
3 The existence of the proscription tends to create a deviant subculture.
4 Widespread knowledge that the law is violated with impunity by thousands every day creates disrespect for law generally.
5 No secular harm can be shown to result from such conduct.
6 The theoretical availability of criminal sanctions creates a situation in which extortion and, on occasion, police corruption may take place.
7 There is substantial evidence that the moral sense of the community no longer exerts strong pressure for the use of criminal sanctions.
8. No utilitarian goal of criminal punishment is substantially advanced by proscribing private adult consensual sexual conduct.

The only countervailing argument is that relaxation of the criminal proscription will be taken to express social approval of the conduct at issue. There is little enough, as we have seen, to that general proposition. It becomes peculiarly vacuous when addressed to this issue, where the social taboo is so much stronger than the legal prohibition. It does not pay a statute much of a compliment, a justice of the Supreme Court once remarked, to say that it is not unconstitutional. It may also be said that it does not express much approval of a behavior pattern to say that it is not criminal.[3]

Because of these widely recognized objections to our present sex laws The American Law Institute, when preparing its *Model Penal Code,* recommended the abolition of all laws governing sexual activities performed in private between consenting adults. The reasoning behind this recommendation is apparent in the comment:

[2]For a detailed analysis of the history and current status of this topic, see Barnett (1973).

[3]Packer (1968), p. 304.

The Code does not attempt to use the power of the state to enforce purely moral or religious standards. We deem it inappropriate for the government to attempt to control behavior that has no substantial significance except as to the morality of the actor. Such matters are best left to religious, educational and other social influences. Apart from the question of constitutionality which might be raised against legislation avowedly commanding adherence to a particular religious or moral tenet, it must be recognized, as a practical matter, that in a heterogeneous community such as ours, different individuals and groups have widely divergent views of the seriousness of various moral derelictions.[4]

A distinction can be made among three general categories of sexual behavior, all of which are subject to criminal sanctions in most of the fifty states at the present time. The first includes the sexual behavior of consenting adults in private. Many, if not the vast majority of, authorities on criminal law believe that such activities should be legalized. Much of the public also believes there should be no laws governing sexual practices. The 1977 Yankelovich survey found that 70 percent of the respondents felt that sexual behavior should not be regulated by laws.[5]

The second category includes offenses involving force or violence (for instance, rape), offenses against children ("child molesting"), and offenses that present a public nuisance (for instance, exhibitionism). Legal opinion is almost unanimous that such offenses should remain under criminal sanctions. No one, obviously, favors the legalizing of forcible rape (though some revision of the laws pertaining to statutory rape may be in order in some states). The third category of offenses is the most controversial at the present time; it includes those offenses that involve commercial exploitation of sex (prostitution and the sale of pornography).

[4]The American Law Institute (1955), Article 207.1, comment.
[5]Yankelovich et al. (1977).

We shall discuss some of the specific offenses included in each of these three categories and compare existing U.S. statutes[6] with those of the American Law Institute's *Model Penal Code* and with some codes from other countries. We shall attempt to describe how existing laws are usually enforced and shall present arguments for and against their retention in our society.

Laws Pertaining to Consenting Adults

In 1962, Illinois became the first state to revise its criminal code along the lines suggested in the *Model Penal Code*. Specifically, oral-genital contacts and anal intercourse between consenting adults (of the same or opposite sex) in private are no longer criminal offenses. More recently, Connecticut, Colorado, Oregon, Hawaii, Delaware, Ohio, California, North Dakota, South Dakota, Washington, New Mexico, Maine, and Arkansas have made similar revisions. Other states, including New York, Kansas, Minnesota, and Utah, have not legalized all consensual sex acts between adults but have reduced such offenses to misdemeanor status.

Fornication

On June 13, 1969, a jury in Paterson, New Jersey, found a man and a woman guilty on three counts of fornication; that is, the defendants were convicted of a crime of sexual intercourse between consenting unmarried adults. According to Municipal Judge Ervan F. Jushner: "I saw a crime being committed when an unmarried woman walked into my courtroom pregnant." There were three counts of fornication in the indictment, for the woman had already borne three illegitimate children.

[6]For convenience we shall refer primarily to the California Penal Code, for in most respects it is typical of the codes in other states as they apply to sexual offenses. When there are wide disparities among states we shall note them, and we shall quote from codes of states other than California in specific instances.

Box 14.1   Prejudice in the Courts: A Case of Incest

In some cases judges allow their prejudices to interfere with the judicial process. The following transcript from a court hearing in California illustrates this point rather vividly. The defendant, a minor, was accused of having committed incest with his sister. This judge's statements are admittedly atypical, and he was duly censored.[1]

IN THE SUPERIOR COURT OF THE STATE OF CALIFORNIA, IN AND FOR THE COUNTY OF SANTA CLARA, JUVENILE DIVISION, HONORABLE XXXXX, JUDGE, COURTROOM NO. 1

In the Matter of xxxxx, a minor, No. XXXX

STATEMENTS OF THE COURT

Sept. 2, 1969   San Jose, California

APPEARANCES:

For the Minor: xxxxx, ESQ., Deputy Public Defender
For the Probation Department: xxxxx, ESQ., Court Probation Officer
Official Court Reporter: xxxxx, C.S.R.

Sept. 2, 1969   10:24 A.M.

The Court: There is some indication that you more or less didn't think that it was against the law or was improper. Haven't

you had any moral training? Have you and your family gone to church?

The Minor: Yes, sir.

The Court: Don't you know that things like this are terribly wrong? *This is one of the worst crimes that a person can commit. I just get so disgusted that I just figure what is the use? You are just an animal.* You are lower than an animal. Even animals don't do that. You are pretty low.

I don't know why your parents haven't been able to teach you anything or train you. [You] people, after 13 years of age, it's perfectly all right to go out and act like an animal [sic]. It's not even right to do that to a stranger, let alone a member of your own family. I don't have much hope for you. You will probably end up in State's Prison before you are 25, and that's where you belong, anyhow. There is nothing much you can do.

I think you haven't got any moral principles. You won't acquire anything. Your parents won't teach you what is right or wrong and won't watch out.

Apparently, your sister is pregnant, is that right?

The Minor's Father, xxxxx: Yes.

The Court: It's a fine situation. How old is she?

The Minor's Mother, Mrs. xxxxx: 15.

The Court: Well, probably she will have a half a dozen children or three or four marriages before she is 18.

[1]This same judge was subsequently reelected to another term.

The couple was convicted under Section 2:133–1 of the *New Jersey Statutes*, which reads:

Any person who shall commit fornication shall be guilty of a misdemeanor, and be punished by a fine not exceeding $50, or imprisonment not exceeding six months, or both.

The defense attorneys argued that this couple was being prosecuted not for fornication but

because they were poor and sought welfare for the support of the children. It certainly seems likely that the prosecution in this case, as in so many others involving sex offenses, was not directed toward eliminating the behavior specified in the charges. The intention was most likely to punish this couple for having had illegitimate children whom it could not support adequately.

Intercourse between unmarried adults

Box 14.1   Continued

The county will have to take care of you. You are no particular good to anybody. We ought to send you out of the country. . . . *You belong in prison for the rest of your life for doing things of this kind. You ought to commit suicide. That's what I think of people of this kind. You are lower than animals and haven't the right to live in organized society—just miserable, lousy, rotten people.*

There is nothing we can do with you. You expect the county to take care of you. *Maybe Hitler was right. The animals in our society probably ought to be destroyed because they have no right to live among human beings.* If you refuse to act like a human being, then, you don't belong among the society of human beings.

Defense Attorney: Your Honor, I don't think I can sit here and listen to that sort of thing.

The Court: You are going to have to listen to it because I consider this a very vulgar, rotten human being.

Defense Attorney: The Court is indicating the whole [ethnic] group.

The Court: When they are 10 or 12 years of age, going out and having intercourse with anybody without any moral training—they don't even understand the Ten Commandments. That's all. Apparently, they don't want to.

So, if you want to act like that, the county has a system of taking care of them. They don't care about that. They have no personal self-respect.

Defense Attorney: The Court ought to look at this youngster and deal with this youngster's case.

The Court: All right. That's what I am going to do. The family should be able to control this boy and the young girl.

Defense Attorney: What appalls me is that the Court is saying that Hitler was right in genocide.

*The Court: What are we going to do with the mad dogs of our society? Either we have to kill them or send them to an institution or place them out of the hands of good people because that's the theory—*one of the theories of punishment is if they get to the position that they want to act like mad dogs, then, we have to separate them from our society.

Well, I will go along with the recommendation. You will learn in time or else you will have to pay for the penalty with the law [sic] because the law grinds slowly but exceedingly well. If you are going to be a law violator—you have to make up your mind whether you are going to observe the law or not. If you can't observe the law, then, you have to be put away.

STATE OF CALIFORNIA, COUNTY OF SANTA CLARA SS.[2]

[2]The italics are added.

is prohibited in many states. Obviously there are millions of offenses under these laws annually. Prosecution, however, tends to be quite selective. One survey of 426 prosecutors[7] indicated a tendency to prosecute welfare recipients as in the case just cited. The same survey described one admittedly unusual midwestern district attorney who had tried 266 fornication cases from 1968 through 1972; of these cases, 260 involved persons from racial minorities.

In those states where fornication is prohibited by law, the offense is usually a misdemeanor punishable by a fine, which may be as small as $10 (Rhode Island) or as large as $1000 (Georgia). In Arizona the statute defines fornication as a felony punishable by imprisonment for not more than three years.

[7]*Playboy* 21:6 (June 1974), 60–61.

The offense is defined as "living in a state of open and notorious *cohabitation*," one of several variations among state statutes defining fornication.[8] In some states, for instance, a single act of intercourse between two unmarried adults is an offense. In other states there must be evidence of repetition or of cohabitation. In such a state a couple living in a stable relationship may be penalized, but the promiscuous individual has not violated the law.

An interesting aspect of some fornication laws is the differences in application to males and females. A married woman who has intercourse with a single man is more likely to be charged with adultery if she is prosecuted. On the other hand, a married man who has intercourse with a single woman is likely to be charged with fornication, a lesser crime in most states and no crime at all in some states. The rationale behind this form of discrimination dates back to Roman law. It reflects concern for property rights; the illicit sexual activities of a married woman were viewed as more serious because they raised the possibility of the introduction of a fraudulent heir into the family. A man might then end up unwittingly supporting a child that was not his own.

The difference between fornication and statutory rape is based on the age of the girl. When the girl is under a certain age (varying from 14 to 21, depending on the state), the crime is defined as statutory rape rather than as fornication; only the male is then considered guilty of the offense, even if the girl has been a willing partner.

Our society is unique in many aspects of its sex laws, particularly those defining sexual intercourse between unmarried consenting adults as *criminal* behavior. Other societies may condemn such activity as immoral; some may set certain limits on it; and others may encourage it; yet most of our states define it as a crime. As we have noted earlier, the majority of men and women in our society do engage in sexual intercourse before marriage.

The American Law Institute has not included a fornication statute in the *Model Penal Code*. Nor has it recommended a seduction statute, which is common in existing criminal codes. The California seduction statute reads:

268 Seduction.—Every person who, under promise of marriage, seduces and has sexual intercourse with an unmarried female of previous chaste character, is punishable by imprisonment in the State prison, or by a fine of not more than five thousand dollars ($5000), or by both such fine and imprisonment.

It should be noted that the male can usually escape prosecution for seduction by marrying the female. If she is under age, however, he may still be prosecuted for statutory rape, even though a legal marriage may have occurred since the offense.

Marital Sexual Activities

Most people assume that whatever varieties of sexual activities a married couple engages in at home in private are legal. This assumption is incorrect. Almost all sexual activity that may occur between husband and wife—with the exception of kissing, caressing, and vaginal intercourse—is defined as criminal in many states of the union. Oral-genital contacts (cunnilingus and fellatio) and anal intercourse (sodomy), in particular, are so defined. In the majority of states they are felonies and carry severe penalties.

In some states oral-genital contacts, anal intercourse, and intercourse with animals are all included under single sodomy laws and are labeled "crimes against nature." The rationale for these laws should be clear from the discussion of "crimes against nature" in Chapter 15, which we can anticipate here: The natural purpose of sex is reproduction,

[8]Arizona Code, Section 43–402.

and therefore any sex act that does not include the potential for conception is a sin (crime) against the laws of nature. A few states even include mutual masturbation or sex with dead bodies under sodomy, presumably for the same reason.[9]

We have already presented data from the Kinsey and other studies to show that many married couples do practice forms of sexual expression other than vaginal intercourse either as part of foreplay or for occasional variety. It is unlikely that the average married man suspects that his marital sexual activity will ever be held against him. Even if he knows that a certain behavior is illegal, as long as he and his wife perform it in private, who can substantiate any charge? It turns out, however, that a wife may offer such evidence in order to win a divorce on grounds of cruelty. Or, in rare cases, she may simply be angry at her husband and looking for vengeance. In 1965 a woman in Indiana had a major quarrel with her husband of ten years. In the heat of anger she filed a complaint of sodomy against him. She did not accuse him of having used force. Before the case came to trial the woman changed her mind and sought to withdraw the charge. She was not allowed to do so because sodomy is an offense against the state, and the state proceeded to prosecute. The husband, stunned by the whole affair, was convicted and sentenced to a term of from 2 to 14 years in state prison. After serving three years of his sentence he was released when the U.S. Seventh Circuit Court of Appeals overturned the conviction on a technicality in the proceedings. The law itself was not challenged. So far the

only landmark decision involving the constitutionality of laws governing the activities of married couples has been the 1965 decision by the U.S. Supreme Court in the case of *Griswold* v. *Connecticut.* The court ruled that a law prohibiting the use of birth control devices by married couples was unconstitutional on the grounds that the right to marital privacy excludes such prohibitions. The *Model Penal Code* recommends the legalizing of all private consensual marital relations.

The laws have also covered frequency of intercourse between a married couple. At one time, when the law of the Roman Catholic Church was enforced by civil law in Europe, the timing of intercourse and the position to be used (face-to-face, with the woman on her back) were prescribed. All intercourse was forbidden during Lent, for three days before taking communion, and during various religious holidays. In early North America the Puritans forbade intercourse on Sundays. The birth of a child on a Sunday was considered evidence that the parents had had intercourse on a Sunday. Such a child was viewed as "conceived in sin" and not eligible for baptism.

Today's laws also deal with the frequency of intercourse between a married couple. For example, if no intercourse at all has occurred, the law provides for annulment of the marriage on these grounds. A man's impotence or a woman's refusal to engage in sexual intercourse with her husband has long been held sufficient grounds for divorce or annulment, though the historical reasoning is somewhat different in the two instances. The impotent male's inability to have intercourse has been held to nullify the reproductive purpose of marriage. To some extent the same notion applies to the unwilling female, but there is also an additional reason. Wives have been traditionally viewed as a "remedy for the sexual lust" of the husband. This concept is reflected in the specific exclusion of rapes of wives from the rape laws in most states.

---

[9]Several states include "carnal knowledge" with "any animal *or bird*" in the statutory definition of sodomy. Indiana includes: "Whoever entices, allures, instigates, or aids any person under the age of twenty-one years to commit masturbation or self pollution, shall be deemed guilty of sodomy." *See Indiana Statues* 10–4221 (1956). Almost all sodomy laws proscribe oral and anal intercourse between *any* persons, regardless of marital status.

Even though the husband may have used force and the wife may have been an unwilling partner on a given occasion, legally rape has not been committed (although the husband can be charged with assault and battery in some instances).

During the last several decades there were an increasing number of divorces granted to women on the grounds that their husbands' demands for frequent intercourse were unreasonable and constitute cruelty.[10] Judges seem to follow highly personal standards (reflecting their generally advanced age?) in rendering opinions on the "normal" frequency of intercourse for a married couple. For instance, Kinsey has described an opinion upheld by the Supreme Court of Minnesota, in which it was ruled that intercourse on the average of three to four times a week represented an "uncontrollable craving for sexual intercourse" on the part of the husband![11]

Abortion

Because U.S. laws reflect a particular point of view about the purpose of sex and marriage, it is not surprising that the right *not* to have children has been limited, until recently, by statute. We have already mentioned the decision in *Griswold* v. *Connecticut,* which in 1965 finally legalized contraceptives in the one state that still prohibited their use.

In the late 1960s a number of states modified their abortion laws to provide for abortions when there was a risk that continuation of the pregnancy would impair the physical or mental health of the women, or when the pregnancy was a result of incest or rape. Many legal abortions were done in these states in the ensuing years, almost all of them under the mental health provisions of these statutes.

[10]See Kinsey et al. (1953), p. 369, for a listing of some examples.
[11]*Dittrick* v. *Brown County,* 1943: 9 N. W. (2d) 510; quoted in Kinsey et al. (1953), p. 370.

In July 1970 a New York abortion law went into effect which removed all restrictions except the requirement that abortions must be performed within 24 weeks of conception (that is, before the third trimester of pregnancy). On January 22, 1973, the U.S. Supreme Court declared unconstitutional all state laws that prohibited or restricted abortions during the first trimester of pregnancy. The Court also limited state intervention in second trimester abortions to the regulation of medical practices involved (certification of hospitals, licensing of physicians, and so forth) insofar as they affect the woman's health. The Court left the prohibition of third trimester abortions to the separate states. The Supreme Court ruled in 1976 that a woman may have an abortion without the consent of her husband or her parents. This also applies to women under 18.

Although women may now legally seek an abortion anywhere in the United States, there are areas of the country where the lack of inexpensive clinics may make it difficult to obtain an abortion. The majority of counties, for instance, do not have a single facility that provides abortions, and the large-scale providers are overwhelmingly concentrated in large cities on the East and West coasts. Furthermore, physicians and nurses are not required to perform abortions, if this action would violate their personal moral or religious principles.

Legal abortions for all women who want them were by no means guaranteed by the U.S. Supreme Court decision of 1973. Many attempts to limit abortions are being made in the United States at the present time. The most common tactical approach is in the direction of restricting or prohibiting the use of public funds for abortions at both the state and federal levels. This approach has been very successful. Presently, federal funds to pay for abortions are available to Medicaid recipients only under a few circumstances: when the woman's life is endangered by the

Figure 14.1   People marching in support of the right for a woman to obtain a legal abortion if she chooses one. Wide World Photos. Reprinted by permission.

Figure 14.2 A march by people seeking a constitutional amendment that would make abortion illegal. Wide World Photos. Reprinted by permission.

pregnancy, when she would suffer severe or longlasting damage to her physical health, or when the pregnancy is the result of rape or incest. Some states continue to fund abortions for women who cannot afford to pay for one. Abortions are available to those with sufficient funds, just as they were available when abortions were illegal in the United States and a woman with money could obtain one by flying to Sweden or Japan.

There have been burnings, bombings, and vandalism of abortion clinics in some parts of the country. There are also efforts under way to amend the U.S. Constitution in such a way as to either greatly restrict or prohibit abortions. The most common legal doctrine in the numerous constitutional amendments that have been proposed is the doctrine that the constitutional rights to due process and equal protection should apply to fetuses. Supporters of these measures are most often motivated by moral and religious concerns (*see* Chapter 15).[12] Fifteen states have requested Congress to call a Constitutional Convention to develop an amendment to the Constitution that would make abortion illegal.

[12]For a detailed history of the evolution of laws governing birth control (including abortion) in the United States *see* Dienes (1972).

Nineteen more requests are needed before Congress must call the convention.

Sterilization

Sterilization for birth control purposes is now, like abortion, legal in the United States within broad limits. Unlike abortion, there is no Supreme Court ruling that defines the limits for state laws on the subject of sterilization. Thus, some states (Utah) expressly forbid the sterilization of someone who is mentally incompetent to give consent, whereas other states (California) have laws that expressly allow for *involuntary* sterilization of the mentally retarded and mentally ill.

Sterilization, except for reasons of medical necessity, has been illegal until recently for a variety of reasons. Under English law male sterilization was considered a crime of *mayhem,* a category that included any "maiming" of the body that would (allegedly) render a man unfit to fight for the king. In the United States until the last decade there was concern about *underpopulation.* As recently as 1950 the Attorney General of California declared that sterilization operations were "violative of the state's social interest in the maintenance of the birth rate." In addition there was the horror of selective sterilization of Jews and mental defectives during World War II, which added an understandable emotional element to the subject of sterilization. Ironically, it was groups such as the Human Betterment Association of America that advanced the cause of legalized sterilization for reasons such as the presence of known hereditary disease or "physical, mental or emotional defect which may seriously impair the patient's functioning as an adequate parent and/or which causes the physician to conclude that parenthood, at any future time, would be hazardous."[13]

Recently, some states have enacted laws requiring informed-consent forms to be signed well in advance of the procedure. This allows people time to change their minds before the operation and helps to avoid sterilizations that are performed because of pressure from the physician or other person. For federally funded sterilizations the Department of Health, Education, and Welfare requires a 30-day waiting period after signing consent forms before the procedure can be performed.

Divorce Laws

Everyone is aware of the high and steadily increasing divorce rate. Some jurists blame the high divorce rate on the fact that "our marriage laws and administrative procedures make it far too easy for the immature, the mentally and physically unfit, and the legally disqualified to become married."[14] Some states recognize common-law marriages, which do not require licenses or ceremonies. Under English common law (still applicable in some states) a boy over 14 years and girl over 12 years have only to agree that they take each other as husband and wife. Some states require that they live together a certain length of time and require parental consent for marriage if the male is under 21 or the female under 18. If the partners falsify their ages and manage to obtain a license and marry, however, there is usually nothing that the parents can do to annul the marriage.

Obtaining a divorce is usually far more difficult. Most of the 50 states require proof of a "marital offense," resulting in the usually unrealistic finding that one party (most often the woman) is not at fault and that one party is "guilty" of the offense, which provides both grounds for the divorce and a basis for awarding property to the "innocent" party. The most common offenses acceptable as grounds

[13]Donnelly and Ferber (1959).

[14]Ploscowe (1951), p. 8. See also Slovenko (1965), pp. 16ff. Slovenko has noted: "It is easier to obtain a marriage license than a driver's license."

for divorce are adultery, insanity, conviction of a felony, conviction of a sex crime, imprisonment, alcoholism, drug addiction, desertion, nonsupport, impotence, general cruelty, physical cruelty, and mental cruelty. Residence requirements vary from six weeks (Nevada) to five years (Massachusetts, though only three years are required if the person suing was a state resident when he or she married). Many states have restrictions on remarriage, particularly for the "guilty" party. South Dakota, for instance, prohibits the remarriage of an adulterer during the lifetime of the ex-spouse. Such restrictions can be evaded by remarrying in another state and then returning home, for the courts recognize a marriage as valid as long as it is valid in the state where it was performed.

The first exception to the divorce laws requiring proof of marital offense occurred in California, where the law provides for dissolution of a marriage on the basis of irreconcilable differences. There are no "guilty" and "innocent" parties, and the property must be divided evenly. This law provides for divorce by consent of both partners, a concept that goes back to Roman law but was abolished when marriage came under the jurisdiction of the Roman Catholic Church. Several other states have adopted "no-fault" divorce laws.

Adultery

Our laws on sexual offenses reflect several sources, but the Judeo-Christian tradition is most prominent. In particular, the early American settlers brought with them the traditions of the English courts, which had a long history of attempting to regulate sexual behavior. From the thirteenth century until the time of Oliver Cromwell and the Puritan Revolution (1640), sexual offenses were handled by the English ecclesiastical courts. Although they condemned all imaginable forms of "illicit" sexual behavior and punished offenders with fines or jail sentences, the ecclesiastical courts were notably ineffective in modifying the sexual activities of the general population.

(They did not always receive support from royalty either, for at times the kings and their courtiers were the most notorious offenders.) The English Puritans abolished the ecclesiastical courts and made sexual offenses like adultery and incest capital crimes punishable by death in the common-law courts (adultery had not previously been a common-law offense).[15] The Puritans of the Massachusetts Bay Colony also made adultery a crime punishable by death, but as the limited colonial population might have been nearly decimated by enforcement of this law, it was rarely invoked; in 1694 the death penalty was replaced by public whipping and the enforced wearing of the letter "A," a punishment immortalized by Nathaniel Hawthorne in *The Scarlet Letter*. Connecticut went a little farther and prescribed that adulterers should have the letter "A" branded on their foreheads with a hot iron. Pennsylvania took a middle course, providing for branding only after the third conviction (prison sentences of one year or more were prescribed for the first and second offenses).

The penalties have diminished over time, but adultery is still a criminal offense in most states. It is a misdemeanor punishable only by fines in some states, but elsewhere it is a felony punishable by lengthy prison terms varying from one to five years. The penalties for adultery tend to be more serious than those for fornication, presumably because of the threat to the family that extramarital affairs pose. Adultery is also the only offense that is considered sufficient grounds for divorce in every state in the union where an offense is required.[16]

[15]The ecclesiastical courts were restored by Charles II of England in 1660, but their power and influence were gradually curtailed.

[16]In New York, where adultery was the only legally acceptable grounds for divorce until recently, it was common practice to arrange fraudulent evidence of adultery in order to obtain a divorce. A witness would be hired to give false testimony about an affair with the husband, or a situation staged with "another woman" would be witnessed by someone hired to do so. (Professional "other women" were available for fees of $10 and up.)

We have already noted that under Roman law (and also under English common law) adultery was defined only as intercourse with a married woman. A married man who had intercourse with a single woman was not guilty of adultery. U.S. courts have tended to hold the view adopted by the English ecclesiastical courts that either a married man or a married woman having intercourse with someone other than his or her spouse is guilty of adultery. At least this definition is applied in divorce cases. But paradoxically, perhaps, this law is almost never applied to prostitution. A married man having intercourse with a prostitute is rarely prosecuted for adultery.

The *Model Penal Code* does not include adultery as a criminal offense, although certain extramarital contacts involving minors (under 16 years old) or seduction ("a promise of marriage which the actor does not mean to perform"[17]) are still included as offenses.

Homosexuality

Homosexuality as such is legal in all the states. It is only specific homosexual *acts* that are defined as crimes (*see* Box 14.2). It is no crime to be sexually attracted and oriented toward members of the same sex. In fact, the laws defining various common homosexual acts (oral-genital contacts, anal intercourse, mutual masturbation) as crimes do not specify the sexes of the participants. These acts, as we have already noted, are crimes under the laws of many states, whether performed by a man and a woman, two men, or two women.

The penalties for these offenses can be quite severe, but in practice relatively few homosexuals are arrested and convicted under these laws because most homosexual acts are performed in private and are thus protected by the search-and-seizure provisions of the U.S. Constitution. When an arrest is made for a specific homosexual act, the latter

usually has occurred in a public place (rest room, park, automobile, theater); and in about 90 percent of instances the act is oral-genital contact. Although this offense is often defined as a felony, judges in some states have the discretionary power to reduce the charge to a misdemeanor. Judges do not have this prerogative when the offense is anal intercourse. In general, and for a first offense in particular, the individual convicted of a homosexual act is fined, given a suspended jail sentence, and placed on probation.

But only a minority of homosexual arrests are made for specific sexual acts; the majority are for solicitation or loitering in public places. The pertinent California statutes read:

647. *Disorderly Conduct Defined—Misdemeanor.*—Every person who commits any of the following acts shall be guilty of disorderly conduct, a misdemeanor:
  (a) Who solicits anyone to engage in or who engages in lewd or dissolute conduct in any public place or in any place open to the public or exposed to public view.
  (b) Who loiters in or about any toilet open to the public for the purpose of engaging in or soliciting any lewd or lascivious or any unlawful act.

650 ½. *Injuries to Persons, Property, Public Peace, Health or Decency; False Personation for Lewd Purpose.*—A person who willfully and wrongfully commits any act which seriously injures the person or property of another, or which seriously disturbs or endangers the public peace or health, or which openly outrages public decency, . . . for which no other punishment is expressly prescribed by this code, is guilty of a misdemeanor.

One survey conducted in the Los Angeles area indicated that 90–95 percent of all homosexual arrests were for violations of section 647(a) of the California Penal Code.[18] The most controversial aspect of these arrests is the use of policemen as "decoys." In most

---

[17]The American Law Institute (1962), Section 213.3(1)d.

[18]Hoffman (1968), p. 84.

Box 14.2 Should Homosexual Behavior Be Legal?

There is a growing trend toward legalizing homosexual behavior. It is no longer a criminal offense in 19 states. *The Wolfenden Report,* based on a ten-year study by Great Britain's Committee on Homosexual Offenses and Prostitution, was issued in 1957 and provided powerful impetus to this trend. The document has been so widely discussed and has had so much influence that it seems appropriate to quote directly some of its crucial arguments and recommendations.

53. In considering whether homosexual acts between consenting adults in private should cease to be criminal offenses we have examined the more serious arguments in favor of retaining them as such. We now set out these arguments and our reasons for disagreement with them. In favor of retaining the present law, it has been contended that homosexual behavior between adult males, in private no less than in public, is contrary to the public good on the grounds that—
(i) it menaces the health of society;
(ii) it has damaging effects on family life;
(iii) a man who indulges in these practices with another man may turn his attention to boys.

54. As regards the first of these arguments, it is held that conduct of this kind is a cause of the demoralization and decay of civilizations, and that therefore, unless we wish to see our nation degenerate and decay, such conduct must be stopped, by every possible means. We have found no evidence to support this view, and we cannot feel it right to frame the laws which should govern this country in the present age by reference to hypothetical explanations of the history of other peoples in ages distant in time and different in circumstances from our own. In so far as the basis of this argument can be precisely formulated, it is often no more than the expression of revulsion against what is regarded as unnatural, sinful or disgusting. Many people feel this revulsion, for one or more of these reasons. But moral conviction or instinctive feeling, however strong, is not a valid

basis for overriding the individual's privacy and for bringing within the ambit of the criminal law private sexual behavior of this kind. It is held also that if such men are employed in certain professions or certain branches of the public service their private habits may render them liable to threats of blackmail or to other pressures which may make them "bad security risks." If this is true, it is true also of some other categories of person: for example, drunkards, gamblers and those who become involved in compromising situations of a heterosexual kind; and while it may be a valid ground for excluding from certain forms of employment men who indulge in homosexual behavior, it does not, in our view, constitute a sufficient reason for making their private sexual behavior an offense in itself.

55. The second contention, that homosexual behavior between males has a damaging effect on family life, may well be true. Indeed, we have had evidence that it often is; cases in which homosexual behavior on the part of the husband has broken up a marriage are by no means rare, and there are also cases in which a man in whom the homosexual component is relatively weak nevertheless derives such satisfaction from homosexual outlets that he does not enter upon a marriage which might have been successfully and happily consummated. We deplore this damage to what we regard as the basic unit of society; . . . We have had no reasons shown to us which would lead us to believe that homosexual behavior between males inflicts any greater damage on family life than adultery, fornication or lesbian behavior. These practices are all reprehensible from the point of view of harm to the family, but it is difficult to see why on this ground male homosexual behavior alone among them should be a criminal offense.

56. We have given anxious consideration to the third argument, that an adult male who has sought as his partner another adult male may turn from such a relationship and seek as his partner a boy or succession of boys. We should certainly not wish to countenance any proposal

Box 14.2 Continued

which might tend to increase offenses against minors.

57. We are authoritatively informed that a man who has homosexual relations with an adult partner seldom turns to boys, and vice versa, though it is apparent from the police reports we have seen and from other evidence submitted to us that such cases do happen.

58. In addition, an argument of a more general character in favor of retaining the present law has been put to us by some of our witnesses. It is that to change the law in such a way that homosexual acts between consenting adults in private ceased to be criminal offenses must suggest to the average citizen a degree of toleration by the Legislature of homosexual behavior, and that such a change would "open the floodgates" and result in unbridled license. It is true that a change of this sort would amount to a limited degree of such toleration, but we do not share the fears of our witnesses that the change would have the effect they expect. This expectation seems to us to exaggerate the effect of the law on human behavior. It may well be true that the present law deters from homosexual acts some who would otherwise commit them, and to that extent an increase in homosexual behavior can be expected. But it is no less true that if the amount of homosexual behavior has, in fact, increased in recent years, then the law has failed to act as an effective de-terrent. It seems to us that the law itself prob-ably makes little difference to the amount of homosexual behavior which actually occurs; whatever the law may be there will always be strong social forces opposed to homosexual behavior. It is highly improbable that the man to whom homosexual behavior is repugnant would find it any less repugnant because the law permitted it in certain circumstances; so that even if, as has been suggested to us, homo-sexuals tend to proselytize, there is no valid reason for supposing that any considerable number of conversions would follow the change in the law.

60. We recognize that a proposal to change a law which has operated for many years so as to make legally permissible acts which were formerly unlawful, is open to criticisms which might not be made in relation to a proposal to omit, from a code of laws being formulated *de novo,* any provision making these acts illegal. To reverse a long-standing tradition is a serious matter and not to be suggested lightly. But the task entrusted to us, as we conceive it, is to state what we regard as just and equitable law. We therefore do not think it appropriate that consideration of this question should be unduly influenced by a regard for the present law, much of which derives from traditions whose origins are obscure.

61. Further, we feel bound to say this. We have outlined the arguments against a change in the law, and we recognize their weight. We believe, however, that they have been met by the counter-arguments we have already advanced. There remains one additional counter-argument which we believe to be decisive, namely, the importance which society and the law ought to give to individual freedom of choice and action in matters of private morality. Unless a deliberate attempt is to be made by society, acting through the agency of the law, to equate the sphere of crime with that of sin, there must remain a realm of private morality and immorality which is, in brief and crude terms, not the law's business. To say this is not to condone or encourage private immorality. On the contrary, to emphasize the personal and private nature of moral or immoral conduct is to emphasize the personal and private responsibility of the individual for his own actions, and that is a responsibility which a mature agent can properly be expected to carry for himself without the threat of punishment from the law.

62. We accordingly recommend that homosexual behavior between consenting adults in private should no longer be a criminal offense.[1]

[1]*The Wolfenden Report* (1963), pp. 43–48.

of the cases a young police officer dressed in casual clothes loiters in a public rest room or similar location for the express purpose of enticing homosexuals to solicit "a lewd or lascivious" act. The arrest is usually made by a second police officer stationed nearby. The decoy then serves as witness against the defendant. The controversy revolves around the accusation that police decoys are involved in *entrapment;* that they induce people to commit illegal acts that they would not otherwise commit. Certainly most homosexuals would not knowingly solicit police officers, but that point is irrelevant under the law. If an individual has a predisposition to commit a particular offense, it is not illegal for a police officer to *entice* that person to commit the offense.

In addition to the issue of enticement versus entrapment, there is the question of whether or not police decoys serve a useful function and represent a worthwhile investment of police manpower. As most homosexual soliciting that does occur in public places is quite subtle—achieved through certain signals, gestures, or brief remarks that have significance only to other homosexuals (or to policemen trained in the jargon of the gay world)—it seems unlikely that such behavior constitutes a significant enough offense to the public decency to justify such measures. Hoffman, in fact, has argued "that putting out as decoys police officers who are young, attractive, and seductively dressed, and who engage in enticing conversations with homosexuals is itself an outrage to public decency."[19] We can argue that the use of police decoys serves to deter public homosexual soliciting, but the argument is unconvincing because the express purpose of using decoys is to promote such behavior in order to achieve arrest, rather than to prevent the behavior.

We have so far been discussing only homosexual activities between males, for, as we noted in Chapter 11, female homosexuals are not usually subject to the same sanctions. With only a few exceptions, the laws do not distinguish between male and female homosexuals, but in actual practice females are almost never arrested or prosecuted for homosexual activities. The Kinsey study reviewed all the sodomy convictions in the United States from 1696 to 1952 and failed to find a single one involving lesbians. In a review of all the arrests in New York City over a period of ten years the Kinsey researchers found "tens of thousands" of arrests and convictions of male homosexuals, but only three arrests of females for homosexual offenses; all three cases had been dismissed.[20] Many factors contribute to this difference in treatment; some of them have been touched on in Chapters 11 and 15. Lesbians tend to engage in less public sexual behavior; lesbian activities are not considered as "sinful" as are male homosexual activities; and the law in general tends to be more protective of female sexual activities (with the exception of prostitution).

For poorly substantiated reasons, male homosexuals are regarded as more threatening to society than are lesbians. Police officers seem to think that homosexuals are more likely to commit crimes of violence and crimes against children than are other individuals. Although massive studies, like that conducted by Gebhard and his associates at the Institute for Sex Research,[21] have not confirmed this belief, it is still commonly held. One result is the practice of requiring the registration of convicted homosexual offenders with the law enforcement agencies in the communities where they reside.

This requirement renders the convicted homosexual susceptible to being "picked up for questioning" whenever a "sex crime" is

---

[19]Ibid., p. 87.

[20]Kinsey et al. (1953), p. 485.
[21]Gebhard et al. (1965).

committed in the area in which he is living. Identified homosexuals are also subject to "purges," like that in the U.S. State Department and other government agencies in the 1950s. In 1978 an attempt was made in California to keep homosexuals from teaching in public schools, but the proposal was defeated by the voters. Homosexuals are generally prohibited from holding jobs that require security clearance or involve the handling of "sensitive information." This requirement is based not simply on the idea that "perverts" are unreliable but also on the belief that homosexuals are more vulnerable to extortion and blackmail. Legalizing homosexual acts between consenting adults would not necessarily change this situation. Homosexuals would probably still be vulnerable to blackmail because of the probable effects of public disclosure of their activities: Whether criminal or not, homosexuality is still widely condemned in our society.[22] This point was made quite clearly in 1977 when the residents of Dade County, Florida—after a nationally publicized and highly emotional crusade by singer Anita Bryant—voted to repeal an ordinance outlawing discrimination against homosexuals in housing, employment, and public accommodations.

Consensual Sex Laws in Other Countries

Kinsey once remarked: "There is no aspect of American sex law which surprises visitors from other countries as much as this legal attempt to penalize pre-marital activity to which both of the participating parties have consented and in which no force has been involved."

The Napoleonic Code, adopted in France in 1810, contains no criminal laws re-lating to sex acts between consenting adults in private. Spain, Portugal and Italy adopted similar codes long ago, as did Belgium (1867) and the Netherlands (1886). In the twentieth century Denmark legalized consensual adult sex in 1930, Switzerland in 1937, Sweden in 1944, Hungary and Czechoslovakia in 1962, England and Wales in 1967, East Germany in 1968, West Germany and Canada in 1969, Finland in 1970, Austria in 1971, and Norway in 1972.

These same sexual acts constitute crimes in the Soviet Union, Rumania, Bulgaria, Yugoslavia, Ireland, and Scotland. Of all the countries of Europe and North America, the United States has the most severe penalties for proscribed consensual sex acts. Even in the Soviet Union, considered by many to be equally as repressive as the United States in its sex laws, the maximum penalties for consensual sodomy are considerably less (5 years versus 10 to 20 years in prison in some states of the U.S.).[23]

Laws Pertaining to Other Sexual Activities

Public Nuisance Offenses

Those acts subsumed under the general category of public nuisances include exhibitionism, voyeurism, and transvestism. They do not involve physical contact with victims, and indeed the victims of voyeurism may be totally unaware of the crimes and of the people committing them. These acts are viewed as criminal on the grounds that they offend public decency, disturb the peace, and tend to subvert and corrupt the morals of the people. The greatest controversy over this general category of offenses involves exhibitionism.

There are various problems in the wording of laws dealing with exhibitionism. One is that a person can be convicted of indecent exposure for an offense that occurs in

---

[22]Although this argument is commonly used by employers, particularly federal and state civil service agencies, it seems to overlook the fact that heterosexuals who perform criminal sex acts (for example, adultery) are also susceptible to blackmail.

[23]Barnett (1973), chap. 10.

Box 14.3 The Law and Sexual Psychopaths

It is generally agreed that sex offenses that involve force or children or that constitute some sort of public nuisance should continue to be prohibited by law. The authors of *The Wolfenden Report* and the *Model Penal Code* of the American Law Institute, for instance, support this view. There is disagreement among legislators, psychiatrists, and other professionals, however, on how offenders should be dealt with under the law. People who commit offenses of the sort to be described in this section are generally designated legally as *sexual psychopaths.* It should be made clear that the term "sexual psychopath" does not correspond to any particular disease constellation generally recognized by psychiatrists. Rather, it is a legal term that poses some of the same problems as does the legal term "insanity," which also does not correspond to any particular form of mental illness. The elements that seem to constitute sexual psychopathy under the law include compulsiveness, repetition, and a certain bizarre, or disconcerting, quality in sexual behavior. Under most relevant statutes, then, a man who commits a single rape is much less likely to be considered a sexual psychopath than a man who has exhibited his genitals in public on several occasions.

Thirty of the 50 states and the District of Columbia now have laws applicable to sexual psychopaths. There are two very significant aspects to these laws. First is the *indeterminate sentence,* under which the sexual psychopath can be imprisoned or hospitalized for the rest of his life (or for any lesser period). The indeterminate sentence is apparently acceptable on the grounds that society must be protected from habitual sex criminals. The procedures for imposing such a sentence, however, pose problems related to the constitutional rights of the offender.[1] The law assumes that the prison or hospital superintendent and the courts will release the sexual offender when there is no longer reasonable cause to believe that he constitutes a menace to society, but this assumption is not always justified. The duration of the sex offender's incarceration is subject, among other variables, to the personal attitudes of the prison warden, hospital superintendent, or judge. The official desire to put a sex offender away indefinitely is based at least partly on other mistaken assumptions, one of which is that sex offenders have a high rate of recidivism. This is not the case. The only group of individuals convicted of major crimes that has recidivism rates lower than those of sex offenders are those convicted of homicides. Among the 7 percent of sex offenders who do repeat their offenses the majority are nonviolent offenders: voyeurs,

[1]Bowman and Engle (in Slovenko, 1965, pp. 757–778) discuss such legal problems as denial of due process and equal protection, especially the rights to counsel, jury trial, and appeal, as well as the rights to notice of a hearing, personal attendance at the hearing, subpoenaing of witnesses, and cross-examination.

comparative privacy, as long as someone present claims to have been offended. There have also been instances in which no one present was offended, yet the person or persons involved were convicted of "indecent exposure." These cases have usually involved people bathing in the nude at nudist camps or sunbathing in their own backyards.[24]

[24]Ploscowe (1951), p. 160. In recent years a number of "streakers" have been arrested for violating similar statutes. In 1974 the Louisiana legislature passed a bill that would exclude from prosecution streakers who did not attempt to arouse the sexual desires of their viewers.

Box 14.3 Continued

exhibitionists, and homosexuals.[2] Furthermore, every study of sex offenders has shown that, contrary to another popular notion, they rarely show patterns of progression to more serious or more violent sex crimes. Exhibitionists do not eventually become rapists, nor do child molesters eventually become "sex killers." When a rapist has a record of previous criminal offenses, it often consists of nonsexual crimes like assault and burglary. Those rare individuals who commit the sort of highly publicized sex murder and mutilation that may lead to general crackdowns on all "sex perverts" are usually extremely disturbed or psychotic.

The second significant aspect of the laws on sexual psychopaths is their recognition of sex offenders as mentally ill, in some sense, and in need of treatment or rehabilitation rather than punishment. Particularly when the earlier sexual psychopath laws were enacted, this recognition was quite revolutionary. Provisions for treatment are usually tied to the indeterminate sentence, so that the sex offender is sentenced to confinement and treatment until he is no longer considered a menace to society.

Although many states have laws covering sexual psychopaths, these laws are seldom applied. One reason is the way in which many of them are written. The potential for double jeopardy is frequently

[2]Report of the New Jersey Commission on the Habitual Sex Offender, quoted in Slovenko (1965), p. 140.

so great that courts are reluctant to enforce such laws, especially when the statutes provide that an individual need only be accused of or charged with a sex offense to be institutionalized as a sexual psychopath.[3] Under these laws the individual may, after his release from a state hospital where he has been committed for treatment, be tried and sentenced to prison for the same offense for which he was committed to the hospital. Under postconviction laws the individual must be tried and convicted of a sexual offense *before* sexual-psychopath proceedings may be instituted; the latter then come under civil, rather than criminal, law. If the convicted sex offender is deemed a sexual psychopath, as the result of examination by expert witnesses (usually two psychiatrists), he may then be committed to a state institution for treatment. Even under most of these postconviction laws, however, the individual can still be sentenced to prison for the original offense after a period of involuntary hospitalization.

California has made the greatest use of the legal concept of sexual psychopathy and has established a special institution (Atascadero State Hospital, Atascadero, California) for the treatment of offenders. Most other states do not offer special facilities for sex offenders and do not have professional personnel specifically trained to treat such individuals.

[3]Ten of the 30 states with laws pertaining to sexual psychopaths do not require conviction of a sex offense before commitment as a sexual psychopath. The individual, if arrested, may be committed without trial.

There has also been some controversy in the courts over what portions of the anatomy constitute "private parts." Most courts draw an absolute line at the limits of pubic hair (which has led some "bottomless" dancers in California to shave their pubic hair in an effort to circumvent this definition). Traditionally a woman's breasts, with the exception of the nipples, have not been considered "private parts" under the law; hence the use of "pasties" by strip teasers. Court decisions in several states, however, have declared that the breasts, including the nipples, do not constitute "private parts," thus affirming the legality of "topless" dancers in certain jurisdictions.

The *Model Penal Code* does not differ significantly from present laws, except that the word "genitals" is substituted for "private parts."[25]

Crimes against Children

Sexual offenses involving minors are subject to severe sanctions in every state, though prosecution is often difficult because the only witnesses are children, who are not always able to provide the reliable, consistent evidence necessary for conviction. Although the following California statute is typical in providing for long prison sentences for child molesters, in practice the disposition in California courts is usually made under the provisions of the laws related to sexual psychopaths:

288. *Exciting Lust of Child Under Age of Fourteen.*—Any person who shall willfully and lewdly commit any lewd or lascivious act including any of the acts constituting other crimes provided for in part one of this code upon or with the body, or with any part or member thereof, of a child under the age of fourteen years, with the intent of arousing, appealing to, or gratifying the lust of passions or sexual desires of such person or of such child, shall be guilty of a felony and shall be imprisoned in the State prison for a term of from one year to life.

The definition of a child or minor in these statutes varies somewhat from state to state. The American Law Institute proposes that minority be defined as being less than 16 years, provided that the offender is at least four years older than the other person.[26]

Although child molesters are almost always males, the children involved may be either male or female, depending on the orientation of the pedophiliac. The behavior involved most often consists of fondling the

genitals, but may also include mutual masturbation, oral-genital contacts, intercourse, or pederasty (*see* Chapter 11).

A special type of sexual offense against a minor is incest. The law usually treats incest in special statutes prohibiting marriage or sexual activity between immediate family members and relatives of varying degrees of consanguinity. The offense is a felony and punishable by as much as 50 years in prison in some states. Incest is probably the least commonly reported of all sex offenses, accounting for 3–6 percent of the total reported sex offenses in various jurisdictions. The actual incidence is probably significantly higher, however, at least among certain segments of the population. In one study of delinquent adolescent girls, the incidence of sexual relations with fathers or stepfathers was found to be 15 percent.[27] For obvious reasons, people are more reluctant to report family members than strangers to the police, particularly if they are the primary or sole source of support for the family.

Rape and Related Offenses

Sexual intercourse with a woman other than a spouse under conditions of force or threat of violence is considered the most serious of all sexual offenses under the criminal law. It is also the sex crime that has been subject to the most serious charges of racism and sexism, particularly in regard to procedures and penalties. Federal courts finally recognized the racial discrimination involved in the administration of the death penalty for this crime when it was pointed out in a series of cases in the late 1960s that of the 455 persons executed between 1930 and 1964 in the United States for rape, 405 were blacks.

Discrimination against men in general is said to exist in the sense that the courts have rather consistently held that a man who is subjected to forcible anal intercourse in

---

[25]The American Law Institute (1962), Section 213.5.

[26]Ibid., Section 213.3(1)a.

[27]Halleck in Slovenko (1965), p. 683.

prison, for instance, has not been raped. Rape laws were written solely to "protect" women, but in reality this has not been the case.

Most cases of rape do not result in a conviction. For example, of the 63,020 reported rapes in 1977, the presumed offender was arrested in 51 percent of the cases.[28] Of those cases in which there was an arrest, 65 percent were prosecuted. Of the prosecuted cases, 40 percent resulted in acquittal or dismissal of the charges. The defendant was found guilty of a lesser offense in 13 percent of cases. In the remaining 47 percent of cases he was convicted of rape. Thus, fewer than 16 percent of the reported rapes in 1977 ended in conviction for rape. (If it is correct that only 1 out of 5 to 10 rapes is reported, the actual percentage of rapes ending in convictions is 5 to 10 times smaller.) It has often been difficult to get a conviction for rape due to questionable requirements for obtaining a conviction. The burden of proof has been on the woman to prove that she was actually raped. In the last decade the procedures and laws governing rape have changed in many states. One of the areas where change is occurring is in the procedures involved in the prosecution of rape cases. Many rapes go unreported, in part, at least, because of the humiliating and accusatory sort of interrogation procedure that women have come to expect at the hands of the police. This problem is being remedied in some areas by such reforms as the establishment of rape investigation units (New York) staffed by women who are trained in counseling rape victims, as well as obtaining the evidence necessary for apprehension, trial, and conviction of the offender.

Another important area where reform is occurring is in the presentation of the victim's sexual history in detail in open court. This is usually just as traumatic as the inves-

tigation. The woman often feels as if she, rather than the accused, is on trial. Courts have traditionally considered such inquiry proper on the questionable grounds that a history of prior "fornication" (most rape victims are unmarried women) is relevant to the question of her likelihood of consenting to intercourse with the accused. While the woman's sexual history is still admissible in some states, the majority of states have changed their laws in this area. These new laws have restrictions on the presentation of the victim's past sexual history and thereby often make it inadmissible.

An unresolved issue in rape cases involves the weight to be given as to how much, if any, resistance was shown by the victim. The rules of evidence vary under the laws of the different states. A few courts require evidence of considerable physical resistance, but most do not on the grounds that a woman may have been paralyzed by fear or may have realized that resistance was useless and might even have brought greater injury to herself.

Serious disagreements exist over the appropriate penalty for rape. Some jurists believe that lighter sentences will increase the conviction rate for rapists, since juries may be reluctant to convict if the penalty is severe (for example, life imprisonment). Other jurists favor stiffer sentences—mandatory prison terms or restoration of the death penalty for rape. The present trend in rape penalties in many states is toward lighter sentences in general, but stiffer penalties for more violent rapes.

Certain rapes are viewed by some police authorities as "victim-precipitated." These include cases where a woman initially consents to intercourse and then retracts her consent prior to the act, and other instances where a woman places herself in a "vulnerable" situation (for example, hitchhiking or walking alone at night in an isolated area or a "rough" neighborhood). There is an obvious difference in the perception of some

[28]Federal Bureau of Investigation (1977).

men and most women with regard to the kind of behavior that constitutes sexual "solicitation." A small percentage of men delude themselves into thinking that the woman who hitchhikes or walks alone is "asking for it," but most women are rightfully offended by this interpretation of such behavior. It is ironic that present attitudes toward rape make it such that women, the victims, are the ones who must restrict their behavior and thus limit their freedom to be in certain places at certain times.

A classic example of the attitudes of some males toward women in the area of rape was seen in a 1977 rape case in Madison, Wisconsin. A 15-year-old male was convicted of raping a high-school girl in the school stairwell, but the judge let him off with a probation sentence. The male judge said: "Whether women like it or not they are sex objects. Are we supposed to take an impressionable person 15 or 16 years of age and punish that person severely because they react to it normally?" Apparently not everyone agreed with the judge's attitude. He was voted out in a recall election and replaced by a woman.

Michigan, which revised its laws dealing with rape in 1974, provides a good example of the current trends in rape laws. Other states have modeled their rape laws after the Michigan reforms. In Michigan, rape is treated without reference to sex. Rape is dealt with as criminal sexual conduct involving sexual penetration or sexual contact. *Sexual penetration* includes cunnilingus, fellatio, vaginal and anal intercourse, and the insertion of an object into the vagina or anus. *Sexual contact* includes deliberate touching of the person's intimate parts for purposes of sexual arousal or gratification. The charge is divided into four degrees. First-degree rape deals with the cases involving *sexual penetration* in which the offender has a weapon, injures the victim, or is helped by another person. A second-degree charge is used where *sexual contact*

occurs under the circumstances just described. Third- and fourth-degree charges apply to cases of less severity. Mention of the victim's past sexual behavior is admissible only under certain circumstances. For example, it is allowed if she has had past consensual relations with the accused. Proof of resistance is not required, nor is corroborating evidence. The punishment varies from a fine to life imprisonment, depending on the degree of the offense.

As mentioned earlier, in almost all states a man cannot be charged with the rape of his wife even when force is used. But this, too, is changing in a few states. Oregon, New Jersey, Delaware, Nebraska, Iowa, Massachusetts, and California now permit such cases to be prosecuted. The first conviction in the United States of a wife by her husband occurred in Massachusetts in 1979. The husband and wife had been living apart, and were in the process of obtaining a divorce. He broke into her home and raped her.

Statutory Rape

The crime of statutory rape includes any act of intercourse with any female under the specified "age of consent" in a given state, as we have noted. For reasons that are not obvious the age of consent has been repeatedly raised in some jurisdictions. For instance, in California it was raised from 10 to 14 years in 1889, to 16 years in 1897, and to 18 years in 1913. This paternalistic protection of the law means that no female under this age is capable of consenting to intercourse—and consent, if given, is rendered meaningless for legal purposes.

The age of consent varies from state to state, but 16 and 18 are most common. In Tennessee the age of consent in this connection is 21, yet a girl can obtain a marriage license when she is 16. If a married woman under 21 has an affair with a man not her husband, he may be prosecuted for rape rather than for adultery. (There are such cases on record.) The law often fails to recognize that a girl of 17 or even younger may be quite experienced and assertive sexually. She may even lie about her age and say that she is 18, especially if she also looks much older than she is. None of these factors can be used as a defense against a charge of statutory rape in most states. In a few states, however, a girl's promiscuity or the fact that she is a prostitute may be used as a defense against such a charge.[29]

The American Law Institute recommends that the age for statutory rape be less than 10 years.[30] A male who had intercourse with a girl under 16 would be guilty of the lesser offense of "corruption of minors," provided that he were at least four years older than the girl.[31] These recommendations would eliminate the present possibility that a boy involved in an adolescent love affair could be convicted of a felony and sentenced to a long prison term.

Commercial Exploitation of Sex

Prostitution

The only sexual offense for which women are prosecuted to any significant extent is prostitution. In itself this phenomenon is interesting, for prostitution, as we shall define it for purposes of this discussion,[32] is a profession of women who perform sexual acts with men who pay for them—and for the most part men write and administer the law in our society. Prostitution can exist only because of the demand for such services by men; and its extent is obviously correlated with the size of

the male population without other readily available sexual outlets, as is attested to by the large numbers of prostitutes near military bases.

The history of prostitution has been the subject of many volumes,[33] and we shall not attempt to cover it here. Suffice it to say that prostitution has always existed, despite repeated attempts to eliminate it. In various ancient cultures prostitution was associated with religious rites—so-called "sacred" or "temple" prostitution. Commercialized prostitution, as we know it today, goes back at least to ancient Greece. Solon is credited with having been the first public official to establish, in 550 B.C., licensed public houses of commercial prostitution. The taxes from these brothels were used to build a temple to Aphrodite.

The term prostitute comes from the Latin *prostituere,* meaning "to expose" and implying the offering of one's body for sale *passim et sine dilectu* (indiscriminately and without pleasure), in the words of Roman law.

Despite various dissenting voices, the prevailing opinion in our society is still that prostitution is a social and moral evil and should be subject to criminal sanctions, especially when young women and men are involved. In recent years a wave of child prostitution—involving both girls and boys, some as young as 12 years of age—has struck large cities and even small towns across the United States. New York City police estimated in 1977 that as many as 20,000 runaway youngsters were on the streets of that city, many of them available for commercial sex. There are no simple remedies for this situation, but the usual response has been to stiffen the penalties, especially against the pimps.

Prostitution is illegal everywhere in the United States except in some counties of Ne-

---

[29]In some states, such as California, a similar defense may be used against a charge of seduction.

[30]The American Law Institute (1962), Section 213(1)d.

[31]The American Law Institute (1962), Section 213.3(1)a.

[32]Other less common forms of prostitution include provision by men of paid sexual services for women and homosexual prostitution (*see* Chapter 11). See also Gandy and Deisher (1970).

[33]See, for instance, Henriques (1962–1963).

vada. The laws dealing with prostitution are many and encompass various types of behavior and many individuals connected with organized prostitution beside the "solo practitioner." The most common form of prosecution by far, however, is for the offense of soliciting. Soliciting is often quite broadly defined to include a wide range of activities, as in this Colorado statute:

> Any prostitute or lewd woman who shall, by word, gesture or action, endeavor to ply her vocation upon the streets, or from the door or window of any house, or in any public place, or make a bold display of herself, shall be guilty of a misdemeanor, and shall be fined not more than $100, or imprisoned in the county jail for not less than ten days nor more than three months, or both.[34]

Most arrests are made when prostitutes solicit customers or plainclothes police officers on streets or in public places like bars or hotels (*see* Figure 14.3). The experienced prostitute is very careful in the wording of her offer in order to avoid arrest. She will mention no sexual activity at all but will speak vaguely of "wanting to have a good time," "some fun," or "having a date." She will also be wary of speaking directly of fees for services to be rendered. Instead, she may mention that she needs a certain amount of money for some new clothes or to support her sick mother. These ploys are not always successful, and courts have sustained convictions when there was sufficient reason to believe, on the basis of circumstances and general behavior, that the woman had been soliciting, regardless of whether or not she specifically "offered her body for hire." Usually a convicted prostitute is fined and then released to resume her occupation. This system obviously does not deter the prostitute much. Instead it functions as a sort of excise tax, the cost of which is passed on to the customer.

[34]*Colorado Statutes Annotated* (1935), Chapter 48, Section 214.

Figure 14.3   A streetwalker in New York City surveys a potential customer.   Photo by Burt Glinn, © Magnum Photos, Inc. Reprinted by permission.

It has often been suggested that the customer should be arrested along with the prostitute as an accomplice to an illegal act. Customers are rarely arrested, however; in most states using the services of a prostitute is not a specific crime, though it may fall under the provisions of more general statutes covering fornication or adultery, for example. There is strong resistance to penalizing customers.

Others besides the prostitute and her customer are usually involved in the enterprise of prostitution. They are often the ones who profit most from the business and are usually viewed as the major exploiters of prostitutes. They include procurers, pimps, operators and "facilitators" of houses of prostitution, and those who "traffic in women."

The activities of all these individuals are generally prohibited by either state or federal law.

The procurer, or panderer, coerces women into houses of prostitution or otherwise entices them into becoming prostitutes. The coercion need not be physical but must involve some element of intimidation or fraud, to distinguish it from pimping, which involves soliciting customers for a prostitute or receiving her earnings. The relationship between the prostitute and the pimp is superficially voluntary, but the prostitute who attempts to sever the relationship is apt to be threatened or intimidated to such an extent that she quickly changes her mind.

Those who operate houses of prostitution or in any way contribute to the running of such enterprises are subject to prosecution in most jurisdictions. This category may include madams or business managers, landlords, taxicab drivers on commission to transport customers, and any other employees of such operations. Enforcement of these laws has led to an apparent decline in the number of brothels in the United States in recent years, but many continue to operate under the guise of massage parlors, "nude photography" studios, "nude counseling" centers, escort services, and other seemingly legitimate businesses. (Not all massage parlors, escort services, and so on are fronts for prostitution. Some are strictly legitimate, and others only offer these services to selected customers who request them.) In addition, there has been an apparent increase in the number of call girls operating out of apartments "by appointment only," available at higher prices than those of "streetwalkers" who "turn tricks" in motel rooms, cars, or less private places.

Bringing women into the country or transporting them across state lines for the purpose of prostitution is now a federal offense under certain provisions of the Immigration and Nationality Act and the Mann Act (also known as the Federal White Slave Act).

The Mann Act (U.S. Annotated Code, 1925, Title 18, Section 398) defines as a felony any act of transporting or aiding in transportation (for example, furnishing travel tickets or means of transportation) of a female for prostitution "or for any other immoral purpose."[35] The latter clause provides for prosecution when no prostitution is involved. Men have been convicted under the Mann Act for crossing state lines with women friends and then having intercourse. Lovers who live near state borders are obviously particularly susceptible to such offenses.

There are those who argue that criminal sanctions against prostitution have obviously not eliminated it any more than Prohibition eliminated the consumption of alcohol, that the law has simply forced prostitution underground and into the hands of gangsters and the criminal underworld. It can also be argued that, if prostitution were legal, there could be regular medical supervision and licensing of prostitutes, leading to lower venereal disease rates. Contact with a prostitute is still the usual source of venereal infection among military personnel, but not among the civilian population.

Among the male civilian population, contacts with prostitutes account for a relatively small percentage of total sexual outlet. Kinsey found that only 3.5–4 percent of the total sexual outlet of his male sample involved sexual relations with prostitutes. About 69 percent of the white male sample in the Kinsey study had had contact at some time or other with prostitutes, but these were often only isolated experiences. About 15–20 percent had had relations with prostitutes more than a few times a year during a period of up to five years at some time in their lives.

But even though prostitution represented only a small *percentage* of the total sexual activity of the population, the *absolute*

---

[35]The offense is punishable by a $5000 fine, five years in prison, or both.

number of contacts with prostitutes was enormous. Kinsey estimated a total of 1,659,000 such contacts per year per million population in the United States. Put in terms of a community of 500,000 people, this figure comes to about 16,000 acts of prostitution a *week*. The magnitude of the problem that these figures present for law enforcement officials is staggering. Full-scale enforcement of the laws governing prostitution is obviously doomed to failure, yet it seems unlikely that any major change will be made in the direction of more enforceable laws. In general, The American Law Institute recommends maintenance of the status quo.[36] The *Model Penal Code* supports the concept that prostitution, whether carried on in private or in public, is criminal.[37] It also appears to reaffirm the concept of prostitution as a "status crime"; that is, one in which the individual does not have to commit an act of prostitution to be guilty of an offense but has only to be identified as a prostitute to be considered guilty.

Pornography

Whereas relatively little public sentiment on regulating prostitution is apparent today, the public concern about pornography[38] and pornography laws, both pro and con, is considerable. This is particularly true when pornography involves the use of children ("kiddie porn"), a phenomenon that has grown recently along with child prostitution. Efforts are being made to curb child pornography by treating it as child abuse. Another area of growing concern is the violence against women

being depicted in some pornography. Women are shown being brutalized, coerced, and victimized in various types of pornographic materials. The public is becoming increasingly desirous of restrictions on pornographic materials. In 1974, only 42 percent of Americans wanted more government control of pornography in movies, books, and nightclubs. However, the Yankelovich survey found that 74 percent of Americans felt this way in 1977.[39] Of these, 54 percent has strong feelings on the subject.

Pornography laws have a relatively short history, dating back only to the nineteenth century. The concern of the law with obscenity seems to be correlated with the development of mass communications, widespread literacy and availability of books, and the invention of the camera. In the United States the single most significant law designed to prevent the dissemination of pornographic materials is Section 1461, Title 18, of the U.S. Code, adopted in 1873. This law has been named for its primary advocate, Anthony Comstock, then secretary of the New York Society for the Suppression of Vice.[40] Under the Comstock Act it is a felony knowingly to deposit in the U.S. mail any obscene, lewd, or lascivious book, pamphlet, picture, writing, paper, or other publication of an "indecent character."[41] Enforcement of this act comes

---

[36]The American Law Institute (1962), Sections 251.2, 251.3.

[37]The *Model Penal Code* does specifically except private mistresses supported by their lovers.

[38]Pornography is also known as "obscenity," "smut," "filth" and in Judge John M. Woolsey's words "dirt for dirt's sake." Judge Woolsey ruled that James Joyce's *Ulysses* could be admitted through U.S. Customs because it seemed to offer more than "dirt for dirt's sake." "In spite of its unusual frankness, I do not detect anywhere the leer of the sensualist. I hold, therefore, that it is not pornographic." *United States* v. *One Book Called Ulysses*, 5 Fed. Supp. 182 (S.D.N.Y. 1933).

[39]Yankelovich et al. (1977).

[40]Comstock was an active crusader. His annual report in 1881 showed that in the first eight years of the existence of the Society for the Suppression of Vice he had confiscated 203,238 obscene pictures and photographs; destroyed 27,584 pounds of books; seized 27 framed obscene pictures from the walls of saloons; confiscated 1,376,939 obscene circulars, catalogues, songs, and poems plus 7400 microscopic pictures designed for use in pocket charms and knives; and obtained mailing lists used in the distribution of pornography with a total of 976,125 names and addresses (Kilpatrick, 1960, p. 243).

[41]The question of whether or not first-class mail, particularly personal letters, is exempt from this act has been the subject of several Supreme Court opinions. Although the Court has ruled that first-class mail is private, it has also ruled that the mailing of an obscene letter is a violation of the law.

Figure 14.4   Some targets of the campaign against child pronography. The recent emergence of children as the stars of pornographic movies and magazines has shocked some social agencies and citizens' groups into an increased resistance to pornography. Wide World Photos. Reprinted by permission.

under the Inspection Service of the U.S. Postal Service.

In all the rhetoric on pornography it is not always clear exactly what sort of material people are including under the term. In the history of American literature we can note that Hawthorne's *The Scarlet Letter,* Mark Twain's *Huckleberry Finn,* and Henry Miller's *Tropic of Cancer* were all condemned as obscene at the time of their publication. Furthermore, some people distinguish between erotic works of art, literature, and the cinema that have potential cultural merit and those produced purely for commercial exploitation and "utterly without redeeming social value" (sometimes called "hard-core pornography"). These and other issues led the U.S. Supreme Court to provide a new definition of obscenity in the landmark case of *Roth v. United States.*[42] The Roth case also addressed itself

[42]354 U.S. 476 (1957).

to the question of whether or not the Comstock Act violates the First Amendment provision that "Congress shall make no law . . . abridging the freedom of speech, or of the press." On the constitutional question, the Court clearly stated that "obscenity is *not* within the area of constitutionally protected speech or press."

In defining obscenity the Court laid down four essential elements: First, the material must be viewed in terms of its potential appeal to *the average person* (a modification of earlier definitions that included material which admittedly might affect only certain "susceptible" individuals). Second, *contemporary community standards* are to be applied. (The court acknowledged that standards vary from generation to generation.) Third, *the dominant theme* of the material and the content must be *taken as a whole,* rather than out of context. It had previously been customary simply to present isolated

Box 14.4 Pornography: The Black Plague?

There is particular concern about material sent by mail because it is believed that this provides the "smut peddlers" with easy access to children. Concern about this issue among legislators can be sensed from this excerpt from *The Congressional Record:*

There is a black plague sweeping the Nation more devastating than the one that ravaged Europe in the Middle Ages. Its principal victims are children and adolescents, although like its ancient predecessor, it destroys adults as well. Clergymen, educators, sociologists, city, State, and Federal law-enforcement agencies are hard pressed to curb it—and often disagree as to method.

The children's plague is pornography. Its name, however, is legion: obscenity, sexual depravity, sadism—the entire spectrum of carnality usually in printed or photographic form, or both. It is sold by the ton primarily to elementary and high school boys and girls. Approximately 1 million children are being solicited by mail order pornographers each year, according to the U.S. Post Office Department, which last year received 70,000 separate complaints from parents. The commercial filth by mail is estimated to be a half-billion-dollar-a-year racket and growing more lucrative by the day, thanks to hobbling court decisions, light prison sentences and fines, and public apathy.

Side by side with the mail-order smut peddlers are the incredibly prolific publishers of obscene paperback books and magazines considered to gross at least a billion dollars annually.

Those concerned declare that no act of

subversion planned by the Communist conspiracy could be more effective in shredding the Nation's moral fabric than the lethal effects of pornography. While it is not impossible that some of the material now sold is Kremlin inspired, ironically the Reds need not work too hard at this. They are well aided by thousands of amoral, dollar-crazed Americans, many of them militant in defense of their constitutional rights to pander to man's baser passions and their consequent fallout: perversion and depravity. . . .

Its effect in a classroom is electric. One nun in a midwestern suburb said: "We can always tell when this stuff is making the rounds. You can sense it in the room. When this happens we question each pupil individually until we uncover the rotten truth." . . .

The advertising copy of most mail order rot plainly is intended to produce one return first of all: names. Names and addresses. "The racket will take the willing sucker for just as much as the sucker can be taken," writes Kilpatrick. "Preying upon adolescents, curious girls, sex-hungry old men, the pornography factories will fill any order that promises a ready profit." The filth merchants aim the bulk of their garbage at the so-called normal male animal. However, should he tire of photos and movies he can readily obtain novelties, playing cards, peephole viewers, jigsaw puzzles, erotic recordings, suggestive statuettes, and lewd chinaware. . . . [1]

[1]From a report introduced by Senator Kenneth Keating of New York, *Proceedings and Debates of the 87th Congress, First Session*, vol. 107, no. 150 (August 29, 1961).

"vulgar" quotes or pictures from a book, for example, without reference to the overall theme; under such a rule the Bible itself could be found obscene because of its descriptions of women's breasts, as in "The Song of Solomon," and of episodes of adultery, like that of King David. Pictures of nudes in a magazine extolling the virtues of nudism for health purposes have become legal under this new definition.

Fourth, the *appeal* must be *to prurient interest*. (This requirement is applicable to content as well as to the *intentions* of authors, publishers, and so on.) A typical obscenity statute—that of California—written since the Roth case defines "prurient interest" as "a shameful or morbid interest in nudity, sex, or excretion, which goes beyond customary limits of candor in description or representation of such matters and is matter which is utterly

Table 14.1 Sexual Response in Normal Subjects to Various Forms of Erotica

		Definite or frequent	Sometimes	Never	Number of subjects in study
Viewing portrayals of nudes	Male	18%	36%	46%	4,191
	Female	3%	9%	88%	5,698
Viewing commercial films	Male	6%	30%	64%	3,231
	Female	9%	39%	52%	5,411
Viewing burlesques and erotic floor shows	Male	28%	34%	38%	3,377
	Female	4%	10%	86%	2,550
Observing portrayals of sex acts	Male	42%	35%	23%	3,868
	Female	14%	18%	68%	2,242
Reading literary materials for example, (romantic novels)	Male	21%	38%	41%	3,952
	Female	16%	44%	40%	5,699
Reading erotic materials for example, (specifically sexual stories)	Male	16%	31%	53%	4,202
	Female	2%	12%	86%	5,523

Source: Compiled from data in Kinsey et al. (1953), chap. 16.

without redeeming social importance."[43] Publishing, distributing, selling, and various related offenses are also considered crimes if the material involved is judged to be obscene by these standards.

The justifications for obscenity laws are generally three. Legislators and judges declare that pornography is damaging to children, causes increases in the numbers of sex crimes, and has deleterious effects on the morals of the population by causing sexual arousal in otherwise normal peope. We shall comment briefly on each of these three issues.

There are no significant scientific data that either prove or disprove the notion of possible damage to children from pictures or books portraying or describing sexual activities. Although few argue seriously in favor of distributing "hard-core pornography" to children, the question of the benefits and dangers of early exposure to material dealing with sexual functioning, anatomy, reproduction, and so on in sex education classes at the elemen-

tary-school level is one that must, for the present at least, be settled by common sense. There are no reliable empirical data on this subject.

There is a substantial body of knowledge on the relation of pornography to sex crimes, particularly as reported in the Gebhard study,[44] which has confirmed the reports of police officers and other law enforcement officials that sex offenders often have pornography in their possession or admit to having seen pornographic materials. The cause-and-effect relation that so many have assumed, however, has not been established. In the Gebhard study the use of pornography by sex offenders was compared to the experiences of a normal control group and to those of a group of prisoners who were not sex offenders. There were *no differences* among the three groups in use of, possession of, or exposure to pornography. Within each group variations in use and exposure to pornography were related primarily to age, socioeconomic class, and educational level. A further important finding was that sex offenders were not prone to greater sexual arousal from viewing pornography than were other groups of males.

[43]The *Model Penal Code,* Section 251.4(1), uses similar wording but omits the phrase "without redeeming social importance." A federal court declared the California statute unconstitutional in 1974 in a case involving the film *Deep Throat.* The ruling is being appealed.

[44]Gebhard et al. (1965), chap. 31.

This point leads us to the third and final issue: How susceptible are normal individuals to sexual arousal from various forms of erotica, and is such arousal an evil that should be prohibited by law?[45] There is no doubt that viewing or reading erotic materials is sexually arousing for a significant percentage of the population, particularly males. The Kinsey data on this subject are typical of the findings of other investigators (*see* Table 14.1). Should this fact be a source of concern for those responsible for criminal law? It has been the source of such concern because of the assumption that sexual stimulation may lead normal individuals to commit illegal sex acts. But there is no particular reason to believe that sexual stimulation of a normal individual will lead to anything other than fantasies and normal sexual activity. If we accept the notion that there is nothing inherently wrong or criminal in the expression of human sexuality, then this argument is without substance.

Children are continually exposed to the graphic details of fighting, violence, and killing on television and in other media. It is paradoxical that our laws seem to be more preoccupied with prohibiting the stimulation of sexual activity than with prohibiting the stimulation of aggressive or violent behavior.

[45]For a review of more than 250 articles on this subject see Cairns and Wishner (1962), pp. 1008–1041.

Chapter 15

Sex and Morality

So far we have confined ourselves mainly to a factual and analytical presentation of such topics as the biological structure and function of the sexual organs and the expression of human sexuality in a wide variety of sexual behavior. We turn now to moral questions, questions about what we *should* do. Morality involves value judgments and questions of right and wrong. It is one thing to discuss how an abortion is performed, but quite a different thing to evaluate the moral questions: whether or not a woman should be allowed to have an abortion on request; whether or not abortion should be limited to victims of rape or incest, or women whose lives or health would be endangered by pregnancy or childbirth; whether or not it should be allowed under any circumstances.

The general impression is that a significant change in attitudes toward sex and morality has been occurring in recent years. We noted in Chapter 11 that very few Americans currently consider homosexuality to be a sin, whatever else they may think of it. In Chapter 6 we reported the shift in attitude of U.S. Roman Catholics toward approval of contraception, particularly in recent years. Similar data are either available or could be readily obtained to tell us what the prevailing current attitudes are toward every aspect of human sexuality. We could base a set of moral principles on such data if we were willing to subscribe to the notion that what is right is defined by what most people believe is right, just as some social scientists define "normal" sexual behavior by the behavior patterns of the majority of people. But even in a democratic society majority opinion is not always right in the moral or ethical sense. There are standards, to which we all refer at some time or other, that go beyond the consensus and reflect belief in certain principles or moral guidelines, whether the specific issue is sexual behavior, business practices, or war.

In Western societies the religious traditions most influential in shaping sexual morality have been Jewish and Christian. Whether or not we agree with these traditions, we simply cannot deny their tremendous influence, even in the present-day United States. Most of our current laws governing sexual behavior reflect these views, and many people who flatly reject the "Judeo-Christian ethic" on intellectual grounds find themselves still subject to it at an emotional level. It is not at all unusual, for instance, to talk to unmarried young people of both sexes who are engaging in premarital intercourse and see nothing wrong in their behavior and yet find themselves *feeling* guilty about it.

In recent years there has been heightened interest in the philosophies and religions of the East. Some Western thinking and practices have been introduced in Asian countries, largely through movies and contact with our armed forces. There has also, however, been

471

strong resistance, in both East and West, to new or different standards of behavior, particularly those in the emotionally charged areas of sexuality. Passionate kisses and nudity on the screen have caused Western movies to be censored in India, and women have been arrested for wearing short skirts in Taiwan. Western dances have been condemned as "vulgar" by the Nationalist Chinese government. Conversely, mixed nude bathing, an old custom in Japan, is not common in the United States yet, nor is the practice of legalized prostitution that exists in some countries in the Orient.

In this chapter we shall examine the historical development of Jewish and Christian ethics in connection with sexual and related behavior. We shall then discuss a series of specific sexual issues and try to show how we approach these issues in moral or ethical terms. It is not our aim to espouse one set of values over another but rather to describe the kind of reasoning that culminates in a widely held moral principle.

The History of Western Sexual Morality

The Jewish Tradition

Attitudes toward Marriage and Family

A high regard for marriage and children is a prominent theme in early Hebraic teachings. In particular, the notion of procreation as a primary obligation of humans is fundamental to the Old Testament and the Talmud, and this notion has been preserved to the present day by the Roman Catholic Church. Probably no other single doctrine has had as many ramifications for sexual behavior as has the doctrine that the purpose of sex and marriage is reproduction. In the very first chapter of the first book of the Old Testament it is written:

So God created man in his own image, in the image of God he created him; male and female he created them. And God blessed them, and God said to them, "Be fruitful and multiply, and fill the earth and subdue it; and have dominion over the fish of the sea and over the birds of the air and over every living thing that moves upon the earth."[1]

The belief among the ancient Jews that they in particular should multiply in order to propagate God's chosen people is repeatedly mentioned in the Old Testament. For example, God tells Abraham, "I will indeed bless you, and I will multiply your descendants as the stars of the heavens and as the sand which is on the seashore."[2] Similar promises were made to Abraham's son Isaac and to Isaac's son Jacob.

The Talmud stresses the religious obligation to marry and to raise a family. The unmarried person was at best pitied, and for a man to remain single indefinitely was considered unnatural and immoral. A Jewish woman was expected to bear children, and, indeed, if she failed to do so after ten years of marriage she could be divorced on those grounds alone. Furthermore, a man had an obligation to see that the family name was carried on:

If brothers dwell together and one of them dies, the wife of the dead shall not be married outside the family to a stranger; her husband's brother shall go in to her, and take her as his wife, and perform the duty of a husband's brother to her. And the first son whom she bears shall succeed to the name of his brother who is dead, that his name not be blotted out of Israel.[3]

Marriage was to be entered into early but not lightly. Eighteen was the recommended age for males, and shortly after age 12 (at which age minority status ended) for

[1]Genesis 1:27–28.
[2]Genesis 22:17.
[3]Deuteronomy 25:5–6.

girls. Jews had a particularly high regard for the institution of marriage (and still do, if judged by the low divorce rate among Jews compared to that among adherents of other faiths, especially Protestants). They were encouraged to be cautious and to give a great deal of thought to the selection of marriage partners. In contrast to the prearranged marriages, often with partners never seen in some Oriental cultures, rabbinic law stated: "A man is forbidden to take a woman to wife without having first seen her, lest he afterwards perceive in her something objectionable and she becomes repulsive to him."[4] Furthermore, marriages were believed to be divinely arranged and sanctioned.

The Jews were apparently very supportive of newlyweds and favored a sort of extended honeymoon. "When a man is newly married, he shall not go out with the army or be charged with any business; he shall be free at home one year, to be happy with his wife whom he has taken."[5]

Attitudes toward Women

Although Jewish women were accorded great respect in their roles as wives and mothers, males had the upper hand in property rights and divorce. A woman could be divorced by her husband without her consent on the grounds that he found something "unseemly" or "indecent" about her,[6] but a woman could not divorce her husband without his consent. There was a division of opinion on the interpretation of this law, and by the first century A.D. there were two fully developed schools of thought. The School of Shammai took the view that the law applied only in instances of adultery by the woman, but the School of Hillel took a much broader

view, which encompassed such grounds as poor cooking and less beauty than that of another woman. Gradually, however, Jewish women were accorded equal rights under Jewish law regarding divorce and property ownership.

Boys were clearly preferred to girls as offspring, however. Some of the reasons for this preference are given in the Talmud:

In a quotation from Ben Sira, which the Talmud preserved: "It is written. A daughter is a vain treasure to her father. From anxiety about her he does not sleep at night; during her early years lest she be seduced, in her adolescence lest she go astray, in her marriageable years lest she does not find a husband, when she is married lest she be childless, and when she is old lest she practice witchcraft." The same thought is contained in the explanation of the words of the Priestly Benediction: " 'The Lord bless thee and keep thee'—bless thee with sons, and keep thee from daughters because they need careful guarding."[7]

Nevertheless, feelings of tenderness and responsibility toward all children prevailed, as did a belief that all children were truly gifts from God.

Rules Governing Sexual Morality

Sexual behavior was strictly regulated by Jewish laws, and the penalties for infractions could be quite severe. Adultery, incest, homosexuality, and bestiality were forbidden, and punishments ranged from social ostracism to death.[8] The early Jews were opposed to abortion and considered it an abomination. Contraceptive practices were totally forbidden for men and generally for women as well, though some exceptions were made for the latter: "A minor lest pregnancy prove fatal, a pregnant woman lest abortion result, and a nursing mother lest she becomes pregnant

---

[4]Kiddushin, 41a (Babylonian *Talmud*), in Cohen (1949), p. 164.
[5]Deuteronomy 24:5.
[6]Deuteronomy 24:1; Mishna Gittin, chap. 9, no. 8, in Cohen (1949), p. 167.

[7]Sanhedrin, 100b (Babylonian *Talmud*), in Cohen (1949), pp. 171–172.
[8]Leviticus, chap. 18–20.

Box 15.1   Christianity and Sexuality

The Jewish and Christian attitudes toward sexual intercourse within marriage have been quite different. The following passage by St. Augustine, an influential early Christian theologican, is an example of the negative view toward sexual intercourse that has been part of the Christian tradition.

18. Of the shame which attends all sexual intercourse

Lust requires for its consummation darkness and secrecy; and this not only when unlawful intercourse is desired, but even such fornication as the earthly city has legalized. Where there is no fear of punishment, these permitted pleasures still shrink from the public eye. Even where provision is made for this lust, secrecy also is provided; and while lust found it easy to remove the prohibitions of law, shamelessness found it impossible to lay aside the veil of retirement. For even shameless men call this shameful; and though they love the pleasure, dare not display it. What! does even conjugal intercourse, sanctioned as it is by law for the propagation of children, legitimate and honourable though it be, does it not seek retirement from every eye? Before the bridegroom fondles his bride, does he not exclude the attendants, and even the paranymphs, and such friends as the closest ties have admitted to the bridal chamber? The greatest master of Roman eloquence says, that all right actions wish to be set in the light, i.e., desire to be known. This right action, however, has such a desire to be known, that yet it blushes to be seen. Who does not know what passes between husband and wife that children may be born? Is it not for this purpose that wives are married with such ceremony? And yet, when this well-understood act is gone about for the procreation of children, not even the children themselves, who may already have been born to them, are suffered to be witnesses. This right action seeks the light, in so far as it seeks to be known, but yet dreads being seen. And why so, if not because that which is by nature fitting and decent is so done as to be accompanied with a shame-begetting penalty of sin? . . .

21. That man's transgression did not annul the blessing of fecundity pronounced upon man before he sinned, but infected it with the disease of lust

Far be it, then, from us to suppose that our first parents in Paradise felt that lust which caused them afterwards to blush and hide their nakedness, or that by its means they should have fulfilled the benediction of God, "Increase and multiply and replenish the earth''; for it was after sin that lust began. It was after sin that our

St. Augustine in his studio. Painting by Simon Marmion. The Bettmann Archive.

Box 15.1   Continued

nature, having lost the power it had over the whole body, but not having lost all shame, perceived, noticed, blushed at, and covered it. But that blessing upon marriage, which encouraged them to increase and multiply and replenish the earth, though it continued even after they had sinned, was yet given before they sinned, in order that the procreation of children might be recognized as part of the glory of marriage, and not of the punishment of sin. But now, men being ignorant of the blessedness of Paradise, suppose that children could not have been begotten there in any other way than they know them to be begotten now, i.e., by lust, at which even honourable marriage blushes.[1]

[1]Augustine (1934 ed.), parts 18 and 21.

and prematurely wean the child so that it dies."[9]

There seemed to be a very positive feeling among Jews about sexual intercourse, within the confines of marriage at least, which contrasts rather sharply with the attitude prevalent in the early Christian Church, an attitude that has persisted to some extent until very recent times: that sex as such is intrinsically evil and tinged with guilt.[10] (See Box 15.1)

The Christian Tradition

Origins

Since Jesus and his 12 disciples were all Jewish, it might seem reasonable to assume that Jewish sexual traditions were largely shared by them. Inasmuch as Jesus radically departed from some of the major religious tenets and practices of his contemporaries, however, we cannot carry this assumption very far. We shall restrict ourselves to inferences from the biblical record.

Jesus was chaste and celibate, yet he did not shun the company of women from any walk of life, even in a culture in which heterosexual contacts were more or less restricted to members of one's own family. Because of the special circumstances of his life, we cannot assume that he necessarily intended his celibate existence to serve as a model, nor did he ever indicate that he meant it so.

What did Jesus say about sex specifically? We have only a fragmentary record of his teachings, and there is relatively little on this subject. His most restrictive statements are those in the Sermon on the Mount:

You have heard that it was said, "You shall not commit adultery." But I say to you that every one who looks at a woman lustfully has already committed adultery with her in his heart. If your right eye causes you to sin, pluck it out and throw it away: it is better that you lose one of your members than that your whole body be

[9]Cohen (1949), pp. 170–171.

[10]This is one of several areas in which the traditional Jewish and Christian views differ. Hence, the term "Judeo-Christian ethic" does not describe a homogeneous viewpoint but two related viewpoints that arose in the Western world and are based in part on the same authorities (the books of the Old Testament, particularly the Mosaic code).

thrown into hell. And if your right hand causes you to sin, cut it off and throw it away: it is better that you lose one of your members than that your whole body go into hell.[11]

What did Jesus actually mean by these remarks? It is highly unlikely that he was suggesting that one literally blind oneself rather than cast adulterous glances. Such a prescription simply does not fit the overall context and meaning of his sayings. It is relevant that earlier in the same sermon Jesus equally condemned the nursing of anger.[12] Since it is evident that no human being can avoid feeling angry at one time or another, it seems that Jesus was using these examples not as actual standards of behavior but rather as illustrations of how wretched and helpless man is apart from God. A minor yet significant point is that Jesus was speaking in a language and idiom that happen to be rich in metaphor.

As far as we know, Jesus made no statements extolling the virtues of sex. In view of the fragmentary record, however, such negative evidence is inconclusive. He did deal with a woman caught in adultery (the Mosaic penalty for which was death by stoning), and he said to her accusers: "He that is without sin among you, let him first cast a stone at her."[13] No one cast a stone. Then Jesus told the adulteress that he did not condemn her and that she should not sin again. Jesus was criticized by his pious detractors for consorting with sinners, including prostitutes. It is interesting that none of the three great temptations of Jesus was related to sex.[14]

From this fragmentary record theologians, as well as other believers and nonbelievers, have reached all feasible conclusions, casting Jesus in roles ranging from stern ascetic to proponent of free love to "Jesus Christ Superstar."

[11]Matthew 5:27–30.
[12]Matthew 5:21–22.
[13]John 8:1–11 (King James version).
[14]Matthew 4:1–11.

Christianity was based on the teachings of Jesus, but did not limit itself to them. Even in the early Church a variety of interpretations and points of view on all matters began to be incorporated into Christian doctrine.

Greek and Roman Influences

Very early in the history of the Church (the first century A.D.), and particularly under the influence of St. Peter and St. Paul, gentiles (non-Jews, especially Greeks and Romans) were incorporated into the Church.[15] They brought with them the thinking of Greek and Roman culture about sexuality and morality. On one basic premise the Greeks, Romans, and Jews were agreed, however: that the purpose of marriage was to produce legitimate offspring (the Greeks and Romans on behalf of the state, the Jews on behalf of God).

Both the Greeks and the Romans held women to be inferior and subservient to men. In the early days of the Roman Empire women were treated with perhaps more respect than Greek women had been, but they remained subservient and dependent on their fathers until they married, after which time they were legally subject to their husbands. By the second century A.D. a gradual lessening of the husband's authority over his wife had occurred, but, rather than improving the quality of married life, it seems simply to have reflected the general breakdown of social life during the period just before the ultimate downfall of the Empire. Divorce rates and hedonism greatly increased, and, concomitantly, family life degenerated. In both Greek and Roman cultures, the double standard was traditional. Men participated in extramarital sexual liaisons (both heterosexual and

[15]St. Peter, considered by Roman Catholics to be the first head of the Christian Church, had a vision, subsequent to which he preached that God had spoken to him on the integration of the Church: "Truly I perceive that God shows no partiality, but in every nation anyone who fears him and does what is right is acceptable to him" (Acts of the Apostles 10:34–35).

homosexual, especially among the Greeks), and prostitution was condoned.

Although hedonism prevailed in the gentile world at the time of Christ (at least in the large cities of Greece and Rome; the outlying provinces tended to be more conservative), there were schools of thought that condemned the common sexual practices of the time and extolled the virtues of asceticism. Particularly in Greece, the Cynics and the Stoics alike tended to renounce the world—including material possessions and marital and sexual relationships—in favor of purity (poverty and chastity, according to some). This ascetic tradition, rather than the hedonistic one, was quite influential in the thinking of the early Christians, as we shall see.

The Teachings of St. Paul

St. Paul was the first important Christian teacher on issues of sexual behavior. As discussed earlier, Jesus himself had had relatively little to say on such issues, although we have the distinct impression that he was quite understanding toward those who had been condemned or ostracized for offenses like adultery and prostitution. St. Paul, on the other hand, appears to have considered marriage and sexuality inferior to chastity and celibacy. Defenders of St. Paul point out that he wrote in the belief that the world would end within his lifetime. If the Kingdom of God was at hand, why worry about marriage and family when one should be preparing for the end? Nevertheless, for whatever reasons, St. Paul clearly elevated the single, celibate state to a status of greater purity than that of the married or sexually active state. This elevation was the beginning of a tradition that became very influential in Christian thought over the centuries. St. Paul saw marriage as a relationship to be entered into in order to avoid the sin of fornication, and thus appropriate only for those too morally weak to resist venereal temptations. In one of his best-known statements on this subject he said:

"To the unmarried and the widows I say that it is well for them to remain single as I do. But if they cannot exercise self-control, they should marry. For it is better to marry than to be aflame with passion."[16]

Regardless of St. Paul's motives, the important point is that he provided a basis for future elaboration of the notion that sex is to be avoided, that abstaining from sexual activity *of any kind* leads to a higher moral state, and that marriage is a concession to the body that should be made only by those deficient in willpower. St. Paul suggested that celibacy is not only more pleasing to God but also less anxiety-provoking.[17]

St. Paul advised those who did marry: "Wives be subject to your husbands, as to the Lord. For the husband is the head of the wife as Christ is the head of the Church. . . . Husbands, love your wives, as Christ loved the Church.[18]

The Patristic Period of the Church: St. Augustine

Theologians call the several centuries following the time of St. Paul and extending through the fall of the Roman Empire "the patristic age" because in that period formulation of the doctrines of the new religion was dominated by a small group of men who are known as the "Fathers of the Church." Included in this group were St. Ambrose, St. Jerome, and St. Gregory (the Great), but the one who most influenced Christian doctrine on human sexuality was St. Augustine.

St. Augustine's personal struggle with his own sexual nature is recorded in his *Confessions*. In brief he "sowed his wild oats" during the first 30 years of his life; then he was converted to Christianity and, in effect, renounced all sexual activity. We find a similar pattern in the lives of St. Jerome and

---

[16]Corinthians 7:8–9. The King James version reads, "It is better to marry than to burn."

[17]I Corinthians 7:32–38.

[18]Ephesians 5:22–25.

the theologian Tertullian, but the contrast be-tween "before" and "after" is not nearly as striking as in the life of St. Augustine. He was born in 354 A.D. of a Christian mother and a non-Christian father. While still a minor he fathered a child and began a 13-year sexual liaison with the mother of his son Adeodatus ("by God given"). During this time Augustine was involved in turn with Manichaeanism (which took a dim view of marriage and even of sexual intercourse), then with Skepticism, and, just before his conversion to Christianity, with Neo-Platonism. Having reached the con-clusion that he could not successfully control his own sexual desires, St. Augustine decided to enter a legitimate marriage, and his mis-tress of many years was exiled to Africa in order to avoid complications. Even while be-trothed and awaiting his marriage, however, he found himself taking another mistress to satisfy what seemed to him base but uncon-trollable instincts. His conflict during this pe-riod is reflected in the oft-repeated prayer of his younger years: "Give me chastity—but not yet."

The turning point in St. Augustine's life came in his thirty-second year, when he read the writings of St. Paul, which convinced him that the highest calling in life was celibacy and total abstinence from sexual activity. He broke his engagement, renounced his mis-tresses, and was baptized into the Christian Church, much to the delight of his mother with whom he had been living.

Following his conversion, St. Augustine quickly became an influential member and ultimately a bishop of the Roman Catholic Church. Later in his life, beginning three years after Rome had been sacked by the Vandals in 410 A.D., St. Augustine spent 13 years writing his monumental *The City of God.* Whereas his autobiographical *Confes-sions,* in the words of Lord Byron, "make the reader envy his transgressions," St. Augus-tine associates guilt rather than pleasure with

sexuality in *The City of God.*[19] He acknowl-edges that coitus is essential for human prop-agation but argues that the act itself is tainted with guilt because of the sin of Adam and Eve. Sexual intercourse was thus transformed from something pure and innocent to some-thing shameful—"lust"—by the original sin of Adam and Eve, which was passed on from generation to generation.

As lust (the Latin *concupiscentia*) is inextricably involved in all sexual acts be-cause of original sin, it then follows that chas-tity is a higher moral state than is marriage—and is certainly a prerequisite for priests and nuns.[20] This view is being seriously ques-tioned today by certain members of the Ro-man Catholic Church, as it was by Martin Luther during the Reformation. Whereas St. Paul had viewed the married state as inferior to celibacy on the grounds that it was distract-ing for those who truly wanted to dedicate themselves to God, St. Augustine went a step further and labeled intercourse, even within marriage, as sinful. Although he recognized that the act of copulation is essential for pro-creation—the subject of a divine command-ment—he believed that the behavior and emotions that accompany intercourse make it shameful. Such behavior and emotions he took to be signs of man's degradation since the Fall. Although one could minimize the sin-fulness of coitus by performing it only as part of fulfilling one's *duty* to have children (a no-tion that even today is not foreign to many people), one could not totally ignore the fact that a child conceived under these circum-stances is the product of an act of sexual lust. Hence the need for infant baptism in order to wash away the guilt of lust as well as of Original Sin. The fact that an aborted fetus usually dies before it can be baptized and is

---

[19]Augustine (1934 ed.), parts 18 and 21.
[20]During the first four centuries A.D. priests were allowed to marry, although marriage was not encour-aged.

therefore condemned was at one time a major argument against abortion.

The Middle Ages:
St. Thomas Aquinas

The early centuries of the medieval period were the Dark Ages as far as significant new thoughts about sexual ethics are concerned. But, as the Church ultimately assumed jurisdiction over marriage and divorce, previously a function of civil authorities, there ensued a lengthy controversy over the conditions, if any, under which divorce and remarriage could be allowed. Church authorities in Rome held that a lawful, consummated marriage could not be dissolved under any circumstances. Elsewhere, particularly in England, divorce was allowed to Roman Catholics for adultery, and remarriage was allowed when a husband had died or was presumed dead in battle.

By the twelfth century, however, the Roman Catholic Church had clarified and consolidated the official view that it still takes today that marriages are final.[21] There were a few loopholes, however. A Christian spouse could obtain a divorce from a non-Christian on the grounds that the latter would not convert: the so-called "Pauline privilege" based on St. Paul's statement, "If the unbelieving partner desires to separate, let it be so, in such cases the brother or sister is not bound."[22] Also, in practice, marriages outside the Church did not have quite the same binding force as did marriages performed within the Church. Another loophole involved "consummation" of the marriage; that is, sexual intercourse. Although a marriage was formed by mutual consent as expressed in the marriage vows, it did not become indissoluble until the couple had had intercourse. Consequently, if both

---

[21]It was not until the Council of Trent (1545–1563) that marriage became an official sacrament of the Catholic Church.

[22]I Corinthians 7:15.

parties wanted "out" of a Roman Catholic marriage they could (and still can) seek an annulment on grounds that it had never been "consummated."

By far the most influential writer in the Church during the Middle Ages was the thirteenth-century scholar and theologian St. Thomas Aquinas. An unusually systematic thinker and author, Aquinas spelled out the position of the Roman Catholic Church on questions of sex and morality in such minute detail that essentially nothing new has had to be added since. There is virtually no form of sexual behavior to which Aquinas did not address himself. In his massive work *Summa Theologica* he has included dissertations on touching, kissing, fondling, seduction, intercourse, adultery, fornication, "nocturnal pollution" (wet dreams), marriage, virginity, homosexuality, incest, rape, bestiality, prostitution, and related topics.

The question of abortion was also addressed by Aquinas. From the earliest days of the Catholic Church abortion at any stage of pregnancy was equated with murder. But Aquinas and other Church philosophers of the Middle Ages held that abortion was permissible in the early stages of pregnancy. Aquinas reasoned that the fetus was not "formed" and was not "infused" with a soul until the time of quickening—around the end of the fifth month of pregnancy. Others argued that the fetus was fully formed by the fortieth or eightieth day of pregnancy, and only abortions performed after that time were murder. In 1588, Pope Sixtus V declared that all abortions were a form of murder, but in 1591, Pope Gregory XVI reversed that and allowed abortions up to the fortieth day. That position held until about 100 years ago. In 1869, Pope Pius IX again declared that abortion at any stage is murder—a position that is still held today by the Catholic Church, with two exceptions, (see page 494).

In addition to his comprehensive treat-

Box 15.2 The Problem with Illegitimacy

Some of the arguments from nature made by St. Thomas Aquinas in the thirteenth century are still quite compatible with modern professional thinking. Consider, for instance, the argument against coitus by an unmarried couple.

In essence, Aquinas argued that offspring should have both mother and father for optimal upbringing and that, since fornication involves the possibility that a child will be born without defined parents to care for it, fornication is morally wrong *because of the potential deleterious effects upon the child* who may be conceived.[1] Many recent studies have shown higher rates of juvenile delinquency, emotional disturbance, and suicide among young people who have grown up in "broken homes"—that is, in homes from which one or both parents are absent because of divorce, death, separation, or other reasons.

Most people in the United States believe that children should be born to married couples. In the 1977 Yankelovich survey 70 percent of the respondents disapproved of having children out of wedlock. In spite of people's beliefs, the number of illegitimate births is increasing among most age groups. In 1960 only 5 percent of births occurred outside of marriage. By 1976 this number had increased to about 15 percent.[2]

One might think that the current availability of reliable contraceptives would have nullified the Catholic argument against fornication. Pope Paul VI, in 1968, addressed this issue with the following admonitions:

Not much experience is needed in order to know human weakness, and to understand that men—especially the young, who are so vulnerable on this point—have need of encouragement to be faithful to the moral law, so that they must not be offered easy means of eluding its observance. It is also to be feared that the man, growing used to the employment of anticonceptive practices, may finally lose respect for the woman and, no longer caring for her physical and psychological equilibrium, may come to the point of considering her as a mere instrument of selfish enjoyment, and no longer as his respected and beloved companion.[3]

This position was reaffirmed in 1976. In a document called a "Declaration on Certain Questions Concerning Sexual Ethics," prepared under a mandate from Pope Paul VI, it was stated that all forms of premarital sex, homosexual activity, and masturbation are contrary to Church teaching.

[1]Aquinas (1911–1925 ed.), Second Part of the Second Part, Question 154, Article 2; italics added.
[2]National Center for Health Statistics (1978).
[3]Pope Paul VI (1968), p. 11.

---

ment of issues involving sex and morality, which helped to consolidate the position of the Roman Catholic Church on these questions, Aquinas is noteworthy for his reliance on the notion of Natural Law, or "rules of nature." Aquinas based his arguments partly on the Bible, but also on the writings of the Fathers of the Church and the use of "right reason." In addition, he held the view that God had created the natural world and that with the exception of the human species, which had been corrupted by the Fall (original sin) and subsequent willful misdeeds, the natural order of things is representative of the way that God had originally intended the world to be. Consequently it is possible to observe the sexual behavior of animals, for instance, and to derive conclusions about what is natural and therefore "right" for man. It is particularly striking, as we shall discuss later in this chapter, that a similar argument is currently being put forth by various eminent anthropologists and ethologists; the major difference is that the behavior of animals (particularly of the subhuman primates) is being viewed today as a standard of *normality* rather than of *morality.*

Attempts to suppress sexual activity have not been entirely negative in their approach. Throughout the Middle Ages a positive virtue was ascribed to chastity; that is, total abstinence from sexual activity. The chaste person was often characterized as happy, content, and someone to be envied rather than pitied. It is somewhat difficult to appreciate today how widespread this view has been for many centuries, not only in the Christian world but also in other developed cultures and in some preliterate societies. The glorification of virginity, as in the cult of the Virgin Mary, was long a popular subject for both secular and religious writers.

Havelock Ellis has written an interesting history of the "chastity movement" during the Christian era from the beginnings of the Church to the twentieth century.[23] He pointed out that the romantic aspects of chastity were not as mysterious as might appear at first glance—underlying this movement was an element of female protest against subjugation in the traditional marriage arrangements of the times. He has noted that chastity was advocated not simply as a source of rewards after death or "because the virgin who devotes herself to it secures in Christ an ever-young lover," but also because "its chief charm is represented as lying in its own joy and freedom and the security it involves from all the troubles, inconveniences, and bondages of matrimony.[24]

The Reformation

Both Luther and Calvin, from the earliest stages of their revolt within the Church, attacked the prevailing notions of chastity, celibacy, and marriage. One of Calvin's arguments sounds not at all dissimilar to those being put forward by certain Roman Catholic priests today: The argument is that since marriage was permitted for clergymen in the early days of the church, it is surprising that this practice has not had greater weight in determining present policy.[25]

Luther's arguments against celibacy were somewhat different from those of Calvin. Luther seems to have drawn from his own emotional experiences in formulating his doctrines, as had St. Augustine. Luther's childhood in Germany had been replete with visions of demons and witches and with severe beatings for the most minor offenses. In 1505, caught in a terrible thunderstorm, he vowed to St. Ann that he would become a monk if his life were spared. He entered an Augustinian monastery and reflected on his sins. But, in contrast to St. Augustine, he came to the conclusion that the desires of the flesh could be neither conquered nor atoned for by good works, penances, and the like. On the specific issue of celibacy Luther argued, in the style of Aristotle and Aquinas, that celibacy is not a natural state for man and, indeed, that those who are prone to practice it are inclined to be peculiar. Luther viewed marriage not only as normal but also as a secular arrangement that should fall under the jurisdiction of civil authorities rather than of the Church. Luther himself set an example by being married in his home rather than in a church. He felt strongly that marriage is not a specifically Christian sacrament but rather an institution for all men, established at the time of man's creation, long before the founding of the Christian Church. Although this notion ultimately led to more flexible divorce laws in Protestant countries, Luther himself did not condone divorce and remarriage except in instances of adultery or "desertion" (the latter term came to be interpreted more and more broadly with time).

---

[23]Ellis (1942), vol. II, part 3, pp. 143–177.
[24]Ibid., p. 158.

[25]Calvin (1960), Book IV, chap. XII, section 27.

The Reformers were influential not only in elevating the status of marriage but also to some extent in removing the onus of sin from sexual intercourse. Calvin departed farther from tradition than did Luther. Whereas Luther viewed the sexual appetite as natural, on the order of hunger and thirst, he still shared some of St. Augustine's feeling that sexual behavior has a certain intrinsic shamefulness. Calvin, on the other hand, viewed sex as something holy and honorable, at least within the confines of marriage. He also challenged the long-standing notion that the purpose of marriage is procreation and put forth the idea that marriage should be a social relationship, in which the wife provides companionship for her husband rather than serving simply as the mother of his children and as a source of relief for his sexual tensions. Nevertheless, both Luther and Calvin held the notion that women should be subject to male authority, within both marriage and the Church. Underlying this teaching was a belief that women are the inferior of the two sexes. This was hardly a uniquely Christian, or even religious, doctrine. It is seen in Aristotle's description of women as ''deficient males'' and various other secular writings that preceded the Christian religion.

The Reformation was an extraordinary challenge to established beliefs and traditions. Yet exceedingly important changes were actually being brought about throughout the Renaissance as well. This transitional period between medieval and modern times began in Italy in the fourteenth century, spread to other parts of Europe, and continued into the seventeenth century. It was characterized by the revival of classical influences and humanistic attitudes, expressed through an unprecedented outpouring of the arts and literature. Medieval asceticism was rejected in favor of full expressions of romantic and physical love, and the human body was glorified. It was also a period of considerable confusion in sexual morals and of sharp contrasts even in the behavior of the popes. Alexander VI (1492–1503), for example, was well known for his worldly interests and illegitimate children. Yet 50 years later Pope Paul IV judged Michaelangelo's nude frescoes in the Sistine Chapel indecent and had clothes painted over the figures in *The Last Judgment.*

It would be impossible to trace here all further developments of sexual morality during succeeding centuries. However, two movements will be discussed briefly because of their direct bearing on present-day beliefs.[26]

Puritanism

The Puritan movement for religious reform began early in the reign of Queen Elizabeth of England in the sixteenth century. Calvinist in theology, the early Puritans felt that the Church of England was too political and too Catholic. During the intermittent periods of persecution throughout the next two centuries large numbers of Puritans emigrated to New England in search of religious freedom.

To the Puritan, man was by nature weak and sinful and therefore in need of constant self-examination, unremitting self-discipline, and hard work. The Puritan sexual ethic, although severe and uncompromising, was primarily concerned with regulating behavior that threatened the stability of the family unit. Apart from their biblical faith, as newcomers to a harsh land the Puritans were concerned with survival, and protecting the integrity of the family as the basic social unit was felt to be vital to that end. Therefore, the Puritans were unforgiving of adulterers and quite concerned about sex that might lead to the birth of illegitimate children.

In their eagerness to discourage sexual laxity the Puritans imposed rigid codes of dress and behavior. Activities appealing to the

---

[26]The authors acknowledge the suggestions of Bryan Strong in the preparation of this section.

senses were frowned upon. Women accused of witchcraft or of partaking in sexual orgies with Satan faced torture and sometimes death. However, despite these excesses, sexual activity within marriage was not strictly regulated. In fact, the Puritans in the seventeenth century were quite open about sex and viewed it as a natural and joyous part of marriage. One James Mattock was expelled from the First Church of Boston for refusing to sleep with his wife. Puritan maidens with child were married by understanding ministers, as is indicated in the town records of the time. The Puritans were therefore not "antisexual" in principle but rather were opposed to sexual behavior outside of the bonds they believed to have been ordained by God and society.

The Victorian Era

The reign of another English queen, Alexandrina Victoria (1819–1901) is referred to as the Victorian period. During the two centuries separating the reign of Victoria from that of Elizabeth important changes seem to have taken place in sexual attitudes. For instance, whereas the Puritans were content with restricting sex to marriage, Victorians attempted to restrict sexual behavior within marriage as well. Even the stated basis for the restrictions had changed. The Puritans were concerned with piety: Adultery was a sin against God and a violation of community trust. The Victorians were concerned with "character," health, and how best to harness sex and rechannel it to loftier ends. Men and women could not visit art galleries together in Philadelphia because of the potential embarrassment that classical statues would cause. Prudery was carried to extraordinary lengths, and Victorian standards of decorum seem to have been more oppressively enforced in this country than even in England.

How did this remarkable change come about? Since Victorian society was considerably more secular than Puritan communities, religion can hardly be responsible for it. There is some evidence that the more indiscriminate antisexuality within Victorian morality was based on the erroneous medical and scientific beliefs of the time.

Victorian sexual ideology revolved around a theory in which semen was viewed as a vital substance and its spillage a grievous and potentially lethal waste. In principle, it mattered little if a man ejaculated into his wife or into some other woman, although procreative necessities required that some concessions be made in this regard.

This semen theory did not originate in the Victorian period. Such notions were current long before the nineteenth century. But from this starting point Victorian morality evolved into a code of sexual behavior as well as a theory of human sexuality. In this scheme, men were the sexual beings who victimized women and were in turn victimized by them. In the first instance, men imposed their "beastly" sexual urges on innocent women who were "pure," asexual beings. In the second case sexually provocative women lured men into wasting their seed. A "moral" man abstained from sex outside of marriage and was highly selective and considerate in sexual expression within marriage. "Moral" women endured these sporadic ordeals and did nothing to encourage them. Pleasure was not an appropriate goal for either sex, but especially not for women.

So far as noncoital sex was concerned, the ideas of Victorian morality are predictable. Since these acts served no procreative purpose, they were without any redeeming value whatsoever. Masturbation was particularly bad since it involved the young and, being unrestrained by the need for a partner, most readily led to excessive indulgence.

The semen theory of human sexuality has not been entirely abandoned, even today. It is impossible to say, however, to what extent such attitudes rule people's sexual lives. Even during the Victorian period countless thousands undoubtedly paid no heed.

Box 15.3 The People's Republic of China

More than one billion people live in the People's Republic of China. Although China is in the process of creating major social changes, old established ways are often difficult to eliminate; thus, there is a difference between official policy and common practices.[1] In general, people in the countryside (where 85 percent of the people live) are more traditional than people in the cities.

Some young adults date in China, especially in the cities, but they do not always ask for a date directly. Instead, a friend may act as a go-between in arranging the date. In this way there are fewer hurt feelings if the date is refused. Men almost always ask for dates. In some areas it is considered very improper—even immoral—for a woman to request a date. When a young couple spends time alone together, this signifies romantic involvement. Holding hands in public is frowned upon, as is any more personal contact. Masturbation is officially discouraged. Premarital sex is unethical and is reported to be rare, as is illegitimacy. Chinese are expected to postpone marriage until

they are in their mid-twenties for females and late twenties for males. In reality, some women are likely to marry in their early twenties and men in their mid-twenties.

Arranged marriages and the payment of money or goods for a wife are now against the law, but in actuality both practices sometimes occur, especially in the countryside. When marriages are arranged by parents, young people are consulted before official commitments are made. The Chinese do not endow the male-female relationship with the same romantic associations and special significance that people in many Western cultures do. Even though women have gained many rights, the husband is still the head of the household. Both men and women can initiate a divorce, but the divorce rate is reported to be very low. Divorce is considered immoral and is strongly discouraged. Before obtaining a divorce a couple

[1]For information relating to sexuality, marriage, and sex roles, see Hsü-Balzer et al. (1974), Sidel (1974), Curtin (1975), Watson (1975), *Family Planning Perspectives* Digest (1977).

Some people today see the shadow of "Puritanism" or "Victorianism" behind any attempt to regulate private or public sexual behavior. Others pine for bygone days when men were gentlemen, women "pure," and so on, with total disregard for the realities of those periods.

Modern concepts of sexual morality, which allow that pleasure is a legitimate sexual goal, probably date back most immediately to the post–World War I era (and may, in fact, have been influenced by it). We shall next examine some of the important changes that have been occurring since then.

The Twentieth Century and Situation Ethics

Theoretical Background

Rather than attempt to review contemporary scholarly thinking in sexual ethics, we shall concentrate on examining some of the forces that have helped shape present-day morality and will discuss the works of a few writers who have reached a wide readership, particularly among the young.

At least two major forces have had a profound influence on Western ethics in the

Box 15.3   Continued

must try to overcome differences during several months of discussion with the head of each person's work unit, the head of the Revolutionary Street Committee, or the like. A few married couples experience forced separation because the government may assign the spouses to work in different parts of the country or because it is difficult to obtain permission to change localities (especially to move from the country to the city). Even among couples that live together, there seem to be limited opportunities for privacy due to crowded living conditions. Couples are supposed to limit their family size to one or two children. There is considerable pressure to use contraception. Birth control, abortion, and sterilization are widely available and are free or very inexpensive.

This husband and wife live with their child in a one-room apartment and share a kitchen with another couple. From Hsü-Balzer et al., *China Day by Day* (New Haven: Yale University Press, 1974), p. 27. Reprinted by permission.

twentieth century: science and technology, and World War II.

What can serve as foundation for ethics in an age dominated by an ethically neutral discipline, science? The belief that truth is to be found by means of the scientific method is widespread; and belief in the discovery of truth, moral or otherwise, through divine revelation combined with "right reason," in the tradition of Aquinas and other theologians, has apparently waned as people have glorified the scientific method and the products of technology. Science affects values in several ways. First, by creating new technologies, it can alter social practices and people's values about those practices. For example, the development of reliable contraceptive methods made it possible for people to separate sex from procreation. As people began to explore higher frequencies of marital and premarital sex, values about sex began to change. Today, most Americans under 25 believe that premarital sex is acceptable. The generations who grew up with access to the pill and other effective contraceptives have new values that are not commonly shared by the people in the age groups that were raised with a different, prepill morality.

The advent of new scientific breakthroughs and technologies may change values, but are the changes right or wrong? Can science answer these questions? There has been some attempt to use scientific observations (broadly defined) in arriving at moral judgments—that is, in deciding what is right and wrong. In 1929, Margaret Mead published her anthropological study of adolescence and sex in primitive society, *Coming of Age in Samoa.*[27] She drew certain implications from her study of sexual behavior patterns in another culture: A nonpunitive attitude toward sexual experimentation (premarital intercourse) among adolescents leads to happier and healthier acceptance of sexuality in the culture as a whole; and, since happiness and health are legitimate goals for any society, we should adopt such standards in our own culture.

More recently, Wolfgang Wickler, in *The Sexual Code,* has used scientific data to critique the fundamental position of the Catholic Church on sex—that sexuality which is not for procreation is contrary to Natural Law.[28] The Catholic position has assumed that the sole biological function of sex is procreation; thus Natural Law presumably dictates that sex not be done for any purpose other than procreation. However, there are ample biological and anthropological data showing that throughout the animal kingdom sexual organs and sexual behavior are used for nonreproductive functions, such as in greetings, friendliness, play, pair formation, threats, dominance, and territorial marking. Recent studies on primates demonstrate that sexual intercourse is used to establish bonds of friendship, not merely to produce offspring.[29] Thus scientific research reveals that certain moral arguments cannot be substantiated by the data. On the other hand, arguments about topics like sex education can be

[27]Mead (1929).
[28]Wickler (1972).
[29]Lancaster (1979).

clarified by scientific data. The data demonstrate that teenagers who receive adequate sex education have fewer unwanted pregnancies. In addition, women who do not become pregnant as teenagers exhibit lower rates of divorce, less reliance on welfare, and higher rates of completing their education. To the degree that people concur that unwanted pregnancies, divorce, being on welfare, and disrupted education are undesirable, the research data confirm that sex education is valuable. Also, it has not been demonstrated that sex education leads to an increase in premarital sexual behavior. Before these data were available, people often took sides in heated arguments about the value of sex education, without recourse to solid data about the consequences of various courses of action. In fact, discussions about sex education have been among the most fiery of the issues debated in many school districts.

Even though science does not pretend to offer a set of moral values, it does provide data by which moral arguments can be evaluated.

The second major force that caused twentieth-century individuals to rethink traditional morality was World War II. Death camps, atomic bombs, and the Nuremburg trials raised anew many moral questions that are still unresolved. At what point do responsibility and loyalty to the law and the state end, and at what point does one choose other, higher standards? Conventional religious principles were found wanting, as Miller found in interviews with Christians who had participated in the French and Dutch Resistance forces:

If the Christian men of the Resistance did not know before they committed themselves, they very soon learned that to participate in the anti-Nazi struggle was to be plunged into a moral maelstrom, in which no rules would help. For to resist one must stay alive, and to stay alive one must forge and cheat. Ration books and passports must be forged or stolen. Even within the Christian group, the traitor or the potential traitor must be liquidated without hesitation if not without compunction, since not only might the lives of the group members depend upon it, but the good cause itself. But drive this to its logical limit, and where does it take us? Presumably if a man may be liquidated as a danger to the good cause, the same man may be tortured to make him yield information vital to the good cause. If he resists torture himself, might it not be effective and therefore necessary to torture his children before his eyes? Forgery, lying and liquidation: they had had a hand in all of them. Then, said I, is *everything* permitted? The reply was quite clear and quite crucial: "Yes: everything is permitted—and everything is forbidden." In other words, if killing and lying are to be used it must be under the most urgent pressure of social necessity, and with a profound sense of guilt that no better way can presently be found. . . . But notice that the dire decisions which are here involved, while they are not held under the neat restraint of any moral formula, are held under the restraint of Christian compassion. And what good in any event would a formula do?[30]

We have taken a slight detour here to demonstrate the background that has led to contemporary rethinking of traditional Judeo-Christian morality. To put it briefly, the notion of a moral rule book that one can follow to the letter, rather than simply conforming to its spirit, may lead to immoral behavior, in the view of many modern theologians. The Ten Commandments say, "Thou shalt not kill" and "Thou shalt not bear false witness [lie]," yet there are specific *situations* in which strict obedience to these principles seems likely to lead to evil consequences, as in the Resistance during World War II. The Vietnam War and, more recently, the "Watergate era" raised similar dilemmas for many people—for instance, the problems of violating a confidence or disobeying a lawful order in order to attain some presumably higher ethical

goal. Should rules be discarded, so that people can be free to decide for themselves what is right or wrong each time they are confronted with a moral decision? Opinion is divided on this point. No ethical system, no matter how complete, can possibly cover every situation. Every individual human being is in a sense unique and will be confronted sooner or later with a situation that does not fit the rules or in which the rules conflict. For instance, should an unmarried college woman who is pregnant and plans to have an abortion tell the truth to her overprotective father, who has just had a major heart attack, knowing that the news might kill him? According to the Danish Christian existentialist Sören Kierkegaard, certain special situations call for "suspension of the ethical"—that is, a break with the usual universal ethical principles. But such variations, he advises, should be made with "Fear and Trembling" (the title of his essay on the subject). The latter advice seems well founded, especially when we look at the consequences of the flexible approach as put forth in a different way by Friedrich Nietzsche. Conventional moral rules can be put aside by superior individuals when it is necessary to advance their own power, said Neitzsche—and Hitler took that seriously.

And so we come to twentieth-century "situation ethics,"[31] the first attempt in a long time to rethink our approach to ethical questions, particularly those relating to human sexuality. We have chosen to focus on situation (or contextual) ethics here, and particularly on the writings of Joseph Fletcher, for several reasons. Situation ethics appears to be a logical outgrowth of the life and experience of humans in the twentieth century, and consequently has achieved, in a relatively short period of time, widespread popularity and acceptance (uncritical acceptance, some thinkers say). In addition, Fletcher, the prin-

[30]Miller (1955), pp. 99–101.

[31]Situation ethics is also called "the new morality"; indeed, the full title of Joseph Fletcher's book on the subject is *Situation Ethics: The New Morality* (1966).

cipal popular spokesman for situation ethics, addresses himself particularly to questions of human sexuality.

Situation ethics appears deceptively simple—undoubtedly another reason for its popularity. There is only one fundamental principle: "whatever is the most loving thing in the situation is the right and good thing."[32] Fletcher sees right and wrong in terms of its effects on interpersonal relationships and love as the one and only guiding principle for moral decisions. "Christian situation ethics reduces law from a statutory system of rules to the love canon alone."[33] That is, people's *attitudes* or *intentions* in a given situation determine whether or not their behavior in that situation will be right or wrong. Behavior should be motivated by love of a particular kind (the Greeks distinguished several different kinds)—not *eros*, the passionate love, or desire, commonly associated with sexuality; not *philia*, the brotherly sort of love between friends, which is also emotional to some extent; but *agape*, the spiritual love manifested by an attitude of concern for fellow human beings with no expectation of receiving something in return. The person who is motivated by *agape* can do no wrong, and therefore has no need of rules or laws. Fletcher believes that this teaching is the essence of Christianity. Whether or not it is so is a question for theologians to debate. We shall address ourselves to the question of how this approach works in practice.

Specific applications will be discussed later in this chapter, but at this point we can offer two generalizations. First, in situation or contextual ethics *any means* is justified by the end (love). According to this approach, even killing may conceivably be the most loving thing to do in a given situation—for instance, killing a baby whose crying endangers the lives of an entire party traveling through hostile territory and facing certain death if dis-

covered. Presumably, then, there are also instances when almost any form of sexual behavior is justified. Fletcher has declared:

Whether any form of sex (hetero, homo, or auto) is good or evil depends on whether love is fully served. The Christian ethic is not interested in reluctant virgins and technical chastity. What sex probably needs more than anything is a good airing, demythologizing it and getting rid of its mystique-laden and occult accretions, which come from romanticism on the one hand and puritanism on the other.[34]

The second general consideration has to do with the inherent difficulties in applying situation ethics:

A common objection to situation ethics is that it calls for more critical intelligence, more factual information, and more self-starting commitment to righteousness than most people can bring to bear. We all know the army veteran who "wishes the war was back" because he could tell the good guys from the bad guys by the uniforms they wore. There are those who say situationism ignores the reality of human sin or egocentricity, and fails to appreciate the finitude of human reason.[35]

The demands that situation ethics places on the individual are tremendous, and perhaps unrealistic, when applied to the general population. This point seems particularly valid in connection with sexual behavior, for situation ethics calls for rational, unemotional appraisal of each situation and its short- and long-term ramifications, a prodigious accomplishment for those who are, by definition, involved in extremely emotional situations. That is, we suggest that even two people who are not in bed may have some difficulty in achieving *agape* while discussing whether or not they *should* go to bed together. Fletcher has cited the following instance:

A young unmarried couple might decide, if they make their decisions Christianly, to have intercourse (e.g., by getting pregnant to force a

---

[32]Fletcher (1966), p. 65.
[33]Ibid., p. 69.

[34]Ibid., pp. 139–140.
[35]Ibid., p. 81.

selfish parent to relent his overbearing resistance to their marriage). But as Christians they would never merely say, "It's all right if we *like* each other!" Loving concern can make it all right, but mere liking cannot.[36]

Sexuality involves powerful emotions— not only love (*eros*) but also feelings of guilt. The former tends to predominate before and during the sexual encounter, it seems. When a question of morality is involved, however, feelings of guilt tend to appear the following day or even months or years later. Guilt feelings may be regarded as the "voice of conscience," but actually their origins are extremely complex and may be totally unconscious and irrational. Again, we shall leave debates over whether or not conscience is a God-given faculty to the theologians, but we cannot deny the reality of guilt feelings. Situation ethics emphasizes the processes that occur before an act. That the individuals believe *at the time* that what they are about to do is right is the important variable. But what of the potentially painful aftermath of guilt feelings, irrational as they may be?

It seems that the current generation of young people is living in a transitional period, in which there is an overlap between two phenomena. One is the belief that guilt feelings associated with sex are a heritage from past generations and are acquired in childhood. The other is the new morality, involving intellectual acceptance of the premise that sex in the proper context is good and should not be associated with feelings of guilt. Those who find it difficult to shake their feelings of guilt sometimes seek psychotherapy, implying that the feelings of guilt, rather than the behavior that engendered them, are bad and must be dispelled so that these people will be free to act according to their reason.

The Roman Catholic Church has its own method for dealing with guilt—the confessional. It may work as well as psychotherapy in relieving guilt feelings, but the un-

derlying assumptions are quite different. Take, for instance, the devout woman, who after due consideration participates in sexual intercourse with a young man whom she deeply loves and plans to marry. She goes to confession, and the priest, if he is true to the tradition of the Church (as he may not be nowadays), acknowledges that the woman has committed a wrongful act (fornication, which is always wrong in the Roman Catholic view, regardless of the situation) but offers absolution in exchange for a specific penance.

One thing that can be said about the Roman Catholic confessional and any other "legalistic" system of ethics, secular or religious, is that the individual knows where he or she stands in terms of right and wrong. There is no need for the element of "fear and trembling" that Kierkegaard describes, and there are those who argue that the average person either does not want or cannot cope with the vagaries of an unstructured approach like situation ethics. It is an age-old problem, the responsibility that accompanies freedom of choice. The more rules or laws that there are to follow, the less freedom we enjoy—but the lighter is our burden of responsibility.

Application to Sexual Behavior: Specific Issues

We shall now describe a few of the most common issues of human sexuality on which different approaches to moral questions seem to clash. The disagreements, as we have tried to demonstrate, are bound up in traditions rooted not only in specific religions but also in culture and in certain underlying assumptions that have persisted in the West for several thousands of years. Perhaps the best example of the latter is the assumption that women are inferior to men. This attitude is reflected in many of our customs, our sex laws (written to "protect" women against men, though they deprive women of certain rights as well), differential opportunities in jobs and professions, and attitudes toward sexual gratification (the secondary impor-

---

[36]Fletcher (1966), p. 104.

Box 15.4   Sweden

Sweden is an example of a sexually liberal society. Premarital sex among those who are in love is an accepted and expected part of growing up. A study involving a representative sample of the population revealed that whereas 20 percent of married women over 30 years of age had waited until marriage before engaging in sex, only 9 percent of women under 30 did.[1] In Sweden 93 percent of those polled found it acceptable for people who are "going steady" or engaged to have sexual relations. One study of young people reports that about 90 percent of males and 75 percent of females have had intercourse by the time they are 17.[2] The young sometimes have sexual relations in their own homes with their parents' knowledge. Cohabitation is common in Sweden. In fact, trial marriage is permitted by law. Many Swedes do not feel that it is necessary to formalize their relationship with marriage until after the woman becomes pregnant. Approximately one-half of the brides are pregnant. Some people would rather have

[1]Moskin (1971). Unless otherwise stated, all statistics in this box are from this survey.
[2]Elliott (1970), p.9.

tance granted to female orgasm, for instance, and even the notion that there is something intrinsically wrong in a woman's expecting the same degree of sexual gratification as her male partner achieves).

We shall emphasize here the contrast between the "new morality" and the traditional theological-legalistic approach best exemplified by the teachings of the Roman Catholic Church (called simply the "traditional position"). These two approaches to sex and morality represent opposite ends of a continuum, and the reader will probably be able to infer and extrapolate from these two poles where and how other viewpoints fit in. We are well aware that many Roman Catholics disagree with the official position of the Church on questions of sex and morality and are striving for change. Nevertheless, even though the Church's official position may change in the near future, the influence of its traditional attitude can be expected to persist for some time to come.

Sexual Intercourse

The new morality clearly approves of intercourse for unmarried people under certain conditions. Fletcher has offered two principles or guidelines for deciding whether or not the conditions are being met.[37] First, another person must not be hurt or exploited by the sex act. (We wonder if there is not a contradiction in Fletcher's example, cited earlier, in which an unmarried couple might deliberately have intercourse and conceive in order to force the parents into consenting to a marriage—is there not an element of manipulation here?) Second, the decision should be based on concern for the welfare and happiness of those involved. Despite the emphasis on eliminating traditional criteria of right and wrong, notions like "happiness" seem to crop up frequently among exponents of the new morality. Probably one of the major practical difficulties with the new morality is how easily it is perverted into the notion that "as long as you like each other and feel happy about what you're doing, it's all right." Fletcher carefully points out that "liking" does not equal "loving" in the sense of *agape*, but it seems that many individuals find the distinction either spurious or too difficult to make.

The traditional point of view on pre-

[37]Fletcher (1967), p. 138.

Box 15.4   Continued

children outside of marriage. The illegitimate child and the unmarried woman have equal rights with legitimate children and married women. Illegitimacy is not stigmatized.

Swedes generally have small families, usually one or two children. Contraceptives are not only readily available, but are approved of and used by almost everyone. In addition, abortion is legal and available. The divorce rate is considerably lower than that in the United States. In 1976 the rate was 2.7 per 1000 people in Sweden, whereas in the United States the rate was 5.0 per 1000.[3]

A primary guideline for sexual behavior is mutual responsibility. There is an emphasis on equality in relationships and a concern that people do not get hurt by exploitative sex. Men are encouraged to carry their share of contraceptive responsibility. As in the United States, love and romantic commitment play an important role in the serious relationships of women and men in Sweden. The survey in Sweden

[3]Glick and Norton (1977).
[4]Herman (1972).

found that even though people are beginning sex earlier and having more partners than the previous generations, both men and women have a strong commitment to their sexual partners whether married or not. Seventy-seven percent of Swedes felt that a partner should not hurt a good relationship.

The vast majority felt that promiscuity is not right. In the early 1970s the National Association for Sex Education produced a poster for use in subways and factories saying "You don't have to go to bed together."[4] The survey results indicated not only that 93 percent disapproved of extramarital sex, but that extramarital sex had not increased in the younger generation. Most Swedes were happy with their sexual relations. Generally those who were in love were more pleased with their sexual life than those who were not in love. Having a steady partner also resulted in more satisfaction than having a short-term partner. In general, people wanted more intercourse than they were having (but that is true in the United States and in many other countries too).

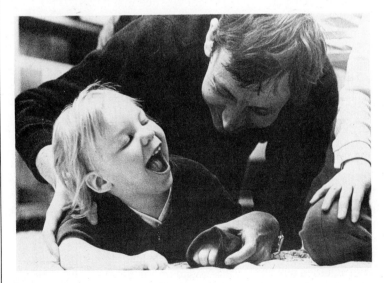

Men are encouraged to participate in child care in Sweden; and many men do share part of the joys and responsibilities of child-rearing. From the Swedish Information Service. Reprinted by permission.

marital or extramarital intercourse has been quite clear and simple: It is wrong. The very term "premarital" implies an act in anticipation of marriage (as the term "extramarital" implies an act outside of marriage) that should be reserved for marriage itself. We have noted earlier in this chapter some reasons why moralists and theologians have traditionally argued that sex and marriage must go together. It is no coincidence that the church most opposed to contraception is also firmly opposed to premarital intercourse. The traditional objection to premarital intercourse was based on the fact that the resulting child may be deprived of legitimate family life and parental devotion.

Aquinas made it quite clear that premarital intercourse as such (fornication, in his terminology) is not a sin, for heterosexual intercourse properly performed is a natural act and thus does not offend God. In Roman Catholic writings the arguments against fornication until recently were not that the act is offensive to God or harmful to the partners involved but that "the postulated offspring explains why fornication is sin."[38] However, we noted earlier in this chapter that Pope Paul VI's 1968 encyclical made it clear that he was concerned about deleterious effects other than unwanted offspring, and he therefore condemned the use of contraceptives, in part, in order to maintain the presumed inhibitory force of fear of pregnancy, particularly among young people. The major burden in this approach falls on women, since they are the ones who may become pregnant. Many parents of teenage daughters express this dilemma: "Should we offer to help our daughter obtain contraceptives knowing that there is the possibility that without them she may have intercourse with her boyfriend and become pregnant? Or should we refuse to help her in this way (even if she asks) on the principle that the fear of pregnancy will discourage her from engaging in intercourse?"

There is no easy answer. Even when the avowed aim of the parents (or the university health service) is to discourage fornication by not providing contraceptives, the large annual number of illegitimate pregnancies and abortions in this country demonstrates that this approach is not effective. Yet it is conceivable that offering birth control pills to a young woman might encourage her to engage in sexual intercourse when she is not ready to do so in terms of her emotional maturity. The availability of reliable contraceptives, among other factors, has certainly led to a rethinking of the traditional views on intercourse outside of marriage in our culture, and at the present time even the theologians, not to mention parents and young people, are having some difficulty in trying to decide what is "right." And they are arriving at different answers. The 1977 Yankelovich survey found that among the 35–49 age group, 72 percent believed that it was morally wrong for teenagers to have sexual relations. Eighty percent of the people over 50 felt it was morally wrong. On the other hand, 60 percent of those under 25 believed that sexual relations among teenagers was not morally wrong (compared with 34 percent who felt that it was).

Contraception

The use of contraceptives has ramifications in many areas—economic, social, political, and ethical. It is well known that the main ethical opposition to their use comes from the Roman Catholic Church. Almost all Protestant and Jewish denominations approve of the use of contraceptives. The official position of the Catholic Church has been made quite clear: "Catholics regard the use of contraceptives as an objectively defective moral act so that even when they are used with the right motives (spirit), the action remains immoral."[39] The primary Roman Catholic argument against the use of contraceptives is based on the belief that any *unnatural*

---

[38]Noonan (1967), p. 292.

[39]Thomas (1965), p. 114.

act is sinful. Contraceptives interfere with the natural purpose of intercourse, which is procreation. The rhythm method of birth control (*see* Chapter 6) is permissible because it does not interfere with any "natural" processes (but it is clearly designed to frustrate the natural processes, as defined by this tradition). The Catholic Church now permits the use of contraceptives in special circumstances. If a woman takes the birth control pill not to prevent conception, but is prescribed them in order to remedy certain conditions such as painful or excessive menstrual bleeding or endometriosis (*see* Chapter 6), this is morally correct even though contraception occurs as a "side effect" of the treatment. (But do not medicines interfere with the laws of nature? The reply is, "No; it is lawful to correct the defects of nature.") In our experience, some Roman Catholic physicians have tended to broaden the definition of "diseases" treatable by the pill to include menstrual irregularity and premenstrual tension, so that almost any woman who wants to use the pill may do so.

Although the Roman Catholic Church is still struggling with the morality of contraception and clinging to its view that downright "sterilization"—whether by chemical, surgical, or other means—is immoral, diametrically opposed points of view have become increasingly popular. The situational view has been summed up as:

1. *Making babies is a good thing but making love is, too,* and we can *and should* make love even if no baby is intended. There ought to be no unintended or unwanted babies.
2. The best way to make love without making babies is to prevent their conception; the next best way is to prevent fertility itself; and the least desirable way is to end a pregnancy already begun. *But any of these methods is good if the good to be gained is great enough to justify the means.*[40]

Some experts propose investing the state with the authority to enforce the use of

[40]Fletcher (1967), p. 123.

contraceptives, yet these same people condemn the Roman Catholic Church's stand against contraception as rigid, authoritarian, and an invasion of individual human rights. Again the question of individual freedom and responsibility, which we discussed earlier in this chapter, arises. There are always those who claim in the name of God or in the name of Science to have the gift of truth and prophecy; they are all too willing to impose the principles of their "truth," by force if necessary, for "the good of the people." An alternative approach is to provide people with the knowledge, means, and *freedom* to exercise a variety of options and then to let them choose for themselves. This approach is based on the assumption that, given adequate information about birth control methods, access to contraceptives at reasonable cost, and freedom from sanctions for or against the use of contraceptives, most people will make the "right" choices.

Abortion

As has been noted, abortion is approved within contextual ethics "if the good to be gained is great enough to justify the means." The Catholic view set forth by Pope Paul VI is quite different: " . . . we must once again declare that the direct interruption of the generative process already begun, and, above all, directly willed and procured abortion, even if for therapeutic reasons, are to be absolutely excluded as licit means of regulating birth."[41] The Catholic view rests primarily on two propositions, one generally held and one quite controversial.[42] The first proposition is that human beings do not have the right to take the lives of innocent human beings. The second is that human life begins at conception. Obviously it is the latter statement that is the most controversial. If accepted, it leads to the inescapable view that abortion constitutes murder, and this is the position of many

[41]Pope Paul VI (1968), p. 8.
[42]For a comprehensive discussion of the Catholic view on abortion see Callahan (1970).

right-to-life groups in the United States and elsewhere. The question of whether or not an embryo or fetus is a human being cannot be answered by science. Biologists have provided information about chromosomes that supports the statement that the embryo is a *potential* human being and this is what many Protestant and Jewish denominations believe. For that matter, *every* egg and sperm, by virtue of the information stored in their genes, is a potential human being. But when can we say that this potential has been realized? This is the question that is currently being so hotly debated. The 1977 Yankelovich survey found that 48 percent of those polled believed abortion was not morally wrong while 44 percent said it was. Sixty-four percent felt that a woman should have the legal right to abortion if she wants one.[43] But other polls find different results. In a 1979 representative survey 73 percent of those polled believed that the decision about abortion in the first trimester should be between a woman and her physician.[44] The question concerning the morality of abortion will continue to be unresolved for some time.

The Catholic Church allows two exceptions to its rule against abortion: ectopic pregnancy and cancer of the uterus. The justification in these situations is that an operation performed to save the life of a pregnant woman is morally correct because the death of the fetus is an unintended, unavoidable, indirect result of the procedure.[45]

Other Issues

Traditional views of the morality of various forms of sexual behavior are currently being reexamined in the light of new knowledge, new ideas, and new circumstances. The view of homosexuality is one. We have discussed the current trend toward legalizing homosexual activities conducted in private

between consenting adults (*see* Chapter 14), which reflects, among other things, a changing morality. In the Christian and Jewish traditions homosexuality was considered immoral because it clearly frustrated the procreational purpose of sexual behavior. In an era when procreation that contributes to population pressures is coming to be viewed as immoral, there is a tendency to view nonreproductive sexual behavior more leniently. This view seems implicitly to have removed some of the onus from certain previously condemned practices. The Yankelovich survey found that up to 70 percent of people favor the right of homosexuals to live where they want, run for elective office or serve in the army.

To some extent moral attitudes have been influenced by studies like the Kinsey reports, which revealed that large percentages of individuals were performing sexual acts in private that were publicly condemned as perversions. The best example of this influence is the changing attitudes toward masturbation, particularly among males. After condemning it for centuries because it involved ''wasting'' sperm—which, according to Natural Law, is meant for reproductive purposes—moralists made the awkward discovery that virtually every male is guilty of mortal sin!

Certain taboos may well remain with us for a long time to come, but the reasons for observing them may change. The moral quality of behavior cannot be dissociated from motives, regardless of the consequences. As T. S. Eliot has said:

The last temptation is the greatest treason:
To do the right deed for the wrong reason.[46]

But there is an equal danger inherent in the new morality—that we may too readily justify doing the wrong thing for the right reason.

[43]Yankelovich et al. (1977).
[44]Harris (1979).
[45]Callahan (1970), p. 423.

[46]Eliot (1935), part I, p. 44.

Selected Bibliography

A research questionnaire on sex. *Psychology Today*, 3, no. 2 (July 1969), 64–87.

A research questionnaire on sex. *Psychology Today*, 6, no. 2 (July 1972), 55–87.

Abraham, K. *Selected papers of Karl Abraham.* London: Hogarth Press and Institute of Psychoanalysis, 1948.

Advisory Committee on Obstetrics and Gynecology, Food and Drug Administration. *Report on the oral contraceptives.* Washington, D.C.: Government Printing Office, 1966.

————. *Report on intrauterine contraceptive devices.* Washington, D.C.: Government Printing Office, 1968.

————. *Second report on the oral contraceptives.* Washington, D.C.: Government Printing Office, 1969.

Ainsworth, M. *The effects of maternal deprivation: A review of findings and controversy in the context of research strategy.* World Health Organization, Public Health Paper no. 14. Geneva: WHO, 1962.

Allen, C. *A textbook of psychosexual disorders.* 2nd ed. London: Oxford University Press, 1969.

Amelar, R.D. *Infertility in men.* Philadelphia: F.A. Davis Co., 1966.

American Law Institute, *Model penal code: Tentative draft no. 4.* Philadelphia, 1955.

————. *Model penal code: Proposed official draft.* Philadelphia, 1962.

American Psychiatric Association. *Diagnostic and statistical manual of mental disorders.* 2nd ed. Washington, D.C.: APA, 1968.

Amir, M. *Patterns of forcible rape.* Chicago: University of Chicago Press, 1971.

Amos, S. *Laws for the regulation of vice.* London: Stevens & Sons, 1877.

Anati, E. *Camonica Valley.* New York: Alfred A. Knopf, 1961.

Anderson, G.G., and L. Speroff. Prostaglandins, *Science* 171:502–504.

Aquinas, St. Thomas. *The summa theologica.*

Fathers of the English Dominican Province, trs. New York: Benziger Bros., 1911–1925.

Ard, B.N. Percentage of women who experience orgasm. *Medical Aspects of Human Sexuality* (April 1974), 35–39.

Arey, L.B. *Developmental anatomy.* 7th ed. Philadelphia: W.B. Saunders Co., 1965.

Arnstein, R.L. Virgin men. *Medical Aspects of Human Sexuality*, 7, no. 1 (January 1974), 113–125.

Athanasiou, R. A review of public attitudes on sexual issues. In *Contemporary Sexual Behavior: Critical Issues in the 1970's*, Joseph Zubin and John Money, eds. Baltimore: Johns Hopkins University Press, 1973, Ch. 19.

Augustine, St. *The city of God, book XIV.* J. Healey, trs., E. Baker, intro. London and Toronto: J.M. Dent & Sons, Ltd.; New York: E.P. Dutton & Co., 1934.

————. *Treatises on marriage and other subjects.* C. Wilcox et al., trs., R.J. Deferrari, ed. New York: Fathers of the Church, Inc., 1955.

Austin, C.R., and R.V. Short. *Reproduction in Mammals.* Vol. 1: *Germ cells and fertilization.* Vol. 2: *Embryonic and fetal development.* Vol. 3: *Hormones in reproduction.* Vol 4: *Reproductive patterns.* Vol. 5: *Artificial control of reproduction.* London: Cambridge University Press, 1972.

Bailey, S. *Sexual relation in Christian thought.* New York: Harper & Row, 1959.

————. *Sexual ethics: A Christian view.* New York: Macmillan Co., 1963.

Bāna (Banabhatta).*Kādambari.* C.M. Ridding, trs. Bombay: Jaico Publishing House, 1956.

Bandura, A. *Principles of behavior modification.* New York: Holt, Rinehart and Winston, 1969.

Bandura, A., and R.H. Walters. *Social learning and personality development.* New York: Holt, Rinehart and Winston, 1963.

Bardwick, J. *Psychology of women.* New York: Harper & Row, 1971.

Barnes, R.W., R.T. Bergman, and H.L. Hadley. *Urology.* Flushing, N.Y.: Medical Examination Publishing Co., 1967.

Barnett, W. *Sexual freedom and the constitution.* Albuquerque: University of New Mexico Press, 1973.

Barrett, N.S. Women in industrialized society: An international perspective. In *Economic independence for women.* Beverly Hills, Calif.: Sage Publications, 1976, 77–111.

Bartell, G.D. *Group sex.* New York: Peter H. Wyden, 1971.

Barry, H., M.K. Bacon, and I.I. Child. A cross-cultural survey of some sex differences. *Journal of Abnormal and Social Psychology* 55(1957):327–332.

Bates, M. *Gluttons and libertines.* New York: Vintage Books, 1967.

Baudelaire, C. *Les fleurs du mal.* Paris: Société des belles lettres, 1952.

Beach, F. A review of physiological and psychological studies of sexual behavior in mammals. *Physiological Review* 27, no. 2 (1947):240–305.

Beach, F.A., ed. *Sex and behavior.* New York: John Wiley & Sons, 1965.

Beckett, S. *Malone dies.* London: Penguin Books, 1962.

Bell, A.P., and M.S. Weinberg. *Homosexualities.* New York: Simon & Schuster, 1978.

Bell, R.R., and M. Gordon, eds. *The social dimension of human sexuality.* Boston: Little, Brown and Company, 1972.

Belliveau, F., and L. Richter. *Understanding human sexual inadequacy.* New York: Bantam Books, 1970.

Belt, B.G. Some organic causes of impotence. *Medical Aspects of Human Sexuality.* New York: Hospital Publications, Inc. VII, no. 1 (January 1973), 152–161.

Bem, S.L., and D.J. Bem. Case study of a nonconscious ideology: Training the woman to know her place. In *Beliefs, attitudes, and human affairs,* D.J. Bem. Belmont, Calif.: Brooks/Cole, 1970, 89–99.

Benedek, T. The functions of the sexual apparatus and their disturbances. In *Psychosomatic medicine,* F. Alexander, ed. New York: W.W. Norton & Co., 1950, 216–262.

———. *Psychosexual functions in women.* New York: Ronald Press, 1952.

Benson, R.C. *Handbook of obstetrics and gynecology.* 3rd ed. Los Altos, Calif.: Lange Medical Publications, 1968.

Beral, V., and C.R. Kay, Royal College of General Practitioners. Mortality among oral contraceptive users. *Lancet* 2(1977):726–731.

Berelson, B. Beyond family planning. *Science* 163(1969):533–543.

Bergstrom, S., M. Bygdeman, B. Samuelsson, and N. Wiqvist. The prostaglandins and human reproduction. *Hospital Practice* 6 (February 1971): 51–57.

Bernard, J. *The future of marriage.* New York: Bantam Books.

Bieber, I., et al. Homosexuality—A psychoanalytic study. New York: Basic Books, 1962.(Paperback edition entitled *Homosexuality*: New York: Random House, Vintage paperback).

Billings, E.L., and J.J. Billings. *Atlas of the ovulation method.* Collegeville, Minn.: The Liturgical Press, 1974.

Bishop, N. The great Oneida love-in. *American Heritage* (February 1969) 20: 14–17, 86–92.

Blakeslee, A. The role and responsibility, 1975, of the mass media in the U.S.A. In *Sexually transmitted diseases,* R.D. Catterall and C.S. Nicol, eds. New York: Academic Press, 1976, 250–256.

Blough, H.A., and R.L. Giuntoli. Successful treatment of human genital herpes infections with 2-deoxy-D-glucose. *Journal of the American Medical Association* 241(1979):2798–2801.

Boccaccio, G. *The decameron.* John Payne, trs. New York: The Modern Library, n.d.

Bohannan, P. *Love, sex and being human: A book about the human condition for young people.* Garden City, N.Y.: Doubleday & Co., 1969.

Bonaparte, M. *Female sexuality.* New York: International Universities Press, 1953.

Bonsall, R.W., and R.P. Michael. Volatile odoriferous acids in vaginal fluid. In *The human vagina,* E.S.E. Hafez and T.N. Evans, eds. New York: Elsevier, 1978, 167–177.

Borell, U. Contraceptive methods–their safety, efficacy, and acceptability. *Acta Obstet. et Gynecolog. Scand.* 45, Suppl. 1 (1966): 9–45.

Bower, D.W., and V.A. Christopherson. University student cohabitation: A regional comparison of selected attitudes and behavior. *Journal of Marriage and the Family* 39(1977):447–452.

Bowlby, J. *Maternal care and mental health.* World Health Organization Monograph Series no. 2. Geneva: WHO, 1951.

———. *Attachment. Attachment and loss,* vol. 1. New York: Basic Books, 1969.

———. *Separation. Attachment and loss,* vol. 11. New York: Basic Books, Inc., 1973.

Brecher, E.M. *The sex researchers.* Boston: Little, Brown & Co., 1969.

Brecher, R., and E. Brecher. *An analysis of human sexual response.* New York: New American Library, 1966.

Brenner, C. *An elementary textbook of psychoanalysis.* Garden City, N.Y.: Doubleday & Co., 1957.

Brim, O.G., Jr., D.C. Glass, J. Neulinger, and I.J. Firestone, *American beliefs and attitudes about intelligence.* New York: Russell Sage, 1969.

Brod, M. *Franz Kafka: Eine biographie.* New York: Schocken, 1946.

Broderick, C.B., and J. Bernard. *The individual, sex, and society: A SIECUS handbook for teachers and counselors.* The Johns Hopkins Press, 1969.

Brodie, H.K. *et al.* Plasma testosterone levels in heterosexual and homosexual men. *American Journal of Psychiatry* 131(1974):82–83.

Brown, W.J. *et al. Syphilis and other venereal diseases.* Cambridge: Harvard University Press, 1970.

Brownmiller, S. *Against our will.* New York: Simon & Schuster, 1975.

Brunner, H.E. *The divine imperative.* O. Wyon, trs. Philadelphia: Westminster Press, 1947.

Burgess, A.W., and L.L. Holmstrom. Rape trauma syndrome. *American Journal of Psychiatry* 131(1974):981–986.

Burgoyne, D.S. Factors affecting coital frequency, *Medical aspects of human sexuality* 8, no 4 (April 1974): 143–156.

Burroughs, W. *Naked lunch.* New York: Grove Press, 1959.

———. *The ticket that exploded.* New York: Grove Press, 1968.

Burton, R. *The anatomy of melancholy.* London: J.M. Dent & Sons, 1932.

Burton, R.F., trs. *The thousand and one nights.* n.d. Luristan, ed. n.p.: "Printed by the Burton Club for subscribers only."

Butler, S. *Conspiracy of silence.* San Francisco: New Glide Publications, 1978.

Byron (George Gordon, Lord Byron). *The poetical works of Lord Byron.* London: Oxford University Press, 1912.

Cairns, R.B., J.C. Paul, and J. Wishner. Sex censorship: The assumptions of antiobscenity laws and the empirical evidence. *Minnesota Law Review* 46(1962):1008–1041.

Calder-Marshall, A. *The sage of sex.* New York: G.P. Putnam's Sons, 1959.

Calderone, M.S., ed. *Manual of contraceptive practice.* 2nd ed. Baltimore: Williams & Wilkins Co., 1970.

Callahan, D. *Abortion: law, choice and morality.* New York: Macmillan Co., 1970.

Calverton, V.F., and S.D. Schmalhausen. *Sex in civilization.* New York: Citadel Press, 1929.

Calvin, J. *Institutes of the Christian religion.* J.T. McNeill, ed. London: S.C.M. Press, 1960.

Caprio, F., and D. Brenner. *Sexual behavior: Psycholegal aspects.* New York: Citadel Press, 1961.

Casanova de Seingalt, G.G. *Memoires.* Paris: Gallimard, 1958–1960.

Chafetz, J.S. *Masculine, feminine or human?* Itasca, Ill.: F.E. Peacock, 1978.

Chall, L.P. The reception of the Kinsey report in the periodicals of the United States: 1947–1949. In *Sexual behavior in American society,* J. Himelhoch and S.F. Fava, eds. New York: W.W. Norton & Co., 1955, 364–378.

Chamove, A., H.F. Harlow, and G. Mitchell. Sex differences in the infant-directed behavior of preadolescent rhesus monkeys. *Child Development* 38(1967):329–335.

Chang, J., and J. Block. A study of identification in male homosexuals. *Journal of Consulting Psychology* 24, no. 4(1960): 307–310.

Changing morality: The two Americans, a *Time*-Louis Harris poll. *Time* (June 6, 1969):26–27.

Chertok, L. Psychosomatic methods of preparation for childbirth. *American Journal of Obstetrics and Gynecology* 98(1967):698–707.

Chilman, C., and D.L. Meyer. Single and married undergraduates measured personality needs and self-rated happiness. *Journal of Marriage and the Family* 28(1966):67–76.

Christenson, C.V. *Kinsey: A biography.* Bloomington: Indiana University Press, 1971.

Churchill, W. *Homosexual behavior among males.* New York: Hawthorn Books, 1967.

Chvapil, M. An intravaginal contraceptive diaphragm made of collagen sponge: New old principle. *Fertility and Sterility* 27(1976):1387–1397.

Clark, L. "Is there a difference between a clitoral and a vaginal orgasm?" *Journal of Sex Research* 6, no. 1 (February 1970):25–28.

Clayton, R.R., and H.L. Voss. Shacking up: Cohabitation in the 1970's. *Journal of Marriage and Family* 39(1977):273–283.

Cleaver, E. *Soul on ice.* New York: Dell Publishing Co., 1968.

Cleland, J. *Memoirs of a woman of pleasure.* New York: G.P. Putnam's Sons, 1963.

Cochran, W.G., F. Mosteller, and J.W. Tukey. *Statistical problems of the Kinsey report of sexual behavior in the human male.* Washington, D.C.: American Statistical Association, 1954.

Cohen, A. *Everyman's Talmud.* New York: E.P. Dutton & Co., 1949.

Colby, K.M. *A primer for psychotherapists.* New York: Ronald Press, 1951.

Colette, S.G. *Claudine à l'école.* Paris: Le Fleuron, 1948–1950.

Collis, J.S. *Havelock Ellis: Artist of life.* New York: William Sloane Associates, 1959.

Comfort, A. *The anxiety makers.* New York: Delta Publishing Co., 1967.

Comfort, A. *The joy of sex.* New York: Crown Publishers,1972.

Comfort A. *Likelihood of human pheromones. Nature,* 230(1971):432–433.

Comfort, A. *More Joy.* New York: Crown Publishers, 1974.

Conroy, M. *The rational woman's guide to self-defense.* New York: Grosset & Dunlap, 1975.

Cooper, J.F. *Technique of contraception.* New York: Day-Nichols, 1928.

Cory, D.W. *The lesbian in America.* New York: Citadel Press, 1964.

Crandall, V.C. Sex differences in expectancy of intellectual and academic reinforcement. In *Achievement-related motives in children,* C.P. Smith, ed. New York: Russell Sage, 1969.

Crawley, L.Q., J.L. Malfetti, E.I. Stewart, and N. Vas Dias. *Reproduction, sex, and preparation for marriage.* Englewood Cliffs, N.J.: Prentice-Hall, 1964.

Culliton, B.J. Penicillin-resistant gonorrhea: New strain spreading worldwide. *Science* 194 (1976):1395–1397.

Curtin, K. *Women in China.* New York: Pathfinder, 1975.

Curtis, Helena. *Biology: The science of life.* New York: Worth Publishers, 1968.

Daly, C.B. *Morals, law and life.* Chicago, Dublin, London: Scepter Publishers, 1966.

Daly, M., and M. Wilson. *Sex, evolution & behavior.* Belmont, Calif.: Wadsworth Publishing Co., 1978.

Danté Alighieri. *The inferno.* J. Ciardi, trs. New York: American Library, 1954.

Davenport, W.H. Sex in cross-cultural perspective. *Human sexuality in four perspectives,* F.A. Beach, ed. Baltimore: The Johns Hopkins University Press, 1976, 115–163.

David, D.S., and R. Brannon. *The forty-nine percent majority: The male sex role.* Reading, Mass.: Addison-Wesley, 1976.

Davis, J.E., and D.T. Mininberg. Prostatitis and sexual function. *Medical Aspects of Human Sexuality* 10(August 1976):32–40.

Deaux, K. *The behavior of women and men.* Monterey, Calif.: Brooks/Cole, 1976.

De Beauvoir,S. *The second sex.* New York: Alfred A. Knopf, 1952.

Defoe, D. *The fortunes and misfortunes of the amorous Moll Flanders.* New York: The Modern Library, 1926.

Delaney, J., M.J. Lupton, and E. Toth. *The curse.* New York: E.P. Dutton & Co., 1976.

Dement, W. An essay on dreams. In *New directions in psychology II.* New York: Holt, Rinehart and Winston (1965): 135–257.

Denfeld, D., and M. Gordon. The sociology of mate swapping: Or the family that swings together clings together. *Journal of Sex Research* 6(1970):85–100.

Dengrove, E. The mecanotherapy of sexual disorders. *The Journal of Sex Research,* 7, no. 1 (February 1971):1–12.

De Rougemont, D. *Love in the western world.* New York: Pantheon Books, 1956.

Deutsch, H. *The psychology of women.* 2 vols. New York: Grune & Stratton, 1944–1945.

———. *The psychology of women.* Vol. 1. *Girlhood.* New York: Bantam Books, 1973. (First published in 1944.)

Devereux, G. Institutionalized homosexuality of the Mohave Indians. In *Human biology*, 9. Detroit: Wayne State University Press (1937): 498–527.

DeVore, I., ed. *Primate behavior: Field studies of monkeys and apes*. New York: Holt, Rinehart and Winston, 1965.

DeWald, P.A. *Psychotherapy: A dynamic approach*. 2nd ed. New York: Basic Books, 1971.

Dewey, J. *Theory of the moral life*. New York: Holt, Rinehart and Winston, 1964.

Diamond, M., ed. *Perspectives in reproduction and sexual behavior*. Bloomington: Indiana University Press, 1968.

Dickinson, R.L. *Atlas of human sex anatomy*. 2nd ed. Baltimore: Williams & Wilkins Co., 1949.

Dienes, C.T. *Law, politics, and birth control*. Chicago: University of Illinois Press, 1972.

Dienhart, C.M. *Basic human anatomy and physiology*. Philadelphia: W. B. Saunders Co., 1967.

Djerassi, C. Birth control after 1984. *Science* 169(1970): 941–951.

Djerassi, C. *The politics of contraception*. New York: W.W. Norton, 1979.

Dmowski, W.P., Manuel Luna, and Antonio Scommegna. Hormonal aspects of female sexual response. *Medical Aspects of Human Sexuality*, 8, no. 6 (June 1974): 92–113.

Do marriage manuals do more harm than good? *Medical Aspects of Human Sexuality* 4, no. 10 (October 1970): 50–63.

Dodson, A.I., and J.E. Hill. *Synopsis of genitourinary disease*. 7th ed. St. Louis: C. V. Mosby Co., 1962.

Don Leon/Leon to Annabella: An epistle from Lord Byron to Lady Byron (Attributed to Byron). London: The Fortune Press, n.d.

Donnelly, R.C., and W.L. Ferber. The legal and medical aspects of vasectomy. *Journal of Urology*, 81(1959): 259–263.

Doshay, L.J. *The boy sex offender and his later career*. 2nd ed. Mount Prospect, Ill.: Patterson Smith, 1969.

Dostoyevsky, F. *The brothers Karamozov*. Constance Garnett, trs. New York: Random House, 1950

Doty, R.L., M. Ford, G. Preti, and G.R. Huggins. Changes in the intensity and pleasantness of human vaginal odors during the menstrual cycle. *Science* 190(1975):1316–1318.

Dumas, A. *La dame aux camélias*. Paris: Calmann-Levy, 1956.

Eastman, N.J., and L.M. Hellman. *Williams obstetrics*. 13th ed. New York: Appleton-Century-Crofts, 1966.

Edwards, J.N., ed. *Sex and society*. Chicago: Markham Publishing Company, 1972.

Egerton, C., trs. *The golden lotus (Chin p'ing mei)*. London: Routledge & Kegan Paul, 1939.

Ehrhardt, A.A., and J. Money. Progestin-induced hermaphroditism: I.Q. and psychosexual identity in a study of ten girls. *Journal of Sex Research* 3(1967):83–100.

Ehrlich, P., and A. Ehrlich. *Population, resources, environment*. 2nd ed. San Francisco: W.H. Freeman & Co., 1972.

Ehrlich, P.R. *The population bomb*. New York: Ballantine Books, 1968.

Eichenlaub, J.E. *The marriage art*. New York: Dell Publishing Co., 1961.

Eliot, T.S. *Murder in the cathedral*. New York: Harcourt Brace Jovanovich, 1935.

Elliott, N. *Sensuality in Scandinavia*. New York: Weybright and Talley, 1970.

Ellis, A. *The art and science of love*. New York: Dell Publishing Co., 1965.

————. Healthy and disturbed reasons for having extramarital relations. In *Extramarital relations*, G. Neubeck, ed. Englewood Cliffs, N.J.: Prentice-Hall (1969):153–161.

Ellis, A., and A. Abarbanel, eds. *The encyclopedia of sexual behavior*. New York: Hawthorn Books, 1967.

Ellis, H. *My life*. Boston: Houghton Mifflin Co., 1939.

————. *Studies in the psychology of sex*. 2 vols. New York: Random House, 1942.(Originally published in 7 volumes, 1896–1928.)

Engel, G.L. *Psychological development in health and disease*. Philadelphia: W. B. Saunders Co., 1962.

Englemann, G. *Labor among primitive peoples*. St. Louis: J.H. Chambers and Co., 1883.

Epstein, L.M. *Sex laws and customs in Judaism*. Rev. ed. New York: Ktav Publishing House, 1968.

Erikson, E.H. Identity and the life cycle. *Psychological issues*. 1, no. 1. New York: International Universities Press, 1959.

————. *Childhood and society.* New York: W.W. Norton & Co., 1963.

————. *Identity: Youth and crisis.* New York: W.W. Norton & Co., 1968.

Eroticism: The disease of our age. *Films and Filming* (January 1961).

Eysenck, H.J., ed. *Behavior therapy and the neuroses.* New York: Pergammon Press, 1960.

Falkner, F. Body composition. In *Puberty: Biologic and psychosocial components,* S.R. Berenberg, ed. Leiden: H.E. Stenfert Kroese B.V., 1975, 123–131.

Farnsworth, D.L., and G.B. Blaine, Jr., eds. *Counseling the college student.* Boston: Little, Brown & Co., 1970.

Feather, N.T. Attribution of responsibility and valence of success and failure in relation to initial confidence and task performance. *Journal of Personality and Social Psychology* 13(1969): 129–144.

Federal Bureau of Investigation. *Uniform Crime Reports,* 1977.

Fenichel, O. *The psychoanalytic theory of neurosis.* New York: W.W. Norton & Co., 1945.

Ferenczi, S. Male and female: Psychoanalytic reflections on the "theory of genitality," and on secondary and tertiary sex differences. *Psychoanalytic Quarterly* 5(1936):249–260.

————. *Sex in psychoanalysis.* New York: Basic Books, 1950.

Fidell, L.S. Empirical verification of sex discrimination in hiring practices in psychology. In *Women: Dependent or independent variable,* R.K. Unger and F.L. Denmark, eds. New York: Psychological Dimensions, 1975, 774–785.

Fink, P.J. Dyspareunia: Current concepts, *Medical Aspects of Human Sexuality, VI,* no. 12 (December 1972):28–47.

Finkle, A.L., *et al.* How important is simultaneous orgasm? *Medical Aspects of Human Sexuality* 3, no. 7 (July):86–93, 1969.

Finler, *J.W. Stroheim.* Berkeley, Calif.: University of California Press, 1968.

Fisher, S. *The Female Orgasm.* New York: Basic Books, 1973.

Fisher, C., *et al.* Cycle of penile erection synchronous with dreaming (REM) sleep. *Archives of General Psychiatry* 12(1965):29–45.

Fiumara, N.J. Gonococcal pharyngitis. *Medical Aspects of Human Sexuality* 5, no. 5 (May 1971): 195–209.

Fletcher, J. *Situation ethics: The new morality.* Philadelphia: Westminster Press, 1966.

————. *Moral responsibility: Situation ethics at work.* Philadelphia: Westminster Press, 1967.

Fleuret, F., and L. Perceau, eds. *Le cabinet satyrique.* Paris: J. Fort, 1924.

Ford, C.S. *A comparative study of human reproduction.* Yale University Publications in Anthropology no. 32, 1964.(Reprinted: New York: Taplinger Publishing Co., 1964).

Ford, C.S., and F.A. Beach. *Patterns of sexual behavior.* New York: Harper & Row, 1951.

Foster, J.H. *Sex variant women in literature.* Chicago: Muller, 1958.

Fowlkes, D.M., G.B. Dooher, and W.M. O'Leary. Evidence by scanning electron microscopy for an association between spermatoza and T-mycoplasmas in men of infertile marriage. *Fertility and Sterility* 26(1975):1203–1211.

Fowlkes, D.M., J. MacLeod, and W.M. O'Leary. T-mycoplasmas and human infertility: Correlation of infection with alterations in seminal parameters. *Fertility and Sterility* 26(1975): 1212–1218.

Fox, C.A., and B. Fox. Blood pressure and respiratory patterns during human coitus. *Journal of Reproduction and Fertility* 19, no. 3 (August 1969):405–415.

Fox, C.A., and B. Fox. Uterine suction during orgasm. *British Medical Journal* 1 (February 4, 1967):300.

Fox, C.A., A. Ismail, *et al.* Studies on the relationship between plasma testosterone levels and human sexual activity. *Journal of Endocrinology,* 52(1972):51–58.

Fox, C.A., H.S. Wolff, and J.A. Baker. Measurement of intra-vaginal and intrauterine pressures during human coitus by radio-telemetry. *Journal of Reproduction and Fertility* 22, no. 1 (June 1970):243–251.

Fraiberg, S.H. *The magic years.* New York: Charles Scribner's Sons, 1959.

Frank, E., C. Anderson, and D. Rubinstein. Frequency of sexual dysfunction in "normal" couples. *New England Journal of Medicine* 299(1978):111–115.

Frank, Gerald. *The Boston strangler.* New York: The New American Library, 1966. (Also available as a Signet paperback.)

Franklin, J. *Classics of the silent screen.* New York: Citadel Press, 1959.

Frazer, J.G., trs. *Pausanias's description of Greece.* New York: Macmillan, 1898.

Freedman, M.J. Homosexuality among women and psychological adjustment. Ph.D. dissertation, Case Western Reserve University, 1967.

Freeman, L. *Before I kill more.* New York: Crown Publishers, 1955. (Also available as a Pocket Books paperback.)

Freud, S. Letter to an American mother. *American Journal of Psychiatry* 107(1951):787.

―――. *The standard edition of the complete psychological works of Sigmund Freud,* James Strachey, ed. London: Hogarth Press and Institute of Psychoanalysis, 1957–1964.

Frisch, R.E. Critical weight at menarche, initiation of the adolescent growth spurt, and control of puberty. In *Control of the onset of puberty,* M.M. Grumbach *et al.* eds. New York: John Wiley & Sons, 1974. chapter 15.

Fromm, E. *The art of loving.* New York: Harper & Row, 1956.

Gagnon, J.H., and W. Simon, eds. *The sexual scene.* Chicago: Aldine Publishing Co., 1970.

Gagnon, J.H., and W. Simon. *Sexual conduct: The social sources of human sexuality.* Chicago: Aldine Publishing Co., 1973.

Gandy, P., and R. Deisher. Young male prostitutes. *Journal of the American Medical Association,* 212(1970):1661–1666.

Ganong, W.F., and L. Martini. *Frontiers in neuroendocrinology,* Vol. 5. New York: Raven Press, 1978.

Gebhard, P.H. Factors in marital orgasm. *Medical Aspects of Human Sexuality* 2, no. 7 (July): 22–25.

Gebhard, P.H. Human sexual behavior: A summary statement. In *Human sexual behavior,* D.S. Marshall and R.C. Suggs, eds. Englewood Cliffs, N.J.: Prentice-Hall, 1971, 206–217.

Gebbhard, P.H., J.H. Gagnon, W.B. Pomeroy, and C.V. Christenson, *Sex offenders.* New York: Harper & Row, 1965.

George Washington University Population Report. *Oral contraceptives.* Series A, no 1(April). Washington, D.C.: George Washington University Medical Center, 1974.

Gerassi, J. *Boys of Boise.* New York: Macmillan Co., 1967.

Gessa, B.L., *et al.* Aphrodisiac effect of p-chlorophenylalanine. *Science* 171(1971):706.

Giarretto, H. Humanistic treatment of father-daughter incest. In *Child abuse and neglect: The family and the community.* R.E. Helfer and C.H. Kempe, eds. Cambridge, Mass.: Ballinger Publishing Co., 1976, chapter 8.

Gilder, G.F. *Sexual suicide.* New York: Quadrangle/The New York Times Book Co., 1973.

Gilmartin, B.G. Swinging: Who gets involved and how? In *Marriage and alternatives: Exploring intimate relationships,* R.W. Libby and R.N. Whitehurst, eds. Glenview, Ill. Scott, Foresman and Co., 1977, 161–185.

Ginsberg, G.L., *et al.* The new impotence. *Archives of General Psychology* 28(1972):218.

Girodias, M., ed. *The Olympia reader.* New York: Grove Press, 1965.

Glick, P.C., and Norton, A.J. Marrying, divorcing, and living together in the U.S. today. *Population Bulletin* 32, no. 5 (1977):1–39. Washington, D.C.: Population Reference Bureau.

Gold, A.R., and D.B. Adams. Measuring the cycles of female sexuality. *Contemporary Obstetrics and Gynecology* 12(1978):147–156.

Goldberg, I. *Havelock Ellis.* New York: Simon & Schuster, 1926.

Goldberg, P. Are women prejudiced against women? *Transaction* 5, no. 5(1968):28–30.

Goodall, J. *See* Van Lawick.

Goodlin, R.C. Routine ultrasonic examinations in obstetrics, *Lancet* (September 11, 1971): 604–605.

Goodlin, R.C., *et al.* Orgasm during late pregnancy—possible deleterious effects. *Obstetrical Gynecology,* 38(1971):916.

Gordon, S., and I.R. Dickman. *Sex education: The parents' role.* New York: Public Affairs Pamphlets no. 549; 1977.

Gorer, G. *Himalayan village.* London: Michael Joseph Ltd., 1938.

Gortvay, G., and I. Zoltàn. *Semmelweis: His life and work.* Budapest: Akadémiai Kiadó; 1968.

Goy, R.W. Organizing effects of androgen on the behaviour of Rhesus monkeys. In *Endocrinology and human behavior,* R. Michael, ed. London: Oxford University Press, 1968:12–31.

Grabstald, H., and W.E. Goodwin. Devices and surgical procedures in the treatment of organic impotence. *Medical Aspects of Human Sexuality.* 7, no. 12 (December 1973):113–120.

Graves, R. *The Greek myths.* New York: George Braziller, 1959, 2 vols.

Greenblatt, R., E. Jungck, and H. Blum. Endocrinology of sexual behavior. *Medical Aspects of Human Sexuality* 6, no. 1 (January 1972): 110–131.

Greene, F.T., R.M. Kirk, and I.M. Thompson. Retrograde ejaculation. *Medical Aspects of Human Sexuality*, 4, no. 12 (December 1970):59–65.

Grumbach, M.M. *et al.* Hypothalamic-pituitary regulation of puberty: Evidence and concepts derived from clinical research. In *Control of the onset of puberty*, M.M. Grumbach G.D. Grave, and F.E. Mayer, eds. New York: John Wiley & Sons, 1974, chapter 6.

Guerrero, R. Type and time of insemination within the menstrual cycle and the human sex ratio. *Studies in Family Planning* 6, no. 10 (1975): 367–371.

Gulevich, G., and V. Zarcone. Nocturnal erection and dreams. *Medical Aspects of Human Sexuality* 3, no. 4 (April 1969):105–109.

Guthrie, D. *A history of medicine.* London: Thomas Nelson and Sons Ltd., 1958.

Guttmacher, A.F. *Pregnancy and birth: A book for expectant parents.* New York: Viking Press, 1962.

Guttmacher, A.F., W. Best, and F.S. Jaffe. *Planning your family.* New York: Macmillan Co., 1964.

Guttmacher, A.F., and B.L. Nichols. Teratology of cojoined twins. *Birth Defects Original Article Series* 3 no. 1 (1967):3–9.

Hall, R. *The well of loneliness.* New York: Covici Friede, 1928.

Hamburg, D.A., and D.T. Lunde. Sex hormones in the development of sex differences in human behavior. In *The Development of Sex Differences*, E. Maccoby, ed. Stanford, Calif.: Stanford University Press, 1966:1–24.

Hampson, J.L. Determinants of psychosexual orientation. In *Sex and Behavior*, F.A. Beach, ed. New York: John Wiley & Sons, 1965, 108–132.

Hare, E.H. Masturbatory insanity: The history of an idea. *Journal of Mental Science* 452 (1962):2–25.

Harkel, R.L. *The picture book of sexual love.* New York: Cybertype Corp., 1969.

Harlow, H.F., J.L. McGaugh, and R.F. Thompson. *Psychology.* San Francisco: Albion Publishing Co., 1971.

Harris, F. *My life and loves.* New York: Grove Press, 1963.

Harris, L. ABC News-Harris Survey release. New York, March 6, 1979.

Hart, R. *Children's experience of place.* Irvington, N.Y.: Halsted (John Wiley & Sons).

Hassett, J. A new look at living together. *Psychology Today* 11, no. 7 (1977):82–83.

Hatcher, R.A. G.K. Stewart, F. Stewart, F. Guest, P. Stratton, and A.H. Wright. *Contraceptive technology 1978–1979.* New York: Irvington Publishers, 1978.

Hastings, D.W. *A doctor speaks on sexual expression in marriage.* Boston: Little, Brown & Co., 1966.

Heath, R.G. Pleasure and brain activity in man. *Journal of Nervous and Mental Disease* 154, no. 1 (January 1972):3–18.

Henley, N.M. Power, sex, and nonverbal communication. In *Language and sex*, B. Thorne and N. Henley, eds. Rowley, Mass.: Newbury House, 1975, 184–203.

Henriques, F. *Prostitution and society: A survey.* Vol. 1: *Primitive, classical, oriental.* Vol. 2: *Prostitution in Europe and the New World.* Vol. 3: *Modern sexuality.* London: MacGibbon & Kee, 1962–1968.

Henry, G.W. *All the sexes.* New York: Holt, Rinehart and Winston, 1955.

Herman, R. Sex-roles and sexual attitudes in Sweden: The new phase. *The Massachusetts Review* 13, no. 1–2 (1972):45–64.

Hewes, G.W. Communication of sexual interest: An anthropological view. *Medical Aspects of Human Sexuality* 7, no. 1 (January 1973):66–92.

Hilgard, E.R. *Theories of learning.* New York: Appleton-Century-Crofts, 1956.

Hilgard, E.R., R.C. Atkinson, and R.L. Atkinson. *Introduction to psychology.* New York: Harcourt Brace Jovanovich, 1971.

Hill, A.B. *Principles of medical statistics.* London: Oxford University Press, 1966.

Hiltner, S. *Sex ethics and the Kinsey reports.* New York: American Book-Stratford Press, 1953.

Hinde, R.A. *Animal behavior: A synthesis of ethology and comparative psychology.* New York: McGraw-Hill, 1970.

Hite, S. *The Hite report.* New York: Macmillian, 1976.

Hobsbawm, E.J. Revolution is puritan. In *The new eroticism*, P. Nobile, ed. New York: Random House, 1970:36–40.

Hoffman. M. *The gay world: Male homosexuality and the social creation of evil.* New York: Basic Books, 1968.

Hollister, L. Popularity of amyl nitrite as sexual stimulant. *Medical Aspects of Human Sexuality,* 8, no. 4 (April 1974):112.

Hooker, E. The adjustment of the male overt homosexual. *Journal of Projective Techniques* 21, no. 1 (1957):18–31.

Hooker, E. An empirical study of some relations between sexual patterns and gender identity in male homosexuals. In *Sex research—new developments,* J. Money, ed. New York: Holt, Rinehart and Winston, 1965:24–25.

Horos, C.V. *Rape.* New Canaan, Conn.: Tobey Publishing Co., 1974.

Houston, P. *The contemporary cinema.* London: Penguin Books, 1963.

How does premarital sex affect marriage, *Medical Aspects of Human Sexuality, 2,* no. 11 (November 1968):14–21.

How frequently is sex an important factor in divorce? *Medical Aspects of Human Sexuality,* 4, no. 6 (June 1970):24–37.

Hsü-Balzer, E., R. Balzer, and L.K. Hsu. *China day by day.* New Haven: Yale University Press, 1974.

Hudson, J.W., and L.L. Hoyt. Campus values in mate selection: forty years later. Unpublished manuscript.

Hunt, M. *Sexual behavior in the 1970's.* Chicago: Playboy Press, 1974.

———. Sexual behavior in the 1970's. *Playboy.* 20, no. 10 (October 1973):84–88, 194–207.

———. Sexual behavior in the 1970's. *Playboy.* 20, no. 11 (November 1973):74–75.

———. Sexual behavior in the 1970's. *Playboy.* 20, no. 12 (December 1973):90–91, 256.

———. Sexual behavior in the 1970's. *Playboy.* 21, no. 1 (January 1974):60–61, 286–287.

———. Sexual behavior in the 1970's. *Playboy.* 21, no. 2 (February 1974):54–55, 176–177.

Hunt, M. Special, today's man: Redbook's exclusive Gallup survey on the emerging male. *Redbook* 147, no. 6 (1976):112ff.

Hursch, C. *The trouble with rape.* Chicago: Nelson-Hall, 1977.

Hyde, H.M. *A history of pornography.* New York: Dell Books, 1966.

Inkeles, G., and M. Todris. *The art of sensual massage.* San Francisco: Straight Arrow Books, 1972.

International Planned Parenthood Federation medical handbook. London, IPPF, 1968.

Israel, S.L. *Menstrual disorders and sterility.* New York: Harper & Row, 1967.

"J." *The sensuous woman.* New York: Lyle Stuart, 1969.

Jackson, H. *Antifertility compounds in the male and female.* Springfield, Ill.: Charles C Thomas, 1966.

James, A.G. *Cancer Prognosis manual.* 2nd ed. New York: American Cancer Society, 1966.

James, J., and J. Meyerding. Early sexual experience and prostitution. *American Journal of Psychiatry* 134(1977):1381–1385.

James, W.H. The distribution of coitus within the human intermenstruum. *Journal of Biosocial Science* 3(1971):159–171.

Janis, I.L., G.F. Mahl, J. Kagan, and R.R. Holt. *Personality: Dynamics, development and assessment.* New York: Harcourt Brace Jovanovich, 1969.

Jawetz, E., J.L. Melnick, and E.A. Adelberg. *Review of medical microbiology.* 9th ed. Los Altos, Calif.: Lange Medical Publications, 1970.

Jay, K., and A. Young. *The gay report.* New York: Summit Books, 1977.

Jay, P.C., ed. *Primates: Studies in adaptation and variability.* New York: Holt, Rinehart and Winston, 1968.

Jones, E. *The life and work of Sigmund Freud.* 3 vols. New York: Basic Books, 1953.

Jones, E. *On the nightmare.* London: Hogarth Press, 1949.

Jones, H.W., Jr., and W. Scott. *Hermaphroditism, genital anomalies and related endocrine disorders.* Baltimore: Williams & Wilkins Co., 1958.

Jong, E. *Fear of Flying.* New York: Holt, Rinehart and Winston, 1973.

Joyce, J. *Ulysses.* New York: Random House, 1934.

Juhasz, A.M., ed. *Sexual development and behavior: Selected readings.* Homewood, Ill.: The Dorsey Press, 1973.

Jung, C.G. General aspects of dream analysis. *Structure and dynamics of the psyche,* Vol. 8. R.F.C. Hull, trs. New York: Pantheon Books, 1960.

Juvenal (Decimus Junius Juvenalis). *Satires.* G.G. Ramsay, trs. London: William Heinemann, 1961.

Kahne, H. Women's roles in the economy: Economic investigation and research needs. In *Economic independence for women.* Beverly Hills, Calif.: Sage Publications, 1976, 39–76.

Kallmann, F.J. A comparative twin study on the genetic aspects of male homosexuality. *Journal of Nervous and Mental Disease* 115(1952): 283–298.

Kameny, F.E. Gay liberation and psychiatry. *Psychiatric Opinion* (February 1971):18–27.

Kantner, J.F. Teens and sex: A national portrait? *Family Planning Perspectives,* 5, no. 2 (Spring 1973):124–125.

Kantner, J.F., and M. Zelnik. Contraception and pregnancy: Experience of young unmarried women in the United States. *Family Planning Perspectives,* 5, no. 1 (Winter 1973):21–35.

———. Sexual experience of young unmarried women in the United States. *Family Planning Perspectives,* 4, no. 4 (October 1972):9–18.

Kaplan, H.S. *The New Sex Therapy.* New York: Brunner/Mazel, 1974.

Karim, S.M.M., and G.M. Filshie. Therapeutic abortion using prostaglandin F_{2a}. *Lancet* 1(1970):157–159.

Karlen, A. *Sexuality and homosexuality.* New York: Norton, 1971.

Karpman, B. *The sexual offender and his offenses.* New York: Julian Press, 1954.

Katchadourian, H. *The biology of adolescence.* San Francisco: W.H. Freeman, 1977.

———, ed. *Human sexuality: A comparative and developmental perspective.* Berkeley: University of California Press, 1979.

Kaufman, I.C., and L.A. Rosenblum. The waning of the mother-infant bond in the species of macaque. *Determinants of infant behavior,* Vol. IV. B.M. Foss, ed. London: Methuen & Co., 1969:41–59.

Kaufman, R.H., and W.E. Rawls. Herpes genitalis and its relationship to cervical cancer. *CA-A Cancer Journal for Clinicians* 24, no. 5 (1974):258–265.

Keeton, W.T. *Biological science.* New York: Norton, 1967.

Kepecs, J. Sex and tickling. *Medical Aspects of Human Sexuality.* 3, no. 8 (August 1969):58–65.

Kessel, J. *Belle de jour.* Paris: Geoffrey Wagner, trs. New York: Dell Books, 1967.

Kessler, S., and R. Moos. The XYY karyotype and criminality: A review. *Journal of Psychiatric Research,* 7(1970):153–170.

Kilpatrick, J.J. *The smut peddlers.* Garden City, N.Y.: Doubleday & Co., 1960.

King, A.J., and C. Nicol. *Venereal diseases.* 3rd ed. Baltimore: Williams & Wilkins, 1975.

Kinsey, A.C., W.B. Pomeroy, and C.E. Martin. *Sexual behavior in the human male.* Philadelphia: W.B. Saunders Co., 1948.

Kinsey, A.C., W.B. Pomeroy, C.E. Martin, and P.H. Gebhard. *Sexual behavior in the human female.* Philadelphia, W.B. Saunders Co., 1953.

Klaus, H., J. Goebel, R. Woods, M. Castles, and G. Zimny. Use effectiveness and analysis of the *Billings ovulation method. Fertility and Sterility* 28(1977):1038–1043.

Klausner, S.Z. Islam, sex life in. In *The encyclopedia of sexual behavior.* Vol. 1. A. Ellis and A. Abarbanel, eds. New York: Hawthorn Books, 1961.

Kleitman, N. *Sleep and wakefulness.* Chicago: University of Chicago Press, 1963.

Knight, A., and H. Alpert. The history of sex in cinema. *Playboy.* I. The original sin (April 1965); II. Compounding the sin (May 1965); III. The twenties: Hollywood's flaming youth (June 1965); IV. The twenties: Europe's decade of decadence (August 1965); V. Sex stars of the twenties (September 1965); VI. Censorship and the Depression (November 1965); VII. The thirties: Europe's decade of unbuttoned erotica (February 1966); VIII. Sex stars of the thirties (April 1966); IX. The forties: War and peace in Hollywood (august 1966). X. The forties: War and peace in Europe (September 1966); XI. Sex stars of the forties (October 1966); XII. The fifties: Hollywood grows up (November 1966); XIII. The fifties: Sex goes international (December 1966); XIV. Sex stars of the fifties (January 1967); XV Experimental films (April 1967); XVI. The nudies (June 1967); XVII. The stag film (November 1967); XVIII. The sixties: Hollywood unbuttons (April 1968); XIX. The sixties: Eros unbound in foreign films (July 1968); XX. Sex stars of the sixties (January 1969).

Knight, R.P. Functional disturbances in the sexual life of women: Frigidity and related disorders. *Bulletin of the Menninger Clinic* 7(1943):25–35.

Kohlberg, L. A cognitive-developmental analysis of children's sex role concepts and attitudes. In

The development of sex differences, E.E. Maccoby, ed. Stanford, Calif.: Stanford University Press, 1966, 82–173.

Kolata, G.B. Gonorrhea: More of a problem but less of a mystery. *Science* 192(1976):244–247.

Kolodny, R., W. Masters, *et al.* Depression of plasma testosterone levels after chronic intensive marijuana use. *New England Journal of Medicine.* 290, no. 16 (April 18, 1974):872–874.

Kracauer, S. *From Caligari to Hitler: A psychological history of the German film.* Princeton, N.J.: Princeton University Press, 1966.

Kronhausen, E., and P. Kronhausen. *Pornography and the law.* New York: Ballantine Books, 1964.

Kuchera, L.K. Stilbestol as a "morning-after" pill. *Medical Aspects of Human Sexuality* 6, no. 10 (October 1972): 168–177.

Kupperman, H.S. Treating climacteric men. *Medical World News* (June 28, 1974):42–44.

Kyrou, A. *Amour, érotisme, et cinéma.* Paris: Le Terrain Vague, 1957.

Lancaster, J.B. Sex and gender in evolutionary perspective. In *Human sexuality: A comparative and developmental perspective*, H.A. Katchadourian, ed. Berkeley: University of California Press, 1979, 51–80.

Landis, J.T., and M.G. Landis. *Building a successful marriage.* 6th ed. Englewood Cliffs, New Jersey: Prentice-Hall, 1973.

Landtman, G. *The Kiwai Papuans of British New Guinea.* London: Macmillian, 1927.

Laub, D.R., and P. Gandy, eds. Proceedings of the second interdisciplinary symposium on gender dysphoria syndrome (February 2–4, 1973).

Lawder, S.D. Film: Art of the twentieth century. *Yale Alumni Magazine* (May 1968).

Lawrence, D.H. *The tales of D.H. Lawrence.* London: William Heinemann, 1948.

———. *Lady Chatterly's lover.* New York: Grove Press, 1957.

Laws, J.L. A feminist review of marital adjustment. The rape of the locke. *Journal of Marriage and the Family* 33(1971):97–137.

Legman, G. *Love and death: A study in censorship.* New York: Hacker Art Books, 1963.

———. *The horn book: Studies in erotic folklore and bibliography.* New York: University Books, 1963.

LeGrand, C.E. Rape and rape laws: Sexism in society and law. *California Law Review* 61(1973):919–941.

Lehfeldt, H. Coitus interruptus. *Medical Aspects of Human Sexuality* 2, no. 11 (November 1968): 29–31.

Lever, J. Sex differences in the games children play. *Social Problems* 23(1976):478–487.

Levinger, G. Husbands' and wives' estimates of coital frequency. *Medical Aspects of Human Sexuality* 4, no. 9 (September 1970):42–57.

Levy, R. *The social structure of Islam.* London: Cambridge University Press, 1957.

Lewinsohn, R. *A history of sexual customs.* New York: Harper & Row, 1958.

Lichtenstadter, L. *Islam and the modern age.* New York: Bookman Associates, 1958.

Liddon, S.C., and D.R. Hawkins. Sex and nightmares. *Medical Aspects of Human Sexuality.* 7, no. 1 (January 1972):58–65.

Lippes, I.J., H.J. Tatum, D. Maulid, and M. Zielezny. A continuation of the study of postcoital IUDs. Paper presented at the annual meeting of the Association of Planned Parenthood Physicians. San Diego, October 25–27, 1978,*qv Family Planning Perspectives* 11(1979):195.

Li Yü. *Jou-p'u-t'uan (The prayer mat of flesh).* H. Lowe-Porter, trs. London: Penguin Books, 1955.

Lloyd, C.W. *Human reproduction and sexual behavior.* Philadelphia: Lea & Febiger, 1964.

Loth, D. *The erotic in literature.* New York: Macfadden, 1962.

Lunde, D.T., and D.A. Hamburg. Techniques for assessing the effects of sex hormones on affect, arousal and aggression in humans. *Recent Progress in Hormone Research* 28:627–663.

Lynn, D.B. The process of learning parental and sex-role identification. *Journal of Marriage and Family* 28(1966):466–470.

"M." *The sensuous man.* New York: Lyle Stuart, 1971.

Maccoby, E., ed. *The development of sex differences.* Stanford University Press, 1966.

McCance, A.A., M.C. Luff, and E.C. Widdowson. Distribution of coitus during the menstrual cycle. *Journal of Hygiene*, Cambridge 37(1952):571–611.

McClintock, M.K. Menstrual synchrony and suppression. *Nature* 229(1971):244–245.

McConnell, J.V. *Understanding human behavior.* New York: Holt, Rinehart and Winston, 1974.

McCormack, W.M. Sexually transmissible conditions other than gonorrhea and syphilis. *Practice of medicine.* Vol. 3. New York: Harper & Row, 1975, chapter 20.

McQuarrie, H.G., and A.D. Flanagan. Accuracy of early pregnancy testing at home. Paper presented at the annual meeting of the Association of Planned Parenthood Physicians, San Diego, October 24–27, 1978, *qv Family Planning Perspectives* 11(1979):190–191.

Macdonald, D. *On movies.* Englewood Cliffs, N.J.: Prentice-Hall, 1969.

Macdonald, J.M. *Rape: Offenders and their victims.* Springfield, Ill.: Charles C Thomas, 1971.

Macklin, E.D. Cohabitation in college: Going very steady. *Psychology Today* 8, no. 6 (1974): 53ff.

Maisch, H. *Incest.* London: Andre Deutsch, 1973.

Malinowski, B. *The sexual life of savages in north-western Melanesia.* New York: Harcourt Brace Jovanovich, 1929.

Malla, K. *The ananga ranga.* R.F. Burton and F.F. Arbuthnot, trs. New York: G.P. Putnam's Sons, 1964 ed.

Mann, T. *Death in Venice.* H. Lowe-Porter, trs. London: Penguin Books, 1955.

Manvell, R. *New cinema in Europe.* London: Studio Vista, 1966.

Marcus, S. *The other Victorians.* New York: Basic Books, 1966.

Marmor, J. Some considerations concerning orgasm in the female. *Psychosomatic Medicine* 16, no. 3 (1954):240–245.

Marmor, J., ed. *Modem psychoanalysis: New directions and perspectives.* New York: Basic Books, 1968.

————. ed. *Sexual inversion: The multiple roots of homosexuality.* New York: Basic Books, 1965.

Marshall, D.S. Sexual behavior on Mangaia. In *Human sexual behavior*, D.S. Marshall and R.C. Suggs, eds. Englewood Cliffs, N.J.: Prentice Hall, 1971.

Marshall, D.S., and R.C. Suggs, eds. *Human sexual behavior.* Englewood Cliffs, N.J.: Prentice-Hall, 1971.

Marshall, W.A. *Human growth and its disorders.* New York: Academic Press, 1977.

Martial (Marcus Valerius Martialis). *The epigrams.* Loeb Library trs. London: William Heinemann, 1920.

Martin, D., and P. Lyon. *Lesbian/Woman.* San Francisco: Glibe Publications, 1972.

Martin, M. Kay, and B. Voorhies. *Female of the species.* New York: Columbia University Press, 1975.

Marx, J.L. Birth control: Current technology, future prospects. *Science*, 179(1974): 1222–1224.

Masters, W.H., and V.E. Johnson. The aftermath of rape. *Redbook* 147, no. 2 (1976):74ff.

Masters, W.H., and V.E. Johnson. *Homosexuality in perspective.* Boston: Little, Brown, 1979.

Masters, W.H., and V.E. Johnson. *Human sexual inadequacy.* Boston: Little, Brown & Co., 1970.

————. *Human sexual response.* Boston: Little, Brown & Co., 1966.

Mathews, D.K., and E.L. Fox. *The physiological basis of physical education and athletics.* 2nd ed. Philadelphia: W.B. Saunders, 1976.

May, R. *Love and will.* New York: Norton, 1969.

Mayo, J. The new black feminism: A minority report. *Contemporary Sexual Behavior: Critical Issues in the 1970's*, J. Zubin and J. Money, eds. Baltimore: Johns Hopkins University Press, 1973, Ch. 9.

McGaugh, J.L., N.M. Weinberger, and R.E. Whalen. *Psychobiology*—The biological bases of behavior, readings from Scientific American. San Francisco: W.H. Freeman and Co., book published in 1966.

Mead, M. *Coming of age in Samoa.* New York: William Morrow & Co., 1929.

————. *Male and female.* New York: William Morrow & Co., 1949.

————. *Sex and temperament in three primitive societies.* New York: William Morrow & Co., 1935.

Meleager, Strato of Sardis, *et al. The Greek anthology.* W.R. Paton, trs. London: William Heinemann, 1918.

Menninger, K. *Whatever became of sin?* New York: Hawthorn Books, 1973.

Mernissi, F. *Beyond the veil: Male-female dynamics in a modern Muslim society.* Cambridge, Mass.: Schenkman Publishing Co., 1975.

Messenger, J.C. Sex and repression in an Irish folk community. In *Human sexual behavior*, D.S.

Marshall and R.C. Suggs, eds. Englewood Cliffs, N.J.: Prentice-Hall, 1971, 3–37.

Meyer, A.W. *The rise of embryology.* Stanford, Calif.: Stanford University Press, 1939.

Meyer, M.B., and J.A. Tonascia. Maternal smoking, pregnancy complications and perinatal mortality. *American Journal of Obstetrics and Gynecology* 128(1977):494–502.

Michael, R.P., R.W. Bonsall, and P. Warner. Human vaginal secretions. Volatile fatty acid content. *Science* 186(1974):1217–1219.

Michael, R.P., R.W. Bonsall, and D. Zumpe. The evidence for chemical communication in primates. *Vitamins and Hormones* 34(1976): 137–186.

Michael, R.P., and E.B. Keverne. Pheromones in the communication of sexual status in primates. *Nature,* 218(1968):746–749.

Millar, J.D. The national venereal disease problem. *Epidemic Venereal Disease: Proceedings of the Second International Symposium on Venereal Disease.* St. Louis: American Social Health Association and Pfizer Laboratories Division, Pfizer, Inc. (1972):10–13.

Miller, A. *The renewal of man.* Garden City, N.Y.: Doubleday & Co., 1955.

Miller, H. *Tropic of cancer.* New York: Grove Press, 1961.

Miller, W.B. Sexuality, contraception and pregnancy in a high-school population. *California Medicine,* 119(1973):14–21.

Millett, K. *Sexual politics.* Garden City, N.Y.: Doubleday & Co., 1970.

Minuchin, P. Sex-role concepts and sex typing in childhood as a function of school and home environments. *Child Development* 36(1965): 1033–1048.

Mirbeau, O. *Le jardin des supplices.* Paris: Les Editions Nationales, 1935.

Mischel, H. Sex bias in the evaluation of professional achievements. *Journal of Educational Psychology* 66(1974):157–166.

Mischel, W. A social-learning view of sex differences in behavior. In *The development of sex differences,* E.E. Maccoby, ed. Stanford, Calif.: Stanford University Press, 1966, 56–81.

Mitamura, T. *Chinese eunuchs.* Tokyo: Charles E. Tuttle Co., 1970.

Mittwoch, U. *Genetics of sex differentiation.* New York: Academic Press, 1973.

Moghissi, K.S. Accuracy of basal body temperature for ovulation detection. *Fertility and Sterility* 27(1976):1415–1421.

Money, J. Ablatio penis: Normal male infant sex-reassigned as a girl. *Archives of Sexual Behavior,* 4, no. 1 (1975):65–77.

Money, J. Human hermaphroditism. In *Human sexuality in four perspectives,* F.A. Beach, ed. Baltimore: The Johns Hopkins University Press, 1976, 62–86.

Money, J. *Sex errors of the body.* Baltimore: The Johns Hopkins Press, 1968.

Money, J., and D. Alexander. Eroticism and sexual function in developmental anorchia and hyporchia with pubertal failure. *Journal of Sex Research* 3(1967):31–47.

Money, J., and A.A. Ehrhardt. *Man and woman, boy and girl.* Baltimore: The Johns Hopkins University Press, 1972.

Money, J., J.C. Hampson, and J.L. Hampson. An examination of some basic sexual concepts: The evidence of human hermaphroditism. *Bulletin of Johns Hopkins Hospital* 97(1955):301–319.

Montagu, A. *Life before birth.* New York: New American Library, 1964.

———. *Sex, man and society.* New York: Tower Publications, 1969.

Montanelli, D.S., and K.T. Hill. Children's achievement expectations and performance as a function of two consecutive reinforcement experiences, sex of subject, and sex of experimenter. *Journal of Personality and Social Psychology* 13(1969):115–128.

Moos, R., D.T. Lunde, *et al.* Fluctuations in symptoms and moods during the menstrual cycle. *Journal of Psychosomatic Research,* 13(1969): 37–44.

Morin, E. *The stars.* Richard Howard, trs. New York: Grove Press, 1960.

Morris, D. *The human zoo.* New York: McGraw-Hill, 1969.

Morris, J. *Conundrum.* New York: Harcourt Brace Jovanovich, 1974.

Morrison, E.S., and V. Borosage, eds. *Human sexuality: Contemporary perspectives.* Palo Alto, Calif.: National Press Books, 1973.

Moskin, J. Sweden: The contraceptive society. In *Family in transition.* 1st ed. A.S. Skolnick and J.H. Skolnick, eds. Boston: Little, Brown, 1971, 187–193.

Mostofi, F.K. Carcinoma of the prostate. *Modern Trends in Urology,* Sir Eric Riches, ed. New York: Appleton-Century-Crofts, 231–263, 1970.

Murdock, G.P. Comparative data on the division of labor by sex. *Social Forces* 15(1935):551–553.

Murdock, G.P. *Social structure.* New York: Macmillan Co., 1949.

My secret life. New York: Grove Press, 1966.

Nabokov, V. *Lolita.* Greenwich, Conn.: Fawcett Books, 1959.

National Center for Health Statistics, DHEW. Advance report: Final natality statistics, 1976. *Monthly Vital Statistics Report* 26, no. 12 (1978):1–27.

Navran, L. Communication and adjustment in marriage. *Family Process* 6(1967):173–184.

Nefzawi. *The perfumed garden.* R.F. Burton, trs. New York: G.P. Putnam's Sons, 1964 ed. (London: Neville Spearman Ltd., 1963.)

Netter, F.H. *Endocrine system.* The Ciba Collection of Medical Illustrations, Vol. 4. Summit, N.J.: Ciba, 1965.

———. *Reproductive system.* The Ciba Collection of Medical Illustrations, Vol. 2. Summit, N.J.: Ciba, 1965.

Neubardt, S., and H. Schulman. *Techniques of abortion.* Boston: Little, Brown, 1972.

Neubeck, G., ed. *Extramarital relations.* Englewood Cliffs, N.J.: Prentice-Hall, 1969.

Newton, N. Interrelationships between sexual responsiveness, birth, and breast feeding. *Contemporary Sexual Behavior: Critical Issues in the 1970's.* J. Zubin and J. Money, eds. Baltimore: Johns Hopkins University Press, 1973:77–98.

Nilsson, A.L., *et al. A child is born.* Boston: Seymour Lawrence, Inc., 1965.

Noonan, J.T., Jr. *Contraception: A history of its treatment by the Catholic theologians and canonists.* New York: New American Library, 1967.

Novak, E.R., *et al. Novak's Textbook of Gynecology,* 8th ed. Baltimore: The Williams & Wilkins Co., 1970.

Novak, E.R., and G.S. Jones. *Novak's textbook of gynecology.* Baltimore: Williams & Wilkins Co., 1961.

Nunberg, H. *Principles of psychoanalysis: Their application to the neuroses.* New York: International Universities Press, 1969.

Olds, J. Pleasure centers in the brain. *Scientific American* 193(1956):105–116.

Oliven, J.F. *Clinical sexuality.* Philadelphia: J.B. Lippincott Co., 1974.

O'Neill, N., and G. O'Neill. *Open marriage.* New York: M. Evans and Co., 1972.

O'Neil, R.P., and M.A. Donovan. *Sexuality and moral responsibility.* Washington and Cleveland: Corpus Publications, 1968.

Opler, M.K. Cross-cultural aspects of kissing. *Medical Aspects of Human Sexuality* 3, no. 2 (February 1969):11–21.

Ovid (Publius Ovidius Naso). *Heroides and Amores,* G. Showerman, trs. London: William Heinemann, 1914.

Packer, H.L. *The limits of the criminal sanction.* Stanford, Calif.: Stanford University Press, 1968.

Paige, K.E. Women learn to sing the menstrual blues. *Psychology Today* 7, no.4 (1973):41–46.

Paige, K.E. The declining taboo against menstrual sex. *Psychology Today* 12, no. 7 (1978):50–51.

Parke, J.R. *Human sexuality.* Philadelphia: Professional Publishing Company, 1906.

Parker, E. *The seven ages of woman.* Baltimore: The Johns Hopkins Press, 1960.

Parran, T. *Shadow on the land—syphilis.* New York: Reynal & Hitchcock, 1937.

Patten, B.M. *Human embryology.* 3rd ed. New York: McGraw-Hill, 1968.

Paul, G.L. Outcome of systematic desensitization. C.M. Franks, ed. *Behavior therapy: Appraisal and status.* New York: McGraw-Hill, 1969.

Pavlov, I.P. *Conditioned reflexes: An investigation of the physiological activity of the cerebral cortex.* London: Oxford University Press, 1927.

Peck, E. *The baby trap.* New York: Pinnacle Books, 1971.

Pedersen-Bjergaard, K., and M. Tønnesen. Sex hormone analyses. II. The excretion of sexual hormones by normal males, impotent males, polyarthritics and prostatics. *Acta Medica Scandinavica* 131(1948):284–297.

Peterson, H. *Havelock Ellis, philosopher of love.* Boston: Houghton Mifflin Co., 1928.

Pfeiffer, E., *et al.* Sexual behavior in aged men and women. *Archives of General Psychiatry* 19(1968):753–758.

Pheterson, G.I., S.B. Kiesler, and P.A. Goldberg. Evaluation of performance of women as a function of their sex, achievement, and personal history. *Journal of Personality and Social Psychology* 19(1971):114–118.

Pierson, E., and W.V. D'Antonio. *Female and*

male: Dimensions of human sexuality. Philadelphia: J.B. Lippincott Co., 1974.

Piotrow, P.T., W. Rinehart, and J.C. Schmidt. IUDs—Update on safety, effectiveness, and research. *Population Reports*, Series B, no. 3 Washington, D.C. Population Information Program (May 1979:49–98.)

Pirages, D., and P. Ehrlich. *Ark II*. San Francisco: W.H. Freeman and Co., 1974.

Playboy. What's really happening on campus. *Playboy* 23, no. 10 (1976):128ff.

Pliny, S. *Natural history*. Vol. 2 Trans. H. Rackham, Cambridge: Harvard University Press, 77 A.D. [1961], book 7.

Ploscowe, M. *Sex and the law*. Englewood Cliffs, N.J.: Prentice-Hall, 1951.

Pohlman, E.G. *Psychology of birth planning*. Cambridge: Shenkman Publishing Co., 1968.

Pomeroy, W.B. *Dr. Kinsey and the Institute for Sex Research*. New York: Harper & Row, 1972.

Pope Paul VI. *On the regulation of birth: Humanae vitae* (Encyclical Letter). Washington, D.C.: United States Catholic Conference, 1968.

Potts, M., B. Chir, T. van der Vlugt, P.T. Piotrow, L.J. Gail, and S.C. Huber. Advantages of orals outweigh disadvantages. *Population Reports*, Series A, no. 2 Washington, D.C. Population Information Programs (March 1975:29–51.)

Pouillet, T. *L'onanisme chez la femme*. Paris: Vigot Freres, 1897. (Originally published in 1876.)

Pound, E. *Personae*. New York: New Directions, 1926.

Prévost, A.F. *Manon Lescaut*. Paris: Garnier Frères, 1965.

Pribram, K.H. The neurobehavioral analysis of limbic forebrain mechanisms: Revision and progress report. *Advances in the Study of Behavior*, Vol. 2. New York: Academic Press, 1969:297–332.

Proust, M. *Cities of the plain*. D.K.S. Moncrieff, trs. New York: Random House, 1932.

Rabelais, F. *Works*. T. Urquhart and P. Motteux, trs. London: The Abbey Library, n.d.

Rainwater, L. Marital sexuality in four "cultures of poverty." In *Human sexual behavior*, D.S. Marshall and R.C. Suggs, eds. Englewood Cliffs, N.J.: Prentice-Hall, 1971, 187–205.

Rawson, P., ed. *Erotic art of the East*. New York: G.P. Putnam's Sons, 1969.

Reich, W. *The discovery of the orgone*. Vol. 1: *The function of the orgasm*. New York: Orgone

Institute Press, 1969. (Originally published in 1942.)

Reichlin, S., R.J. Baldessarini, and J.B. Martin. The hypothalamus. New York: Association for Research in Nervous and Mental Disease/Raven Press, 1978.

Reichlin, S. Relationships of the pituitary gland to human sexual behavior. *Medical Aspects of Human Sexuality* 5, no. 2 (February 1971):146–154.

Reik, T. *Of love and lust*. New York: Farrar, Straus & Giroux, 1970. (Originally published in 1941.)

Rein, M.F. Gonorrhea. In *Practice of medicine*. Vol. 3. New York: Harper & Row, 1975, chapter 19.

Rein, M.F., and T.A. Chapel. Trichomoniasis, candidiasis, and the minor venereal diseases. *Clinical Obstetrics and Gynecology* 18(1975):73–88.

Reiss, I.L. How and why America's sex standards are changing. *Trans-Action*, 5(1968):26–32.

———. *Premarital sexual standards in America*. Glencoe, Ill.: The Free Press, 1960.

Repairing the conjugal bed. *Time* 95 (May 25, 1970):49–52.

Rheingold, H.L., and K.V. Cook. The content of boys' and girls' rooms as an index of parents' behavior. *Child Development* 46(1975):459–463.

Riess, B.F., J. Safer, and W. Yotive. Psychological test data on female homosexuality: A review of the literature. *Journal of Homosexuality* 1, no. 1 (1974):71–85.

Riess, C. *Erotica! Erotica! Das Buch der verbotenen Bücher*. Hamburg: Hoffman & Campe, 1968.

Rinehart, W., and P.T. Piotrow. OCs—Update on usage, safety, and side effects. *Population Reports*, Series A, no. 5 (January 1979):134–186. Washington, D.C. Population Information Programs.

Robbins, S.L. *Textbook of pathology*. 3rd ed. Philadelphia: W.B. Saunders Co., 1967.

Robertiello, R.C. The "clitoral versus vaginal orgasm" controversy and some of its ramifications. *Journal of Sex Research* 6, no. 4 (November 1970):307–311.

Roberts, E.J., D. Kline, and J. Gagnon. *Family life and sexual learning*. Vol. 1. Cambridge, Mass.: Population Education, 1978.

Rose, R.M. Androgen excretion in stress. *The psy-*

chology and physiology of stress, P.G. Bourne, ed. New York: Academic Press, 1969: 117–147.

Rosenbaum, S. Pretended orgasm. *Medical Aspects of Human Sexuality* 4, no. 4 (April 1970):84–96.

Rosner, F., trs. *Mishneh Torah*, "Hilchoth De'oth," Ch. IV, no. 19. *Annals of Internal Medicine* 62(1965):372.

Rossi, A.S. Maternalism, sexuality, and the new feminism. *Contemporary Sexual Behavior: Critical Issues in the 1970's*, J. Zubin and J. Money, eds. Baltimore: The Johns Hopkins University Press, 1973, Ch. 8.

Rossman, I. *Sex, fertility and birth control*. New York: Stravon Press, 1967.

Rothballer, A.B. Aggression, defense, and neurohumors. *Brain Function*, Vol. V: *Aggression and defense*, C.D. Clemente and D.B. Lindsley, eds. Berkeley, Calif.: University of California Press, 1967:135–170.

Roth, P. *Portnoy's complaint*. New York: Random House, 1967.

Roth-Brandel, U., M. Bygdeman, N. Wiqvist, and S. Bergstrom. Prostaglandins for induction of therapeutic abortion. *Lancet* 1(1970): 190–191.

Rothschild, L., F.R.S. Human spermatozoon. *British Medical Journal* 1 (February 8, 1958):301.

Rowell, T. *The social behaviour of monkeys*. Baltimore: Penguin, 1972.

Rowse, A.L. *Homosexuals in history*. New York: Macmillan, 1977.

Rubin, E., ed. *Sexual freedom in marriage*. New York: New American Library, 1969.

Rubin, T.I. *Understanding your man*. New York: Ballantine, 1977.

Ruble, D. Premenstrual symptoms: A reinterpretation. *Science* 197(1977):291–292.

Ruch, F.L., and P.G. Zimbardo. *Psychology and life*. Glenview, Ill.: Scott, Foresman and Co., 1971.

Rudel, H.W., F.A. Kincl, and M.R. Henzl. *Birth control: Contraception and abortion*. New York: Macmillan Co., 1973.

Ruitenbeek, H.M., ed. *The problem of homosexuality in modern society*. New York: E.P. Dutton & Co., 1963.

Russell, B. *Marriage and morals*. New York: Bantam Books, 1968. (Originally published in 1929.)

Russell, M.J., G.M. Switz, and K. Thompson. Olfactory influences on the human menstrual cycle. Delivered at the American Association for the Advancement of Science, San Francisco, 1977.

De Sade, D.-A.-F. *Justine. The Marquis de Sade: Three Complete Novels*. New York: Grove Press, 1965.

Saegert, S., and R. Hart. The development of environmental competence in girls and boys. In *Play: Anthropological Perspectives*, M.A. Salter, ed. West Point, N.Y.: Leisure Press, 1978, 157–176.

Safilios-Rothschild, C. *Love, sex and sex roles*. Englewood Cliffs, N.J.: Prentice-Hall, 1977.

Saghir, M.T., and E. Robins. *Male and female homosexuality: A comprehensive investigation*. Baltimore: Williams & Wilkins, 1973.

Salzman, L. Female infidelity. *Medical Aspects of Human Sexuality* 6, no. 2 (February 1972):118–136.

———. Sexuality in psychoanalytic theory. *Modern psychoanalysis*, J. Marmor, ed. New York: Basic Books, 1968: 123–145.

Sanger, M. *Margaret Sanger: An autobiography*. New York: W.W. Norton, 1938.

Sappho of Lesbos. *Lyra Graica*. J.M. Edmonds, trs. London: William Heinemann, 1922.

Scanzoni, L., and J. Scanzoni. *Men, women and change: A sociology of marriage and the family*. New York: McGraw-Hill, 1976.

Schally, A.V. Aspects of hypothalamic regulation of the pituitary gland: Its implications for the control of reproductive processes. *Science* 202(1978):18–28.

Schlesinger, A., Jr. An informal history of love U.S.A. *Medical Aspects of Human Sexuality*, 4, no. 6 (June 1970):64–82. (Originally published in *The Saturday Evening Post*, 1966.)

Schmidt, G., and V. Sigusch. Sex differences in responses to psychosexual stimulation by films and slides. *Journal of Sex Research* 6, no. 4 (November 1970):268–283.

———. Women's sexual arousal. *Contemporary Sexual Behavior: Critical Issues in the 1970's*, J. Zubin and J. Money, eds. Baltimore: Johns Hopkins University Press, 1973, Ch. 7.

Schneider, R.A. The sense of smell and human sexuality. *Medical Aspects of Human Sexuality*, 5, no. 5 (May 1971).

Schofield, C.B.S. *Sexually transmitted diseases*. Edinburgh: Churchill Livingstone, 1972.

Schroeder, L.O. New Life: Person or Property? *American Journal of Psychiatry* 131 (1974): 541–544.

Schroeter, A.L. Rectal Gonorrhea. *Epidemic Venereal Disease; Proceedings of the Second International Symposium on Venereal Disease*. St. Louis: American Social Health Association and Pfizer Laboratories Division, Pfizer, Inc. (1972):30–35.

Schwarz, G.S. Devices to prevent masturbation. *Medical Aspects of Human Sexuality*, 7, no. 5 (May 1973):141–153.

Schwartz, L.B. Morals, offenses and the model penal code. *Columbia Law Review* 63 (1963):669.

Serbin, L.A., and K.D. O'Leary. How nursery schools teach girls to shut up. *Psychology Today* 9, no. 7 (1975):56–58ff.

Sexton, P.C. *The feminized male*. New York: Vintage Books, 1969.

Shah, F., M. Zelnik, and J.F. Kantner. Unprotected intercourse among teenagers. *Family Planning Perspectives* 7(1975):39–44.

Shapiro, H.I. *The birth control book*. New York: Avon Books, 1977.

Shaver, P., and J. Freedman. Your pursuit of happiness. *Psychology Today* 10, no. 3 (1976):26–32ff.

Sherfey, M.J. the evolution and nature of female sexuality in relation to psychoanalytic theory. *Journal of the American Psychoanalytic Association* 14, no. 1 (1966):28–128.

———. *The nature and evolution of female sexuality*. New York: Vintage Books, 1973.

Shettles, L.B. Predetermining children's sex. *Medical Aspects of Human Sexuality* 6(June 1972):172ff.

Shiloh, A., ed. *Studies in human sexual behavior: The American scene*. Springfield, Ill.: Charles C Thomas, 1970.

Sidel, R. *Families of Fengsheng*. Baltimore: Penguin, 1974.

The significance of extramarital sex relations. *Medical Aspects of Human Sexuality* 3, no. 10 (October 1969):33–47.

Silber, S.J., and R. Cohen. Normal intrauterine pregnancy after reversal of tubal sterilization in the wife and vasectomy in the husband. *Fertility and Sterility* 30(1978):606–608.

Simon, P., J. Gondonneau, L. Mironer, A. Dour-len-Rollier, and C Levy. *Rapport sur le comportement sexuel des français*. Paris: René Julliard/Pierre Charron, 1972.

Singer, I., and J. Singer. Types of female orgasm. *Journal of Sex Research* 8, no. 11 (November 1972):255–267.

Singer, J. The importance of daydreaming. *Psychology Today*, 1, no. 11 (April 1968):18–27.

Skinner, B.F. *The behavior of organisms: An experimental analysis*. New York: Appleton-Century-Crofts, 1938.

Slovenko, R. *Sexual behavior and the law*. Springfield, Ill.: Charles C Thomas, 1965.

Smith, D.R. *General urology*. 6th ed. Los Altos, Calif.: Lange Medical Publications, 1969.

Somadeva. *Vetalapañcavimsati*. C.H. Tawney, trs. Bombay: Jaico Publishing House, 1956.

Sorensen, R.C. *Adolescent sexuality in contemporary America (The Sorensen Report)*, New York: World Publishing, 1973.

Spiro, M.E. *Kibbutz: Venture in utopia*. Cambridge: Harvard University Press, 1956.

Spock, B. *Baby and child care*. New York: Pocket Books, 1970.

Stearn, J. *The grapevine: A report on the secret world of the lesbian*. Garden City, N.Y.: Doubleday & Co., 1964.

———. *The sixth man*. Garden City, N.Y.: Doubleday & Co., 1961.

Stein, A.H., S.R. Pohly, and E. Mueller. The influence of masculine, feminine, and neutral tasks on children's achievement behavior, expectations of success and attainment values. *Child Development* 42(1971):195–207.

Steiner, G. Night words. *The new eroticism*, P. Nobile, ed. New York: Random House, 1970: 120–132.

Stekel, W. *Auto-eroticism*. New York: Liveright Publishing Corp., 1950.

———. *Sexual aberrations*. 2 vols. New York: Liveright Publishing Corp., 1930.

Stephenson, R., and J.R. Debrix. *The cinema as art*. Harmondsworth, Middlesex: Penguin Books, 1965.

Stern, C. *Principles of human genetics*. 2nd ed. San Francisco: H.H. Freeman & Co., 1960.

Stoller, R.J. *Sex and gender: On the development of masculinity and feminity*. New York: Science House, 1968.

Student Committee on Human Sexuality. *Sex and*

the Yale Student. New Haven, Conn.: Yale University Press, 1970.

Sturdy, D.E., and G. Lyth. *Essentials of urology.* Bristol: John Wright & Sons, 1974.

Suitters, B. *The history of contraceptives.* London: International Planned Parenthood Federation, 1967.

Sullivan, P.R. What is the role of fantasy in sex? *Medical Aspects of Human Sexuality* 3, no. 4 (April 1969):79–89.

Tarabulcy, E. Sexual Function in the normal and in paraplegia. *Paraplegia,* 10(1972):202–204.

Tavris, C. The sex lives of happy men. *Redbook* 150, no. 5 (1978):109ff.

Tavris, C., and D. Sadd. *The Redbook report on female sexuality.* New York: Delacorte Press, 1977.

Taylor, G.R. *Sex in history.* New York: Harper & Row, 1970.

Tepperman, J. *Metabolic and endocrine physiology.* 3rd ed. Chicago: Year Book Medical Publishers, 1973.

Terman, L.M. *Psychological factors in marital happiness.* New York: McGraw-Hill, 1938.

Thielicke, H. *The ethics of sex.* J.W. Doberstein, ed. New York: Harper & Row, 1964.

Thomas, J.L., S.J. *Catholic viewpoint on marriage and the family.* Garden City, N.Y.: Image Books, 1965.

Thomlinson, R. *Demographic problems: Controversy over population control.* Belmont, Calif.: Dickenson, 1967.

Thompson, G. *Sex rackets.* Cleveland: Century Books, 1967.

Tietze, C. Unintended pregnancies in the U.S., 1970–1972. *Family Planning Perspectives* 11(1979a):186–188.

Tietze, C. The pill and mortality from cardiovascular disease: another look. *Family Planning Perspectives* 11(1979b):80–84.

Tjio, J.H., and T.T. Puck. The somatic chromosomes of man. *Proceedings of the National Academy of Sciences* 44(1958):1222–1237.

Tucker, S.J. The menopause: How much soma and how much psyche? *JOGN Nursing* (Sept./Oct. 1977):40–48.

Tyrmand, L. Permissiveness and rectitude. *The New Yorker* 46 (February 28, 1970):85–86.

Udry, J.R., and N.M. Morris. Distribution of coitus in the menstrual cycle. *Nature* 220 (1968):593–596.

Ullrich, H.E. Caste differences between Brahmin and non-Brahmin women in a south Indian village. In *Sexual stratification: A cross-cultural view,* A. Schlegel, ed. New York: Columbia University Press, 1977, 94–108.

U.S. Bureau of the Census. Marital status and living arrangements: March 1978. *Current Population Reports,* Population Characteristics Series P–20, no. 338 (May 1979):1–63.

U.S. Department of Health Education and Welfare, Food and Drug Administration. Medical Device and Drug Advisory Committees on Obstetrics and Gynecology. Second report on Intrauterine contraceptive devices. Washington, D.C., U.S. Government Printing Office, December 1978.

Van de Velde, T.E. *Ideal Marriage.* New York: Random House, 1965.

Vanek, J. 1974. Time spent in housework. *Scientific American* 231, no. 5 (1974):116–120.

Van Lawick-Goodall, J. Mother offspring relationship in free-ranging chimpanzees. *Primate ethology,* D. Morris, ed. Chicago: Aldine Publishing Co., 1967: 207–346.

Vatsyayana. *The Kama Sutra.* R.F. Burton and F.F. Arbuthnot, trs. Medallion ed. New York: G.P. Putnam's Sons, 1963.

Vergil (Publius Vergilius Maro). *Works.* H.R. Fairclough, trs. London: William Heinemann, 1965.

Verwoerdt, A., *et al.* Sexual behavior in senescence. *Geriatrics.* (February 1969).

Vessey, M. Remarks at "Workshop on risks, benefits and controversies in fertility control," sponsored by the Program for Applied Research on Fertility Regulation, Arlington, Virginia, March 13–16, 1977,*qv Family Planning Perspectives* 9(1977):136.

Vessey, M.P., K. McPherson, and B. Johnson. Mortality among women participating in the Oxford/family planning association contraceptive study. *Lancet* 2(1977):731–733.

Vidal, G. *Myra Breckinridge.* Boston: Little, Brown & Co., 1968. New York: Bantam Books.

Vierling, J.S., and J. Rock. Variations in olfactory sensitivity to exaltolide during the menstrual cycle. *Journal of Applied Physiology,* 22 (1967):311–315.

Von Krafft-Ebing, R. *Psychopathia sexualis.* C.B. Chaddock, trs. Phildelphia: F.A. Davis Co., 1899. (Reprinted: New York: G.P. Putnam's Sons, 1969.)

Wade, M.E. A randomized perspective study of the use-effectiveness of two methods of natural family planning: an interim report. *American Journal of Obstetrics and Gynecology* 134 (1979):628–631.

Wade, N. Bottle-feeding: Adverse effects of a Western technology. *Science*, 184(1974):45–48.

Waelder, R. *Basic theory of psychoanalysis.* New York: International Universities Press, 1964.

Wagner, N., and D. Solberg. Pregnancy and sexuality. *Medical Aspects of Human Sexuality.* 8, no. 3 (March 1974):44–79.

The way of a man with a maid. New York: Grove Press, 1968.

Watson, A. *Living in China.* London: B.T. Batsford, 1975.

Weinberg, M.S., and C.J. Williams. *Male homosexuals: Their problems and adaptations.* New York: Oxford University Press, 1974.

Weinberg, S.K. *Incest behavior.* New York: Citadel Press, 1963.

Weiss, H.D. Mechanism of erection. *Medical Aspects of Human Sexuality,* 7, no. 2 (February 1973):28–40.

Weiss, R.S., and H.L. Joseph. *Syphilis.* Camden, N.J.: Thomas Nelson, 1951.

West, C., and D.H. Zimmerman. Women's place in everyday talk: Reflections on parent-child interaction. *Social Problems* 24, no. 5 (1977):521–529.

West, D.J. *Homosexuality re-examined.* Minneapolis: University of Minnesota Press, 1977.

West, D.J. *Homosexuality.* Chicago: Aldine, 1968.

West, N. *Miss Lonelyhearts.* New York: Avon Publishing, 1933.

Westoff, C.F., and E.F. Jones. The secularization of U.S. Catholic birth control practices. *Family Planning Perspectives* 9(1977):203–207.

Westoff, C.F., and L. Bumpass. The revolution in birth control practices of U.S. Roman Catholics. *Science,* 179(1973):41–44.

Westoff, C.F., and R. Parke, Jr., eds. Sexuality, contraception and pregnancy among young unwed females in the United States. *Demographic and Social Aspects of Population Growth,* Washington, D.C.: U.S. Government Printing Office, 1972.

Westoff, C.R., and R.R. Rindfuss. Sex preselection in the United States: Some implications. *Science,* 184(1974):633–636.

Westwood, G. *A minority: A report on the life of the male homosexual in Great Britain.* London: Longmans, Green & Co., 1960.

Weyranch, H.M. *Life after fifty: The prostatic age.* Los Angeles: Ward Ritchie Press, 1968.

What are the effects of premarital sex on the marital relationship? *Medical Aspects of Human Sexuality* 7, no. 4 (April 1973):142–167.

What do you tell parents who are concerned about their children's masturbation? *Medical Aspects of Human Sexuality* 1, no. 3 (November 1967): 12–24.

What is the chief cause of marital infidelity? *Medical Aspects of Human Sexuality* 8, no. 1 (January 1974):90–110.

The Whippingham papers. London: Privately published, 1888.

Whiteman, R.M. Multiple orgasms. *Medical Aspects of Human Sexuality* 3, no. 8 (August 1969): 52–56.

Whyte, L.L. *The unconscious before Freud.* New York: Basic Books, 1960.

Wickler, W. *The sexual code.* Garden City, New York: Doubleday, 1972.

Wiesner, P.J. Gonococcal pharyngeal infection. *Clinical Obstetrics and Gynecology* 18(1975):121–129.

Wilkins, L. *The diagnosis and treatment of endocrine disorders in childhood and adolescence.* 3rd ed. Springfield, Ill.: Charles C Thomas, 1965.

Wilkins, L., R. Blizzard, and C. Migeon. *The diagnosis and treatment of endocrine disorders in childhood and adolescence.* Springfield, Ill.: Charles C Thomas, 1965.

Williams, F.E. *Papuans of the Trans-Fly.* Oxford: Clarendon Press, 1936.

Willson, J.R., C.T. Beecham, and E.R. Carrington. *Obstetrics and gynecology,* 4th ed. St. Louis: C.V. Mosby Co., 1971.

Wilmore, J.H. Inferiority of female athletes: myth or reality. *Journal of Sports Medicine* 3, no. 1 (1975):1–6.

Wilmore, J.H. *Athletic training and physical fitness.* Boston: Allyn and Bacon, 1977.

Wilson, M.L. and R.L. Greene. Personality characteristics of female homosexuals. *Psychological Reports* 28(1971):407–412.

Wilson, W.C. The distribution of selected sexual attitudes and behaviors among the adult population of the United States. *Journal of Sex Research* 11(1975):46–64.

Witkin, H.A., S.A. Mednich, F. Schulsinger, E. Bakkestrøm, K.O. Christiansen, D.R. Goodenough, K. Hirschhorn, C. Lundsteen, D.R. Owen, J. Philip, D.B. Tubin, and M. Stocking. Criminality in XYY and XXY men. *Science* 193(1976):547–555.

Witkowski, J. *Anecdotes sur les accouchements.* Paris: Steinheil, 1892.

Winick, C.The desexualized society. *The new eroticism*, P. Nobile, ed. New York: Random House, 1970:201–207.

The Wolfenden report. New York: Stein & Day, 1963.

Wolpe, J., and A.A. Lazarus. *Behavior therapy techniques.* New York: Pergamon Press, 1966.

Wolpe, J. *The practice of behavior therapy.* New York: Pergamon Press, 1969.

———. *Psychotherapy by reciprocal inhibition.* Stanford: Stanford University Press, 1958.

Women on Words and Images. *Channeling children: Sex stereotyping on prime time T.V.* Princeton, N.J., 1975.

Women on Words and Images. *Dick and Jane as victims: Sex stereotyping in children's readers.* Princeton, N.J., 1972.

Wood, H.C., Jr. *Sex without babies: A comprehensive review of voluntary sterilization as a method of birth control.* Philadelphia: Whitmore, 1967.

Woolf, V. *A room of one's own.* New York: Harcourt Brace Jovanovich, 1929.

World Health Organization. *Hormonal steroids in contraception.* World Health Organization Technical Report no. 386. Geneva: WHO, 1968.

———. *Intrauterine devices: Physiological and clinical aspects.* World Health Organization Technical Report no. 397. Geneva: WHO, 1968.

World Health Organization, *Special programme of research, development and research training in human reproduction: Seventh annual report.* Geneva, November 1978.

Yalom, I.D., *et al.* Postpartum blues syndrome. *Archives of General Psychiatry* 18(1968):16–27.

———. Prenatal exposure to female hormones: Effect on psychosexual development in boys. *Archives of General Psychiatry*, 28(1973): 554–561.

Yankelovich. Raising children in a changing society. The General Mills American Family Report, 1976–1977.

Yankelovich, Skelly, & White. The new morality. *Time* 110, no. 21 (1977):111–116ff.

Yates, A.J. *Behavior therapy.* New York: John Wiley & Sons, 1970.

Young, W.C., ed. *Sex and internal secretions*, 2 vols. Baltimore: Williams & Wilkins Co., 1961.

Zelnik, M., and Kantner, J.F. Sexual and contraceptive experience of young unmarried women in the U.S. 1976 and 1971. *Family Planning Perspectives* 9(1977):55–71.

Zelnik, M., and J.F. Kantner. Sexuality, contraception and pregnancy among young unwed females in the United States. C.F. Westoff, and R. Parke, Jr. eds. *Commission on Population Growth and the American Future, Research Reports*, Vol. 1. Demographic and Social Aspects of Population Growth. Washington, D.C.: Government Printing Office, 1972.

Zelnik, M, Y.J. Kim, and J.F. Kantner. Probabilities of intercourse and conception among U.S. teenage women, 1971 and 1976. *Family Planning Perspectives* 11(1979):177–183.

Zichy, M. *The erotic drawings of Mihaly Zichy.* New York: Grove Press, 1969.

Zimmermann, A.A. Embryologic and anatomic considerations of cojoined twins. *Birth Defects Original Article Series* 3, no. 1 (1967):18–27.

Zimmerman, D.H., and C. West. Sex roles, interruptions and silences in conversation. In *Language and sex*, B. Thorne and N. Henley, eds. Rowley, Mass.: Newbury House, 1975, 105–129.

Zola, E. *Nana.* Paris: Fasquelle, 1938.

Zuckerman, S. *The social life of monkeys and apes.* London: Routledge & Kegan Paul, 1932.

Glossary

abortion Termination of pregnancy, usually during the first 12 weeks, by expulsion of the fetus.

adrenocorticotrophic hormone Pituitary hormone that stimulates secretion of hormones by the adrenal glands.

afterbirth The discharge of the placenta, along with the fetal membranes, during the third stage of labor.

amniocentesis Procedure for testing the chromosomal makeup of the fetus when an abnormality is suspected or for determining the sex of an unborn child.

ampulla In the female, the second portion of the fallopian tubes located between the infundibulum and the isthmus. In the male, the terminal enlargement of the vas deferens before it joins the ejaculatory duct.

anal intercourse Intromission of the penis into the anus.

androgens Male sex hormones produced by the adrenal glands in both males and females and by the testes in the male; may be related to the female sex drive.

anterior pituitary The front portion of the pituitary gland.

anus The opening of the alimentary canal located between the buttocks.

aphrodisiacs Substances believed to enhance sexual drive or potency.

areola The area surrounding the nipple.

autoeroticism Solitary sexual behavior consisting of erotic fantasies, masturbation, and erotic dreams.

axillary hair Underarm hair which appears at puberty; a secondary sex characteristic.

Bartholin's glands Two small glands located behind the vestibular bulbs which are the female counterpart of the male Cowper's glands; also called bulbourethal glands.

behavior therapy Approach to the treatment of emotional problems, including sexual dysfunctions, based on the principles of learning theories.

bestiality See **zoophilia.**

birth control Prevention of pregnancy by artificial or voluntary means.

bisexual Term applied to individuals who engage in both homosexual and heterosexual activities.

blastocyst The fluid-filled structure that develops about five days after fertilization of the egg cell and that attaches itself to the lining of the uterus, eventually to become a fetus.

body of the uterus The main part of the uterus.

bulb of the penis The expanded inner end of the corpus spongiosum, or spongy body, of the penis; with the crura makes up the root of the penis.

bulbocavernosus A muscle surrounding the bulb of the penis which aids in ejecting urine and semen through the urethra; see also **ischiocavernosus.**

cardiac prominence By the end of the fourth week in the development of the embryo the upper bulge on the front side of the trunk representing the developing heart.

castration Removal of the testes, which in a young boy prevents the development of secondary sex characteristics. The term is also used to mean amputation of the penis.

cephalic position The head-down position

of the fetus in the final trimester of pregnancy, the most common position for delivery.

cervical caps Contraceptive devices similar to diaphragms, popular in Europe.

cervical dilation The first step in a method of abortion used in the first trimester of pregnancy involving the expansion of the cervix and the scraping of the uterus.

cervix The lower part of the uterus which projects into the vagina.

cesarean section Surgical operation through the walls of the abdomen and uterus for the purpose of delivering the baby.

chancre The hard, round ulcer at the site of sexual contact that characterizes the early stages of syphilis.

chancroid Venereal disease marked by a soft, painful chancre.

childbirth (puerperal) fever A contagious disease which spreads among pregnant women unless antiseptic practices are instituted to prevent it.

chromosomes Rodlike bits of material in the nucleus of each cell which are the site of genes and which provide information to guide cells in their division and multiplication.

cilia Tiny hairlike structures that line the fallopian tubes.

circumcision The surgical cutting off of part of the foreskin of the penis, leaving the glans exposed.

climacteric The period, usually between the ages of 46 and 50, during which women experience the physiological changes associated with menopause.

clitoral orgasm Culmination of sexual excitement achieved through direct stimulation of the clitoris.

clitoridectomy Removal of the clitoris.

clitoris A small, highly sensitive organ within the minor lips of the female; the developmental counterpart of the penis.

coitus Heterosexual intercourse, or copulation; the coupling of the penis and the vagina.

coitus interruptus The birth-control measure involving withdrawal of the penis from the vagina just before ejaculation.

coitus reservatus Coitus without ejaculation.

common-law marriages Marriages effected by agreement between couples without licenses or ceremonies.

condom Thin, flexible sheath worn over the erect penis to prevent sperm from entering the vagina.

contraceptive Device or drug to prevent pregnancy.

corona The extremely sensitive rim, or crown, of the glans penis.

corpora cavernosa The cavernous bodies, two of the three cylinders of spongy tissue which make up the penis.

corpus luteum Small structure that develops out of the ruptured ovarian follicle during the secretory phase of the menstrual cycle.

corpus spongiosum The spongy body, one of the three cylinders of spongy tissue which make up the penis.

Cowper's glands Glands which secrete a sticky, alkaline fluid that appears on the glans penis during sexual arousal.

crura The inner tips of the corpora cavernosa, or cavernous bodies, of the penis which are attached to the pubic bones; with the bulb make up the root of the penis.

culdoscope Instrument used by physicians to see inside the abdominal cavity.

culdoscopy A method for sterilization of the female involving locating the fallopian tubes through a puncture in the closed end of the vagina.

cunnilingus Oral stimulation of the female genitals.

curette In abortions involving cervical dilation, the metal instrument used to scrape the tissue off the inner walls of the uterus.

cystitis Infection or inflammation of the bladder.

desensitization Therapeutic approach to emotional problems, including sexual dysfunctions, based on gradually leading patients to confront their problem situations without anxiety.

detumescence Partial or total loss of erection of the penis.

diaphragm A thin rubber dome positioned over the cervix to prevent sperm from entering the cervical canal.

dildo Artificial penis used for sexual stimulation.

douching Washing out of the vagina.

ductus deferens See **vas deferens.**

dysmenorrhea Painful menstruation.

ectopic pregnancy Implantation of the fertilized ovum in the wall of the fallopian tube, a condition resulting in the death of the fetus and sometimes the rupturing of the tube.

ejaculation The ejection of semen in male orgasm.

ejaculatory impotence Failure of the erect penis to ejaculate.

embryo The organism resulting from the fertilized ovum approximately one week after fertilization; after the eighth week of pregnancy is termed the fetus.

embryonic disk Early in pregnancy a disk-shaped layer of cells which forms across the center of the blastocyst and from which the fetus grows.

endocrine glands Glands, including the thyroid, parathyroid, pituitary, and adrenal glands, that secrete hormones into the bloodstream.

endocrinology The study of the secretions of the endocrine glands.

endometrium The lining of the uterus shed during menstruation. See **mucosa.**

epididymis Mass of ducts at the back of the testes through which sperm first pass on leaving the seminiferous tubules.

episiotomy An incision of the perineum that is sometimes performed to ease the passage of the baby's head at birth.

erectile dysfunction See **impotence.**

erection The state in which the penis is engorged with blood and becomes firm and erect.

erogenous zones Areas of the body that are particularly sensitive to erotic tactile stimulation.

erotic fantasies Daydreams with a sexual focus that may be accompanied by sexual arousal; see **autoeroticism.**

estrogen Female sex hormone produced by the ovaries.

eunuchs Castrated males.

exhibitionism Male sexual deviation involving the exposure of the genitals to involuntary observers.

fallopian tubes The tubes through which ova are transported from the ovaries to the uterus; also called uterine tubes.

false labor Contractions of the uterus at irregular intervals in the ninth month of pregnancy which are sometimes taken as the beginning of actual labor.

fellatio Oral stimulation of the male genitals.

fetishism A sexual variation in which the sexual object is an inanimate article, such as a piece of clothing.

fetus A developing human being in the uterus from about eight weeks after conception until birth.

fimbriae Projections fringing the infundibulum of the fallopian tube.

flush See **hot flash.**

follicle (retention) cyst A common form of ovarian cyst resulting from failure of the graafian follicle to rupture.

follicles The many capsules, each containing an ovum in various stages of development, embedded in the tissues of the ovaries.

follicle-stimulating hormone One of the two pituitary hormones that stimulate the gonads.

follicle-stimulating releasing factor Chemical factor secreted by the hypothalamus which has a reproductive function.

foreplay Period of sexually arousing activity preceding coitus.

foreskin The skin covering part of the glans penis; see also **prepuce.**

fornication Sexual intercourse other than between husband and wife.

frenulum In the male, the thin strip of skin on the underside of the glans penis stretching from the glans to the body of the penis. In the female, the fold of skin beneath the clitoris formed by the lower portions of the minor lips.

fundus The rounded part of the uterus which is located above the fallopian tubes.

gender identity The recognition of one's individuality as male or female as experienced through self-awareness and behavior; see also **gender role.**

gender role All that one says and does to indicate to the self and others that one is male, female, or ambivalent; see also **gender identity.**

glans penis The smooth, rounded tip of the penis.

gonadotrophins The two pituitary hormones (follicle-stimulating hormone and luteinizing hormone) that stimulate the gonads.

gonads The paired reproductive glands; testes in the male and ovaries in the female.

gonorrhea A contagious venereal disease caused by a bacterial infection which affects mucous membrane tissues.

graafian follicle The spherical structure encasing the egg within the ovary.

Granuloma inguinale Venereal disease marked by spreading lesions.

gynecomastia Temporary enlargement of the breasts in males during puberty.

Hegar's sign The softening of an area between the cervix and the body of the uterus; a good indicator of pregnancy.

hepatic prominence By the end of the fourth week in the development of the embryo the lower bulge on the front side of the trunk representing the growing liver.

hermaphrodites Individuals with the gonadal and genital characteristics of both sexes.

Herpes Simplex Virus Type 2 Common viral infection characterized by blisters in the genital area.

hot flash Symptom of the climacteric characterized by the sensation of waves of heat spreading over the face and upper half of the body; also called **flush.**

homosexual An individual who engages in sexual activity with members of the same sex; the term is usually applied to males.

human chorionic gonadotrophin (HCG) The hormone measured in pregnancy tests which is produced by the placenta.

hypospadias Condition in which the opening of the urethra is located under rather than at the tip of the glans penis.

hypothalamus Site in the brain that regulates the pituitary gland; secretes the chemical factors follicle-stimulating hormone releasing factor and luteinizing hormone-releasing factor, among others

hysterectomy The surgical removal of the uterus resulting in sterilization.

impotence Failure of the male to achieve erection during sexual activity.

incest Sexual relations between an individual and close relatives.

infundibulum The fringed, ovarian end of the fallopian tubes.

inguinal hernia A condition in males in which loops of the intestine make their way into the scrotal sac; also called **rupture.**

intercourse. See **coitus.**

interstitial-cell-stimulating hormone Term for the luteinizing hormone in the male.

intrauterine device (IUD) A device, usually plastic, inserted into the uterus by a physician in order to prevent pregnancy.

introitus The opening of the vagina within the minor lips.

ischiocavernosus A muscle attached to the bulb of the penis which aids in ejecting urine and semen through the urethra; see also **bulbocavernosus.**

isthmus of the fallopian tubes The third segment of the fallopian tubes located between the ampulla and the uterine border.

laminaria sticks Sticks made from compressed seaweed which when inserted into the cervix expand to cause cervical dilation, the first step in a method of abortion; see **cervical dilation.**

lanugo Fine hair that appears on the scalp and above the eyes in the developing fetus during the fifth or sixth month.

larynx The voice box, which in males enlarges as a secondary sex characteristic.

lesbianism Female homosexuality.

luteinizing hormone One of the two pituitary hormones that stimulate the ovaries.

luteinizing hormone-releasing factor Chemical factor secreted by the hypothalamus which has reproductive function.

Lymphogranuloma venereum Venereal disease characterized by tenderness of the lymph glands.

major lips (labia majora) Two elongated folds of skin that run down and back from the mons pubis and constitute the outermost portion of the female genitalia.

mammary gland The milk-producing part of the breast.

mammograms Special X-rays for diagnosing breast cancer.

masochism Sexual deviation in which an individual must experience pain in order to achieve sexual gratification.

mastalgia In females painful swelling of the breasts associated with cyclical hormone changes and the buildup of body fluid.

mastectomy Surgical removal of the breast.

masturbation Self-stimulation for sexual pleasure usually involving genital manipulation.

meiosis The process of reduction division by which male and female germ cells each end up with 23 chromosomes, or half the normal number.

menarche The first menstruation.

menopause In females the end of the reproductive period characterized by various physiological changes.

menstrual extraction Suction method of removing menstrual tissue and fluids to alleviate painful menstruation.

menstrual migraines Headaches associated with menstruation.

menstruation In females the periodic uterine bleeding that accompanies the ovarian cycle and involves the shedding of the lining of the uterus.

mesonephric duct One of paired ducts present in the early stages of development of the reproductive system from which develop the genital ducts in males. Also called **Wolffian duct.**

middlepiece The cone-shaped portion of the sperm lying between the head and the tail.

minor lips (labia minora) In the female two hairless folds of skin located between the major lips.

miscarriage The termination of pregnancy by natural causes.

mitosis The process of cell division.

mittelschmerz Unexplained intermittent cramps in the lower abdomen that sometimes occur during ovulation.

mons pubis The soft, rounded mound of fatty tissue that covers the female pubic symphysis; also called the **mons veneris.**

mons veneris See **mons pubis.**

morula A round mass of smaller cells, resulting a few days after fertilization, from the original fertilized egg cell.

Müllerian ducts See **paramesonephric duct.**

mutual orgasm The simultaneous experiencing by a couple of the sexual climax during intercourse.

myometrium The second, muscular layer of the uterus which gives it elasticity and strength.

myotonia The increased muscle tension that accompanies sexual arousal.

necrophilia Sexual deviation involving the sexual use of corpses.

neuroendocrinology The study of the role of the brain in hormone secretion.

nipple The prominent pigmented tip of the breast.

nocturnal emissions Nocturnal orgasms, or those that take place during sleep, among males; also called **wet dreams.**

nocturnal orgasms Orgasms that take place during sleep, usually accompanied by dreams; see also **nocturnal emissions.**

no-fault divorce Divorce by consent of both partners with property divided evenly.

nongonococcal urethritis A venereal disease that may result in infections of the eyes in infants of women so affected; in males causes inflammation of the urethra.

nubility The final stage of puberty, during

which full fertility is achieved.

ophthalmia neonatorum A gonorrheal infection, acquired by infants during passage through infected birth canals, which can cause blindness.

orgasm The climax of sexual arousal consisting of the discharge of neuromuscular tension accompanied by feelings of intense pleasure.

orgasmic platform The congestion of the walls of the outer third of the vagina which appears during the plateau phase of the sexual response cycle.

orgasmic unresponsiveness In females repeated failure to attain orgasm.

ova Germ cells, or eggs, produced by the ovaries (Singular, "ovum")

ovarian cortex The surface of the ovary.

ovarian cysts Fluid-filled sacs in the ovaries.

ovarian ligaments Bands of tissue that attach the ovaries to the sides of the uterus.

ovarian medulla The central portion of the ovaries, rich in blood vessels.

ovaries The pair of reproductive glands, or gonads, of the females that produce ova (eggs) and the sex hormones estrogen and progesterone.

ovum The egg, the germ cell produced in the ovaries.

ovutimer A device that when inserted into the vagina determines the time of ovulation by measuring the stickiness of cervical mucus.

oxytocin A pituitary hormone which in the late stages of labor causes contractions that expel the fetus and which also causes the ejection of milk from the breast to the nipple during breast feeding.

paramesonephric duct One of the paired ducts present in the early stages of development of the reproductive system; from which develop the female genital passages. Also called **Müllerian ducts.**

pedephile Individual who uses children for sexual gratification.

pederasty A sexual deviation involving anal intercourse with a child.

Pediculosis pubis Infestation of the pubic hair by lice, usually sexually transmitted.

pelvis The basin-shaped bony structure made up of the sacram and the two hip bones which contains and protects the internal sex organs.

penis The external male sex organ for copulation and urination.

perimetrium The external third layer of the uterus; also called the **serosa.**

perineum The skin and deeper tissues between the openings of the vagina and anus which is sometimes torn or cut purposefully during childbirth.

petting Erotic caressing, basically similar to foreplay, but not leading to coitus.

phallus The Greek name for "penis".

pharyngeal gonorrhea A form of gonorrhea characterized by an infection of the throat transmitted during fellatio.

Pill, the Popular name for a number of commonly used oral contraceptives.

pituitary gland Complex endocrine gland located at the base of the brain.

placenta The organ through which nutrients are passed from the mother to the fetus growing in the womb.

polar body The result of the first, mitotic division of the egg, containing 46 chromosomes, which later disentegrates.

posterior pituitary The rear portion of the pituitary gland.

pregnancy The state of carrying a developing child in the womb.

premature ejaculation In males orgasm before or right after vaginal entry.

premenstrual tension Fatigue, irritability, and other discomforts that signal the onset of menstruation.

prepuce In the male the skin covering part of the glans penis; see also **foreskin.** In the female the single fold of skin covering the clitoris.

priapism A rare condition in males marked by persistent erection.

primary oocytes The several hundred thousand immature ova contained in the ovaries at birth.

progesterone A female sex hormone produced in the ovaries.

progestogens A group of synthetic compounds, which because of their ability to inhibit ovulation, are used as a contraceptive drug.

prolactin   Pituitary hormone that stimulates milk production.

prolactin-inhibiting factor   Secretion of the hypothalamus that controls milk production by preventing prolactin production except after childbirth.

prostaglandins   Chemicals known to stimulate the muscles of the uterus as well as muscles of the gastrointestinal tract.

prostitution   The performance of sexual acts by women with men who pay for them.

prostate gland   A glandular body at the bottom of the bladder that contributes most of the fluid to the ejaculate.

pseudohermaphroditism   In females the enlargement of external sex organs caused by a defect in the functioning of the adrenal glands.

puberty   The biological stage of development that begins with the appearance of secondary sexual characteristics and lasts until the start of reproductive ability.

pubic hair   Hair that appears at puberty in the pubic area of the lower abdomen; a secondary sex characteristic.

pubic symphysis   The point in the lower abdomen at which the hip bones of the pelvis are attached to each other.

quickening   Fetal movements, a positive determinant of pregnancy, which usually appear by the end of the fifth month.

rape   The use of force on an unwilling victim to achieve sexual gratification.

rectal gonorrhea   A gonorrheal infection of the rectum transmitted during anal intercourse.

retrograde ejaculation   A condition in which the semen is ejaculated into the urinary bladder rather than flowing out normally.

rhythm method   Method of birth control based on avoidance of intercourse during a woman's fertile period.

rubella   German measles virus.

rupture   See **inguinal hernia.**

sacrum   The end of the spinal column which forms a part of the pelvis.

sadism   Sexual deviation in which sexual gratification is derived by inflicting pain.

sadomasochism   A form of behavior in which sex and pain are pathologically linked.

saline abortions   Abortions induced by injection of a salt solution into the uterus; used during the second trimester of pregnancy.

scrotum   The external sac that contains the testes.

secondary oocyte   The result of the first, mitotic division of the egg, containing 46 chromosomes.

secondary sex characteristics   The physiological changes that accompany genital and reproductive maturity.

secretory phase   In the menstrual cycle the period after ovulation.

semen   The whitish fluid which contains the sperm. Also called ejaculate.

seminal vesicle   Paired sacs in the male reproductive tract which are believed to contribute fluids that activate the movement of sperm.

seminiferous tubules   The tubes within the testes that are the site of sperm production.

serosa   See **perimetrium.**

sex hormones   Chemicals produced by the sex glands that play a role in reproduction and sexual behavior.

sexual deviations   Departures from standard coital practice; also called **sexual variations.**

sexual variations   See **sexual deviations.**

situation ethics   Approach to ethical decisions in which the individual determines what is right or wrong on the basis of the situation itself rather than in terms of a universal moral law.

smegma   The cheesy substance secreted between the glans penis and the foreskin.

spermatids   The cells resulting from reduction division, or meiosis, of the spermatocytes, that eventually become mature sperm.

spermatocytes   The second stage of development of sperm cells.

spermatogenesis   The process of sperm formation which takes place within the seminiferous tubules of the testes.

spermatogonia Cells that lie along the internal linings of the seminiferous tubules; the first stage of development of the sperm.

spermatozoa The male germ cells produced in the testes; often shortened to sperm.

spermicidal substances Contraceptive jellies, foams, creams, and suppositories which are inserted into the vagina to kill sperm on contact.

sphincters Muscular rings that surround body openings, for example, the vaginal sphincter and the anal sphincter.

Spirochaeta pallidum The microorganism that causes syphilis.

spontaneous abortion Miscarriage, or the unwanted termination of pregnancy.

statutory rape The crime of intercourse with a girl under a certain age, varying from 14 to 21, depending on the state.

steroids Group of chemical substances including the sex hormones estrogen, progesterone, and testosterone.

suction curette The instrument used to perform a vacuum aspiration, or abortion.

syphilis An infectious venereal disease characterized by lesions in various parts of the body.

testes The pair of external reproductive glands, or gonads, of the male which produce testosterone and sperm; the singular is "testicle."

testicle See **testes.**

toxemia A condition that occurs only in pregnant women in which a poison produced by the body can, if uncontrolled, lead to infection, hemorrhaging, and death.

transsexual Term applied to individuals—usually males—who wish to be members of the opposite sex.

transvestism Sexual variation in which sexual gratification is obtained through wearing the clothing of the opposite sex.

troilism Sexual relations among three people, one of whom is of the opposite sex.

tubal ligation For sterilization of females the procedure that involves tying or cutting the fallopian tubes.

urethra The tube running through the corpus spongiosum of the penis that carries both urine and semen out of the body. In the female the urethra, the opening of which is located just to the rear of the clitoris, carries only urine.

urethral meatus The opening of the urethra to the outside.

urethral sphincter Mass of muscle fibers that make possible the voluntary control of urination.

uterine mucosa The inner layer of the uterus consisting of numerous glands and blood vessels; also called the **endometrium.**

uterus The womb, the organ in which the developing organism is sustained until birth.

vacuum aspiration A simple method of abortion involving the use of suction to withdraw fluids and tissues from the uterus.

vagina The copulatory organ of the female.

vaginal orgasm Orgasm reached through stimulation of the vagina.

vas deferens Duct which conveys sperm from the epididymis to the ejaculatory duct.

vasectomy The surgical cutting of the vas deferens in the scrotal sac which results in male sterilization.

vasocongestion During sexual arousal the overfilling of the blood vessels and the increased flow of blood into body tissues; for example, the erection of the penis.

vestibular bulbs Masses of erectile tissue which surround the vaginal opening.

voyeurism A sexual variation that focuses on seeing, or "peeping" at a naked person without the person's knowledge.

vulva The external female sex organs.

wet dreams See **nocturnal emissions.**

Wolffian duct See **mesonephric duct.**

womb See **uterus.**

zona pellucida The gelatinous capsule surrounding the mature egg.

zoophilia Sexual deviation involving sexual contacts between humans and animals; also called **bestiality.**

Name Index

Subject Index